The
Church of England
1900–1965

The
Church of England
1900-1965

Roger Lloyd

SCM PRESS LTD

First published 1966
by SCM Press Ltd
56 Bloomsbury Street London

© *SCM Press Ltd 1966*

Printed in Great Britain by
Western Printing Services Ltd
Bristol

To
MARGARET
friend and critic
I gratefully dedicate this book

Contents

8 *Contents*

PART THREE · 1939–1965

The Church of England
1900–1965

Preface

THIS book has a long and a rather complicated history behind it, and it is necessary to say something, by way of explanation and not of excuse, of what that history is. Some of its readers may remember that in 1946 Longmans, Green published the first volume of my *Church of England in the Twentieth Century*, and followed it with a second volume in 1950. The two volumes were reprinted several times, but eventually they went out of print and have been unobtainable now for a good many years. They told the Church of England's story from 1900 to 1945.

In January 1963 the Rev. David L. Edwards of the Student Christian Movement Press invited me to add a third volume to carry on the story from 1945 to the present day, and offered to publish all three volumes together in a single book, with the present and new title.

But he hoped, as I did, that the resultant amalgam would not be three separate volumes but one single book, a unity in itself, with the thread of narrative flowing continuously from the first page to the last. This has only been made possible by a heavy revision of the two earlier volumes, to remove inconsistency, inconsequence, reduplication, and to correct errors of fact. Some of the judgements which seemed so obvious in 1946 or 1950 time has shown to have been mistaken, and these have been tempered. Some passages have been deleted altogether, others have been abridged, and some new ones have been added.

This revision has been an exacting task. What has made it possible has been the unselfish help, the continuous criticism, and the shouldering of the greater part of the burden by my friend Margaret Duggan. If any inconsistency or jerkiness of narrative are now left, it is no fault of hers. She also read, chapter by chapter, both the first and second drafts of all the chapters which take the story from 1945 to the present day. Much of what merit they may possess I owe to her penetrating criticism.

In the original preface I called the book a Meditation on an Historical Theme, and I cannot now find better words to describe it. It is not a professional history. If it was, many things would have to be included which I have omitted. But the time for that will not come for many years yet. A meditation is personal, and can therefore be arbitrary. If it builds itself on the history of a Church, then its form must be a picture of this Church at work, now in this field and now in that. The theme of this meditation is the title of the book. To read and think around it gradually kindles a vision of what the characteristic mission of the Church of England in this century has been and must be. Whether true or false, such a vision can only be the fruit of historical study. But in the presentation of the fruits of this study, arbitrariness of choice is not amiss in a meditation as it would be in a formal and professional history. The principles of selection which I have followed will, I hope, become apparent, but far more is left out than is included.

But I must turn to the paying, or at least the acknowledging of my debts. No one has ever refused or given grudgingly of their help when I asked it. In the prefaces to the two earlier volumes—not now reprinted—I thanked a representative sample of my then benefactors. The lapse of years has not dimmed the generosity I have received over the third part. First of all I must thank my friend and colleague Canon David Maundrell who read through the book in typescript, corrected my grammar and punctuation, saved me from several errors of fact, and made many helpful suggestions. It cost him many hours of work and I am deeply grateful. Mrs Edna Blake of Winchester typed it all for me with speed and accuracy. The Archdeacon of Capetown was kind and patient in answering many questions about the Church in South Africa. The Rev. Philip Bell, one time chaplain of Tristan da Cunha in the diocese of Capetown, told me much about Archbishop Clayton which only someone who knew him well could have known, and allowed me to quote from one of his personal letters to him. Bishop Wand has helped me forward in many ways by his encouragement and his answers to my questions. The Church Information Office has never failed me in any enquiry I made of it. I owe a heavy debt to my publisher, David Edwards, to whose initiative this present book has its existence, and for his constant but critical encouragement.

The list is already long, but though it is still incomplete I must make an end. What it amounts to is a testimony to the kindness of his fellow Christians which anyone who undertakes a task of this kind may confidently hope to receive. I now send this completed book forth with the prayer that in spite of all its blemishes it may still be used for the good of the Church of England which bore me, bred me, trained me, and taught me everything I know of God, and which I am so thankful and so proud to belong to and to serve.

Winchester   ROGER LLOYD
All Souls' Day 1965

PART ONE

1900–1919

1

The Divine Society

I · *The Dilemma of the Church Historian*

IN ALL its branches the Christian Church is a religious society and a divine organism. It has its work in history and beyond it; its interests in the eternal no less than in the material world; and its root and its goal in heaven. Therein lies the fundamental and the hardly soluble dilemma of all its historians. Their calling as historians first of all requires them to give an account of the Church's action within history, as it goes about its business of telling it out among the heathen that the Lord is King, and of claiming the kingdoms of this world to the obedience of our Lord and of his Christ. But so objective a description of men and narrative of events in the space-time world can easily become seriously misleading. To tell the story of the Christian action within and upon history is not necessarily to have given the least account of what the Church is in itself. But no account of what an institution does can really be intelligible to those who have no idea of what it is.

To consider what is the real function of religion, and therefore of the Church, only deepens the historian's perplexities. It is the business of religion to conduct research into mystery: therefore the Church must provide for this research, and find out how best to give expression to its results in terms of life. Thus the mystical quest is the purest of all religious activities, and the celebration of a sacrament is the most fundamental of all religious rites. The institution which provides for both forms of religious devotion, and within which both are chiefly conducted, does so as an expression in terms of the space-time world of the deep springs of its own being. The note of mystery is inescapable; and, to the chagrin of the historian, the essence of mystery is that it remains mysterious. Against the background and in the atmosphere of mystery the whole life and work of the Church takes place. A visible, definable organization in the world, the Church is yet rooted and grounded in heaven. The home and the organ of

the Holy Spirit, it is from eternity and to eternity. No one has ever satisfactorily placed the date of its birth at any single point within the historical
scheme of things: short of the pre-existent Word of God we can find no
point within history where we can stop and say, 'This is the beginning of
the Church.' To predicate any satiety of its quest in this world is philoso-
phically an absurdity of the grossest kind. It can find complete fulfilment
of its purpose only in the joy of God over its own perfection. 'Christ so
loved the Church and gave himself for it . . . that he might present it to
himself a glorious church, not having spot, or wrinkle, or any such thing.'
St Paul also spoke constantly of the Church as the Body of Christ. It is a
phrase which every considerable school of Christian theology has endorsed.
As such the Church is part of the eternal self-revelation of God. It becomes
that part of heaven, set within the physical universe, which exists to be for
history the divine energy, and to perform within history the divine will. It
is the fullness of him that filleth all in all. It is a divine society, and its
children form the fellowship of a deep mystery.

As we contemplate its actual work in the space-time world, which ought,
on the face of it, to be a simpler study for the historian, the note of mystery
persists. It has a world to win for Christ. It seeks to win it by bearing witness in every age and in every place to the resurrection of Jesus, and by
exhibiting in, and proclaiming through, its own organism the liberating
affirmations and the revolutionary simplicities of the Gospel. But these are
contained in such words as Judgement, Repentance, Forgiveness, Conversion, and Atonement. Every single one of them leads straight back into the
heart of the very realm of mystery from which the Church emerges, and
within which it is nevertheless contained. The very quality and power of
sacrifice through which alone in the last analysis each of these promises can
be proclaimed, has meaning only because it asserts the spiritual nature of
man, and the Spiritual is itself one of the categories of mystery. Nor do the
Church's claims, already staggering, stop there. They include nothing less
than the claim that it is an extension of the Incarnation; that, as the Body
of Christ and the organ of the Holy Spirit, it is, in a profoundly mysterious
but a most real sense, God himself at work; that through it are mediated
all the processes of the divine redemption. The fact that over and over again
the Church's actual behaviour seems to be, and indeed is, a gross travesty
of claims so august and pretensions so illimitable, makes no difference to
the serene assurance with which the Church urges them. They are there,
implicit in the Church's scriptural title-deeds. Not even the awful and most
true contrast between what Christians claim for the Church and what they
actually make of it can undo claims thus grounded. Built on the rock and
into the heart of mystery, and enshrining in the core of its own being the
surging energy of God himself, the Church is armoured against all the
normal consequences of failure. It is indestructible, and the gates of hell
cannot prevail against it.

The historian is bound to view such material as this with discomfort. He knows that if he is to accept such categories as valid for the institution whose life he is to describe, his task must be the depressing one of putting on record the facts of a constant failure. But he cannot judge the Church by any standards less exacting than those which Christians themselves claim for it. Only very rarely, therefore, can the joy of describing success be his. Nor can he escape from his embarrassment by passing over to the theologian the duty of grappling with the meaning of these great affirmations of divine mysteries made flesh in visible societies. He is the servant of the theologian, but he cannot abdicate from the bearing of his own distinctive charge. He cannot put out of his mind the world of dogma, and dismiss it as irrelevant to his purpose. For, in the last resort, the history of the Church is neither more nor less than the history of its theology which is hardly less the concern of the historian than is history itself. He cannot escape from his material, however awkward it may make his task as an artist. He can abdicate from neither spiritual nor worldly throne. He must keep his feet on the solid earth, and lift his head above the clouds.

II · *The Nature of Anglicanism*

This book is a study of the Church of England in the last six decades of its history. But by spreading over many parts of the world the Church of England has given birth to the Anglican Communion of Churches, and thus to a Christian entity called Anglicanism, which, as a field of study, has difficulties all its own.

Anglicanism is a way of corporately following Christ. It is a way which bears the marks both of catholicism and of protestantism, for Anglican Churches are catholic and they are also reformed. The biggest achievement of Anglicanism is the worldwide Anglican Communion of Churches. Starting from the Church of England Anglicanism spread slowly over the globe. For the most part it followed the flag, and where British colonists or governments went the English Church went with them, to the Americas, to India, to Africa, to the Arctic, to West Indian plantations. Where the colonized or annexed lands won their independence, the British flag was pulled down, but the Anglican Church has remained, as in India after 1947, and in many parts of Africa today. Its position in any newly independent country, which, like Malaysia or Ceylon, may not be Christian at all, is necessarily uneasy, and the more so if by the time of independence it has not established a truly indigenous ministry. But it always stays on, and functions as best it can until easier days come. Anglicanism has spread also to many lands; such as China and Japan, where the British flag has never flown. Wherever this way of following Christ has spread, there it has taken root, and it has been proved to be a way which can be followed by peoples of every race, every colour, every level of culture and civilization. Always its essential spirit has been missionary, and every Anglican Church founded has looked to see what others it could establish. Anglicanism may have been begun and long sustained by the Church of England, but it is as wide as humanity because there is in it that which all humanity can adopt and make its own.

The achievement is impressive, and leads one to ask questions about what the Anglican spirit really is. The heart of Anglicanism ought to be found in whatever it is that successfully holds all the Anglican Churches in the world, from Japan westwards to California, in living communion with each other, and makes possible the decennial gathering of all their bishops in the Lambeth Conference. What is this tie? It is not our loyalty to the Scriptures, for they are not the exclusive possession of any Church. Neither establishment, nor any other particular relationship to the state has anything to do with it: the Church of England is the only Anglican Church which is established, and a Church may be in a nonconformist position, as is the Episcopal Church in Scotland, and still be Anglican. It is not that Anglican Churches are pervaded by the spirit of England. Tell that to the members of the Episcopal Church of the U.S.A. and see what they would say. The Anglican Church in Japan grows steadily more Japanese and eastern, that in Uganda steadily more African. Wherever the Anglican Church is planted it becomes all the time more native to its new soil and less native to the soil of the land whence it came. Yet all these Churches, African, Australian, Indian, and Chinese remain in formal and living communion with each other, cherish their Anglicanism, and regard Canterbury as their focal point and its archbishop as the natural chairman of their assemblies.

The tie that binds them is the Book of Common Prayer as the norm of their worship, and with its implications as the criterion of their corporate living of Christianity. The revisers of 1662 dimly foresaw something like this when they wrote that the new service for the baptism of those of riper years 'may always be useful for the baptizing of natives in our plantations'. The revisers of 1928 had the same thought in mind when they prefixed to their revision a preface which brought together the thought of a whole world to be won for Christ, and the thought of the Book of Common Prayer. 'We are living in a new world; it is ours, if we are true to the faith that is in us, to seek to make it a better world.' The book of Common Prayer has been retained, with slight modifications, by all the Anglican Churches as their official service book. In all of them, from Westminster Abbey to the tiny mission station on stilts in a Malayan jungle or the igloo church in a snowfield in the Arctic, the liturgical worship follows the same familiar Anglican pattern, with the same epistles, collects and gospels.

The common use of the Prayer Book Ordinal registers for the whole Church the continuance of the visible notes of catholicity, and the threefold ministry, given within the apostolic succession, ensures that the shape of the Church shall be the same in all its provinces in every land. Everywhere there is the ministry of bishops, priests, and deacons; and in every Anglican Church the Communion is celebrated by ministers who have been episcopally ordained. The admission to Communion is always by Confirmation by a bishop. This has the result of securing uniformity in outward shape between the different Anglican Churches, and without this it is hard to see how the whole Communion of Churches could be held together. But the Ordinal, the apostolic succession in the ministry, and the rite of confirmation, are not jealously preserved chiefly as a piece of mechanism which secures unity, but because all Anglicans believe that this church order is a part of the will of God for all Churches which prize their catholic status. This status is embodied still further in the ineradicably sacramental tone and emphasis of the Book of Common Prayer.

All this the Anglican Communion shares with the Roman Catholic and the Orthodox Churches. But where our system, as exemplified in the Book of Common Prayer and enshrined in centuries of history, differs most strongly from theirs is in the tremendous emphasis it places on the spiritual freedom of the individual. Throughout the whole range of our worship and our life the permissive 'You may' or 'You should' predominates over the dominical 'You must'. The Prayer Book says 'You must' to the clergy in the ordering of public worship, and in the recitation of the daily Offices of Morning and Evening Prayer. It says 'You must' to the laity only in the matter of communicating three times in the year, including Easter Day. This emphasis has coloured the whole expression of Anglicanism, and there is no Church in the world which so passionately believes in freedom and which so positively demands it from clergy and laity alike. Anglicanism is an assertion of spiritual freedom, and there is nothing of which the Anglican Communion is more completely convinced. As a result no priest in all Christendom is as free as an Anglican priest, and his freedom is more nearly absolute, safeguarded as it is at every turn and point, than that of any other stipendiary in any other profession in the modern world.

So strongly does Anglicanism believe that the best work is done and the best lives are lived when clergy and laity are trusted with freedom as nearly absolute as makes no matter that it faces squarely the fact that many will abuse that freedom, and that in consequence, some scandals, many inconsistencies, and much wastage must mar its picture. Anglicanism knows very well that it carries a higher proportion of spiritual passengers to weaken its witness than any other Church does. It knows too that the wastage under a system which so exalts freedom must be heavy. But its belief in freedom is so fundamental that it deliberately rates these considerable dangers as less than the gain which freedom brings. It is a sign of the maturity of Anglicanism. But the dangers of freedom are real, and though we cease to be Anglicans in heart and mind if we say they are more real than the benefits of freedom, we must never forget them. There are some words of Archbishop William Temple which put this gravely and clearly:

The whole desire of the Church has been to offer the fullness of God's help to every soul but never to dictate to any soul precisely how that soul may best receive the benefit. It sets a high standard for the individual member. No doubt it involves comparative failure for very many who might, by a more strict and more military discipline, have been led to a fuller use of all the means of grace than in fact they practise under the Anglican system. None the less I believe the Church of England did deliberately adopt that attitude and I believe it did so rightly. For with all the dangers—in fact, humanly speaking with all the certain loss involved —there is made possible in this way for all the members of the Church a fullness of individual apprehension and appropriation which is almost impossible and is certainly discouraged under a system which so marks out for men quite clearly their religious duties so that when they have performed these they feel that their duty is done.[1]

From this basic principle of freedom an important corollary follows. It is that in the Anglican system, or scale of values, the average counts for more than the exceptional. Anglican Churches have produced great men and women in abundance, and the Church of England in this century has been served by a long list of people of high eminence and uncommon ability. No one underestimates the value of heroism or disputes the immensity of our debt to their leadership. But in the Anglican way of life what really counts is the cumulative pressure upon society of the anonymous host of the average; and certainly the Anglican Communion believes that its own particular part of the Kingdom of God will best be occupied and won for Christ by the rank and file membership of the Church. Our real heroes are those whose names can never be known, the ordinary parish priest, and most of all the small band of the faithful who make the congregation at the Eucharist on weekdays. On their continued and obscure fidelity the entire worldwide Anglican Communion of Churches ultimately rests. If that were everywhere withdrawn for only one generation the Church would collapse and no amount of specially gifted leadership by those in places of eminence and authority could save it.

In the forefront of the Anglican array of battle, then, we place the average, the rank and file member of the Church. Our leaders are like the generals in a modern army—absolutely necessary for victory, but they do their leading from behind. Side by side with this tradition of Anglicanism, therefore, there has grown up another distinctively Anglican characteristic, the emphasis on the office of a pastor, and the primacy of this office over that of the prophet, the scholar, or the administrator. One could argue for ever whether this scale of comparative values is just or unjust. The point is that this is how Anglicans instinctively think or feel—how they *must*

---

[1] *Essays in Christian Politics* (Longmans, Green), 1927, pp. 201, 202.

think or feel if they are to lay all the responsibilities of heroism upon the anonymous and obscure average of churchpeople of all races and languages. For this emphasis on the pastoral is the only thing which could save the Anglican spiritual economy from the heresy of rating the collective above the individual, of preferring to deal with crowds and herds, of laboriously estimating power in terms of mass trends and tendencies, rather than the dealing with individual people, individual families, and small groups one at a time. The Anglican Church is essentially and fundamentally pastoral. It cannot be said too often for nobody will ever understand Anglicanism who ignores this basic fact. It is always the great pastors who remain beloved heroes for one generation after another. It is possible that Archbishop Laud did more for the Church than George Herbert, but through the centuries it is Herbert who is loved while Laud is at best admired. Those bishops are loved best who know their sheep and are known by them, like Chavasse the universally beloved 'Little Bishop' of Liverpool. Frank Weston, Bishop of Zanzibar, was known to have a passionate and sacrificial love for each one of his dear native spiritual children. His tiresomenesses, which were many, will all be forgotten but he will live on in Anglican memories because he was a wonderful pastor. Tell any Anglican priest in any part of the world that he is no prophet and he will cheerfully agree that this is indeed so. Tell him that he has no gifts of leadership and while he may not like it he will not greatly resent it. But tell him that he has no pastoral sense and he will be really hurt, and feel deeply wounded and insulted in the house of his friends. For he will feel, and rightly, that if it is really true he is without excuse. Few can be leaders, and fewer still prophets, but everybody can be a faithful pastor. The gift is utterly commonplace; anybody can have it who pays the price, and the price is heavy. For nine-tenths of the prosecution of its worldwide mission Anglicanism relies on the most commonplace of all spiritual gifts, the gift of the pastoral sense. Failure elsewhere can be redeemed, but failure there is for Anglicans absolute, and the dominical injunction which the Anglican Church has taken more deeply than any other is, 'Her sins which are many are forgiven for she loved much.'

No Church in the world is so completely Anglican in mind, temper and spirit as the Church of England for, after all, she is the mother of all Anglican Churches. This passion for freedom, this vision that real heroism lies in the average and the unknown, this belief that effectiveness lies in the slow cumulative pressure of community upon a society, this exaltation of the unspectacular pastoral office—all these mark the Church of England. No one who does not know this will ever understand her. No one who does not share this scheme of values will ever succeed in adequately explaining her to others. But undeniably it makes the process of explanation difficult. It is so much easier to write about the famous men and the resounding events. They are indeed part of the scene and cannot be ignored if the portrait is to be true. But if they occupy the stage all the time, as in so many ecclesiastical histories they do, the result is not a portrait but a cartoon.

III · *The Hero of Anglican History*

Through most of its history the Church of England has rested its case for existence and its hope of vindication on this principle, which takes organizational shape as the Parochial System. It is the method of ministry which the Church has always understood best. But if the primacy of the parish has been usual throughout the centuries, it has not been invariable. Periods have come when the parish lost some of its high standing, and its functions had to be rescued and re-established by being transferred to a variety of ancillary, non-parochial ministries. This happened in the eighteenth century when much of the basic work of the Kingdom of God was laid on the shoulders of the newly formed church societies; and since 1939 it has begun to happen again.

The Church of England is always parochial in the sense that all its ministries of every kind and in every place depend in the last resort on the worship offered and the teaching given in the parish church. It is usually, but not invariably, parochial in the sense that the mechanism of the parish provides nine-tenths of the ministry of the whole. The parochial system requires a period of comparative repose for its full working. In a period of great perplexity and restlessness, such as we entered in 1945, it begins to lose its primacy in the economy. It still remains there, so to speak, but functioning at less than its full power, and waiting for the day of its renewal.

But if the Church of England is parochial in outward shape and in normal methods of working, it has no limited vision. No one who knows it from within could reasonably urge such an accusation. The record and scope of its missionary enterprise down the centuries would be a sufficient answer to the charge. Of all human societies the Anglican and the Roman Catholic Churches are probably those which bring the most truly international mind and outlook to bear on the history of today. But though there are few parts of the world where the Anglican voice of praise cannot be heard, the Church of England remains fundamentally parochial. The whole range of its activity is built on the foundation of its parishes. The great majority of its priests are drafted at once into parish work, and most of them stay in that work until they retire or die. Most of its children are taught the love of God and man through their earlier, and more easily grasped, love of their own parish churches. By a thousand ties of tradition, sentiment, economics, and, deepest of all, by the common human need to learn the art of love by loving first of all the thing you can see, the Church of England is wedded to the parochial system. There is certainly need to put the marriage on rather a better basis, but no divorce is possible.

This gives to its parish priest a position as commanding as it is responsible. It means in practice that he and his band of faithful workers are the corner-stone of the entire building. The vicar can, if he chooses, block any reform, however urgent, and stifle any appeal, however august the authority which lies behind it. No movement in the Church has the ghost of a chance of success unless and until it wins the sympathy and commands the enthusiasm of the average parish priest. Against his verdict, which he slowly arrives at in the quiet of his study, and as he visits in his parish, where he finds out what his people are likely to think about it, there is really no appeal. He, with his workers, wields, in an absolute of freedom such as can hardly be seen anywhere else in the modern world, a power which is collectively overwhelming. If he is not interested in the missionary cause, it goes by default in that parish. If he has no vision of the hand of Christ stretched out in blessing over a world quarrelling, fighting, starving, and dying for lack of what God could do through a regenerated Church to redeem and save it, then the work and worship of his people is turned inward upon itself, and the Body of Christ in that parish quickly becomes little more than a society for mutual admiration. The level of the whole Church can never rise higher than the level of its parish clergy.

The real history of the Church of England is therefore mostly made in its parish churches, and the parish priest is the pivot on which that history turns. The Church might possibly survive a whole generation of impossible bishops and dead cathedrals. Not even in the worst days, happily, has this test been laid upon it. But it could not possibly survive a whole generation of bad vicars and lethargic parish churches. For the parish church is the centre of the Church's life, and 'the main stream of Anglican piety flows, as it has always flowed, through the parish churches: and therefore it is the parishes that are the exciting thing. The life of the parish is Church History.'[1]

IV · *The Ministry of Frustration*

It is, however, the distance separating worship from life as actually lived which sets the formidable problem of Christian witness. It is endemic in every age of Christendom, but in the twentieth century we see it in a very acute form. As the ministry of the Church of England unfolds itself and wanders down the many tortuous paths of its expression in the lifetime of the older among us, the perpetual dilemma, partly hidden from view in ages of comparative repose, becomes apparent, and presses for a resolution which it cannot find because in this world none exists.

In every age and in all circumstances it is the business of the Church to win souls for glory. This it does by the use of the timeless ministries of

[1] Charles Smyth, *A Study of Church History*. An Essay in the composite volume (ed. H. S. Box), *The Priest as Student* (S.P.C.K.), 1939, pp. 274–5.

worship, personal devotion, and pastoral fidelity. In England most of this work has always been done, and still is, by the parish. But it is also its business to claim the kingdoms of this world for the obedience of our Lord and of his Christ. This, though constantly attempted, is seldom accomplished; and it is a work which lies beyond the compass and the competence of the parish. It has to be done by the Church as a whole. It has never been more sedulously attempted than in this century, and seldom with less success. It is one thing to save a soul, and this is a constantly achieved fact. It is quite another thing to recall a nation, a civilization, a culture from the evil of its ways. Any Church which believes it is the Body of Christ is bound to attempt it, but it is a prophetic enterprise usually attended by failure.

The Old Testament prophets tried to do it. By rebuke and by persuasive pleading they set themselves to recall the people from their wickedness and infidelity, and to cause the makers of national policy to hear the word of God and to desist from their disastrous courses. They succeeded in other ways even more important, but in this almost all of them failed. Jesus himself warned the Jews many times of the consequences of their national defiances of God, and he—even he—failed too. The revolt against Rome took place; the siege of Jerusalem followed; his prophecy that the Temple would be utterly destroyed was fulfilled; and the dispersion of the Jewish people was completed for nearly two thousand years.

When it is face to face with what the Liturgy of St James centuries ago called 'the wanton insolence of the nations' in any of its forms, the Church can, and must, put on the garments of the prophet. It must protest, warn, and rebuke. It can suggest more creative policies. The powers that be, even if they do not attempt to silence the inconveniently critical voice, will seldom take any notice of it. They will almost never change their ways because of it. Frustrated though it is, the Church must continue to bear its witness. But after that there is nothing more that it can do. The prophet has failed and the pastor must take his place. The day of nemesis comes and the Church must stand by the nation which refused to heed its warning voice, take its share of the suffering, and help the people to bear creatively the inevitable punishment.

When 1900 dawned the Anglican prophets were, as we shall see, almost as full of foreboding as Jeremiah himself. They saw a lowering darkness ahead. But none of them dreamed for a single moment that before the century had run half its course the whole shape of the world would be changed by two major wars. It did not enter their heads even as a nightmare that in less than fifty years practices abandoned for hundreds of years as utterly uncivilized would become the normal, hardly noticed procedures of enlightened modern governments. Yet by 1950 imprisonment without trial, the slavery of prisoners of war, the deportation of whole populations into exile, and the use of torture to extract confessions had not only become commonplace among supposedly civilized nations, but were tolerated, and even defended, by their progressive citizens. Nor was this just the exceptional expediency of wartime. It is still the usual practice of several modern nations, and in several continents.

Frustration is a fact of the Church's life. It is very noticeable in this century but there is nothing new about it. Racial tolerance has to be preached to heedless governments. The rights of minorities have to be defended and the wickedness of aggression denounced to potentates and powers who have no intention whatever of hearkening to either. Prophetic voices must cry without ceasing but they do it in a wilderness where, as it almost seems, there are none to hear. The wielders of power, corrupted by what they have wooed, change few of their ways until disaster constrains them. Christian nations, embarked on unchristian courses, do not reverse them at the bidding of any Church.

The Church is always a relatively frustrated society. More than half its policies fail. A notorious example is the failure of every Church to reach the working masses of an industrialized society. Yet throughout the century the Church has tried harder and more consistently in this matter than in any.

The historian, then, who looks at the life of a great Church over a long sweep of time, is conscious of the fact that he must describe a society always in process of making great efforts, most of which are bound to fail. There are naturally success stories to be told, and plenty of them. But in a Church, just because it is what the state is not—a divine society—success is always superimposed upon a basic pattern of failure, and hope is kindled and kept alive on a foundation of frustration. The story of a Church which is true is a tale of sadness lit by gleams of joy, not a narrative of joyfulness overcast now and then by streaks of sadness. In and by some other world these balances are set right and made just; there is the communion of saints and the Church invisible. But the historian can take no cognizance of them because it is his business to describe the known, not to theorize about the unknown.

But because he describes a Church he has his being in the temple of doctrine. It is by faith that a Church keeps alive and the doctrines of a Church are the definitions of its faith. He cannot therefore forget that there is such a thing as a doctrine of necessary frustration, and that this bitter but constant experience has often proved itself to be the necessary condition of Christian progress. Here, as elsewhere, the Jewish prophets chart the course of all the centuries. They had to grapple with the fact of total national disaster. All that they had hoped to do for Israel lay in ruins about their feet. But out of this failure they created one of the most formative moments in the history of the world. The greatest of them all, whose name we do not even know, drew out of the agony the doctrine of the Suffering Servant. They had failed, but precisely through their failure they were able to go forward to the most glorious of successes. There is in fact a principle written into our human affairs that frustration can often be the condition of a triumph which, without it, would not have been possible. The historian who accepts this must not therefore shrink from paying full heed to the disappointed hopes, even to the failures, as well as to the successes of his Church.

2

The Victorian Legacy

I · *Rediscovery of Catholicity*

THE HEALTH of the Church of England during the fifty years before the
Oxford Movement has not yet ceased to be a controversial issue. Thus,
to the question, How dead or how alive was the Church of England in
the eighteen-thirties? there is no universally agreed answer. We see, for
example, how the Swedish Professor Yngve Brilioth protested against the
Anglo-Catholic historian's overdrawing of the darkness of the pre-
Tractarian Church. 'Since Dean Church,' he wrote, 'under the influence of
inferior spirits, a Vulgate has gradually been formed in the High Anglican
writing of history as regards its representation of the time before 1833.'[1]
He quoted many statistics to refute this picture. The next historian of the
Movement, C. P. S. Clarke, at once felt it necessary to contradict Brilioth,
and to bring once more out of the cupboard all the hoary cautionary tales.[2]

But it is now possible to answer some of the secondary questions raised
by such a theme with a confidence which few are likely to question. The
state of Anglican religion as a whole may have been at once more vigorous
than the Anglo-Catholic and more lethargic than the Protestant historians
are yet prepared to admit. But both parties now agree that certain of the
aspects and needs of the Christian religion, on which it is at all times the
business of the Church to insist, were hardly emphasized at all in the years
immediately before the Oxford Movement. Every one of the leaders of that
Movement, for example, insisted that its work was largely to remind the
Church of England of a clause in the creed, 'I believe in the Holy Catholic
Church', which for years had been almost forgotten. No one now doubts
that their charge was accurately and soberly drawn. None of the great
leaders, however, formulated the indictment in words as vivid and prophetic as those used by Dr Thomas Sikes, Rector of Guilsborough, in

[1] *The Anglican Revival* (Longmans, Green), 1925, pp. 6–11.
[2] *The Oxford Movement and After* (Mowbray), 1932, pp. 22–31.

Northamptonshire. In 1833 he was talking with Pusey, who afterwards wrote down what his friend had said, and, in 1834, included them in a report which he submitted to the Archbishop of Canterbury.

Wherever I go about the country [he said to Pusey] I see amongst the clergy a number of very amiable and estimable men, many of them much in earnest and wishing to do good. But I have observed one universal want in their teaching: the uniform suppression of one great truth. There is no account anywhere, so far as I can see, of the one Holy Catholic Church.

Sikes then went on to speak of the seriousness of this omission, saying that religious teaching in England was inevitably lopsided because of it; and he ended by giving utterance to a most remarkable prophecy, which the fullness of time exactly fulfilled:

Our confusion nowadays is chiefly owing to the want of it; and there will be even more confusion attending its revival. The effects of it I even dread to contemplate, especially if it were to come suddenly. And woe betide those, whoever they are, who shall, in the course of Providence, have to bring it forward. It ought especially of all others to be a matter of catechetical teaching and training. The doctrines of the Church Catholic and the privileges of Church membership cannot be explained from pulpits; and those who will have to explain it will hardly know where they are, or which way they are to turn themselves. There will be one great outcry of Popery from one end of the country to the other. It will be thrust on minds unprepared, and on an uncatechized Church. Some will take it up and admire it as beautiful; others will be frightened and run away and reject it; and all will want a guidance which one hardly knows where they shall find.[1]

Sikes had put his finger on the real weakness of the Church of England as Newman knew it in his Anglican days. He forecast exactly the task lying before its theology and its worship throughout the years of the century. 'I believe in the Holy Catholic Church'—in 1800 hardly any Anglicans perceived the significance or rejoiced in the glory of this claim. In 1900 the catholicity of the Church of England was eagerly asserted by all instructed churchpeople. In the religious sphere, this was one of the two great achievements of the Victorian era. The other, of course, was its missionary expansion.

The rediscovery of the catholicity of the Anglican Church as the main task of its witness and theology throughout the nineteenth century is the thread by which the enquirer can guide himself through the maze of vexed questions about the health or sickness of the Church of that day. By using it he can come to a reasonable judgement about the real nature and the value of the legacy which Victorian Anglicanism bequeathed to the present century. Grasping that thread, then, let us boldly enter the maze, and ask

[1] Quoted in S. C. Carpenter, *Church and People* (S.P.C.K.), 1933, pp. 82–4, from the Life of Pusey, vol. I, p. 257. Partly quoted also in C. P. S. Clarke, *op. cit.*, p. 12. Sikes belonged to the 'Hackney Phalanx' of pre-Tractarian High Churchmen. He knew of what he spoke. His views and teaching had already made him very unpopular (Clarke, p. 12).

the difficult questions about the health of the Church in the first half of the nineteenth century; remembering always that it is in the average parish, the average cathedral, and the average mission station that we must look for an answer.

II · *Four Average Parishes*

The average parish—where and what is it? We must not look first at the statistics or the visitation returns. They tell but a tenth of the story, or less than that. Still less reliable is the testimony drawn from the speeches, books, and letters of contemporary ecclesiastical reformers. These always look first for evidence of the state of affairs which it is their mission to remedy. They describe what they see, but, being human like the rest of us, their vision has its limits, and its blind spots. They tend to see the evils they are looking for, and to miss the faithfulness which lies too close to be as easily discerned. Nor must we go to the formal histories. None of them has really done justice to the parish life of the Church from 1750 to 1850, and the then vicars of England have been forced to share the evil reputation which their bishops had earned. These histories are dealt with very faithfully, if somewhat summarily, in a devastating judgement by a modern Church historian and parish priest, Canon J. E. W. Wallace:

The Church has had interested critics and a bad Press for over a century. On the one side, the Romans, and on the other, the Methodists in religion; and the Whigs and Liberals in politics, were all determined to blacken the National Church as much as they could. Add to this such difficulties as arose from a reliance on Church Rates for money, and from such consequences as the formation of civil parishes whenever new ecclesiastical parishes were created, and the prospect of a new Peer of the Realm for every new bishoprick. Add to this the tendency of any new movement to arrogate to itself not merely novelty, but also, and perhaps chiefly, reform of its wicked and effete predecessor. Thus the Evangelicals are found pouring contempt on the Hanoverians, and the Anglo-Catholics in turn on the Evangelicals. Add the obvious attraction to such writers as Dickens, with a strong vein of caricature, of such a broad, easy target as the National Church. Add finally the quiet and unadvertised character of the work of the parish priests in town and country. Add all these together, and you will see that those who like to puff themselves up by knocking others down can have a grand field-day against the Church of the Napoleonic and post-Napoleonic periods without over-exerting their wits or their historical acumen.

The last sentence is a little severely phrased, but the whole judgement is nearly as accurate as it is vivid. It is at any rate a good and sufficient warning not to go hunting for the average parish in the average historical work. To disregard these obvious streams of evidence, and yet to find examples of the average parish of the day is not the easiest of tasks. So few ordinary parishes are articulate. But the quest is by no means impossible, for indirect evidence does exist in printed form. It is not as plentiful as we could wish, but what there is of it is both interesting and significant. From this evidence we will choose four samples. Each one of the four is a perfectly typical, perfectly ordinary parish.

HAWORTH, YORKSHIRE

No parish could be more ordinary than Haworth was in 1820 when Patrick Brontë was instituted as its vicar. Yet no parish has ever bequeathed to posterity a greater mass of the most valuable of all kinds of evidence about its health. Its rectory is the most celebrated parsonage in existence. But its fame was almost wholly posthumous for it rested on the three sisters and their brother who lived there. From a religious point of view it was simply one parish among scores of others all over Yorkshire and Lancashire, in no way inherently distinguishable from them. Yet there is none about which we know more. The patient and most exhaustive research into every detail of that famous household has rarely been conducted by those who were much interested in the spiritual health of the parish. Hence it is the best evidence we could desire.

The research has provided us with a portrait of the rector of Haworth hardly less clear and vivid than the portraits of his children. It is the picture of a priest who did his duty according to his lights as well as he possibly could. Faithfully and constantly he visited his people. He knew his sheep and was known of them—all of them. He looked carefully after his church day school. His Sunday school had many scholars, and was regularly supplied with an adequate number of voluntary teachers, whom his daughters periodically entertained to tea at the rectory. His sermons were thoughtful rather than commanding. They always lasted for half an hour, neither more nor less: not even when he became too blind to see his watch did his time vary. The parish was always furnished with curates on what now seems a rather lavish scale. At one time there were three. Perhaps it was then that Charlotte Brontë was moved to begin *Shirley*, that classic scourge of curates, with the words, 'Of late years an abundant shower of curates has fallen upon the north of England; they lie very thick upon the hills.'

Charlotte's dislike of curates had experience behind it. Her father's curates were the weak spot in the work of Haworth parish church. Probably they were not quite so much of a 'self-seeking, vain, and empty race' as *Shirley* suggests. Nor were they at all times so exasperating as on the day when Charlotte was hot and tired with baking, and they all rushed in, uninvited, for tea. 'I would have served them out their tea in peace', she wrote, 'but they began glorifying themselves and abusing Dissenters in such a manner that my temper lost its balance, and I pronounced a few sentences sharply and rapidly, which struck them all dumb.'[1] It is not surprising. No ordinary curate could be expected to appear at his best in that house, with

[1] Quoted in Ernest Dimnet, *The Brontë Sisters* (Cape), 1927, p. 108.

one daughter glowering at him, and the other surveying his littleness with a terrific, paralysing disdain. But make whatever allowances we may for Charlotte's notorious views about all curates but one, it remains true that the Haworth curates were poor specimens. They had misunderstood Dr Pusey's teaching, but had greedily sucked in all his fanaticism. They had none of his balance, and little of his knowledge. They were always making trouble with the Dissenters by their tirades in the pulpit; and in a parish half full of Baptists and Methodists this did not noticeably serve the cause of Christian charity. The sort of thing that could, and often did happen is illustrated by the episode of the militant and reverend Mr Weightman, who was promptly nicknamed Miss Celia Amelia by Charlotte and Emily. He made the parish church ring with the fury of his attacks on the local non-conformists; and they, not to be outdone, visited their wrath on Mr Brontë by holding indignation meetings in his study, and by refusing to pay the church rates. With very great skill the rector calmed them sufficiently to persuade them to close their chapels the next Sunday, and to come to the church to hear the explanation of Mr Weightman's conduct. The Sunday came and the pews were filled with Baptists and Methodists. In the morning a fellow-curate of Weightman's 'crushed them with a terrible sermon. In the evening Mr Weightman, without mercy for his poor, defenceless listeners, finished them by a discourse so learned, violent and eloquent that even Charlotte, hostile as she was to the idea of Puseyism, was filled with admiration.'[1]

Poor Mr Brontë! Plainly he was less strong than dutiful. Why did he not preach himself? But even such a display as this was a sin of vigorous religion, not a symptom of languid indifference. And even among the Haworth curates there was always the exception. He was Mr A. B. Nicholls, who won universal praise, and, at last, the hand of Charlotte. 'He has greatly promoted the interests of the National Sunday Schools', wrote his rector to the S.P.G., when Nicholls was toying with the idea of becoming a missionary; while a lay schoolmaster who knew his work testified, 'for uprightness and steadiness of Conduct, Activity in the prosecution of his pastoral labours, and especially successful management of the parochial schools, there is not to be found his equal'.[2]

At Haworth, in fact, the people were visited; the children were taught on weekdays and Sundays; all the parochial ministrations were regular and devoted; and the people went to church. In many ways, no doubt, religion was misdirected and misrepresented—it always is. But it was alive and not dead; and Haworth was remarkable among parishes only in the daughters who lived in the parsonage, and in no other way.

[1] Dimnet, *op. cit.*, p. 73.
[2] 'The Nicholls Correspondence with the S.P.G.' An article published in *The Times* on October 18, 1937, by the Rev. W. F. France.

GREAT HARWOOD, LANCASHIRE

Another example of parochial obscurity, on which the accidents of time have bestowed a flicker of limelight, comes from the other side of the Pennines. On the county border between East Lancashire and the West Riding of Yorkshire under one of the ribs of the backbone of England, the Pennine Chain, lies the town of Great Harwood. Its pride is still, and always has been, its ancient parish church, which dates back to eight hundred years ago, and, which like so many others of the same date in the district, was built originally to serve the spiritual needs of nomad bands of charcoal burners who plied their trade in the vast Pendle Forest.

It happens, however, that it is possible to lift a corner of the curtain of obscurity which hides the life of Great Harwood parish, and to show a few glimpses of a Lancashire church in characteristic action from a hundred to a hundred and fifty years ago. A stroke of sheer luck makes it possible. In 1819 a new vicar was appointed, Robert Dobson by name. He died in 1861. In his own person he happened to combine mildly antiquarian leanings with a methodical and businesslike bent of mind. The former quality prompted him to collect all the documents he could lay his hands on about the earlier history of his parish; the latter habit caused him to keep the drafts of the more important letters he wrote. With a touching care for the curiosity of his successors, he generally wrote these drafts (in what must certainly be one of the world's most difficult handwritings) on the backs of such letters as they were intended to answer. He must have died before he had the chance to arrange and edit these papers. A hundred years later they were found by one of his modern successors (who happens to be the present writer), quite by chance, in a small black oak chest, lying under a bench in a dark corner of the tower.

These papers covered two periods fairly fully, 1790 to 1800, and 1820 to 1830. In the first of these periods the vicar was Borlaise Willock. There is plenty of other evidence to prove that he really was the vicar; and that is just as well, for anyone who reads these papers might very well come to the conclusion that he was the town clerk. There was a local quarrel going on about a toll bar on the new road to Whalley. The town was in danger of losing a safe and easy revenue of £250 a year. But not if Willock could help it! He called public meetings of the 'respectable inhabitants'; he canvassed most of the county notabilities; he skilfully contrived to win the support of Lord Derby—then, as now, the sure way of guiding a Lancashire enterprise to success; he even appointed a private parliamentary agent in London to pilot a special amendment to the relevant bill through the House of Commons. In the end the townspeople kept their toll bar and their £250. They owed it solely to the vicar. His tradition was plainly that of the old episcopal statesman of the Middle Ages. He was in the line of pastoral succession which makes fullest proof of its ministry by immersion in public work. The papers in the box had nothing to say about what sort of parish priest he was. But in his day, whether the parish church counted for the right things or not, it certainly counted for something. It was alive and not dead.

In Dobson's day, 1819 to 1861, the parish church still counted—and for more and better things. Dobson did not leave behind him many written memorials of his ministry, but he did leave a legend of pastoral faithfulness, which, after more than a hundred years, is still green in that parish. There is a portrait of him hanging on the vestry wall. It shows a man about sixty years old, with a clean-shaven, firm chin resting on a puffy cravat, a wide mouth drawn down at the corners, clear resolute eyes, and a rather dour but determined expression.

He needed all his resolution, and his dourness too. In his time the parish church was faced by a desperate and grim crisis, the cotton famine of the thirties and forties. In that day Lancashire was in the throes of the change from handloom to powerloom weaving. Great Harwood had been a laggard community in the race. Its people still lived on handloom weaving, which is only another way of saying that they could hardly live at all. All over East Lancashire the distress was great, but in Great Harwood it was desperate beyond anything known in Blackburn or Burnley, a condition of affairs to be exactly repeated a hundred years later. In London a committee was formed to administer a great public distress fund for Lancashire. Dobson was its local almoner. As such he wrote copious and innumerable reports to the committee on the condition of the people, on how he spent their grants, and requesting more.

I will now endeavour [he wrote on one typical occasion] to give the Board the necessary information, so far as I am able. I am sorry to inform you that the distress in this place is not abated at all, but on the increase. There is no advance in wages for handloom weavers. The present wages for a weaver will not be more than 3s. or 3s. 6d. for an able bodied man, and that will not do more than keep himself. When two or three children are dependent on him for support there is nothing for them except what must come from the poor rate and the relief fund. I could mention many cases of the above kind. During the last six months a large calico printworks where a great number of the inhabitants of Great Harwood used to have regular employ have not had more than two days' work in a week, and the poor fellows come begging for a day's work or two in a week to keep them alive. I have made a personal visit from house to house in the last fortnight, and have found the articles the poor had received still in their possession, and have also enquired into their wants of clothing. I have since distributed the committee's grant, and in so doing I have exceeded the grant of £60 by nearly £30. That deficit I trust the liberality of the London Committee to make up. When I say I spent the grant [? two words indecipherable] I wish to be understood as acting with a very sparing hand. I require more than 20s. a family for many families to make them at all comfortable.

To their everlasting credit the reply of the committee to this confession was to send back not £30 but £50, and that without a single word of reproach.

Dobson wrote a large number of reports of this kind; and the material for them was gathered by incessant pastoral visiting throughout what was then a fairly large parish. One of these reports stated the facts statistically. Out of a population of 2,000, only 150 were in full work. Their average week's wages was 3*s*. 4*d*. Relief was needed for 1,400. Had it not been for the vicar very few of those 1,400 would have got any relief. As it was, some men did fall dead in the streets from starvation. If the vicar's energy could have saved them, they would have been saved. His life and work became one long struggle against destitution, and he saved the situation. This was his life's work, his chief claim to his people's gratitude. He must himself have set this value on it. He left behind him hardly any evidence of how he discharged his spiritual ministry; but he carefully preserved every scrap of paper dealing with his work during the Cotton Famine. Perhaps it is significant, as it is certainly interesting to add, that the one document still remaining which casts any light on his work as a priest is a set of *Questions Preparatory to Confirmation*, which he composed and had printed for his confirmation candidates. The first answer disposes very firmly of any popish idea that confirmation is a sacrament. It is a reasonable inference that in this parish serious, if mistaken, preparation was attempted.

A recent historian has said of the Diocese of Chester in 1824, in which all Lancashire was then included, that it was 'sadly out of order. The prevalence of hastily admitted ordinands and of ill-paid, non-resident, idle, secularly employed, or even vicious clergy, irregularity and scandal in the matter of Church Services, short tenure of the see by bishops, had made the diocese a byword.'[1] Yet here was at least one of its obscurer parishes and parish priests to whom not one of those epithets could at that time be applied. Is it reasonable to suppose that this one stood alone?

CAMERTON, SOMERSET

In 1800 John Skinner entered upon the possession of the rectory of Camerton, near Bath. His preferment was due to an unabashed piece of nepotism, for his uncle, the rector of Bennington, in Hertfordshire, purchased the advowson in order to be able to present to him a comfortable independence. In practice, however, the position turned out to be far from comfortable: to a conscientious man the incumbency of Camerton was as exhausting and exacting a task as the Church had to offer; and no one can read a single page of Skinner's diary[2] without realizing that he was extremely conscientious. Skinner was among the company of clerical diarists, such as Cole, Woodforde, and Kilvert, who have become famous in our own day. His diary, however, is sad and gloomy. He seemed chronically

---

[1] S. C. Carpenter, *op. cit.*, p. 90.

[2] *A Journal of a Somerset Rector*, John Skinner A.M. Antiquary, 1772–1839. British Museum MSS., Nos. 33673–33728. Edited by Howard Combs and the Rev. Arthur N. Bax, M.A. (John Murray), 1930. See also an essay on Skinner by Virginia Woolf in *The Common Reader*, Second Series (Hogarth Press), 1932.

unable to like either his children or his people, and he could not conceal the irritation they caused him. Thus as both father and parish priest he was a failure; and he ended his life by shooting himself in the wood behind his house. This was in 1839. His diary, or at least the published parts of it, began in 1822, when he had been rector for twenty-two years, and it ended suddenly, in the middle of an unfinished sentence, ten years later.

It would not have been easy for an archangel to be a good rector of Camerton. The parish lay on the edge of the Somerset coalfield. Its population had lately trebled, and the majority of the people were colliers. Feudalism and industry proved a bad mixture. It produced oppression and fickleness in the gentry, and chronic drunkenness in the people. The choir would come drunk to church. Skinner would then forbid them to sing the service; whereupon they would noisily and defiantly leave the church. Then Skinner would use the most extraordinary methods to end the impasse. On one occasion he had resort to bad doggerel verse:

> Some merry musicians quite fresh from the barrel
> Last Sunday resolved with Religion to quarrel,

and so on for twenty lines or so, and ending:

> Whilst the oaths they have sworn, and vile songs they have sung,
> Will add fuel abundant to the flame on their tongue.

This he sent anonymously to the inn where the choirmen went in the evenings; and, incredibly, it worked, for a few days later the drunken singers

called to say they were very sorry for their behaviour in leaving the Church in the manner they did, and would never be guilty of such bad conduct again, and hoped I would permit them to sing in future.[1]

Among the farmers and gentry there was not seldom a real conspiracy against Skinner's authority. The Bishop of Wells protected him from it as much as he could, and Skinner never approached him in vain. Tithe was a constant irritant; and tithing-time was wont to produce violent scenes, with farmers running at their unhappy rector 'like a wild bull and bellowing as such'; and ending with an unseemly rough and tumble between the rector's agents and the farmer's men.[2] Camerton, in fact, was anything but a desirable living to have. Skinner never found the way to its heart. Perhaps he could not find it through his own defect: perhaps in that generation the people themselves fenced every way.

But if diligent faithfulness and an absolute sincerity could have found the way, Skinner would not have had to endure the wretched life which was his. These qualities he had to the full, and Camerton was emphatically a well-shepherded parish. Hardly a day passed without an entry in the diary about sick visiting; and no sickness ever came to his knowledge and was then neglected. When he took the sacrament to a house of sickness

[1] *Journal*, pp. 8, 10, 22.   [2] *Journal*, p. 167.

he did one of the few things which gave him real and deep joy. In his church the sacraments were regularly and reverently administered; and the Word of God as carefully and systematically preached. It is true that Skinner, by the evidence of his own words, convicts himself of preaching *at* particular individuals during public services. But while nothing excuses that, it is certainly true that he put a high value on the ministry of the word. There seem to have been regular and properly conducted confirmations in that part of Somerset. On July 21, 1823, at the curious hour of nine o'clock in the morning, there was a confirmation at Frome, at which the Bishop of Gloucester acted for the Bishop of Wells. 'There were about five hundred confirmed, and an impressive charge was afterwards delivered by Dr Ryder; I mean impressive because it came from the heart.'[1] The day before Skinner had valiantly done a very difficult thing, from which every parish priest in every age shrinks; he had turned down fourteen out of his fifteen confirmation boys. 'Two classes of the collier boys attended to say their Catechism after dinner, but could not recollect what they had formerly learned, and when I explained it to them they were so very ignorant and ill-behaved that I did not think I could in conscience give them tickets for Confirmation.'[2]

Skinner had as strong a social as a pastoral conscience, and was fearless in fighting against powerful oppression. In Camerton feudalism was still trying to maintain itself; and the feudal magnates, being frightened for their position, were merciless. Skinner never allowed himself to be in the least daunted by their power; and the diary quotes more than one letter like this to a feudal magnate:

> *Camerton Parsonage,*
> *January 25th, 1831.*
>
> Sir,
>   As the Minister of this Parish I have a right to ask whether you can reconcile it to your conscience that your old servant, Swift, and his wife, who have served you and your relatives for fifty years, should die destitute of every comfort, being in more absolute want than any paupers in the place? I could scarcely believe my ears last Easter Vestry, when you desired the parish pay of 5s. a week (for two people each more than 80 years of age) should be lowered. For your own sake before you die, Sir, I hope you will think and act differently.
>
> JOHN SKINNER[3]

From a country vicar to a local magistrate that is strong and brave language.

HOLY TRINITY, BRIGHTON

One of the most remarkable parishes in England during this period was, however, in Brighton. The town had recently received a new vicar, Robert Anderson. Strictly speaking, he was not an incumbent so much as a perpetual curate or 'proprietor' of Trinity Chapel, which had been taken over

---

[1] *Journal*, p. 57.   [2] *Journal*, p. 56.   [3] *Journal*, p. 269.

from the dissenters in 1826; and which was later to provide F. W. Robertson with his pulpit. Anderson was an instance of how a most remarkable man may none the less remain hidden in obscurity, both during his own time and after his death, until an accident happens which reveals his greatness. In his case the accident was the chance discovery by Dr Lowther-Clarke, the editorial secretary of the S.P.C.K., of an old book, which Anderson's widow had published with Rivingtons, called *Practical Religion exemplified by Letters and Passages from the Life of the late Rev. Robert Anderson, Perpetual Curate of Trinity Chapel, Brighton*. Dr Lowther-Clarke made it the subject of an article in the March 1940 number of *Theology*.[1]

The greater part of the book is devotional in tone and intent, being concerned with the way in which Anderson found expression of his personal life of religious devotion. But his letters and diaries also give a vivid picture of the state of the parish life of Holy Trinity, Brighton, in the eighteen-thirties. Unquestionably, Anderson worked with splendid and untiring devotion; and his people expected this work from him and responded to it. He said his daily services at home. He held frequent and regular celebrations of the Holy Communion on weekdays as well as on Sundays. He had a weeknight service every Wednesday evening. All his Sunday school teachers were expected to attend a weekly preparation class. At these classes Anderson read them 'passages from the most approved divines, Leighton, Hooker, and others of the same kind, and closing with an exposition of Scripture and a prayer'.[2] Most of his mornings were given to the work, the really hard and difficult work, of listening to the troubles of those who came to consult him; there might be as many as thirty in a morning. In the afternoon he would visit an average of fifteen homes; and he often continued his visiting in the evening, ceasing always at ten o'clock, the time for his family prayers. Probably there was hardly another parish in England where as much time and trouble was given to the preparation of confirmation candidates, and to their spiritual care when they had been confirmed. Dr Lowther-Clarke quotes with the greatest emphasis a passage from his wife's book bearing on this point. 'Lastly,' writes Dr Lowther-Clarke, 'I must transcribe a passage on Confirmation which is strikingly different from the usual account of pre-tractarian ways.'

The mention of our Bishop (Otter, 1836–1840) brings me to the subject of the Confirmation which took place yesterday at St. Peter's church. Though only two years have elapsed since our last Confirmation, there were 830 candidates for that holy rite: and nothing could be more admirable than the order with which the whole was conducted. The vicar, in full canonicals, walked at the head of each file, as they approached the table, and his curate, also in full canonicals, headed

[1] Dr Lowther-Clarke quotes from the sixth edition of 1855. The book thus enjoyed an exceptionally long and popular life; which makes the forgetfulness of Anderson the stranger.
[2] Anderson, p. 222.

each file as they returned to their seats. The effect was very striking, as we followed these shepherds with their little flocks, moving silently along the different aisles of that beautiful church; while the good Bishop, as the representative of our Lord, stood with love in his heart, and blessings in his hands, to animate and encourage these followers of the Lamb, for their approaching encounter against the enemies of their salvation! I am greatly in hopes that, of the ninety-nine whom I examined and recommended for Confirmation, almost, if not entirely, all will approach the Lord's table next Sunday; and after having thus completed this blessed portion of my ministerial labours, which has occupied me for nearly two months . . .[1]

Holy Trinity, Brighton, was obviously a parish unknown to Dr Thomas Sikes. There the Holy Catholic Church was much more than a forgotten clause in the creed. It was the subject of a living body of teaching, and the daily inspiration of a whole congregation.

III · The Sacramental Test

The story of these four parishes is sufficient to show that the Tractarians did not find quite so universally dry and dusty a soil for their seed as their historians have generally claimed. It would of course be absurd to claim too much and generalize too fluently from the evidence provided by only four parishes. But there is plenty of other evidence, and that of the most trustworthy kind, to show that in the days immediately before the Oxford Movement the standard of pastoral faithfulness in those parishes which were blessed with conscientious vicars was very high.[2] On the other hand, there is also plenty of evidence, far more frequently produced, to show that in many other parishes the standard of pastoral faithfulness was low. Where it was low, it was probably lower in that day than it has ever been before or since.

The evidence, taken as a whole, leaves no doubt that in 1830 a concealed but serious disease was gnawing at the heart of the Church of England. To recite the well-known symptoms of absenteeism, pluralism, and the rest does not constitute a sufficient diagnosis. It is necessary to ask what were the limitations which the high standard of faithfulness accentuated or concealed. At Haworth and Great Harwood the parish church was alive, and each vicar was devoted. Each was as good as the average best of his day. At Camerton the vicar was just as devoted as they, but the parish was

---

[1] Anderson, p. 211.

[2] Brighstone, in the Isle of Wight, is another sample of the healthy parish life to which this abundant evidence points. When Samuel Wilberforce was its vicar, the people had two sermons every Sunday, and the children were catechized every Sunday afternoon. There was one service with a sermon on a weekday evening, to which hymns were added on Saints' Days. Three hamlets were included in the parish: each one had regular cottage services. At one of these hamlets, as, of course, at Brighstone itself, there were constant classes for confirmation candidates, and for the communicants. See A. R. Ashwell's *Life of the Rt Rev. Samuel Wilberforce* (Murray), vol. I, 1880, pp. 56–7.

passing through so difficult a phase in its history that he could do but little, for he lacked the one thing needful. Holy Trinity, Brighton, on the other hand, was a very exceptional parish, rising far above the best of its time. It is true that it depended too completely on the strength of its vicar, though in this it was true to the Anglican system as a whole, which has always been endangered by precisely this defect.

What, then, is it which the Brighton parish possessed, and the others lacked? It is, of course, the note and the atmosphere of corporate holiness. The records give no hint or suggestion that in these parish churches, or in thousands of others, where really good work was being steadily done, anyone dreamed of applying to their lives the standards of a true church suggested by St Paul in Ephesians. All their energy was being poured into duties of real but none the less secondary importance. They were often real communities. They did much good. Many had ample reason to bless their names. But they missed 'the many splendoured thing'—no doubt because they had never been taught to value it and did not know how to find it. These parishes, in fact, had not become the very thing which it is the chief business of every parish church in every age and clime to become, a redeeming society of Christian holiness. They did not think of the people of the parish church as the Body of Christ; and they left behind them but little trace of any understanding that they were in fact a part of the Holy Catholic Church. They energetically immersed themselves in the social work of the neighbourhood, and in the necessary mechanism of parish life. But of their true status as Households of Faith, they showed but little trace of any awareness.

In the parish of Holy Trinity, Brighton, on the other hand, there were at least the rudiments of such an awareness. They appear most clearly in Anderson's account of a confirmation, for this shows the great part which sacraments played in the worship and witness of the parish. Where sacraments are properly valued and regularly received there is churchmanship: where they are lightly valued and little used, there is none. The great weakness of the Church of England was that a parish like Holy Trinity, Brighton, and a parish priest like Anderson, were extremely exceptional. Thus the Church had lost sight of the value of churchmanship; and the lessons which Hooker, Laud, and Jewel had taught had been largely forgotten. (Anderson's Sunday school teachers, it will be remembered, had Hooker regularly read to them.) This forgetfulness was due to the fact that all English non-Roman Christians had almost ceased to value sacraments, and wholly failed to perceive the essentially sacramental structure of life. This is the real burden of the indictment of the Anglo-Catholic historians. The familiar cautionary tales they tell—and copy from each other—of the Bad Old Days are nearly always tales of horrible confirmations, casual ordinations, and disgraceful communions. Some of the early leaders of the Oxford Movement were themselves infected by the prevailing sacramental apathy,

though they did not know it. It took Newman himself some years to learn
that to be a high churchman involved becoming a practising sacramentalist. In his Anglican days he was hardly a sacramentalist at all. He was
ordained priest on May 29, 1825, and he did not celebrate his first Communion until August 7. In his parish church he did not institute a weekly
Eucharist until 1837, having taken no less than four years to 'consider'
this revolutionary step. Nor did he say his matins in church till 1834, in
spite of the perfectly clear direction in the Prayer Book.[1] It may be said
that the early Tractarians mistook the natural order of things, in that
they emphasized churchmanship first, and stumbled upon its foundation
of sacramentalism afterwards. Even Dean Church, it has been said, very,
very rarely gave his Somerset country parish an early Eucharist. But once
they had learned to put the two together they sowed the seed of a rich
flowering of stately and beautiful public worship, of a renewed sense of
Christian social obligation, of our Lord's desire for his children to desire
and find the beauty of holiness through their membership of the Catholic
Church, his Body and his instrument.

IV · *The Hardened Arteries of the Establishment*

The nineteenth century was one of swift and urgent change in every field
of human life. From 1815 to 1900 almost every phase of this development
was led, and, in a sense, controlled by Great Britain. If all this new life was
to be saved from materialism and won for Christ, the giant's share of the
spiritual burden must necessarily fall on the Church of England. But the
Church entered the century with palsied limbs and hardening arteries. Its
heart was beating strongly, for at the centre still lay, as it had always lain,
the ideal of faithfulness in the parochial ministry. Because the heart of the
body was still robust and healthy, it was possible to quicken the limbs, and
restore to the arteries their freedom. But that took time: it is not wholly
accomplished even today. In the meantime the pace of the development of
the secular machinery of life was faster than the pace of reform in the
Church. Throughout the nineteenth century the Church was always trying
to catch up with its better equipped secular rival, and never quite succeeding. Thus the history of the Church in that century is a story of growth,
change, and reform, all of them focused upon and held together by the
urgent need to quicken the motion of its sluggish pulse.

The handicaps, which, at the beginning of the century, forced upon the
Church a gait far too lethargic to meet the challenge of the times, were
many. The long lack of any clear and systematic teaching about catholicity
and churchmanship had given a fillip to that fissiparous sectarianism which
is the eternal bane of protestantism. The last great religious movement in
England, the Evangelical Revival, had driven Wesley and his followers into

[1] Carpenter, *op. cit.*, p. 123.

action which necessarily involved their schism. In the Anglican congregations which it affected, it had done much to save their souls, but it had done hardly less to foster the sectarian habit of mind. Most of the great Anglican figures of the Revival, Simeon of Cambridge, Venn of Huddersfield, Cadogan of Reading, and Berridge of Everton, had staked their all on their personal genius in the pulpit leading to individual conversions among the people. Only Simeon stood for any maintenance of definite church order. The others habitually thought, wrote, and spoke as if one entered the Church by conversion, not by the sacraments of baptism and confirmation.[1] Cadogan's great congregation at Reading was utterly dispersed by schism and split into no less than four separate sects, within forty years of his death.[2] When Venn retired from Huddersfield, he was succeeded by a minister not to his taste. He then urged the malcontents in his old congregation to withdraw from the parish church, and to set up their own bethel. He sent subscriptions, and personally canvassed for the building fund of the new chapel.[3] When, to the changes and chances of an utterly unpredictable system of patronage, there was added the profound error of building a congregation around a specially gifted man, rather than around the Church with its worship and sacraments, that sort of thing was bound to happen. But it happened so frequently, during, and immediately after the Evangelical Revival that schism had almost ceased to wear the appearance of sin.

Moreover, those who, like the Haworth curates, regarded all schismatics not merely as sinners but also as national traitors, and thought of every dissenter as a schismatic, did not give people any good reason to suppose that they themselves were in a state of grace. The evangelicals were very zealous for the Lord. They were devoted and self-sacrificing. They mostly had an urgent sense of social responsibility, which had already become the haft of the axe which was chopping at the roots of the tree of slavery. But it was a limited sense. They passionately objected to black slavery, but were not much moved by near-slavery in Lancashire. And if the dissenters and sectaries were apt to pick and choose between the relative importance of the different parts of the New Testament, reading Romans with an eager acceptance and Ephesians with what now looks like a positively wilful negligence, at least they did read, know, and value their Bibles. Those who were foremost in condemning them were the old pre-Tractarian High Churchmen, and they had neither social conscience, biblical knowledge, nor evangelistic fervour. Their condemnation of many of the forms which 'enthusiasm' had taken had both righteousness and common sense behind it. But it was neither righteous nor sensible when uttered by men who had nothing to

---

[1] Throughout this paragraph and the next I am very heavily indebted to Canon Charles Smyth's *Simeon and Church Order: The Birkbeck Lectures for 1937–8* (Cambridge University Press), 1940. See p. 258.

[2] Smyth, *op. cit.*, pp. 233–6.   [3] *Ibid.*, pp. 240–1.

offer, and only disliked it because it disturbed their own lethargic complaisance. In any case, what most of them condemned was not merely the perversions of 'enthusiasm,' but 'enthusiasm' as such.

The old High Churchmen certainly stood for what churchmanship then existed, but it was not an inspiring or a sacramental churchmanship. Only too often it was typified and expressed by the action of Cadogan's successor at Reading, who 'signalized his ecclesiastical prejudices by preaching in the parish church of St Mary's, Reading, on July 30, 1798, at the visitation of the Bishop of Salisbury, a sermon entitled *A Dispassionate Enquiry into the Probable Causes and Consequences of Enthusiasm*, in which, with insufferable condescension, he alluded to the "well-meant" piety of his predecessor'.[1] But whereas this 'well-meant piety' had at least provided services in church to which many people delighted to come, those who protested against it, and the far larger number of clergymen who simply ignored it, had little to offer to their own congregations. At no time in the history of the Church was the level of parochial worship so low, and its state so dead. Reverence hardly existed: it was too 'enthusiastic'. The services were deadly dull and inordinately long. A certain amount of comic relief might be provided by the privileged eccentricities and uncertain pronunciations of the parish clerk, and those who were members of the village band and accompanied, from the gallery, the singing of the psalms had a certain proprietary interest in the proceedings. But for the most part the worship of the parish church was pedestrian and uninspiring to an altogether shocking degree.

Pluralism and absenteeism were commonplace, especially among bishops and superior clergy. The shockingly low level of subsistence on which the mass of unfortunate curates were expected to maintain themselves and their families inevitably had a deadening effect on the whole range of the parochial system. At no time in all its history has the Church distributed its endowments quite so iniquitously as it did then. It seems to have occurred to extremely few clergymen to protest, or to do more than vaguely pity their unfortunate brother clergy in distress. This blindness on the part of otherwise good and merciful men, in a generation which the events of the French Revolution had made acutely aware of the challenge of poverty and the need of progress, is at first sight astonishing. The disrepute into which the sacraments had fallen was a part of the cause: to be concerned for the honour of the Church as a whole is a function of a sense of churchmanship, and a sense of churchmanship depends on the proper valuation of sacraments. But it was due even more to the increasingly shadowy relationship between a stationary theological study and a fast developing change in scientific knowledge and social equipment. For any parish priest, moreover, to inform himself of the real state of the Church, or to make any estimate of what progress the Church was making in its mission to the

---

[1] Smyth, *op. cit.*, p. 232.

world was very difficult. The Church had no voice which he could hear, for the only voice it had was that of a bench of desperately worldly and socially blinded bishops, the convocations having ceased long since to be called together. Not until 1855 were they revived.

V · *Churchmanship and the Cathedrals*

Any judgement which in 1830 pronounced the Church to be dead and called for the undertaker to carry out the corpse was thus as inevitable as it was superficial. Many shouted that judgement, and who should blame them? How should the hooligan in the Bristol riots or the radical Member of Parliament know what was being done at Haworth or Great Harwood? So the Bishop of Bristol's house was burnt by the mob in 1831; and other bishops were pelted with dead cats through the incautiously opened windows of their carriages. All this violence was one way of uttering a judgement. The atheist-radical M.P. Joseph Hume found another and more decorous way, but it was just the same judgement which he echoed, when he thundered in the House of Commons in 1831:

> I had hoped that these foolish ordinations would terminate. Though it would doubtless be unjust that a corporation like the Church, set up by Parliament nearly three hundred years ago, and older therefore than either the East or West India companies, should be abolished without adequate compensation to those who have wasted their youth in its service, yet by those who enter this body now, when its charter is on the eve of being cancelled by those who gave it, when it is admitted on all hands to be not only useless but absolutely detrimental, neither indulgence nor compensation can fairly be expected.[1]

There is something rather perverted, because deliberately wounding and cruel, about a judgement so phrased. That did not alter the fact that many said Amen to it, and others echoed it.[2] The Church provided only too much evidence to justify them. The Evangelical Revival had done very little to transform this evidence. Yet the judgements were all faulty. They had missed the two most important pieces of evidence. They forgot that the heart of the Church is always in its obscure parishes, beating where only a few can see its motion. They overlooked the fact that the Church Catholic is divine, and the gates of hell cannot prevail against it.

Perhaps the greatest, and certainly the most attractive of all the Victorian bishops, King of Lincoln, thus summarized the ecclesiastical significance of his era. 'At the beginning of the era, the Church seemed effete, worn out, useless; at its end, it had passed through strange and marvellous revivals,

---

[1] *Church Congress Report:* 1890, p. 40. Also quoted in L. E. Elliott-Binns, *Religion in the Nineteenth Century* (Lutterworth Press), 1936, p. 41.

[2] See, for example, the contemporary attack on pluralism and on every other real and imaginary evil which the not inconsiderable wit of John Wade, the author of *The Black Book of Corruption Unmasked*, could discover, or even invent. He spoke of ordination as 'a gross and beastly absurdity'. Quoted in Carpenter, *op. cit.*, p. 55.

and was once more on its trial, facing a new world,' The telling of that story has to be woven around the great names of its heroes, Newman and Keble, Kingsley and Maurice, Pusey and Hook, Church and Benson, and so many others. Truly that century had an abundance of giants. But most of all it is a story of the revival of churchmanship, the recovery of the arts and poetry of worship, and the revaluation of sacraments. The rebirth of a Christian social conscience, the great advances in theological learning and biblical study, the refashioning of the convocations—all these strengths of nineteenth-century church history, these items in the rich legacy it bequeathed to us, rested upon and moved side by side with the recovery of a sense of elementary catholic loyalties in one parish after another. For this, and only this, was able to set the feet of the common pastoral faithfulness in a larger room.

But it all took time, nearly a hundred years. Perhaps it took more time than it really need have done because the cathedrals, so peculiarly fitted and even designed, as it seems, by a divine providence to lead the way in such a recovery, lagged behind the parish churches. In 1845, for example, it was still true of Ely that

> There was only one sermon for the whole of Ely, which was preached by the canon-in-residence. There were two parish churches where prayers were said, after which the parishioners, if they pleased, came into the Cathedral to hear the sermon, and waited until the service was over. The cathedral was not then warmed, and was wonderfully cold in winter. The poor, whilst waiting for the sermon, used to go into one transept, and the better class into another: the rest of the people chose the nave. The farmer class talked a little business between themselves, and the others walked up and down the nave to keep themselves warm. Persons had to provide seats for themselves.[1]

Salisbury was almost as moribund. In 1840, writes the most attractive of its historians, 'it had touched bottom'.[2] The level was lower than that of Ely, for even its fabric was in a bad way. The cloisters needed restoring, and the chapter house rebuilding. The music was lamentable. A new canon noticed that the lay vicars (*i.e.* the choirmen) were in the habit of simply absenting themselves from the services whenever they felt so disposed. He enquired of the organist, and was told, 'Well, sir, you must know that the rule at Salisbury has always been "let everybody get off everything he can".'[3] This new canon bore one of the great names in cathedral history. He was Walter Hamilton, who later became Bishop of Salisbury. He went there in 1841, and flung all his great energies into the work of cathedral reform. In 1853 he outlined his plan for this in a famous letter to his dean.

---

[1] A speech by Archdeacon William Emery, canon-residentiary of Ely to the Church Congress of 1900. *Report*, p. 109.
[2] Dora H. Robertson, *Sarum Close* (Cape), 1938, p. 284. Mrs Robertson's book, although primarily a history of the Sarum Choir School, is a mine of information about every aspect of the life of Salisbury Cathderal down the ages.
[3] Robertson, *op. cit.*, p. 284.

The backbone of his plan was to make the cathedral a real centre of educational and musical life, and to give the cathedral clergy, both canons and vicars-choral, important duties in the city. He was in favour of abolishing all distinctions between the two types of clergy, and wished that the vicars might hold prebendary stalls and have their place in chapter.'[1]

He also managed to have the cathedral opened each day to the public between the hours of matins and evensong and he instituted a weekly celebration of Holy Communion.

The London public who were so ill-advised as to wish to enter St Paul's Cathedral in 1858, still had to 'pay twopence at the door to enter a vast and dreary area abandoned to dust and damp uselessness';[2] while at Chester, as late as 1860,

> The manservant from the Deanery would arrive early, unlock the dean's stall, and place his books in readiness. Galleries were perched high behind the canopies of the choir stalls to which the first comer was admitted by a verger, he or she retaining the key until all the privileged had taken their places, the door being carefully locked between each arrival. When additional seating was required, forms would be placed down the choir aisles, on which the worshippers would sit sideways and back to back. At that time the nave was colour-washed yellow; and the choristers had the right to fine any man coming into the cathedral with his hat on, and they seemingly found the custom profitable.[3]

Many years later, Chester, under Dean Bennett, was to have the honour of taking the greatest of all steps forward to the full revival of cathedral life and usefulness. But Bennett's genius—in its own field perhaps the fullest and purest genius England has ever produced—stood upon the earlier cathedral revivals of Benson at Truro and Church at St Paul's. In 1873 Benson wrote to his friend Canon Crowfoot of Lincoln:

> I do not know whether cathedral life and cathedral work are at present attractive to you, but to me it is so unspeakably important in the present age of the Church of England, that I have given up the dearest work of my life (the headmastership of Wellington) to surrender myself to cathedral work.[4]

Benson and Church founded a new tradition of capitular devotion to match the expanding parochial devotion; and, as a result, Archdeacon Emery, whose impressions of Ely in the bad days were quoted above, could sum up a debate on cathedrals at the Church Congress at Newcastle in 1900—a body traditionally suspicious of all capitular pretensions—by a glad acknowledgement of charity and hope, 'I was afraid I should hear some strong denunciations of the cathedral, but the general result as to the cathedral system seems to be that of friendliness.'[5]

[1] *Ibid.*, p. 287.
[2] *The Guardian*, March 1878. Quoted by Carpenter, *op. cit.*, p. 294.
[3] Elma K. Paget, *Henry Luke Paget* (Longmans), 1939, p. 277.
[4] *Church Congress Report, 1900*, p. 91.
[5] *Report*, p. 110.

VI · *The Missionary Pioneers*

It is universally agreed that of all the centuries of Christendom the nine-teenth is the supreme period of missionary expansion. During those hun-dred years the religion of Jesus Christ was spread over a larger part of the earth's surface than was achieved in all the earlier centuries added together. This flinging of the Name of Christ to all the scorched and frozen ends of the earth was, to a very large extent, the work of English-speaking Chris-tians. No Church capable of accomplishing so much abroad could be completely effete at home; and nothing like it could have been done if the work of the Church overseas had not been perceived to grow just as naturally and inevitably out of the Gospel as did the work of the Church at home.

The story has been told statistically over and over again—how in one continent after another pioneers were martyred, or had their hearts broken by the lack of interest shown at home, or were forced against the blank hard wall of hostility on the part of vested interests. The secular enmity of the directors of the East India Company had become specially notorious. In 1793 the directors had adopted this resolution, and formally entered it into their minute book, 'That the sending of missionaries into our eastern possessions is the maddest, most extravagant, and most unwarrantable project that was ever proposed by an enthusiastic lunatic.'[1] Nor was this line of vehement opposition confined to secular committees. It could be found in Christian circles, and could be just as violently expressed. At a meeting of Baptist ministers in 1786, Robert Carey proposed this resolu-tion, 'The command given to the Apostles to teach all nations is obligatory on all succeeding ministers to the end of the world.' At once the chairman jumped violently to his feet and cried, 'You are a miserable Enthusiast for asking such a question. Certainly nothing can be done before another Pentecost.' The ministers endorsed not Carey's view but the chairman's.[2] The same sort of attitude was often taken by white settlers in the dominions. In 1820 the S.P.G. offered £500 towards the cost of a church in Cape Town, there being none. The Local Government Board thanked the society kindly, but said that 'such a building was not wanted'.[3]

It was in the face of such opposition as this that the pioneer missionaries opened the way of the Lord. In their wake came priests and teachers, doctors and nurses, the catechists and the colporteurs of the Bible Society and, trailing along a considerable distance behind everyone else, bishops to administer the new dioceses. The figures which tell the story form a statistical variation, worked out in cool and lucid counterpoint, on the

[1] H. H. Montgomery, *Foreign Missions* (Longmans, Green), 1902, p. 6.
[2] *Life of Carey*, by Dr Smith, p. 31. Quoted by B. R. Wilson in *Church Problems*, edited by H. Hensley Henson (Murray), 1900, p. 361.
[3] Cecil Lewis and G. E. Edwards, *Historical Records of the Church of the Province of South Africa* (S.P.C.K.), 1934, p. 14.

eternal theme: the blood of the martyrs is the seed of the Church. They have been set out, and are available in a dozen different places. Broadly speaking, the spring of progress rose about 1840, and in ten years the trickle had become a steadily flowing stream. It was God's answer to the chaos of the Napoleonic wars. This unprecedentedly urgent and swift spreading of the Gospel among people of every race and colour, reflecting, as it did, the creative impulse of a Church at home, itself labouring in the throes of a process of home development hardly less swift, and perhaps even more devastating, naturally created tremendous problems in every sphere, social, cultural, ethical, tribal, and economic of the individual and communal lives of the peoples thus evangelized. These problems the Church of the twentieth century inherited; and it had to grapple with them and solve them as best it could.

The nineteenth-century missionaries wasted but little time over any problems. They just ignored them. Until the century's closing years, and at the London Missionary Conference of 1894, they hardly even bothered to make much effort to define them. The missionaries of that century had more urgent things to do. They had to catch up and redeem the wasted opportunities of centuries, and atone as best they might for the behaviour among the natives of so many of their own countrymen, who had often created a new secular hell even more horrifying than the native hell of false religion. They generally set to work alone, and they seldom had anyone to advise them. They made their own policy as they went along, each one for himself; and they dealt with their problems by the light of such wits and character as God had given them. Under the circumstances, and because missionaries, like other men, are fallible, it was not surprising that their adventurous zeal created almost as many problems as it solved.

They needed episcopal oversight, and could not get it, for they were nearly always in the territory far ahead of any bishop or effective diocesan organization. In 1840 there were still only ten bishops serving abroad, and these were wholly or partly financed by the state.[1] It was really very little use for a missionary in Masulipatam to seek the guidance of his bishop in Calcutta; and the diocesan bishop of the missionary in North America still lived at Fulham Palace. But 1841 saw the birth of the Colonial Bishoprics Fund, and thereafter things began to move. It was time, for, in the absence of episcopal control, some astonishing things had happened. In colonies where there were many white settlers and no bishop, the state of church affairs was really startling. When Bishop Gray arrived at Cape Town in 1848 he found chaos, which for some years baffled even him. The chaos was doctrinal as well as administrative. When he arrived, and had looked round, he wrote despairingly home:

As to our church here, the only two clergy belong to a little evangelical alliance. In the cathedral last Sunday a school was taught from an American catechism,

[1] W. F. France, *The Overseas Episcopate* (Colonial Bishoprics Fund), 1941, p. 8.

wherein the definition of a Sacrament was in total contradiction to that of our own catechism. There is a debt of £7,500 on the church which the shareholders (who before now have increased their dividends out of the Sacrament money) want the government to purchase.[1]

This church was the cathedral. It was virtually a joint-stock company 'in which some of the proprietors are Jews and some atheists'. The theological chaos had been created by a body of Anglo-Indian laymen who had settled in Cape Town in 1840.

They found out what a pleasant place the Cape was to live in, and the names of the streets and houses are reminiscent of their Indian days. Their churchmanship was undefined. They taught in the church Sunday school, but refused to teach the Church catechism with its definite sacramental doctrine. They attended morning service and communicated at church, and preached in nonconformist chapels in the evening. To these men an offertory, a surplice, or the singing of chants was distasteful.[2]

But all that does nothing to alter or mar the splendid achievement of the lonely pioneer priests. A picture, however episodic, of some of them at work during the decade 1850–1860, will show something of the greatness of their achievement, and demonstrate how, all unknowing, they were creating problems all the time as they went along, which were presently to grow into baffling proportions.

First of all, a man had to get to the field of his choice. While this did not usually involve him in an imitation of the arduous heroisms of a Livingstone in Central Africa, his journey was likely to be most tedious and difficult. The famous Hoernle, for instance, landed at Calcutta after a long voyage of mingled discomfort and terror. From there he had to travel by barge to Agra; and his barge was towed by idle and obstinate boatmen, whose idea of providing entertainment for themselves was constantly and deliberately to ground Hoernle's party for hours on shoals and sandbanks, while they departed to visit their aunts and cousins in the local villages. The journey by barge from Calcutta to Agra took them two and a half months.[3]

Having at last got to his station, the missionary found that the word 'station' was often no more than a purely courtesy title, and consisted merely of a plot of virgin country, quite innocent of either building or tillage. The missionary of a Red Indian station near Hudson Bay in Canada draws an idyllic picture of 'the neat church and parsonage, the nice laid-out garden and premises, the village and its Christian Indians coming down to welcome the bishop with their pastor at their head'. But this leads him to remind himself of a day when Lac-la-Rouge was not at all like that, the

---

[1] *Records of South Africa*, pp. 35–6.   [2] *Ibid.*, p. 25.
[3] J. F. D. Hoernle, *Memoir of the Rev. G. P. Hoernle* (Simpkin, Marshall), 1884, p. 78.

day when he first arrived to begin his mission, and discovered that before he could begin to preach the Gospel he must set about the task of farming the land. He had to drain swamps to dry the heavy clay, to clear the ground of huge clusters of fir-tree roots, to ferry load after load of sand across the lake to mix with clay for building, and to cut reeds for manure. Not until then could the crops of potatoes, oats, and barley be sown on which the missionary's household were to live.[1]

In those palmy days the missionary had to be a man of many parts and uncovenanted resources. In Central Africa he might have to exhibit, quite on the spur of the moment, a pretty talent for military tactics. On one occasion the missionary at Abeokuta suddenly found himself involved in a battle. The formidable and dreaded Amazon warriors of Dahomey came sweeping to the attack in an undeclared war, and the missionary, unperturbed, assumed command of the defences, and inflicted upon these Amazons one of the first defeats they had ever known. He might also have to become a combination of diplomatist and courtier. In 1850 Archdeacon Merriman arrived at a native village near Grahamstown in South Africa:

We reached the Kraal, and Umhalla, a dirty, scrubby-looking savage in an old blanket crawled out. After eyeing one another for what seemed an age, he asked where I came from, and I told him from the bishop he had seen at Kingwilliamstown a year before, and that I bore a message to ask if he would receive two teachers, protect them, and see that they did not starve. He thanked me and asked if I would give him a blanket. I told him not to look for gifts from the teachers; that we were quite poor men; that he had hundreds of cattle and was Sukosi, I had none and was no Sukosi. I said, too, that the missionaries who came to confer a benefit on him must be paid, given food, and if they had cattle must not be robbed, and that he must provide a good hut for them; to all of which he agreed, and then said that I was the man he wanted, and the bishop must send me. I explained that I was wanted elsewhere, but he insisted. 'Tell the bishop you are the man I want.'[2]

In pure evangelism, India was perhaps the most interesting, as it was certainly the most promising field. By 1845 Indian missions had advanced beyond their pioneering, rough-and-ready stage. A good many of the missionaries in the country were by then being drafted to special tasks of administering the tiny settlements of native Christians, which the pioneers had founded. One of the best established of these was at Burdwan, near Calcutta, which had been in existence since 1819. In 1850 it consisted of a house for the missionaries, a school for orphan boys and another for orphan girls, a church, an infant school, a playground, and a native village, all built 'along two sides of a noble tank'.[3] But missionaries who were engaged on such tasks of administration seem generally to have hated them. Hoernle spoke for most of his brethren when he launched into a tirade

[1] *Church Missionary Gleaner*, 1850–51, p. 239.
[2] *Records of South Africa*, p. 240.   [3] *Gleaner*, p. 177.

about the folly and waste of sending a missionary to do a district commissioner's job. He was always trying to escape from the fetters of having to administer the Agra settlement. They were all the time breaking their hearts to do genuinely and directly evangelistic work; and in their spare time they generally did it. Their perception of the realities of the spiritual situation in India went deeper than the wisdom of the home authorities, who were more and more tending to think of them as handy administrators of institutions which, having once been founded, must somehow be kept going. For in many parts of India the old paganisms were beginning to flag and wane because the native was ceasing to have much real belief in many of the customs and symbols connected with them. Many of them, the missionaries eagerly reported, had no real reverence either for rituals or for idols. In some places the local religious customs were kept up only because they were unique in one village or another, which brought to the village a more than local renown, and, if the ritual was sensational enough, a regular financial contribution from idle Europeans looking out for a new kind of entertainment.

The village of Pedlana, near Masulipatam, held each year a cruel and degrading Swinging Festival. A man had a set of meathooks gaffed through the loose skin of his back, and then was swung high, to and fro, backwards and forwards, on the end of a great pole. A missionary, H. W. Fox, of Durham, who was much loved in the district, many times protested. But he always got the same reply: 'Why should *we* give it up? The Company have hitherto encouraged us in it. Till a few years ago the Collector used to give money to the festival, and gentlemen used to come out from Masulipatam and sit down on their chairs to look at it along with us. Why should *we* give it up? Let the Government forbid it, and we will stop it at once; but till they do, why should we take any step in abandoning it?' A religious faith thus defended is already mortally stricken. This foreboding of mortality was perhaps the reason why peripatetic missionaries in India were accustomed to make very free with the idols they preached against. One of them arrived 'on progress' at Hajipur. He put up his tent in the village, and preached to three hundred people in the afternoon. 'In the evening they conducted me to a Shib temple, and requested that I should preach from its steps. I always like such a spot. It is like carrying the lamp of the Gospel into Satan's dark corners. I had the honour to sit before the nose of the idol.' The next day, at Kamapuka, he preached 'in a shop in which a decrepit old Brahmin was sitting and chanting verses from the Ramayun', and he violently denounced a dirty image of Kali nearby. These peripatetic, almost free-lance missionaries travelled about from village to village, putting up a tent, accepting supper from the people, and then preaching to anyone who would listen, telling them the Stories of Jesus, and his parables, by a curious antiphonal method of question and answer.

And so the tale might go on, in one continent after another. It has been a tale of the average missionary labouring unknown and little rewarded side by side with the great heroes, Livingstone of Central Africa, Patteson of Melanesia, Selwyn of New Zealand, whose praise is gone out into all the world. But the inexorable rule of the home Church is also the rule of the mission field— in the long run the work of the average counts for more than the heroism of the exceptional. Many mistakes had been made. That was inevitable in a day when happy-go-lucky, improvised methods of evangelism were all that was really possible. But the ground had been occupied, and that was the main thing. In the overseas work of the Church, the nineteenth century story had been a saga, as consistently heroic as anything in the past. St Boniface would have saluted his Victorian fellow-countrymen and Christians. They were of his spirit.

3

The Field of Battle: 1900-1914

I · *The Spirit of Edwardian England*

TO MAKE a journey of the imagination back to the England of our grandfathers is an odd, disturbing adventure. The traveller at once knows himself a stranger in a foreign and a distant land; and the more deeply he tries to steep himself in it the more of an alien he feels himself. Yet the land he is exploring is not foreign and not distant. It is his own land. His own dimly remembered grandparents lived in it and shaped it. There is an elusive secret to be found, and a desultory, random wandering does not disclose it. So he turns to study. He sets himself to master its politics, its economics, its sociology, its international relationships; he systematically tries to enter into its general culture. As a result, his historical knowledge may be increased, but his sense of strangeness is stamped yet the more uncomfortably upon him. How could they feel so secure? How could they innocently think that their wealth, their safety, and their progress must continue indefinitely for ever? What possible grounds could they have for their apparently sincere belief that the long ceaseless elegy of the world's tragedy, sin, and misery had suddenly become a spring song in their day, and would not, could not ever again lose its joy? All the time the seeds of wakefulness from all such opium dreams are plainly evident to us and should have been to them. Why did they never see? It is very difficult for a generation twice led through the shambles of hell, twice guided through the valley of the shadow of death, to be even patient, much less to understand the complacent Edwardians. Such a journey invites a wry cynicism.

It is easy enough to make it. Many of the essential documents and state papers of the period have now been collected and published, and authoritative histories are abundantly available. They can be supplemented not only by the newspapers and reviews of the time, but also by many efforts which the Edwardians made to explain their own society to themselves and to their successors. Among these perhaps the most noteworthy is the prophecy (in the Old Testament sense) of C. F. G. Masterman, whose book, *The Condition of England*,[1] is certainly one of the most able and outstanding essays of its kind to be found in English literature. To read these documents, however, is merely to have that sense of strangeness brought still further into the forefront of consciousness, and to turn it into a positive emotion of exasperation. But it is also to pin down and define that in which the sense of exasperated strangeness consists. It was not so much the icy finality of their caste system, and the deep gulf between their classes, for, though considerably softened, these curses are with us still. It was the absurd and intolerable spiritual complacency, leading to an assured optimism, now seeming merely comic, which really builds the barrier between our grandfathers and ourselves.

It was to that generation and not to ours that the famous remark about modern man and his sins belongs. Oliver Lodge coined it in 1904:

> The higher man of to-day is not worrying about his sins at all. As for Original Sin or Birth Sin, or other notion of that kind, that sits lightly on him. As a matter of fact it is non-existent, and no one but a monk could have invented it.[2]

The really significant phrase in that sentence is 'the higher man of to-day'. Superman and Overman are concepts belonging to the thought of Edwardian England. Bernard Shaw mocked, but he was not then accepted as a prophet. The idea that humanity had climbed so high up the mountain of Parnassus that upon that generation the fullness of the times and the heritage of the prophecies had come was accepted so readily by most people that there seemed nothing strange in the belief that they themselves were a new and a much higher type of human being than anything the world had seen before. They counted the instruments of progress, applied science, universal education, a smoothly organized state machine, and a colossal self-confidence. They had them all. It was a new age, with progress at last set in automatic motion.

> England has shaken man's authority and founded freedom. Free England has shaken nature's authority and founded industrialism.[3]

Having decided to go in for industrialism, England had set herself the aim of prosperity. 'Will industrial revolution yield a prosperity reasonably diffused?' It did not take Mr Peel more than a few lines to answer Yes. Masterman, a far more acute and knowledgeable observer, was more cautious, but he began his survey in very similar terms, and bore witness to the spirit of complacent optimism which surrounded him:

> Today, perhaps too complacently, we assume that history will sharply distinguish our particular period of security from such troublous upheavals of Birth or Death [as in the Middle Ages]. We see ourselves painted as a civilization in the

---

[1] Published in 1909 (Methuen).   [2] *Hibbert Journal.*
[3] The Hon. George Peel, *The Future of England* (Macmillan), 1912, pp. 29, 31.

vigour of early Manhood, possessing contentment still charged with ambition; a race in England and Europe full of energy and purpose, in which life, for the general, has become more tolerable than ever before.[1]

Optimism is the impetus, and despair the nemesis of all purely secular dreams for humanity; and the ground of such an optimism is the ability to ignore the lessons of history. Only a self-conscious pride in modernity as such—the instinctive judgement that everything new and up-to-date must necessarily be superior to, and so supersede, everything old and out-of-date—is able to carry such an optimism with dignity. But the Britain of the first decade of the twentieth century entertained this pride, and espoused this optimism. It is significant that the historian of that day who spoke to scholars with the voice of accepted authority was Professor Bury, and he, examining the centuries of the past with the microscope of his encyclopaedic knowledge, declared that at last the victory of liberty had been won, and its enemy Christianity, stricken with a mortal disease. He was saying, in effect, that the history of two thousand years had come to its fulfilment, that it had taught the last of its lessons and conferred the last of its benefits upon western civilization. But the mood which is prepared to ignore, and even fiercely to repudiate both history and the religion which is its essential theme, is always a mood of brittle morale, and the return of history to claim its inevitable meed of acknowledgment always brings despair to the society which has cast it out.

Any society of which this self-sufficiency is the dominant characteristic offers a field of peculiar difficulty to Christian evangelism. Taken as a whole, the England of 1900 to 1914 persisted in disqualifying itself from receiving the greatest of all blessings. Redemption is a gift offered to all, but some are not able to receive it. Their self-sufficiency makes them helpless. First there must be an acknowledgment of the need for it, and a renunciation of the humanist error that humanity, if it needs salvation at all, can save itself by itself. Where there is complacency, redemption cannot be offered. The gospel of God's indiscriminating and fathomless love holds no syllable of comfort for the complacent and the proud. There has seldom existed a generation of English people which more needed and less desired the Christian redemption.

II · *The Edwardian Social Structure*

The picture of the Edwardian society in all its parts was very fully drawn by Masterman, and all the mass of incidental evidence coming from other sources confirms the accuracy of his drawing and of his judgement.

He began his book with an acid description of the upper classes. He called them the Conquerors. They were those who had done well out of the Skin Game of an essentially competitive order, who had found their

[1] *Ibid.*, p. 2.

commanding positions and their wealth ready made by being born into the hereditary aristocracy, or who had fought their way into the five-figure class by commercial intrigue. It was one of the most ominous facts of that society that between these two types there was ceasing to be any visible distinction. England had drifted into a fatal alliance between the aristocratic principle and financial cleverness and the monarch himself had done much to blur the distinction by his unhappy and unconcealed liking to have financial magnates of mediocre minds as his intimates. This alliance gradually spread and developed into the entanglement of political conservatism with money power, which in our own day has done so much to make every appeal to tradition suspect to the generous minded.

These people, the possessors of tremendous wealth, had but little knowledge of the morality of the New Testament, and what they had they repudiated. The typical figure, perhaps, was the 'Edwardian Hostess', and of her one who knew her well has composed this portrait:

The 'famous Edwardian hostesses' were not as a rule very human beings. They were often hard, ambitious, and greedy for money; they wore high collars of tulle, tautened with little sticks of whalebone, and their laughter was as high and ambitious as their tiaras. Their sympathies were restricted and their emotions concealed; they lacked impulse: even their amusement expressed itself in a dry cackle at the solecisms of those who had not learned their drill. These hostesses were hard and cold and slightly clammy, as the jade fish upon the mantelpiece.[1]

They had to be greedy for money, and importunate for tips on the stock exchange, for their extravagance was immense, almost heroic, and it needed a lot of support. No part of it could be allowed to go, for this extravagance was the badge of the tribe, a kind of certificate of belonging to it. One who was born and lived rebelliously in the tribe has memorably described the extent and the vulgarity of this extravagance:

Those meals! Those endless, extravagant meals, in which they all indulged all the year round! Sebastian wondered how their constitutions and their figures could stand it; then he remembered that in the summer they went as a matter of course to Homburg or Marienbad, to get rid of the accumulated excess, and then returned to start on another year's course of rich living. Really there was very little difference, essentially, between Marienbad and the vomitorium of the Romans. How strange that eating should play so important a part in social life! They were eating quails and cracking jokes. That particular dish of the Chevron chef was famous: an ortolan within the quail, a truffle within the ortolan, and *pâté de foie gras* within the truffle; by the time all the disembowelling had taken place, there was not much left of any of the constituents. From his place at the head of the table, Sebastian watched the jaws going up and down, and wished that he did not always see people as though they were caricatures. There was Sir Harry Tremaine, the perfect courtier, with his waved white hair, turning his head rigidly above his high collar, rather like a bird; there was Mrs Levison, with her

[1] Harold Nicolson in *The Spectator*, July 23, 1943.

raucous voice and her hair like a frizzled yellow sponge. They were all people whose names were familiar to every reader of the society titbits in the papers. Sebastian saw them suddenly as a ventriloquist's box of puppets. Fourteen down one side of the table, fourteen up the other; with himself and his mother at either end, that made thirty. Then his vision shifted, and he was obliged to admit that they were very ornamental. They seemed so perfectly concordant with their setting, as though they had not a care in the world; the jewels glittered, the shirt-fronts glistened; the servants came and went, handing dishes and pouring wine in the light of the many candles. The trails of smilax wreathed greenly in and out among the heavy candelabra and the dishes of grapes and peaches. Yes, he must admit that his mother's friends were ornamental; he liked the bare shoulders and piled hair of the women, their pretty hands and the bracelets round their wrists; the clouds of tulle, and the roses clasped by a brooch against the breast. His mother herself, whom he had so lately seen as a mask within her mirror, looked young and lovely now, so far away down the table; for a curious instant he imagined her, no longer his mother, but his wife. Then leaning towards her he saw the long nose of the Jew. 'A tip for the Stock Exchange!' he thought; for his mother had explained to him, with unusual candour, exactly why she wanted him to be polite to Sir Adam. This passion for money was a thing Sebastian could not understand; he was rich; his mother practically controlled the spending of his fortune until he should be twenty-one; where was the need for more? It was simply part of her creed and the creed of her friends.[1]

Not for nothing is the possession of great wealth stigmatized in the teaching of Jesus as the most dangerous of all states of existence. To possess it involves the need to guard it and the power it brings. The next stage is the phobia of fear; fear of those who would take that wealth away. For them the object of their fear was not the revolutionary anarchist or syndicalist, whom they never took seriously, but the politically organized socialism of the Parliamentary Labour Party, and the Trades Unions. They feared it, but did not understand it, for socialism presented itself to them not as a philosophy of life, but in revolutionary form,

an uprising of the uneducated, suddenly breaking into their houses; their clumsy feet on the mantelpiece, their clumsy hands seizing and destroying all beautiful and pleasant things. So they lie awake at night, listening fearfully to the tramp of the rising host: the revolt of the slave against his master.[2]

John Galsworthy, surveying the tribe in novel and play, with sympathy but with flat repudiation, fixed upon an over-developed and a wilfully cherished sense of property as the real agent of its spiritual corruption. For it was corrupt: the virtue had gone out of it. It could vigorously obstruct, but it had nothing to give. The story of its obstruction of the people's will as expressed in successive Liberal budgets in the House of Commons forms the main theme of the nation's political story in the five years before 1914. It could obstruct just as persistently, and much more skilfully, in

---

[1] Violet Sackville West, *The Edwardians* (Hogarth Press), 1931, pp. 43–5.
[2] Masterman, *op. cit.*, p. 64.

smaller matters. When the London County Council, housed in conditions such as to make its work difficult, proposed to build the present County Hall, the tribe of the super-wealthy was moved to make outraged protests against the extravagance, and the building was postponed for years.[1] Nor had they any benefactions to bestow. Their extravagance was dogged by a nemesis of barrenness.

The super wealthy give little leadership to the classes below them. Never were fairer opportunities offered to the children of wealthy families for the elaboration of a new aristocratic Government of a new England; and never were those opportunities more completely flung away. Their chosen leaders can offer nothing but a dialectic, or perpetual criticism of other men's schemes, clever, futile, barren as the east wind.[2]

It is a stern but a justifiable indictment.

It was in Edwardian times that the nation as a whole first became aware of, and first took into its reckoning, a new class which had been gradually developing during the previous fifty years. This class was the inhabitants of Suburbia, the endless series of trim, neat rows of semi-detached small houses, each with fifty or a hundred square yards of garden, which, by 1900, were to be found on the outskirts of every great industrial city. It was a new class, coming below the level of the commercial managers, and above that of the skilled artisan. The industrial revolution had created it by its demand for men of fair education to write up the ledgers and send out the bills, and girls to do the typing. Nothing like these endless reduplications of Acacia Villas and Magnolia Avenues had been seen in England before, and those who lived in them gradually became a new type in English society. Their occupation, essentially sedentary and unadventurous, helped to graft into them a deep-seated passion for security, for respectability, for privacy. Gathered together in new districts, even in whole new townships, were these hundreds of thousands of rootless folk, always tending to move on to a new address as one suburb got the reputation of being a trifle more socially select, just a touch superior in privacy and prestige than another.

The new suburbia presented a unique problem: it still does. In its new form of the Housing Estate, the essential problem of suburbia is as insoluble as ever. The problem is that there is nothing in all the world's history or at any point on the earth's surface to correspond with the essential aloofness of English suburbia. Desiring privacy more than all things, and having uprooted themselves from the pattern of immemorial social community, the suburbans presented the great, apparently insoluble problem of all churches, all political parties. They wouldn't be organized, and the Church's ancient parochial system was ill adapted to deal with these novel districts and types of mind, hardly envisaged by the Book of Common Prayer. They were impossible to bring into any genuinely Christian community, or any fellowship even momentarily classless, for they were

[1] *Ibid.*, p. 23. [2] *Ibid.*, p. 28.

conscious only of separations, not of kinships. They tended to identify themselves with Kensington or West Didsbury, being only too conscious of the gulf which separated Tooting or Levenshulme from either; their optimistic priests tended to identify them with Bethnal Green or Newton Heath, the very milieu they had escaped and regarded with horror.

Because they could neither organize nor co-operate, no one feared them, or seriously regarded their interests. But there was in them a deep fear of organized labour, and a corresponding envy, set so deep as to be virtually unperceived by themselves, of the wealthy.

The rich despise the working people; the Middle Classes fear them. . . . As feverish hordes, the suburbs swarm to the polling booth to vote against a truculent proletariat. The Middle Class elector is becoming irritated and indignant against working class legislation. He is growing tired of the plaint of the unemployed and the insistent crying of the poor. The spectacle of a Labour Party triumphant in the House of Commons, with a majority of members of Parliament apparently obedient to the demand of its leaders, and even a House of Lords afraid of it, fills him with profound disgust.[1]

In 1908 Suburbia, thus driven, served notice upon the wealthy and the proletariat alike, upon governments and politicians, that it existed, and that it counted. For in the municipal elections of that year its votes utterly defeated the long triumphant reign of the Progressive Party over the London County Council.

Every circumstance of their lives worked together to drive the inhabitants of suburbia into a materialistic view of life. Where comfort and security are the supreme ends, where the struggles of creative ambition are directed not towards living but towards attaining, and where all life is passed far away from the open-air world of nature with its incalculable benignancies and dooms, a thin, poor soil for the growth of the spiritual interpretation of life is all that can be scratched up. When the Lambeth Conference of 1908 optimistically asserted that 'Men's minds are more and more set towards the spiritual', the assembled bishops must momentarily have forgotten the millions of citizens of the new suburbia, whose minds were being fast driven away from all contact with spiritual realities, and whose manners and customs and shape of living presented to a parochially organized Church a field of quite peculiar difficulty. Masterman's eye saw much more clearly:

It is losing its old religions. . . . The whole apparatus of worship seems archaic and unreal to those who have never seen the shaking of the solid ground beneath their feet or the wonder and terror of its elemental fires.[2]

The stately houses of the aristocrats, the blackened brick palaces of commerce, and the jerry-built villas of suburbia were all superimposed over and erected upon a basis of the cramped thatched cottage of the country-side

---

[1] Masterman, p. 71.   [2] *Ibid.*, p. 75.

and the slums and back streets of the manufacturing districts. These, as always in history, paid the price and offered the possibility of elegant living to the few. As for the country-side, it was in its usual, and apparently chronic, state of 'ruined villages, and dwindling population'.[1] If the artisan had not quite so bleak an age to live in as he had had, it was still grim, as the various social surveys of that time, and the statistics of birth, death, and disease clearly show. Lady Bell, for example, held a thorough survey of the conditions in Middlesbrough, a typical industrial centre. It had the highest birth-rate in the kingdom—and nearly the highest infant mortality rate. Its population of 100,000 were nearly all artisan workers, for who would live in the Middlesbroughs of England except that need made them? The whole social structure and economy of the place was geared into the service of the blast-furnaces of the iron trade, and the impression it gave to the visitor was of an all-embracing devastating greyness. Men were spent before they were fifty; at fourteen years of age boys were treading the path of the iron worker, which, in Lady Bell's vivid phrase, runs 'along the sandy platform, that narrow path that lies between running streams of fire on the one hand and a sheer drop on the other'.

A good many attempts were made to survey one corner or another of this field of insecurity and greyness, which gave England nearly all her wealth. Lady Bell wrote of Middlesbrough, and Mr Charles Booth of London, while others told of life in a Devon colony of fishermen, in a Camberwell tenement, and the Rowntrees saw to it that the condition of the York workers should not be forgotten. In terms of physical condition the sum of these documented impressions and social habit is well known. Masterman used the surveys, made lively by his own great experience, to draw for his readers a more difficult and a less customary picture—a portrayal of the minds and spirits of those whom society thus exploited. He was, of course, forced to conclude that their first expressible desire was simply to be let alone, especially by the spreading government organizations for social welfare, and even by their would-be helpers, the enthusiasts for the Trades Unions, and the compilers of social surveys. But if that was one side of the medal, there was also the other; and it was this other which caused Masterman to see in the manual workers the real hope for the future. What he saw was a certain attitude towards life as a whole, healthier than the attitude of any other class in the national community:

They are not afraid of life. They keep something of the adventure which takes all risks: the resolute action which cannot even see the risks it is taking. With the original Christian axiom, as Renan saw it, they reveal that 'the heart of the common people is the great reservoir of the self-devotion by which alone the world can be saved.'[2]

This had much in common with the reservoir of spiritual courage out of

---

[1] *Ibid.*, p. 12.   [2] *Ibid.*, p. 118.

which the Christian gospel came. But it was not a religion, only the raw material of one. 'Religion counts for little in their scheme of human affairs.'[1]

Nevertheless the chief hope for the triumph of the Christian cause in England at that time lay in the working people. They had a fullness of idealism, and a sense of human brotherhood transcending the barriers of class, culture, race, and colour which no other section of the nation so completely shared; and that vision they were always prepared to serve even though that service should be to their hurt. The discussions of the inner ring of the Labour Party, Keir Hardie dominating and Arthur Henderson taking a junior part in them, had something of the flavour of a prayer meeting; and the speakers at local rallies of the party on Parker's Piece in Cambridge or the Bull Ring in Birmingham were accustomed to deliver harangues hardly distinguishable from the sermons preached in church by radical minded curates. An instance of this semi-political and semi-Christian idealism was afforded by the response of all the workers to the challenge of 'Chinese Slavery' in the Transvaal Diamond mines. In 1903 there was a great shortage of Kaffir labour to work in the mines, and the mine owners applied to the Government to be allowed to import Chinese coolies—not as free men, for reasons of South African racial policy forbade it—but indentured for a period of years, and confined in compounds day and night for the whole span of their contracted time of service in the country. The result was a scandal and a horror,

> To ship tens of thousands of Chinese young men overseas to perform for long years the hardest underground toil, and coop them up for their leisure in horde-compounds with no society but each other's, meant deliberately creating, as in the sequel it did create, moral sinks of indescribable human beastliness.[2]

Worst of all, it was the Balfour Conservative Government which had sanctioned it—an error which cost them the 1906 election. But it was in the workers' hearts that the horror really lodged and burnt. They were partly moved by their resentment against the commodity view of labour, but still more by a real sense of brotherhood with the Chinese coolie, who was thus enslaved. They championed him as their grandfathers had championed the suffering Italians, as their fathers had championed the persecuted Armenians, and as their children in Lancashire were presently to sympathize with and even champion the illiterate Indian cotton weaver who in the time of the Indian Nationalist Agitation had put them on the unemployment register.

[1] Masterman, p. 115.
[2] R. C. K. Ensor, *England: 1870–1914* (Oxford University Press), 1936, p. 377.

III · *Christianity and the 'Modern Cultivated Man'*

At the end of his book, Masterman paid a tribute to the energy of the Church in its work among the different classes of the people he had described. But for any Christian the tribute was wry reading:

> The Churches are extraordinarily active, endeavouring in this way and in that to influence the lives of the people. Their humanitarian and social efforts are widely appreciated. Their definite dogmatic teaching seems to count for little at all. They labour on steadily amid a huge indifference. The very material of their appeal is vanishing. Fear which is the beginning of wisdom no longer terrifies a society which sees orderly arrangements everywhere, accepting the secure as the normal. It cannot believe that, even if any future world exists at all, of which existence it is becoming increasingly doubtful, that future world will not in essence re-establish the decencies and commonplaces of the modern city state. . . . The fleeing from the city of Destruction, the crying out against the 'burden' of sin, the vision of the flames of hell drawing close to the Celestial City, represent an apparatus of experience that is alien to the present.[1]

On the showing of Masterman's own social analysis, the strategy of the Church should have been to concentrate all its strength upon the evangelizing of the workers. But throughout this period its best minds had to be turned towards the growing menace of philosophical materialism in the universities. Their influence had created, and their prestige had caused to be accepted the deadly fiction of the Superman, fit at last to be charged with his own destinies and those of a world. They usually called him the Modern Cultivated Man. Intellectual Christianity accepted the title, and sent its pleading to that address. Twice in the course of a letter to the Archbishop of Canterbury, seeking his support for the modernists, did Dr Sanday use the phrase.[2]

The Modern Cultivated Man of modernistic evangelism may have been a lay-figure, but he was not made of straw. He really existed as a type, and his influence over society was very great. Boundlessly confident in his belief in a quasi-automatic progress towards a kingdom of universal happiness, thinking that he had at hand in scientific techniques the one instrument needed to hasten that progress, he was fast casting off every garment which traditional and classical religion had taught him to wear. The Higher Man was in that stage of development in which everything which could be called traditional was automatically offensive. As he did not wear the garments of repentance, so he would not put on the robe of praise except for the worship of science. For him God was a back-number, as God must always be to any who are content to be labelled Higher Man or Super Man.

As a considerable number of the public figures of Edwardian England,

---

[1] *Ibid.*, p. 267.
[2] G. K. A. Bell, *Randall Davidson, Archbishop of Canterbury* (O.U.P.), 1935, vol. I, p. 678.

men such as Lowes Dickinson among the humanists and Oliver Lodge among the scientists, gave their authority to the belief that the Higher Man really existed, and was the characteristic product of the age, the Christian modernists were certainly wise to accept the fiction as truth, and they heroically set themselves to preach the Gospel to them. But what appeal could the Gospel make to them? Its promises were embedded inextricably within a story depending at every turn upon belief in the miraculous. They were offered to humanity from within the framework of a series of very ancient documents. They were formulated by means of many types and forms of traditional worship and devotion. They were themselves of such a nature as to stand far above the auditing power of any scientific technique of measurement. They constituted in themselves a tradition, the oldest, the widest, and the most persistent of any in the world. How could such promises, set in such a Gospel, appeal to a communal mind which prided itself on nothing so much as its repudiation of and emancipation from tradition of any kind, and one which had never experienced the discipline of communal catastrophe?

This turning away from all the old paths and guides just because they were old, and this eager attachment to what time was to show to be a profoundly false utopianism of perpetual and automatic progress, was the commonplace of the mental leaders, and the thrilling adventure of the ardent young of Edwardian England. Nor did it content itself with repudiating supernatural religion in general and the Church of England in particular. It was an attitude towards life which did not stop short at the figure of our Saviour himself. He also was made to abide the questions and the balances of the scientists. Father Neville Figgis was unquestionably right when, in 1909, he declared to a rather startled Cambridge audience, 'In the last generation men were unable to take Jesus as Lord, and were sad. Now they are choosing other masters, and are glad.'[1] It is true that these new masters were still disembodied ideas: they had to wait for nearly thirty years before they passed through the processes of personification and became adult. But these ideas mastered that society almost as thoroughly as they have mastered our own.

The vital task of the Church was therefore clear. It had to break the loyalty commonly devoted to these new and powerful gods which could not save. This it could only do by winning a fair hearing and a glad acceptance of a set of spiritual ideas embedded in a classical tradition, and inseparable from it. These ideas, and even the Person of Jesus in whom they were all found and by whom they were perpetually sustained, were opposed at every point to the really influential ideas of the day. Thus its task in an age which wore a self-sufficient garment of scientific modernity, and despised more sober clothing, was immensely difficult. The whole impetus of the doctrinal struggle within the Church during the first quarter of the

[1] *The Gospel and Human Needs* (Longmans, Green), 1909, p. 8.

twentieth century lay in its consciousness of this initial and crucial difficulty. The violence and bitterness with which the struggle was waged was due precisely to the urgency of the Church's need to find the way of escape from this impasse. Father Neville Figgis was the Christian thinker who saw this dilemma more clearly than anyone else, though it was never far from the mind of Randall Davidson, the new Archbishop of Canterbury. Figgis was also, perhaps, the only Christian spokesman who would speak with any authority to both parties. In lecture after lecture he urged on his contemporaries the starkness of the choice between Christ and Christ's enemy which society had now to make. But he nowhere precisely delineated nor identified this rival. Perhaps he was too much of an artist to bring himself to use the only accurate, but also the cumbersome and most ugly name of Secular Utopianism.

But now there was a new age in which at last progress was assured. What made it new was the prestige and authority of science. The sciences, with their new methods of study and the tremendous power of their new techniques, constituted at once the mould and the magnet of Edwardian imagination. It is not easy for us to realize quite the novelty, and therefore the emotional force of science; but G. K. Chesterton, in an inspired piece of mockery, came near to finding contemporary words for it:

Anyone who has read Mr Blatchford's very interesting book knows perfectly well that scientific authorities are quoted in the most miscellaneous way conceivable. It does not seem to matter to Mr B. whether he quotes Darwin or Professor Israel K. Poggins of Pocahontas College. It is all science and therefore all truth.[1]

To science the resources of popular imagination were fastened. From religion they were increasingly withdrawn. But the life-blood of a living religion is always popular imagination: as religion was increasingly starved of its life-blood it naturally became increasingly anaemic. 'Only when science captures the imagination, and seeks to subdue history, philosophy, and the individual life does she conflict with our religion,' said Figgis.[2] But that was precisely what was happening. A conflict was inevitable, and this must be a conflict in which the weight of educated people was thrown almost wholly in science's favour. On every side there was not merely an intense development of scientific research, but also, and even more significantly, a vast extension by universal education in the knowledge of scientific conclusions. When, as so often happens, these conclusions were only tentative, and afterwards proved to be completely erroneous, a great mischief was done to religion, because the correction of error very rarely overtook the enunciation of the initial conclusion.

Religion was emphatically held to lie within the limits of the territory

[1] Church Congress, 1904. *Report*, p. 98.
[2] *Civilisation at the Cross Roads* (Longmans, Green), 1913, p. 7.

which modern science was thought properly to occupy and control. It was thought right and sensible, even by some Christians, that Christianity should submit itself to science for its reinterpretation. This attitude of secular humanism and scientific utopianism towards religion was most worthily voiced in the writings of that splendid humanist, Lowes Dickinson, by common consent one of the most high-minded thinkers of his day. In 1905 he published his book *Religion: A Criticism and a Forecast*. In the course of it he easily and quickly disposed of every kind of ecclesiasticism, on the ground that while a Church may save a people from revolution and the collapse of law, it must always do this by keeping them pure and unspotted from all knowledge of new discovery and secular progress, just as the Roman Church had indeed tried to do in Italy before the Risorgimento. But salvation from revolution can be bought at too high a cost if the price of it is, as Dickinson said it must be, intellectual petrifaction. Then he turned to Christian belief, as it is in itself, and as apart from its social action. He dismissed it as of no practical effect or value. His ground for this judgement was remarkable and significant. It is valueless because it is untestable and unknowable, and the Faith itself is then agnostic because the dogmatic statements of Creeds and Gospels about the nature and the miracles of Christ cannot be scientifically proved and therefore cannot rank as real knowledge. 'Religious truth, like all other truth, is attainable, if at all, only by the method of science.'[1] It is a most remarkable statement, but it was phrased in the authentic accents of the intelligentsia of 1905. However, Lowes Dickinson went on to twist the dagger in the wound. Once the claim that Christian 'truths' must submit to the results of scientific investigation was conceded, then at once every vital statement of fact in the Gospel became thoroughly dubious:

Those who are acquainted with the nature of historical enquiries, the uncertainty of testimony, the prejudices of witnesses, the doubtfulness of documents, and have watched in other religions than the Christian the growth of myths and the creation of fictitious personalities, may easily assure themselves, without entering far into the laborious enquiry, that its results are bound to be in the highest degree laborious and uncertain.[2]

The trick, for such it is, is very obvious—to us, but it was not at all obvious to the young undergraduate of 1905, nor yet to Dickinson himself. He was just as blinded as his hearers were by his slavish adulation of science and modernity for their own sweet sakes. There was of course no difficulty in criticizing the critic. The fact that throughout his book he had virtually nothing to say about the life or death of Jesus Christ was itself sufficient to demonstrate his unfitness to pronounce judgement about the truth of Christianity. But at that time it was merely a waste of breath to point out elementary facts such as this. Science had spoken, and the matter was closed.

[1] *Religion: A Criticism and a Forecast* (Dent), 1905, p. viii.
[2] Dickinson, *ibid.*, p. 37.

Only perception, and inference, and logic; only, in the broadest sense, science can teach us anything, about the constitution of the universe, and our place in it; can teach us whether or no there be anything corresponding to what we have called God; whether or no the individual soul survives death; whether or no the process of things moves towards a good end.[1]

If, however, no knowledge worth calling by that name can come to men by any other road than that of scientific induction and logic, then the mind which accepts this limitation can take no cognizance of pure mystery, must deny the validity of the universal human sense of numinous awe, and can give no evidential credence to the subjective experience of forgiveness and redemption. Nor can it believe that sin is the vital matter which Christian teaching makes of it. The consequences for militant Christianity were serious and the outlook was most formidable. To teach Christianity to those whose outlook on life Lowes Dickinson expressed (and they included nearly all who held to the intellectual fashions of the day) was difficult nearly to the edge of impossibility. They would not listen: indeed, they could not. To offer them the forgiveness of God through Christ was to use language conveying no meaning whatever. For good or ill they had cast away all that was not scientific, all that came to them by tradition.

IV · *Idealism and Hysteria*

The closing years of this period, 1910 to 1914, added a new complication and embarrassment to the evangelistic work of the Church. They were marked by a rising passion of hysterical excitement in every sphere of public life, and by August 1914 the growth of this spirit had brought the nation to the very edge of civil war. Had it not been for the German invasion of Belgium in that month, civil war in Ireland and violent social revolution in England and Scotland could hardly have been prevented. Nothing less catastrophic and emotionally cooling than the outbreak of the first world war could have caused the gun-running partisans in Ireland to use their weapons against a common enemy instead of against each other, nor could any challenge less appalling have induced the newly founded alliance of the trade unions of miners, transport workers, and railway men to lift their hands from the preparations they were even then making for a general strike. In those years it seemed as though no issue could be raised without everybody bawling insults, and no argument conducted without threats and weapons.

Few of the great strikes took place without riots: often the troops were called in, and sometimes there were deaths. The suffragettes ousted the suffragists, and courted the public approval of their cause by the new policy of slashing pictures, setting fire to cathedrals, and maiming racehorses.

[1] *Ibid.*, p. 57.

The Government replied in kind by the tortures and degradations of forcible feeding of women in the prisons. Twice the Conservative Party violently struggled to overturn the constitution. Its leaders openly encouraged and some of the senior generals secretly conspired with those who were preparing to levy private war against the state. It was a malady, an infection which spread far beyond the political and industrial spheres of its origin. Presently, as was inevitable, the Church caught the disease of hysteria, and ecclesiastical controversialists too began to argue only at the tops of their voices, and to be persuaded that all who differed from them must be moved by motives of treachery and fraud. It was not the appropriate atmosphere in which to persuade people to accept Christ's gifts of serenity in personal living and charity in all social relationships.

Fundamentally, the growth of this atmosphere of hysterical violence was all a function, or a consequence, of the growing domination of the idea that man is sufficient for his own salvation. The flooding optimism which this idea bred seemed to find its political opportunity in 1906, when Liberals utterly routed the Conservatives in the General Election, and came into power under the most talented administration of modern times. It is impossible to exaggerate the force of the wave of optimism which swept over all those sections of the nation with demands to make. Even so cautious a historian as Mr R. C. K. Ensor emphasizes it in what is for him unwontedly emphatic language.

The 1906 House of Commons was at the outset a difficult body to lead. It was rich in inexperienced idealists. Radicalism and socialism alike, released from the suppressions of two decades, were radiant with sudden hopes of a new heaven and a new earth. No leader not alive to that morning glory could have carried the house with him; and that was where Campbell-Bannerman in his kindly and generous old age gave the parliament an incomparably better start than the efficient but earth-bound Asquith could have done. One marked trait in common, however, they had; both shone more in office than in opposition. Campbell-Bannerman had been particularly handicapped since 1898, because he was never able to speak with a clear authority. Now he could, he was a different man. The change appeared strikingly, when Balfour upon reappearing at Westminster attempted to repeat at his expense the logic-chopping which had served to humble him in the past. The Premier retorted with a single phrase—'Enough of this foolery!'—so perfectly expressing the new House's sense that politics was a task for men and not a sport for gentlemen that for long afterwards even Balfour's golden tongue could not win its ear.[1]

The social achievements of this new ministry were very considerable. It overhauled the system of taxation, and by laying heavier burdens on the wealthy began to equalize the distribution of wealth. It gave workmen compensation for injuries, pensions to the aged, medical inspection to all children, an eight-hour day to the miners. It passed a Sweated Industries Act, a National Health and an Unemployment Insurance Act. It made

[1] Ensor, *op. cit.*, p. 391.

town planning possible, and began to provide garden allotments for all who desired them. Never before had quite so much social legislation of the first importance been passed within four years. But in 1910 all this beneficence came to a full stop: the quarrels over the Parliament Act and Irish Home Rule, and the growing menace of Germany left Parliament neither time nor energy to continue the beneficent record.

As a result almost nobody was satisfied, and the disillusion was made the harder to bear by the extravagance of the hopes with which the last of the Liberal Governments had been greeted. Organized Labour was dissatisfied. The Government had attempted to melt the grievances of the Trades Unions over the incredible judicial decision in the Taff Vale case, by which every Union was made actionable for every damage caused or loss sustained in a strike of its members. But the Trades Disputes Bill was so 'unintelligible to anybody but a trained lawyer',[1] that the Labour Members of Parliament introduced a Private Member's Bill of their own, directly exempting Trades Unions from all actions for tort, and this Bill was eventually passed into law. It was a significant episode, for it seemed to show that the right way to get what you wanted from the Government was to become a rebellious nuisance. Others who wanted things the Government seemed slow to grant thus interpreted it. Women wanted votes. Workers wanted that sharing of the wealth they had created which would give them a rise in real wages, instead of the steady drop they were experiencing. The Irish wanted Home Rule, and the Ulstermen wanted separation from the rest of Ireland. There was hardly an end to the accumulated wants of so many sections of the people, and the long list of beneficent social legislation had done very little to assuage the general appetite. All these things were demanded in vain by constitutional action, and after 1911 they were demanded by force. Strike succeeded strike, each being more violent and devastating than the one before, and more often than not the workers came out in defiance of their own trades unions, for they were passing over from the socialism of Ramsay Macdonald to the syndicalism of Tom Mann. The Conservatives themselves were the foremost in defiant law-breaking. The Suffragettes were more violent and destructive than all the others. In the House of Commons there was scene after scene, blows given and taken, books flying through the air, as the legislators shouted insults at each other about Ireland, about Welsh Disestablishment, and about educational reform. The whole air of the nation was turgid with hysteria, and passion rather than reason dictated every response. All these demands had been presented in the form in which responsible parliamentary government, as the Liberals interpreted it, could hardly grant them, and by or on behalf of groups who wanted these things far too strongly to allow themselves to be deflected from them by the ordinary processes of the accepted parliamentary game.

[1] Ensor, *op. cit.*, p. 392.

4

The Anglican Array

I · *The Task Ahead*

CHRISTIAN doctrine, proclaiming, as it does, a realistic rather than an idealistic view of the world, forbids the Church to take refuge in any kind of exaggerated utopianism. Thus the Church greeted the opening of a new century with sober, even with sombre expectations. Most of the sermons, pronouncements, and pamphlets, which came from the various spokesmen in 1900, were either estimates of the work lying ahead of the Church, or else laments over its manifest unfitness to discharge the duties which God seemed to be laying upon it. The Church has always been exceedingly eloquent on the dual theme of its great tasks and its crippling defects; and the impetus of a closing and an opening century brought to birth a considerable body of the literature of ecclesiastical stocktaking.

Two samples of this may aptly be given. In 1900, Hensley Henson, at that time the warden of St Mary's Hospital in Ilford, marked the turn of the century by editing a composite book of essays called *Church Problems*.[1] He and his contributors set themselves the task of making a survey of the stresses of the moment and the challenges of the future, as they affected the Church and the Church affected them. Unquestionably, the most notable contribution was the editor's own introductory essay on *The Church of England*. In this, he began with a thoroughly blistering account of the Church, and he embellished it with an ample series of quotations from as many uncomplimentary opinions as even his pertinacity of research could discover. But he then arrived at the considered and stimulating judgement that 'events do seem to be visibly converging to one result, and that an immense demand on the Church of the English people'.[2] In front of the Church as Henson saw the situation, there lay four main tasks. First, the imperial mission of Great Britain carried with it the spiritual implication of a charge to convert the world; and he quoted with emphatic assent the

[1] Published by John Murray, 1900.　　　　[2] *Ibid.*, p. 25.

challenge of Archbishop Benson to the London Missionary Conference of 1894, 'The Church of England is now charged with the world's Christianity.'[1] Secondly, there came the discharge of the responsibilities to Christendom as a whole which were involved in the unique position of the Church of England as a bridge between the Catholic and Protestant conceptions of Christianity.[2] Thirdly, there was an urgent need for the intellectual restatement of the Christian Faith. Here, while gladly acknowledging all that *Lux Mundi* had accomplished, Henson still judged it to be not enough, and was convinced that

if Christian doctrine is to be successfully restated in terms acceptable to the modern intellect and the modern conscience, it seems no extravagant assumption that the Church of England must take a leading part in the great work.[3]

Finally, there were the heavy sociological responsibilities of the Church, and a great charge ahead to work out, and to implement in terms of national social structure and daily industrial life 'the tendency which shows itself in every part of Western Christendom, and which insists on holding Christianity very close to the actual course of human life'.

Canon Charles Gore viewed the future with grimmer forebodings than these. He looked back over the many years of the Queen's reign, and he thanked God for them. He saw them as a great period of history for the Church because in them its corporate life had been revived. In 1837, he said, the Church had been generally regarded as merely a department of the civil administration; and there was no consciousness of the truth that the Church, though national, was part of a Society older and still more important than the state. Reasoning from this recovery, he saw three existing tendencies making for spiritual health and vitality. The growth of the Church's corporate consciousness should surely lead to more, and yet more, corporate action. The state, on the other hand, was showing an increasing disinclination to touch purely spiritual and religious affairs. In this the state was moved by something more positive than any desire to let sleeping dogs lie, because Gore discerned on the state's part an increasingly high valuation of the services the Church was rendering to society as a whole.

But that was in 1898, two years before the end of the century, and before the Boer War had begun, On the last day of 1899 Gore preached in Westminster Abbey a 'most despondent sermon on the hollowness of modern progress'.

The nineteenth century was closing with a widespread sense of disappointment and anxiety among some who cared most for righteousness and truth. In all departments of life there was a lack of conspicuous leadership. There had been a great diffusion of popular education, but it was doubtful if this had promoted either thought or character or skill. Literature was singularly uninspired. There

---

[1] *Ibid.*, p. 26.   [2] *Ibid.*, p. 27.   [3] *Ibid.*, p. 29.

was little belief in intelligence or study among the young. Visions of peace, which had fascinated the minds of men in the middle of the century had retired out of view. The grinding of mere commercial competition heralded no better prospect for mankind than did military strife. Imperialism was dominant, but it was 'poor in moral quality, and appeared, behind only too thin a veil, as the worship of our unregenerate British selves without morality or the fear of God.'

But, on the other hand, he did see some dim signs of a reasoned hope.

The lack of rival enthusiasms gave an opportunity to the Church to appeal to every man's conscience. They were on the eve of a fresh understanding of Christianity. The old Bible was being read afresh with new power. If there is for the moment silence, it may be only the hush before the wind of the divine spirit blows.[1]

Thus there was a contrast already existing between the optimistic idealism of the humanist and the more sober realism of the Christian. They surveyed the same scene, and estimated the work of the same past, and drew from this wholly different conclusions. As the years unfolded this contrast was to become a serious clash. At that moment, the dawn of 1900, a wise observer might perhaps have noted that the Church was at least armouring itself against the onslaughts of disillusion, which were so soon to become a potent and fatal cause of disunion and feud in the body social and political.

The story of Church and state in England from 1900 to 1914 is the same story, but told, so to speak, from both ends at once. In the affairs of state, 1900 saw a virtually united people suffused with a great hope for the future : and 1914 saw a hopelessly disunited, quarrelling people, filled with gloomy apprehensions. But the Church has never been more disunited than it was in 1900, and in consequence looked forward to its twentieth-century tasks with fear and trembling. By 1914 it had recovered much of this unity. The theme of these fourteen years is the effort to bring to fulfilment the words of the Prayer for the Church Militant, asking for the Church, 'truth, unity and concord', and for its people 'that all they that do confess thy holy name may agree in the truth of thy holy Word, and live in unity and godly love'.

II · Barriers to Harmony

The chief barriers to this godly union and concord in the Church from 1900 to 1914 were the activities of the Modernists and the Anglo-Catholics respectively. These were so important that each must have a full-length chapter to itself, and thus will come to be described in later pages. But there were other barriers as well.

The reunion of Christendom was ironically destined to be one of them. In 1894 Lord Halifax and the Abbé Portal had begun their conversations in the hope of laying the foundations of a better understanding between the Roman and the English branches of the Catholic Church. Not much had

---

[1] G. L. Prestige, *The Life of Charles Gore* (Heinemann), 1935, p. 225.

come of them as yet, except a snub from Rome in the form of the bull *Apostolicae Curae*, and the firm rejoinder of the Lambeth Conference. But neither Halifax nor Portal considered their work fatally compromised by these events; nor did they abandon their efforts. The fact that these conversations continued intermittently until they led up to the Malines Conversations in 1921 is a testimony to their pertinacious and righteous zeal; but they helped to keep alive the latent suspicion of Rome in most sections of the Church, and to make harder the task of those who supposed that the first of all needs was unity within the Church of England itself.

The other endeavour which was to excite controversy in the new century was the effort, led by Gore and his friends, to secure reform in the Church by the method of claiming the freedom of the Church from parliamentary control in things spiritual. The terms of this controversy were largely fixed by a very successful volume of essays by different authors, edited by Gore, and published in 1898,[1] What Gore chiefly hoped would come from the movement, whose bible at that time was *Essays on Church Reform*, was four principal acts of liberation—the end of the sale of advowsons, the end of the particular form of Establishment which so tied the Church that she had no freedom to manage even the affairs committed to her by Christ himself, the power of the laity to stop improper appointments to benefices and to secure the removal of incompetent or lazy clergy, and the protection of the clergy from the tyranny of wealthy parishioners.[2] On all these things, and on their imperative urgency every contributor to this book was agreed. As most of them were lawyers, this agreement was impressive. They judged that the right moment for pressing forward with the self-govermnent of the Church had come; and they regarded this as being the only practical alternative to disestablishment. The immediate scandals lying behind the book, and which the Church was powerless to remedy under the existing systems, were, in Gore's words, 'the traffic in the cure of souls, the apparently needless reduction of the Confirmation of Bishops to the merest farce, and the miserable lawlessness which characterizes our Church'. They saw that for this there must necessarily be lay representation on the councils of the Church; but they differed as to whether a competent layman for this purpose was any baptized adult, or those who had been confirmed. This collection of essays was very influential, and it attracted a swarm of hostile pamphlets.

III · *Parishes and Parsons*

It is one of the unfortunate but constant traits of the Church of England that it realizes the acid facts of its situation in contemporary society about twenty years after they become apparent to most other social observers. What few, if any, of its accredited leaders of 1900 seem to have realized

[1] *Essays on Church Reform*, edited by Charles Gore (John Murray), 1898.
[2] *Ibid.*, p. 29.

was that the mission field of the most urgent importance lay within the shores of England herself. For twenty years and more the Church overseas had been making a tremendous impression on the heathen world, but the Church at home had made practically no discoverable impression upon the secular world. While church people were wasting their strength in fighting the most violent battles against each other, their great enemies, rationalism and indifference, were winning one engagement after another. The war between a Christian and a secular view of life, which, from 1920 onwards, was to become as bitter as it was inescapable, had already begun, though there are not many traces of this realization in the correspondence of the foremost church leaders in the early years of the century.

The parish priests in the great cities knew it, for in 1900 they were already lamenting a slow but steady decline in church attendance. It betokened a coming alienation, if not a divorce, between the mass of the English peoples and their national Church. The majority still claimed its services for baptisms, weddings and burials; but so meagre a claim cannot constitute church membership in any effective and real sense.

When Davidson went to Lambeth, a careful census had just been compiled in London by Mudie Smith, and published in the *Daily News*. It was exact and scientific in method, for it was taken Sunday by Sunday for a year. It included all services, and it did not omit the smallest chapels of the the most obscure sects. Comparing the results with the admittedly much less exact census taken by Robertson Nicholl in the same area in 1886,[1] the population area having increased by half a million in the meantime, the results were startling:

It showed a drop from a gross total of 1,167,321 attendances to one of 1,003,361. Attendances at the Anglican Services (including missions) had actually fallen from 535,715 to 396,196; nonconformist attendances (excluding missions and the Salvation Army) only from 369,349 to 363,882. As Mudie Smith obtained figures showing how many persons attended more than one service, he was able to give the net number of persons worshipping. They were only 832,051 in a resident population (outside institutions) of 4,470,304, or a little over two in eleven.[2]

Still more startling were these figures when compared with the census taken by Mr Horace Mann in 1851. This had been a rather inexact census, but it represented that about half the total population of England were churchgoers. In 1882 there had been a series of private investigations in a number of large towns, from which it was estimated that the following percentages of the population went regularly to church or chapel: Sheffield 23, Nottingham 24, Liverpool 26, Bristol 31, Southampton 38, Hull 41, Portsmouth 41, Bath 52. Of these, about 37 per cent of the attendances

---

[1] Nicholl took the whole of his census in one day, and excluded all services before 11 a.m.

[2] Ensor, *op. cit.*, p. 308.

were made in the parish churches—a considerable drop from the 50 per cent of Mr Mann's census of 1851. The only city outside London for which statistics as exact as those of Mr Mudie Smith are available was Liverpool. The *Liverpool Post* took a census on much the same lines as Mr Mudie Smith's in 1881, in 1891 and again in 1902. The figures of church and chapel attenders in those three years were: 1881: 146,469; 1891: 157,846; and 1902: 178,477. There was actually an increase, but it was not in proportion to the much more rapid increase of the population of Liverpool during those thirteen years; and the growth in churchgoing was due to the evening and not to the morning congregations, which had slightly declined.[1]

On the other hand, the communicant statistics were more encouraging. The Dean of Norwich, in his contribution to *Essays on Church Reform* quotes these figures of communicants:

1891–1892	1,437,719	1894–1895	1,778,361
1892–1893	1,607,930	1895–1896	1,840,351
1893–1894	1,701,499	1896–1897	1,886,059

But these figures are really a testimony to the devotion of the Anglo-Catholic movement.

Such were the statistical facts. They reflected a changing state of mind about religion. No longer was there any generally agreed core of religious belief to which the Churches could appeal; and every Church was losing ground fast. England was just as truly a mission field as China or India, and the clergy would have to become missionaries again. Some of them realized this necessity, and realized with it that the Church at home was not suitably organized to meet it. They made their protests and offered their suggestions in pamphlets and letters to the newspapers, producing in this way quite a considerable amount of literature, mostly relating to conditions in London, which underlines the facts revealed by Mudie Smith's census.

On May 22, 1899, *The Times* printed 'An Appeal from South London Incumbents to the English Church'. Fifteen of these incumbents signed it; and their parishes ranged from Lambeth to Greenwich.

South London [they wrote] presents a problem to the Church which is rare even in the foreign mission field. It is the problem of dealing with vast masses of the people in whom the religious sense, once more or less active, is now seldom exercised, and from whom it seems in real danger of dying out. Clergymen who have laboured in the foreign mission field have borne witness that the so-called 'heathen' of India have more religious feeling in them, and perform the religious duties of prayer and worship more generally than the masses in South London. And therefore we are forced to the humiliating suggestion that there is less habitual turning of manhood and womanhood towards religious subjects and religious duties among the two million souls in South London than exists among the similar masses of struggling poor in non-Christian lands.

[1] *Report of Church Congress, Liverpool, 1904*, pp. 59, 60.

A week later, on May 29, 1899, the Bishop of Stepney wrote a letter to *The Times* to endorse all this as applying also to East London.

The next *cri-de-cœur* came from St Pancras in North London. In 1900 an anonymous writer brought out a pamphlet,[1] the immediate intention of which was to protest against the unintelligent method which had been followed in dividing the unwieldy parish of St Pancras, but which gave an account of the spiritual health of North London which was no less alarming than that which *The Times* letter had given of conditions on the other bank of the Thames. The district, he said, was now as fully populated as it ever could be. Every inch of the ground was now built on; and many old houses were being demolished to make room for railway extensions. The people, yearly turning more and more completely into slum dwellers, and living as best they could on casual labour, were wholly out of touch with organized religion, and constituted one vast mission district.

The writer wanted it organized as such. But this, he complained, was not being done. What was being done was to tear old parishes into pieces to make new ones in a wholly arbitrary and mechanical way. 'Hitherto our authorities have argued that whenever a parish arrives at a population of 10,000 or 15,000, it is ready and fit for sub-division.'[2] This policy, which had already ruined the Church in St Pancras, was in fact being carried out everywhere, but mechanically, and on the cheap. Writer after writer complained of it.[3] The bishops had produced new parishes furnished with the cheapest possible churches, no money for a curate, and a bare minimum of necessary equipment, with the slick fertility of a conjuror delivering rabbits out of a top hat. In St Pancras, for instance, four ancient parishes had given birth to thirty new ones. The inevitable result was the gradual sinking into a state of contented dejection of very many vicars of these new parishes, who were simply left alone in an impossible position with an impossible job.

The author of the St Pancras pamphlet then went on to say what he did want, namely, a system suitable to the 'huge mission district' which North London had become.

Evangelization must proceed from strong and fully equipped centres. Instead of the poor and sickly churches in out-of-the-way corners, we sorely want a few large Basilicas which will show up well in open spaces, capable of holding 2,000, with a strong staff of five or six clergy, each carefully selected, not to be a sort of jack of all trades, but for his particular vocation and ministry. Let these weak and feeble parishes with their mean, dilapidated, and ill-placed churches be boldly thrown together.[4]

This view was warmly endorsed by those all over the country who knew

[1] *The Organisation of the Church in Large Centres of Population, with Special Reference to the Church in St Pancras, London, 1900.*
[2] Pamphlet, p. 4.
[3] See the essay on the parochial system by Edgar Gibson, Vicar of Leeds, in Henson's *Church Problems.*
[4] St Pancras pamphlet, p. 6.

the facts, and particularly by such men as Edgar Gibson, Vicar of Leeds, who pleaded the same cause, and pointed to the great success of those lamentably few centres of population which were worked in that way, Yarmouth, Portsea, Leeds, and Stepney.[1] What was really needed, as most people saw, was a new system of pluralities. But here the archaic state of the law stood in the way, for by the Act of 1838, which still held good, the only benefices which could be held in plurality were those within four miles of each other by the nearest road, and the annual value of which did not exceed £200. To get any exemption meant the promoting of a special Act of Parliament for each separate case.

Although the bishops seemed strangely indifferent to the problems of parochial reorganization, urgent though they were, they devoted careful attention to another pressing problem, that of the maintenance of the supply of candidates for ordination. In 1900 the position was becoming serious. All through the nineteenth century there had been a steady increase in the number of deacons ordained each year, though it was not an increase which kept pace with the rapid growth of the general population. This process came to its peak in the years 1886 to 1888, during which 2,324 men were ordained. Ten years later, in the period 1896 to 1898, the number had dropped to 1,994. But in these ten years the general population had grown by 300,000 a year, that is, a net increase of 3,000,000. This increase should have been met by a yearly increase of a hundred ordinations; but it was in fact met by a yearly decrease of 110. The position can be made still more clear by taking the figures over a slightly longer term of years, and by reckoning in longer periods. Thus, from 1872 to 1899, 19,747 deacons were ordained, that is, 705 a year. In 1885 to 1899, an average of 738 deacons were ordained a year. This seems to suggest that the decline did not begin to set in until 1894, and had begun to become serious in 1897. But whenever it may be held that the falling process had begun, it had become sufficiently serious by the end of the century to cause the Church to set up more than one commission to enquire into it.[2] It was felt most seriously in the great cities and towns outside London, and particularly in Cardiff, Birmingham and Manchester.

The type of man offering himself for ordination was also beginning to change. The candidates from Oxford and Cambridge were decreasing—in 1899 they were only 61 per cent of the whole—while those from the great provincial universities with a theological faculty, especially Dublin and

[1] Gibson, *Church Reform*, p. 125.
[2] In 1899 the Convocation of Canterbury set up a committee under the chairmanship of Archdeacon Sandford of Exeter. It produced a report, *The Supply and Training of Candidates for Holy Orders* (Paper 343, The National Society, London). In 1900 the Bishop of Winchester set up an independent diocesan committee on the same subject, under the chairmanship of the Bishop of Southampton. It produced a report, which was published in Winchester. All the figures in the paragraphs are arrived at by a collation of these reports.

Durham, were steadily rising. In the view of those best qualified to judge, the Church had lost nothing by this change. The intellectual qualifications of the candidates were steadily rising, and though some complaints were heard that the candidates generally showed too little sense of vocation, there has never yet been a time, from the days of St Paul onwards, when the older priests did not make that complaint about their juniors. If this complaint was justified, then it was one which could easily be remedied in the theological colleges—given the right principals to rule over them. But the rarest of all vocations is that of the good principal of a theological college: there are never more than a handful of them in any one generation of priests. It was therefore all the greater luck that one of the very greatest in any generation came to his life's work in 1899. He was B. K. Cunningham, who was appointed by Randall Davidson to be the first Warden of Bishop's Hostel, Farnham. In the last year of his life, Davidson wrote this tribute to him in his Farnham days:

> We were, I think, very fortunate in the men who came as students, but we owe profound thanks to Cunningham for the teaching he gave. He was absolutely free from any partisan allegiance in the Church, and attracted men of widely differing sentiments and attainments. True, he was very deaf, but he possessed the power more than I have known in any other deaf man of overriding it by his beaming power of affection and sympathy. The men did a good deal of theological work for him, and, so far as I could judge, his teaching was really excellent.[1]

This appointment did more than any other single act to keep up a high standard in the ordination candidates during the years 1900 to 1940.

But the main difficulties in the way of increasing the numbers were not so simply overcome. They were the financial difficulties, and the unsatisfactory status of all the unbeneficed clergy. It was very expensive to be ordained. The cost was at least £500 after the boy left school; after the university, the annual charge of the theological colleges varied from £70 to £120.[2] And after ordination, there was no certainty of becoming an incumbent after a reasonable period of years as an assistant curate. In 1896 there were 200 more curates than benefices, and in 1898 the position was still worse. Besides that, most incumbencies had a wholly insufficient income, and even that income was dropping. The figures for the ancient parish of St Pancras are illuminating, and they constitute only one instance among many. The ancient parish had been divided into thirty parishes. Their incomes varied from £700 to £173. Only nine of them had an income of £400 or above; and the average was £355.[3] Well might the anonymous pamphleteer complain:

> Nothing could be more discreditable to the Church of England than the way she treats her unbeneficed clergy. At present the almost universal qualification

[1] Bell, vol. I, p. 251.　　　　　　　　[2] Winchester report, p. 6.
[3] St Pancras pamphlet, p. 14.

for a benefice is the possession of private means. Hundreds of appointments are made on this sole recommendation. The unfortunate curate who does not possess any private means cannot accept a benefice. His lot in any Church but ours would still be a happy and honourable one. But it is notorious that with us his career is practically at an end at forty years of age : the Church which has impressed on him her indelible orders has no further need of his service.[1]

The indictment was exaggerated, but it exaggerated a truth, as all contemporary evidence testifies.

As the new century dawned, the Church was entering upon forty of the most difficult, exacting, and discouraging years of all her history. In many ways she was not adequately equipped to meet the strain which was coming; and, as the coming pages will show, in matters of organization she was continually forced to improvise changes to meet urgent needs as they arose. The tasks ahead were enormous and the dangers immense. That it has survived them, and emerged spiritually the stronger for the testing, is due to two great assets which have never deserted it, the chronic faithfulness of the average parish priest, and the theological realism which causes it to reject all the utopian visions held out by politicians and sociologists.

IV · *The Church's Leaders*

In this period the leadership of the Church counted for a great deal. Lambeth Palace mattered more to the whole Church than it had done for centuries. In part, this was because the Church could no more than the state escape the growing tendency to centralize power and authority in a single cell of energy. It was in Davidson's primacy that Lambeth became what the Vatican has always been to the Roman Communion. Today, every Anglican bishop recognizes the Archbishop of Canterbury as providing the one centre of cohesion for all the scattered dioceses, and as being in a real though an undefined sense his chief. But there was more than this; and the acknowledged importance of Lambeth rested chiefly on the remarkable personality of the particular archbishop who lived there during the reigns of Edward VII and George V.

Any decision and any public action of his quickly affected the remotest parish, and deflected the courses of the clergy. But it was not only of him that this was true, though it was naturally more immediately true of him than of any other. There were, however, at least two other men of whom it could be said that every word they uttered was widely listened to, and really counted. They were Charles Gore, bishop first of Worcester and then of Oxford, and Hensley Henson, first canon of Westminster, and then Dean of Durham, and Bishop of Hereford, and later of Durham. No one else, not even Talbot of Winchester, or Percival of Hereford, or, among the laity, Lord Halifax, counted as these three men did. Each in his own sphere

[1] *Ibid.*, p. 15.

was indubitably great, but none were possessed of the powerful personalities of Davidson, Gore, and Henson. Their names march through all the histories and biographies. Their judgements on all the issues of the day had to be taken into account and weighed, for they would sway the balances; and the combinations, dissensions, and the differences between them did much to condition and colour the most ordinary, day-to-day ministry of Church to people.

Randall Davidson was certainly one of the most remarkable of all the Archbishops of Canterbury, and the only one up to then whom all alike agreed to be indispensable. Again and again the fiery reformer and the cold logician were restrained from carrying through a course of action to its proper end because of the fear that this end might be the resignation of the Archbishop. Until the last years of his long primacy there was nobody at all in sight who could be thought of as an adequate successor. There were indeed other great men among the bishops: it is at least arguable that Gore was a greater man than Davidson. But none of them could do the real work of Davidson, not one could bring his particular gifts. These gifts were the art of inspiring the trust of those who agreed but little with his policies (and this gift he had to an altogether unusual degree), and his genius for cohesion. Not many archbishops can have consulted so many and so various people when he was making up his mind on some big problem. He might, and he usually did follow his own judgement in the end; but he always made each one of those he had called in for consultation feel that he had made an invaluable contribution. As the years passed, this habit of 'finding out what so-and-so thinks' grew on him. He deliberately let it grow, with the result that when the war came, and he bravely gave public utterance to many opinions which were far from popular, he had reached the unusual position in public life that he himself was invariably trusted, and his words heeded. He had also very great skill in organizing the daily work of Lambeth. He found it in some chaos, and when he left it, Lambeth was the centre of a network of filaments stretching out to every part of the world, with a daily average output of scores of letters, the writing of all of them having been dovetailed into an endless stream of public engagements and private interviews, and all working as smoothly and serenely as a tempered machine.

The regard in which he was held by the bishops, and by such of the clergy as had dealings with him, was universal and unvarying. Yet in many ways he seemed to have so little in common with so many of them. The habit of his mind was utterly unsacerdotal: his interests lay outside all narrowly priestly things. Over and over again the issues with which the ecclesiastical controversialists forced him to deal did not greatly interest him, and their detail he had laboriously to 'get up', not having of his own natural volition paid much heed to it. Essentially his was the mind of a very great Christian layman, with an utterly simple and an apparently unquestioning faith. In most controversies with which he had to deal (and no archbishop has had more, or they more tormenting) he saw the issues much as a Christian layman would see them, and he brought to his conduct of them an inspired power of compromise, and the balm of a wise and benignant judge of the high court. At the beginning of his primacy two very different observers diagnosed his danger as that of paying too much heed to the views of the great lay administrators. One of them was Scott Holland, who wrote:

Bishop Davidson's point of danger is not the Court. He has survived its perils with a singular simplicity. Rather is it to be sought at the Athenaeum. There dwell the sirens who are apt to beguile and bewitch him. They have ceased to be mermaids with harps and have adopted the disguise of elderly and excellent gentlemen of reputation, who lead you aside into corners and, in impressive whispers, inform you what will not do, and what the intelligent British public will not stand. The Bishop has a deep veneration for the judgement and the wisdom of important laity of this type. Yet the Athenaeum is not the shrine of infallibility. Its elderly common sense has no prophetic afflatus.[1]

The other was Lord Halifax, who wrote Davidson a terrific letter of seventy-six pages, the moral of which was in one emphatic sentence: 'I do entreat you, do everything that is needed for the good of the Church on your own inherent authority and that of the bishops.'[2]

His policy was framed so as invariably to further two out of his three chief aims. He believed completely in the constitutional connection between Church and state, and at nearly any cost he would preserve the establishment. He tried his very hardest to hold the Church together in godly love and concord. Let there be unity between us, and as for schism, let it not once be named among us. Such was his watchword; and time after time he used the whole weight of his tremendous authority to bring the quarrelling partisans to a state of compromise. The last weapon in his armoury, the threat of resignation, was always sufficient to quell the most turbulent. It even quelled men like Charles Gore and Frank Weston, Bishop of Zanzibar, and that took some doing. The third great purpose of his life really grew out of the first, but he was never allowed to pursue it as he would have wished. He cherished and at no time lost the vision of what a united, a peaceful, and a harmonious Church could do to set forward all the causes of private and public righteousness in the nation. No man can ever have struggled harder than he did to hold the Church to its true purpose, but it was his fate to be forced to grapple with one interior discontent and controversy after another, and very few of them were much concerned with the right action for a Church in an increasingly pagan world. Doctrine, creeds, sacraments, appointments—with these his life was spent; and he wanted to give it to lead the Church in an onslaught on slums, prostitution, and drunkenness. This constant thwarting he accepted with an inspiring

---

[1] Bell, vol. I, p. 406. [2] *Ibid.*, p. 390.

humility, and he brought to his charge a wisdom and a penetration of judgement, intensified to the point where these pedestrian accomplishments become heroic virtues. During the course of his long primacy there were many who disagreed with him, but there was not one who wished to see anyone else as Primate of All England.

All his life he was astonishingly accessible to all who wished to see him to urge on him this or that scheme or panacea. But he did not easily catch fire, and to be granted an interview with Davidson was something of an ordeal. He had (and it is the common failing of the Anglican priesthood in every age) a much clearer view of difficulties than of opportunities. To go to see him with a scheme only partly thought out was to invite an unhappy half-hour. But to an enthusiast who really knew his subject and its worth, and could communicate the practicality of his conviction, an initially chilly Archbishop would quickly thaw. There is a lovely story about the American John R. Mott's first talk with Davidson which exactly illustrates his method, his formidability, and his charm. In 1905 Mott came to England to collect information about university men as candidates for the ministry. He sought out Tissington Tatlow, the Secretary of the Student Christian Movement, to ask for his help; and together these two, in a state of considerable trepidation, sought and were granted an interview with Davidson. Tatlow tells the story of their reception:

On arrival at Lambeth we were greeted by a chaplain, and in a few minutes were in the Archbishop's presence. I recall the scene vividly. The Archbishop shook hands, motioned us to a couch, and seated himself at his writing table across which he looked at us. He wasted no time but immediately asked that we should state our business. Mott explained that he was making an enquiry on the recruiting of the ablest young men for the ministry, and was anxious to have the opinion of the Archbishop on the subject. The Archbishop interrupted to explain that he had just appointed a committee on this very subject, and that until the committee reported he felt it impossible for him to say anything official on the subject. The interview showed every sign of an early end, but Mott's prearranged strategy was ruthlessly put into operation.

He hurled himself into the awful silence, and simply talked and talked about his experience in foreign universities, especially in Tokyo, addressing Davidson just like a public meeting. Within five minutes 'his Grace's interest began to be aroused. He had his face in his hands with both elbows on the table, and his gaze fixed on Mott with a concentrated frown of interest.' Then he gave Mott everything for which he had asked.[1]

At the end of his biography of Charles Gore, Dr Prestige has a passage in which he asks himself if Gore was to be regarded as a saint, and he cannot decide his answer. He prefers to call him a very great Englishman. To accept that title may be flattering to one's sense of national pride, for if that is

[1] Tissington Tatlow, *The Story of the Student Christian Movement* (S.C.M. Press), 1933, pp. 254, 255.

what Englishmen are meant to be like, and can become, the native stuff and genius of the race cannot be wholly unsatisfactory. Gore was a rigorist, an ascetic, and a disciplinarian, and yet no one who knew him failed to love him. He was a scholar in the pure academic sense of the word: only Darwell Stone knew more of the Fathers, and no one knew more of the Prophets. But all his scholarship went to feed his passion for social righteousness, and his desire for the good of his fellow-men. His generosity was on the heroic scale; his individuality so spirited that it created a rich deposit of legend and story as his life went on. Almost alone among the great churchmen of his day, disciples gathered round him and he kept them. To this day one constantly comes across priests up and down the country, who at some point in their lives were brought into contact with Gore, whose lives began again on that day, and who have ever since looked to him as their chief inspiration on earth. His counterpart in history was St Bernard of Clairvaux. The same vehemence, the same logical relentlessness, the same glow of pastoral and evangelistic love were to be found in both men. For most of his life he was fighting in one cause or another, and most of his fights were with personalities. But they were his friends, and he never lost one of them as a friend. The tolerance shown towards and the understanding of the Anglo-Catholic cause in the Church of England today, and the fact that in the last twenty years the Church has steadily grown more Anglo-Catholic, is due primarily to the fact that in the first twenty years of this century it was Gore who was its chief exponent.

The one really formidable antagonist Gore had, and the only one who carried a sufficient weight of conviction and armoury of intellectual power to stand up to him, was Hensley Henson. From the day when Henson came to Westminster as canon until the day when Gore resigned the bishopric of Oxford, the two were nearly always in conflict, and there were few problems before the Church on which they did not stand on opposite sides. This meant that every problem had to be a battlefield, for neither Gore nor Henson knew what compromise meant. Yet, through it all, they remained the firmest and the closest friends. Henson was born with the eighteenth-century mind. He held firmly to it because he believed in it. He had always hated what he called fanaticism, and he meant by that term many of the things for which Gore stood. He fought them with every power he possessed, and he brought to the fight great courage, complete tenacity, and a barbed pen such as Gibbon himself would not have despised. He stood outside all parties in the Church, and said over and over again that he valued independence above all else. In an age of communal thinking and feeling, he was an individualist. Led to espouse unpopular counsels, he himself had no gift for popularity, and he had to be known over a long period to be loved. Only a great mind was likely to be able to weigh him at his true worth: only a high generosity and a true humility could fight against his causes without fighting against his person. There were not many such minds among Henson's opponents, and from the rest Henson had an unhappy knack of provoking the very worst. There is no chapter in the long story of Anglo-Catholic controversy quite so discreditable as that which tells of the weapons which these partisans used to fight Henson. He saw the defeat of nearly every cause he believed in but nothing ever quenched his fiery spirit, and he never once sought popularity. Without him the Church would have been immeasurably the poorer, but his paths were in stony places.

5

New Testament Criticism and the
Doctrinal Crisis

I · *The Effects of Albert Schweitzer*

ON SEPTEMBER 27th, 1910, the Annual Church Congress met at Cambridge. It was its fiftieth meeting: the first had been in 1861, also at Cambridge. Although the Congress had never been, and was never to become an official function, yet it had won for itself a recognized place in the life of the Church, and it fulfilled a necessary purpose. Year after year, ecclesiastics and the more leisured lay-people from all over the country met for a week in one or another of the great centres of population. They assembled in their hundreds, they listened to episcopal sermons, they received civic welcomes, they were assured of true sympathy and deep fellowship by nonconformist deputations, they listened to the reading of carefully prepared papers and to the delivery of less well prepared speeches until their heads ached. The Church Congress was certainly not the least exhausting of the events in the Church's year. Its function was to consider the chief spiritual and social problems of the day, to provide a platform for the most thoughtful and active churchpeople to have their say about them. Most of the leading prophets of the day could be heard in the Congress, and the quality of the papers read frequently reached a very high level. To go to the Church Congress in its golden days was to make a fruitful, not a wasteful, use of time; and there is a good deal of scholarship and prophecy of permanent value buried between the dingy brown covers of its annual Reports.

The Congress of 1910 at Cambridge was perhaps the most impressive and valuable of the whole series. What made it so was the contribution made to it by a great Christian scholar, Albert Schweitzer. He was not himself present at the Congress. While it was being held, he was still in his native Alsace, laboriously learning medicine so that he might make his life the more fit to be offered for the healing of diseased and dispirited negroes in the Congo forests. But in absence he so dominated the proceedings at Cambridge that week that ever since the Congress has been nicknamed the Schweitzer Congress.

His book had shaken the world of biblical scholarship, for *The Quest of the Historical Jesus* was one of the few works which in the writing of history made history. It was written and published in German in 1906 under the title *Von Reimarus zu Wrede*, and an English translation was published in 1910.[1] The book took the form of an examination of the results of many generations of work of German critical scholars on the synoptic Gospels— a vast critical apparatus which Schweitzer, though about to argue that its results were almost valueless, yet proclaimed as constituting one of the great achievements of the human spirit.

When, at some future day, our period of civilization shall lie, closed and completed, before the eyes of later generations German theology will stand out as a great, a unique phenomenon in the mental and spiritual life of our time.

Such is the opening sentence. He felt it so deeply that he contrived to saturate the whole of his long description of the work of Reimarus, Strauss, Bauer, Weiss, and all the rest, with his recognition of their great courage and its momentous importance. Never had victims been more sincerely saluted before being despatched. But they were to be despatched, none the less. Of that evident duty there could be no doubt. For the sum total of their highly destructive work was to obscure and not to clarify the historical Jesus, and to make nonsense of his teaching. Taken together, these critics formed the Liberal Protestant School. They had at last produced a Christ whose teaching was limited almost solely to an interest in ethical philosophy and social reform. Their criticism had been both so ruthless and so misdirected that they had virtually made nonsense of the Gospels, producing complete scepticism not only about the Gospels themselves, but also about all critical methods of treating them. They had left modern historical theology 'with only a torn and tattered Gospel of Mark in its hands'.[2] Out of all this labour not even a fragment of the unquestionably authentic life of Jesus had emerged. Under such treatment, he had remained yet the more enigmatic.

We are experiencing what St Paul experienced. In the very moment when we were coming nearer to the historical Jesus than men had ever come before, and were already stretching out our hands to draw Him into our time, we have been obliged to give up the attempt. We must be prepared to find that the historical knowledge of the personality and life of Jesus will not be a help but perhaps even an offence to religion. The truth is, it is not Jesus as historically known but Jesus as spiritually risen within men, who is significant for our time and can help it.[3]

---

[1] *The Quest of the Historical Jesus*, trans. W. Montgomery (A. & C. Black), 1910. All following quotations from edition of 1922.
[2] *Quest*, p. 307.   [3] *Ibid.*, p. 399.

As the last sentence hints, Schweitzer had his own solution to propose and this made his assault on his predecessors all the more devastating.

A vivid passage in his autobiography describes his methods of workmanship.

> When I had worked through the numerous Lives of Jesus, I found it very difficult to group them in chapters. After attempting in vain to do this on paper, I piled all the Lives in one big heap in the middle of my room, picked out for each chapter I had planned a place of its own in the corner or between the pieces of furniture, and then, after thorough consideration, heaped up the volumes in the piles to which they belonged, pledging myself to find room for all the books belonging to each pile, and to leave each undisturbed in its own place till the corresponding Chapter in the Sketch should be finished. And I carried out my plan to the very end. For many a month all the people who visited me had to thread their way across the room along paths which ran through heaps of books. I had also to fight hard to ensure that the tidying zeal of the trusty Wurttemberg widow who kept house for me came to a halt before the piles of books.[1]

It was an odd genesis of an indubitable literary masterpiece. Schweitzer somehow contrived to put into his work the force of his own tremendous personality, and—a still rarer feat—his translator managed to keep it there. His devastating account of the work of his predecessors was itself exciting, coming, as it did, from a radical scholar at least as extreme as any of them. His own proposed solution of the Christological problem was so radical and so novel that it seemed to strike at the roots of the whole catholic tradition of Christian doctrine. No wonder, then, that when his book, freshly and vividly written and worlds away from the traditional dullness of the German dryasdust theologian, could at last be read in English, it created a storm.

Strauss and the other German critics had made a social reformer and an ethical philosopher out of Jesus. They had drained him of his spiritual and supernatural content. Schweitzer denied almost everything they had said. For him, Jesus was not a teacher but a prophet, not the Messiah but his forerunner in terms of time, for, on his return in glory he became the Messiah. Until then he was another John the Baptist, but deluded, as John was not, for he had from the first the Messianic consciousness, and this was mistaken. There was indeed a Kingdom of God coming, as the synoptic writers said, but Jesus had no part in founding it. It was to be founded by the Tribulation of which Mark and Matthew wrote; and it was to come quickly. The key to the consciousness and the mission of Jesus lies in the Matthean text, 'Ye shall not have gone through the cities of Israel till the Son of Man be come.' But it tarried in coming. Could the necessary Tribulation be forced, could the eschatological grace be wrung from God? Yes, if he, the suffering servant of Isaiah, should bring the Tribulation on him-

---

[1] Albert Schweitzer, *My Life and Thought*, trans. C. T. Campion (Allen and Unwin), 1933, p. 58.

self, that would suffice, and would open the channels of grace. Thus Jesus succeeds in bringing about his own condemnation. But in this he miscalculates utterly, and dies in the depth of despair, thus having destroyed at the same time both his own life and the eschatological view of the energy of God.

At that last cry upon the Cross the whole eschatological supersensuous world fell in upon itself in ruins, and there remained as a spiritual reality only that present spiritual world which Jesus by His all-powerful word had called into being within the world which He contemned. That last cry, with its despairing abandonment of the eschatological future, is His real acceptance of the world. The 'Son of Man' was buried in the ruins of the falling eschatological world; there remained alive only Jesus 'the Man'.

This theory was exceedingly alarming. That it was argued persuasively, from a background of deep and wide knowledge, and with the greatest literary skill, made it still more alarming. For if Schweitzer's portrait of Jesus, and his reconstruction of the processes of his consciousness was right, then the whole of Christendom was wrong, and had always been wrong. He had struck at the creeds, and at the roots of all popular devotion, for the Jesus he described was in grim fact deluded, and a true fanatic. Those who married these two terms, deluded and fanatic, in their anger, were logically right. He had also laid an axe to the root of the idea of Christian morality, for he described Jesus as having taught an ethic possible to be practised only by a few and then but for a short time until the world should end, but utterly unfitted to be the moral guide of whole civilizations throughout the ages of time. And if his work was hardly likely to be acceptable to the general body of his fellow Christians, it would not even be likely to find a welcome among the modernists, whether of the German or Anglican variety. For although on most things German and Anglican modernism differed widely, yet they were agreed that the humanitarian and ethical Christ which their researches seemed to be producing was the Christ whom they wanted. Adolf von Harnack was the prophet of both, and his book *What is Christianity?* answered the question virtually in terms of social reform, ethical training, and political liberalism, amid the cheers of the modernists all over Europe. But if Schweitzer was right, von Harnack was completely and ludicrously wrong, and the whole body of his followers was wrong with him. Thus Schweitzer was just as perturbing to the modernists as to the traditionalists; and even today modernist scholars are apt to write of him sourly.

For all these reasons it was a matter of some moment that the first considerable Christian body to meet after the English translation of Schweitzer's book had been published should worthily answer the challenge. This body happened to be the Cambridge Church Congress, and its proceedings in the matter of Schweitzer were conducted at a very high level indeed. The prepared papers contained much which was of a permanent value, and the unprepared speeches were worthy both of a Christian and a scholarly assembly. Once only did a speaker slip for a moment into a personal attack on the man whose work, after all, seemed to constitute a deadly threat to the personal faith of every person in the Congress hall, whether Protestant, Anglo-Catholic, or Modernist. This was when Archdeacon Charles, at the end of a long paper, qualified his appreciation of the 'brilliant young writer', by adding that 'the bizarreness' of his work 'is only equalled by its cocksureness. He reminds one of the old Epicurean teachers, who, according to Cicero, spoke with as much assurance as though they had just come down from the Council Chambers of the Gods'.[1] It was the one and the only personal remark made that day; and this one was immediately answered by Professor Burkitt, in a moving and glowing testimony to Schweitzer's personal holiness.

The personal charity which the Congress showed to Schweitzer was in keeping with the fact that it was after all a Christian assembly—a fact which on other occasions, particularly when ritual was under discussion, it only too frequently forgot. Not less in keeping with its duty of Christian charity was the onslaught made upon Schweitzer's arguments. They were examined by two great scholars, J. H. Bernard, Dean of St Patrick's, and R. H. Charles, at that time an Oxford don, and later Archdeacon of Westminster. Bernard was a New Testament scholar of the front rank, whose special field was the Fourth Gospel, while Charles had made for himself a European reputation with his work upon Jewish Apocalypticism. Both of them examined Schweitzer's work with great sympathy and absolute fairness, but agreed in rejecting his main, and hence all his subsidiary, conclusions. Bernard accused him of building almost his whole case upon Matthean corruptions of the original Marcan text, and of virtually neglecting the entire witness of Luke. Could anyone who had taken a full and just account of such parables as the Good Samaritan and the Prodigal Son really dismiss our Lord's ethical teaching as a mere *Interimsethic*?[2] Archdeacon Charles, moving happily and skilfully in his own chosen field, had no difficulty in convicting Schweitzer of a chronic failure to distinguish between Eschatology and Apocalyptic, and of giving an inadequate meaning to the latter. 'Schweitzer's reconstruction of the teaching and life of our Lord appears to me therefore wrong in most of its positions. This teaching and life cannot be made intelligible by a school which sees nothing but eschatology in the Gospels, any more than it can be by the school which rejects the permanent

---

[1] *Official Report of the Church Congress* (Allen and Unwin), 1910, p. 74.
[2] This is a clumsy German technical term, a piece of theological jargon, for an ethical system so extremely idealistic that no one could hope to live faithfully by it for more than a short time. But the earliest Christians supposed that the world's life was very brief, and Christ's return in glory very near. Hence it was once supposed by many critics that this expectation of a quick end of the world coloured and distorted the reporting of the Lord's ethical teaching, making it at once more idealistic and 'impossible' than it really was. Today few would hold that view. It is generally accepted that for the most part Jesus meant exactly what he said.

nature of the apocalyptic element in the teaching of our Lord.'[1] Broadly speaking, the verdict of the Congress was that Schweitzer's book had not only destroyed the almost legendary credit and authority of the earlier German critical examination of the Gospels, but that it had also undermined the very solution it had been written to sustain. After Schweitzer, no one could doubt the immense and even crucial importance of eschatology in the life and the teaching of Jesus; but he himself, by his own vehemence and mishandling of textual evidence, had put out of court the theory that in the interpretation of the life of Jesus only the eschatological passages in the Gospels were credible evidence. The Cambridge Church Congress, by its mingled charity, learning, and fairness, had given the impression of having passed a righteous judgement, based upon a cool and competent examination of the evidence, and had done a great service to the whole Church. It had steadied it at a moment of incipient doctrinal panic.

For Schweitzer himself there was reserved a more glorious reputation than that of the *enfant terrible* of biblical criticism. That tremendous personality could not be expressed within the negatives of his theology. He was to become not the least inspiring of all the long roll of the great saints of God. From time to time people are born who seem successfully to defy all the ordinary rules of logic. Schweitzer was one of them. When his readers complained that he had reduced the Jesus of the Gospels to the level of a deluded and rather pathetic fanatic; when they reproached him for having set about his iconoclastic task almost in a spirit of high enthusiasm, they were plainly right. This is exactly what Schweitzer had done with his hero. And yet, illogically, inconsistently, Jesus was to him the Lord of all his life. The careful reader of his book could find in it many signs of what Professor Burkitt, at the Cambridge Church Congress, called a passionate enthusiasm for Jesus[2]—for the Jesus of history not less than for the Christ of his own experience. There were, moreover, little pieces of the most profound spiritual wisdom woven here and there into the texture of his pages, comments which could only have been made as a result of years of the richest prayer and meditation. There was, for example, to be the coming Kingdom of God, but neither Jesus nor the apostles were to found it. It was the 'host of penitents' who were 'wringing it from God'. This was the interpretation he put upon the phrase 'The Kingdom of heaven suffereth violence, and the violent take it by force'[3]—a strange, even bizarre interpretation, but only a saint and a mystic could have thought of it.

To his soul, Jesus was the Lord of all life. Both in his autobiography and his account of his work in the Congo forests, he writes frequently of Jesus, so near and so real to him, and when he does so, he uses the language of absolute devotion, and sets it in a music of phrasing which might almost be that of Julian of Norwich. And this attitude to his Master was his from the beginning: the writing of his great book made absolutely no difference

---

[1] *Report*, pp. 60–75.   [2] *Report*, p. 85.   [3] Matt. 11.12.

to what his soul had found in Christ. It was in 1906 that his book was first published, and it was in 1904, while he was taking the utmost pains to prove the pathetic and fallacious delusions of Jesus, that he was ardently welcoming the never questioned authority of this same Jesus to dispose of all his life. Thus he describes the divine call to give his life to the healing of sick negroes in the Congo:

Many a time already had I tried to settle what meaning lay hidden for me in the saying of Jesus, 'Whosoever would save his life shall lose it'. Now the answer was found.

One morning in the autumn of 1904 I found on my writing table one of the green-covered magazines in which the Paris Missionary Society reported every month on its activities. That evening, in the very act of putting it aside that I might go on with my work, I mechanically opened this magazine. As I did so, my eye caught the title of an article, 'The Needs of the Congo Mission'. It was by Alfred Boegner, the President of the P.M.A., an Alsatian, and contained a complaint that the mission had not enough workers to carry on its work in the Gaboon, the northern province of the Congo colony. The writer expressed his hope that his appeal would bring some of those 'on whom the Master's eyes already rested' to a decision to offer themselves for this urgent work. The conclusion ran, 'Men and women who can reply simply to the Master's call, "Lord, I am coming", those are the people whom the Church needs.' The article finished, I quietly began my work. My search was over.[1]

The rest of his story has become one of the modern glories of Christian discipleship. Schweitzer's name will always live in the history of biblical scholarship and in the missionary annals of Christendom. But not the least of the services he rendered to Christendom was to prove in his own person that a man may be the most radical and disturbing of modernist scholars, and at the same time a saint made free of all the riches of spiritual experience.

II · *Continental and Anglican Modernism*

The book with which Schweitzer smashed a whole school of German biblical criticism—for neither in Germany nor anywhere else did the 'Liberal Christ' fully recover from his defeat—had the further effect of seriously disturbing the hitherto confident march of the Anglican modernists. It did not in the least undermine the general modernism of their attitude both to the scriptures and to the creeds, and it did not cause them to swerve from their essential purpose, but it did strike out of their hands one of the chief of the instruments which they had been using to achieve it.

No one has ever described the essential purpose of Anglican modernism so briefly and so well as did William Sanday, Regius Professor of Divinity at Oxford, in the course of his famous controversy with Charles Gore. It

---

[1] *My Life and Thought: an Autobiography*, trans. C. T. Campion (Allen and Unwin), 1933, pp. 103, 106, 107.

was a battle of pamphlets that they fought; and each of the contestants wrote with one eye fixed on the inscrutable Archbishop at Lambeth, for the prize would not be so much the support of the general body of Christians as success in forcing Davidson to undertake or persuading him to disallow disciplinary action against the modernists. The crucial pamphlet of the whole series was Sanday's *Bishop Gore's Challenge to Criticism*, and one paragraph of it laid down clearly just what it was that the modernist movement in the Church of England was trying to do.

If it is said that what I have written is Modernism, I would reply that I believe —I emphatically and hopefully believe—that a sound and right modernism is really possible; that the Saviour of mankind extends his arms towards the cultivated modern man just as much as He does towards the simple believer. I believe that the cultivated modern man may enter the Church of Christ with his head erect—with some change of language due to differences of time, but all of the nature of re-interpretation of old truths, and without any real equivocation at his heart. I believe he can afford to say what he really thinks—provided only that his fellow Christians of more traditional types are willing to greet him with the sympathetic intelligence which he deserves, and do not turn towards him the cold shoulder of suspicion and denunciation.[1]

'The Cultivated Modern Man'—the phrase is twice repeated, and it was to him that the Anglican modernists believed that they had a distinctive apostolate. It was generally believed that such a person existed, and that he stood at the centre of the whole kaleidoscope of the structure of English society in the early twentieth century, giving to it its characteristic pattern and form, while it revolved round him.

Once given belief in this premise, the effort to win the 'cultivated modern man' to belief in the Christian religion and membership of the Christian Church obviously had to be made. There seemed, thought the modernists, but one way to do it. This was to accept the form of criticism which Lowes Dickinson later wrote down and to pick up the challenge, 'Religious truth is attainable, if at all, only by the method of science.' Let it be so. Let the process be undertaken. Let scientific research have free play to criticize the biblical documents and to censor the creeds. If they are, as Christians claim, the eternal Truth, they can emerge from even this test. And when all this has been faithfully done, what is left must be a Gospel which speaks to modern man in his own language. Such was the faith of the modernist.

Where should the process begin? Obviously with the Gospels themselves. In this field there were precedents to follow, and the virgin country of interpreting the historical Gospels by the methods and the certitudes of the modern scientific spirit had already been well mapped by the continental scholars, particularly those in Germany. They had started by taking for granted the most fundamental of all contemporary scientific assertions about religion—miracles do not happen. If the documents describe mir-

[1] Pp. 30, 31. Quoted in Bell, vol. I, p. 678.

acles, then either their authors were deluded, or they were exaggerating and falsifying the evidence, or the documents themselves were corrupt. To say that miracles, however well attested, can actually have happened was treason to the scientific spirit. The continental theologians were most aggressive and assertive about this. The French Renan could write: 'The clear scientific view of a universe where no free will superior to that of a man is at work in any appreciable manner became since 1846 the immovable anchor whence we have never departed.'[1] In Germany, Strauss spoke for a whole succession of radical theologians when he wrote: 'What has been gained from biblical criticism is only that the exclusion of miracle from our view of history has been universally recognized as a principle of criticism, so that miracle no longer concerns the theologian either positively or negatively.'[2] Among English modernists this rejection of the whole category was much less violent, and most of them were prepared to halt the process before it reached the mystery of our Lord's nature, though not before it had dealt with the tomb of Christ in the same manner as with the sepulchre of Lazarus. But English modernism, too, was ill at ease in the presence of miracle. Dr Inge, probably the most judicious and cautious thinker among them, warned the Church not to be so touchy and so scrupulous about miracle. If it was, it would 'date' its message. No reputable ecclesiastic or theologian would spend five minutes in investigating a modern miracle. 'It would be assumed that it must be ascribed to some obscure natural cause.'[3] He did not therefore deny the New Testament miracles; flat denials were not the way of Anglican modernism. He simply said that they were 'isolated as they never have been before'; and for 'isolated' we may read 'irrelevant' without any falsification of his real meaning.

Although English modernism never developed either the ruthlessness or the thoroughness of its continental models, the writings of the Germans were its models none the less, and a thinker like Strauss was regarded with real veneration. Thus English modernists were always skating on the edge of the two great errors which Schweitzer had detected in the German theologians, and they had missed. The first of these has already been mentioned in this study, namely, that the scholars were cutting away the dead wood of the Synoptic Gospels so ruthlessly that in fact they had virtually destroyed their whole authority, and with it the very basis of their own radical studies. The second was a no doubt unconscious but very real addiction to force all theological study into the service of German nationalism. Nationalism was the heresy to which Europe was then most addicted, and the nerve centre of European nationalism lay in the Germany which

---

[1] Quoted in Charles Gore, *The Reconstruction of Belief* (John Murray), 1921, p. 217.
[2] Quoted in Gore, *op. cit.*, p. 219.
[3] W. R. Inge, *Outspoken Essays* (Longmans, Green), vol. I, 1919, p. 123. This essay, 'Bishop Gore and the Church of England', was written in 1908.

Bismarck had created. Every vital movement and current of thought and expression within Germany worked, whether consciously or not, for the furtherance and the strengthening of German nationalism. Theological modernism, whose true home was in the German universities, was no exception. The long stream of German biblical criticism had tried, and failed, to lay bare the Jesus of history. In the process it had certainly destroyed its own creation, the Liberal Christ, but only to create a monstrous Germanic Christ. Schweitzer brought the charge, and dryly commented: 'This Jesus is not alive, however Germanic they make him.' He went on:

This German critical study of the life of Jesus is an essential part of German religion. As of old Jacob wrestled with the Angel, so German theology wrestles with Jesus of Nazareth, and will not let Him go until He will consent to serve it, and will suffer Himself to be drawn by the Germanic spirit into the midst of our time and our civilization. Since the 'sixties the critical study of the Life of Jesus in Germany has been unconsciously under the influence of an imposing modern religious nationalism in art.[1]

The vast apparatus of Schweitzer's learning, and the extreme literary skill with which he displayed it, gave to him a position of unquestionable authority when he came to survey and assess the achievements of continental critical theology. His conclusion was that it had completely destroyed the basis of its own existence, that it had smashed its own idol, the Liberal Christ, into pieces, and erected in its place another, the Germanic Christ. This meant that the Anglican modernists were also wounded. They had stood on the ground which the Germans had cleared. They had eagerly accepted the Liberal Christ. And now the ground turned out to be a quicksand, and the Liberal Christ was broken, and in its place all that was on offer was a Germanic Christ which nobody outside Germany could possibly want, or an eschatological, deluded Christ in whom nobody except Schweitzer believed. Schweitzer's book certainly disturbed the modernists at least as greatly as the traditionalists themselves. Anglican modernism was at that moment torn up by the roots, and it has never again found the ground to nourish them.

III · *Hastings Rashdall*

With that introduction it is now possible to turn to the story of Anglican modernism from 1900, and of the strife which dogged its steps.

In 1900 two Anglican priests were causing much apprehension by the radicalism of their theological opinions. The first was Canon T. K. Cheyne, the Oriel Professor of Exegesis. He was an old Oxford friend of both Gore and Scott Holland, and had been a constant though distinctly timorous visitor to their annual 'Holy Party' in Illingworth's rectory at Longworth, being drawn there no doubt by some obscure form of the attraction of

---

[1] Schweitzer, *op. cit.*, p. 310.

opposites. Certainly Cheyne can have had very little in common with men like Illingworth and Scott Holland. They loved him but they also shook their heads dolefully over him. And well they might. He was constantly uttering speculative opinions about the New Testament which were neither consistent with any known principle of evidence, nor with each other. He had composed an *Encyclopedia Biblica* which was sufficiently destructive of all Christian belief in biblical inspiration to be gladly published in a cheap edition by the Rationalist Press. 'Where he will end at last, I cannot say', wrote Holland.[1] In the fullness of time, a too consistent trafficking with biblical and theological negations, a too specialized concentration on the parish of the Modern Cultivated Man, and an absence of any sort of pastoral responsibility had their inevitable effect. He became an arrogant intellectualist of the most barren kind; and by 1911 Holland's question had been grimly answered, for Cheyne had 'landed' at the position where he thought it honourably consistent with his priestly Orders to write such sentences as these:

That the God-man, whose cult in ceremonial Jewish circles was probably pre-Christian, was called by a name which underlies Joshua, *i.e.* Jesus, has become to me, on grounds of my own, very possible: and it is to me much more than merely possible that Jesus of Nazareth was not betrayed or surrendered to the Jewish authorities, whether by Judas or by anyone else. The 'Twelve Apostles' too are to me (and, I should think, to many critics), as unhistorical as the Seventy Disciples.[2]

And again:

As the critical enquiry stands at present, one may reasonably hold that an extraordinary teacher and healer called Jesus incurred the displeasure of the Roman authorities, and suffered the extreme penalty as a rebellious and unrecognized 'King of the Jews'. But is it not possible that the statements of the Messianic claims of Jesus, and consequently also of the intervention of the procurator may be imaginary?[3]

The goodness and the piety which Scott Holland had discerned in Cheyne in 1900, had by 1911 become something else. Cheyne, however, stood by himself. He illustrated a disturbing tendency, it is true, but he did so by violently exaggerating it, like a cartoonist. He was too eccentric and too extreme to attract much of a following. The real head and tail of Anglican modernism in 1900, and for many years to come, was not Cheyne but Hastings Rashdall.

Rashdall was a very different and a far nobler man. He completely avoided succumbing to the inevitable moral snare of all modernists, who must deal so much with negations that they always tend to shed humility

---

[1] Quoted in G. L. Prestige, *The Life of Charles Gore*, p. 33.
[2] *Hibbert Journal*, July 1911. Quoted in Figgis, *Civilisation at the Cross Roads*, pp. 132, 133.
[3] *Hibbert Journal*, April 1911. Quoted in Figgis, *op. cit.*, p. 287.

and gather arrogance. His spirit was profoundly, ineradicably Christian. He was of that wing of the modernist movement which has always been the salt of the whole, seasoning and purging it by the power of sustained mental prayer. The two most characteristic features of his character were a deep sense of holiness, and a vivid realization and hatred of sin. These led him to live with a consistent austerity. In the long list of his University Sermons, carefully scrutinized by all his opponents for the heresies they were said to contain, the many passages in which he proclaimed the need and painted the beauties of living the austere and sacrificial life within a university not noticeably addicted to it, are still moving to read. It was wholly characteristic of him that what time has shown to be his most permanent contribution to religious thought should have been made in the spheres of the doctrine of the Atonement and of Christian Ethics. Thus he attracted a considerable number of disciples to himself, and although not all of them shared his views on creeds and scriptures, all revered him, and knew he had much to teach them. When he lay ill in 1923, Dr William Temple spoke for all of these in a moving letter:

I feel specially conscious of all your help to me when I was an undergraduate, both on our delightful walks and at other times—help which I continued to receive until I left Oxford for Repton. If we did not then always agree and have not always done so since, I am often aware of wider sympathies than would have been possible to me apart from your influence. And I know that at a rather critical time in my life that influence, rooted in your combined love of truth and personal devotion to our Lord, was of supreme value.[1]

He went from Oxford first to Lampeter, and then to Durham; but all the time the Oxford bells rang in his ears. Yet when, in 1895, the post he had dreamed of was at last his for the taking, and he was offered a fellowship of New College, he was characteristically in an agony of doubt. Ought he to accept a position on which he had set his heart? Was not the strength of his personal desire itself a reason for saying No? It needed the robust commonsense of Gore to persuade him that to say Yes would not be an act of treason to his conscience.[2] To Oxford, and to the rest of his work for the Church, he brought a mind which was academic at bottom, but which contained also a deep love for humanity, and even for individual human beings —by no means always the same thing. His feeling for humanity led him into membership of the Christian Social Union. He retained this membership all his life, and he interpreted its obligations ardently. He had a most genuine admiration for the Cultivated Modern Man, and he regarded it as his chief work in life to re-interpret the Christian Faith so as to make educated modernity comfortably and sincerely at home in the Church.

But his love for people was not matched by his understanding of them,

---

[1] P. E. Matheson, *The Life of Hastings Rashdall* (Oxford University Press), 1928, p. 223.
[2] Prestige, p. 192.

and he had but little knowledge of the odd complexities of human nature. Thus he was always quite as surprised as he was grieved when his fellow-Christians resented some of the things he said, and when they could not dissociate controversies as readily as he could himself from the particular personalities who conducted them. For him, the idea was everything. That ideas have to be urged and argued by persons was quite incidental—an instinctive judgement which had unfortunate fruit when he was putting forth his theory of the relationship of the Teaching of Christ to the Person of Christ. It was this curious contradiction which cost him the friendship and earned him the antagonism of Gore.[1] Perhaps Rashdall would have been happier if it had been possible for him, as it was for men like Kennett and Burkitt, to remain simply a don, and address the world through sermons, lectures, and books. But he was the acknowledged, and the only possible leader of the Anglican modernists, and he could not escape the charge. Eventually, he even had to become a dean. Thus he had many times to come into the open, to fly to the succour of this modernist priest and that who had said more than his bishop could stand, and to immerse himself in the hardly congenial subscription controversy. Steeling himself to perform a dreaded duty, he naturally performed it with a rather rough vehemence. Fearing to be found wanting in his leadership, he treated those who asked his protection as though they were all swans, and all suffering from grave injustice, whereas in fact some were geese, and the bishops were at least as often right as they were wrong. As Dr Inge said of him, he had on these occasions 'a combative disposition' which impelled him 'always to seize the poker by the hot end'.[2] His real weakness, however, was his lack of any sense of humour; and no humourless person can successfully command his cause or conduct himself in the give and take of democratic discussion. That is why he, who withstood successfully all the grave, cultivated anger of scholars, was defenceless against the darts and jibes of Puck. The Puck in question was G. K. Chesterton: he it was who really blew Rashdall's whole position to smithereens.

Rashdall's position as a religious teacher was governed by his fundamental judgement of the character of his generation. He believed that broadly speaking it was theistically dubious in proportion as it was educated. It is a different, and a far more serious state of mind than a mere agnosticism about the particular interpretations of theism contained in Christian theology. It was dubious about the being and the relevance of God because the intellectual fashions of the day were woven round an initial prejudice against whatever was classical and traditional and pre-scientific. God could be held to lie under all three condemnations. The whole scheme of Christian theology and ethics was ineradicably supernatural, and claimed to be independent of all purely scientific scrutinies. Rashdall shared to the full the liberal delusions about progress, and he was as hostile to traditionalism

[1] *Ibid.*, p. 196.   [2] W. R. Inge, *Vale!* (Longmans, Green), 1934, p. 54.

as any empty sceptic. He was always saying that the attempt to win his generation of educated men back to the Faith by eloquent appeals to the Christian tradition was hopeless from the start. In any case, he said, only dishonesty or ignorance could make such appeals for:

The assumption that there is a certain body of Christian faith which has always been taught from the first, and taught universally, cannot outlive serious study.[1]

To win the Modern Cultivated Man, the Christian teacher must stand on the same ground, talk the same language, and share something of the same outlook on life. Thus equipped he must translate such supreme mysteries as the Incarnation and the Redemption of Jesus into modern thought-forms and speech. Both language and method must be scientific through and through, and the application of scientific techniques to Christian theology was a proceeding full of danger. But that could not be helped.

There was thus all the difference in the world between theological destructiveness for its own delightfully shocking sake, which had been the sign-manual of the early German critics and of Cheyne, and the sincere and genuinely noble attempt of Rashdall to set his hand to the pruning. The first thing to be pruned was of course the category of miracle. It was not that he flatly stated that miracles did not and could not occur, for he said no such thing. What he did say—again and again—was that it was no longer of any avail to try to use the alleged miraculous events in the New Testament as evidence for the claims which the Church made for Jesus. But these claims did not rest, and had never been rested, on the miracles of healing, or on any of what the evangelists called his mighty works. They rested on miracles of a still sublime and even more staggering order, the miracles of Christ's own Person, his birth, his resurrection, and on what he was in himself. Of these, the Incarnation is the heart, and the miracles of the Virgin Birth and the Empty Tomb are part of the testimony. Even if the German critics had not written, the Christological issue would still have been the chief battle-ground of English theology from 1900 to 1914. The publication of *Lux Mundi* had raised issues about the human knowledge of Christ, and raised them very publicly; and when Gore published his *Dissertations on Subjects connected with the Incarnation* in 1898, and gave there a full-length treatment of the 'Kenotic' theories about Christ, he defined and limited the battle-field of the conflict which was to come, and in which Rashdall was one of the chief warriors. It was in fact quite impossible to separate the doctrinal issues from those of the literary criticism of the Gospels. But very few men are equally at home in both fields. Not the least of the misfortunes of the Church in the twentieth century has been the fact that modernism was led by the literary critics, not by the doctrinal scholars or theologians. Rashdall was an historian and a philosopher as well as a textual critic: most of the others were textual critics who had

[1] *Ideas and Ideals* (Blackwell), 1928, pp. 108–9.

enjoyed but little training in dogmatic theology. But the goal which modernism had set itself to achieve needed both—and the second even more than
the first. Neither Rashdall, nor indeed any other religious teacher, could
escape from the need to attempt the restatement of the doctrine of the
Incarnation, which must necessarily elude every attempt at formal definition, into the terms of thought of the society in which he moved. After all,
there is no other way in any age of convincing the agnostic. But he had to
do it by the light of the principle he had laid down for dealing with the
theistic dubiety of his generation. Theism was true, but not defensible by
appeals to tradition or to the scriptural miracles. In the same way, the Incarnation of Jesus was blessedly true, but its truth did not in any way hang
upon either the Virgin Birth or the Empty Tomb. About even these a rever-
rent suspension of judgement, a virtual agnosticism, was perfectly compatible with a true assertion of the central article of the creed. More than
this, it was morally consistent with the position of an accredited, pledged
teacher of the creed.

But from this position, it was only one step to another and a still more
dangerous one. That was to say that Christianity might, in a sense, be even
independent of its own Founder, that it might exist even if it could be
shown that Christ had never existed in history. Rashdall did move towards
this position. He himself seems never to have doubted the actual historical
existence of Jesus, nor yet that he did and said substantially what is attributed to him in the Synoptic Gospels. But his tenderness to agnosticism
was so sensitive, and his realization of the revolution wrought by the continental criticism of the New Testament was so vivid, that he was prepared
neither to deny the full title of Christian to those who believed that Jesus
had never lived, nor to affirm that the Christian religion was completely
dependent on its Founder, and lived or died with him. He put this clearly
in a passage in *Conscience and Christ*:

I think it should be very distinctly realized that the truth and value of the
Christian Ethic does not depend on the fact of its having been taught by Jesus
Himself—still less upon its having been taught by Jesus exclusively. If it could be
shown that the sayings which we have been in the habit of regarding as most
characteristic of the historical Jesus were in reality none of His, if it could be
shown that there never was an historical Jesus, or that we know nothing to speak
of about His teaching, the truth and the value of the teaching attributed to our
Lord in the Gospels would not be one whit diminished.[1]

In *Ideas and Ideals* the same approach is found:

The Christian ideal of life is present in the New Testament however it got there.
If conscience tells us that the words of Christ are true, they would be true even
if those words were wholly the creation of the Church, and none of them were
really uttered by the historical Jesus.[2]

[1] *Conscience and Christ* (Duckworth), 1916, pp. 274, 275.　　　[2] *Ibid.*, p. 112.

These two brief quotations make Rashdall's general purpose and position quite plain. He was trying to guard what he conceived to be the vital heart of Christianity from the three main lines of attack of the day. They were the criticism of the Gospels, the rejection of the category of miracle, and the researches into comparative religion which had revealed earlier examples in other religions of many of our Lord's moral sayings. Rashdall himself carefully guarded his statements by plentiful use of the word 'if'. The two quotations given above stop far short of any affirmation by Rashdall that he himself believed that Christianity could ever be independent of its Founder. In fact, he never did believe it. But some other modernists did. His opponents saw two deadly dangers looming ahead. The first was that the modernist approach to the historical Jesus was one in which his ethical teaching was all important, and his supernatural acts and spiritual authority much less important. The modernists, in fact, were busy producing the Liberal Christ, and the Church as a whole wanted none of him. The second danger was that to take away from Christian ethics the support of scripture and divine authority was to leave them suspended in a void. Catholic Christendom as a whole was quite sure that it does make every difference by whom a set of moral precepts is uttered. The Beatitudes, they argued, are true not because our conscience accepts them but because the Incarnate Son of God uttered them. If Rashdall's interpretation were allowed to stand, it would mean that there was really no reason why men should pay any more heed to the injunctions of Jesus than to those of Socrates. Christianity stakes its whole claim to absoluteness of truth and universality of realm on the historicity of its Founder. It was precisely this citadel that the modernists seemed to many to be surrendering; and therefore it was necessary to consider how best to defend it.

IV · *The Battle Joined*

Those who wished to stem the tide of critical views of the Bible and the creeds had the choice of two battle-fields. They could fight on either of them, or on both of them at once. The one battle-field was the question of formal heresy; the other was the question of public subscription to creeds and formularies. On the continent, and throughout the Roman Catholic Church, the orthodox theologians attacked Modernism with the battle cry of Heresy. But in England, though a charge of formal heresy certainly lay against such writers as Cheyne, the defenders of traditional orthodoxy preferred not to make much use of this weapon, but instead made their attack on the ground that the modernists' handling and interpretation of the creeds was inconsistent with their solemn oath of subscription to them. How could a man honestly recite the Creed, and how could he take his ordination vows, when in fact he did not believe, and loudly said he did not believe, that our Lord was virgin-born, did not accept the traditional and biblical doctrine of the physical resurrection of the Lord's body, and whose attitude to very many of the Gospel narratives was a perpetual question mark? In this strategical contrast, the continental theologians undoubtedly saw more deeply into the realities of the issues raised. The modernists were in fact teaching much heresy, and logically speaking, besides this vital, fundamental fact, the question of whether they were honest or dishonest when they recited the creeds was of quite secondary importance. The English defenders of the Faith, in concentrating as they did upon the subscription issue, were certainly less logical than their continental counterparts. But, as so often happens, they did far less harm. The continental modernists were driven out of the Church and excommunicated. Even mildly scholarly views of the Bible were ruthlessly proscribed. The Roman Church itself was driven by the very vigour of its persecution into espousing a theological conservatism of the most rigid kind.

There is something horribly final about charges of heresy. If they are successful, they must carry with them sentences of punishment which can be appropriate only to the gravest crime; and where there is humiliating condemnation of the honest heretic, there will be in the end embarrassment for the condemning, punishing body. For many reasons, such a method of dealing with the modernist challenge did not commend itself to English ecclesiastical authority. Indeed, it could hardly have done so, not only because persecution for matters of individual beliefs is quite alien to the English temperament, but also because the Church of England had been so built through the centuries as to make every method of regimenting and proscribing freely uttered opinion almost impossible to apply. Hensley Henson attributed this to the Church's

inability to legislate secured by its subordination to the State, the relative moderation of its denominational confession, and the tradition of clerical independence distinctive of its legal system. The first disarmed the orthodox resentment which would otherwise have found expression in coercive action; the second so mitigated the burden on clerical consciences that repugnance to the doctrinal tradition was comparatively slight and infrequent; the third so weakened authority as to secure practical immunity for individual aberrations from conventional orthodoxy. The Erastian establishment, the Thirty-Nine Articles as imposed by the Clerical Subscription Act of 1865, and the parish parson's freehold in his benefice, however open to adverse criticism from the point of view of spiritual religion, of intellectual liberty, and of pastoral efficiency, did render the important service to the Church of England of providing a breakwater against the impetuous reactions of panic-stricken orthodoxy.[1]

In religion as in politics, there is always a certain rawness in the air of the continent which the sea softens before it reaches our shores. English

---

[1] Herbert Hensley Henson, *The Church of England* (Cambridge University Press), 1939, p. 112.

bishops, moreover, have never been notable for plucking nettles before counting the cost. They always prefer to let sleeping dogs lie, even when the dogs are in fact barking their heads off and disturbing all the neighbours. And this is partly due to the further fact that in no Church in Christendom are proceedings for heresy made so extremely tortuous, difficult, chancy, and expensive as they are in the Anglican Church. Nor could the only courts legally competent to try such a charge be regarded by anybody, other than their own members, as sufficiently informed on the nature of all the scholastic and historical detail which would have to be put in as evidence. Besides all this, there is always the reaction of the general public as well as the mass of churchpeople to bear in mind. It is poor tactics to brand and punish a man as a heretic when that very fact and title would automatically make him a hero, and the prosecuting bishop a bigot and a tyrant, to nine-tenths of the people. But inconsistency was a charge everyone understood, and set at its proper value. Thus in English the questionable position of modernists who publicly recited creeds in which they only partly believed, and on the articles of which they put their own glosses and private interpretations, was plainly the right point at which to join issue. It meant in practice that the excommunications and proscriptions which were so marked a feature of the struggle abroad were kept out of the story of the conflict in England. Thus in the end that which was creative in Anglican modernism was able to find its place within and make its contribution to Anglican doctrine.

Inconsistency in subscription to the creeds and the formularies was a real charge, and the modernists found it difficult to reply convincingly to it. Consider three short quotations:

As we may believe with St Mark that Jesus was born of human parents, and yet call Him divine; so we may believe with St Paul that His human body remained in the grave, and yet worship Him as risen and alive.[1]

It is to me much more than merely possible that Jesus of Nazareth was not betrayed or surrendered to the Jewish authorities, whether by Judas or anyone else.[2]

I believe . . . in Jesus Christ his only Son our Lord, who was conceived by the Holy Ghost, Born of the Virgin Mary, Suffered under Pontius Pilate, Was crucified, dead, and buried: The third day he rose again from the dead, according to the scriptures.

Those who said that a priest could not consistently write the first two sentences, and then recite the third in an act of worship, made a charge to which an answer had to be returned. The modernists sincerely held them-

---

[1] J. M. Thompson, *Miracles in the New Testament*, p. 211. Quoted in *The Church and the Twentieth Century*, edited by G. L. H. Harvey (Macmillan), 1936, p. 413.
[2] Cheyne, see above, p. 93.

selves justified, but they had to justify themselves to their critics. How did they do it?

Although Dean Inge stretched forth a hand to help, it fell mainly to Rashdall to defend the honesty of those who recited and taught the creeds while yet giving to certain of the articles therein a very tentative intellectual assent. In 1897, Rashdall had first stated his case in answer to Professor Henry Sidgwick's article in the *International Journal of Ethics*, in which the Professor, a master of unbiased fairness, had said:

There is one line of thought which is not compatible with the creeds and that is the line of thought which, taught by modern science and modern historical criticism concludes against the miraculous element of the gospel history, and in particular rejects the story of the miraculous birth of Jesus.[1]

To this Rashdall replied that because strict and complete veracity was plainly impossible in all circumstances, nor yet always to be desired, so there should be a corresponding latitude of interpretation of an ordination vow, and that this should extend to a point which would regularize the ordained ministry of those who 'believed in God and immortality' but did not believe in miracles, nor yet in the virgin birth of our Lord.[2] It was this not very fortunate reply which attracted to Rashdall Gore's wrath, and such a wrath was formidable. Rashdall was never to be free of it again as long as he lived. Whatever explanations and justifications casuistry might bring forward, common sense and ordinary opinion would plainly require a good deal of converting to a view so finely drawn of credal obligations upon accredited Christian teachers. Thus in 1908 Rashdall set forth his apologia at fuller length in a composite work called *Anglican Liberalism*. In his essay he advanced five principal justifications for his attitude. First, latitude in the interpretation of ecclesiastical formularies had after all a long and respectable tradition, in which the seventeenth-century Platonists, Tillotson, Jeremy Taylor, and the Oxford Movement itself—especially the celebrated Tract Ninety—were the landmarks. 'The inevitable progress of theological opinion practically extended the limits generally recognized as compatible with honesty long before the growth of modern liberalism.' Second, no man who takes an oath of allegiance before entering some secular or professional appointment means by it what would have been meant in Tudor days, but nobody thinks him dishonest. Third, any radical Member of Parliament must take an oath of allegiance to the Crown, but he may none the less be an honest and consistent republican both before his oath and after it. Fourth, no one who is ordained can honestly and literally mean just what the ordination oath says when it pledges him to an unfeigned belief in all the canonical scriptures: Gore himself, in his *Lux Mundi* essay, had shown very plainly indeed that he had no belief of that

[1] Prestige, p. 193.   [2] *Ibid.*, p. 194.

kind. Fifth, everybody liberalizes the creeds, whether consciously or not; and especially the Athanasian Creed, yet the Church does not explicitly give to it a lower authority than that of the other two.[1]

This was really no more than a codification of what Rashdall had been saying for years, and an indication of the ground on which the modernists were prepared to give battle to the traditionalists. The latter, led by Gore, were no less ready to accept the Subscription Issue as the battle-field. But then they would find it embarrassing to fight on any other. They needed Gore to lead them, and his contribution to *Lux Mundi* on the limitations to our Lord's earthly knowledge was still fresh in memory. It would not do for him to be too lavish or shrill in accusations of heresy.

When great forces, having selected a battle-field, and agreed to fight it out, are sparring for an opening, it is always more than a little unfortunate for the individual whose indiscretions provide them with a *casus belli*. They rush to battle over the individual's body, they clinch and sway, and when at last they recoil for breath, the victim is pounded into the earth and quickly forgotten. Such a rôle was played by the Rev. C. E. Beeby, Vicar of Yardley Wood, Birmingham, then a parish in Gore's diocese. He had claimed publicly the moral and legal right to retain his benefice and yet to disbelieve in the Virgin Birth. The article in which he claimed it contained also an attack on the idea that the category of Miracle was at all necessary for, or even relevant to the idea of divine revelation. All this Beeby had argued at greater length in a book he had written some years before. The Chancellor of the diocese advised Gore that the book might more easily sustain a formal charge than the article, but Gore would not take action on what happened before he came to be Bishop of Worcester. He wrote to Beeby setting out his views at length, and he interviewed him. But just when he was meditating over whether he must inhibit him or not, Beeby resigned his living, and Gore accepted his resignation. Thereafter Beeby lasped into the darkness of obscurity so far as his own person was concerned. But he was no longer a person: he had become a cause, and as such he was championed by Rashdall with some acerbity. He made this cause the subject of his address to the annual meeting of the Churchmen's Union, and he accused Gore of 'worrying' poor Beeby into resignation. There followed a correspondence, and Rashdall in part, but only in part, withdrew his accusation of bullying. On the main issue he was as adamant as ever

It was a preliminary skirmish, and as indecisive as most such occasions are. Gore then carried the battle straight to the seats of the mighty. Davidson had not been enthroned as Archbishop of Canterbury for so much as one day when Gore opened fire. 'Can we not in this Convocation', he wrote to the Archbishop, 'do something to reassure a great number of people that the Bishops would not connive at men being ordained who do not believe in the Articles of the Creed; particularly the Virgin Birth.' He

[1] *Anglican Liberalism* (Williams and Norgate), 1908, pp. 77–134.

enclosed the draft of such a declaration as he would desire to see. But the Archbishop was very cautious. He pointed out that such a step would be 'virtually an addition to our formularies', and he wrote of his perplexity, not to say his impatience, to a friend. 'If we say that we hold the Creed and wish others to do the same, we surely do what is worse than useless. If, on the other hand, we attempt to define its terms in a particular way, the Church at large may well ask: (1) by what right we do so, and (2) what claim our definition has on the faith of Churchmen.' Those that were for Gore were naturally more than those that were for either the Archbishop or the modernists; and they were sufficiently heavily represented on the benches of Convocation to force the bishops 'to do something'. It was decided to ask the two Archbishops to write a joint pastoral letter on the subject. Probably they never meant it to do more than quell the clamour of Convocation, for this letter was never actually written. Such a procedure would in fact have been quite violently uncanonical: it is the bench of bishops as a whole, and not the two chief bishops among them, which is the guardian of doctrine and sacraments. If indeed such a step was really being seriously contemplated by Davidson—which is unlikely—it was killed in advance by Armitage Robinson, Dean of Westminster, who chose that moment to add to his new book on the Incarnation a Prefatory Letter to the Archbishop of Canterbury, in which he used his very great authority to administer the *coup de grâce* to the proposal in the following devastating sentences:

If the Bishops were asked to declare that the Incarnation is a cardinal doctrine of the faith, such a statement would be superfluous indeed, but it would be true. But to say that the historical fact of the Virgin Birth is a cardinal doctrine of the faith is to use language which no Synod of Bishops, so far as I am aware, has ever ventured to use. It is to confuse the Incarnation with the special mode of the Incarnation in a way for which Christian theology offers no precedent.[1]

Thus ended the first round of the battle. It had been an inconclusive skirmish, except of course for the unfortunate Mr Beeby. But it pointed a clear tactical moral, which Gore had kept instinctively in mind but the eager and rash members of Convocation had forgotten, namely that if you want to deal with modernism in England you must do so on the ground of subscription to the creeds and not on the ground of pure doctrine.

The Roman Catholic Church was, as is its habit, far less cautious and circumspect. The modernist infection had spread and attacked its tough, experienced body; and a group of its foremost scholars, headed by the Abbé Loisy and George Tyrrell had been publicly teaching very much the same kind of naturalistic interpretation of the Scriptures, the Gospel, and the Church which were the commonplaces of advanced theology in English universities. For a time they staved off the inevitable condemnation by

[1] Bell, vol. I, pp. 396–8.

ingeniously putting their arguments into the form of replies to such strongly anti-catholic writers as von Harnack. Moreover, as an English Roman Catholic historian disapprovingly remarks, 'by the dexterous use of pseudonyms the modernists were able to create the impression that they had a larger following than actually appears to have been the case'.[1] In 1907 they were condemned root and branch in the Papal Encyclical *Pascendi*. Loisy and Tyrrell were excommunicated as heretics and rebels, and apparently von Hügel narrowly missed the same fate. An anti-modernist oath was imposed on all clergy; and as Rashdall indignantly wrote: 'All modernist priests had to choose between absolute silence and expulsion from the Roman fold. Modernist periodicals ceased to appear. Modernist books could no longer be published. Those who submitted were silenced—forbidden to preach, or write, or lecture, and compelled to occupy themselves with harmless functions such as the elementary education of children.'[2] It was certainly a more vigorous way of dealing with the challenge than that adopted by the Anglican Archbishop, but he was at least able to save the Church of England from the most deadly of all charges against a Church, that it could maintain uniformity and order only by persecution, and the denial of the primary law of liberty.

Those who were hoping that the Lambeth Conference of 1908 would be able to still a controversy so radical and pull together the edges of a divergence so complete were blind optimists. There was no possibility of peace, except on conditions of persecution from which the Anglican episcopate invariably, and rightly, shies away as from the skirts of the devil himself. To cry doctrinal peace at such a moment would have been a proceeding far less principled than deliberately to connive at an extension and a deepening of the conflict. The Lambeth Conference, of course, did neither. It placed *The Faith and Modern Thought* at the top of its agenda, and its report reaffirmed the doctrinal position of the Church of England as standing by the historical statements of the Apostles' and the Nicene Creeds. That Lambeth Conference undoubtedly made a true contribution to the Anglican Church's understanding of its own mission. But it made it in the context of recalling the Church to the fact that it stood among the people as their servant for Christ's sake, and not in the context of doctrinal development. In that sphere its deliberations were quite unimportant.

The controversy then proceeded briskly. The new storm centre was the (then) congregationalist minister, R. J. Campbell, who was packing the City Temple in London by the picturesque vividness of his sermons on what he called the New Theology. There was in fact very little, if there was anything, new in what he was teaching. Most of the classical heresies, particularly Pelagianism, duly reappeared; and its general effect was to lower doctrinal standards by assaulting the sense of universal evil or

[1] H. J. P. Johnson, *Anglicanism in Transition* (Longmans, Green), 1938, p. 72.
[2] *Ideas and Ideals*, p. 98.

'Original Sin', by claiming for man a status a little higher than the angels, and by consequently devaluing the uniqueness of Jesus. But he did it so vividly that it all seemed novel, and it was sensationally successful in attracting crowds and creating argument. He possessed an undeniable sense of the historic present, quite untempered by any corresponding but hampering sense of the historic past. A Roman Catholic historian has wittily and accurately, though unkindly, defined Campbell's whole attitude in a single phrase: 'The preacher had persuaded himself that he was adapting the Christian message to the minds of the generation which had elected the Parliament of 1906–10.' A single sentence of Campbell's, which his historian quotes, undoubtedly justifies the diagnosis, 'Go with Keir Hardie to the House of Commons, and listen to his pleading for justice to his order, and you see the Atonement.'[1]

In 1908 England was wearing its liberalism with emotion and passion. Nearly all scholarship and thoughtfulness was backing liberalism, and most of it was working for the Liberal Party. A Liberal, even a politically Liberal, Christ seemed urgently needed, and it was precisely such a Christ which the new methods of textual criticism seemed to be wrenching out of the old pages of the synoptic Gospels. Then came Schweitzer. He failed to win acceptance for his own apocalyptic Christ, but he did shatter to bits the Liberal Christ, just as he also shattered the German nationalist Christ. After the Cambridge Church Congress the purely disintegrating progress of modernism in England was stayed. Naturally it took time—a long time —for this to become apparent. At that moment no seer seems to have remarked what had really happened, and certainly the modernists themselves showed no signs of any consciousness that they had received a shattering blow.

A source of their serenity was their complete confidence in the methods of textual criticism which they took over from the Germans, and such Frenchmen as Loisy and Renan. They thought of themselves as essentially scientific workers in the sphere of New Testament scholarship, and they were no more immune than British scientific workers in other spheres from an altogether excessive adulation of all German scholarship. This was, before 1914, the commonplace attitude of the rest of the European world of scholarship; and there was indeed something dazzling, and even bemusing, about the incredibly voluminous patience and industry of the typical German research student. The English modernists, as a whole, had no doubt whatever that however disconcerting the incomplete results of their critical research might be, in the end the method they followed would infallibly lead them to the uncovering of the actual Jesus of history, and that his figure, when at last uncovered, would be sufficient to bear the whole weight of the devotional life of Christendom.

[1] Johnson, *op. cit.*, p. 70. Campbell, *The New Theology* (1907), p. 173. See also Prestige, p. 304.

On the long view Schweitzer had shattered this illusion, but on the short view the Catholic party had to make some reply to the series of negations which modernist literature was propagating, and when the propagators were clergymen, that reply must sometimes be disciplinary. Their difficulty was to secure united episcopal action. Gore had failed to secure it in the case of the Rev. J. M. Thompson, and he had no chance of securing it in either of the next two issues which arose. The first of these was the publication in 1912 of a collection of theological essays called *Foundations*. Only one of the essays really created much stir. It was by the editor of the volume, Canon B. H. Streeter, and it concerned the Resurrection of Jesus. It was, and was intended to be, a challenge to Gore and his friends; for though it was in tone humble, though it put forward its conclusions as being merely tentative and personal, it did deliberately raise the question of whether scholarship in the Church was to be free or bound. 'If episcopal action denies to Churchmen the necessary conditions of genuine historical investigation, thoughtful men in future will inevitably conclude that if they wish to know the truth about the Life of Christ, they must seek it from scholars outside the Church.'[1] Gore considered the possibility of cancelling Streeter's licence, but his friends, headed by his beloved Scott Holland, persuaded him to refrain.

The second challenge was more devastating, and much more unhappy. Professor William Sanday, a holy and universally beloved Oxford scholar with a European reputation, and one of Gore's warmest friends, privately announced that he had lost his faith in the miraculous element in the Gospel, and that he was no longer able to affirm his belief in the Virgin Birth or the Resurrection, not, at least, in their traditional form. This was all the more serious, not only on account of Sanday's authority and personal charm, but also because there was in him no trace of the excessive confidence of the typical modernist, but, on the contrary, his scholastic reputation was that of one who can never bear to publish the fruits of his research and thought until it has been checked, and tested, and rechecked, and then checked again. For such a one so momentous a pronouncement was indeed a portent. There was of course no chance at all of episcopal action against Sanday, and, in consequence, for a whole year Gore prayed and debated, opening his heart in letter after letter to the Archbishop, as to whether it was his duty to resign his see. This the Archbishop prevented for the moment, but the real crisis was still to come.

The situation was by now unbearably tense. A great explosion was plainly not far away. The long battle of books and pamphlets, conducted with no thought of a strategic plan, had so developed as to drive both sides into a position from which no retreat seemed possible, and the suffering and cost of which could hardly be alleviated by compromise. The modernists felt that they were struggling to fend off an imminent divorce between the

[1] Prestige, p. 345.

intellect of Europe and the whole catholic tradition. The divorce had already taken place on the continent. Should it also happen in Britain then the decree of *Nisi Prius* must be made absolute and final for the whole world. The modernists therefore considered themselves to be more catholic than the catholics. In a sense, so they were. Nothing could be more un-catholic than the cheerful and reckless contemplation of a cleavage between scholarship and faith, and of this recklessness the rank and file of the Anglo-Catholics were at that time certainly guilty. They saw the real danger, they reached out their hands to draw it nearer, and they turned their controversial methods so as to exacerbate it. They were in a thoroughly intransigent mood. This they had caught like a plague, from the corresponding intransigence towards themselves of almost every section of English society, and neither their faith nor their devotion, deep and sincere though both were, had done them the service of saving them from the common infection.

Yet when they asked the question, For what did the Church of England stand? they had the right on their side. Any man might well have been excused in 1914 for not knowing what was the answer. Bishop Weston of Zanzibar's answer, given in 1918 after long reflection, that it stood for the correction of its Master, had a certain justification. He it was who loosed the storm. Books can pack ecclesiastical bombshells with powerful explosives, but they rarely cause the explosion. For that there has to be something more open, more irrevocable—a clear charge of indictment, publicly preferred in such a manner that authority cannot possibly evade it, but is bound to take action. Bishop Frank Weston of Zanzibar provided what was needed. He wrote a famous open letter to the Bishop of St Albans, and he followed it by writing formally to the Archbishop of Canterbury on 30th September, 1913, charging his brother bishops of Uganda and Mombasa with disobedience to church order. After this, there could be no smoothing over or drawing back, and the battle had begun. Weston's choice of the Bishop of St Albans seems curious at first sight. He had been ordained by a previous Bishop of St Albans, Festing; and though Festing had now been succeeded by Jacob, Weston regarded St Albans as his own home diocese. Jacob, moreover, had just appointed Canon Streeter as an examining chaplain, and Streeter had been not only the editor of *Foundations*, but also the author of the most notorious essay in the book, that on the Resurrection.

Thus, says Henson, 'the storm broke where it could least have been expected'.[1] But by those who knew what manner of man the Bishop of Zanzibar was, as Henson at that time did not, it was by no means unexpected that such a one as he should publicly raise the fighting standard of the Church Militant and Catholic, and the distance between Zanzibar and

[1] Herbert Hensley Henson, *Retrospect of an Unimportant Life* (Oxford University Press), vol. I, 1942, p. 159.

London had nothing to do with it. Weston had a great impetuousness and more than a lion's heart. He was the kind of Anglo-Catholic who is utterly unyielding on any point of principle, and to whom the principle of church order expressed in the theory of Apostolic Succession was not one particle less important than the doctrine of the inerrancy of Christ in the Gospel, but whose unfathomable fountain of pity for all sufferers and hunger for souls redeems him from the cruel rigidity of the doctrinaire. As a missionary, his episcopate in Zanzibar was one of the outstanding glories of the Church in this century. But the story to be told now exhibits Weston in his less attractive character: all the more reason, then, for prefacing it by a sketch of Weston written by that one of all his opponents whom Weston regarded with a holy horror, Hensley Henson:

> He was in my belief a very good unselfish Christian, with all a fanatic's sincerity and all a fanatic's injustice, but by nature entirely lovable. It was impossible not to feel his charm even while one execrated his bigotry. On the whole I think that represents my considered verdict. Something should be added about his practical sagacity which I think was quite conspicuously great whenever his fanaticism did not influence his judgment: and something more should be said about his passionate love for souls, which lifted him above his fanatical obsessions, and carried him into the company of the greater saints.[1]

There were two other reasons, besides the personal character of a particular Bishop of Zanzibar, for supposing that the doctrinal storm might break not in England, but in either Africa or India. In England, Christianity was in possession, but in Africa and India it was not. There it had to fight for its kingdom against great classical religions such as Islam or Buddhism. In England the academic dubieties about the miraculous element in the Gospels were the data of scholastic debates, but in Zanzibar or Delhi they were triumphantly hawked about the streets in Islamic pamphlets.

> In the streets of Zanzibar you can buy Arabic tracts emanating from Cairo, with information about the destructive criticism of the Bible in Europe and with comments appropriate for Mohammedan readers,. These tracts are read by the literate, they are read to the illiterate, they are discussed in the streets, and they provide the weapons to resist missionary propaganda.[2]

Weston had seen this happen again and again in his diocese, as it had also happened in many others, and he spoke for more African and Indian bishops than himself when he wrote in his *Open Letter*:

> I do not hesitate to say that a Church which has two views in its highest ranks about the trustworthiness of the Bible, the authority of the Church, and the infallibility of the Christ has surrendered its chance of winning the Moslem; for his dependence upon his Book, his tradition and his Prophet will not be broken by a

---

[1] Henson, vol. I, p. 173.
[2] H. Maynard Smith, *Frank, Bishop of Zanzibar* (S.P.C.K.) 1926. p. 171.

debating society, but by the living, speaking Church of the Infallible Word incarnate.[1]

The second reason why the storm might have been expected to break in the mission field rather than at home was that missionary dioceses are inevitably the grounds where experiments which infringe on the niceties of church order are bound to be tried first. To the Anglo-Catholic, the doctrine of the Apostolic Succession is just as much and just as necessary a part of the ineluctable Christian Faith as the doctrine of the Incarnation. But to the missionary the divisions and separations of Christendom are a sin which hinders and embarrasses him every day. Even where in a missionary diocese there is a gentleman's agreement between the missions of different Churches to work in different districts and to refrain from sheep stealing—an agreement which the Roman Catholics have never made, and, given their theology, could not make—it is obviously impossible to explain to the negro in the Congo Forest the nice shades of difference between a Baptist and a Methodist church; and it is dreadful to have to tell him that his loyalty to the Anglican Church of his baptism must involve him in a certain separation from other Christian Churches. Islam is united and Christendom is divided. The missionary in close contact with Islam cannot be expected to share the calm acceptance of such things by his brother at home.

Moved by such considerations as these, the Bishops of Uganda and Mombasa held a conference of all missionaries working in East Africa at Kikuyu in June 1913. They proposed a union in their several Churches, and in this proposal they urged 'Recognition of common membership between the Societies in the federation'. This they held to involve that 'recognized church members of the different Societies would be allowed to communicate in the churches of other Societies', and that 'a common or public worship should be used with sufficient frequency to enable the members of all the churches to become familiar with a common order'.[2] It was no more than a proposal and it committed nobody. But at the end of the conference all the missionaries present, from whatever Church they came, joined together to receive the Holy Communion, in the Presbyterian Church at Kikuyu, at which the Bishop of Mombasa was the celebrant.

Weston had just been sent *Foundations* and Hensley Henson's *The Creed in the Pulpit* in a parcel of books from home, and now he had before him, and on his own doorstep, the defiance of catholic order committed at Kikuyu. He saw very clearly that both these events were symptoms of exactly the same disease. The action of the bishops at Kikuyu offered him an opening which the publication of books, however 'advanced', in England could hardly give. It constituted an issue possible of open ecclesiastical arraignment, and one which could be stretched to cover an indictment of the whole range of the liberal devaluation of Christian dogma. Accordingly,

[1] Maynard Smith, p. 172. [2] Bell, vol. I, pp. 691, 698.

in a letter to the Archbishop of Canterbury, he charged the Bishops of
Mombasa and Uganda with having committed not one but seven ecclesiastical offences by their conduct at Kikuyu:

> I am the nearest Bishop to Mombasa and Uganda, and I tell you, my leader
> and Father in God, that the remedy which will alone touch the disease is a public
> admission on their part that they have not faithfully emphasized:
>
> 1. The Athanasian Creed.
> 2. Confirmation.
> 3. Absolution.
> 4. Infant Baptism.
> 5. Holy Communion as different from Communion administered in Protes-
>   tant bodies.
> 6. The broad difference between Church doctrine and that of the Protestant
>   bodies, so that it is impossible:
>
>   *a.* to communicate at each other's Altars;
>   *b.* to preach in one another's pulpits;
>   *c.* to prepare men of all these bodies with Church candidates either for
>   Baptism or Ordination.
>
> 7. The need of Episcopacy in the Church.

So that unless they will so 'recant,' I most humbly and respectfully urge my plea
for a 'Synodical' Court, or, so far as I see it today, resign my See on the ground
that heresy has been condoned in the sight of my missionary Churches in East
Africa.[1]

But it was not a plea but a demand for a Synodical Court that he made, for,
in order to make sure that the whole issue was brought so prominently
before the public that the Archbishop could not possibly shelve it or smooth
it, Weston solemnly added to his letter a formal and public arraignment of
the two offending bishops. This document was all magnifical with legal
language and capital letters, and it ended thus:

> Therefore We, Frank, by Divine Permission Lord Bishop of Zanzibar and East
> Africa, do by these presents accuse and charge the Right Reverend Father in God
> William, Lord Bishop of Mombasa, and the Right Reverend Father in God John
> Jameson, Lord Bishop of Uganda, with the grievous faults of propagating heresy
> and committing schism:
>
> And We do hereby most humbly implore Your Grace to obtain from them for
> publication in East Africa and Zanzibar a complete and categorical recantation
> of the errors which they have taught in word and action:
>
> Or failing that We do hereby request Your Grace to appoint us a day or place
> in which conformably with Catholic precedent We may appear before You and
> not less than twelve of Your Grace's comprovincial Bishops sitting with Your
> Grace as Judges in this cause, and to permit us there and then to meet the afore-
> said Lord Bishop of Mombasa and Lord Bishop of Uganda, and in open Assem-
> bly to allow us to make and sustain our charges and accusations against them.[2]

<hr/>

[1] Bell, vol. I, p. 693.   [2] *Ibid.*, p. 694.

From the publication of this indictment there followed, as Weston had plainly intended, a public controversy more prolonged and more excitable than any raised on an ecclesiastical issue for years past. All three East African bishops rushed to London, Already many church leaders, headed by Gore on the one side and Hensley Henson on the other, had hurled themselves into the fray, recklessly exacerbating a situation already dangerous enough. Every public controversy on any conceivable subject held seeds of danger in the hysterical summer of 1913. Meetings were held, many sermons preached, and the letter-bags to and from Lambeth were overloaded. Only Davidson refused to lose his head. Only he seemed to realize the inevitable consequences of allowing the controversy of Kikuyu to be pushed to its logical judicial conclusion. Neither to this, nor to any action which would drive the whole body of the modernist clergy out of the Church would he be a party, and because at this juncture all alike agreed that his continuance in his office was utterly essential, his will for compromise prevailed. For nearly twelve months a series of extremely complicated negotiations followed. It would be as tedious as it is fruitless to describe them in any detail here : the full tale has already been told by Dr Bell, in his biography of Davidson. The archbishop set himself two goals. The first was to secure such a declaration from Convocation as would placate Gore and his friends without driving even men like Rashdall and Henson to forsake their Orders. The second was to arrive at such a judgement on the Kikuyu issue that both Weston and Willis of Uganda would be able to continue their splendid work as missionary bishops, untroubled on either side by suspicion and controversy. In this he came nearer to complete success than any other living man could have done. For on April 29th, 1914, Convocation passed the form of resolution submitted by the Bishop of London and endorsed by Davidson in a weighty speech, which admitted the perplexity of church opinion, asserted the determination of Convocation to uphold the faith in its fullness, and shied away from the need to restrain the modernists by any form of penal method.

At the same time [the resolution ended] recognizing that our generation is called to face new problems raised by historical criticism, we are anxious not to lay unnecessary burdens upon consciences, nor unduly to limit freedom of thought and enquiry, whether among clergy or among laity. We desire, therefore, to lay stress on the need of considerateness in dealing with that which is tentative and provisional in the thought and work of earnest and reverent students.[1]

Rashdall and his friends not unnaturally welcomed this resolution : Gore accepted it, but hardly with an enthusiastic gladness. The Kikuyu affair Davidson submitted to a consultative committee consisting of eleven bishops. They met for the first time at Lambeth at the end of July 1914. It was not therefore surprising that their labours should have passed almost

---

[1] *Ibid.*, p. 683.

wholly unnoticed. At that time people had grimmer and more desperate things to think of. It was not until Easter 1915 that the Archbishop found time to issue his own judgement, which inevitably endorsed that of his consultative committee. It was to the effect that what had taken place at Kikuyu was irregular in form but meritorious in motive, and it should not be repeated. The judgement satisfied neither side. For that very reason it the more commended itself to the Archbishop.

V · *The Fundamental Failure of the Modernists*

There is of course no doubt at all that between 1900 and 1914 Anglican modernism never came within the most distant sight of success in the field which it had set itself to conquer. It had set itself the task of winning back to practising Christianity the Modern Cultivated Man, and there is absolutely no evidence to suggest that it succeeded. Nor was real success possible because the problem was shallowly analysed and the disease defectively diagnosed from the very beginning. In choosing only one particular section of the community as its parish it was necessarily untrue to the principles of both catholicism and the establishment. Neither a catholic nor a national Church has any business to rate the religious interests of any one section of the community as being more important than those of any other: on either theory the Church is responsible for the souls of all alike and all equally, and its first pastoral duty is to bind communities consisting of representatives of every rank of society around its creed. The one thing it must not do is precisely what modernism did: it suggested to one class of the catholic or the national community that it was evangelistically more important than any other.

Nor did it truly diagnose the real need even of this class. Before all else the highly educated Edwardian citizen needed what he did not want, redemption; and in the processes of redemption the heart has a greater part to play than the intellect, and the imagination than the will. Neither to the heart nor to the imagination did even the best of the modernists make the least effort to appeal: they would have considered it rather indecent. Throughout the whole range of Edwardian society the Gospel was being reproached, but this reproach lay not so much because the new knowledge had made it intellectually difficult to believe in it, as in the fact that it seemed so generally impotent to produce the ethical blessedness which it promised. This was the point stressed in the most impartial and far from unsympathetic contemporary estimate of the significance of modernism, the Bampton Lectures of 1907 by Canon H. J. F. Peile. The following paragraph contains the heart of his judgement:

The hope and purpose of Liberal Theology have been, and are more than ever today, to make Christianity a possible religion for the intelligent man of the world. It makes its appeal to common sense by submitting the dogmatic and historical tenets of the Churches without reserve to the tests of critical investigation; and ultimately by presenting Christianity not as a creed but as a life, and faith as the result not of an intellectual surrender which is felt to be repugnant to sincerity, but of the normal intellectual processes which apply in the sphere of practice and secular knowledge. In the first stage of its endeavour it has been to a great extent successful. Whatever may be our opinion of Liberal Theology we must at least admit that its methods and results have compelled the educated intelligence of Europe to reconsider most seriously the truth and importance of that which, seventy years ago, it was preparing to dismiss as unworthy of consideration. But in its further purpose of facilitating the wide acceptance of Christianity it has largely and unexpectedly failed.[1]

Even in the first sphere, the success of modernism was a great deal more patchy than the charity of Peile suggested; and in the second sphere the failure was absolute, and, after all, the second sphere was what mattered, not the first.

The real religious needs were not what the modernists supposed, and the real field of battle they never approached. What was at stake was not the intellectual integrity of the few but the faith of millions: what was on offer was not a new academic theory leading to self-satisfaction but the grace of humility, leading through penitence to joy. The evidence of those who really knew the mass of the people by living and working among them, which is the only way in which such knowledge can be gained, leaves no doubt of the pathetically ludicrous insufficiency of the modernist diagnosis. Canon Barnett, for example, who for thirty years had worked in every class of English society, at the end of his life summed up his impressions, by saying that he saw all round him 'Morality without faith; kindliness and devotion with no consciousness of a divine inheritance or of the sin by which it is lost.'[2] It was true that people had better manners, and were more sober, but they had less idealism, less joy, and life was losing its savour.

In all generations of which it is true to say that the Gospel lies under the two reproaches of ethical insufficiency and doctrinal ineffectiveness (two aspects of exactly the same disease) the remedy is identical. The people have to be taught afresh the facts of history on which the ethic and the doctrine stand; and the dogma has to be more adventurously and imaginatively presented. Modernism set itself to neither task. There was a great need to meet a terrible ignorance of the historic facts of both Old and New Testaments. The state of the knowledge of public school boys and ordination candidates is generally a sound indication of the knowledge of society as a whole; and the evidence is that both these classes were startlingly ignorant. This was brought into the open in the Church Congress of 1908. The Headmaster of Charterhouse, Mr Frank Fletcher, said:

---

[1] J. H. F. Peile, *The Reproach of the Gospel* (Longmans, Green), 1907, pp. 125, 126.
[2] Masterman, pp. 274, 275.

Schoolmasters in both preparatory and public schools will tell you that there is among boys an astonishing and increasing ignorance of the simple facts of the biblical narrative, of old Testament stories, and even of the main incidents of the Gospel. Now I believe that early neglect at home is in the main responsible for the ignorance, and I think that the neglect is partly due to a feeling on the part of the parents that old views of the Bible have altered, and that they hardly know what is taking their place.[1]

Almost immediately afterwards Professor E. M. Kennett of Ely Theological College rose to add his testimony:

Judging from what I have seen in those who come to Cambridge from school, and my experience is founded almost entirely on those who may be expected to have the best knowledge of the Bible, inasmuch as they are intended to take Holy Orders—it seems to me, speaking generally, that the rising generation shows an ignorance of Holy Scripture which is perfectly appalling. There is a class of men, far more numerous than is generally supposed, consisting of those who have left school practically without any knowledge of the Bible, and who imagine that, to a great extent, the Bible—the old Testament at any rate—is an exploded book, and one which, so to speak, the Church may put away in its lumber room.[2]

Here plainly was revealed a failure which the characteristic attitudes of modernism could do nothing to alleviate but could only exacerbate, and by both speakers modernism was blamed for being a prime cause of the evil they deplored.

The other great task, that of so presenting Christian dogma to the people as a whole that it was a militant challenge with imaginative power was, on the whole, ill performed. In essence it involved an appeal to the human sense of mystery, for, as Figgis once said, 'Mystery is the very root of the religious sense . . . for Christ appeals to this sense and He takes it for granted.'[3] It is true that the work of Dr Inge and Evelyn Underhill were attempts to transfer the Christian strategy to this field of battle, but inevitably they spoke only to the educated, and they needed a great body of popularizers, and this they lacked. Only two ever set themselves with any real success to treat the Christian dogma as a challenging trumpet to be blown far and wide so that all must hear. They were Father Neville Figgis and G. K. Chesterton. Both saw the true need, both set themselves to fulfil it, and both regarded the negations of modernism as an enemy within the camp. Chesterton was by far the more effective controversialist. His *Heretics* (1905) and his *Orthodoxy* (1908) were immensely successful and quickly ran through many editions. His method was to laugh the modernists out of court, and his entertaining and persuasive puckishness concealed a considerable theologian and philosopher. Figgis had the mastery of the striking phrase, and did a fine work in commending dogmatic religion to undergraduates.

---

[1] *Record*, p. 40.   [2] *Ibid.*, p. 55.   [3] *The Gospel and Human Needs*, p. 41.

But in the end the task of making Christian mystery relevant to life, and perceived as such by the people as a whole, depends not on lectures and books, but on what the parochial clergy make of the lectures and books, and on how they reinterpret them in the pulpit, the Bible class, and the study group. Modernism had made their task overwhelmingly difficult. Again and again the complaint was made by them that, to take but one example out of many, 'Working as I do among working men, I unhesitatingly say that a paper like the one read at this Congress the other day by Professor Burkitt will cause me more difficulty in my ministerial work than all the writings of Mr Blatchford.' The superiority complex of modernism did, moreover, make for a corresponding inferiority complex in hundreds of pulpits. If as a system of thought it was negligible, as a prevailing atmosphere it was most influential. It had the effect of making hundreds of priests hesitate over their message. They began to apologize for the Gospel instead of proclaiming it; and throughout the whole period 1900 to 1914 preaching was weakened by this note of uncertainty. The trumpets gave an uncertain sound, so no one prepared himself for the battle.

VI · *A More Creative Way*

Underneath the tempestuous surface of all this storm and stress, another seed, planted at the turn of the century, was quietly growing. Its flowering was a rebirth, or rather, a restatement of something basic in all religious experience, the approach to the fundamental reality of God by the mystical path. This had never been forgotten—how could it be?—but it was long since it had been seriously studied. Its revival was overdue, and was fostered by three notable scholars, W. R. Inge, von Hügel, and Evelyn Underhill.

Dr W. R. Inge was the pioneer in the revival of interest in the mystical approach to God. In 1899 he was invited to give the Bampton Lectures, and he chose as his subject Christian Mysticism. The choice was bold and novel. In 1899 the Church was not thinking much about mysticism. The very name sounded foreign and even hostile to the confident utilitarian ethos of the Victorian interpretation of Anglicanism which had for so many years held the field. Not since the days of William Law had Anglican scholarship seriously explored the mystical fields. But the lectures were phenomenally successful.

The sensation of Oxford soon became that of thoughtful churchpeople, and Dr Inge was widely acclaimed. He was well qualified for his task. Today it is accepted as a commonplace that no one should write about mysticism who does not know the classics as well as the Christian mystics. It is not enough, for example, to know Julian of Norwich, St John of the Cross, and Jacob Boehme. One must also know Plotinus and the neo-Platonists of Alexandria. But it was Dr Inge who made this assertion a commonplace. Many scholars before him had known well one or the other of these primary sources. He was the first to know both equally well, and to use both equally freely. In the interpretation put upon Christian mysticism by an earlier classical mysticism, he had found 'a philosophy and a rule of life which would satisfy my mind and conscience'.[1]

Not only did he claim for mysticism its own characteristic excellence and define wherein it consisted, but he also convinced many who heard his words that its rewards were really open to all who were ready to pay the price of self-discipline, patience, and faith. He stressed again and again the power of mysticism to show to the Church of that day, so full of strife, the paths which would lead her to peace. Both the sacraments and the scriptures were, alas! battle-fields. But to search for the mystical vision of God was to enter a fresh religious pathway into a divinely created garden where all Christian parties could unite in fellowship and be at peace.

A more general acquaintance with mystical theology and philosophy is very desirable in the interests of the English Church at the present time. I am not one of those who thinks that the points at issue between the Anglo-Catholics and the Anglo-Protestants are trivial; but I do not so far despair of our Church, or of Christianity as to doubt that a reconciling principle must and will be found. Those who do me the honour to read these lectures will see in what quarter I look for a mediator.[2]

The time was ripe for a revival of interest in mysticism, and Dr Inge's treatment seized the tree and shook down much of the fruit. While he had necessarily to use thousands of words in examining the different systems of the great mystical writers of the past, and in making clear the always rather shadowy distinction between mysticism and pantheism, he most cunningly contrived to commend the following of the mystical path to his fellow-churchmen. He made it crystal-clear that, historically speaking, mystics are hardly ever unhealthy and unpractical dreamers, dabbling for curiosity's sake in forbidden things, but on the contrary wise and far-sighted people. As a form of religion mysticism is as 'practical' as any other. Just because this is so, it could be convincingly shown that mysticism is a form of the knowledge of God, and that it leads to the enjoyment of the fruits of religion, wisdom, fairness, and charity; it had the rôle of reconciling quarrelling partisans. It could thus be commended as appealing both to the typically Anglican desire for a working compromise of peace, and, even more important, to the secret poetic impulse always native to the English spirit.

The torch which Dr Inge had lit was taken up on the Roman side by Baron von Hügel, and on the Anglican side by Evelyn Underhill. In her *Mysticism* (1911) Evelyn Underhill started from a different point of view

---

[1] W. R. Inge, *Christian Mysticism* (Methuen), 1899, pp. vii, viii.
[2] *Ibid.*, p. xi.

from that of Dr Inge: her sub-title—*Study in the Nature and Development of Man's Spiritual Consciousness*—suggests the extent of her likeness to and her difference from her predecessor. Her work was more concerned with the growth and the healing of the spiritual consciousness than with the history of mysticism. Thus her book formed the perfect colophon to Dr Inge's. Together they form a landmark in the history of Anglican theology. More English churchpeople than can be counted owe to them a progressive intensifying and enriching of the life of prayer and the power of sacraments.

Dr Inge had made far more than Evelyn Underhill did of the power of mysticism to heal divisions and end feuds. She had a deeper appreciation than he of the fact that wherever there is mysticism there too conflict and tension will be found. This she had learned from the great book of mysticism which, in point of time, separated her work from that of Dr Inge. This was Baron von Hügel's *The Mystical Element in Religion* which was published in 1908. She learned it also directly from the Baron in person. He was for years her spiritual director.

From time to time one branch of the Catholic Church seems to lend one of its great sages and teachers to another. There is more than one example of an eminent Roman Catholic whose influence is greater outside than inside his own communion. Lord Acton was one, but the supreme example is Baron von Hügel, whose influence upon Anglican theology was as deep, and perhaps deeper than that of any Anglican of his day. No one, for example, has written more profoundly and movingly than he about the great problem of how to suffer with and in Christ; and there must be many now living who in recent bitter years have reached for the Baron's *Essays and Reviews* to renew in an hour of desperate unhappiness their memories of his two most moving and yet most serene essays on human suffering, and who have again found in them peace of mind and steadiness of soul. This power that he wielded through the written word is the more remarkable, for his prose has all the involved tortuousness, the essential outlandishness, of one who always thought in German and wrote in English. Not even his most devout admirers have ever dared to claim that von Hügel is easy to read. But somehow he did contrive to get into his writing the vital, radiant quality of his own soul. He was a most learned philosopher and theologian, and a thorough intellectual.

The Baron was as anxious as any modernist to appeal to the Modern Cultivated Man, and he believed that this could best be done by an exposition of mysticism. But he knew that this would by no means get rid of the conflict. To deal with it in a mystical setting would indeed be to intensify it. In mysticism the very soul of the individual seeks for immediate knowledge of the Absolute. Hence just in proportion as such a soul is loyal to the many-sidedness of revealed truth it must suffer, and the fact of this suffering is the test of health in the soul's following of the mystic way. Mysticism in itself, the Baron pointed out again and again, is deeply immanentist. A phrase like 'The flight of the alone to the Alone' shows it. The transcendence of God is a vital part of the truth about God, but the temptation of the mystic must always be to forget or to minimize just this truth. It was because the Baron so deeply realized this that he set himself to preach the idea of Divine Transcendence precisely through his study of mysticism. He collected long quotations from St Theresa of Avila and St John of the Cross to show how

mysticism was necessarily immanentist in general tendency. Neither speculation nor feeling is satisfied with a pure Transcendence of God; and hence the whole effect of a true mysticism, while not abolishing His Transcendence, is to embrace and experience God, His living Presence, in the innermost soul, that is to insist in some way or other upon the Immanence of God.[1]

It followed that mystics had usually shunned the 'social spirituality which finds God in our neighbour and in great human organizations'.[2] From the deep immanence of this religious attitude towards God and life, so characteristic of much Christian devotion since the Renaissance, no small part of the ineffectiveness of the Church in social relationships can be shown to spring. But to combine mysticism with transcendence, the Baron continually insisted, involves tension and suffering. He quoted instance after instance, and finally clinched it with a tremendous sentence from Kierkegaard:

> To tear the will away from all finite aims and conditions requires a painful effort, and this effort's ceaseless repetition. And if, in addition to this, the soul has, in spite of its striving, to be as though it simply were not, it becomes clear that the religious life signifies a dedication to suffering and self-destruction. What wonder then that for the Jew death was the price of seeing God; or that for the Gentile the soul's entering into closer relations with the deity meant the beginning of madness.[3]

None the less von Hügel bade the mystics suffer. It was the price of spiritual health for them. They could be healthy only when they cleaved to learning, to self-discipline, to the obligations of loyalty to the Church, and to deep, demanding fellowship with ordinary, simple folk. He showed them the way, and because he had followed it himself, they too were gradually brought to follow it with him.

'In the last twenty years', wrote Evelyn Underhill in 1930, 'the study of mysticism has been almost completely transformed.'[4] She then proceeds to catalogue the notes of this transformation. Each one is a consequence of the great change which has come over the theological scene since the century began. This change consists in the fact that the idea of the transcendent

---

[1] Baron Friedrich von Hügel, *The Mystical Element in Religion* (Dent), 1908, vol. II, p. 325.
[2] *Ibid.*, p. 365.   [3] *Ibid.*, p. 345.
[4] In the Preface to the twelfth edition of *Mysticism*, p. vii.

supernatural and its commanding relevance was in 1900 profoundly suspect, and even disreputable, but is now the starting-point of all thinking
about and devotion towards God. There is at last 'a growing recognition
of the distinctness and independence of the Spiritual Order'.[1] The recognition of the Transcendence of God is now as much taken for granted among
us as is the divine Immanence. No doubt the terrible political events of this
century have done more to bring about this more healthy balance of emphasis. But no small part of the gain is due to the lives and labours of these
three scholars—to Dr Inge whom, curiously enough, Evelyn Underhill does
not mention in her 1930 preface; to her own work, so much more influential
than she would ever admit; and supremely to Baron von Hügel, who, with
all the tremendous authority attaching to his name, did more than any
other scholar to deliver mystical studies, and the search for the mystical
vision of God, from their immanentist and subjectivist trends. We owe
much to the insight and perception of the scholars who, in the early years
of the century, perceived that the study of mysticism was the path to health.

[1] *Ibid.*, p. vii.

6

The Anglo-Catholic Movement

I · *Testimonial from a Broad Churchman*

THE REV. H. L. Jackson, who was the vicar of St Mary's, Huntingdon at the end of the nineteenth century, had formed the engaging habit of issuing a solemn pastoral letter to his people at Ascensiontide each year. He seems to have been a perfectly typical vicar of his day, and his parish was the ordinary country town parish, of which England could show hundreds of examples. In 1899 Mr Jackson devoted the whole of his pastoral to the 'Ritual Controversy'. His considered judgement upon the Anglo-Catholics echoed that of the fast increasing number of clergy, who refused their loyalty to anything less than the Church of England as a whole. He made a great effort to be strictly fair and honestly impartial in his estimate. As he explained to his people, he was no Puseyite: the only label he could wear was a 'Liberal Broad Churchman'. But though he did not like this or that element in High Church Anglicanism, he could no longer conceal from himself or from his people the evident fact that on balance the Anglo-Catholics stood in a position of great strength.

The High Churchman has, as I think, deserved to win. Very patiently, very courageously has he worked. Most of the opposition he has met with has been fatuous to the last degree. The High Church position is largely warranted by our Church's formularies. It is, so it seems to me, only malice and ignorance that can determine otherwise.

This vicar was evidently led by his reason. Having conceded the victory to the Anglo-Catholics, he must do what he could to give them the fruits of it. They fought for complete loyalty to the Prayer Book, and had beaten all their enemies. So he publicly undertook that in his church there should be no more small lawlessness in worship. In future two or three must be present to communicate with the priest: if not, there would be no Communion. Not Matins only, but Evensong also would be said daily in church.

The Athanasian Creed, though to him most unattractive, should be duly recited on all the proper occasions. Because the Ornaments Rubric does command the wearing of the eucharistic vestments,

You have from me hereby an expression of my perfect willingness to adopt the aforesaid Vestments *when they shall be provided by the parish, and presented through the Parochial Council.*

The Anglo-Catholic victory in that particular parish was weakened by the fact that the letter made no reference to confession, but otherwise it was complete in all essentials.[1]

II · *The Opposition to the Anglo-Catholics*

What a single obscure vicar says may not matter much to the historian. What he represents may matter a great deal. Jackson represented the average; and his pronouncement meant that the average and fair-minded opinion in the Church had in 1899 come to the point when it was ready to admit the victory of the Anglo-Catholics. Yet this was no concession, but merely a recognition of evident fact. By the end of the century, that interpretation of English Christianity which Newman had proclaimed, Pusey had argued, Keble had lived, and a host of obscure priests had valiantly laboured and suffered to bring to victory, had once and for all won its place. The Anglo-Catholics had won, and in 1899 it was evident that they had won. They had out-thought, out-lived, and out-suffered all their opponents. But, in spite of this, with the turn of the century they had to suffer a second phase of bitter hatred, more hysterical than anything they had yet encountered. This was because three sets of people, the bishops, those in high places in the state, and the mass of the unreflecting laity, flatly refused to concede the victory.

So it was that with the dawn of the new century, the chief barrier to godly union and concord in the Church was the intemperance of partisanship and the violence of opposition excited by the Anglo-Catholics. They were, as Hensley Henson said, in 'an exasperated and exasperating mood'.

Even within the Church, the Anglo-Catholics did not find many defenders outside their own ranks; and most of the bishops were dubious to the point of hostility. They had to administer the organization, and, like most bishops in every age, they valued a smooth and steady functioning of the organism above almost everything else. But the very possibility of this smoothness was denied to the Church by the mere existence of Anglo-Catholicism, and the violent acerbities it caused. This was partly due to the disloyal extravagances of their own extreme wing, who would publish

[1] *Liberalism and Loyalty: or Some Plain Words on the (so-called) Crisis in the Church.* A letter addressed to his parishioners by H. L. Jackson, Vicar of St Mary, Huntingdon, Ascensiontide, 1899.

devotional manuals for children with sentences like this, and then complain most bitterly when the bishops denounced them:

In the evening before you make your communion, be careful to wash your mouth well. If you leave it till the morning, you might accidentally swallow a drop of water. If you swallow even a drop of water, that is breaking your fast. To make your Communion after breaking your fast dishonours Jesus: it is a sin against God and the Church; it is a sin against the Holy Ghost; and if done wilfully and against the light, it is a mortal sin.[1]

But the bishops, though bound by their consecration oath to drive out this sort of idolatry from the Church, actually paid far more attention to the growing practice of auricular confession, which, if done as a matter of free choice, they should have guarded and fostered as being in accordance with the perfectly plain provisions of the Book of Common Prayer. For the most part, they did nothing of the sort. In his charge of 1898, Temple, Archbishop of Canterbury, spoke more than coldly about it. He let drop a few sentences which accurately estimated the strength of the opposition to confession as lying in the fear of the Victorian paterfamilias lest his prerogative of absolute family authority should be undermined.[2] Randall Davidson, Bishop of Winchester, was still more definite. In his charge of 1899 he turned to confession, quoted a very extensive catalogue of citations about it, and added, 'After quiet and anxious thought and prayer I feel it to be my duty, as your Bishop to exhort you to beware of the insidious growth of a usage fraught, as I believe, with much that is perilous to the healthy and robust development of the Christian life.'[3] Add to all this chronic misapprehension of the quite plain formularies of the Church on the part of those who should have known better, the uncertainty of a priest's position before the courts, both spiritual and secular, and the fact that the Anglo-Catholics entered upon the new century in an exasperated, and in an uncompromising mood, is not remarkable. It would have been strange indeed if they had shown no trace of the resentment they could not possibly help feeling.

They were, however, also exasperating. Whether they meant to be or not, they were perpetually the cause of exasperation in others; and strife followed them wherever they went. This strife, whether it took the form of violent controversy or mild rioting, was of a kind which neither ecclesiastical nor parliamentary administrators could ignore. It might start with a debate on the Real Presence in the Eucharist, or the practice of Fasting Communion; but presently its effects would be sure to be felt in the spheres of party politics in the House of Commons and of public order in the streets

---

[1] Quoted in *Charge to the Diocese of Winchester* by Randall Davidson, Bishop of Winchester (Macmillan), 1899, p. 99.

[2] *Charge to the Diocese of Canterbury* by Frederick Temple, Archbishop of Canterbury (Macmillan), 1898, pp. 20–4.

[3] *Ibid*, p. 47.

of the cities. The Anglo-Catholic challenge, as it was called, was answered by the militant protestants who showed all their customary skill in organizing great bodies of ecclesiastical hooligans under such titles as 'The Manchester Protestant Thousand', and in utilizing every resource of legal tyranny under the aegis of the Church Association. Every resource offered by the ugly chaos of the patronage system was also employed to the full. The hectic activities of Sir William Harcourt helped to fan the flames. He was incorrigible and persistent; and he had the attention of the public through being made free of the correspondence columns of *The Times*. There, almost every morning, some new bitter violence of his on 'The Mutiny of the Priests' was to be read. He was for wholesale prosecution in the secular courts; and his views were admirably expressed in the course of a letter to his weary and long-suffering diocesan, Randall Davidson:

I confess I am getting rather sick of the 'good and earnest men' who violate the law and break their oaths. It really does not melt my heart, when a man is discovered to be a swindler or a pickpocket, to be told that he is an admirable family man and goes to church twice on Sunday.... Half a dozen deprivations of contumacious law-breakers will do more good than all the 'talky-talky' of well-meaning and weak-acting people and might tranquillize the public mind. If these gentlemen take themselves off to the place where they properly belong so much the better—until these bacilli are got out of the system there will be no health in the Church.[1]

Harcourt was just as Erastian as most other Christians who rejoiced to call themselves Protestants; but he was what they were not—a master of parliamentary tactics with few, if any, scruples to restrain him. Thus the strife of parties within the Church became one which the Prime Minister himself could not possibly escape; and as the Prime Minister of that day was no less a refugee within philosophic detachment than Balfour, and found himself not in the least aided by the bishops, it is not surprising that he took a gloomy view of the Church's future. This he was wont to express in letters to his greatest friend among the bishops, Talbot of Rochester. On February 6th, 1903, he wrote:

I confess to entertaining the gloomiest apprehensions as to the future of the Church of England. I can hardly think of anything else. A so-called 'Protestant' faction, ignorant, fanatical, reckless, but every day organizing themselves politically with increased efficiency. A ritualistic party, as ignorant, as fanatical, and as reckless, the sincerity of whose attachment to historic Anglicanism I find it quite impossible to believe. A High Church party, determined to support men of whose practices they heartily disapprove. A laity divided from the clergy by an ever deepening gulf, and exercised by religious problems which the clergy cannot help them to solve. An Episcopate—but I will not pursue the subject; my sheet of paper is finished, and I should weep for very soreness of spirit if I went on.[2]

[1] Bell, vol. I, p. 335.
[2] Blanche E. C. Dugdale, *Arthur James Balfour* (Hutchinson), 1936, vol. I, pp. 284–5.

He might well weep in soreness of spirit for all this was intertwined with politics, and was exercising no small effect on the balance of power in the House of Commons. It is significant that when Randall Davidson became Archbishop of Canterbury in 1902, and discussed with his chaplain the issues lying ahead, the talk was almost wholly of politics.[1] The Khaki Election had brought a strong Conservative Government into existence at home, which was already weakening itself by disputing over the chronic problem of tariff reform. The traditional alliance between the Church and the Conservative party was therefore needed at that moment more by the politicians than by the ecclesiastics; but the day was not far off when it might be needed more by the ecclesiastics than by the politicians, for they had the educational reform question to deal with, and the prospect of a Liberal Government ahead. But the Conservatives were strong protestants for the most part, and the ascendancy of Anglo-Catholicism within the Church made the alliance daily more precarious and uneasy. It looked as though disestablishment would soon become a living issue, for the dissenters were conducting a raging and tearing campaign for it; and it seemed as though they might find their best political backing in the most unlikely of all places, the Conservative benches in Parliament. Already Balfour had hinted this to Davidson. Writing to him, through his secretary, on December 15th, 1900, he had said:

> No one denies that the resources of Parliament are equal to the task of enforcing 'Law and Order' in the Church by means of the lay arm; but I know that there are statesmen (and I have some reasons for thinking that Mr Balfour may be numbered among them) who hold the view that this result will probably be attended by the severance of the tie which unites Church and State at the present moment.[2]

The traditional alliance, in fact, was fast being broken to pieces; and it was the Anglo-Catholics who were doing the breaking. Many will now hold this to be one of their great claims on the regard of posterity; but no one could reasonably expect either Balfour or Davidson to see it like that.

It would be neither fair nor accurate to say that the Anglo-Catholics had turned the Church into a field of battle: it would be both to say that it had become one because of them. Meanwhile the general body of informed opinion, both clerical and lay, cursed the strife and peered uneasily into the future. Their point of view was put up by one of the great pamphlets of the language, Hensley Henson's *Cui Bono*, which, in forty-eight pages of rolling Gibbonian prose expatiated on the theme, 'the National Church, torn with dissensions, invites attack. What can be the outcome of the amazing agitation, which has spread sacrilege and blasphemy from one end of England

---

[1] Bell, vol. I, pp. 389–90.
[2] Dugdale, *op. cit.*, vol. I, p. 281.

to the other?'[1] the pamphlet was cast in the form of an Open Letter to Lord Halifax. It reminded him that he was the leader of a party which was in a considerable minority in the Church; 'Only one clergyman in every six is a High Churchman, only one layman in twenty can be so described';[2] and it invited him to compromise for the sake of peace, and to ensure the continuance of the Establishment of the Church. But this appeal came too late —if, indeed, it could ever have been in time.

III · *The Unpopularity of the Catholic Movement*

The governing fact in the situation was the popular detestation of the Anglo-Catholics. It was to this dominant and quite irrational emotion that Erastians like Harcourt, the militant Protestants, and the stout guardians of family tyranny were all making appeal.

Why was the Anglo-Catholic still so bitterly hated? Their historians have seldom given full value to the fact of this hatred, or seriously investigated the reasons for it. They always put it down to sheer malice, to bigoted ignorance, to vested interests of many kinds, to the chronic dislike most men cherish towards those they have wantonly injured. The judgement is undoubtedly just as far as it goes. The dealings of the public with the Anglo-Catholics had always exhibited just those sins. But the strength and extent of the hatred is not thus completely explained. There was something deeper and less disreputable in it.

By all the normal precedents of English public life, the Anglo-Catholics ought by 1900 to have emerged from the period of unpopularity and persecution; and the views of the vicar of St Mary's, Huntingdon, ought to have prevailed throughout the Church. If it was simply a moral conflict between them and their opponents, they had all the victories. As between them and their more reputable opponents among the churchmen who were determined to keep Christianity safely and comfortably lethargic, let Stubbs decide, for he was easily the most level-headed bishop of the day. He examined their complaints with absolute impartiality, and passed a judgement which placed not them but their opponents in the dock. The Protestant opposition, said Stubbs in his pastoral charge of 1899 to his diocese of Oxford, professed

to regard the Anglo-Catholic movement as a reactionary, disloyal, underhand, intriguing conspiracy of a few not very able but very pertinacious traitors to lead us on, or lead us back to the state of sacerdotalism, Jesuitry, antiquarian dogmatism, effete ritualism, immoral dependence on exploded ordinances, false

---

[1] H. Hensley Henson, *Cui Bono: An Open Letter to Lord Halifax on the Present Crisis in the Church of England* (Skeffington), 1898, p. 16. At the time Henson was Master of St Mary's Hospital, Ilford; but he had an ample experience behind him, parochially as Vicar of Barking, academically as Fellow of All Souls. This pamphlet had a vast circulation.

[2] Henson, *ibid.*, p. 29.

morality, and venal repentance, and that system of direction and discipline which ages of corruption had devised to make the world comfortable in sinning.

Such was the charge. It was not difficult to answer. But it was not so much its content as the spirit in which it was constantly urged which gave the whole struggle the flavour of a war for victory

between the moral forces of charity and intolerance, hatred and love, obstinate wrongheadedness and intolerant assumption, the spirit of controversy and the spirit of peace, Christian civilization and unchristian barbarism.[1]

The Anglo-Catholics, in fact, had the angels on their side. They had a roll of martyrs, a list of battle honours. They could, and rather too incessantly they did, say that they had saved the Church, a claim which, if they had included a few other movements in it, was obviously justified. For spiritual treasure it all availed much. The whole history of the Church in this century shows that. But for a fair judgement by the mass of the people, and for a free admission into an honoured place within the religious organism of England, all this had, in 1900, availed nothing. It is a fact which needs to be examined.

For many years the Anglo-Catholic movement had suffered the hatred and been discomposed by the attacks of two enemies, as influential as they were virulent. The first was Queen Victoria. Her letters and her diary leave no doubt of what her views were. For the Anglo-Catholics she had a sincere, a violent, and a never-ending hatred; and when she had occasion—or made occasion—to write of them, she lost all her sense of proportion, and rolling phrases of abuse, heavily underscored, spouted from her pen. She seems never once even to have tried to discover what they really taught, or what there might be to be said for their practices. In 1900 her letters were still unpublished, but her opinions on church affairs were widely known: she had never taken much trouble to hide them. There had once been a time when the Queen was most unpopular with her subjects, and what she thought mattered but little to them. But in 1900 she was a legend, and her people paid to her a homage which did not fall far short of worship. To hold opinions opposed to hers, to do the things she was well known specially to detest, was to commit an act of eccentricity of a highly unpopular kind. It was right thinking to think as Queen Victoria thought, and anything else was anti-social, even anti-national, thinking. The eccentric enormities of the Anglo-Catholics could therefore be brought under the charge of a failure in patriotism by an easy association of images. Of all the terms of abuse which were flung at them, un-English was the commonest. This taunt was hurled again and again. It was almost comically silly, but it was most damaging.

The royal heats and passions were echoed for years with a suavity yet

[1] William Stubbs' *Visitation Charges to the Dioceses of Chester and Oxford, 1886–1899*, edited by E. E. Holmes (Longmans, Green), 1904, pp. 315–16.

more deadly by *Punch*.[1] Week after week for years on end it had sneered at and misrepresented those whom it was pleased to label the Puseyites; and by joke and cartoon had succeeded in implanting their inherent treacheries deep in the imaginations of its wide, influential body of readers. The campaign of abuse reached a climax about 1851. Nine out of the first thirteen cartoons for that year were anti-Puseyite. They were much more brutal and vulgar than funny. A fair example of how far *Punch* carried this malice is this jingle which was published in 1850:

Parody for Puseyites

Though crosses and candles we play with at home,
To go the whole gander there's no place like Rome;
We've statues and relics to hallow us there,
Which, save in museums, you'll not find elsewhere.
Rome, Rome, sweet, sweet Rome!
For all us Tractarians there's no place like Rome!

This sort of thing, repeated steadily week after week and year after year, must have had an immense influence. Any cause which *Punch* consistently ridiculed had but little chance of escaping the enmity and none of winning the approval of the real rulers of England.

The hostility of Queen Victoria and *Punch* had succeeded in fastening the epithet un-English to the movement; but was there really anything about the Anglo-Catholics in 1900 and the following years alien to the native air of England? Their articulate opponents never ceased to proclaim it at the top of their voices; and there is no doubt that those who did not approve of the movement, but took no active steps in the matter, really thought so. But what these two groups said and thought can hardly be accepted as evidence. On the other hand, the historian cannot simply dismiss the charge unheard. The manner of formulating it might be over-hysterical, just as it was, in turn, itself un-English. But in the charge itself there was a certain substance.

The evidence comes from three main sources. First, there is the testimony of the satirical novelists, which, just because they wrote satires, needs to be handled with great caution. But a satire exaggerates a truth and caricatures a real aberration. In its own limited way it is evidence. Compton Mackenzie is the most celebrated of these novelists. His trilogy, *The Altar Steps*, sets out to depict the manners and morals of the most notorious wing of the movement at the turn of the century. His hero, Mark Lidderdale, was successively curate of a country town in Hampshire, of a very 'advanced' London church, and vicar of a Cornish village, where eventually he came to a bad end. The reader is taken right in to the inner circles of the revolutionaries among the Anglo-Catholics. He hears the priests talking in their

[1] See, e.g., S. L. Ollard, *A Short History of the Oxford Movement* (Mowbray), 1915, p. 134.

studies, planning to outrage their bishops. He is made free of all the secrets of the confessional. He reads the private correspondence of all the leaders. Character after character in the book was taken straight from living models, and disguised with a coat of paint so thin that the portraits are hardly decent. Any reader with the least knowledge of the period is bound to recognize Lord Halifax; Canon Hensley Henson, whose conversion to Christianity the saints of Margaret Street decided was a task too exacting even for the Holy Ghost; Father McKay of All Saints, Margaret Street; Father Dolling of Portsmouth; and Bishop Davidson of Winchester. Perhaps it was significant that Father Stanton of Holborn did not appear in the gallery. His life was not one that lent itself to satire. The trilogy leaves a nasty taste. It applied to only a very few among the priests of the movement, but it did apply to some. The Anglo-Catholics had their Mark Lidderdales, and even a very few of them were enough to give the enemies of the movement munitions for their warfare. The wrong sort of Anglo-Catholic layman also found his satirist in Shane Leslie's *The Anglo-Catholic*, a novel still more unpleasant than *The Altar Steps*. Its heroes are a group of young laymen who have taken up the movement as a hobby or a game, and who at no time have come into contact with the living realities for which it stands. Their whole interest—and it is a passion of interest—is with all those matters of ecclesiastical politics which are completely trivial; and this they balance by a morbid and even diseased preoccupation with the various problems of sex. Perhaps it is significant, as certainly it is a relief, that it is not possible to fix the label of any historical person to any of Shane Leslie's horrible young men. The novel is quite unimportant as a contribution to history, but the type it satirized did have a scanty and fugitive existence in the movement, and did the cause immense damage.

The movement had added to itself a party, and all the equipment of a party—a newspaper to announce its policies and a society, the English Church Union, complete with organizing secretaries and a London office, to protect its interests. This step is generally risky to a spiritual movement. Its publicity gets into the hands of its party Society, and the true cause becomes considerably shop-soiled in the process. Protestantism is not so paltry, bad tempered, and negative a thing as the Church Association's behaviour inevitably suggests; and the Anglo-Catholics suffered a great deal from the light cast upon them by the English Church Union and the *Church Times*. The leaders and the writers of these organizations, which were accepted as speaking for the whole movement since the movement itself had created them, seemed to be un-English at least in this that they had no sense of proportion, and not enough sense of scruple. They gave the impression of being quite irresponsible. Unless they were in the throes of a crisis they seemed never to be happy. If no true crisis existed at any particular moment they adroitly magnified and publicized some trivial incident, and then dealt with it at the tops of their voices until it had the artificial life of the rushing, raving crisis in which their souls delighted. It was a mere manœuvre in the party game, but they even deceived themselves with it. It was a very strong supporter of the English Church Union who wrote of it:

> The Union has always existed in an atmosphere of crisis. The Church was always in danger, the Catholic Movement on the brink of disaster. The unguarded utterance of a bishop, the latest heresy of the New Criticism, or the impropriety of a clergyman who had married a divorced couple were denounced as the precursors of catastrophe.[1]

So it was with the movement's weekly paper, *The Church Times*. It was edited with very great journalistic skill, but at that time it was not conspicuous for its scruples or its charity. There, week by week, the faithful found the catholic cause urged, the protestants vilified, and the episcopate denounced.

Where the party society and the party journal set such a standard of bellicosity, many of the party members fell into line, and denounced their Christian brethren with a fervent freedom of phrase such as they would never have dreamed of applying to a Moslem imam. Bishops were the natural target for this kind of abuse. A bishop dared to disapprove of Percy Dearmer's *English Hymnal*, whereupon that 'artist of the catholic movement' promptly wrote of him as 'that scoundrelly bishop'. When Archbishop Temple gave judgement that the law of England, as it then stood, did not permit the reservation of the Sacrament in churches, Lord Halifax pleasantly remarked, 'The Archbishop must be demented.'[2] On another occasion he allowed himself publicly to compare Sir William Harcourt to Titus Oates.[3] This miniature anthology of such gems of courtesy could be almost indefinitely extended; and the general public were not wholly to be blamed if they drew the conclusion that whatever virtues Anglo-Catholicism produced, a temperate judgement and a Christian courtesy were not among them. There was, moreover, a contrast too obvious to pass unremarked between the Anglo-Catholics' preaching of the merits of authority and obedience, and their actual practice of the same. No doubt the Anglo-Catholics were at that time extremely irritated. They had good reason for that, as for years they had been unscrupulously misrepresented and cruelly mishandled. But after all it is the business of a Christian not to let himself get irritated, and more especially when that Christian receives the Blessed Sacrament, with all its Grace, every day of his life.

Perhaps the best piece of evidence for a certain aptness in the cry of 'un-English' comes from the autobiography of a priest calling himself A. F. Webling (the name is a pseudonym), which he entitled *Something Beyond*.

---

[1] J. G. Lockhart, *Viscount Halifax, 1885–1934* (Geoffrey Bles), 1936, vol. II, p. 128.
[2] *Ibid*, p. 128.   [3] *Ibid.*, p. 126.

He had seen the very best and the very worst of the movement within the compass of a few years in the Portsmouth parish of which he was curate. When he went there as a deacon the parish was dead, and to all appearances beyond hope of resurrection. Then the vicar died, and his fellow curate was appointed to succeed him. This curate, Hallam by name, was the sort of priest that any parish dreams of, and one which only the Anglo-Catholic movement could have produced. He was a young saint, glorious, understanding, human, energetic, but a rigorist only with himself. Starting from much less than scratch, he had in a few years built up a vast congregation which really had become an arm of the authentic Body of Christ. Further, and much, much more difficult, he had built it into and around the whole Church, and not merely around himself. To read the book is to realize that nothing but Anglo-Catholicism could possibly have done it: nothing else has quite the virtue which can make deserts blossom. But the day came when he went to Africa as a missionary, there to die a martyr's death; and two very different priests came to take up his charge, bringing with them a very different interpretation of Anglo-Catholicism. The new vicar

was determined to bring to an end the irregularity of communicating several persons at the Sung Mass. He preached a sermon in which he quoted from the Councils and the Fathers, and, having established his case, he proceeded to make the practical application. Henceforward any who desired to communicate at the late service must first satisfy him that it was impossible for them to do so at any other time, and, further, must give a written assurance that they would be fasting. Such persons would be given a badge which they must wear at the altar rails, and only they would be communicated. The plan was duly carried out, but it so happened that from time to time persons unacquainted with the rule approached for Communion. Wearing no badge they were passed over, and in shame and bewilderment crept back to their seat.[1]

This is by no means an exaggeration of a rare incident. It happened again and again. People were refused the Sacrament if they were known not to be fasting. An incident was reported to Gore where a priest refused to celebrate for a man injured in a street accident, and at the point of death. He could not do so, he said, for he had taken food that day. Gore of course was outraged by this pharisaic rigorism. It happened again and again that candidates for confirmation were ordered, not merely recommended, to make their confessions to a priest before they were confirmed. Sometimes their presentation was made conditional upon that. The services of this parish church or that were often arbitarily altered in tone and type, and the parishioners had no redress. Yet it was their church, not the priest's, or even the patron's. The extremists of the movement had a maddening facility in inventing sins which no one had ever supposed to be sins at all, and which in any case seemed to matter very little, if indeed they could be said to

---

[1] A. F. Webling, *Something Beyond* (Cambridge University Press), 1931, pp. 177, 178.

matter at all to the Christ of the Gospels. They were apt to make much more fuss about marriage with a deceased wife's sister than about adultery, more heavy weather about communicating after a cup of tea than about receiving the Sacrament while in a state of moral worthlessness. They seemed to many to have invented a queer sacerdotal land of moral topsy-turvy, and to have learned their ethics in very odd places.

These things gave rise to a general feeling that there was indeed something in the movement neither healthy in itself, nor native to this country, and caused an instinctive fear of a renewed tyranny in the sphere of religion. This fear, or phobia, nine English people out of every ten secretly entertain, and to those who seem to justify it public opinion is always so hostile as to be quite indiscriminating in its anger. In 1900 and the following years there were those in the Anglo-Catholic movement who caused this fear to rise in many hearts. They were few, but they were voluble, and they caused the hatred which in those years pursued the whole movement.

IV · *The Anglo-Catholic Priest at Work*

The Oxford Movement 'began, continued, and is today a strenuous attempt to preach Jesus Christ as for many years He had not been preached in England'.[1] This is the considered conclusion of Canon Ollard, one of the movement's greatest historians. He wrote the sentence in 1915. Ten further years of reflection did but set the same judgement in italics in his mind, for in 1925 he ended a course of lectures in All Saints, Margaret Street, in London, with a solemn recitation of virtually identical words: 'The Anglo-Catholic Revival began, continued, and is today an attempt to preach Jesus Christ as He had not been preached for many years.'[2] That this was true in what may be called the Tractarian period of the movement's life, say, up to the death of Pusey in 1882, Canon Ollard amply demonstrates. Can it be said also to be true in the next period, 1882 to 1914? If so, the movement needs no further justification, and such aberrations and absurdities as were described in the last section are merely as one discoloured drop in a whole fountain of living water.

Perhaps the greatest strength of the Anglo-Catholic movement was that it produced a type of Christian sanctity which had not been seen in England for centuries, and to this day has never been seen anywhere else. What was the common ground of its great heroes of the past, men like John Keble, Dolling, Church, and Marston? They all had deep convictions. They lived a most austere and disciplined life. They had all the evangelists' love for human souls, and they kept that passion human by their lively affection for human beings, more especially the frail ones. They lived, and no one could possibly doubt it, in daily, and even hourly intimacy with all the hosts of

[1] Ollard, *op. cit.*, p. 272.
[2] S. L. Ollard, *The Anglo-Catholic Revival* (Mowbray), 1925, p. 94.

the unseen spiritual world; and they were sufficiently at home in the stored learning of Christendom, in the fields of liturgy, sacrament, and devotion, to know exactly how to keep that intimacy healthy and constantly refreshed. To be in the company of any one of them was to know beyond doubt that the unseen world is the real world, that there is really no penalty of uselessness but actually the strength of a perpetual usefulness in this world attaching to affirmation of the nearness and the relevance of the spiritual order. Christianity is caught more often than it is taught (for so the famous epigram should be written); and from them and their like, it was certainly caught, and taught as well. Such a manner of life is indeed a preaching of Jesus, and perhaps the most effective of all. Many there were, hundreds certainly, and it may be thousands, who had been won for Christ and his Church by being brought for a little into contact with holiness of this order.

Yet to write this is not to indicate the very distinctive quality of the evangelistic holiness of life which the Anglo-Catholic movement so successfully brought to birth. It was built, as holiness must always be built, upon the strength and richness of the interior devotional life. But the Anglo-Catholics never left their personal devotions to chance or momentary inspiration; they studied them, they systematized them, they regulated them, and yet the best of them always contrived to keep the quality of freshness and spontaneity in their prayers, their sacraments, and their meditations. They laboured over them infinitely, but they did not stale in the process. This great achievement was very largely due to the fact that they knew exactly where to go for help. One of the greatest, and the least acclaimed, gifts which the earliest leaders of the movement had bestowed on all English Christendom was to bring back into common circulation and to make easily available the inexhaustible store of wise experience in the writings of the Fathers, and, with them, the accumulated devotional wisdom of the sages of the two other great branches of the Catholic Church. Being English, they were apt synthesists, and fine anthologists; and they had woven the jewels of this huge treasury into a pattern so creative as to have become new. They had made the whole of it relevant to the varied needs of their own devotional lives, and had so arranged this treasure that they had only to look to find just what they needed to nourish this mood and to correct that danger of their devotional practices.

Vivid pictures of them crowd the biographies: Darwell Stone, incessantly poring over the serried tomes of the Fathers, and spending hours in rich prayer before the reserved Sacrament in Pusey House Chapel; Gore's anguished and humorous serenity, and his dying murmur, 'Transcendent Glory'; Evelyn Underhill, rapt as the sacramental drama unfolds, and all the treasuries of the ancient liturgies wrought into her mind and at her instant command to give words to her crowding thoughts. One more detailed picture must stand for them all. It is the picture of old Lord Halifax at the end of his long life receiving the Blessed Sacrament in the parish church of Hickleton; on week-days, in the chapel of his own house.

I do not think [wrote his vicar] that when possible he ever missed assisting at daily Mass. The picture rises up before me of many an early Mass in that rather dark, private chapel at Hickleton which he loved so well. I always found that, however early I went to the chapel to say my preparation before Mass, there was always kneeling in the front row of seats on the right, and wrapped in the French cloak which he always wore, quite still, and almost invisible, the venerable figure of Lord Halifax. Perhaps there was the light of a pocket torch if he was using a book; otherwise only the gleam of the white hair of the bowed head. There was an intensity about him and the sense of entire recollection when he was praying (it was always easy to be recollected oneself if he was there); he made no movement and was utterly absorbed. During Mass he made the responses quietly but audibly; he received the Holy Communion with deep devotion, and, returning to his prayer desk, knelt again and remained quite still. I have known him not to leave the chapel for his frugal breakfast for two hours after he had received our Divine Lord.[1]

Truly, a lifetime of self-discipline in the devotional life has its rewards.

This Tractarian determination to be made free of the ancient knowledge of devotional principles and practices was certainly one of the things which gave the movement its Roman tinge. The Anglo-Catholics were constantly accused of being the Holy Father's fifth column within the Anglican citadel. The accusation was silly, but believed.

In a later generation this ubiquitous and over-sensitive consciousness of Rome had to be fought by the newer leaders in the movement. Darwell Stone was probably the last of the Tractarians who had it, and he was perhaps more deeply rooted in it than any who had gone before him. Stone, significantly, had to spend a large part of his energies all his life in controversy not with protestants, not even with bishops, but with other leaders of the Anglo-Catholics. Men like Gore and Frere were steadily moving far from Rome, and taking most of the movement with them. This they were doing because they had been impelled to add to the characteristic Anglo-Catholic treasury of discipline two elements, which fitted ill with papal Christianity. One was an acceptance of the new learning about the Bible. The other was a renewed sense of the obligations owed by catholic order to social order. These men and their fellow-workers were founding a new kind of Anglo-Catholicism, but they themselves carried on the really vital tradition of the movement, an austere care for holiness, leading to sanctity. Gore and Frere at Mirfield, Kelly at Kelham, Francis Underhill at Birmingham and Oxford, and, still later, Basil Jellicoe at Somers Town in North London—all of these were typical in their several ways of the newer spirit in the movement, its care for freedom of scholarship and its passion for social justice, but all had inherited that painstaking and knowledgeable

---

[1] Lockhart, *op. cit.*, vol. II, pp. 357, 358.

cultivation of the interior spiritual life for which the movement has always stood. The men and women thus trained may have been odd in some ways, and even perverse in others, but grew up into characters of irresistible evangelistic power.

As was natural, not more than a few of the Anglo-Catholics became saints, and so were able to preach Jesus by the mute attraction of their sanctity. But what all could do and (in those days) most did, was to preach him by their toil. The Anglo-Catholic priest might commit many kinds of mistake and folly. His hours were long, his endeavour was ceaseless, and he knew the technique of his job. He had a clear goal before him and he knew exactly how he meant to get there.

The Anglo-Catholic curate normally went to a slum parish. By 1900 that had become a tradition. Twenty years earlier, he would have known perfectly well that not only would he start his ministry in Bethnal Green, but he would be left there till he retired or died. Twenty years earlier still, he had to reckon with the extreme probability that he would serve his entire ministry as assistant curate in the same parish. Such was the tradition which the 1900 Anglo-Catholic ordinand inherited. It was indeed in process of being a little extended, and even humanized. He might start in the slums, but would very likely be drafted later on to those parts of the mission field which had the worst possible climates. Alternatively, he might be given a parish of his own—in another slum. Either way, he still held passionately to the splendid code of all his kind, that you asked for nothing—nothing whatever, you did what you were told (always provided that it was not a bishop who was giving the order), you went where you were sent, and you worked till you dropped.

But this aversion from promotion and passionate loyalty to duty is nothing like the whole story. Any stoic, any puritan might claim as much, and the Anglo-Catholic parish priest was much more than either. He was thoroughly interested in people; he understood them, and he generally liked them. He had a knack of identifying himself with them, so that his talk about his people was not of I and They, but of We. He knew exactly what he wanted to do with them, and that was to bring them regularly to the Mass. He had an extraordinary fertility of intention in dealing with one type and another, and he was commonly blessed with a strong sense of humour, and a shrewd appreciation of the evangelistic power of a certain unconventionality. A sinner did not need to put on the garments of an agonizing and unnatural piety of manner if he wanted to talk to the curate. For all these reasons, an afternoon's visiting by an Anglo-Catholic slum priest was always purposive, often lively, and quite frequently fruitful. A series of confirmation classes did produce good communicants, even if the said communicants were still exceedingly hazy about certain other elements of the Christian life. In the right sense of the word, they were professionals: they knew their job through and through. Called out to visit the sick or the dying, they knew exactly what to do, and did not waste time on trivialities or non-essentials. They were uniformed priests on active service. They commonly wore their cassocks in the streets of their parishes, and were content to be marked men, since that fact would the better help them to fulfil the ideal of the priestly ministry described by our Lord, 'I know my sheep, and am known of mine.' All this was being done not by the giants but by the average among the priests of the movement in scores and scores of parishes up and down the country. In many square miles of dreary town streets in many cities, it was largely from the clergy of the 'High Church' parish that this sort of gay and sacrificial ministry was to be had. Too many of the others just plodded on in the old pedestrian way, while the Anglo-Catholic church was crowded and alert. When these qualities were wielded by the giants of the movement, Dolling of Portsmouth, Lowder of London Docks, and their peers, an instrument of conversion was at work the like of which that generation had never seen.

Evangelism is an art practised best by those who have inventive minds, and the Anglo-Catholics were very original thinkers and planners in this sphere. It was one of them, Canon Body of Durham, who had invented the evangelistic instrument of the ten-day Parochial Mission. That was in an earlier generation: in a later one the movement gave birth to two adaptations of the parochial mission in the Teaching Mission (or Convention, as many prefer to call it) and the Liturgical Mission. Such parochial adventures as these had a great vogue in the first twenty years of the century, and were adapted to their own conditions by many parishes of a quite different churchmanship. They did a great deal of good, as, indeed, they still do. But the success of any venture depends just as much on the suitability of the missioner as on the preparation of the parish; and another enterprise of the Anglo-Catholic movement had, without exactly intending or planning it, furnished the Church with a sufficient supply of trained and competent priests to take missions.

This was the revival of the Religious Order in a new form. The Community of the Resurrection, founded at Radley and established at Mirfield by Gore, attracted a most notable company of priests. They gave themselves very largely to the parochial mission movement, and they were skilled directors of souls. The Society of the Sacred Mission at Kelham has been not less important. Its chief work has been the maintenance of a remarkable and thorough school for testing a boy's vocation for the priesthood, and giving him a seven years' training. More recently Kelham has become a very important centre of Anglican sociology. The Cowley Fathers at Oxford were more monastically cloistered than either Mirfield or Kelham, but both in India and among undergraduates at Oxford they did the great work dreamed of by their great founder, Father Benson; and they provided a centre for retreats and a body of retreat conductors which has splendidly served the whole Church. At Cambridge, much of the same sort of work has been done, though in a very different way, by the Oratory of the Good Shepherd. Perhaps the most difficult and exacting field of labour of all has been claimed and gloriously occupied by the Anglican Franciscans, who made it their business to bring the Gospel to the rootless social outcastes. Among women, probably the outstanding Order is that of the Wantage Sisters, which now has many houses in different parts of England, and which sustains the Christian cause by a creative division of labour between the life of intercessory prayer, the maintenance of really good schools, and the serving of all kinds of unfortunates.

Taught in all these ways, the good Anglo-Catholic priest nearly always knew more about the art of curing souls than his brother of equal virtue who belonged to the evangelicals or the Broad-Church party. If any Anglo-Catholic of that day had claimed all this he would have said at once that the credit should go to the three great contributions which he and his fellows were trying to make to the whole life of the Church. In theology, they were insisting on the doctrine of the authoritative catholicity of the Church, and so were offering certainties and not dusty answers to the problems of life. In ethics, they were trying to show that absolute holiness was really possible to man because it was native to man, and that only they were truly fulfilled and completely natural who were seeking after it. In the arts of conversion, they were struggling to demonstrate in the eyes of a still largely sceptical Church that there is an intimate and direct connection between conversion and ceremonial in church.

Anglo-Catholics were known as such by the general public not by the narrowness of their collars but by what they did in church. In their ritual they did undoubtedly go very far beyond what the Prayer Book allowed and what most of their parishioners relished. But, as one of their number explained, 'In going beyond what the Prayer Book allows we do get the results which the Prayer Book intends.' They aimed to revive and to call into new life the whole liturgical wealth of the Early and Medieval Church. But they were not moved in this by mere ancientry or antiquarianism, nor yet, as a rule, by the desire to annoy bishops. The real lovers of souls among them were not even thinking first of all of the need to assert the continuity of one generation of the Church with another, though this was always in their minds. They wanted the revival of the ancient forms because they believed that they were the most evangelistically effective forms. Nobody ever demonstrated that they were wrong in this belief, and they themselves frequently demonstrated that they were right. All history, whether 'secular' or 'ecclesiastical', underlines and endorses that belief. The soul is approached through the eye, and the heart moved by appropriate pageantry, for these speak things to the sub-conscious faculty of imagination which it can hold and return to the will in the form of concentrated power. By their ceremonies they were trying to make the spiritual known to be the real, and when they said that they had another sanction, more authoritative than this pragmatic sanction, in their fidelity to the spiritual insights of the earliest years of Christendom in the undivided Church, they made a claim which history endorses.[1] But let the final judgement be uttered by a German Lutheran theologian, who had deliberately rejected the Roman Catholic allegiance of his birth and youth to become an evangelical pastor. From such a source it comes decisively:

The renaissance of evangelical Christianity is to be sought neither in modern Liberalism, nor in its anthithesis, the 'catastrophic' theology of the 'dialectic' theologians, but in the revival of the Catholic spirit. And in point of fact, the Catholic spirit (which is not to be confused with the Roman Catholic) has for the last hundred years been engaged in reconquering the Reformation Churches. The Anglican Church, which of all the Protestant Churches has retained the closest connection with the Old Church, made the beginning. . . . Today there has arisen, out of the Oxford Movement, which aimed at the recovery of the full Catholic tradition, the mighty movement known as the Anglo-Catholic. Nearly one half of the members of the Anglican Church think of themselves as Catholics, not Protestants. . . . Anglo-Catholicism is one of the most hopeful and fruitful movements in the Western Church of the present day.[2]

If, in 1926, such a judgement could come from such a source, between 1900 and 1914 the Anglo-Catholics were worth all the hatred they got, and much more than a match for it. They had something to offer; their opponents generally had not.

V · *The Ritual Commission*

From the windows, first of Farnham Castle and then of Lambeth Palace, Randall Davidson had been watching all this counterpoint of assertion and protest with alarm. It all spelt trouble, and much of the trouble would certainly fall upon him. But he was in a better position than most other bishops to know how deeply the Protestant emotions of the Church were wrought into and expressed by the Conservative members of Parliament; and he knew far better than the House of Commons how fundamentally immovable the Anglo-Catholics were, and that, let the irresponsible freakishness of some of them be what in fact it was, they were none the less bearing far more than their share of the Church's real burden. But all he could do was to watch, and wait, and prepare himself for the coming storm. It was impossible for him to precipitate it in any way.

The storm broke in 1904. The Rev. Mr Bowen of the Church Association wrote a more than usually violent and abusive pamphlet and sent it to members of Parliament. Among them it had an explosive effect, and they began to demand from Balfour that because the bishops had not succeeded

[1] See, e.g., Friedrich Heiler, *The Spirit of Worship* (Hodder and Stoughton), 1926, p. 47.

[2] Heiler, *op. cit.*, p. 185.

in curbing ritualistic excesses, and because Parliament had a legal control over a state Church, that a Select Committee of the House of Commons must be appointed to consider and to remedy clerical lawlessness. Unless this was granted, Balfour's own party threatened to vote against him, and to bring down the Government. But to this proposal Davidson could not possibly consent. It was nakedly Erastian, and, as he said himself, it would not be only the 'eccentric' men who would violently resent it. Lord Halifax called the proposal 'a gross piece of impertinence';[1] and H. W. Hill, the Secretary of the English Church Union, lost no time in letting his chief know what he would do if this impudence came to pass:

I have been enquiring into the methods of Select Committees and if that expedient were resorted to I think our best course would be to let them go to the devil their own gait, and treat them with absolute contempt. If they sent for one one would have to go, but if I found myself before a Committee made up of such rascals as Austen Taylor I would pretty quickly let them know what I thought of them, clock-tower or no clock-tower.[2]

Hill was indeed capable of behaving exactly as he wrote; and in so doing he would have enjoyed the support and stimulated the imitation of very many clergy and laity not of his own party. Almost certainly the appointment of a Select Committee would set in motion a process which must end at one place only, the disestablishment of the Church.

At all times it was a major aim of Davidson to avoid this, and he therefore brought his full powers of negotiation to bear upon Balfour in order to persuade him to appoint not a Select Committee but a Royal Commission. There is a nice shade of difference between the two instruments. The former judges and the latter enquires; the former has the authority of the House of Commons, and the latter that of the King. Davidson had taken soundings, and had discovered that while the Anglo-Catholics did not much relish even a Royal Commission, they would put up with it, and refrain from treating it with open disrespect, if they could be saved from a Select Committee. An outburst from Balfour during an interview shows the Archbishop's difficulties:

It is now clear to me that all the clergy, of whatever school, are equally stupid. I had thought the range of stupidity more limited. I cannot appoint a Royal Commission: it would not satisfy the House of Commons. They would vote against me if I urged it.[3]

By the strength of two of his most weighty letters—they were masterpieces such as no other public figure could have composed—Davidson's will prevailed, and in March 1904 Balfour announced to the House of Commons that he would appoint not a Select Committee but a Royal Commission. The Royal Commission on Ecclesiastical Discipline was appointed in

[1] Lockhart, vol. II, p. 143.   [2] *Ibid.*   [3] Bell, vol. I, p. 459.

April 1904. It had fourteen members—the Archbishop of Canterbury, the Bishops of Oxford and Gloucester, Sir F. H. Jeune, Sir L. Dibdin, Mr Drury, Mr J. G. Talbot, Sir John Kennaway, Sir Samuel Hoare, Mr G. Harwood, Mr George Prothero, the Marquess of Northampton, Sir Edward Clarke, Lord Alverstone, with Sir Michael Hicks Beach as Chairman. Thus it was nicely divided between 'High' and 'Broad' and 'Low'; and laymen heavily outnumbered clergymen. The Commission met 118 times, and in the end produced a vast Report.

It is probable that nobody now reads the Report. It is almost inconceivably tedious to a modern reader—a very large, fat volume, immensely long and printed in microscopic type. The examination of innumerable witnesses began with the Rev. Mr Bowen of the Church Association. He introduced to the commissioners each of his paid agents in turn, and one by one they described how they had played the spy at various Anglo-Catholic churches, having been sent by their paymasters to find matter for accusation while purporting to be worshippers of God. Incredibly, neither these creatures, nor the *agent provocateur* who employed them were censured by any member of the commission. Mr Bowen and his henchmen were, indeed, treated with astonishing forbearance, for their behaviour had by any decent standards been appalling. Scores of pages of the Report are filled by their evidence of how in this church and that the archaic law was being broken by, for example, the wearing of vestments and the use of incense. A copy of this evidence was sent to the vicar of each church concerned, and the Report prints their replies in black type. Each of these vicars had evidently been briefed by the English Church Union, for they all replied in the same way and used almost exactly the same words. Each one claimed that in his services, he was following the instructions of the Ornaments Rubric, and added that if the decision of the Judicial Committee of the Privy Council had interpreted that rubric differently, it was for him quite irrelevant since he could not accept the authority of that secular tribunal.

Presently it came to the turn of the Anglo-Catholics, and they proceeded to make very merry at the expense of the Commission. They were headed by Lord Halifax and Athelstan Riley, and they exactly copied the tactics of the Protestants, producing endless examples of churches which had broken the law by not reciting the Athanasian Creed when the Prayer Book ordered it, by providing hymns at Matins and Evensong, which the Prayer Book does not sanction, and examples of clergy breaking the law by *not* wearing the eucharistic vestments when they celebrated the Holy Communion. With these witnesses the commissioners dealt far less patiently than with the intolerable Mr Bowen. They were in fact not a little provoked, as the following impression of the evidence given by the secretary of the English Church Union shows:

Hill was so bluff, debonair, and confidential that the Committee [*sic!*] can hardly have known what to make of him. He seized any chance that offered of plunging into digressions, in the course of which, with an air of innocence, he would throw out a few facts likely to be injurious to his adversaries. Ecclesiastical disorders? Yes, unhappily they existed. Low Churchmen—he would like to think them honest—were such strange people. 'Of course, they are troublesome sometimes when they talk of turning us out, which is rather like the lodger threatening to turn the landlord out; but of course everyone knows what is going on in the way of disorder. Only the other day, I was told of a case in an eastern diocese where the black bottle was drawn out. . . .' The Chairman hurriedly intervened.[1]

By far the greater part of the Report is devoted to what was of no more consequence than this kind of slanging match between the Church Association and the English Church Union; and it is this fact which makes the Report so insufferably tedious to read today. A solemn and portentous assembly wearily listening to a succession of pert and aggressive children, and all of them together using day after day of precious time upon matters, in themselves of vital importance, but so presented that only their trivialities were to be seen—that is the impression given to anyone who now sets himself to read through the evidence.

In two very different ways, however, the Commission did something to justify the extravagant hopes set on it and the heavy sacrifices of time and energy its members made. The first positive good which came out of it was the Archbishop's really profound historical survey of the rise of the Anglo-Catholics. It is strange that it has never been printed separately from the Report, for it is probably the best introduction to its subject which has ever been written, and an undoubted contribution to history. The second real benefit which came out of all this labour was that the leading laymen were at last brought to see that the objections of the Church at large to recognizing the Judicial Committee of the Privy Council as the ultimate authority in matters and causes spiritual were so wide, so deep, and so determined that it would never be possible to overcome them. This mute recognition meant a final abandonment of the old attempt to force conformity and stamp out variety in public worship by the threats of secular courts for deprivation and imprisonment. Since 1906 these threats have never again been seriously made, and in part we owe it to the realism of these royal commissioners.

Davidson began by recognizing in his historical introduction the 'consolidation of High Churchmen in a more solid and deliberate disallowance or distrust of the Privy Council as the ultimate court in ritual matters'.[2] Witness after witness underlined this during the course of the evidence. It all had its effect because the unanimous recommendations of the Commission contain these significant sentences:

> Bishops and others have naturally been slow to appeal to a court the jurisdiction of which was so widely challenged; clergymen have claimed the liberty, and

[1] Lockhart, vol. II, p. 144.   [2] Bell, vol. I, p. 468.

even asserted the duty, of disobedience to the decisions of a tribunal the authority of which they repudiate; and judgments of the Judicial Committee, though at least the reasoned statements of very eminent judges, are treated as valueless because they are Privy Council judgments. A court dealing with matters of conscience and religion must, above all others, rest on moral authority if its judgments are to be effective. As thousands of clergy, with strong lay support, refuse to recognize the jurisdiction of the Judicial Committee, its judgments cannot practically be enforced.[1]

This pronouncement was the most important of all—a real contribution to setting the Church free to concentrate on its true task. But the rest of the labours of the Commission, when seen in the perspectives of thirty years of subsequent historical experience, were of but little account; and upon the vagaries and the usages of the Anglo-Catholics they had no effect whatever.

[1] *Ibid.*, p. 471.

7

The Church and the People: 1900–1914

I · *The Challenge of Secularism*

MOST of the Christian pronouncements of the first fifteen years in the twentieth century were laments. Whether uttered by the parson in his pulpit, by the reader of a paper, or by the more impromptu speaker towards the end of the session of a Church Congress, or, more weightily, by the assembled bishops in Convocation or the Lambeth Conference, still the elegiac undertone coloured most utterances. At a superficial level, the vicar lamented the gaps in his congregation where the men and youths should have been, and were not. At a deeper level, the thinkers and the sages announced that a tide of great strength was flowing against Christianity; and they gave to that tide the name of 'secularism'. At the deepest level of all, rather occasional prophetic voices (contrary to popular assumption, they were nearly always either episcopal or monastic voices) sounded a more bracing note. Acknowledging the threat of the secular spirit, they perceived that the real task was the integration of Christianity with the passion for social righteousness which underlay so much secular preaching, that this diagnosis furnished the Church with its true policy, which must be to take the whole culture of the age, the spiritual ethos and the social organization of its civilization as its field of action.

Bishops Gore and Percival (of Hereford) were constantly preaching this, as were men like Figgis and Kelly, among those who had taken monastic vows. From a very different point of view, their pleas were echoed and most ably reinforced by such residentiary canons as Hensley Henson and Barnett of Westminster Abbey; and also by the already influential voice of William Temple in Oxford. About what tactics were necessary to pursue this general strategy there was certainly no agreement in the Church. There never is—or will be. But those who thought most deeply had least doubt that a central feature of it must be the embracing by the Church of the idea of democracy. To put it more shortly, democracy was limping because it was too seldom conscious of its soul: the task of the Church in the twentieth century was to give to democracy that knowledge in order that it might be saved. Secularists were all known to be democrats. They loudly said so. They said further that Christians were not, that they could not be, and that the most undemocratic Christians of all were those who, as Roman Catholics or Anglicans, set a value on their catholicity. Inevitably, the Anglican Church had to reckon with the secular assault.

Holyoake, one of the more celebrated expounders of what twentieth-century secularism stood for, defined his creed as a system of thought which

relates to the present existence of man and to actions the issue of which can be tested by the experience of this life. It deals with the moral duty of man as deduced from considerations which pertain to this life alone, and proposes to regulate human affairs by considerations purely human.[1]

There could plainly be nothing but war between Christianity and such a view of life, for there is hardly a single article of the Christian creed which is not attacked by it. But it could not be an easy war or a short. A good many streams of thought, which for centuries had moved along separate courses, had by now converged into a deep and turbulent river of troubled waters. It all might be said to have begun with John Locke, two hundred years before. He had given the *imprimatur* of his immense authority to the view that there is no contradiction between the Christian way of life and the competitive ordering of society, and since then the idea of acquisitive man set in a competitive social order had not found many voices to challenge it. The imperturbable secularism of Gibbon had been by no means uninfluential. The researches of Charles Darwin, given to the world in *The Origin of Species*, and immediately popularized by a host of commentators and controversialists, had seemed to bestow the benediction of nature herself upon the consequences of competitive capitalism, that the fit must survive and the unfit perish. This had been a powerful vindication of the way in which society was in fact organized, both nationally and internationally, to be a field of battle between competing centres of power.

If the Edwardian citizen looked out upon his world at home he saw the slums and the workhouses, the long succession of violent, bitter strikes and lock-outs, and the unscrupulous and unsocial behaviour of a dozen pressure-groups, ranging from the die-hards in Parliament to the militant suffragettes. If he looked ahead he saw the unfinished tale of German aggression, and the resultant competitive armaments race. If he looked across the water to his own 'other island', he saw a scene of perpetual and, apparently, incurable strife. Let Locke say what he might, this was a hell. Godlessness in the ordering of society and in the framing of industrial and international policy had made the hell. But, perversely and illogically, the

[1] *Church Congress Record* (1908), p. 587.

Edwardian citizen tended more and more to call in a new kind of secularism to cure the hell which secularism had made.

All classes and sections of society were tinged with this delusion that secularism alone could reclaim what secularism had perverted. This was no doubt partly due to the fact that the Church seemed rather helpless. Her vital message seemed to have been compromised by the very ill-digested success and prestige of the German criticism of the Scriptures and by the modernist movement in the universities. She was ill equipped to denounce the competitiveness of the secular world, for she herself was split into competing parties; and in her interior organization, in her handling of 'success' and 'failure' among the clergy, she was far from having kept herself unspotted from the competitive world. If the citizen's great hope lay in the prestige and progress of democratic government, he was again disappointed. For he saw that in so far as democracy tended towards the egalitarian fellowship of true socialism it was opposed far more often than it was commended by the mass of the Anglican laity. Every circumstance was suggesting to him that salvation lay in the triumph of the secular mind, and he did not let the lack of logic in this conclusion disturb him.

The man in the Mechanics' Institute and the secretary of the local branch of the Trade Union, though propelled in that direction by the very able polemics of Robert Blatchford, had more or less drifted into the secular frame of mind. But in the student world, which is ultimately the most influential world, secularism was always a militant and aggressive creed. Many pronouncements by priests like Neville Figgis, who were in a position to know the facts, testified to this; and the experience of the Student Christian Movement in many universities both at home and abroad confirmed it. As far back as 1893 one of their travelling secretaries had tried in vain to get Christian work started in the university of Bristol. He could find no Christians to start it. 'I asked several men if they knew a Christian man in college to whom I could go. They answered that they did not think there was one.'[1] He went on to Nottingham and to Manchester, and found much the same state of affairs.

The drift of the English student world away from the loyalties of organized religion was very evident; and the superstition that religion is an opiate to make people dreamingly content with their lot was canvassed and often believed in English universities as in others. The secretary of the Student Christian Movement, who was in the right position to have true knowledge of the facts, had no doubt of the cause.

More and more students studied science. None of them was prepared intellectually for this study. Many of them had never heard the word evolution mentioned until they came to college, and discovered with a shock that there were

---

[1] Tissington Tatlow, *The Story of the Student Christian Movement*, p. 52.

some among their teachers who believed that evolution, which was made so much of by teachers of science at this period, cut at the roots of Christianity.[1]

If the bias of most higher education was scientific—and most of the newer universities had developed out of science technical colleges—it followed automatically that the broad movement of education must be towards the forsaking of the classics and the liberal arts. The results were the swift spread of materialist thinking, and an increasing identification in the popular mind of the scientist with the progressive. They had not yet experienced two world wars in a single lifetime to teach them the crassness of any such assumption. Progress, democracy, the secular spirit, the revolt against the Church, the tacit assumption of a materialist view of life—no reputable thinker associated all these together, but the unthinking did somehow receive and very frequently adopt the impression that these ideas formed a synthesis, and that those who resolutely pursued them would arrive at the freedom to which they seemed to point.

Only half of this was perceived at the time by the Church's leaders. The Lambeth Conference of that decade took place in 1908. The encyclical letter with which it introduced and commended its resolutions was an absurdly optimistic document. It began by hailing the spirit of service which the bishops claimed to have descried, and it passed on to this extraordinary judgement:

We are bound by our principles to look with confidence and hope on the progress of thought. But we mark in the present day special reasons for such confidence. Materialism has not for the minds of our generation the strength or the attractiveness that once it had. Science displays in an unprecedented way the witness of nature to the wisdom of God. Men's minds are more and more set towards the spiritual, even when they are set away from Christianity.[2]

The bishops cannot possibly have had any real evidence. But the other and more positive half of the Church's situation they saw with the clearness of prophets. They realized something of the first importance which was soon after forgotten again, and to which Christian eyes were to be closed until the agonies of our own day forcibly opened them. This was that one of the two chief duties of the Church is always to flavour or to pervade a whole culture, a whole system of organized life. In 1908 to pursue such a duty necessarily involved a declaration of the relationship of Christianity to democracy. To this the Lambeth Conference committee on the Moral Witness of the Church at once turned, and its report might have been, as it deserved to be, a really influential document if only it had been translated into ordinary speech and popularized. The committee saw that democracy was a problem, not an achievement. They realized that the democratic

---

[1] *Ibid.*, p. 425.
[2] *The Five Lambeth Conferences*, compiled under the direction of the Most Reverend Randall T. Davidson, Archbishop of Canterbury (S.P.C.K.), 1920, pp. 301, 302.

organization of government in this country was fast changing in its nature as well as in its form. They firmly stated that democracy was in great danger of becoming secular in proportion as it was self-regarding. They were clear that if this should happen, the Church must bear no small part of the blame for having been blind for so many years to the fact that if democracy was not the only possible form of Christian government, it was far more Christian than any other.

Why [they asked] does the Church fail to win the sympathy and regard of those who seek an ideal so largely in accord with the Lord's own principles, since it is plainly wrong to suppose that this democratic movement is in itself atheistic and anti-Christian?[1]

They answered that it was because of the divisions among Christians, and because there was too much autocracy and too little democracy in the domestic organization and system of the Church. There was, however, another and a more immediately relevant answer which escaped them.

This was the attack upon the Church which both organized and unorganized secularism was making. Two or three militant and well-financed societies of rationalists and freethinkers existed, each one with its weekly newspaper; and the whole output of at least one well-conducted publishing business was given to the discrediting of Christianity. Then there was Bernard Shaw who, with cheerful and infectious impudence, was hammering away at the orthodox presentation of the Christian Gospel. He devoted one of the most persuasive of all his long prefaces—the preface to *Androcles and the Lion*—to an attack on the doctrine of the Atonement, which, more than any other single dogma, makes Christianity a Gospel. More effective by far than any of these was Robert Blatchford, whose weekly paper *The Clarion* was to be found in every working-men's club or mechanics' institute, and in a vast number of working-class homes, particularly in Lancashire, to which Blatchford belonged. It was one of the most ably edited weeklies which had ever existed. It was popular without being cheap, deadly serious and yet most readable, its circulation manager was certainly a genius, and on every page it carried the unmistakable imprint of a most remarkable personality. The Church had nothing, nothing whatever, to put against it. The only interesting Church weekly papers were too busy denouncing other Christians to give much space to answering attacks on Christianity as such, and the other Church papers were scholarly but dull. Only G. K. Chesterton seemed to see and tried to meet the need, but his allusive impishness was miles above the heads of Blatchford's audience.

Blatchford perceived more clearly than anyone else the particular weakness of the Church in conflict with secularism, and in consequence he had a strategy to offer to the secularists. The secular spirit was growing, and was on the march. It was implicit in the materialistic and competitive ethos

[1] *Five Lambeth Conferences*, p. 410.

of international and industrial relationships. About this social disorder, and its awful results for human lives, thinking workers complained bitterly that the Church had all too little to say, and they contrasted this quasi-silence with the vigorous eloquence of the socialists. This dissatisfaction was the real opportunity of the secularists, but only Blatchford really seized it. He was always hammering just that nail, and the result for the pastoral work of the Church was neatly estimated by a rather bewildered Manchester curate in a speech to the 1908 Church Congress:

> I have read the *Clarion* ever since it came out. I thought it was my duty to do so, because I was going to be a worker amongst the poor. Now Mr Robert Blatchford is a Manchester man, and Manchester working men admire him. They crowd up at the Free Trade Hall to hear Mr Blatchford speak in a way in which they would not crowd to hear a man like myself; yet Mr Blatchford does not pretend to be a Christian and I do. Although I believe I have the spirit of my Master helping me in my work, I do not get the people to come and listen to me in the way Mr Blatchford does.[1]

But the other secularists must have annoyed Blatchford almost as much as Christians did. Their business was to organize and to make militant the rather vague and individualistic secular spirit. Mercifully they were very bad tacticians. Although they took as their motto, 'To establish morality on grounds independent of Christianity,' and should therefore have been hammering all the time at the social issue, what they actually did was to weary people by confining themselves to incessant and negative detraction of the Church and Christianity. It was as though they had learned only one tune, and could sing to no other. The tune was catchy, but it palled with repetition and no other ever took its place. Too much negation had made them 'too old at forty', and the membership of the rationalist societies was now very middle-aged, and was apt to be drawn from only one class or social group.

II · *The Position of the Parochial Clergy*

At every stage in the history of the Church the pace of Christian expansion is the pace at which the clergy are willing to move. It is quite impossible to do without the clergy, and any Church which endows them with the Parsons' Freehold, gives to them an ultimately commanding position. In the last analysis, it is they—the vicars and rectors in their parish churches—and not their bishops, who are the real arbiters, sitting in judgement on any appeal for action which authority makes. If they say No, there is nothing more to be said until they change their minds. There is certainly no way of coercing them.

During the first decade of the twentieth century the parochial clergy were a harassed body of men. To be harassed is automatically to lack both

[1] *Record*, pp. 604, 605.

judgement and initiative, or at least to have these qualities blunted. It is quite possible to be both harassed and faithful, and at no time has a quiet faithfulness ceased to be the rudimentary virtue of the Anglican priesthood. But even faithfulness can retire within itself and become unseeing and pedestrian outside the limits of a very small circle, and there was very little sign that the rank and file of the parochial clergy perceived the true nature of the challenge which secularism was sounding.

There were not enough clergy to minister fully to the people; and while the population was increasing the number of deacons ordained was getting less. The first meeting of the Canterbury Convocation in the new century, in February 1900, devoted long attention to this problem. The debate took place on a motion to reintroduce the sub-diaconate, a device whereby selected lay people might be authorized to administer the chalice at Holy Communion. The discussion was lengthy and learned but it got nowhere, for it soon lost itself in a vain effort to decide just exactly what the sub-diaconate historically was, and to define the nice shade of distinction between a sub-deacon and a lay reader. But nevertheless some interesting and significant facts about the way in which this situation was developing were brought out into the open. It was not only the Church which was suffering from a decline in the number of candidates for service in its ministry. Other learned professions were feeling the same draught, particularly medicine and education. Between 1889 and 1894 the medical profession had suffered a drop of 19 per cent of candidates; and the figures for the teaching profession were even more serious. Neither profession, it was said, was any longer drawing the best men from Oxford and Cambridge.[1] But although this decline was common to several vocations, it was the Church which suffered most, for it was making the least effective use of the clergy it had. In 1900, for instance, there were 33,500 ordained men in England, and of these only 29,000 were at work; 4,000 held no appointment. This is an astonishing and a grave proportion, for out of the 4,000 men who held no appointment, only 1,800 were retired incumbents. What had happened to the 2,200 left? Besides this, there was a most serious disproportion between the number of retired clergy and of assistant curates, for there were 500 more of the one than the other.[2] Statistics such as these were incomplete and sketchy, but they were sufficient to give ground for the constant complaints that too many curates could never become vicars, and too many vicars could get no curates. By 1906, 424 curacies were vacant; and in the diocese of Liverpool alone there were thirty-eight vicars hunting for curates whom they could not find.

The Lambeth Conference of 1908 appointed a commission to examine the supply and training of the clergy. Its chairman was Winnington Ingram, the Bishop of London. This commission collected and published the statis-

[1] *Chronicle of the Convocation of Canterbury* (1901), pp. 129, 130.
[2] *Ibid.* (1900), p. 109.

tics of the problem and put them in a form which made the figures talk. The peak year for ordinations had been 1886 when 814 deacons had been ordained. Since then the figures had steadily dropped to 569 in 1901, and thereafter had very slightly risen to 587 in 1907. If the standard of 1886 had been maintained the number of deacons ordained between 1886 and 1907 would have been 17,808. It had actually been 14,784. Thus there was a deficit of 3,024. But to get a true picture one had to take into account the movement of the general population figures, which was annually increasing at the rate of 260,000. This, by the standards of clerical staffing of 1886, demanded an increase of 100 clergy a year. A simple sum gives the total deficit of clergy in 1908 as 5,024.[1]

A dozen reasons could be—and were—produced to explain these unhappy facts, but there was no real doubt that the real trouble was the Church's archaic financial system, which made the worst possible use of an income already far too small for its needs. The would-be ordinands and curates—those who were financially the least able—had to carry the heaviest part of the burden. The Additional Curates Society, which made grants to 1,400 parishes if a curate was employed, and ear-marked these grants to these parishes, calculated that the number of these parishes which did not claim the grant because they employed no curate rose from 10 per cent to 19 per cent of the whole 1,400 between 1903 and 1907. Other parishes which could have produced the money to pay a curate could not find one. Thus, in 1906, 6,925 curates were at work, but there were 400 parishes which wanted one but could not find him; and in 1907 there were 93 fewer curates at work, and 24 more parishes which wanted them, Nor do these figures take any account of the shortage of clergy for overseas work. Here too the position was becoming serious. In 1907 the Church Missionary Society and the Society for the Propagation of the Gospel calculated that between them they were 259 priests short.[2]

At that time there were not many ways in which a candidate for ordination could be financed and helped when his family resources were not sufficient to see him through his training. Those who came from poor homes had the scales very heavily weighted against them, and the figures show that a lamentably high proportion of those who had a genuine vocation for the ministry, and who were, or could have become sufficient for it, must have been denied the chance to answer their call simply for lack of means. The Central Ordination Candidate Fund received about 300 enquirers each year, and definitely accepted as candidates an average of 120 of them; but of these 120, only 45 were eventually ordained. The colleges at Mirfield and Kelham received respectively 300 and 400 enquiries a year. They approved 100 each, but could only accept twelve each year, having at that time no room for more. The theological college of the Community of the Resurrection at Mirfield had been begun precisely to meet this discreditable challenge.

[1] *Five Lambeth Conferences*, pp. 358, 359.   [2] *Ibid.*, p. 36a.

A chapter was held in the parlour. Gore sprawled in an armchair. Bull said that he had some fifteen boys from poor homes who wanted to be priests in the so-called National Church. They could not become priests because their parents lacked the means for an expensive education. A boy at Halifax had told him that if he forsook the Church, became a Unitarian, and denied the deity of Christ, he would be given six years' thorough education for the ministry without any cost to his parents. The same would follow if he joined the Wesleyans or the Baptists. If the parents of a boy in the Church of England had £1,000 to spare, he would be sent to Oxford or Cambridge, and be ordained in due course. Another boy who might have heard God's call, and be pre-eminently fitted for the priesthood would find the door to the sanctuary locked, bolted, and barred, just because his parents had not £1,000 to spare for his education and could not afford to dispense with the weekly wage he was bringing into the home. 'We have invented a class priesthood with a money qualification.'[1]

The Community took immediate action. They begged money and they transformed the old stables of their house into a theological college for boys without this world's means. They gave these boys a long and very thorough pre-graduate and post-graduate training; and it was not long before they were able to establish their own hostel at Leeds for the young men they had sent to the University there. The Society of the Sacred Mission at Kelham, near Newark, had preceded Mirfield in the same field by a year or two, and these two communities still offer a more prolonged and probably a more thorough religious education and testing of vocation than an ordination candidate can find elsewhere in the Church. It was a great achievement. But although the original buildings Mirfield used for the purpose have since been doubled and trebled in size, at no time have they been in a position to accept more than a proportion of their applicants. There are at least some scandals which time mends. Today, neither in theory nor in practice is any acceptable candidate debarred from the priesthood because he cannot produce the money for his training.

What was then required of a candidate was a university degree (though soon after 1900 some bishops were beginning to waive this requirement), a knowledge of Latin and Greek, and a sufficiency of scriptural and theological knowledge to pass the examination of deacons. But this knowledge need only be intellectual and theoretical. There was no such thing as a universal requirement of residence for a given period at a theological college, and a man could be ordained without any training whatever in how he should do his job as curate in a parish, and even without any guarantee that he had learned to say his prayers and to read his Bible, not as a subject for examination but as the Word of Life. In 1907 almost exactly half of those ordained had never spent one day in a theological college, and although the bishops had recently agreed among themselves to demand at least one year's residence in a theological college after the

[1] Prestige, *The Life of Charles Gore*, p. 218.

winning of a university degree from all their ordination candidates, they postponed the implementation of this decree until 1917.

The theological colleges themselves were also causing a good deal of perturbation. The criticisms fell under two heads. First it was urged that a theological college course was too academic, too severely detached from the actual conditions of the world and of the daily routine of work in an ordinary parish. Vicars complained that their young deacons had not been taught anything about their job; that they had not been told how to prepare or deliver a sermon, what to do when visiting the dying, or how to teach religion to young children in the parish school. On the other hand, they rather illogically entertained a deep suspicion of the two theological colleges, Mirfield and Kelham, which were really thorough. They took boys at sixteen and kept them until ordination at twenty-three, by which time they were properly and competely trained. Yet they were called seminary priests, and regarded with apparently ineradicable suspicion by most incumbents and a good many bishops too. To know one's job really well was not regarded as obviously commendable. Yet all alike wanted the deacon to know his job better than he did, and were full of suggestions to the theological colleges as to how they might ensure this admirable result without keeping the students for longer than the normal two years, for this would be to fasten the label 'seminary trained' round their necks. The bishops in the Lambeth Conference of 1908 expressed the hope that the theological colleges would add to their present curricula the study of missions, and of the principles of religious education, together with actual teaching practice, a proper training in preaching and in voice production. In addition, they were unhappy about the character of biblical study, and wanted their young men to hear less of the Bible as a series of literary problems and more of it as God's word. They put the coping-stone on their list of requirements by adding that 'instruction should be imparted in social and economic questions, general business principles, applied moral theology, and Church law'.[1] But as the bishops of the Church of England were prepared to postpone until 1917 the compulsory residence of an ordination candidate in a theological college, this was no more than a pious opinion.

No institution is more incessantly blamed than the theological college, and none less deserves it. They were—and are—always in the dilemma that they had to do a job hardly possible in the time available, that every critic was clamouring that this or that favourite extra of his own should be added to the timetable but without prolonging the course of study. Vociferous blame was constantly hurled at them because they found it impossible to escape from this dilemma. Moreover, the vocation to be the principal of a theological college is the rarest of all. It is not reasonable to expect that in any generation there will be more than three or four priests who possess

[1] *Five Lambeth Conferences*, p. 354.

the right gifts in their right proportion, together with that flair (or vocation) for this exacting task. In that day there were at least two such men, B. K. Cunningham and Father Kelly of Kelham; and though most other colleges were more pedestrian than theirs, hardly any was conspicuously failing. Whatever might be said in criticism, and much was said, the theological colleges of that generation were faithfully serving the Church. Very little of the blame for the threatening situation in which the Church was placed can rightly be laid at their door.

There was a sense in which the theological colleges succeeded too well. They sent their men away with a vision of the greatness of their calling. They at once became assistant curates[1] in this parish and that, and it was less easy for the curates than for any other branch of the ministry to save their vision from being spotted by the world. It was in its handling of curates that the ecclesiastical machine approached most closely to the thoughtless cruelty of worldliness. It was not a heedless cruelty. The scandal was recognized. It was debated again and again. But without far more money than the Church possessed, and in an era when Parliament would neither let the Church legislate for itself, nor grant the time to debate and pass ecclesiastical bills, it was very hard to see what could be done.

The average curate's situation was far from promising. An indignant headmaster correctly described the curate's position as

hardly worth calling a position at all. It begins fairly well; it often ends in bitterness, disappointment, and despair. He has no security of tenure. In theory he is the bishop's curate; but when friction arises, it is the exception for the curate to be supported.[2]

He might work for years for £120 a year, and he had, on the average, to wait thirteen years before he was given a living of his own. He had no pension. Because he was not an incumbent he did not qualify for any help from the Queen Victoria Clergy Fund. He could not plead his case in the councils of the Church for he had neither vote nor place in Convocation. As he aged, his market value steadily decreased; and the number of elderly curates who had had no luck in the patronage lottery—the 'system' was just that—and were out of work was a crying scandal. Worst of all, in his own eyes, was the heartless way in which an incoming incumbent could, and often did, make a clean sweep of the curates of his predecessor, casting them out upon the world to sink or swim. It was at this point that the curate was apt to protest. A curate who spoke at the Church Congress of 1908 voiced the feelings of thousands of others, and denounced

a system which allows it to be possible for a man in holy Orders some twenty-seven years to be ousted from his sphere of work by incoming incumbents no less

---

[1] Technically, the assistant priest is the assistant curate, and his vicar is the curate, for he has the care of souls. But it is less cumbrous to use the common terminology.
[2] *Church Congress Record* (1908), p. 495.

than five times during such a period; accompanied indeed with expressions of goodwill and best wishes; yet the act is done.[1]

It was done because it was inevitable in a system where a parish could be quite independent of the diocese, and where one class within the ministry was protected by the absolute security of the parson's freehold and another class was given no security at all. Yet curate and vicar were priests and priests equally, fellow-workers rather than masters and servants, a fact constantly asserted by the theologians and as constantly derided by the practical facts of the situation.

Dr Guy Warman, then principal of St Aidan's Theological College at Birkenhead, acknowledged all these facts, bent fierce eyebrows at those vicars whose conduct towards their curates denied the equality of the priesthood, and gave it as his considered judgement that if the patronage system could be made to work with fairness, the majority of the curates' grievances would disappear. There is an old and a noble tradition among Anglican priests that a man should never ask for any appointment, never even pull strings behind the scenes, or seek in any way to bring his name to the favourable attention of patrons. The fact that many a curate remained a curate for fifteen or twenty years shows that the majority faithfully observed this tradition. But it was made woefully hard for them. Here Mr 'Webling's' experience illustrates the position. A new vicar came to his parish when he was still curate, and after a time the relationship became so strained that Mr Webling, no longer a young man, decided he must go.

It is quite a mistake (said another priest to him) to suppose that in the Church of England, as by law established, merit automatically meets its reward. It is necessary for merit to get up on a tub and draw attention to itself with piercing cries. The Crown is patron of a large number of livings. Place your name on the waiting list for anything suitable that may become vacant.[2]

His archdeacon was of exactly the same opinion:

You must watch the weekly clerical obituary, he explained, and as each suitable Crown living falls vacant, you must apply for it and bring to bear all the influence you can command to support your endeavour.[3]

Mr Webling had extremely little taste for this sort of thing, and happily it turned out not to be necessary. The curate who saw his youth slipping away, and had a foreboding that he might spend all his working days in a series of subordinate positions, leading at the age of fifty to unemployment without any pension, had to be heroic if he was to put away this archdeacon's advice, to avoid complaint, and to endure hardness. He often was heroic, far more often than the Church deserved or had any right to expect; and among all the clergy of that day he had the best right to wear laurels.

[1] *Ibid.*, p. 504.   [2] *Something Beyond*, p. 237.   [3] *Ibid.*, p. 238.

III · *Public Worship and 'The English Hymnal'*

In England when people see a great unhappiness, an injustice, a tyranny, or a scandal, they always ask 'What is the Church doing?' In the palmy days of King Edward VII there were plenty of blemishes to make people ask the question. Long after the king had been gathered to his fathers, after some three million young Englishmen had prematurely followed him, the only right answer to this question was suggested. 'What is the Church doing?' 'The most obvious thing that the Church does, what every onlooker can watch it doing, is to gather people together for worship.'[1] It is not a soft answer, and it is most unlikely to turn away wrath. But it is a real answer. At least half, and much the more important half of the Church's witness in the world to its Master is to be found in the quality of its worshipping life. The impact which it makes upon the people as a whole begins and ends with what is done within the four walls of the parish church. It begins there because it is by joining in common acts of worship that the clergy and congregation are welded into a militant community: it ends there because no work which they undertake is thoroughly done until it has been gathered up, expressed, and offered to God within the compass of liturgical worship. What supremely matters in any parish is what it does on Sundays, and if Sunday is inert and dull weekdays will certainly be lifeless. A congregation which does not worship cannot offer the Gospel to the parish.

The true history of the Church is therefore the history of its worship, and the best way of weighing the effect upon the whole Church of any party or section within it is to discover the answer to the question: What influence upon the worshipping life of the Church did the party exercise? By 1910 the Oxford Movement and its aftermath, the Anglo-Catholic Movement, had enjoyed nearly eighty years of life, and in that time had marched through persecution and abuse from strength to strength. But its effect was not to be weighed in the peculiar balances which the zealots of the party liked best to provide—counting the number of parishes which had a sung Mass for the chief Sunday morning service. Nor was it only to be found in the deepened and widened sense of the reverence which is fitting in church. It was much more in the popularizing of those acts through which a sense of reverence is expressed—the bowing of the head, the act of genuflexion, or the making of the sign of the Cross. It had produced in fact a large number of congregations which were properly drilled, and in many parish churches where its immediate influence upon the type of service provided had been negligible, the congregation was no longer averse to the idea of performing ritual movements together. The Anglo-Catholics had in fact provided the whole Church with a very greatly needed *mimesis*, a ritual drill. It was not the least of their services to English Christianity, for without this joining together at the same time in the due performance of the same

[1] F. R. Barry, *The Relevance of Worship* (Nisbet), 1935, p. 117.

movements and acts it is hardly possible for a very mixed body of people to become a unity. Only when this kind of 'drill' becomes an instinct does it find that little by little it is being provided with a common mind and a unified purpose, and so turning into an organic community which God can use.

It was therefore natural that one of the foremost places in the history of the development of public worship during this period should be occupied by a priest who owed almost everything to the catholic revival, and yet was strongly opposed to many of its latter-day manifestations. This priest was Percy Dearmer, Vicar of St Mary's, Primrose Hill, in London. An odd creature, and always a rebel, an individualist with an inconsistent but real passion for order and reverence for tradition, he had the two expressions of real genius which gave him a commanding place in the revival of worship as a fine art. He had the gift of persuading the most unlikely people to work together, and of holding them to the task until it was done; and he was a true artist, with an artist's selective enthusiasm and the gift of taking endless pains over matters of detail. At the beginning of the century he had written *The Parson's Handbook*, and his appointment to be Vicar of St Mary's, Primrose Hill, gave him a sphere of his own in which all his principles could be worked out and tried in the actual conditions of parish life. The result was that not only his parishioners, but also many pilgrims from all over the country could see an order of worship which was genuinely English and correctly catholic. In hardly another church could just the same thing be seen, for Dearmer was unique in his knowledge of the principles and precedents of worship. Those who wanted to know what was the liturgically correct shape and size of a chalice veil, or how the procession at a solemn evensong should be managed, had to go to him. Nobody else had anything like his knowledge of the details. It is quite true that he succeeded neither in reclaiming the more unruly Anglo-Catholics from their tiresome copying of incorrect Roman models, nor in persuading other churches to adopt the exact ceremonies of St Mary's. But he made his own church a Mecca for artists, who found there a satisfaction they could find nowhere else, and he did successfully impress upon the clergy as a whole that half the secret of worship that is alive lies in a scrupulous, tireless attention to small details.

Although Dearmer made a mark which will not fade in the sphere of the ordering of worship, his name will be held longest in memory for what he did for Christian hymnology. *The English Hymnal* did even more for the Church than *The Parson's Handbook*. It was three years in the making. In the spring of 1903, Dearmer and a few friends (A. Hanbury-Tracy, D. C. Lathbury, T. A. Lacey, Athelstan Riley) had the idea of issuing a supplement to *Hymns Ancient and Modern*, but before they began seriously to work upon it, the proprietors of this hymn-book published a supplement of their own. In the autumn of 1904, however, they took up the idea again.

W. J. Birkbeck and W. H. H. Jervois joined them; and early in the next year they brought off their greatest stroke by persuading Vaughan Williams to join them as musical editor. At that time they intended to publish 150 hymns not to be found in other collections, and to call the book *English Hymns*. But they soon realized that it must be 'all or nothing', and that what the situation called for was not less than 'a companion to the Book of Common Prayer for use in the Church',[1] even though this must mean the issuing of a tacit challenge to *Hymns Ancient and Modern*, which held the field. The plan grew and grew until on Ascension Day, 1906, when the book was published, it contained more than 700 hymns. It was an immediate and a huge success, and its publication forced Anglican hymn singing into new and more creative paths. The collection showed a strong sense of liturgical worship. It offered among many other novelties of arrangement, a complete set of Office hymns for the saints' days and Sundays of the Church's year. It recovered many ancient treasures of hymnody which had been forgotten, and it brought into constant use many fine new hymns by living authors. No fewer than thirteen, for instance, were taken from the *Yattendon Hymnal* of Robert Bridges. Something of the greatness, and the freshness too, of Dearmer's achievement can be realized by the mere citation of the following nine hymns, old and new, which for the first time were made readily available to English congregations. The list could easily be doubled and trebled in length:

> He who would Valiant be.   *Bunyan*
> Dear Lord and Father of Mankind.   *Whittier*
> Wilt Thou Forgive?   *Donne*
> The Lord will come and not be Slow.   *Milton*
> In the Bleak Midwinter.   *Rossetti*
> O God of Earth and Altar.   *Chesterton*
> Judge Eternal.   *Scott Holland*
> Jesu Good above all other.   *Dearmer*
> Rejoice, O Land, in God thy Might.   *Bridges*

The collection owed almost as much to Vaughan Williams as to Dearmer. He saw to it that no unworthy tune appeared in the body of the book. The tunes he scorned but could not, for old times' sake, utterly cast away, he hid in the cupboard of an appendix at the end. He transposed the tunes into a key which brought them easily within the vocal compass of ordinary people, and any one of the 744 hymns could be sung without an aching throat. Above all, perhaps, the editing of this collection drew from him his great tunes to 'For all the Saints', 'Come down, O Love Divine' and 'Hail Thee, Festival Day'. A hymn-book had at last been offered to the Church freed from any taint of vulgarity or sentimentality in either words or music, and which, as the editor justly said, spoke throughout of the

[1] *The English Hymnal* (Oxford University Press and A. R. Mowbray), 1906, p. iii.

'conviction that duty lies at the heart of the Christian life—a double duty to God and to our neighbour'.[1]

It was quickly discerned by the more percipient admirers of the hymn-book that it had a deeply democratic tendency, and thus could become not the least of the instruments in the hand of a Church which was struggling to find means of expressing its necessary kinship with a growing democracy built upon fundamentally Christian presuppositions. There were, for instance, a good many hymns in it with verses like,

> Tie in a living tether
> The Prince and Priest and Thrall,
> Bind all our lives together:
> Smite us and save us all.   *Chesterton*

or this,

> When wilt thou save the people?
> O God of mercy, when?
> The people, Lord, the people,
> Not thrones and crowns but men!
> Flowers of thy heart, O God, are they;
> Let them not pass, like weeds, away—
> Their heritage a sunless day.
> God save the people!   *Elliott*

But these are isolated instances of a general tendency. The firm insistence on congregational, unison singing, and the pitching of tunes so that they could be so sung, all suggested in and through the most powerful of all means of suggestion, the democratic ideal. But the compilers of the hymnal, being artists, held out to congregations the best form of democracy, a trust in the instincts of ordinary people to choose the best when they were shown it, and the willingness to endure a measure of self-discipline in pursuing it. The most deeply democratic utterance in the preface was made by Vaughan Williams:

No doubt it requires a certain effort to tune oneself to the moral atmosphere implied by a fine melody; and it is far easier to dwell in the miasma of the languishing and sentimental hymn tunes which so often disfigure our services. Such poverty of heart may not be uncommon but at least it should not be encouraged by those who direct the services of the Church; it ought no longer to be true anywhere that the most exalted moments of a churchgoer's week are associated with music that would not be tolerated in any place of secular entertainment. . . . The average congregation likes fine melody when it can get it, but it is apt to be undiscriminating, and will often take to bad melody when good is not forthcoming.[2]

He also sternly bade all congregations to sing the melody, and only the melody, of any tune, and to leave the harmonies to the choir. When the

---

[1] *The English Hymnal*, p. v.   [2] *Ibid.*, p. xi.

most convinced democrat happens to be a great artist, he is also very much of an autocrat.

The English Hymnal was such an immense service to the worshipping life of the Church that it is the more melancholy to record that the serried ranks of the bishops greeted it with suspicion, and a section of them, headed alas! by Gore, tried to have it forbidden for use in church. They were at that moment in the thick of the semi-political controversy caused by the very aberrations of those extreme Anglo-Catholics whose behaviour Dearmer himself had denounced again and again. If he had supposed that *The English Hymnal* gave any countenance to them he would never have compiled it. Yet it was precisely this that the protesting bishops cried out that it did. Their rather slender reason was that a few of the hymns seemed to take for granted the doctrine of the Invocation of the Saints. Dearmer did not at this point greatly help towards a sweet reasonableness, for he gave his intemperate invective full rein, and denounced 'these scoundrelly bishops' at the top of his voice. Gore himself, not to be outdone, wrote that the editors had deliberately introduced invocations 'into our public services through the medium of hymns', and said that Dearmer's pleading for his book was 'very sophistical and rather immoral and unscrupulous'. He forbade its use in the diocese of Birmingham.[1] The Archbishop of Canterbury took the same line in his diocese. Eventually the language of one or two of the hymns was slightly modified, and the storm subsided. It had after all been only the episcopate's common form. They had greeted *Hymns Ancient and Modern* in just the same way in 1861.

But *The English Hymnal* went through edition after edition and suffered revision after revision for fifty-six years, and by then only Vaughan Williams remained alive to represent the original band of editors. In one way hymn-books are compromised by success. Every revision adds more hymns to the original collection until at last the book becomes padded and bulky. Then the skill of a ruthless pruner has to be called in.

It was in 1960 that the proprietors of the collection decided that the moment had come to face the awkward problem of over fifty years of great success. They dealt with it in a highly original way. Not only did they drastically reduce the number of hymns from 656 to 318, but they added many new features that no previous hymn-book had contained. Those who in 1962 opened *The English Hymnal Service Book* found in it the psalms and canticles ready pointed for them, the sung parts of the Holy Communion set to Merbecke, a collection of nineteen collects for use with processional hymns, and a number of Christmas and Easter carols. The editors of this new book remained anonymous, and the preface they gave it was modest and peaceable. They said it was the steady growth since 1906 of the liturgical movement, and of its characteristic expression in the parish Communion which had decided them to make these changes. What

---

[1] Prestige, pp. 300, 301.

they have done should stimulate its growth. The book is 'High Church' still, but the 1962 meaning of that phrase is very different from its 1906 meaning, and much more healthy. *The English Hymnal* had been not the least potent of the instruments to promote that health, and Dearmer and his original collaborators had given birth to a baby with the attributes of immortality.

IV · *The Working of the Town Parish*

Parish life in this period, however, had its own quite distinctive and identifiable quality. At least, the parish in the town was trying to work by methods which were not the methods of the fathers, and which, in the fullness of time, are now being repudiated by their children and grandchildren. But whether in town or country the parish was still very much its own monarch, and apt to be self-sufficient, and haughtily independent even of diocesan organizations, and much more of such central church organizations as then existed. There was but little diocesan loyalty, and for the clergy there was not much fellowship to be had except in the hivings of their party groups and societies, and the great majority of the clergy preferred to have no dealings with them. The parochial system was still quite unsystematic, and was so shaped as to nurse individualism and hamper co-operation.

It was therefore very illogical that the town parish was more and more tending to put its trust in organization, in system, and, presently, in the grim ideal of efficiency. Not the blindest lover or the most furious enemy of the Church of England, however, has ever suggested that consistent logic is a mark of her life. The various lectures on pastoralia to ordination candidates in the period, the published accounts of life in this parish or that, and chance references in a dozen biographies all tell the same tale. The thing to do was to make the parish a buzzing hive of furious activity, and the way to do it was to organize everything and everybody. Those were the great years of the church organization—the Mothers' Union, the Church of England Men's Society, the Girls' Friendly Society, and, reaching downwards in age, the Band of Hope, and the King's Messengers. The town parish was not considered to be properly equipped if it did not possess a branch of at least all of these.

These societies could be and often were a source of great strength. The parish of St Mary, Portsea, for instance, was deservedly famous for its work among men, and the backbone of this work was the branch of the C.E.M.S. If this Society had not existed, the vicar of Portsea would certainly have had to invent something like it. It had a membership of rather more than two hundred men, and this was a purged and tested membership. The great weakness of all such societies is to rely on social entertainment to attract membership, and to allow the obligations of spiritual discipline to be overlaid. Thus it was always possible to make a fair show in the flesh in the shape of a membership roll which looked very well in an annual report. But where a vicar was alive to such dangers, a C.E.M.S. branch could do a work which could then be done in no other way. There were very few entertainments or socials for the Portsea branch, and no one long remained a member who did not pull his weight both in prayer and work. A monthly prayer meeting was held in the parish church which the men themselves conducted. There they learned how to loose the string of their tongues and to speak plainly of God and their needs. They contrived to make an annual twenty-four-hour retreat, and counted the sacrifice of wages but a small thing. They were expected to give themselves to the service of the parish, to whatever service might be asked of them. They taught in the Sunday schools, they visited in the streets, they preached on soap boxes in the squares and corners, and they undertook every kind of manual job.[1] In degree, the same was true of all other societies which had a place in the field of energy that was St Mary's, Portsea, for there, whether parochial society or assistant curate, you justified your existence, and by pretty high standards, or you speedily ceased to be. St Mary's was a rather fabulous parish, and very far from ordinary or average. Other parishes held it in awe, and regarded it as the example of what a town parish should ideally be. When St Mary's provided a ready hospitality to church societies, and thereby plainly showed that it regarded them as being almost that without which parish work could not be properly done, hundreds of other parishes promptly followed the example. In those days it was good to be a church society's central organizing secretary. You might be run off your feet and bustled in your office, but you were a personage, and you counted in the scheme of things. All these societies which worked through the parochial system deserved the prestige they had, and justified their claim to be the handmaidens of the Church. They were in fact its maids-of-all-work. From one or another of them most of the parish workers were recruited, and on their own account, as separate fellowships, they did extremely good work of the kind which is necessarily unassessable, for it consists in the sweetening of life in a thousand ways at a thousand points of strain. Even if no identifiable advance in the Kingdom of God could be traced to the work they undertook, which it could, still their existence could have been justified by the training in fellowship they provided; and fellowship is always good for its own sake, and quite apart from any activity in which it may engage.

The parochial branches of the great societies organized into fellowship those who were already members of the congregation, or in some way connected with it. They did not cater for the great mass of the parishioners who seemed to be living, more or less contentedly, without God in the world. Yet these were the first responsibility of the vicar and his people, and if together they were trying to be the Body of Christ in the parish, it was a

[1] *The Work of a Great Parish*, edited by C. F. Garbett (Longmans, Green), 1915, pp. 129–32.

charge which weighed upon their souls day and night. Somehow the parish church had to bring before them the challenge of the Gospel, whether they would hear or forbear. Somehow a militant organism of Christian witness must make its impact upon them. There were thousands of parishes in England, and therefore hundreds of experiments in new methods were always being tried. But, speaking generally, the parish priest put his faith in three primary methods—house-to-house visiting, the clubs, and the relief of those in need. All but one of the books of pastoralia belonging to the period agree in emphasizing the importance—even the equal importance —of these three things. Canon Peter Green's *The Town Parson* speaks in a very different voice from Professor Clement Rogers's *Principles of Parish Work*, while neither of them point to quite the sort of thing which is described in *The Work of a Great Parish*, which, though not written as a treatise on pastoralia, none the less takes a very high place among the books which can teach a young deacon the rudiments of his job. Both Green and Garbett were passionately convinced that the clergy must visit. But Rogers, though as convinced as anyone that the people must be visited, was sure that this was primarily a layman's job.

The attempt to 'get to know your people' by 'diligent house-to-house visiting' is, in a large parish, physically impossible, and is too often prosecuted at the cost of neglecting more important duties to (*sic*) those nearer at hand. Many a man will wear himself out by a ceaseless round of visits, and yet remain practically unknown to the members of his choir and the masters of his School. Much of the work which is now wearing out the clergy could be done, and done better, by a tactful, uneducated woman at a pound a week, and they themselves set free to take their place again as members of the governing class that is called to serve God with soul and mind.[1]

It is not an elegant piece of reasoning, and it does not suggest a very exalted view of the priesthood of the laity. But even on these terms, visiting, whoever does it, is regarded as something which must evidently be done. The actual experience of parishes in south and east London, which seems to have been more fully recorded than that of parishes elsewhere, shows exactly the same emphasis and scale of pastoral values.

It was taken for granted and universally accepted that the parson's duty was to visit his people—all his people, and not only the churchgoers. The theological colleges and the books on pastoralia did not argue about it. They assumed it, and set themselves to show how it could be done even in the biggest parish, and how to do it rightly. They were all eloquent about the sort of notes the visiting parson ought to take as he went his rounds, how he should enter them afterwards in more permanent form, and how many hours a week he should give to this exploratory, house-to-house visiting. They counted no parish effective unless every single house in it

[1] Clement F. Rogers, *Principles of Parish Work* (Longmans, Green), 1905, pp. 94, 95.

was visited by a priest at least once in the year, and they gave chapter and verse from their own experience to show that this could really be done without any neglect of other necessary work. But if these books assumed that such visiting was the priest's duty, they did not take it for granted that to visit was also the layman's duty. Most parishes had their zealous bands of district visitors, but generally they were more amateur welfare workers than laywomen (district visitors were seldom men) consciously exercising the priesthood of the laity. Most dioceses, too, had their bishop's messengers, who did receive a quite thorough special training for their work, and would descend upon this parish or that, and visit all the houses in a district most devotedly, though this would generally be in preparation for some special effort, like a parochial mission. Taken all in all, it is probably true that the homes of England were more zealously visited by the Church in the first decade of this century than ever before or since.

If the curate visited in the afternoon, and, several days a week, in the early evening too, he spent most of his nights in one or another of the parish clubs. Few town parishes were considered to be complete in their equipment unless they had at the least a boys' and a men's club; and a parish like St Mary, Portsea, had a bewildering array and variety of these institutions. But it was not only the parish churches which set up social clubs. Every voluntary social organization entered the fray. The universities had their missions, as did each college, and those missions were chiefly clubs, Oxford House at Bethnal Green and Cambridge House at Camberwell setting the standard. Most of the great public schools followed suit, and established their settlements in the slums of London, Liverpool and Manchester. This type of club took its colour from the great days of Oxford House in Bethnal Green, when Winnington Ingram was the head of it. Its essence was the permanent residence of a few, and the week-end visits of many graduates, undergraduates, and boys, in the settlement, to help with the administration and to learn the technique and routine of club work. A vital part of the whole scheme was the organization of visits by club members at public holidays to the particular seat of learning which had caused the club to be. At such times the streets of Oxford and Cambridge were apt 'to be thronged by Cockneys, escorted by undergraduates, who entertain them at lunch, take them on the river, and expound to them the manners and customs of the place'.[1] It was in fact something of a universal principle that wherever a great social problem was discerned, the right thing to do about it was to start the appropriate club. Thus clubs in the greatest profusion were always springing up. One London parish priest, Richard Wilson of St Augustine, Stepney, even went to the length of establishing a club for tramps, who, one would think, are the least clubbable creatures on the face of the earth. What is more, he made it a tremendous success. In this club, a tramp could get a shave, have his hair cut, wash his

[1] Dr W. R. Inge in *Facing the Facts*, p. 187.

shirt, clean his shoes, and have his buttons sewn on—all free of any cost. He ran it after the manner of the Houses of Parliament, with ministerial titles for officials, and regular debates with a Speaker to control them. The tramp progressed from Commons to Lords. The Commons part of the club was for the casual tramp—a place where he went to get a meal and a warm before the fire before resuming his dispirited search for a place to sleep out. The Lords were the men, once tramps but tramps no more, for the club had found them jobs. They lived in the club. They had an obligation to try to find a permanent job for at least one man a year in the Commons.[1]

The vast majority of these clubs existed to serve the young working lad, and his problem, and the Church's problem of its responsibility for him, soul and body, was certainly more urgent than any other. His position in society and in the Church was often heartrending. He came from a home, which, if it was good was heroic, wresting its goodness from the teeth of every material improbability. To be a Christian, even to be a good citizen, took some doing in a back street in Portsmouth or Birmingham. Taken from school when his new adult powers of body were coming upon him and bewildering him, and then flung upon the labour market into the nearest factory, or, more likely, into some blind-alley occupation which threw him out of work at seventeen or eighteen, it was no wonder that he often drifted into vacancy of mind, flabbiness of body, and desperate, noisy unhappiness of soul. From those who were at all vicious by nature the race gangs were recruited. These existed in every great city, and they offered the lad a brutal, gaudy existence, trained him to be handy with a concealed razor, and set his feet on the quickest path to prison. For more ordinary boys life offered a sad wastage of body and soul, expensive to Church and state alike. Every parish church complained of the drift away from the observances of religion of boys who had been confirmed. A very experienced priest spoke for all his brethren, when he told the Church Congress:

When a lad reaches the age of fifteen we had better take off our hat and bid him goodbye for five years—keep him on our list and in our prayers—and at the end of that time we may be able to drag him back, or, as experience often shows, he would turn up again, sobered by his experiences, and wishful for reception again into the company he had left.[2]

But most never did turn up again. Even the boys who had been brought up in the Church uninterruptedly from babyhood, and had never left it even in the crisis years of their lives, fourteen and fifteen, had a very difficult time. More than a few flatly refused to be confirmed, because they knew the moral flavour of their workshop and did not believe they could possibly 'live up to it'. The long-term answer to this challenge was a completely new social system. But that was outside the parish priest's area of competence. The best thing he could do was to start a lads' club as quickly as possible.

[1] Paget, *op. cit.*, p. 167.   [2] *Congress Record* (1908), p. 127.

It was often a formidable undertaking. There is a vivid description of the process in a mission district in the parish of St Mary, Portsea. There were 5,000 people in the district. It had its church, and a good institute. A small room in a house served for an infant Sunday school and a club for little boys. A corner shop became a babies' crèche. A shop became the head-quarters of the curate-in-charge. A disused public house accommodated the 'Shoeblacks' Brigade'. The catalogue of amenities includes nothing for older boys or men; but there was the institute, so let there be clubs!

Now, to commence with, the most useful thing we have found to be the *concert* —and sometimes the *smoking concert.*

On the first night it is a concert for the lads. It is advertised in all the streets. It has been known (shades of the Charity Organization Society) to take the form of a Coffee Supper. The time comes, the doors are opened, and in the hall of the institute an assembly of lads varying in ages from fourteen to twenty takes place. The entertainment lasts for two or three hours. In the middle, the 'authorities' speak. They tell the lads of a jolly club which meets two or three nights a week on the premises; they enlarge on the physical benefits resulting from gymnastics, they picture the delights of the billiards and games room upstairs. And they wind up by inviting all those who care to give their names to the good layman who acts as secretary. Forty or fifty names are given and the first step is accomplished. There is a club in embryo.

With the men similar methods were employed, a house-to-house visitation by pairs of nervous laymen, invitations to a smoking concert, a speech by the authorities.

The virtues of a club for the men, held three nights a week, are expatiated on, and its free and easy character driven home with vigour. The secretary tours in and out the rows and takes as many names as he can—and lo! we have a men's club on the stocks.[1]

Given the juvenile problem, nearly all the most experienced parish priests of the day agreed that the boys' club was the best solution. Canon Peter Green, for example, argued for it at some length in *The Town Parson* and in his *How to Deal with Lads.* But those who had the longest experience in this sort of work were most full of warnings about the sea of difficulties these clubs brought with them.

The chief difficulty was that of discipline. Better no club at all than a club which was a bear pit. Canon Peter Green was full of suggestions to the nervous curate who was told to go to the club and keep order. Indeed, the club nights were often dreaded ordeals. The young curate pitchforked into a really lively boys' club was not the least among contemporary heroes. But as an instrument of the Church, the parish boys' club could do, and very often did, what no other device could have accomplished. A priest as experienced as Luke Paget could look back over his long ministry, and

[1] The Rev. F. O. T. Hawkes in *The Work of a Great Parish,* pp. 191, 192.

declare that in the parish of St Pancras the clubs and guilds were the backbone of the whole life of the parish. And he put the clubs first:

> On a Saturday evening, at the close of the boys' club, you might hear Tom say to Harry, 'I will call for you tomorrow.' It was all so natural. Harry, after making his confession in the chapel below, would come into the club and say to Will, 'They're ready for you downstairs. Let me take your cue,' or 'your hand at whist.'

One of the clergy was always present, and Paget declared, speaking in the name of all town priests:

> Boys' clubs are in no sense separate from the work of the Church. If we are able to play five matches on any fine Saturday afternoon, a great many more than five elevens find their way to the altar on Easter morning.[1]

The club movement was thus something which the Church warmly approved and actively espoused. But its very success caused the parish priest some embarrassment. All sorts of other and non-religious organizations flung themselves into the movement and started their own clubs. But these clubs, if not strictly irreligious, were certainly undenominational, and some of them were militantly secular. The famous Ancoats Settlement in the slums of Manchester was an example of the former type, and Salford had at least one lads' club which was run by the secularists to promote their own view of life. Some towns in East Lancashire also had their lads' clubs, which were generally inaugurated by the local mill owner, managed by his son, and financed by private subscription. Clubs like these were sincere when they said they needed the help of religion, but immovable when they added that it was their club and they would decide what kind of religion they wanted, and who was to impart it. This meant in practice that the religion the boys actually got was limited to occasional prayers, and bright breezy talks on Sunday evenings by the club superintendent on purity, honesty, service, and, perhaps, citizenship. If the *raison d'être* of the parish church club was to teach the boys the whole Christian Faith as the Anglican Church has received it, and therefore to bring them to confirmation and the altar, there was no escaping the conclusion that there must be competition and not co-operation between them. In any case, those were days of violent partisanship, when co-operation was not easily practised in any walk of life.

The third instrument the town parish used to make its impact upon the mass of the people was the work it did to relieve those in need. This was never picked up as a consciously evangelistic instrument, nor did it have much evangelistic result. It was simply one way of expressing the love that Christ had for the bodies no less than the souls of his people, and for years all parish churches had undertaken it because there was so seldom anyone else to do it. In days when there were neither old age pensions nor any public system of sick benefit, a heavy burden fell on the parish churches; and if

[1] Paget, *op. cit.*, p. 132.

they did not look after their poor and impotent folk they were generally left to stew in their own misery. But after 1906 the state began to step in, and soon there was conflict between the voluntary workers of the parish and the professional agents of the state or the local boards. Mrs Luke Paget, who herself saw most of this development in London, gives this picture of the process:

> The big parish churches still continued on tried, traditional lines, amply staffed, well respected, and counting for much in the neighbourhood. School and college missions, and men's and women's settlements flourished and were occupied with the innumerable activities contingent on a busily legislating state. New organizations seemed to spring up daily, and both observations and conscience were awake to a nervous degree. Everyone was finding out some crying need for change and reform. The trend was from parish to platform, from neighbour to committee. Indeed there was already some impatience with older methods. Social workers looked with a little contempt on Church workers; Church workers were a little touchy over interference; and political partisans were irritated by both.[1]

This unfortunate irritation which surrounded a parish's works of love was the fruit of a long historical process, dating back at least to 1840, and which is understood most easily if we look at it as it affected London. The great challenge of the destitution of the Hungry Forties was met in London by the vast and swift increase in the numbers of the London parish churches. Both clergy and laity, in larger numbers than ever before, flung themselves into the work of poor relief. Their work was organized by a new society founded for the purpose by Gladstone and the Bishop of London (Blomfield), called the 'Metropolitan Visiting and Relief Association'. Until 1880 the Church was left to shoulder the burden of all this work alone; but in 1884 the Fabian Society was founded, which did all it could to put pressure on successive governments to drive the Church out of the field of social relief. No government has been known to refuse to listen to those who suggest that it should increase its power, and, with the turn of the century, its own instrument of a wholly mechanized social service was fast overtaking that of the Church. In the Education Act of 1906 there was a clause making the schools rather than the churches responsible for the feeding of hungry children. Two years later, when the first Old Age Pensions Act was being debated, the victorious party in Parliament expressly ridiculed the idea that the parochial clergy might usefully help to administer it. The Church was, in fact, being driven right out of the field of public poor relief, and being confined to the small corner which purely private, unrecognized relief could still occupy. On the whole, the people in need of such services preferred to receive them from the state; and when this rather unpleasant fact was recorded and accepted, the excuse was made that the modern curate had never learned 'to do a decent job of case work'. But a really resourceful parish could still use the very Acts of Parliament which were intended to

[1] *Op. cit.*, p. 169.

freeze the Church out of public work to open up new spheres of relief work. St Mary's, Lambeth, had a particularly fine record. In 1907 it joined forces with St George's-in-the-East, and together they built out of the Notification of Births Act the first really good infant welfare service in England; and in 1910 the same parish church introduced into the area of its own parish, the most complete and human relief services which England had known.

The suspicion, even the competition, between the parish church and the agencies of the state in the work of ministering to the poor in their poverty, had one unsuspected and disconcerting result. It meant that parish church relief had to be a much more organized affair, and if more organized, then more 'business-like'. It was not merely a matter of the proper accounting and auditing of the parish sick and poor fund, for there is no Christian principle which encourages slackness in the use of other people's money. But when the state administered charity through mechanized social services, the Church was also driven to mechanize its own love and mercy. Quite elaborate rules tended to be drawn up to show who might be helped, and who might not. The forbidding distinction between the deserving and the undeserving poor began to be discussed and applied.

Efficiency was becoming very much the quality which the parish priest was being told he should covet. A parish was constantly said to be a kind of spiritual business, and the art of ministering to souls was a matter of regimentation and method. The tradition of George Eliot's Mr Gilfil, with his pockets always full of sweets, wandering along on his eccentric and spontaneous way, was held to be a way of pastoral life quite unfitted to the requirements of a mechanized, science-worshipping England. The old, illogical individualism of parish and parson had treated the ministry of Word and Sacraments as an art, resting for its discharge upon the particular accidents of individual personality. But it was now coming to be thought of just as much a science, a matter of precedent and experimentation leading to exact knowledge, and there was no longer any sanction for the cheerful inefficiency which so many generations of parish priests had brought to it. In any case, pointed out the apostles of the new efficiency, look where it had brought the Church—to the point where the parson can be as idle in his conduct and even scandalous in his behaviour as he pleases and none can touch him, to the point where the vast majority of the people have neither knowledge of the things of Christ nor allegiance to the Church. It was plainly time to make a change. The parish church had in the past relied far too much upon the Vicar's own personality, upon whatever spirit was in him. It had meant in practice that his people were almost wholly at the mercy of the whims of personality. Let him now rely far more upon scientific method, and let his parish be organized like any other efficient business.

This line of development is best seen in the change of emphasis which was creeping over the books of pastoralia put into the hands of ordination candidates and curates. For centuries, ever since the days of George Herbert, such books had always begun with the spiritual life of the priest and how he must make time to feed it. Then they would remind him how great was the treasure of souls committed to his charge. From that they would lead on to such matters as his studies, his visiting, and how he ought to prepare sermons. Such matters as the management of parochial finance were normally relegated to a chapter at the end, or even to an appendix, like a kind of half-apologetic afterthought. But the new books were apt to be not at all like that. The titles of the first three chapters in Clement Rogers's *Principles of Parish Work* were *Parochial Finance, Parochial Councils,* and *Records and the Organization of Church Work.*

The English are considered to be a nation of shopkeepers; in other words they have the reputation of being the most business-like people in the world. The Church of England is probably of all religious institutions the least business-like in her finance. Yet, as long as this is so, can she claim fairly to be the religious interpreter of the character and genius of the nation?[1]

And how was this lack of efficiency in parochial life to be exorcised? By an elaborate card-index system for the management of the people, with a concatenation of forms to be filled in before any ministerial privilege was accorded them, and by a new kind of archidiaconal inquisition to ensure that the parson kept his parish records efficiently:

Mention has been made of the need of a diocesan auditor for parochial accounts: there is similar need of diocesan officers to do for the Church the work that H.M. inspectors do for the nation's public schools. This might be met by the development of the work of archdeacons, or by the creation of an entirely new set of more authorized visitors. . . . Suitable men, however, will hardly be forthcoming until the clergy as a body have realized the necessity of keeping proper records, and of keeping them as official documents. Such 'inspectors' would pay visits both with and without notice.[2]

These extreme suggestions of treating the English parish as though it were the branch of a bank naturally were never carried out. But the mere fact that they could be seriously made showed the way the wind was blowing— towards the upholding of efficiency as an ideal. The priest must in future be efficient. It was a change of ideals which was to have important consequences later on, for while there is certainly nothing to be said in praise of inefficiency, to make efficiency into a god is no remedy.

V · *The Country Parish*

The warning sirens of the efficiency to come had thus been set to wail, but they affected only the town parishes, and these amount to much less than

---

[1] *Op. cit.,* p. 25.   [2] *Op. cit.,* pp. 76, 77.

half of the whole. The regimentation of country parishes might perhaps be a pious hope of the extreme sects of the rationalizers, but there was never a moment's chance of anything of the sort being actually achieved. This world holds few things more tenacious than the determination of the English country parish to go by its own road, and to retain its cherished individualism. Yet with them, too, the process had begun, and by 1914 was well under way, by which many were to lose their separate identity. Already it was not very unusual that one country parish should be merged with the next on the death or retirement of the incumbent. This was in no sense a policy, an attempt to rationalize the ministry of the countryside. As yet nothing had been heard of the idea of deliberately working groups of country parishes together with an adequate staff at the centre. It was simply a counsel of despair, not a policy, dictated partly by the lack of a proper dilapidations scheme, and partly by the fact that church finance was a chaos. It was detested by all it affected, patron, incumbent, and most of all by the people. Voice after voice was raised in protest, but no voice had any practical alternative to suggest.

These country parishes were, as still they are, both the heart and the backbone of English religion, but their spiritual condition was no more healthy than was that of the town parishes. If the town parson could do little more than touch the fringe of his work by reason of the pressure of numbers, the country parson found it just as difficult to do his true work because his numbers were so small. To minister week after week to the same tiny handful for years on end, to wait for years until he really had the trust of his people, to know that every single piece of work from organizing the whist drive to mowing the churchyard must fall to his lot, and to be forced personally to procure and to provide for another priest to take his Sunday duty if ever he wanted a holiday or if he was taken ill—all these were the constant burdens of the country priest, and the town priest avoided them all. To be a country vicar meant constant isolation, reliance upon one's own spiritual resources, and often a poverty more grinding than the town vicar knew. The country vicar had the really hard task. The virtue which above all others he had to bind unto himself was patience, and again patience, and yet more patience.

This virtue, and that of faithfulness, the great majority of country priests brought fully to their charge. Yet they were beset all the time, just as was the town priest, by the menace of an inarticulate but a real secularism of temper. One who had long lived in the conditions he described surveyed the spiritual condition of rural England in 1911, and came to the judgement:

We have seen that the Christianity of the English countryside is far from strong. It is in possession, but in an attenuated form. It is rather a passive acquiescence in traditional religion than a triumphant living faith. No obvious cure can be suggested for such a state of things. The Church of God in the villages must continue to lay patient siege to the few hundreds of alienated souls and to train the young only to lose the best of them to the towns. We cannot be confident that there will be any improvement in the near future.[1]

Where there was a saint as vicar, and even then only if he stayed for many years in the parish, the village church was full and the congregation in it was a true family of God. But the average country parson had a hard and a lonely life, with frustration as his daily tempter.

[1] Lowther-Clarke in *Facing the Facts*, p. 169.

8

Three Handmaids of the Church

THERE has never been a generation in which it was possible for the parish churches of England to undertake every piece of work which the Church had to do. Even in the remote days when most of the people were born, lived out their days, and died in the same parish, there were those—the student world, for instance—whom the parish churches could not touch. In modern times the numbers and variety of the classes and groups of people whom the parish churches cannot possibly reach, and who plainly need a specialized form of ministry, are very large, and they steadily increase. New ways of ministration have to be invented to serve them, and since the middle of the nineteenth century the Church has given birth to societies, guilds, and communities in quite bewildering numbers in order to meet the spiritual needs of this group or that, which the parochial instrument cannot reach. Three of the most famous of them are therefore chosen for commentary.

I · *Student Christian Movement*[1]

There came a day in 1907 when the Rev. Tissington Tatlow, general secretary of the Student Christian Movement, was walking down an Oxford street with A. L. Smith, Master of Balliol. Suddenly the Master stopped dead, turned to Tatlow, and said, 'I like your Movement, Tatlow. I like it well.' 'I know you do, Master,' Tatlow said, 'But tell me why.' To that the Master replied, 'It is sound education. Dons in my college sometimes complain to me that it occupies men's time too much with brown paper and string, but I tell them that it is not true. It widens men's minds and helps them to think.' (301, 302.)

What the Master of Balliol said was certainly true, though most members of the movement would probably have chosen for praise other examples of

[1] Every quotation and reference in this section is from *The Story of the Student Christian Movement*, by Tissington Tatlow. The page numbers are given in brackets in the text.

its excellence. There never was a Christian society more sturdy than this, none which did better work, none which worked out its discipleship with a more attractive air of grace and gaiety. Founded in a very small way as far back as 1892, it had changed its name several times, but had consistently regarded itself as charged with a divine mission to the student world in any and every country, to bind together in evangelistic fellowship all Christian students, no matter to which branch of the whole Christian Church they belonged. Since then it had moved from one strength to another, and by 1908 there were not many universities in the world in which S.C.M. was not at work.

Its interests were primarily missionary, and it had grown to such an extent that the great missionary societies were increasingly dependent on it to find the recruits to man their missionary stations and dioceses. So real had this dependence become that if S.C.M. frowned even S.P.G. trembled. On one occasion S.C.M. wanted S.P.G. to send an official delegate to one of its conferences. But S.C.M. was an interdenominational society, whereas in the charter of S.P.G. there was a clause by which this society was prohibited from having any official relationships with a society not exclusively Anglican. Tissington Tatlow made his request of Bishop Montgomery, then General Secretary of S.P.G. He explained that in effect it meant that S.C.M., which supplied so many of the candidates for missionary work for S.P.G., was asking for the older society's formal recognition and approval of its existence and its work. The bishop looked very troubled, and was about to refuse, when the door opened and another S.P.G. official, who happened to be Tatlow's personal friend, came into the room. 'Ah, Mr Tissington Tatlow,' he said, 'how nice to see you here; I hope you are going to get plenty of student volunteers for the S.P.G.' But Tatlow, seizing his chance, at once replied firmly, 'I am going to do nothing of the kind. The S.P.G. will not perform a friendly act by the Student Movement, and I am just telling Bishop Montgomery that as far as the Student Movement is concerned I am going to wash my hands of the S.P.G.' (308.) The bare threat was quite enough. S.P.G. climbed down at once, and appointed the delegates to the S.C.M. Conference, their inconvenient charter notwithstanding. Bishop Montgomery was privately rather glad to have his hand forced like this, and shortly afterwards wrote of S.C.M.:

It is becoming one of our sheet anchors, since it is bringing to our ranks hundreds of university men, Churchmen, who are the very material we need. (309.)

But of no society which did not enjoy real power and high prestige could that story have been told. To force a body like the standing committee of S.P.G. to climb down by a single threat was an achievement of no ordinary kind.

From the very beginning the movement had steadily nourished itself on every root of healthy growth. It appealed to the generosity and the essential disinterestedness of the young by its spirit of adventure. It had cheerfully taken as its declared aim, 'The Evangelization of the World in this generation'; and what did it matter if it was constantly having to explain what these words did not mean? In the student world a watchword so rich in adventure and imaginative power was worth hundreds of new members a year. But there was nothing in the least reckless about its direction, nor anything static, highly organized, or over-constitutional. A movement drawing its whole life from its rank and file membership rather than from the few who at any time might be in charge of its fortunes, it had been founded by anonymous students for the ordinary student. Its directorate and its officials were constantly changing. Its shape and form were as constantly developing, this department being scrapped or purged as a new department to meet a new need took shape. It was a true democracy. There was probably no other democracy in the country which was so completely democratic and so wholly competent. Town Councils, and even Parliament itself might very profitably have taken lessons from S.C.M. on the practical working of democracy. It was better at this difficult art than they were, and had much to teach them. Its several governing bodies all had a perfect genius for creative compromise, for making the principle of representation life-giving and not wooden, and for drawing up working constitutions for this and that department, which kept them all working to a general policy, and yet encouraged them to be free and fostered all their spontaneous enthusiasms. It was certainly an organization, and a very extensive one, but it was completely organic, and it held no organization sacred for its own sake. Everything was tested by the work it did, and all committees and officials subjected themselves to a really severe self-criticism. None of its secretaries entertained for one moment the idea that they could do their work by sitting on a chair in a London office, dictating letters. They were all travellers, constantly maintaining touch with their members. Above all (rarest of tributes) the movement was never tied to the name of one specially great man. It was never possible for it to be known as 'So-and-so's show'. It never bore the imprint of a giant, and therefore its dynamic qualities persisted from one generation to another in untroubled continuity.

Broadly speaking, the job of the travelling and the branch secretary was to look to the spiritual health of the members, while the extension of the work into other fields was the charge of the members. They were apt to plunge rather wildly into some new venture. Thus a great deal of the general secretary's time had to be spent in ingenious efforts to bring some new piece of work into the general frame of the movement, or in a struggle to prevent the rather heedless and awkward enterprises of some of the members from compromising the movement, but without damping the enthusiasm for Christ which had gone into them. A conference stirred two women members, for example, and they looked round to see what new work they could make their own. They found a tiny corner of the student world, the women art students of London, which S.C.M. had not yet occupied. So they took possession of it. To start a branch among artists was a daunting undertaking, for to them Jesus and the Christian life were 'ideas to be dreamed over and expressed by brush and chisel, but not facts to be lived out in our daily lives'. (285.) These two women made a start in South Kensington, and from them the movement quickly spread to art schools and academies in Bloomsbury, Lambeth, and Blackheath.

This was but one instance among very many. The secretary had to fit a new field of work into the scheme, and very soon would have to find the money to support a new travelling secretary to work among art students, but that was all in the day's work for him. But there were times when the enthusiasms of his young members landed him in real difficulty. The movement was undenominational. Approaches to the Anglo-Catholic clergy had therefore to be made with great tact. In 1906 S.C.M. had developed a piece of work whereby a pair of students would spend the vacation in a caravan moving from village to village, and holding evangelistic services in each one. Two of them proposed to tour the Oxfordshire villages, and one of them, a Plymouth Brother, thought it would be a good idea to ask the Bishop of Oxford for his official blessing. This blessing was refused, and the students were downcast. They came to complain to Tatlow, but it was he who had the right to complain for they had done much to compromise the movement. In a vivid letter to Malcolm Spencer he revealed some of his difficulties:

Now the apple-cart is going to be upset for us entirely in a good many quarters if every student who arranges a campaign is going to write to the bishop of the diocese he would enter. If we could ensure that those who wrote were Churchmen and only asked for the bishop's blessing for Church of England work, it would not matter much, but it is a serious thing for us if men who are not Churchmen are going to ask various bishops to give their blessing to interdenominational work done in connection with the Student Movement.

Think how carefully we angle for bishops, with what care we approach them, and explain what we are trying to do. Our usual way of approach is to get their approval for some distinctively Church piece of work, or else to get them to a conference. We should not dream of letting our first attack upon them be a request to them to give their blessing to an interdenominational campaign conducted by men about whom they knew nothing whatever. It was simply madness to have written to the Bishop of Oxford. I do not see how he could have done anything else but refuse his blessing. . . .

I should think the net result of this episode with the Bishop of Oxford will be that it has made it about fifty per cent more difficult for us to get into touch with Cuddesdon College than it was before. Starr (one of the students concerned) is a Churchman, but evidently has not studied the Anglican position—may the saints forgive him! The man who actually wrote to the Bishop of Oxford, holy Moses, is a Plymouth Brother. O Malcolm, these wild young friends of ours will upset the blessed apple-cart altogether if they go and do this kind of thing all over the country. (243, 244.)

It had been a tiresome episode, but not more than an episode. The movement was becoming so strong, was launching out into so many fields, and had attracted such a wealth of talent of every kind into its service that no bishop cared for long to withhold his glad recognition of it. After all, more than half his ordination candidates were likely to be Student Movement men. They would probably be the best of his candidates, for they had had a full measure of intellectual and devotional training, and were by no means strangers to self-discipline. The movement was a very solid thing. It reared itself squarely on all the classical Christian disciplines—sound learning, theology, a full use of the Holy Scriptures, and a steady training in the life of prayer. And these were bound into the life of the student in such a way that the enthusiasms proper to his years were never dulled but rather intensified and held together. Every travelling secretary made it his first charge to look to the devotional training of his members, and every new piece of work undertaken was promptly anchored to these rocks of permanence. The traditions of the movement were broadly evangelical, and since from the start it took an interdenominational shape, they remained so. It had more to say about prayer and the Bible than about the sacraments. Yet Anglo-Catholics could, and did find themselves perfectly at home in it. Its aim had for many years been missionary, in the limited technical sense of that word. Its eyes were fixed upon China, India, and the Polynesian islands. The evangelism it performed at home, as for example, through the caravans, was primarily regarded as good training for future missionaries. Not until 1903 (and half-way through Prebendary Tatlow's history) does the note of the social responsibility of all Christian movements begin to be sounded. As soon as this charge was perceived, it was at once accepted with characteristic vigour, and one of the important landmarks of the history of the Christian Social Movement in England is the S.C.M. Matlock Conference in 1909, at which its social charge was defined and accepted.

But it was entirely characteristic of S.C.M. to make the first step to be taken the calling of a conference. For it was from its conferences that it received its impetus, and on them that it really fed. These conferences were most carefully prepared. Many months before they were to begin, the whole movement was called to pray earnestly for them. 'Ten months to pray for one week,' remarked one travelling secretary gloomily; and then rallied himself to see to it that the whole of his department did in fact pray steadily and methodically for all that time. (305.) It was typical. The movement undertook nothing unless it was sure that a sufficiency of prayer had gone to its making. Nor did the prayer cease as the conference began. Nearly half the programme every day was given to prayer meetings, and the organized communal expression of the devotional life. Small wonder that

S.C.M. conferences were occasions when startling things happened, and to all the hundreds of young men and women it seemed as though they stood breathlessly, like Cortez, 'upon a peak in Darien'.

One such conference must here stand for all the others. It was the Conishead Conference in the summer of 1907. Its hero was an Indian, Mr S. K. Datta, first of the Punjab University, and then of Edinburgh. In his spare time he had been travelling a little for S.C.M. in England, and he was a great admirer of John Morley, whose fine speeches on India he made it his business to interpret from his Indian point of view wherever he went. At the devotional meeting at the beginning of the conference Datta was moved to make a speech by way of a bidding to prayer for India. His speech was of a kind which forced a passion of prayer out of that great gathering. On the next day, with all the drama of the totally unexpected, a cable from Calcutta came. It was addressed to the S.C.M. Conference at Conishead, and it was read aloud to the gathering.

> India's students her greatest peril and highest hope. Our Movement appeals to yours for leaders.
>
> Azariah, Andrews, Carter.

The Conference immediately authorized this reply and pledge to be sent:

> Cable found British students already deeply stirred in sympathy and prayer for India. We will help you, God willing. Tell us how.
>
> Tatlow, Davies.

At once cards of intercession were printed, and were ready to be distributed at the evening meeting.

A CALL TO PRAYER FROM INDIA

To the Student Christian Movement. India's students her greatest peril and highest hope. Our Movement appeals to yours for leaders.

> Azariah, Andrews, Carter.

CALCUTTA

Let us thank God for this call to prayer and service.

Let us pray that God may show us clearly how we may help our brothers in India.

Let us pray that our people may meet the aspirations of India in the Spirit of Christ.

Let us pray for the people of India, and for the students that they may now be led into the truth of the Gospel and be the means of bringing to their fellow-countrymen the unsearchable riches of Christ.

> Conishead,
> 26*th July*, 1907

The appeal was met. The Student Movement has gone on with the meeting of it ever since. 'That day', writes Prebendary Tatlow, 'was set in motion influences which have drawn hundreds of members of the Student Christian Movement to India.' (297–9.)

Not every S.C.M. conference had moments quite so tense as this; and the Conishead Conference had now to settle down to a week of steady, solid work—prayer, fellowship, and intellectual training. It was remarkable for the numbers of Anglican dons, who came, saw, and were conquered. Among them were B. K. Cunningham of Farnham, Canon Johnston of Cuddesdon, A. J. Tait of St Aidan's, Birkenhead, W. J. Conybeare of Cambridge House, and many others. But the two who were the most completely conquered of all were Scott Holland, who came for one day to lecture, and stayed on to the very end, saying, 'I couldn't go, I loved it so'; and A. L. Smith, Master of Balliol, who wrote: 'No one can have been more impressed than I was by the wonderful spirit of the gathering and by its potentialities.' (301.)

During the last fifty years the Church has never been served better by any of her handmaids, and probably none can approach the record of the Student Christian Movement. For all it has done, and still does, blessed be God!

II · *The Church Army*

Students in universities and colleges were not the only people who needed a specialized ministry of their own and were beyond the range of parochial competence. The morally and economically dispossessed, convict, tramp, and down-and-out, were quite beyond the power of the ordinary parish priest and his people to reclaim and convert, or even materially to help. A parish which included whole colonies of such people, as many slum parishes did, could at best only help one or two here and there. This social challenge could not be answered except by a new and a specialized evangelistic instrument. The Salvation Army had done much to show the way. It was a way by which the Church had never trodden since the days of the Franciscan and other mediaeval Orders, for it involved the recruiting of a trained, disciplined body of workers, a certain picturesqueness, even gaudiness of uniform, and a readiness to preach the Gospel in very odd places and with the help of markedly unecclesiastical accompaniments, such as brass bands and tambourines. In 1883 a Westminster curate, Wilson Carlile, had seen the need and set himself to fill it. Followed by a tiny band of devoted church-people, he had gone out into the worst slums of Westminster—there were none worse anywhere—and night after night he and they had faced stones, bad eggs, and tomatoes, persecution, abuse, and constant riots, with police court proceedings and sarcasms from magistrates next morning.

They called themselves the Church Army, and if its quick growth is to be reckoned as a test of success, this handmaid of the Church has been phenomenally successful. By 1900 it was a very large and a socially important organization. If overnight it had ceased to exist, the authorities, both municipal and parliamentary, would certainly have had to take over all its work the next morning. The work it did was extensive and various, and the abounding energy which its founder had given it, and which his genius for benevolent autocracy had contrived to keep in it, was apparently insatiable. There can have been very few unfortunates who could not find some Church Army institution within easy reach which had been founded just for the likes of them. Convict, out-of-work, prostitute, tramp, and thief, the Army catered for them all; and where there was any peculiarly troublesome social group, and nobody knew how to deal with them, there would be sure to be some Church Army officer who knew what to do. They even trained men and women to work successfully among gypsies, and there is probably no ministry quite so difficult and heartbreaking as that.

The Army specialized in ambulance work and evangelical preaching. Its officers seldom had much theology, and commonly held the sketchiest doctrine of the Church, but they knew their Bibles thoroughly, they lived trained and disciplined lives of prayer, and what parts of the whole Catholic faith they did hold, such as conversion and justification by faith, they held with tenacious passion. Above all, they loved the people for whose sake they worked—always the best preaching of all. As an organization the Army had no particular political or economic views, and it did not hold theories about how the society which made its particular parish what it was could be changed into something less theologically blasphemous. It simply set itself to supply the gross needs it saw, and took no notice of those who said scornfully 'merely ambulance work'. In its life and work it was a living embodiment of the Parable of Judgement.

In the fifty-six prisons of England the Church Army uniform was a sight of daily familiarity; and the bigger prisons all had an Army staff, both men and women, permanently attached to them. They worked under the chaplain, carrying out with him the daily routine of cell visiting. But in one most important part of the work they could do much more than the chaplain. The Army was its own discharged prisoner's aid society, and a most efficient one. They had established a series of Labour Homes, beginning with London, Bath, Stockport, and Derby; and by 1900, twenty-four out of the fifty-six prisons had Church Army Labour Homes close to them. They took in any who asked for admission, whether prisoners or not, and to any of these a prisoner who had served his time could go. However bad a man's past had been, he could still enter a Labour Home, if he would accept this pledge as an agreement, and sign his name to it: 'I hereby undertake to obey cheerfully all the rules and regulations of the Church Army Labour Home, and I enter it with the determination to make an honest endeavour to live a truly Christian life.' The homes were avowedly evangelistic in aim. The men were set to work. They nearly always began by chopping firewood, and, having survived this test of monotony, they graduated to more skilled jobs. Trade rates of pay were given for all the work done, and all the products of that work were sold at ordinary market prices. Their keep was deducted from this, and the balance was banked for them. All the time effort was being made to find regular work for them; and it was not uncommon for a man to draw £100 or more of his own earned money when he left the home to face the world again. These Labour Homes were also recruited from among the unhappy, spiritless wanderers on the Thames Embankment; and every night of the year several Church Army officers tramped the Embankment seeking whom they could help.

Another feature of the Army's work was its caravan missions. They had forty-eight horse-drawn caravans—but with no horses to draw them—which were large enough to serve as rudimentary homes for two men. A van was attached to each diocese whose bishop would welcome it, and a senior and junior officer would spend a whole summer wandering from village to village, spending a week or three weeks in each one, visiting by day and holding a nightly mission service round the van, or in a handy barn or tent. The van was dragged on rather rusty iron wheels from one village to another by a cart-horse borrowed from a local farmer. The two evangelists lived on the country as much as they could, on gifts from benevolently disposed farmers and gardeners; but it was a life which a man had to be hardy to stand. The van had an area of only a very few square feet, but it was the sitting-room, kitchen, and bedroom of two men, their church and their bookshop, all in one. Only the neat, the tidy, and the clean could survive such tests. The day was long. At six o'clock the men must get up. There was room for only one to dress at a time. Then prayers, and then work—folding beds, cleaning boots, lighting the stove, fetching the water. Holy Communion in the village church at 7.30 and then breakfast. Bible study from 9 to 10, and the rest of the morning one evangelist visited and sold books while the other did the shopping and cooked the dinner. Bible reading again and prayers from 1.45 to 2.30; and then both men must go out to visit until tea-time at 5. Thereafter preparation for the evening mission meeting, and finally prayers and bed at 10.30. This routine was followed week after week throughout the summer months. But in the harvest agricultural workers were much too busy to make caravan missions possible. Then the Army would collect all its van officers, and send them marching together from one seaside town to another to hold missions for holiday makers. There was (and is) a stirring vigour and a freshness of enterprise about the Church Army, and though with them we are in an utterly different world from that inhabited by the Student Christian Movement, their faith too has been abundantly blessed.

III · *The Society of the Sacred Mission, Kelham*

The early nineties saw the beginning of the two modern religious communities which have most deeply impressed themselves upon the modern Anglican consciousness. Kelham, the Society of the Sacred Mission, began in 1890, and Mirfield, the Community of the Resurrection, was founded by Gore in 1892. From the very beginning their paths were wholly distinct. Mirfield, which began in Gore's vicarage at Radley, was founded to be a religious community, and the 'works' which at different stages in its life it undertook, its theological college (to which reference has already been made), its retreat house, and even its mission in Africa, were incidental to its main purposes. These were to provide a religious community of professed men, and through this to meet certain intellectual needs of the Anglican situation, as Gore saw them. There was once a meeting at the parish church hall in Mirfield at which one of the Fathers was to try to make clear to some of the puzzled and slightly suspicious citizens of Mirfield just what the Fathers in their big house up the hill were trying to do. The vicar enlarged upon their good works; but when the Father got up to speak he began by brushing these on one side as being after all secondary to their real purpose, which was, he said, to show that 'men can live happily together in fellowship and community under rule. And sometimes,' he added, 'it takes a lot of doing.' The intellectual need which the clear vision of Gore had seen, and which the community was expressly designed to meet, was to be met by 'the founding of a community of a new type, religious in its general character, liberal in its spirit, and sufficiently modern in its outlook and methods to enable it to move freely in the new and still changing conditions of the modern world, while still drawing on its own life for the inexhaustible resources of spiritual consecration'.[1]

Kelham, however, began its life as a college for the training of candidates for the ministry. Though it has developed and branched out in many other directions, it has never once held any other function to be its central purpose, and it is still true to say that Kelham is a theological college in a sense in which Mirfield is not. Its other works, its missionary districts in South Africa and Australia, its work in English parishes, and even the religious community of the Kelham Fathers, all find their centre of gravity in the specialized training of young men for the ministry for which Kelham is now famous throughout the Anglican Church.

Kelham was started in a small house in a back street of South London (Vassall Road, Kennington) by Father Herbert Kelly. He has been called the most distinguished Augustinian of our day, and if one of the marks of an Augustinian is to match dreams with carefully thought-out principles, so that every movement in pursuit of the vision is governed and checked by the prior discovery and quite ruthless application of the appropriate principles, there can be no doubt about his Augustinianism. Before all else, Kelham has been at every stage of its development a rigidly and completely disciplined adventure, in which the generosity of the heart and the hardness of the intellect have been combined in creative synthesis. Father Kelly's

[1] H. L. M. Cary in *Northern Catholicism*, ed. N. P. Williams and C. Harris (S.P.C.K.), 1933, p. 359.

dream was double-sided: it held two subsidiary visions. The first vision came to him long before his ordination, while he was still a cadet at the artillery and military engineering training college at Woolwich. The technicalities of this training gave him a haunting vision of the invulnerability of organized power. But what was true of such matters as ballistics and blast ought to be true also in its own degree of the impact of the Church on the world. There too the supreme need, as he saw it, was for

organized power, in calculated variety of form, but capable of being used in masses; every part large or small grappling with its ever changing and different problems by its own independent intelligence, and yet concentrating its determination under disciplined direction upon the attainment of one simple and common aim.[1]

It was, he thought, just what the Church lacked, and what it could be given only through a new kind of training for its priesthood by which a disciplined, directed enhancement of individuality could take the place of the far too current individualism, and reliance upon purely personal gifts. But this involved finding the right candidates to train, and the eye of his vision saw where they were:

It ran in our mind—as it runs today—that there were multitudes in that normal sunny youth of England, strong and capable, full of fun and games, who would willingly give up their own petty ambitions, suffer a great deal of hardship, labour gladly, die uncomplaining and unrewarded, for the love of God and the good of men, provided only you did not ask them to stop enjoying it all and making fun of everything along the road. As things are, you can get a hundred English boys to be crucified if only they may laugh for one who will do it solemnly. And being what they are, is it not much better that they should? It makes so much less self-importance.

But if they were to be found, one could not afford to look for them only in one class. Nothing less than the full range of society would form an adequate field of search. As things then stood, only the sons of wealthy families stood any chance of being ordained. It followed, then, that the working out of the idea depended upon three main conditions. There must be complete freedom of opportunity; but it must be the opportunity for a really thorough and prolonged education, resting in turn upon a steadily sacrificial life both during and after the course of training. But to provide anything like such a training as this must involve the complete financing of young wage-earners during a course of study lasting at least four years, and often longer, while the reality of their sacrifice must be assured and their motives tested by residence under discipline in a completely servantless house. It was further evident that this kind of experiment could only be kept in being if at some point it was made to rest upon a definite community of professed 'religious' men. A college to train men, and a society

[1] Herbert Kelly, S.S.M., *An Idea in the Making* (Society of the Sacred Mission Press, Kelham), 1927, p. 9.

to organize them when trained—those were the essentials of Kelham; and they were essential in that order of precedence.

The external facts of the history of the society can be quickly summarized, for what is interesting about it is not so much its rate of growth, as the profoundly revolutionary idea behind the growth, and the inspired skill, by which, as the idea developed, it was always clothed by the exactly appropriate body to give it room to develop and to grow still more. It was in 1890 that Father Kelly began at Vassal Road, Kennington, with three students. He had offered his idea to the Bishop of Korea, and was working under the direction of the bishop's English commissary. The plan then was that he should simply train priests for the Korean Mission, and so they called themselves The Korean Missionary Brotherhood. After three years, the beginnings of the second part of the vision became possible of attainment, and Father Kelly and two other priests were professed, and called their community by its present name, The Society of the Sacred Mission.

In 1895 they started to take boys as young as sixteen, for rather bitter experiences with more mature students had shown them they must; and their numbers then began so to expand that in 1897 they moved from Kennington to a large house at Mildenhall in Suffolk. By this time, they had a connection with the Universities' Mission to Central Africa as well as with the Mission to Korea, and in 1902 they added to these responsibilities by undertaking the charge and the staffing of Modderpoort in the Orange Free State. Their numbers were still growing, and Mildenhall could no longer hold them. So in 1903 they moved to Kelham, near Newark, where they had found not only a big house, but ample room for expansion. In that same year they took the vital decision which has made Kelham what we now know it to be. They ceased to be purely and technically a missionary college, and they withdrew from their special connection with Korea. In the future they would prepare men for ordination in England, whereas in the past their men had gone out to Korea or to Zanzibar to be ordained there; and all their men should serve at least the first three years of their priesthood in English curacies. In 1913 they had considerably to enlarge their buildings, for they were receiving ten applications for each vacant place. When this had been done, they could accommodate more than seventy students; and after the war of 1914, this number rose to ninety. Thus, in thirty years, Kelham had become the largest theological college in the Church of England, and the only one of its kind.

Such are the bare numerical and brick-and-mortar facts of the story. But they matter infinitely less than the idea which they clothed and expressed.

The first of these ideas was that if the Church was adequately to discharge its ministry to the world, it could not afford to draw its clergy from an area less wide than the entire range of British boyhood. No single boy with a vocation to the priesthood must be denied the chance to test it because of straitened means at home. But in a theological college there ought to be equality of treatment as well as equality of educational opportunity, and therefore Kelham must completely provide for every single candidate it accepted, and bear the whole financial burden of his maintenance for at least five years.

It was an heroic endeavour, but there were traps in it. The first trap was sentimentality. For whose sake was all this to be done? It was so easy and so natural to think that it was for the sake of the boys and young men who would otherwise never get their chance. Yet to think thus was deeply false. To accept this idea would be to think of Kelham as an institution for social welfare, and not as a handmaid of the Church; and to pander to and encourage the hidden temptation of the young clerk to think of ordination in terms of social advance and economic security. They had therefore explicitly to formulate it as a never-to-be-forgotten principle that Kelham existed for the sake of the Church and not for the sake of its students. This must involve a complete ruthlessness in rejecting unpromising material. 'We neither could nor ought to take any man for any personal reason whatever. We could take him only for the sake of the Church; therefore we could take a man only so far as we believed the Church could not do better than take him, and we could keep him only so long as we believed the Church could not do better than go on with him.'[1]

This was to be treated as a principle, but to apply it meant that first of all another most difficult principle had to be sought out and clarified. It involved the whole idea of God's act in calling young men to offer themselves. Kelham took only such men as believed themselves to have been called by God. It was right that the men should be ready to submit this vocation to the testing. But to apply the first principle that Kelham existed for the sake of the Church and not for the sake of its men, involved the horrid certainty that some of these men would have to be rejected when half-way through the course. It meant also that the Fathers must seem to set themselves up to be the judges of the genuineness of a man's vocation. Would that not mean that the Holy Spirit was abiding their question? Evidently they could not place themselves in that position, and so the fundamental principles had to be thought out yet again. It was the characteristically Augustinian approach to a practical issue. The Fathers found this principle by making a distinction between Vocation and Calling. The spirit bloweth where it listeth: in particular, God marked with his vocation those whom he would, and this was beyond human questioning. But God's direct vocation was a command to a man to offer himself; it was not also a command to the Church to accept that offer. Upon the Church, just because it is the Body of Christ, has been laid the responsibility of calling in or of refusing to call in any one vocation. The man offers, the Church calls, or decides not to call; and in so doing both alike serve God's purpose.

[1] Kelly, *op. cit.*, p. 74.

It took a long time to get that clear, but once it was clear, the Society's complete freedom to accept a man one year and reject him the next had firm legs to stand on.

The first thing to do was to make as sure as one possibly could that the wrong man did not even start the course. Now Kelham was soon taking boys of sixteen, and, later, of fifteen. They were of all kinds—artisans, shop assistants, boys from 'leisured' families—but by far the greater number of them 'were, might have been, or would have been clerks'. The Fathers insisted first on a written letter of application, and they soon became experts at judging a good deal from that. Then the best of these applicants were called up for interview, and each one was seen separately by at least three of the Fathers, one after the other. They did not look for knowledge, but for intelligence, and above all for some sign of that sense of undeviating purpose which is always the heart of true vocation. They also warned them of the spartan severity of life in the college, with its three fourteen-week terms in the year, for at least five years; and of how, at the end of it, they would be expected to do just what they were told and to go exactly where they were sent. Those who survived this scrutiny were brought up to Kelham for one term on trial.

To test a man's vocation, and to decide whether it should be completed by the call of the Church to the priesthood, therefore involved the testing of both his intelligence and of his sense of purpose. The former was a matter of examination and tutorial report, but the latter was very effectively tested by the conditions of disciplined sparseness under which the student must live for perhaps as long as eight years. If there was any hankering after social advance or any desire for economic security, it would not survive the purge of the regime. The students lived hard, played hard, and worked very hard. They had to, for the great majority started from scratch. In more recent years one of them wrote a full description of one average day. It took him several pages to get as far as breakfast time:

The Caller used to be a self-sacrificing person. He gets up earlier. He is not a popular person, and it was not a much-sought office, but it goes now in weekly rotation. About 6.15 A.M. there is a sharp rap; he bustles in, announces the time, and is gone. There is no regular response. Perhaps there ought to be, but we have as few forms as may be; besides we are sleepy. Energetic people—there may be as many as two, both in their first term—jump up. The remainder lean out of bed and light their lamps, placed with careful forethought on a chair within reach (or on an empty packing case or butter tub—chairs are not numerous). The old hand knows to a minute how long it takes to dress, and calculates accordingly. The time has come. There is a rush; a cold bath—the five minutes' bell has gone— and there is the deep boom of the indoor Chapel bell, 6.40 A.M. Where's the girdle? Everybody must be in his place in three minutes or he's late, involving consequences. So we are mostly in time. Some have a dispensation—'crocks', occasionally examinees, and such like. The boys do not come. The Professed have already said Prime at 6.30. The manuals go to the Lady Chapel. In the big Chapel, there is Matins, and we are out by 7.3 or so.

The yard door is just across the passage from the Chapel, so we pick up a slop-pail and race upstairs. One man empties the slops, while his room-mate rakes out the fire and relays it. Then make beds, and get a start at sweeping if you can. Expert hands can do a great deal in twelve minutes, and we all flatter ourselves that we are experts. Bell again; that's 7.15 o'clock. Collar a coal-scuttle and slop-pail, and empty the latter on the way down. No use going downstairs with empty hands. Put the slop-pail back, and leave the coal-scuttle handy. Now it is God's time, and we are ready. Rather distracting? Not the least; it has been a bit of a rush, but we were busy doing God's Will. What is there better to do? Nothing, except to meet Him. So now we are all there—boys, too, this time. Then the Celebration goes on its solemn way, with its communicants. The priest has gone out, and there are a few minutes for prayer—perhaps as much as 10, or less according to the day.

At five minutes to 8, there is a sharp clang of the bell. That is for carrying on. You may get a few minutes to start sweeping your room. There's the breakfast bell; no deep boom this time, but a busy dinner bell, saying 'hurry up', if any bell ever did. A minute and a fraction to catch up your book and get down. Time enough, but nothing to spare. The lock snaps sharply, the far door echoes it, and the Prior says grace. The reader starts the 'Chapter'—about five minutes' reading from the Old Testament, at the conclusion of which we all rise for the Respond. Then we are free—not to talk, but to look at our letters, or to read, or to gaze at the architecture! But there must be no waste of time. Breakfast is a fairly substantial meal; porridge or rice, with bacon, or an egg, or something to follow. Each as he finishes says grace silently and goes out, for his work is waiting. In a few minutes the 'clearers' will be coming in to get started.[1]

This, of course, does not include all the 'chores'. There were plenty more after breakfast before all hands were free to get to their work—and even then the daily cooking and washing up had to be done, the animals and poultry to be tended, and the garden planted and weeded. There was the Greater Silence and the Lesser Silence every day. The Seven Canonical Hours were observed. Games were played each day: if, for some reason, a man was not booked to play he had to do an hour's useful work in the garden instead. The entire labour of the household, inside and outside, was done by the household. No servants of any kind were employed. About six hours of study were expected. In between whiles, though it sounds quite incredible, the men found time to act and to sing. It all formed a searching test, and a man had to be very much in earnest to survive it. Some naturally fell by the way. The rest learned much about the value of life in community, and the treatment might be very hard on the individualists, but it fostered rather than stultified individuality. Above all, it tended to produce the kind of priest on whom the Kelham Fathers had from the beginning set their minds.

The Society of the Sacred Mission was accused of desiring to foist on the

[1] Kelly, *op. cit.*, pp. 118, 119.

Church a 'seminary-trained priesthood', all as alike as peas out of a pod, and all shaped and fitted for the better pursuance of Anglo-Catholic ends. What the society has really had in mind from the very beginning, and what it has actually produced, is something very different, the ideal of a priest, with a thoroughly tested vocation, and who knows his job through and through. There was not to be any professionalism among Kelham trained men, but they were none the less to be professionals, with nothing of the gifted amateur, with his sketchy, slap-dash ways, left anywhere in them. The ordinary traditional methods of training the clergy did not generally achieve this aim : it was the conviction of Kelham that they could not be expected to achieve it because they were wrongly conceived. Normally a boy leaves school at eighteen, and he goes to the university for three years where he takes an arts course, which may or may not be theology. Then he passes on to one of the theological colleges where he spends two years, and so comes to ordination at the age of twenty-three or twenty-four.

In that traditional process, urged the society, three things were funda-mentally wrong. A man came to the study of theology last and not first : if his first acquaintance with it was as a university arts course, he must necessarily tend to think of theology as one art among many, and not as the queen of them all, as the art of all arts, and the science of all sciences precisely because it alone could have a reach and a range which was univer-sal. Then they claimed that their experience showed that when a man's mind had been formed on the normal university arts system, he became thoroughly restless when later he was submitted to the Kelham system, for he was not then at all inclined to think out his world anew from a new direction, and he generally flatly declined to do it. For these reasons Kel-ham soon decided not only to refuse to take university graduates, but also to refuse to send their own men on to universities, except for the very few specially brilliant ones. Finally, they claimed that the normal university and theological college training did not in fact teach a man his job, which, to a university audience Father Kelly defined as that of dealing with the washer-woman in the back street :

In any afternoon's visiting, the first old washerwoman in ten minutes' account of her religious experiences and views will have moved, illustrated, or assumed, more controversial issues in psychology, theory of religions, doctrine of know-ledge, and their resultants in the theological sphere, than four professors will dis-entangle in three terms. Let us consider the young curate. First, he must deal with her himself. She is not acquainted with the professorial views, and further, inasmuch as the professor never met that particular washerwoman, there will be nothing in the treatises which by itself will fit her case. Secondly, fortunately for him, she does not require a carefully balanced answer. She does not go beyond very broad and crude issues, just such as he has learnt to understand—provided he has learnt to understand anything. But, thirdly, there is no possibility of getting that 'adequate knowledge of the facts', which scholars love. No doubt there is an immense deal more which is very important, but then she does not know what it is, and she will lose her temper if he 'badgers'. From what is before him he must make up his own mind what she is really driving at, what it means, how he can help her, and then translate his own notions into a form she can follow, all within five minutes.[1]

Well, let any priest trained in the ordinary way put his hand on his heart and declare that Father Kelly is wrong about himself and the washer-woman—if he dare. On the other hand, it does not automatically follow that every single Kelham man can give to the washerwoman exactly what she needs.

All these convictions brought Kelham into collision with the bishops, who in 1908 declared their intention to accept no candidates for ordination after 1914 who had not a university degree. They brought every kind of pressure to bear upon Kelham, which by this time was far too important to be disregarded, to copy Mirfield's example and send its students to the university, to live there in hostels under the Society's tutelage and regime, but to take the theological arts course like all other undergraduates. Now if the Society was to defy the bishops, and still more, if it was to convince them, it needed once more to discover a really unshakable principle on which to stand. It could make a very good pragmatic case, but it needed to do still better. It was out of this necessity that the famous principle of the Theological Conception was born. The clearest statement of what this means occurs in a letter from Father Kelly to the Bishop of Southwell, who had asked him to make a statement on the bishops' new rules and their effect on Kelham.

. . . It is only during the last five years or so that our experience with graduates brought home to us that the Arts degree did not help a man to gain that grasp on theology which our own men did get. The theory of the Theological Conception only formulated itself in our minds a little over a year ago. We put it first here because it explains all that we have learnt, felt in practice, observed, during nearly nineteen years' experience. The Theological Conception itself, as we teach it, grew in the same way. At the beginning we tried to work out the meaning of the Christianity men would have to teach by co-ordinating the ideas of natural theo-logy, much as Aquinas handles them, with the Maurician treatment of Church and Sacraments—the Incarnation and the Atonement marking the points of transition. By degrees psychology, modern philosophy, logic, the beginnings of politics, sociology and anthropology, the ends of natural science, theories of ethics, individualism and socialism, and many other things forced their way in, sometimes because one's own ideas had expanded, sometimes because the stu-dents would read them and insisted on having them faced. It grew precisely as we believe it will grow wherever men in our position have to do our work.

But no one with an Augustinian mind is ever happy until he can get a fundamental principle defined and captured in writing in as brief and

[1] Herbert Kelly, *The Universities and Training for the Clergy* (Sherratt and Hughes), 1908 .p. 14.

memorable a phrase as possible. It was much to have discovered the need of an X without which no theological curriculum could be really satisfactory. It was still more to have pushed ahead to a successful identification of this X as the General Theological Conception. But what exactly was this Theological Conception? The finding of it, and still more the defining of it, gave trouble. But eventually they arrived at a form of words which satisfied them, and they declared that the General Theological Conception was this:

THE WILL OF GOD AS THE LAW OF THE WORLD.

Here was a formula around which all theology, all devotion, all discipline, and all work could be grouped, and a principle of interpretation which set all free to play their parts in creative and free organism. But to work it out in an educational curriculum meant to accord to theology a primacy over all other branches of study and knowledge, and this was an exaltation of theology ascribed to by no university in the world. Such an educational curriculum, moreover, would plainly require a particular kind of social setting, disciplined, equal, communal, such as neither a college nor even a theological students' hostel at any university could provide. Small wonder, then, that Kelham argued that the idea of the Theological Conception could be worked out only within the Kelham system, and that to adopt the idea as a principle must necessarily involve the refusal to send their students to the university. Given the principle, the system followed. Did any bishop care to attack the principle? None did; and indeed it was always somewhat temerarious to argue about fundamental principles with a Kelham Father.

This controversy with the bishops had forced Kelham to think out its position once more. The principle had been found which clarified it, and, once discovered and defined, it sanctioned the whole of their past in the sense that it clearly showed them exactly what they had been trying to do all along. They had been teaching, and they claimed the right to go on teaching, exactly what most university trained clergy were apt not to possess. This was that 'theologic or Godward side of the world, which is really the clergy's contribution to the thought of the world'. Father Kelly went on to assert that 'the average clergymen have only a very vague idea that there is or ought to be such a thing; and they don't believe the Church has it to teach'.[1]

The Kelham system was designed for the young potential clerk. That is to say it was meant for the average mind and not for the already well-educated mind. It assumed intelligence and a high degree of purpose, but a bare minimum of actual academic knowledge. So the course had to begin with one and a half to three years of elementary work—the teaching of the preliminary Latin and Greek, and the training of the mind to learn how to learn. Then there followed four and a half years of advanced theological

---

[1] *The Training of the Clergy*, p. 23.

study. If a man was to be ordained at twenty-three, he must therefore start the course at fifteen or sixteen.

The theological study is philosophical in method. 'It resembles in some ways the Oxford School of *Literae Humaniores*, with a philosophical theology supplying the place of a philosophy that is not distinctively theological, and with general or Church history in the place of classical history.'[1] There were lectures, but only one each day. Naturally it was compulsory. But for the rest of the day, a man was made free of the very best books, in ample abundance, and was left free to use them, his mind having been trained to do this in the preliminary course. Each student wrote a weekly essay, and throughout the course he had a far greater amount of individual tuition than he would have got at the university, unless he had been quite exceptionally brilliant. In Kelham, all men received exactly the same care, no matter what their natural capacity for thought might be. Their claims for their system were wholly just. They formulated them thus:

We believe that our system of training is particularly well suited to get the best results from the average, as well as from the exceptional, student. The average student does not take naturally to the study of ideas, theories, and principles, but contents himself with a knowledge of facts, and with theories taken on trust at second hand. With us he learns to pass beyond his 'practical' attitude, to see the principles which facts illustrate, and from which they derive their meaning and importance. This is made possible, first by the wide reading which the length of the course opens to him; secondly by insistence on the importance of his thinking his own thoughts; thirdly by the amount of individual tuition he receives; and lastly by the central position held by theology. If 'to see life steadily and to see it whole' is a recognized aim of education, then, from a Christian point of view, theology which deals with what is the ultimate ground and explanation of life, is the most essential part of the process by which this aim can be reached. It guards the clever man from the danger of dealing with theories as matters of merely speculative interest, and the average man from ignoring them as matters of no interest at all.[2]

For years now, Kelham has been giving to the Church a steady stream of men thus trained; and most of them have been men who, without Kelham, the Church would never have numbered among its clergy. It will never be true, nor ought it to be, that every priest in the Church will be trained in this way. But there is no possibility of doubting the uniformly high quality of those whom Kelham has snatched from clerkdom and made free of their vocation. If the Church had no other reason to be grateful to the Kelham Fathers—and it has many other reasons—this reason would be enough to cause an undying thankfulness.

[1] *A Statement of the Aims and Methods of Theological Training at Kelham*, p. 8.
[2] *Ibid*, pp. 3, 4.

9

1910: The Significant Year

1908, the Pan-Anglican Congress in London; 1910, the World Missionary Conference in Edinburgh; 1914, the outbreak of the First World War. The closeness of the dates is very startling. In the long contexts of history they are virtually simultaneous. No one present at the Congress in London or at the Conference in Edinburgh, seems to have had any foreboding of what must happen in a very few years. Thirteen closely printed volumes were needed to contain the papers and the speeches delivered on these two great occasions. The most careful search through them will discover hardly a single reference or hint showing any awareness of the catastrophe to come. There must have been some delegates, John R. Mott for example, who knew in their hearts that war with Germany was sure and near. But they did not allow any trace of this foreboding to be seen, and all alike spoke and planned as if they were the citizens of a secure world in which the only obstacles to the universal empire of Christ were the poverty of human devotion and the lack of human knowledge. They had come from all the fringes of the earth to plan new Christian worlds for old heathen ones, and they had no doubt at all that a new start in world history was really possible. In their waking thoughts they did not foresee 1914: and not in their most terrifying nightmares did they dream of 1939.

To every Christian the world is the stage, and history is the record of God's action. But divine action through history can proceed only from a divine view of all history. The heavenly watch tower is set up in the perspective of eternity, and this view of historic time is simultaneous. Foreknowledge is in it. God knows what must come—the catastrophic unfolding of his own judgement—and because divine judgement is always big with mercy, he was preparing the great new fact in the history of our time, which is now displayed before our eyes, and is today the one true ground of realistic hope. These two great assemblies, meeting on the eve of the first world war, were his instruments. The more they are studied in the light of all which has since come upon us, the less it is possible to doubt that through them God's answer to the chaos to come began to be declared. Every dream the delegates had, every vision they entertained, every plan they made turned to dust and ashes. But when they declared, as they naturally did, that they had been called together by the authentic inspiration of God, they spoke the exact, historic truth; and because they were humble and sincere in their obedience God used their fellowship in ways it was impossible for them even to suspect at the time, to offer to Christendom the new fact which is today our chief hope.

I · The Pan-Anglican Congress of 1908

The preparations for these two assemblies were being carried on at the same time throughout the early years of the century, but in separation—almost in a studied isolation from each other. Their membership, their fields of study, and their methods of conference were different. It is true that both met under the aegis of the world-wide missionary call, but they painted that stupendous panoply with very different colours.

In 1902 Bishop Montgomery, the general secretary of S.P.G., had preached a sermon in St Paul's Cathedral, which ought to be included in any anthology of sermons which caused big things to happen. In it he pleaded for a world conference of Anglican dioceses, in which each one might lay its peculiar problems before the others, and thus the whole folded picture of the world-wide mission of the Anglican Church might be laid out for all to see and to judge. That sermon bore a swift fruit, and very soon Bishop Montgomery and Eugene Stock of the C.M.S. found themselves in charge of a strong committee bidden to arrange it for the summer of 1908. They began by setting in motion a preliminary but a thorough survey of church problems in every part of the world. These three questions were sent to the bishop of each Anglican diocese:

(1) What are the questions of supreme importance for the Church of God in your own regions?

(2) What, in your opinion, are the greatest problems outside your own regions?

(3) What is the chief corporate duty of the whole Anglican Communion at this time?

Every bishop was eloquent in his answer to the first question, and most were voluble in their answers to the second. But 'nobody seemed able to answer the third with confidence'.[1] This was a discovery of supreme importance, but the committee did not at that time mark it. A world-wide series of federated Churches formed in fact one Anglican Communion, but

[1] *The General Report of the Pan-Anglican Congress*, 8 volumes (S.P.C.K.), 1908, vol. I, pp. 2–3.

how could they be a Communion in more than name if none could say what was the chief corporate duty of the totality, the Communion of them all? In a day when every trend was towards ever more widely gathered accretions of power in rigidly centralized authority, and when this universal tendency was being gleefully used by the devil to hurt the earth and attack earth's guardian, the Church of God, how could the Anglican army be more than various bands of guerillas, an easy prey, when none of its leaders could say what was the chief concern of the whole body? At least the Congress would be an essay in the correction of false views of Christian federalism, and an exercise in fellowship on the grand scale; and if it was no more than this, it would still be worth while to bring people to London for it from all parts of the world.

All exercises in Christian fellowship depend to a surprisingly large extent upon the thoroughness of preparation and the unobtrusiveness of excellent organization. The preparation of subjects to be discussed remained in the hands of the first secretaries. Working on the facts revealed in the diocesan answers to their questions, it was they who gave to the Congress the two features which made its deliberations so distinctive, and with which it broke fresh ground in the history of conferences. These were the determination that the best half-hour, the thirty minutes most certain to be the most fully attended, must be occupied by corporate devotions and a period of Bible study, and the decision to attempt full catholicity in the subjects chosen for discussion. There should be first of all a full enquiry into just what the Gospel for the twentieth-century world must be, then an ample examination of economic, social, and industrial problems, and to such vital problems as the challenge of secularism and the right internal organization of the Church there should be accorded an emphasis not less than that to be laid upon the traditional missionary call.

If all this was to be thoroughly prepared it was evidently necessary that the organization of the Congress itself should be entrusted to other hands, and the committee borrowed the vicar of a country parish in the diocese of Bristol, the Rev. A. B. Mynors of Langley Burrell, and gave him, as Bishop Montgomery vividly put it, the task of 'organizing the whole world at a moment's notice'. They put him at first into two tiny Westminster offices, which very soon had to be extended to eight; and they charged him with such duties as arranging that six delegates from every Anglican diocese in the world should be properly accredited by their respective bishops, and duly dispatched to London, the finding of hospitality for six hundred people, and the stewarding of all the meetings. He proved himself the possessor of a real flair for the combining of spontaneity with regimentation, and his was the kind of organization which underpins liberty. If the Congress had any merit in the eternal scheme of things, as undoubtedly it had, Mynor's name should be one of those written in gold across the firmament of heaven.

But what was this merit? What did the Congress actually achieve? The record of its proceedings occupy eight dingy, closely (and badly) printed volumes which are now to be found on the bottom shelves in the darkest corners of libraries, with only spiders for company and the grime of years as embellishment. They enshrine a voluminous spate of dead oratory; for this was a conference after the manner of the traditional Church Congress, at which people delivered speeches to audiences. Perhaps the most significant part of it was not that which dealt with missions, but the morning devoted to the social challenge. 'The Church and Human Society' was given an early pride of place: it is reported in volume two of the Report. To read it is to realize with rather a shock of surprise that the many, and chronically fissiparous, Anglican Societies which had laboured to urge upon the Church the social implications of her Gospel—The Guild of St Matthew, the Christian Social Union, the Church Socialist League, and all the other organized children of Kingsley and Maurice—had done a far more effective work than anybody supposed or even they themselves dreamed. They had beyond question put the idea of Christian socialism on the map of the Anglican consciousness, and the debate showed that they had stamped it deep into this apparently unpromising material. The question which all speakers absolutely insisted on discussing was, 'Does Christianity point towards a Socialist Society, and, if so, ought the Church to be in alliance with the Labour Party?' Speaker after speaker answered yes to both questions. Lord William Cecil, indeed, complained that he felt 'almost out of place in speaking as a person with no belief in socialism'; whereupon the Rev. F. L. Donaldson at once rejoined that Lord William's speech had 'made a good foil to the splendid socialism of the Congress'.[1] By the end of the day, capitalism had been agreed to be immoral or unmoral, or both; the foolish aphorism about the impossibility of making people moral by Act of Parliament had been entombed and sealed by Scott Holland; and Dr William Temple of Oxford had declared for nationalization, and said that 'the Christian is called to assent to great steps in the direction of collectivism'.[2] That in fact none of this happened until 1940, and that nobody could then possibly trace this legislation back to the Pan-Anglican Congress, does not alter the fact that the day of this debate was historic, and that in heaven the spirits of Maurice and Kingsley must have been singing the *Nunc Dimittis* with the heavenly choir.

Not even in this, however, did the real importance of the Congress lie; and it lay far less in what it said about missions, theology, and Bible study. The journalists, trained observers and well experienced in tearing the significant heart of an occasion out of its mountain of blanketing integuments, saw it with the clearest view, and from the vantage point nearest to *sub specie aeternitatis*. They were thoroughly interested. There was no doubt of that. Bishop Montgomery said it was because:

[1] *Report*, vol. II, pp. 102–3.   [2] *Ibid.*, pp. 100–1.

The Anglican Church is considered to be slower in movement than other religious bodies; very respectable, but rather dull and behind the times. Something seemed to have happened to the Church, and the public were anxious to know what it was. Possibly some thought that the Seven Sleepers were about to issue from their cave.[1]

It almost looked like it. But there was another journalist present who was also a priest, Scott Holland of St Paul's. He saw deeper still, and after a pause for reflection wrote down the significance of the Congress as it seemed to him. He wrote it in his own inimitable way, and it forms a long quotation, but to curtail it would be to spoil it. Scott Holland always needed plenty of space to spread his colours.

Romance! We (clergy) don't look like it. It is, no doubt, our coyness that hinders us from displaying this character of ours with better effect. We hush it all up in gaiters and buttons. We creep about in obscure and ugly disguises. The last epithet that even our best friends would think of applying to those who are known as the dignified Clergy, would be 'romantic'. No! Stuffy: fusty: portentous:— all this we are: but not picturesque. We do not wear the air of having often looked out through

> 'Magic casements opening on the foam
> Of perilous seas, in faerie lands forlorn.'

No one would look for us in that sort of spot: or expect to find us engaged in any such occupation. We are very obvious: very ordinary: very usual: very commonplace: rather heavy and tiresome: a bit slow in the wind: with a touch of wet-blanket somewhere about us.

And that is why the Pan-Anglican business was so significant. Suddenly, we all rubbed our eyes, to find that something was up of quite another order. Strange things were all about us. Strange beings from strange places swarmed round every corner. Their titles stretched our spelling powers to breaking point. We had long ceased to remember whether these Dioceses, with their outlandish names, are in Australia or California. Is 'Oluwole' a name or a place? Who can say? Anyhow, there is not one island in the far seas that one or all these men had not touched at: there is not a river that they had not forded: there is not a veldt so wide and desolate that they had failed to cross it: there is no ocean that they had not sailed: there is no people, black, brown, yellow or green, that they had not intimately greeted. They murmured weird sounds from unknown languages: they clicked: they snorted: they dropped liquid vocables, like rain. They carried about, in their names and in their talk, the fragrance of historic memories that had been to us fabulous, but which they had taken possession of. India, Persia, China, and all the wonders of Pacific Island, were to them familiar ground. They had been rocked in bullock carts: wrecked at sea: half-drowned in floods and fords: all but eaten alive by men and beasts. And here they were: and they were ours: and they made themselves quite at home. There was a Canadian Bishop who relieved the tedium of a Lambeth Conference by dropping in, during lunch-time, at a rifle-range to indulge his favourite tastes, by shooting at tin bears

[1] *Report*, vol. I, p. 10.

down a tube: and hitting at every shot. Probably at certain hours in the day, all those gentlemen who were in the habit of taking sliding headers down the shoots in the Westminster Baths were members of the Episcopal Bench.

Ah! And it was very real, this romance. As we looked at those men among us then, we recalled Archdeacon Johnson, blind and worn in Nyassa: and the body of Chancey Maples under the lake water: and Bishop Hannington dying under the malarian tyranny: and the white body of Patteson floating out in the lone boat, with the martyr-palms laid by those who killed him, crossed on his breast. And many a lonely grave of those well known to us, hidden away in far corners of African jungles, came back on the imagination. Here was adventure: here was romance.

And the odd, and the comforting thing is this—that these returning heroes of ours—these, our braves—looked, after all very like us. You could not tell us apart.

It is this English church, snug and smug among the hedgerows, that has done it. That is the astonishing thing. It has thrown feelers out so far and wide. It has overleaped the paddock fence. It has flung out its frontier line. It has set sail with every wind that blows; and planted its feet on every shore that ocean washes. Who would have dreamed it of her? She hardly believes it herself. She finds it difficult to remember as she sits tied up in Elizabethan red-tape; and smothered under the convention of Establishment; and fat with dignities; and very scant of breath. Yet it is all true. For here were the adventurers whom she had sent out, trooping home to din the story into her dim, deaf, ears.[1]

A new and vivid picture of the greatness, the vast extent of the Anglican Church, and a new grasp of the essential unity of its problems and its mission: this was near the heart of the occasion. But it was in the actual gathering together in fellowship of the endlessly scattered members of a great Church that its final significance for history lay. The Pan-Anglican Congress had implanted in Anglicans everywhere a far more vivid consciousness of their membership of the Anglican Communion than most had ever realized before. The storms which were gathering, and which have beaten ceaselessly upon the Church ever since, have never quenched this flame.

II · *Preparing for the World Missionary Conference*

Two years later the World Interdenominational Missionary Conference took place at Edinburgh, and the date of its assembling is one of the really outstanding events in the history of the twentieth century. It had a significance for world politics which was not less but more than its meaning for the ecclesiastical world. It belongs as truly to the history of statesmanship as to that of missions. As the years of the second half of our own century roll away, the historians of the next generation may well judge that the true path of human happiness in the conditions of the twentieth century was first signposted at Edinburgh in 1910. If, as the wisest observers judge, we

[1] Henry Scott Holland, *A Bundle of Memories* (Wells, Gardner and Darton), 1915, pp. 231-3.

are the creatures of a revolutionary epoch which has world unification as its destined goal, then any events which in a sense anticipate this goal, and take it for granted in their own sphere, are historically important. If they are events which take place under the inspiration and in the service of the one world-wide force which can bring mankind to this goal, and yet guarantee the freedom of separate human beings, they are of historically decisive importance. The Edinburgh Conference was such an event. Even in the more limited sphere of technically ecclesiastical history, its influence on the union of the Churches, which it discussed little, was greater than its influence on missions, which was the purpose of its gathering.

The origins of the Edinburgh Conference went back to 1900, to a gathering in New York, rather grandiloquently called the Ecumenical Missionary Conference. It had done some good work, but it was not more than a rather unprepared demonstration. It left behind it a continuation committee under the charge of a famous missionary scholar, Dr George Robson, a minister of the Free Church of Scotland. In 1906 this committee met in Scotland in order to decide whether the second world conference, vaguely suggested at New York, ought to be held or not. The committee was clear that it would be idle to attempt to organize anything of the kind unless the enthusiastic support of the Student Christian Movement could be enlisted, and therefore Dr Robson approached Mr J. H. Oldham, at that time the Studies Secretary of S.C.M., to discuss the matter with him. Mr Oldham consulted his committee, and it was agreed that there would be great gain in holding a conference, provided that two conditions could be satisfied. It must be genuinely world-wide, and it must be the climax of a long period of the preparatory study of missionary problems. It must, in fact, be a gathering of a deliberative kind, composed wholly of thoroughly informed people; it must not be the kind of conference at which a few experts made speeches to a largely ignorant audience. In addition, it must be the fruit of, and it must register, the genuine co-operation of all missionary Churches.

In 1906, however, one event was violently disturbing students of missionary problems all over the world. It was the defeat of Russia by Japan in 1905. The missionaries saw more clearly than either the statesmen or the traders that this was a portent which completely changed the world situation and made all things new. The battle of Moukden was among the few historically decisive world events: the storming of the Bastille and the victory of Waterloo are its peers. For many centuries before our own the tide of human affairs had flowed westward, and the historic rôle of eastern and southern lands had been to serve the purposes of western nations. Only Japan had held aloof, successfully holding off all occidental exploitation. Then a small eastern nation held at bay and smote in battle a gigantic western nation. Her victory was complete and shattering at sea and on the land, and with this mighty portent the twentieth century began. The balance of power between the nations was changed, the calculations of economists and financiers had to be redrawn, and the whole world situation was permanently altered. The west took years to understand how devastating and how complete the change was: in the east the real significance of Port Arthur and Moukden was at once perceived.

Back from the east westwards [wrote one in a better position to estimate the movement of world forces than most statesmen] ran the electric thrill. All talk about the partition of China ceased with astounding abruptness—the world looked awestruck on, as the sleeping colossus roused itself, woke, stood upon its feet. Korea, Manchuria, Malaysia, Ceylon each in its own way felt the thrill. A new thought, a fresh aspiration seemed to give a sense of unity even to racially and religiously divided India. Vague and ignorant might be the talk that went the round of the bazaars of the cities, and even in the villages of India, but it was not the less significant. The same talk might have been heard in Kabul and Teheran, and in the cafés of Constantinople and Cairo, and God only knows how much further west and south. It was more than a mere coincidence that the quinquennium which followed the event saw the rapid development of nationalism in Egypt, and *coups d'état* in Persia and in Turkey. . . . It was evident that the east had awaked, and this not because it was the fussy thunder of western legions that for the hundredth time was annoying her slumber, but because she was for the first time responding to an awakening call of nature from within.[1]

Here was a new challenge to the world, and a new chance for militant Christianity. Evidently the eastern nations must soon assert their full equality with the western nations of privilege, prestige, and independence. But would they go by the western road of war? Would the terrific new forces unleashed all over the world clash or co-operate? The world knew it was becoming one entity, and people everywhere were dreaming of world empire. Would the principle of unity be the god of war or the Prince of Peace, Man or Christ? If this empire was to be claimed for Christ, the Churches everywhere must co-operate in a gigantic new effort. But it must be an informed effort; and to that end the first need was to gather, to pool, to co-ordinate all available expert knowledge of the new world situation. This having been done, it must then be considered in the creative atmosphere of devotional fellowship by a completely international and genuinely interdenominational conference of Christians. It was this prior need which the promoters of 'Edinburgh 1910' set themselves to fill.

The needs of a uniting world could be declared and served only by manifestly co-operating Churches, and the occasion upon which above all others there must be this fellowship of co-operation must be the Edinburgh Conference. The New York committee contained no Anglicans. When it found itself charged with the task of preparing for Edinburgh, it borrowed J. H. Oldham from the S.C.M. to be its secretary (thus fulfilling one of the two conditions of success), and it added to itself Prebendary H. W. Fox of the

[1] W. H. T. Gairdner, *Edinburgh 1910* (Oliphant, Anderson and Ferrier, Edinburgh), 1910, p. 11.

C.M.S. But Fox was fanatically evangelical and a rigidly party man. He and Tissington Tatlow were charged to nominate the right Anglicans to serve on the preparatory commissions. Fox produced a list and read it out to Tatlow with great satisfaction. It contained only the names of known evangelicals, and it blandly omitted everybody connected with S.P.G. Plainly, Fox was not the man to persuade the very suspicious Anglo-Catholics to co-operate in an interdenominational venture. The committee then wrote to Tissington Tatlow, 'We want you to join the committee which has to plan the conference, and we want you to bring the Church of England with you.'[1] Tatlow replied that he would try, but the committee were woefully mistaken if they thought he could make the Church of England do what he wanted. But really it was Tatlow who was mistaken. He may or may not have had much influence in his own person; but he was also general secretary of S.C.M. and in that capacity he had a great deal, for the S.C.M. is the one interdenominational society which the Church of England has really understood.

It proved to be a task requiring great tact and skilled finesse. First, Tatlow persuaded Fox to scrap his list of undistinguished evangelicals. Instead, he proposed to persuade Bishops Talbot and Gore, Father Frere of Mirfield, and Dr Armitage Robinson, Dean of Westminster, and many others hardly less distinguished to serve on the preparatory commissions; and none of the four men whose names are given had ever before agreed to take part in interdenominational conferences. He began with Armitage Robinson. It was a queer conversation. The Dean had the idea that it was an S.C.M. Conference, and with that he was perfectly ready to co-operate.

'But, Mr Dean, it is not a Student Movement Conference.'
'Then whose conference is it?' said the Dean sharply.
'The Missionary Societies are co-operating in its organization.'
'Oh, I don't want to have anything to do with that sort of conference. I don't want to work for a conference of the Missionary Societies. I thought you wanted me to do something for the Student Movement. I am not going to have anything to do with it.'[2]

It was a characteristically Anglican point of view: principles don't matter when you respect and understand the people who want you to break them. But refusing Tatlow was always rather a hopeless gesture, and within an hour the Dean gladly agreed to serve. The Dean was, moreover, a gateway to others. Talbot, Frere, and Gore all followed his example, without much persuasion being needed.

There remained two more difficult fences. A conference of missionary societies without S.P.G. would be maimed to the point of scandal. Yet that society had a clause in its charter to prevent its co-operation with non-Anglican churches, and in 1908 its committee declined the invitation to be

[1] *The Student Christian Movement*, p. 406.   [2] *Ibid.*, p. 408.

represented. But, as has already been told, Tatlow had two years before persuaded S.P.G.—largely by a veiled threat which no missionary society dared ignore[1]—to be represented at a Student Volunteer Missionary Union Conference, so that he was not much impressed by arguments about the clause in the charter. The Society at first refused, but later relented, and in the end was fully represented. This earlier triumph of Tatlow's, however, gave him a great strength in his persuasion of the Archbishop of Canterbury officially to associate himself with the conference, and to go to Edinburgh to give it his blessing. The Archbishop was very anxious. He knew that the Anglo-Catholics were not exactly enthusiastic, and that S.P.G. would probably refuse an invitation. But he received a deputation consisting of John R. Mott, J. H. Oldham, and Tissington Tatlow, and he said to them:

'I am afraid they [S.P.G.] cannot take part in a conference not exclusively Anglican. I believe there is something in their charter which prevents them.'

'I succeeded [rejoined Tatlow] last year in getting an official delegation to represent the society at our S.M.V.U. conference.'

I remember the eager way in which the Archbishop swung towards me and said: 'You had them officially at your conference? I am profoundly thankful to hear it. I am profoundly thankful to hear it.'[2]

But for all his thankfulness he would not at once agree to go to Edinburgh.

I pointed out to them the difficulties of my position: how my going thither might compromise some people who are quite willing to keep silence, although they disapprove of the joint action, but who would not keep silence if they thought that by the Archbishop's presence the whole Church was committed.[3]

He meditated for nearly a year; but eventually he decided to go. Tissington Tatlow had fulfilled his charge up to the hilt. He had brought the Church of England with him, and the conference was to be genuinely ecumenical. Only the Student Movement could have done it: and after it was all over, William Temple, who was in later years to succeed Randall Davidson, wrote: 'Members of the Movement ought to know that without their movement there never could have been held the Edinburgh Conference, which was the greatest event in the life of the Church for a generation.'[4]

While all these difficult negotiations were going on, the work of preparing for the conference was moving steadily in all parts of the world. The Church's real need was to do some deep thinking, and to do it quickly. Not rhetoric but knowledge was wanted; and the members must be well-informed delegates, not an audience. The whole atmosphere was to be deliberative and consultative. There was, therefore, a vital need of a series of preparatory commissions to gather, digest, and sort material from all over the world. Eventually eight of these commissions were chosen and appointed, as follows. The Chairman's name is given in brackets:

---

[1] See above, p. 172.
[2] *The Student Christian Movement*, p. 309.
[3] Bell, *op. cit.*, vol. I, p. 573.
[4] *The Student Christian Movement*, pp. 410f.

(1) The carrying of the Gospel to non-Christian lands. (John R. Mott of the U.S.A.: Secretary of the World's Student Christian Federation.)

(2) The Church in the Mission Field. (Dr J. G. Gibson of the Presbyterian Mission to China.)

(3) Education in Relation to the Christianization of National Life. (Charles Gore, Bishop of Birmingham.)

(4) The Missionary Message in relation to non-Christian Religions. (D. S. Cairns of Aberdeen.)

(5) The Preparation of Missionaries. (Dr Douglas Mackenzie, Principal of Hartford Theological Seminary, U.S.A.)

(6) The Home Base of Missions. (Dr J. L. Barton, of Boston U.S.A.)

(7) The Relations of Missions to Governments. (Lord Balfour of Burleigh.)

(8) Co-operation and the Promotion of Unity. (Sir Andrew Fraser, of the Indian Civil Service.)

Each Commission had twenty members, and the whole team constituted 160 as able men and women as could be found anywhere in the world. Their labours were immense, their chairmen heroic. Could busier men than these eight be found? Yet they gave most lavishly of time and effort to the great task. They would hardly have done so had it not also been great in their own judgement.

Nothing in Temple Gairdner's book is more exhilarating than his account of this great task:

> The bulk of the question papers (sent by each commission to mission stations all over the world) were at last ready. . . . Some missionaries wrote replies in which they embodied all the experience and philosophy of a lifetime. In all, upwards of 1,000 papers, representing a whose case-full of books in print were received by the unfortunate Chairmen of Commissions.

These had to be read, compared, digested; and then the reports must be composed, printed, and sent to delegates:

> And so in railway trains, on P. & O. and Atlantic liners, the spectacle of the long folio printed documents might have been seen in the hands of a thousand delegates, coming from East, West, North, and South, as they tried to accomplish the feat of mastering eight volumes of closest thinking, each averaging from 200 to 300 pages of ordinary print, in a period that amounted to perhaps half a week per volume.[1]

These eight volumes, which every delegate to the conference was sworn to read before he arrived, contain between them an exact and full statement of the Christian position all over the world. Never before had there been a survey as authoritative.

[1] Gairdner, *op. cit.*, pp. 24, 26.

III · *John R. Mott*

What hard and prolonged co-operative toil could do had been done. It was thanks largely to the careful, scholarly pains of the eight preparatory commissions that Edinburgh was not just another successful world conference, but 'the greatest event in the life of the Church for a generation'. But those who were present had no doubt that it was the inspired chairmanship of John R. Mott which, more than any other single factor, made this preliminary effort bear its full harvest.

He was a very silent chairman, but his silence was more forceful than other people's speech. The man was all compact with the power made of immense experience and the authority of a life-long dedication, as fresh and spontaneous as it was disciplined. The American nation seems to specialize in the production of semi-official world ambassadors who, apparently at their own whim, travel over the globe and give themselves to the task of harmonizing its discordant national elements, and binding them together in creative synthesis. Such a one was Colonel House in the first world war; and, sure enough, it was an American General, Dwight Eisenhower, who in the field of inter-allied strategy, performed this vital office for us in the second world war. But of all these indefatigable, purposeful travellers whom the United States has given to the world, none has been so ultimately influential, nor has any done quite so great a work as John R. Mott. It would be quite possible to write the history of Christendom in this century around his name; nor would it be wholly extravagant to treat him as one of the two or three real heroes of the story. On any showing, his life was crucial for the unfolding of God's plan for the world's righteousness.

In 1910, Mott was forty-five years old. The whole of his life had been shaped around a profound sense of vocation, and all his activity for years, in things small as well as great, had been a consequence of conscious obedience to God's will for him. God had a plan for his life. From his earliest years he had never doubted it, and throughout his student days at Cornell University his main purpose had been to discover what that purpose was. In his last year at Cornell he wrote home:

This matter of choosing a life-field is a very serious question. I thought that everything was settled when I determined about a year ago to give up my life to Christian work, but now looms up a question just as vital—what part of Christian work to enter.

He went on to rehearse at length some of the many fields of Christian work for which he might reasonably consider himself to be equipped, and then he ended:

So you see it is a confusing problem to settle. The elements entering into it are so conflicting and complex that I believe that *only God* can lead a man to a right decision. I mean to keep myself open and study the whole field and then go just where God calls.[1]

In the fullness of time God did call clearly to him, laying upon him the burden of presenting Christ to the students of all races and nationalities in the world. This he must do as a layman. The sense of spiritual discipline he had inherited from his family's traditional membership of the American Presbyterian Church, and his training as a leader in the American Y.M.C.A., had thoroughly equipped him.

The obedience to the special call of God once given, there followed for him a life of arduous, prolonged, and almost incessant travel. The annals of Christendom contain no parallel: not even St Paul lived so completely on the move. He had been twice round the world before 1910, and was to undertake this journey twice more. It has been estimated that before he died he had travelled 1,700,000 miles in the service of his Master—the equivalent of sixty-eight times round the globe.[2] The mere recital of figures and records has no meaning in terms of spiritual achievement. But Mott never made a journey which was not one prolonged spiritual achievement. He was a born ambassador. Knowing this, more than one President of the U.S.A. had used him in ambassadorial journeys, when peace-making of special delicacy had to be provided with a mouthpiece. But most of his journeys were to the various universities of the world, and to conferences of students. There was hardly a university in the world which did not know Mott, nor a city in which he had not a host of friends eager to welcome him. His primary purpose was the presentation of Christ to students, and this he tirelessly pursued, with the authority of his office of president of the World's Student Christian Federation behind him, in an endless series of missions in one university after another, in which the traditional evangelical appeal was made with a wisdom, a restraint, and a power not before achieved or since exceeded. A life of perpetual motion is full of temptations and dangers of its own. It can easily become the madcap flight of the spiritual butterfly, settling idly on one flower after another, and shooting off in purposeless tangents in all directions. But his own life was one with purpose behind every movement of it, so unending and remorseless, and yet flexible and spontaneous, was the spartan spiritual discipline he imposed upon himself. His power of sustained industry was immense, he wasted no moment of any day, and he had a genius for understanding the student mind in every nation. His physique stood up to and supported his labours, but largely because he always made the preservation of physical fitness a part of his positive spiritual duty.

No man could live such a life without adding two other burdens, for they followed automatically from the first. He knew as no other man did the heady excitement of ideas in the minds of students, and he alone was in a

[1] Basil Mathews, *John R. Mott, World Citizen* (SCM Press), 1934, p. 78.
[2] *Ibid.*, pp. 137, 138.

position to estimate justly their effect upon the missionary work of the whole Church, and through that their influence upon world politics. The higher strategy of missions inevitably became his field, for was there anyone else who could know as much about it? Nor could a man accept a concern of this kind without being every day confronted by the chaos of divided Christendom. He was bound to give himself to the cause of co-operation among Christian Churches in missionary work, and it was indeed in this sphere that he made his really decisive contribution to history.

Every circumstance of his astonishing life had therefore prepared him for the task of being chairman of the Edinburgh Conference; and in the minds of the committee there was never any question to be argued about that. Of all the people in the world, John Mott was pre-eminently the one man to undertake it. There was nobody else with his exact, compendious knowledge, no one with his range of friendship, and his power of right diplomacy. Probably there was no single statesman who knew as much about the world as Mott did. It was the Oxford undergraduate magazine, *The Isis*, not much given to enthusiasm, which wrote deliberately of him:

Dr Mott is in the true sense a great statesman. He has had unique opportunities of watching the tendencies of the great nations of the world, and has made remarkably good use of them. No one can hear him speak without knowing that he has a complete grip of the great problems now confronting man. . . . It may be doubted whether any man alive has so firm a grip of present-day conditions or so sure an insight into the nature of the forces which are changing the political and social constitutions of almost all the nations under heaven.[1]

Such was the chairman of the Edinburgh Conference. It turned out to be the crown of his life's work—that for which the Holy Spirit had all the time been preparing him.

The conference over which Mott was to preside assembled in the Council Hall on the ridge of the Mound in Edinburgh in June of 1910. There were 1,200 delegates from all over the world. They belonged to every kind of Christian allegiance, except the Roman, and they represented more than 160 different missionary boards or societies. The photograph of the whole assembly in Temple Gairdner's book does less than justice to its colourfulness. It shows a very large gathering of the elderly and the wise. Bald heads and beards seem to fill the floor of the hall, while the young, both men and women, are relegated to the galleries. But Gairdner's prose colours the staid black and white of his photography, and makes clear how vividly romantic an occasion this was. There was ample colour for those who looked for it. A Chinese delegate in 'full Chinese costume, skull-cap and pigtail, and stuffed quilted jacket of richest peacock blue silk' made one vivid figure in the memorable frieze. Another sat by him—'a pure Brahman high-priestly

[1] Tribute of *The Isis* in 1908, after Mott's Mission to Oxford. Quoted by Mathews, *op. cit.*, pp. 165, 166.

figure, with a long silky white beard, tall, upright figure, with aristocratic, gentle features'; and not far away there was to be seen a huge negro from Liberia, the one free negro republic in the world, 'glorying in his African race'.[1] The grey streets of Edinburgh had exotic colours straying all over them that week.

The stamp of a consciously great occasion, and all the penetrating flights of vision, enveloped the conference from the very beginning. There were messages from the King, from Theodore Roosevelt, and even from the German Colonial Office, to be read out; and it all began with a superb speech by the Archbishop of Canterbury, who magnificently caught the greatness of the occasion and set the delegates firmly in that atmosphere of sober, informed vision which they never lost. He began by saying that this conference was 'one which, if men be weighed rather than counted, has, I suppose, no parallel in history of this or other lands'; and he ended:

> The place of missions in the life of the Church must be the central place and none other: that is what matters. Secure for that thought its true place in our plans, our policy, our prayer and then—why then the issue is His, not ours. And it may well be that if that comes true, there may be some standing here tonight who shall not taste of death till they see the Kingdom of God come with power.[2]

The Archbishop had given them an unforgettable start. But the fact that he was there at all—almost the fact that there was a conference at all for him to come to—was due to the small but authentically heroic figure of J. H. Oldham. The Archbishop had long hesitated whether he should come or not, and it was Oldham who had done most to persuade him, just as it had been Oldham, together with Tissington Tatlow, who had brought in the notable Anglo-Catholic leaders of the Church of England. He was the conference's secretary, and on him had fallen the heavy burden of organizing it all.

> He slipped into or out of his place at the table, as one not merely unnoticed but as not meriting notice; . . . From beginning to end he never opened his lips, save to give out formal notices. Why then was it that the first time he rose to give out a notice, the whole conference applauded as though it would never cease? Some did so, perhaps, because they wanted to show their appreciation of a triumph of organization. But those that knew were aware that, more than any other, the spirit that was in this very unobtrusive exterior had been at the back of that great conference, not merely in respect of its organization and its methods, but also of its ideals, its aspirations, and its hopes.[3]

For him, too, as for John Mott, there was a destiny working. He was being prepared for something, a great service, which came to its full flowering twenty years later.

[1] Gairdner, *op. cit.*, pp. 57, 58.   [2] *Ibid.*, p. 43.   [3] *Ibid.*, p. 65.

IV · The Missionary Picture in 1910

The eight reports of the preparatory commissions were documents of formidable length. They constituted the fullest, the most expert, and the most authoritative statement then in existence of the essentials of the missionary problem. They had been circulated well in advance, and every delegate had been put on his honour to read them every one with scrupulous and devout care before he came to Edinburgh. These reports formed the basis of the whole deliberative conference. The reports of experts were discussed by the well informed. Every speech made came from a mind doubly equipped to make it. Every delegate really knew the contents of the reports, and each one brought to the conference a wealth of intimate, detailed knowledge of missionary problems in his own sphere of work. It follows that if one wants to know what the mission field, taken as a single whole, looked like in 1910, the proceedings of this conference give the answer. They draw a map of world Christian strategy so clear that the three vital areas of decision are at once seen in bold outline.

First of all, there is the note of urgency, more urgency, and yet again urgency. Behold, now is the accepted time: now is the day of salvation. 'The evangelization of the world in this generation,' had been the watchword of the Student Christian Movement, from the beginning, and in the Edinburgh Conference it seemed as if that magnificent disdain of caution was at last to be justified. The Archbishop of Canterbury, in the peroration of his speech to the conference, had exactly caught the atmosphere of those historic eight days—'There may be some here that shall not taste of death . . .' This urgency had a special quality. It beat ceaselessly upon the ears of the delegates with a harsh noise like a Chinese gong, incessantly hammering out the words, 'Now, now, now—or else not for centuries.' It was, they judged—and they of all men had the right to judge—the defeat of Russia by Japan which had made the first fifty years of the twentieth century the hour of decision for east and south. But especially was this true of the eastern races. India, Africa, Polynesia, and even the more temperate British Dominions were all in the valley of decision. All alike needed now and at once what might be too late in twenty years. But Japan and China were the real centres of gravity. On their soils must be fought the ultimately decisive battles to make this world in this century the kingdom of our Lord.

Of Japan the report had said: 'Never was richer freight derelict upon the great waters of time,'[1] and every Japanese speaker endorsed it. Japan's freight was indeed derelict, and her new destiny, full of her own and the whole world's unsolved problems, hung in the balances of choice. In a night she had passed from era to era, and had taken up the reversion of the leadership of all the nationalist ideas of the Orient. In a process just as swift, she had abandoned all her traditional individualism of government, and with

[1] *Ibid.*, p. 145.

it her old isolation. Instead of this, she had now fastened on to the back of a still Shinto people a conception of the state which was of Christian shape, but which could become Christian in spirit only when the mass of her people were Christians. There were Christians in Japan, but not many. These few were mostly drawn from the governing classes. The mass of the people still waited and watched. In the meantime, complained an experienced missionary, they would attend Christian meetings only grudgingly, and in tiny numbers. 'No preacher whether missionary or Japanese commonly addresses audiences with as many as forty or fifty unbelievers.'[1] The mind of Japan was an inchoate welter: so much of the old thought abandoned, so little of anything new yet accepted to take its place. Devils might inhabit that vacuum, and they were already hammering at its gates. Count Okuma, a Japanese Prime Minister had warned his people, 'Unfortunately, the ethical instruction given according to the direction of the Department of Education is shallow. It urges patriotism and loyalty without giving a reasonable and fundamental motive for them.'[2] The view of the conference was expressed by many speakers, but the sum of their deliverances was caught and held most fully a year or two later by Dr Tasuku Harada, President of the Doshisha University, and one of the most prominent of Japanese Christians.

Since Christianity assimilated Greek thought and conquered Roman civilization it has never faced a task so stupendous as that of the conquest of the Orient. Japan, with all her progress in the arts and crafts of civilization, and all her friendliness towards Christian standards, is far from being a Christian nation; indeed, she is in some respects more anti-Christian than at any time since the placards proscribing the 'Evil Sect' were removed in 1873. Then there was unreasoning antipathy, now there is reasoned opposition. Yet Japan is a prize worth capturing. The situation in the whole Orient, in fact, constitutes one of the most splendid opportunities, and at the same time one of the gravest crises in the whole history of the Church. With every passing year the opportunity is slipping farther from her grasp. I make bold to say that her victory or defeat in Japan will largely determine the future of Christianity in the whole Far East.[3]

Five years had gone by since the battle of Moukden, and the Church in Japan had but little to show for them. But the conference claimed that there was still time to win Japan for Christ. After all, Japanese-occupied Korea was then one of the bright stars in the Christian firmament, a country, like Uganda, more deeply Christian than any in Europe. But under God the whole enterprise depended upon Japanese benevolence, and Japan had not yet decided for or against Christ, for or against the road of aggression. On that decision the peace of the Orient must, and the peace of all the world might, hang. Before long it must be taken, and the hour-glass had only a

[1] *East and West* (1915), p. 214.
[2] J. H. Oldham, *The World and the Gospel* (U.C.M.E.), 1916, p. 79.
[3] Quoted in Oldham, *op. cit.*, p. 81.

few grains of sand left to trickle through. Well might an American delegate say: 'A million dollar institution in Japan for higher education will count ten times as much as a million dollar institution in America for uplifting the world.'[1]

On China first of all must fall the weight of the Japanese decision, and China too was in spiritual chaos. The commission's report had said that China was 'the chief storm centre of opportunity in the whole world'.[2] This bold judgement was underlined again and again in the speeches made by men in a position to know of what they spoke. Bishop Bashford of North China had one of the largest dioceses in the world, but also one of the most poorly staffed. The number of Anglican mission workers in his diocese did not amount to more than one per cent of the whole number of missionaries in China.[3] He gave it as his considered judgement that

not since the days of the Reformation, not indeed since Pentecost, has so great an opportunity confronted the Christian Church. The Far East as a whole stands at the parting of the ways. No such opportunity is likely to confront the Christian Church again till the day of Judgement.[4]

A Chinese professor, T. Y. Chang, of Pekin University, was still more urgent in his warning:

The people of China are now giving away the old, but they have not yet grasped the new. The minds of the Chinese are now empty, and this is the time for Christ to step in. If you wait four years, *or even three years*, you will find such a change in China that the minds of her people will be blocked. I beseech you to take immediate steps. In five years it will be too late.[5]

It seemed to be the feeling of the conference that in Japan it was already too late, but that there was still a chance in China to claim the largest empire of human souls in the world for Christ. Subsequent history has confirmed the insight. The conference was similarly hopeful about India: over Africa it was thoroughly optimistic. But however widely the discussion ranged over the world, sooner or later it always came back to the Far East, particularly to China. If the world did hold one particular centre of gravity, one particular field of decision for or against Christ, all those well-informed men were sure that China was that field. On what Christian missions made of their chance there the future history of the world would turn.

It was one of the great strengths of this conference that it saw so clearly how inadequate a missionary policy it is to think of the empire of Christ in China, India, or anywhere else, solely in terms of individual souls converted. There is no such empire until the whole culture of a country—the total power exerted upon the imagination by the habits of daily life—is Christian. This must sooner or later involve the deliberate effort to capture and convert governments and other national organs and institutions in their total

[1] Gairdner, *op. cit.*, p. 127.   [2] *Ibid.*, p. 77.
[3] *Report of Pan-Anglican Congress*, vol. V, p. 144.
[4] Gairdner, *op. cit.*, p. 78.   [5] *Ibid.*, p. 78.

community. This insight involved the conference in two other major pre-occupations, the relationship of the mission to governments on the one hand and to the European communities in native states on the other, and the urgent problem of how best to develop a foreign mission brought from Europe into a genuinely native, independent, and autonomous Church.

The preparatory commission on 'The Relation of Missions to Governments' had revealed a very puzzling and inconsistent state of affairs, and the discussion of the conference did but add to its complexity. It had once been true, but was now true no longer, that 'missions and their agents are the most troublesome of all the things which daily vex the statesman'. But this typically East India Company view of the mission nuisance had given place to the general impression that in 1910 'a large area of natural helpfulness existed between missions and governments'.[1] Still, it was no more than a general impression. There was almost as much evidence to contradict as there was to confirm it. The Japanese government was ironically helpful. The government of the Dutch East Indies was more than helpful: it was enthusiastically co-operative, and had set up a missionary consulate at Batavia. On the other hand, the Chinese government was very difficult, and the governments of the Indian native states were thoroughly hostile. The French government exported its home policy of a nationalist secularism into the government of all its colonies. In Madagascar, French Guiana, Algeria, and all other parts of the French empire, all missions other than those of the Roman Church were openly detested by authority. The Roman missions were excepted from this official execration not because of any tenderness towards the Papacy, but because it was supposed that any other kind of Christian mission must automatically be hostile to French nationalism, and so bring with it an anti-French influence. The result was that there were no parts of the world so little evangelized as the French colonies.

The record of British Colonial government was far better in this matter than that of the French. But, viewed as a whole, the conference did not find much to praise in it. In India, neutrality in matters of religion was governmental policy. A former governor of Bengal, Sir Charles Elliott, had avowed it in a speech to the Pan-Anglican Congress:

> There is one field of improvement which the Government is debarred from entering. Its officers are not authorized to speak to the people of religion. They cannot tell them of the love of God or of the risen Redeemer. This is the noble field which it is given to missionaries to occupy.[2]

That was all very well. But the practical results were that a profoundly secular education was fastened upon a people deeply religious by nature, training, tradition, and thought. The educational system as a whole was badly tainted by cramming for success, producing, as was inevitable, the unhappy, frustrated class of the 'Failed B.A.'; and it positively invited the

[1] Gairdner, *op. cit.*, p. 157.   [2] *Report*, vol. V, p. 86.

white community to believe that Indians ought not to be educated at all, and certainly ought not to be converted to Christianity. The government of the Sudan was strongly pro-Islam: they had actually turned the Gordon College into a purely Moslem institution. In Northern Nigeria

there is a real open partisanship of Islam. Practically no attempt has been made in educational work, and that of missionary societies is looked at coolly, or even thwarted. Bolstering up of Moslem duties, reviving of customs which have been allowed to lapse, gradual levelling up of pagan districts so as to accustom them to Islamic law, all show the trend, and make it obvious to Christian and Pagan that the British Government has no use for either of them, but only for the Moslem.[1]

All governments, it was claimed, were hampered by the vested interests of the traders and the far from helpful attitude towards Christian missions exhibited by the various European communities. At their worst the traders were out to perpetuate three great wrongs which Christianity was bound to attack. These were the opium wrong, upon the evil of which the governments concerned were just as convinced as the missionaries; the liquor wrong, which had particularly devastating social results in Africa, and yet the government of Southern Nigeria had set itself to defend and protect the trade, and itself joined in it;[2] and the forced labour wrong, which had scandalously over-reached itself in the Congo, but was continued in East Africa. Traders generally found that heathen natives were a better paying proposition than Christian natives. They often set themselves to keep the people heathen, and they sometimes tried to underpin the more degrading heathen rites by getting themselves admitted to the lower grades of the mystery cults. The institution of the Egbo in Calabar, with the chirpings and mutterings of the wizards and the cruel smelling out of thieves, had plenty of European traders in its lower ranks, who had joined it because they found it an insurance against theft.[3]

The third great concern of the conference was with the autonomous independence of the native Church, and this was the most important of all. How could there ever be a Christian Papuan culture if there was not also a genuinely Papuan Christian Church? Missionaries from European or American missionary societies might first take the Gospel to some virgin field, and then there must be an intervening period while the young Church was being built during which reference must always be made back to the society in London or New York which had undertaken the charge. But this period ought to be as short as possible. The facts which the conference laid bare in this matter were on the whole most encouraging. They showed that native converts very quickly realized that they must also become evangelists themselves. Thus, out of 40,000 baptized Christians in Korea, it was estimated that only some hundreds had come into the Church solely through

---

[1] Gairdner, *op. cit.*, p. 161.   [2] *Ibid.*, p. 171.   [3] *East and West* (1915), p. 169.

the work of foreign missionaries. Uganda was so completely independent that the secretary of the Church Missionary Society could declare to the conference that he knew almost nothing about the finances of the Church in Uganda. Converted Jews were at work. Schereschewszky's Chinese translation of the Old Testament was read throughout the length and breadth of China. The Christians of the South Sea islands were making a big drive to convert the Chinese, Japanese, and Indians who came to the islands. Samoa had a most flourishing mission of its own in New Guinea, founded by the young prince Tamate as far back as 1883:

> From a training college in Mabia some fifty-four Samoans, Tokelan, and Ellice islanders have gone to New Guinea, that savage isle, successors of those first three who, in 1883, sailed to be the colleagues of Tamate, his fellow missionaries in the Gospel of Christ. Chalmers the Scotsman is not the only martyr of New Guinea. The Polynesian is there too. In Papua sleep saints from Scotland and from Samoa.[1]

The report of the preparatory commission had declared in a sentence of tremendous visionary power, 'The evangelization of the world, as we have come to see it increasingly, is not chiefly a European or American enterprise.' But, if so, it tarried upon the creation of genuinely native Churches under their own native bishops. It could only be begun, but never finished, nor ever carried very far, by foreign missions, largely dependent on London or New York for their funds, and having to turn to Tufton Street or Salisbury Square in every crisis. It had for years been the policy of S.P.G. to leave ecclesiastical government wholly to the bishops of the dioceses concerned. But not every missionary board or society had been as scrupulous; and an American secretary of a mission board declared to the conference with grim candour, 'Save in a very few countries, no Church polity is in practice today on the foreign field (*sic*). Too much real power has been exercised by Boards, Societies, and Missions, altogether too much for the conditions which exist today.'[2] What the phrase 'Church polity' may mean is not clear. But if it means what that secretary plainly intended it to mean, then the fact that in all India in 1910 there was no single Indian bishop shows plainly enough how long a distance on this road the missionary strategists had still to travel.

V · *The Ecumenical Movement Begins*

When the conference had ended, a continuation committee was formed with J. H. Oldham as its secretary. The first greeting it received came in the form of a cable from China: 'Hang on to co-operation like grim death.' The Chinese Christians who sent it had exactly grasped the point. They had seized upon the real significance for history of the events of that tremendous week.

[1] Gairdner. *op. cit.*, p. 97.　　　　　　[2] *Ibid.*, p. 107.

If the members of the conference had been asked: What was the really vital thing you did? they would undoubtedly have given their answer in terms of missionary work. It had been a missionary conference. They had been charged to lay bare before any Christians who cared to see the full map of the then missionary situation; and this they had done with a completeness and an authority never before equalled. With their perpetual insistence upon desperate and burning urgency, and their informed judgement on the facts which constituted this urgency, they had laid before all the Churches a watchword and a policy. They had no doubt at all that history was offering to Christendom its supreme chance, that if the Churches could seize that chance, bringing both cool knowledge and passionate devotion to their seizure of it, the Kingdom of God could be brought within the sight of that generation. Mott himself, than whom no one in the world had a more calm and penetrating judgement, went straight away from Edinburgh into retirement in order at once to write a book with the significant title, *The Decisive Hour of Christian Missions.*

We who have seen so much more than those men and women ever dreamed of, find their optimism difficult to comprehend. Christians of that calibre could hardly have subscribed blindly and uncritically to the Edwardian assumptions of necessary and automatic progress. Nor did they. But they had made an altogether insufficient reckoning with the resourceful power of evil; and they certainly thought that with one more stupendous push, with the whole weight of Christendom behind it, the work would be at least in a fair way to being done, and 'the evangelization of the world in this generation' would at last come true. They took for granted the steady continuance of the period of individual enterprise and freedom. Thus their effort was to discover how best the Gospel could be presented to the various cultures of the world. They did not stay to consider what in fact the Gospel for the twentieth century actually was, and still less why it ought to be preached. The Edinburgh Conference was indeed one of the great landmarks in the history of the Church, but its significance was quite other than its members believed, other than what, at that date, it would have been possible for them to perceive. They had thought they were there to serve the cause of Christian missions, as indeed they were, but they were all the time being used for a still more vital purpose, the writing of a very notable chapter in the story of the perpetual Christian struggle to find in the Church the way to unity.

'Hang on to co-operation like grim death' had run the Chinese cable. This they did, and, naturally, it was co-operation in the cause of missions. They formed in London a permanent 'Conference of British Missionary Societies', and they provided a headquarters for it at Edinburgh House, Eaton Gate. True to all the best traditions, they also provided it with a quarterly review and a publishing house. The review, edited by J. H. Oldham, aimed at the scientific investigation of missionary problems. It was a great success from the beginning. No quarterly had more brilliant contributors. For more lengthy writing there was the Edinburgh House Press, which became a power and a portent in the world of missionary publishing. But Edinburgh House, as an institution, was first of all meant to be an experiment in interdenominational fellowship. From this ideal it has never looked back, and from the search for its perfection it has never faltered.

All this was as splendidly achieved as it was urgently needed. But the real achievement of the conference was something bigger still. In its demonstration of the power and the possibilities of co-operation in fellowship among the separated Christian Churches it had, quite by accident, given birth to the Ecumenical Movement; and this, as William Temple chose the occasion of his enthronement in Canterbury Cathedral to say, is the new fact in history, which, under God, is now the chief stay of our Christian hope. In his address Temple said:

> As though in preparation for such a time as this, God has been building up a Christian Fellowship which now extends into almost every nation, and binds citizens of them all together in true unity and mutual love. No human agency has planned this. It is the result of the great missionary enterprise of the last hundred and fifty years. Neither the missionaries nor those who sent them out were aiming at the creation of a world-wide fellowship interpenetrating the nations. . . . Almost incidentally the great world fellowship has arisen: it is the great new fact of our era. Yes, here is the one great ground of hope for the coming days—this world-wide Christian fellowship, this oecumenical movement, as it is often called.[1]

It may, in a sense, go back a hundred and fifty years, to the beginning of the great missionary expansion of the nineteenth century, and this, in turn, was God's answer to the Napoleonic wars. But in another most real sense it all began with the Edinburgh Conference, where, at great personal cost, men of all the Churches but one in the world were gathered. There they found that they could co-operate together in fellowship. They had come together to be used, and being made apt and meet for use by the quality of their fellowship, God used them.

Although none of them seemed ever to suspect it, the great and appalling era of what are called Peoples' Wars was about to begin. To missions their contribution, as things turned out, was far less than they supposed. They and their sons and their sons' sons, would all taste of death, and the Kingdom of God, so far from being nearer, would be much further away. Before they met in Edinburgh the die had already been cast. Both Germany and Japan had decided against the Prince of Peace and for the god of war. But the thing they were really used to achieve remains, and has stood all tests. This Ecumenical Movement has since expressed itself in a series of great conferences. All have followed much the same pattern—the long preparation, the arduous work, the expert, authoritative survey of one sphere

[1] William Temple, *The Church Looks Forward* (Macmillan), 1944, pp. 2, 3.

of Christian work after another. But the sum of the separate significances of them all has been fellowship—a state of being with its own intrinsic excellence, and an ultimate good in its own right and for its own sake. When the League of Nations broke, this stayed. Through all the hatreds and sunderings of two world wars it has grown. It constitutes, as it seems, God's answer to two challenges, of insolent evil and of a sundered Christendom.

10

The Church in the First World War
1914–1919

I · *The Military Chaplains*

IN August 1914 all the plans the Church had been making were effaced for years by the outbreak of the first world war. All lives, and the patterns within which they had been lived, were disturbed, changed, and all too often ended. But no one who exchanged civilian clothing for uniform had to face so violent a disturbance of life and habit as did the parish priest when he became a military chaplain. If he really worked in his parish as most did, his life had never been easy. Generally it had been very hard. But he himself was the arbiter between ease and hardness. He inherited the position of his office. He was used to a nearly absolute authority in his own sphere, and the age-long routine of parish life protected him from any challenge of it. Then the war came, and his conscience, or the suggestion of his bishop, called him away from all that, put him on the London train and brought him to the War Office, where he had one of those legendary interviews with the Chaplain-General, Bishop Taylor Smith, and emerged from that ordeal to find himself a chaplain to H.M. Forces, fourth class. He joined his battalion, lived in a mess where he had to prove himself completely, had to manage without nine-tenths of the instruments of ministry, without which he could hardly have got through a single day in his parish, and was set to represent the Church and God to thousands of men, most of whom had a very slight acquaintance with it. He had now to live and work among crowds. He was a member of a community, not all of it at all like-minded to himself. He was a priest, but the army would always be trying to turn him into a cross between an entertainments manager, a wholesale tobacconist, and a welfare worker. And these functions he must certainly fulfil and yet remain a priest, first, last, and all the time. He was by no means necessary by virtue of office to the existence of the army, as he had been to the life of his parish church. He could indeed become necessary, but he must create the necessity himself.

The great thing was that he had nearly always learned to love both man and God. This carried him over the tall barrier of utterly changed habits of life. No war is good for religion, and that war was desperately bad for it. The work of the chaplain was made more difficult than it was bound to be. It seemed more futile to the men than it really was. Most of his work could not be expected to cause much stir or to show results. It was very seldom conspicuous in the sense of being done so much in the open that notice was bound to be taken of it. The number of men under his care was so great that most men did not come intimately into touch with him, even if he stayed long with the same unit, which he rarely did. The mass of men saw him actually at work only in the less attractive moments of his ministry, at compulsory church parades.

Actually it was not quite so simple a matter to get appointed a Chaplain to the Forces as the foregoing paragraphs suggest. There was but little co-ordination between the Chaplain-General's office and the bishops. It was difficult to get from the War Office an exact statement of how many chaplains were wanted, and the bishops, on their side, were hampered by the continuous threat that the clergy might be called up like all other men. Most of the clergy would have welcomed it, and the bishops did not care flatly to oppose it, but contented themselves by pointing out the self-evident fact that parish churches had a vital part to play in war just as in peace. It was thus difficult to the point of impossibility for a clear, understandable policy to be adopted; and the Archbishop noted in December 1914 that the appointment of chaplains was still 'chaotically unsolved'.[1] Even by 1917 the chaos remained, for the Chaplain-General's Office had no proper system of filing and keeping a record of the applications of the clergy and the recommendations of the bishops.[2] In view of all the difficulties, it was as surprising as it was creditable that whereas in 1914 there were only 113 chaplains (of all denominations) serving with the Forces, in November 1918 the number had risen to 3,480. Of these, 1,937 were Anglican priests. In all, no fewer than 3,030 Anglican priests were commissioned as chaplains during the war, of whom eighty-eight were killed in action, or died on service.[3]

The difficulties of becoming a chaplain were still greater if the priest happened to be a known Anglo-Catholic. Bishop Taylor Smith, the Chaplain-General, was hardly sympathetic to such, and had no glimmering of an understanding of their position. The war was but two months old when Lord Halifax sniffed out the scandal of this discrimination, and he, the English Church Union, and the *Church Times*, started to give tongue. First he tackled Lord Kitchener, who sent him a most cordial but a non-committal reply. Then he wrote to the Chaplain-General. He said that

[1] Bell, *op. cit.*, vol. II, p. 751.   [2] *Ibid.*, p. 848.   [3] *Ibid.*, p. 850.

soldiers were now civilians in uniform, and should have the same religious privileges in the army as they had enjoyed at home. As for those in France:

There must be hundreds and thousands of men who would wish to make their confessions and receive Holy Communion before going into action.[1]

But there were not enough chaplains, and of those there were, all too few were skilled and practised confessors. But the Chaplain-General coldly replied:

Having to cover all sorts and conditions of Churchmen in the army and with a desire to help all and hinder none, I make it a rule to appoint Catholics—men who will not be party men, but loving and considerate to all. An extremist is out of place in the Army.[2]

It was not very reasonable, perhaps, to expect that Halifax's and Taylor Smith's views of what constituted a catholic priest should coincide. By September 1915 Halifax was writing to the Secretary of the English Church Union, '*That* Chaplain-General has got to be got rid of';[3] and the *Church Times* made this its signature tune. It was taken up with strength, but with less violence, by the Bishop of London in Convocation;[4] and the Archbishop himself had no little sympathy. But he solved the problem in his own quiet way of having Bishop Gwynne of the Sudan appointed Deputy Chaplain-General, with full charge of the chaplains in France. After that there was very little more trouble, for Gwynne was loved and trusted by all alike.

The policy of the Chaplain-General's office about the appointment of Anglo-Catholic priests as chaplains did not, however, prevent a high proportion of the priests of such communities as Mirfield and Kelham from becoming chaplains. For them the transition was perhaps less severe than for others. They lived their lives under communal discipline, and they were necessarily more accustomed to the kind of hardness which army life involved. The letters which the Mirfield fathers who were serving as chaplains wrote home were all printed in the community magazine, and its back numbers give a vivid picture of what a chaplain's life was, as its best examples lived it.

In the early days of the war, while the new army was still training in England, the chaplain's main field of action was usually the big marquee tent. Its equipment was rudimentary, scratched together and scrounged from a hundred sources; and if the successful chaplain was not exactly a thief, he certainly had to be expert as a beggar and a borrower. There would be rough tables dotted about, each one covered with green baize, scrounged from somewhere or other, so that they could be used for writing letters or playing cards. Forms encircled the tent, and were placed across it where there was room for them; and there was a stage with a piano, and an empty

---

[1] Lockhart, *Halifax*, vol. II, p. 247.   [2] *Ibid.*, p. 248.
[3] *Ibid.*, p. 248.   [4] Bell, *op. cit.*, vol. II, p. 761.

bacon box for the pianist. Each night there was a concert. There were choruses, and some solos of great sentimentality. Little groups would sit on the platform on their haunches, after the manner of colliers at the street corner in the lunch hour, and chat with the chaplain. At nine o'clock there would be a little service, a couple of well-known hymns, perhaps, and a few prayers.

In France, behind the line, the chaplain also spent his evenings in recreation huts and tents. They were generally Church Army huts. They would arrive in sections, and the chaplain had to get the sections assembled and the hut erected. It meant draining and levelling the ground, and then getting and maintaining a constant, regular flow of stores of every kind, urns, cups, cigarettes, biscuits, writing paper and envelopes, pens and ink, and transport to carry them. 'If once you start this sort of thing', wrote Father King, 'you must see it through to the bitter end at all costs.' Should a chaplain give so much of his time and strength to such work? Father King had no doubt that he should. 'I am more than ever convinced that this is a very real part of the chaplain's work, or rather the Church's work. I think I could see our Lord working in one of these huts. What a hut that would be!'

Experience would seem to endorse the insights lying behind this judgement. Out of such a view of his office came the venture of the Upper Room at Poperinghe, founded in memory of Gilbert Talbot and conducted with so splendid a flair for what was needed by 'Tubby' Clayton; and this in its turn has developed and spread into the world-wide institution of Christian Service known as Toc H. And those who can still bring back to memory the vision of Geoffrey Studdert-Kennedy wearing his chaplain's khaki will picture him most readily in Lady Mabelle Egerton's canteen at Rouen where he presided night after night, beginning always with a spirited version of Mother Machree, and then talking, and talking, and again talking to man after man just back from his leave and pausing to wait for the train back to the line. Then there would be a service, and finally Kennedy would be on the platform as the train for hardship and death waited to start, moving from one carriage window to another with a breaking heart and a smiling face, taking messages, writing down addresses, distributing cigarettes, and bestowing benedictions. Finally the train would pull out, and Kennedy, exhausted, would stagger back to the canteen, slump down into a chair, and Lady Mabelle would have to use every artifice in her considerable repertoire to persuade him to eat. Not all chaplains were giants like these, but the institution of the recreation hut afforded to all of them the essential foundations of a noble ministry.

But in wars men must fight, and where his men go, the chaplain ought also to go. He may not fight himself: but he should be where the fighting is done. Such is his own intense desire, but circumstances, duty and army orders often combine to thwart his desire.

In battle [writes Fr R. L. Barnes of Mirfield, in a handbook for military chaplains] a chaplain has to be in attendance on his aid post. As there are more of these than in trench warfare the assignment of the battle positions of chaplains was placed in the hands of the Senior Chaplain. What generally happened was that the senior chaplains, and chaplains of brigades in reserve served the field ambulance and the casualty clearing stations, and those of the attacking brigades accompanied their battalions. At his aid post from time to time, the padre has to wander off. There may be wounded or dying men who cannot be got down the line; or the stretcher-bearers may be too few, and he can give a hand; or he can be a very careful help and guide to walking wounded, either to or from his aid post; sometimes his presence has a steadying effect on men.[1]

But other pictures of chaplains in action come drifting down the years. There was, for instance, the occasion when the chaplain and the doctor were crawling about no-man's land in the darkness, hunting for wounded men who could not be carried in by daylight. They lost their way, and found themselves in the German lines, whereupon, to their surprised embarrassment, a whole platoon of Germans surrendered to them. They took them back to their own lines, and then resumed their search for wounded men. They found one boy, badly injured, who said, 'Are you our clergy?' Receiving the answer, yes, he put his arms round the chaplain and clung to him; for many hours his world had been painful and friendless.

One of the most memorable pictures of the chaplain in action comes from the letters of Father King of Mirfield. He was with the divisions which first stormed the Gallipoli beaches. In the darkness the soldiers crowded the rails of the transport, waiting in tense silence. No smoking was allowed, nor might they talk. They could only whisper, but they did not, and there was a great hush. How could this hush be used for God? The chaplain passed the word among the thousand waiting men: at a given moment let all join in saying 'Our Father'. The signal was given and as they stood, all prayed. The chaplain said the prayer for pardon and peace, and gave them the 'noble Aaronic blessing'. Then he landed with them, running forward, stumbling, ducking, crouching. 'Now were added the shrieks and groans of the wounded as they fell all around. One feels so helpless, there seems little one can do, so much to be done: a clasp of the hand, a muttered prayer, a drink of water, and that is about all.' The next day the men had to advance over an open plain or be systematically and leisurely slaughtered by shell fire on the beaches. They advanced, the chaplain with them. There was shrapnel all the way, and he had always to be throwing his body flat. They crossed the plain to such shelter as the hills afforded; and there, next day, 'I was able to climb into a crevice of one of the hills and fell asleep from sheer exhaustion.' His battle station was the field ambulance post in the rear, but day after day he made his way across the open plain to get to the front-line trenches. One did the journey by a zigzag crouching

---

[1] R. L. Barnes, C.R., *A War Time Chaplaincy* (Mowbray), 1929, p. 53.

run, for there was always the chance of shrapnel and the certainty of snipers. Having safely arrived at the trenches, there was the journey from bay to bay to talk to the men; and one carried cigarettes and caramels to give them, and the reserved Hosts from which some were communicated. But one put off the return journey across the plain until after dark, reciting Compline by heart as the crossing was made.

All of these, no doubt, were priests of exceptional devotion, enterprise, and ability. But all the evidence suggests that the average level was high, and that the chaplains of the first world war brought to their strange and difficult task the grace of fidelity which their heritage in the Anglican priesthood and their experience of parish life had taught them. They had their just recognition before the war ended. When the Archbishop visited the troops in France:

> I pressed Haig for criticism about the work of the chaplains, but I could not elicit anything except laudation. He was strong on the great value of the changed administrative order which now encourages the chaplains to go forward into the trenches, if they will do so, instead of being, as formerly, kept behind at the casualty clearing stations, or even further back. Haig was enthusiastic about the fine type of young padre now at work in all parts of the line. There was hardly one whom he knew he would wish changed.[1]

But when the war was over they had an undeniably bad press, and a legend grew up uncritically among the writers of war memoirs and war novels that only Roman Catholic chaplains so lived and worked as genuinely to commend their Faith. No doubt chaplains were rather overwhelmed by all that was expected from them. But then who was not, in so dreadful a testing? Did generals or statesmen really match the hour? And who matched it less than the intellectuals who gave themselves so cheerfully and so long to the occupation of fouling their own nest? 'It is only a very limited number of men, *of any sort of class or profession*', wrote Davidson, italicizing the last words, 'who would be fit at such a juncture to do all that is needed.'[2] Taking it by and large, all the evidence suggests that the record of the Anglican chaplains in the 1914–18 war constitutes not the least glorious page of the long history of the English Church. And if this can be shown to be true of the Army chaplains, it was just as true of their naval brothers. These had an easier task in many ways. In battle, they shared exactly the same dangers as their men and had no agonizing choice to make. They did not wear an officer's uniform. And they were generally allowed to stay in a ship far longer than an Army chaplain could stay with a particular battalion or brigade. The fact seems to be that it is not good for a priest to be a chaplain for too long. One of the finest of all chaplains, Father Barnes of Mirfield, reflecting on his experience more than twenty years afterwards, wrote of it:

> May I end with a warning from my own experience. My work at the beginning of my service was far better than at the end. I put much into it and was too young

---

[1] Bell, *op. cit.*, vol. II, p. 783.   [2] *Ibid.*, p. 841.

to know that spiritual power needs replenishing. I steadily became less efficient. I dragged myself round and neglected my prayers. My frequent recreations relieved the sense of strain, but were by no means of a kind to replenish spiritual power. The dead before their Maker who might have been better men if I had been a more faithful priest!—the pity of it grieves me after all these years; and I still plead to God by the Broken Body and outpoured Blood of His Son that He will not count it to their loss and to mine.[1]

If that was true of him, how should it not be true of all others? And it was the latter end, rather than the beginning of the war which was foremost in the consciousness of those who afterwards wrote down what it had meant to them.

There is another side to it. No priest can make himself or his office. He is made by those to whom he ministers just as truly as he is made by the ministrations he brings to them. It is as true of chaplains as of all priests, and perhaps there is a sense in which it must be even more true of them. A priest in a big parish can always fill all his time in ministering to those who are already converted, and can so easily slip into forgetfulness of all those other souls for whom he is responsible before God. But in the army it cannot be so. He lives cheek by jowl with all sorts and conditions, and perhaps very few of them will speak his language, share his thoughts, and accept his values. These constitute his chance, but they are also his cross. In 1914 he stepped straight into a new and often into a spiritually rough world. It would be certain to know nothing of his ecclesiasticism, and to care less; and it was likely that its knowledge of the Christian religion would be slight. By such challenges a Studdert-Kennedy is made, and it is certainly true that the soldiers made him the great priest that he became. Not all chaplains were like him. It was not reasonable to expect it.

The facts about the average soldier's knowledge of Christianity were grim, and the numbers of men in the army who were wholly out of touch with the life of the Church, whether directly or indirectly, were alarmingly high. These facts were made known. In 1916 a committee of the Churches, under the chairmanship of Edward Talbot, Bishop of Winchester, and containing Baron von Hügel as a corresponding member, started to hold an *Enquiry into Religion in the Army*. It was a most painstaking committee and it went about its task in such a way as to make its conclusions trustworthy and authoritative. Evidence was collected from every possible source, and very carefully sifted. The report was published in book form in 1919, but its conclusions were put as adequately and much more briefly in a letter of Bishop Talbot to his son, Neville:

My work is reading the replies to our Interdenominational Questionnaire about the Army and Religion—a saddening and humbling thing enough.

There is an extraordinary unity about the descriptions of the average man; more discrepancy about the numbers, at least, of the superior small minorities.

[1] Barnes, *op. cit.*, p. 9.

One thing that appals me is the mass and bulk of the sensuality (sexual) which seems to lie upon the whole general life of the army; and to make the trenches filthy for good men, with language and obscenity.

I am wondering rather whether some of the Padres have not succeeded more than is reported to us in enlisting the *Comradeship*, of which everyone speaks, as the means of a corporate effort to clear a battalion, say of this generally acknowledged, unrebuked and vile evil.

Our difficulty in the Report in the future will be to be strong enough against this, while yet showing that we realize how 'Christian' in some, and even higher, ways many of these men are by 'natural virtue' and not by Christian profession.

Another thing, of course, is the horrid bulk of evidence that Christianity and the Churches have failed, are disliked, and *not* for righteousness' sake; how extraordinarily little Our Lord is understood, and His 'Grand Entry' into the sinful world and presence in it. The 'deep answering to deep' by Nature and Grace, Conscience and the Spirit of God, man and the Son of Man seems to be so little what it ought to be.

I feel that if I have *any* qualifications for this work it is that I have always had that keynote strong in my mind. It must be the *glory* of a padre's work to put forward some of that; and the *misery* of it to see it so little understood and effective.[1]

In any kind of ministry, whether parochial or military, this glory and misery are mixed in varying proportions. But the experience of this priestly glory and misery is sharper and more intense for the military chaplain in a great war than it is for any but the most saintly among parochial clergy at home. He lives, he rejoices, he suffers with an enhanced intensity. He must the sooner exhaust his spiritual reserves and in the conditions of active service he cannot easily replenish them. This fact was recognized by Bishop Gwynne and the Archbishop of Canterbury, and they set themselves to meet it by setting up, in France, a centre for the resting and renewing of chaplains. It was presided over by Canon B. K. Cunningham and Professor Oliver Quick, and, as might be expected, it was a wonderful success. But there was only one such centre, and there were many chaplains. To them all was given the most difficult job in the world, and only a very few of them had any training for it. The marvel is they did it so well, and throughout the long strain faithfully tended their priesthood.

II · Episcopal Leadership

If the chaplains did not escape criticism, how could the bishops expect to be free? There are not many occasions on which it is allowed to bishops that they are doing as they should. 'We were an assembly of bishops,' once observed Hensley Henson when Bishop of Durham, 'and that circumstance alone sufficed to immerse us in much popular suspicion.' The soliloquy continues: 'I have often reflected on the unpopularity of bishops as a class,

[1] July 24, 1917: Gwendolen Stephenson, *Edward Stuart Talbot* (S.P.C.K.), 1936, p. 228.

and wondered what its true explanation might be.'[1] Both during a war, and in the period of public inquests and post-mortems after the war, it is therefore to be expected that the bishops will become one of the focusing points of the vague resentment and disillusion of a weary and strained people. They are not alone in the company of those who occupy this uncomfortable position, but they are always allotted prominent seats, well in view.

In this respect, the war of 1914 and its aftermath ran true to form. While it lasted, the bishops were accused of being old women, of refusing to fling themselves whole-heartedly into the national war effort, of failing to rage against the Germans with a seemly fury, and of not have a righteous taste for blood. When it was over, the tide of accusation did not cease to flow. Then they found themselves accused of having played false to the mission of their Master to bring peace on the earth. They had fed the fires of hatred. They had done nothing to restrain the nation from meeting atrocity by reprisal. They had used the physical safety of their position to urge young men to join the army, sending them into a hell which they themselves would never suffer. They had joined gladly in the hounding of conscientious objectors to prison. All these charges, and more besides, were included in the indictment which one writer after another drew up.

What is the level of truth and what of falsehood in them? The impression which any fair-minded student of the evidence will get is that during the first world war the Church was blessed with genuinely Christian and unusually wise episcopal leadership, and that hardly ever in history has Lambeth Palace played a more noble part than it did in those dreadful years.

The number of bishops and other church dignitaries who flung themselves into the campagin to persuade young men to join the army seems to have been very small. Every bishop was glad that there should be such recruits, but almost all hesitated themselves to become ecclesiastical recruiting sergeants. Davidson was asked by the Parliamentary Recruiting Committee to join and to sponsor an 'Appeal for Recruits from Religious Leaders', and was dubious indeed as to whether he should do anything of the kind.[2]

When a war begins, and throughout its course, it is a temptation of any well-known Christian spokesman to endorse from a spiritual point of view all the passions of his countrymen. But the bishops as a whole did not shape their speech to add to the fury of the flowing tide, and they said no word to encourage, but very many words to discourage any spirit of national self-righteousness. Gore had no doubt that England fought on the side of the angels, but he entertained even less doubt that this was a perilous position for mortal men. 'If we fought the works of the devil in Flanders, we must remember that a great many of the works of the devil remained

---

[1] H. Hensley Henson, *Disestablishment* (Macmillan), 1929, p. 38.
[2] Bell, *op. cit.*, vol. II, p. 739.

to be destroyed at home.'[1] The war was hardly a month old when he solemnly and publicly warned his diocese:

The thoughts and feelings which patriotism inspires legitimately fill our minds and imagination. But this is not enough. I am sure that if we simply yield our-selves to these thoughts and feelings we shall fall disastrously short of what our Lord would have us think. The Bible is full of patriotic emotion, but even more conspicuously the Bible is full of a great warning against the sufficiency of patriot-ism, against the sufficiency of the thoughts natural to flesh and blood.[2]

Talbot of Winchester took exactly the same line. The judgement had come. And what had called it forth from God? No doubt the Germans had the greater share of the guilt. 'Have we no sin with us, of materialism, of boast-ful confidence in force and wealth of unchristian dislike or contempt for other peoples?'[3] In a charge to his diocese delivered in 1915, he returned to the same theme:

Absorbed in the goodness of its cause, the country was slow to face all that moral championship requires. A good cause may fail for the fault or feebleness of its defenders. Were we prepared to own how much we were responsible, as part of the European Commonwealth, for the odious and unchristian state of inter-national relations which made the war possible and inevitable?[4]

The Archbishop of Canterbury, himself, chose the occasion of a day of Humble Prayer and Intercession in 1915, to preach in St Paul's Cathedral against the danger of 'letting anger—even if it be righteous anger—be fanned and cherished into something like an un-Christian hate'.[5] This single sentence is merely one sample of what the Archbishop was continually say-ing in sermons, speeches, and correspondence throughout the war. When the Cabinet made untrue statements under Government authority about the sinking of H.M.S. *Audacious*, he denounced the Prime Minister to his face.[6] No man did more than he to try to save Roger Casement from the gallows.[7] There never has been an archbishop who was more ready to say and continually to repeat unpopular things.

But these instances are all negatives. There are more positive and much more searching tests. How did the bishops behave when the whole of the press and most of the people were calling for reprisals for the opening of gas warfare, and for the night air-raids on London? And what line did they take about the conscientious objectors to military service—the most detested and the most infuriating group of men in the nation? The occa-sions on which the Archbishop publicly protested against all forms of reprisals were so numerous that it is possible neither to list nor to quote them. He protested most firmly to Asquith in private, and in speeches to

---

[1] Prestige, *op. cit.*, p. 369.   [2] *Ibid.*, p. 370.
[3] Stephenson, *op. cit.*, p. 221.
[4] Edward Talbot, *Aspects of the Church's Duty* (Macmillan), 1915, p. 3.
[5] Bell, *op. cit.*, vol. II, p. 752.   [6] *Ibid.*, p. 753.   [7] *Ibid.*, pp. 786–7.

the House of Lords.[1] He drew upon himself extreme unpopularity, and was the target of violent abuse.

I am regarded [he wrote to Dr R. F. Horton] as the representative mouthpiece of those who object to reprisals undertaken with the deliberate object of injuring non-combatants, and I am in consequence the recipient of a continuous shower of protests, denunciations, and often virulent abuse, from every part of England, especially from London. I am said to be the cause of the Air Raids, to be in league with the Germans, and to be responsible for the death of those who have suffered, and so on. Devout hopes are expressed that I (and occasionally my wife, to whom they sometimes write) may be the next person to be blown to pieces.[2]

The bishops took the same unpopular but Christian line about conscientious objection. Gore, who enjoyed the unique distinction of seeing his commentary on the Sermon on the Mount banned by a zealous Chief Constable, spoke many times in the House of Lords against the treatment of conscientious objectors, though he allowed that many of them were 'among the most aggravating human beings with whom I ever have had to deal'.[3] Davidson gave them all a most sympathetic hearing, and spent day after day trying to help them, and interceding with the Government on their behalf.

There is thus no truth whatever in the charge, constantly and recklessly brought, that the bishops allowed themselves to be Englishmen first and Christians afterwards. The opposite was true, and the war brought hardly a single moral issue in which their leadership failed to be emphatically Christian.

Much of the credit for this must certainly be given to the great Archbishop of Canterbury who, throughout the war, never failed in his judgement of a moral issue, always gave a lead when (and only when) it was needed and never drove the leadership principle to the point at which no voice but his own could be heard. When he took an unpopular stand—and he took very many—he showed the nicest judgement on the right way in which to take it, whether it was an occasion for a sermon, a speech in the House of Lords, a letter to *The Times*, or, in one of those masterpieces of correspondence, a private letter to the minister or official concerned. He neither held his peace about great and complicated issues, nor was he perpetually eloquent about them. All his interventions were carefully considered and dispassionately weighed. For that reason they were immensely influential.

But in that which lay nearest to Davidson's heart's desire during those years, he failed. No one could possibly have succeeded. It is always said of him that the chief end he set himself was to hand over to his successor a united, comprehensive, Anglican Church, not ruined by schism or any

---

[1] Bell, *op. cit.*, vol. II, pp. 757, 777.   [2] *Ibid.*, p. 837.
[3] Prestige, *op. cit.*, p. 389.

such thing. But—united for what? Although fellowship is an ultimate, a good in its own right, quite apart from what can be done with it, the united fellowship of Anglican Christians of which Davidson dreamed was something far more positive than a mere absence of schism. It was for him the fundamental condition of what he always had at heart, his dream of the whole Church giving herself as one to the attack upon evil. That was what mattered to him; and his scheme of values placed the machinations of the devil very high on the list of things which burdened his thoughts and prayers. But evil could only be effectively attacked by a Church uniting in heart and mind to attack it, and the appalling intelligence of the devil could be countered only by a Church set upon that one work and relating every activity to it. A too exclusive concentration of energy upon the domestic differences of the Church of England must not merely withdraw much strength from the assault upon wickedness, but must also go far to deliver the battle into the devil's hands. It was the tragedy of Davidson's life, and especially during the first war, that he could never turn the negative, and, in the circumstances, considerable achievement of avoiding schism into that positive unity of creative fellowship with a scale of values which puts first things first. He tried hard enough, but the parties in the Church would never let him.

This he felt deeply. At a Sunday tea-party at Lambeth in February 1917, the talk took a turn which

started the Archbishop on a very interesting statement as to the important and the unimportant things just then occupying religious minds. He said he could not bring himself to stress the points of liturgical reform and a change in the Canon of Holy Communion as comparable with the fight against evil.[1]

His official letters about such matters, which he was forced to write, were also apt to end with pointed reminders that there were other, and far more important, things to claim ecclesiastical attention. Of the Reservation controversy he wrote to Gore in June 1915:

This particular juncture in national life is quite extraordinarily unfortunate as a moment for our launching upon the Church what would probably be the gravest controversy of our generation. Must it be pressed forward now?[2]

And he followed it with a letter to Bishop Winnington Ingram of London:

I can hardly find words to say how sad I think it to be that men like those advanced skirmishers of yours should force this matter forward at the present moment when our thoughts and prayers are concentrated on other things.[3]

But the most deeply-seated weakness of the ecclesiastical mind was too much for him. It is significant that the two longest of the chapters covering

[1] Bell, *op. cit.*, vol. II, p. 815.   [2] *Ibid.*, p. 808.   [3] *Ibid.*, p. 809.

the first world war in Bell's biography are those dealing with the controversies about the reservation of the Blessed Sacrament and the appointment of Hensley Henson to be Bishop of Hereford. It is unfortunate that the action which forced these issues upon the attention of the people, and worked them up into crises which inescapably claimed for months on end the time and attention of thoughtful Christian people, came from the Anglo-Catholics.

III · *The National Mission of Repentance and Hope*

The first and the greatest fruit of Davidson's anxiety that during the war the Church might put first what mattered most was the preparation and the launching of the National Mission. It was a vast and adventurous undertaking—the most considerable corporate act of the Church of England during the war.

In the first year of the war some of the signs of a coming religious revival had undoubtedly existed. Churches were unwontedly full. In large numbers people came on weekdays to pray silently and on Sundays to worship in them; and several efforts in this diocese and that to hold pilgrimages of prayer, and in other ways to bring people to their knees and to keep them there, had been markedly and significantly blessed. In the autumn of 1915 therefore the Archbishop appointed a committee of twelve priests to consider what ought to be done and to report to him. A proportion of them seemed to be very doubtful whether the signs of the times were to be rightly interpreted as the Archbishop was interpreting them, and very early in the Committee's life, its chairman, Armitage Robinson, wrote to Davidson:

> It was extremely difficult to make any progress in face of the determined pessimism of the Bishop of Oxford and Peter Green. The Bishop maintained that there was a 'rot amongst the clergy' who chiefly desired to flee from their spiritual duties; and that the Church was in such a state that any talk of a Mission to the Nation was quite out of the question. Peter Green was sure that the influence of the clergy on the community was nil.[1]

Such views, however, were not allowed to prevail, and indeed the pessimists themselves changed them, and the committee recommended, and the Archbishops accepted, that in the autumn of 1916 there should be a Mission of witness of the whole Church to the whole people 'to call the men and women of England to earnest and honest repentance of our sins and shortcomings as a nation and to claim that in the Living Christ, in the loyal acceptance of Him as the Lord of all life, individual and social—lies the one sure hope'.[2] It was to take place simultaneously in every village and city in the land, and each diocese was bidden to prepare for it in its own way.

[1] *Ibid.*, p. 768.　　　　　　　　[2] *Ibid.*

The whole Church loyally accepted the charge; and if there were many who doubted in their hearts whether the work of the Holy Spirit could be done in this wholesale way, all but a tiny handful flung themselves into the adventure with all their might. The first thing to be done, the preparation of the clergy, was the duty best performed. Gore, who had been most dubious about the possibility of a whole nation's repenting, and hesitated to use these large words lightly, believed that the phrase 'Corporate Repentance' was something which practising Christians ought to understand, and which the Church very urgently needed. The first stages of the year's preparation must necessarily be devoted to the clergy, and here was a task into which Gore, and all who thought with him could fling themselves with complete enthusiasm. He performed the astonishing feat of taking practically the whole body of his parochial clergy, over six hundred of them, into retreat during the preparation year. He borrowed the school buildings of Wellington, Radley, Bradfield, and Wycombe Abbey for the purpose, and took the retreat at Radley himself. Then, a few weeks later, a fifth retreat was held at Queen's College, Oxford, which Scott Holland took, for such of the clergy as had been prevented by urgent pastoral duty from going to any of the previous retreats. All this greatly encouraged Gore, and he so flung himself into the further work of preparation that he breathed vivid and enthusiastic life into the bones of the whole diocesan organization for the Mission, and through that into the length and breadth of his huge diocese.

The preparation in the diocese of Canterbury was not less thorough. The Archbishop summoned the whole body of his clergy to spend two days and a night in Canterbury, and he gave to them the whole force of his power and the full weight of his grave authority as he spoke to them in the cathedral. His addresses, says his biographer.

were very solemn, very moving, and piercing too. And, as so often with him, a deep note of personal sympathy was struck from the start, with peculiar effect. He felt much, perhaps most of all, for the clergy in the remotest country parishes who found it specially difficult to let the new thoughts, the new conditions, in. 'These parishes make a more anxious, if not a heavier, call on a man's spiritual resources than the busiest town parish makes. . . .' He spoke of the *pathos* of the trust on the nation's part which had led to the exemption from military service of the clergy. . . . He begged his hearers to take strict, deep, most solemn thought, prayer, counsel, as to how far they were answering the trust reposed in them. . . . He brought his clergy face to face with their Ordination vows, and bade them examine themselves as to how far they were faithful messengers—watchmen— stewards in their own immediate work. Looking at the manhood of England, 'what is the proportion of those who feel *active* responsibility as Christians? as Churchmen? When we face these facts, these proportions, is it not a cause of thankfulness, an avoidance of despair, to feel we can say, No, No. It is not that these men are all inaccessible to the stir, the enthusiasm of God's message, or hardened against the Saviour's love, or deliberately deaf to the call. That would be desperate indeed. But it is not so. It is *we*. It is I and I and I who have failed. Give me, by thy grace, O God, power to make a new, redoubled, quadrupled endeavour in Thy strength, and then the Gospel message *can, will* win its way.'[1]

A charge of such quality counts for much, and there is evidence to show how fully the Archbishop achieved his purposes by it. Whether the National Mission as a whole failed or succeeded, there is no doubt that the preparation of the clergy for it gave to them a spiritual power which at the least saw them through the bitter, dark years of the war that were still to come. In point of fact it is impossible cavalierly to write off the National Mission as a total failure, though it has become customary to do so. Certainly the results it obtained fell far short of the hopes of the Archbishop. But it was a great act of witness, undertaken, and at no little cost, by the whole Church at a moment of tremendous crisis in the nation's history.

All this was admirable. But as the year of preparation wore on, two features began to show themselves, and two moods of the Church to disclose themselves, which were as confusing as they were disconcerting. The clergy did indeed repent: there is ample evidence of it. But the subject-matter of this repentance was limited. It did not, for instance, include the sin of partisanship; and this sin, being unshriven, was quickly infused into the efforts made to prepare Church and people. The polemical note had entered in, and though, in the actual Mission it never became the dominant, it could not be struck out, and the harmony was impaired. And if the partisans among the Anglo-Catholics were apt to see the romantic effort of a mission from the whole Church to the whole nation only through their own rather myopic vision, how could it be expected that the various socialist societies could forget their own past and certainly unhappy relations with the 'official' Church? They followed the fashion, and wrote pamphlets for dear life. Many finely stated the obvious facts that the war was the judgement, and the thing judged was the nature of twentieth-century European society. But presently—it was inevitable—these pamphlets turned to the past to regard with some bitterness the failure of Christian Socialist societies to persuade the Church to listen to their prophecies. But it was the Church they blamed, not their own failure to persuade the Church that the things they had said were true:

> The time of criticism is past. The day of action has come. It has been our misfortune to find ourselves in constant opposition to the authorities in the Church, and we have been out of sympathy with our fellow-churchmen. We have been driven for our fellowship outside rather than inside the Church. We have become almost aliens to our Mother's children. Such a state of things is to be deplored. It has been to some of us spiritually disastrous. Thank God the day of better things has come.[2]

[1] Bell, *op. cit.*, vol. II, pp. 771–2.
[2] P. E. T. Widdrington in *The Church Socialist*, April 1916. Quoted from Maurice B. Reckitt *Maurice to Temple* (Faber and Faber), 1947, p. 114.

Again, most natural—but also polemical. Any parochial congregation which prepares for a parochial mission must abstain even from 'natural' controversy during the year of preparation. If, at such a time, it holds inquests on the past, it compromises the present, and it loses the future. The same principle holds good in a national mission.

The scriptural demand for repentance also proved rather disconcerting in its results. The demand was for *corporate* repentance. Individual repentance was well understood among clergy and people alike; and part of this process is a seemly reticence in the formulation of the charges which conscience brings. They are automatically not a subject for casual conversation, still less for any kind of concealed masochism, or inverted self-display. But corporate repentance is not so simple, and in a Church traditionally and dangerously individualist, it is peculiarly difficult to express. What actually happened was that the prophets, and those who aspired to wear their robe, were too often moved to prove the sincerity of their repentance on behalf of the Church—not at all the same thing as corporate repentance, but often passing for it—by 'placarding our clerical failings on every high hill', as Scott Holland grimly remarked.[1] But the uttering of accusations is not the whole stuff of penitence, whether corporate or individual; and an example was set which has been consistently followed ever since, with quite disastrous results. A Church thus constantly abused by those whose first duty to it is love and loyalty is hindered from and not driven to genuine repentance; and the impression is given to the heathen that they will be the better Christians if they stay outside.

On an earlier page it was suggested that the controversies had impaired the harmony of the National Mission. But was that harmony ever there? A mission is an adventure which must be harmonious, but the constituent elements in such a harmony are those who take the mission to the people and the people to whom they take it. In that vital sense there was no harmony between Church and Nation. It was called a Mission of Repentance and Hope. The man in the street understood hope. He had plain need of it. He knew that need. He would accept hope wherever it came from, whether brought by the Church, the astrologers, or the Sunday newspapers. But repentance was quite a different thing. The Christian doctrine of penitence, atonement, and forgiveness is the hardest of all dogmas to explain and to grasp; and the drift of people away from the dogmatic teaching of the Church was so widespread, and had been in motion so long that there could be no real harmony between Church and nation if repentance, on a national scale, and for national sin, was to be in the forefront of the message of the mission. 'What right has the Church to talk to our splendid men about repentance,' demanded Horatio Bottomley in *John Bull*. 'They don't need repentance; they are saints, every one of them. To preach repentance to them is an insult.' The comment was utterly puerile, but that it could be

[1] Paget, *op. cit.*, p. 321.

made, and commonly applauded, was a sign of how little most of the citizens understood of the most fundamental Christian teaching. And if they needed to be taught it, the technique of the huge mission was not the right way of doing it. There were not a few churchmen who realized this, and Hensley Henson's reasons for standing aloof from the National Mission were based on the grim facts of the actual situation. As he gives them in his autobiography they were four:

> It seemed to me that the Church of England was too inwardly divided to make effective corporate appeal to the Nation; that the nature and extent of the indispensable restatement were still too little realized by English Churchmen. . . . Moreover, I did not think that the nation, absorbed by the efforts and distracted by the anxieties and excitements of war, could reasonably be expected to give audience to a religious appeal, however well considered, well informed, and honestly delivered.[1]

In the light of subsequent history it is not possible to gainsay any of these judgements, even though the 'indispensable restatement of the Christian message' has eventually turned out to be quite other than Henson at that time supposed. There is no denying this final comment. 'The slump in religion which the National Mission was designed to arrest has continued.'[2]

Evidence about what had happened during the actual course of the Mission is now strangely difficult to come by. One can still hear stories of the oddities which happened in this church or that; and there were those missioners who whistled up their courage by groaning to their intimates that the whole undertaking had been as ill-managed as possible from above—but, after all, such comments are no more than common form, specimens of that peculiarly Anglican humour which the heathen cannot be expected to understand. But the tremendous preparations, with their concomitant and groaning organization, were duly gathered and expressed in the delivery of the Message in every Anglican pulpit to congregations chiefly composed of the faithful.

And with what result? Before the war ended at least two answers to the question were suggested by those who were in the best position to estimate correctly and to know of what they spoke. In the spring of 1918, the Archbishop of Canterbury wrote:

> Two years ago, in this grave crisis of our nation's history, after much thought and prayer, we called the people of England to a National Mission of Repentance and Hope. . . . The call told: not, of course, universally, but very widely. We found that people were ready to face familiar facts afresh: that a new spirit was breathing upon dry bones: that we must, and could, be up and doing. As we appraised the outcome of the Mission-call five subjects in the life of Church and nation stood out with obvious claim for our rehandling. The character and manner of our teaching: our worship: our evangelistic work: the discovery of

---

[1] Henson, *op. cit.*, vol. I, pp. 177–8.		[2] *Ibid.*, p. 180.

removable hindrances to the Church's efficiency; the bearing of the Gospel message on the industrial problems of today.

Davidson wrote these words in the spring of 1918 in the foreword to the Report of the five commissions he appointed to deal with these five problems. He went on to use language which suggested that the work of these five commissions of enquiry constituted the most abiding result of the National Mission: 'The roadway to right knowledge and effective action is now open.... It is the most important stage of the National Mission.'

Any mission, whether national or parochial, is in some sort an essay in evangelism; and therefore the estimate of the National Mission's success or failure given in the Report of the third of these commissions—on the evangelistic work of the Church—can be regarded as being reasonably authoritative. The members of this commission regarded the mission as 'having been entered upon with the full conviction that it is the will of God'. In its actual course, it proved to be 'not so much a time of harvest as of seed-growing'. Then, on a later page, the Report gives a more considered and deliberate statement of the primary result of the whole venture:

> It is undeniable that during the autumn of the year 1916 (the period of the mission) one idea took possession of the Church of England to a very remarkable degree. There came to the Church a new consciousness of obligation to the service of the nation's highest life.... We now know not only that we of the Church have an imperative duty to our country, but what that duty is. It is to evangelize. ... Upon that evangelistic task the Church must now concentrate its whole thought and activity.

And then, in heavy black type:

> **We desire to see as the means to this concentration a further call from the Archbishops to the Church, summoning it, by the all-powerful aid of the Divine Spirit, to nothing less than the evangelization of England and the English people.**

But, having said that, the Report passed immediately to organization, to ways and means.

> We suggest the establishing in every diocese of an evangelistic council.... These diocesan councils in their turn would be reproduced in miniature in every rural deanery.[1]

It had nothing more to offer—nothing about responding to God's activity, nothing about corporate conversion, no realization of the appalling but relevant difficulty of offering the Gospel not only to individuals but also to corporate concentrations of social power, which in effect characterize the modern state.

---

[1] *The Evangelistic Work of the Church*, The Report of the Archbishop's Third Committee of Enquiry (S.P.C.K.), 1918, pp. 32, 33.

IV · *Life and Liberty*

Thus it happened that the Christian movement which really counted in the Church of England during the war took place in the sphere of organization; and Archbishop Davidson was cheated of his dreams.

The framing and passing of the Enabling Act in 1919, by which the Church Assembly was created and its relationship to Parliament defined, was a very considerable achievement. That is true irrespective of whether one welcomes or distrusts the whole organized ecclesiastical apparatus which the Enabling Act brought into being. What is certain is that the Act was necessary, and of its necessity no one was likely to be so well informed as Archbishop Davidson himself, who spoke thus to a meeting of the old Representative Church Council.

Not once or twice, or five times or perhaps ten times, have I brought before the Ministers in power during the last quarter of a century matters which, big or little, I thought needed attention at the time in the Church's life, and the answer has been again and again the same, 'Probably you are quite right: but with the present pressure upon the time of Parliament and the present attitude of the House of Commons towards the varied work that lies urgently before it, we could never ask the House to give up the days or the weeks that would be necessary.' They did not say, 'We are opposed to it,' or 'We are objecting to what you do,' but rather, 'You are asking a machine to do it, which is already so clogged with work, and work of a different kind, that you are asking an impossibility.'[1]

Thus it was that the sheer pressure upon parliamentary time had again and again made the passage of church legislation—a bill for a new bishopric, perhaps, or for the holding of two adjacent rural parishes in plurality—a matter of not very savoury barter and exchange. In 1913, for example, there was an agreed need to create three new dioceses, Sheffield, St Edmundsbury and Ipswich, and Chelmsford. The money had been subscribed, but the government could not allow time for the proper debating of the Bill, for it had been made clear that it would not be allowed to pass unopposed. But suddenly, to everybody's surprise, and not least the Archbishop's, it was passed during the Archbishop's summer holiday. He asked Lord Hugh Cecil how this had been done, and received answer:

My nephew, Wolmer, on the Friday before the prorogation, suggested that we might oppose, and so prevent the passage of a number of Non-conformist Charity Bills unless we got the Bishoprics' Bill through.

There followed a deal of backstairs work, conducted with great secrecy. The conspirators promised not to oppose fourteen Charity Bills for Nonconformist bodies. They gained Asquith's support. They chose a moment when they knew the chief opponents to the Bill would have already left London for their holidays, and they sprang the Bishoprics' Bill on the

1, *op. cit.*, vol. II, p. 968.

House. Taken by surprise, the members let it through; and thus, as Lord Hugh said: 'The passage of the Bill resulted partly from a Parliamentary deal, partly from the goodwill of the Prime Minister, partly from the absence of the Liverpool members, and of some strong Radical opponents who were abroad.'[1] But it is not thus that dioceses should be created, or by such means that Fathers-in-God should receive their flocks.

The disease which the Enabling Act was designed to cure was as old as the hills, and therefore the story of how the Act came to be framed cannot begin with the activity of the Life and Liberty Movement. It has to go back at least to 1899, when Gore published his book of composite essays, called *Essays on Church Reform*. It was a very influential work, and was much discussed. The vital essay it contained was that by Clement Sturge, who was a barrister, and who attacked the existing system (or the lack of it) primarily from the point of view that it perpetuated the scandal whereby the right of presentation to a benefice was regarded as a piece of property, like a picture or a public house, and could be bought and sold with as little restriction. Sturge himself took the story back to 1870. Many then agreed that the reform of patronage was urgent. Since then

No fewer than twenty-five Bills, dealing with various aspects of the problem, have been introduced into the House of Lords or the House of Commons, only two of which have reached the other House of Parliament. Of these, the most important was the Bishop of Peterborough's Bill, which passed the House of Commons in 1875, mangled and deprived of its most valuable provisions, Mr Stanhope's Bill, perhaps the most statesmanlike and comprehensive of the whole series, introduced into the House of Commons in 1881, the two Bills of the Archbishop of Canterbury, brought forward in 1886 and 1887, and the Benefices Bill of 1896, which, after passing its second reading by a majority of 178, and successfully running the gauntlet of the Standing Committee on Law, succumbed at the report stage to the opposition of a little knot of patronage mongers in the House, aided by some conscientious English liberationists, and the more violent of the Welsh irreconcilables.[2]

The scandal of patronage was thus the chief motive in the minds of many whose vigour was eventually to secure the passing of the Enabling Act. It could not be dealt with unless some such Act was passed; and since the Church Assembly came into being its record in the serious tackling of the patronage scandal has been impressive. The system has not wholly ceased to be scandalous, but, short of disestablishment, as many of its horns and hoofs of wickedness have been shorn as was at all possible.

One effect of all the thought stimulated by Gore's essays was the formation in 1903 of the Representative Church Council. It was a body very similar to the present Church Assembly, with three houses of bishops, priests, and laity; but the power of election was limited to those who had

---

[1] *Ibid.*, vol. I, pp. 644–6.
[2] *Essays on Church Reform*, edited by Charles Gore (Murray), 1899, p. 209.

been confirmed. It was of course a consultative, not an executive body. Its decisions were only recommendations. They had no legal force. But through its agency diocesan conferences had been formed, and parochial church councils existed in many parishes. In the diocese of Winchester in 1915, for example, there were 142 parochial church councils, and the incumbents testified that 136 of them were useful.[1] Few, if any, of the necessary administrative reforms had been wrung from Parliament by the Representative Church Council in the fifteen years of its life. But it had provided an absolutely invaluable training for the whole Church in the working of democratic forms of government, and it had educated the Church to make the habit of consultation before action. Above all, it had provided the necessary pattern of self-government. If there had been no Representative Church Council, there would certainly have been no Enabling Act in 1919.

This Council it was that took the first necessary steps. In 1913 it demanded and secured the appointment of an Archbishop's Commission on the relationships of Church and state. In 1917 this Commission reported, and proposed a scheme for passing church legislation through Parliament which was remarkably like that which the Enabling Act eventually legalized. This report was accepted by the bishops; but the Archbishop, while welcoming it, yet declared: 'it is obvious to anyone that it is impossible to make this a *fait accompli* during the war.'[2]

This warning brought the Life and Liberty Movement violently into the picture, for it was composed of men and women who were not in the least degree convinced of this 'impossibility': far from it.

The Life and Liberty Movement was one of the most remarkable fellowships which have ever changed a Church's history. For this—nothing less—was what they did: without their enthusiasm the Enabling Act would not have been passed. And their enthusiasm was a direct consequence not only of their conviction, but also, and far more, of the high degree of fellowship which bound them together. They were led by William Temple, afterwards Archbishop of Canterbury; H. R. L. Sheppard, then vicar of St Martin-in-the-Fields; and F. A. Iremonger, later Dean of Lichfield. They had first come together as a consequence of the National Mission, united in their conviction that the tasks which the Mission had indicated could not be carried out unless a great measure of legislative liberty was granted to the Church. The report of the Archbishop's commission gave them their chance, and made clear to them their marching orders. They took to themselves a name, the Life and Liberty Movement, and they began operations by holding an enormous meeting in the Queen's Hall in London, on July 26, 1917; at which the following resolutions were urged, and tumultuously carried, with one significant dissentient:

[1] *Aspects of the Church's Duty*, pp. 42, 60.
[2] Bell, *op. cit.*, vol. II, p. 960.

That whereas the present conditions under which the Church lives and works constitute an intolerable hindrance to its spiritual activity, this Meeting instructs the Council (of the Life and Liberty Movement), as a first step, to approach the Archbishops, in order to urge upon them that they should ascertain without delay, and make known to the Church at large, whether and on what terms Parliament is prepared to give freedom to the Church in the sense of full power to manage its own life, so that it may better fulfil its duty to God and to the nation and its mission to the world.[1]

This meeting was historic: it caused things to happen which all subsequent historians are bound to discuss. All the greater pity, therefore, that the only easily accessible account of it which seems to have survived outside the files of the newspapers is the description of it written to Davidson by Hensley Henson. This letter of Henson's, printed in full both in Bell's biography of Davidson and in Henson's *Retrospect of an Unimportant Life*, provides today the only account of the meeting to be easily found by the ordinary student who has neither the time nor the means for proper research.

With a degree of artistry worthy of a better cause, the Dean of Durham set out to make the meeting seem faintly comic, as he reported it to the Archbishop. It was full, but the fullness was composed of 'women' of the 'upper middle class' and 'youngish parsons'. The platform was crowded by headmasters, Rugby, Harrow, and Eton predominating. At the end of the Creed, 'the crowded platform seemed to make the Sign of the Cross unanimously'; and this circumstance 'quite startled' Henson. Nor did the speeches fail to offer him material for denigration. Even Temple had 'not much stuff' in his speech. Maude Royden was 'confused, incoherent, and, when intelligible, irrelevant', Father Carey was 'jocose', and 'Mr "Dick" Sheppard' made 'an ecstatic appeal for enthusiasm'. Being thus very bored, Henson amused himself by mentally sorting the meeting out into its constituent elements. He found them to consist of 'the academic, the feminist, the socialist, the clericalist'; and he commented 'these are not the constituents of an ecclesiastical policy which is likely to be tolerant, or virile, or just, or large'.[2]

The Archbishop himself seems to have written to Temple about the Queen's Hall meeting *before* he saw Henson's letter, for both his letter and Henson's bear the same date. He was far more sympathetic, but hardly more pleased, for he thought that the speeches at the meeting reflected an unjust view of contemporary episcopacy, and complained that they had made 'what the bishops are trying to do a good deal more difficult'[3] by the demand that the present Parliament should be forced either to pass the proposed legislation or to disestablish the Church. A few days later he wrote again to Temple:

[1] *Ibid.*, pp. 961, 962.
[2] Text in Henson, *op. cit.*, vol. I, pp. 207–8, and Bell, *op. cit.*, vol. II, pp. 963–4.
[3] Bell, *op. cit.*, vol. II, p. 962.

Where I think you and the others are mistaken is in your belief that we could, with advantage to the cause of wise reform, take steps at the present moment for propounding schemes to Parliament, or committing thoughtful people who care about the Church's life to a particular and detailed policy. I am mixing for hours on most days of the week with the men prominent in our public life, on whose aid we should have to rely if the changes we want were to be made, and I do not literally know one of them who would share your view as to the practicability of the forward push in an official way at the present moment, when every thought and every ounce of energy is absorbed in England's struggle for its very life.[1]

Thus a triangle of conflicting views on this problem had been disclosed. First, here was the Life and Liberty Movement, echoing most of the views of the Archbishop's Commission, and resting largely on the education of church-people which the mere existence of the Representative Church Council had carried through, but determined to win an Enabling Act for the Church at once and on the spot, wartime or no wartime. Then there were Henson and his friends, no less determined to prevent any such legislation. Finally, there was the Archbishop, whose prestige in the circles of authority was such that each party knew it must win his support or fail. Without him or against him nothing whatever could be done.

The essence of Henson's objections is contained in the one and only constructive remark he made in his famous letter after the Queen's Hall meeting. He called it not 'in any marked degree enthusiastic', and justified his very odd judgement by adding, 'You can't get up much enthusiasm over sectarianizing a national Church.' Historically minded to the depths of his being, and imbued by a curiously formulated but passionate patriotism, what mattered to him was the verdict which history seemed to him to have pronounced on the real meaning and purpose of the Church of England. It was the national Church of the realm, the spiritual home of all true Englishmen; and it was secured in this place by the Reformation, which defined it as both protestant and reformed, and gave to the laity, through Parliament, the final voice in its government. Thus he could write to *The Times* on June 26, 1917:

Is this the way the National Church should be handled? Is the Nation thus to be shut out from concern with the oldest and greatest of its historic institutions? Is the religious settlement which was slowly hammered into shape in the course of 130 years . . . to be hustled out of existence in a few months, during the desperate distractions of a great war, by a handful of enthusiasts who really have but little beyond their enthusiasm to put hand to the task? It is unfair to the Church of England: it is outrageously unjust to the English people.[2]

These are the notes of an appeal which must count for much. Such notes would be heard; there is the stuff of an infectious passion in them. Especially would this be true when it was pointed out—and Henson did not fail to point it out—that when the Enabling Act was passed none but the con-

---

[1] *Ibid.*, p. 965.   [2] Henson, *op. cit.*, vol. I, p. 210.

firmed would have voice and vote in and for the Assembly,[1] and the result must be to catholicize still more ineradicably a Church whose protestant elements were being more deeply overlaid every day. There was, perhaps, but little substance in these complaints. Henson's subsequent change of mind over the necessity of a National Church being an Established Church seems to show it. The first twenty years of the actual working of the Enabling Act, moreover, showed that the fear of a lessening of lay control of the Church was groundless. The real change was to bestow a strong element of democracy upon the ecclesiastical organization. But at the time, none of these developments could be foreseen with any precision; and the stand taken by Henson and his friends looked like constituting, and actually could have erected a barrier so formidable in the path of the reformers that they might not have surmounted it.

As it is, the greatness of the achievement of the Life and Liberty Movement is still insufficiently measured. Their task did not lie in the novelty of what they proposed, except in so far that they never concealed their intentions to lay violent hands on the patronage system. In fact they proposed but little that was new. In a sense they wanted to legalize the long established but voluntary Representative Church Council. The Archbishop's Commission had just urged most of what they were urging. The episcopate unanimously agreed that a way must be found to pass church legislation more expeditiously through the parliamentary formalities; and there were few statesmen in Cabinet, Lords, or Commons who were not ready to concede that this was necessary, and would have failed to look with sympathy upon a workable scheme presented at a feasible moment. So far they were appealing to people already converted.

But they wanted it all done at once. For them, now was the accepted time, now, in wartime, in the life of the coalition Government. Now, not later when things had settled to the slower and less disturbed rhythms of peace, was the moment of salvation. And what they wanted they got. It was a most remarkable achievement—how remarkable can be understood only by someone who considers what the difficulties would have been if a similar piece of important legislation had been proposed in the summer of 1944 by some unofficial group of citizens, with a demand that 1945 must see it all done.

It was a tall order, and in the judgement of those members of the Movement still remaining among us, it would have been utterly impossible to persuade virtually the whole Church to make the demand in tones so loud and prolonged that Parliament was forced to heed them had it not been for one man, William Temple. Bringing to the Movement a reputation already tremendous, moved by a sense of deep conviction of vocation, and resting

---

[1] In fact the suffrage was broadened, and any who have been baptized may have a vote to elect a member of the Church Assembly. This concession to Henson's point of view caused Gore to resign his bishopric.

himself upon the fellowship of very high degree existing among those leading spirits, he 'went out into the wilderness', resigning St James's, Picca-
dilly, £2,000 a year, and one of the foremost pulpits in England, and gave
all his powers and time to the Life and Liberty Movement. It was just the
gesture which was needed, and it *made* the Movement. Thereafter he
travelled incessantly up and down the country, bearing uncomplainingly
the grim discomforts of wartime railway trains, to speak for the Movement
and to stir church-people to demand action. Thus it grew at a pace with
which its members could hardly cope; and they themselves, Dick Sheppard,
Edward Woods (afterwards Bishop of Lichfield), and F. A. Iremonger, and
many others followed Temple's lead, and gave themselves to the work.
By the summer of 1919 they had created such a demand that the Archbishop was able to set himself to use all his unrivalled skill to get a unanimous resolution out of the Representative Church Council, and to pilot,
as only he could have done, the Enabling Act through Parliament. By the
end of 1919 the Act had become law, the New Church Assembly was
formed, and the Church of England had become a tempered democracy.
It had been in fetters, and a framework allowing life and liberty to grow
in the Body of Christ had been constructed. The movement going by that
name had achieved its true aim.

So it happened once again that the contrasting sequences of mood in
Church and state were repeated. Into the period 1900 to 1914 the state
entered with jubilant hope and came to the end of it with the gloomiest
forebodings, while the Church regarded the new century with apprehension
which, by 1914, had changed to a mood of greater confidence. And while
the people as a whole began the war with cheerful optimism and ended
it with all the depression of disillusion; the Church, having from the beginning taken a far more realistic and sober view of what must come, came to
the end of the war with a new hope. In the teeth of every human probability,
a great piece of legislation was on the Statute Book. It must make a great
difference to every parish in the land. There would at least be a real chance
to end the ancient abuses in the Church's organization, to make the position of the parson appreciably less economically intolerable, to offer to the
men returning from the army a Church more fashioned into the ideal of
democracy, and containing within itself more of the elements of institutional
freedom which they had fought so long and endured so much to save. A
wider panorama opened out, and a new and better chance was at hand.

PART TWO

1919–1939

11

The Waste Land after the War

I · *Disenchantment in the Nineteen-Twenties*

THE LONG hurricane of the 1914 war had now blown itself out, but for many years to come there would be little peace in the world and no enchantment in the air. By Great Britain the storm had been ridden, and we had just managed to master it, but at the cost of the sacrifice of the most promising young lives of a whole generation, whose loss crippled the next twenty years. It was a tremendous feat, one of the greatest in this nation's long history, to have survived such a storm, and won such a war. But this achievement was one in which we seemed to take but little pride, and for many years after 1918 those who had voices to speak and pens to write used them to express and deepen the contemporary scene of utter disillusion. Almost at once after the end of the war, and continuously for years, Englishmen steadily mocked their own sacrifices, stripped themselves bare of the laurel wreaths they had won, the politicians and the generals of their reputations, and even the dead of their renown. We were not comfortable with the remembrance of greatness. The strain had been too long and too heavy, and the losses too catastrophic for human flesh to bear and be the same.

Those who were left behind were drained and weary. Almost at once the tide of disillusion came flooding in, its waters stained by the dark froth of a resentful turbulence, and leaving behind it on the shore the dead wreckage of a cynicism which mocked every liberating cause. Soldiers mutinied and workpeople struck. Of the negotiations at Versailles nothing was heard that was good. The General Election of 1918 was most discreditably conducted, and it produced a parliament of which no subsequent historian has ever found a good word to say. A peace to make war certain was made. An ignoble miasma fell upon public life. It was not realized at the time, but in fact we were entering the dark corridor of the twenty shabbiest and most disastrous years of English history.

Everybody was on the make, so everybody believed he had been cheated —by the 'They' who, for the first time in English writing, became the ominous but convenient surrogate for personal responsibility. Demobilized soldiers reckoned they had been done out of the jobs and homes they had been promised. Still serving soldiers felt cheated of the security of their own Service when it came under the axe of economy and retrenchment. The ardent and the generous resented the non-arrival of the better world they had been too glibly promised. The wage-earner saw no improvement in his condition. The intellectuals complained that they had no faith to live by. All alike were made to realize with bitterness that they had won no settled and pacified world in which to bring up their children. Everybody had given up so much for so long that few indeed were inclined to sacrifice any more. 'Of those who survived only a small proportion took to public life; the majority turned resolutely to private business and stayed there.' But the many expected the few to produce at once and on the spot the new world of comfort and plenty with all its appurtenances.

How shallow (remarked one of H. G. Wells' most voluble characters) was our conception of Reconstruction! was every conception of Reconstruction I ever encountered! To most of the hopeful people of that time Reconstruction meant simply—all they wanted—at once. Labour, for example, demanded an immediate shortening of hours and a rise in wages, and was blind to any necessity for intermediate phases or auxiliary constructive effort. In England trade after trade struck vigorously and got its advances, its eight hour day, and crowded off at once to see the cinema and football matches, leaving the working out of the Millennium to anyone else who chose to bother. Nobody chose to bother.[1]

The millennium, therefore, showed no signs of arriving; far from that, England was a more uncomfortable and distressing place to live in during the first five of the twenty inter-war years than it had been for many generations. Widespread disenchantment passed into disillusion, and disillusion into resentment.

It is easy to say that this turbulent bitterness was exaggerated and unfair. So it was. But whether just or unjust, that is how many people were feeling. The literature of disenchantment flooded the presses for some years. Poets and novelists, essayists and historians, all joined together to chant the dirges of disillusion. By their sufferings, their endurances and their achievements in the fighting, many had earned their right to a respectful hearing as they interpreted the nation's mood. But they were followed by a host of imitators whose credentials were less impressive.

Among most ordinary people whose actions were determined more by instinct than by reasoning this resentment showed itself in a dark suspicion of all institutions with long traditions behind them, or which they could identify as belonging to that old world from which they had been promised

[1] *The World of William Clissold*, vol. II, p. 334, quoted in *The Future of the Church*, edited by Sir James Marchant (Longmans, Green), 1926, p. 243.

(or were invincibly convinced they had been promised) an escape. From those who are ridden by a vague but haunting suspicion not much good can be had. The whole social life of England was cursed by an ubiquity of suspicion, while the sense of disillusion, so constantly underlined by the consistently discouraging facts of the political and economic spheres, was a slow poison spreading through all veins and arteries. Two decades which saw the growing impotence of the League of Nations, the resurgence of totalitarian dictatorship, the constantly and evidently fumbling political leadership of the nation, the general strike, the economic crisis and the prolonged mass unemployment it caused, the abdication of Edward VIII, the Munich crisis, and at last the opening of another world war, were evidently overcrowded by disaster. No historian will ever be able to write happily about English history between 1919 and 1939, and it would be hard to find any other period of twenty years in which more people were unhappy, or more people also believed that their unhappiness was neither necessary, nor of their own making, but due to some betrayal of the powers-that-be, the custodians and vested interests of the old order, or to the indifference of God himself. Thus a weary nation which is not given time to rest and recover after long strain is bound to feel.

II · *Restlessness in the Church*

It was a difficult field for the Church of England to sow and reap in; and the Church, being composed of perfectly ordinary English folk, had to perform this husbandry while it was itself hampered by the presence of exactly the same weariness and tensions. The Church was not less embarrassed than the nation by the bitter quarrel between the revolutionaries and the traditionalists. The same suspicion, the same disillusion as was in the nation as a whole ran through the life of the Church. It was mercifully less disastrous, because in the Church there was always the parish church, the service of which claimed the majority of clergy and laity, and in the parish there is a ceaseless pressure of pastoral need hammering at the door day and night, which simply must be met however angry one is with the bishops. This fact it was which kept many clergy and laity going, and gradually laid to rest the bitterness which was in them.

The very first meeting of the new Church Assembly (it was called the National Assembly of the Church of England in those days) on June 30, 1920, proved to be an occasion on which these tensions were exhibited. From the early days of the Life and Liberty Movement there had been a subterranean cleavage between those of its members who desired the Enabling Act because it would facilitate organizational reform and increase efficiency and those who believed it would revitalize the whole Church throughout the entire range of its life and witness. As long as the Movement's purpose was to get the Enabling Act passed this cleavage remained hidden. When it had become law the cleavage came to the surface and in the first meeting of the new Assembly it was plainly seen.

It was an historic moment. 'It is a great hour in the history of the Church and the people of England,' declared the Archbishop of Canterbury. The Assembly might still be in the embryonic stage, but 'the actual pulsing life has already begun, and it is part of the constitution of England.' He then gave them a felicitous quotation:

> there is a day in spring
> When under all the earth the secret germs
> Begin to stir and flow before they bud.
> The wealth and festal pomp of midsummer
> Lie in the heart of that inglorious hour
> Which no man names with blessing: but its fruit
> Is blessed by all the world. Such hours there are

'and this', he said, 'is one of them.' First of all they must shape and fashion the machinery of the Assembly, so they proceeded to appoint a secretary and a treasurer, and, after much argument about its numbers and about the nice meaning of the word 'provisional', a Provisional Standing Committee. On this committee ten laymen were appointed to serve, and of these only two were without titles, Mrs Creighton and Mr T. W. H. Inskip, K.C. The comment made that 'the Old Gang had collected all the positions of influence' may have been over suspicious, but was not unnatural. After that there was some heat about the appointment of the Legislative Committee. The Archbishop of York said that the Lord Chancellor and the Speaker of the House of Commons had declined to appoint the Parliamentary Ecclesiastical Committee (though required to do so by law) until they had seen the character and membership of the Church Assembly Legislative Committee, and, amid loud protests from the floor, it was agreed that the Provisional Standing Committee should choose and present the names.

This put the members of the Provisional Standing Committee in a very strong, even in an almost impregnable position, and very soon members began to protest that this was not what they had meant in their work for the Life and Liberty Movement. Miss Minna Gollock got up and said that if this sort of thing was all that the Assembly had been elected to do then she and many others would never have lifted a finger to bring it into being; and the Bishop of Southwell supported her by bearing witness to the new hope and enthusiasm created in the Church by the passing of the Enabling Act.

Too much can be made of just one meeting of the Church Assembly, and that the very first. But it was symptomatic of the deepest and most inward trouble of the Church in those years. It caused great disappointment, particularly to many of the leaders of the Life and Liberty Movement to whom it owed the fact that it existed at all. They had hoped for a New

Deal for the Church. What it seemed as though they were to be offered was the Old Deal, made slightly more efficient.

The returning military chaplains have sometimes been described as bursting with optimism about the possibilities of reform in the Church, and carrying about with them the delusion that the country was ripe for a great spiritual revival. But the evidence is all the other way. Such as it is, it tells of spiritual fatigue and bewilderment. In January 1919 Archbishop Davidson toured France and Germany to hold conferences with the chaplains. He found an extraordinary mixture of suggestions, on the one hand for equalizing clerical stipends and for covering the land with companies of mission priests, and on the other even for the organizing of a general strike of chaplains who would refuse to come home until their demands for the radical reform of the 'official elements' in the Church were met. Their mood was difficult and suspicious, and although Davidson's sympathy did much to allay their bitterness, they found it far from easy to come home to work again in the still unreformed ecclesiastical system and to fit contentedly into the old routines of parish life.[1] Their deepest loyalties had held them fast and at last brought them home through all the neuroses and complexes caused by their intense spiritual loneliness during the years of war. The treadings of many of them had well nigh slipped, and were not to be steady for some years. But what saved them from slipping completely were, under God, two things, the wonderful work done in Flanders by Toc H under P. B. Clayton, and also the work, the friendship, and the love of B. K. Cunningham in the Chaplains' School at Blendecques. In two years, nine hundred chaplains had passed through it and 'recovered their sense of proportion . . . and their obsessions fell into place'.[2] Without Clayton and Cunningham the situation would have been twenty times more difficult than it was when the war was over and the chaplains made the hard transition to peace, an embittered country and an archaically organized home Church.

Many plans were in the air to ease the situation. The reports of the Archbishop's several Committees of Enquiry after the National Mission had been published, and had done much to point out the ways in which the Church must go. The Church Assembly existed, and held out the hope that at least the grossest of the archaisms of organization would be swept away. The setting up of the Knutsford Test School for Service Ordination Candidates promised a relief in due time to heavily over-driven incumbents. There were paper schemes for doing away at last with the age-old scandal of grinding clerical poverty and for some equalizing of clerical incomes. The Lambeth Conference of 1920 served the Church magnificently in its Appeal for Unity, which stirred the imagination of Christendom at the moment when all Churches alike found imaginative enthusiasm the hardest

[1] Bell, *op. cit.*, vol. II, p. 943.
[2] John R. H. Moorman, *B. K. Cunningham, A Memoir* (SCM Press), 1947, p. 92.

of virtues. In the first years of the peace these things were promised, and the instruments for fulfilling their promise were in process of being fashioned. In the pages which follow we shall see how far all these promises came to fruition. Most of them did. But at that moment in the Church, as in the state, it was not easy to persuade men to believe much in promises; and everybody could see that time, much time, must pass before they could be fulfilled.

The spirit which specially characterized the rank and file clergy and laity of the Church throughout the period was perhaps most correctly suggested by the title of a celebrated book by a famous priest, Dick Sheppard, *The Impatience of a Parson*. It is true that there were more radically impatient souls among those who staffed and served the Church than there had been for many generations. Thus the air rang for year after year with criticisms of the Church uttered by those who were its members and of this denigration *The Impatience of a Parson* was a comparatively mild example. As the years passed it almost seemed as though some Anglicans had been born with a spiritual muck-rake in their hands, and were never tired of proclaiming how dead and stinking the Anglican Church was, and of accusing it of every sort of betrayal of its Master. Yet they rarely left it. They carried on their campaigns of vituperative denigration at the tops of their voices, and though it was all very unseemly, yet they did it because there was a fire burning within them. It is, in fact, a strain to belong to the Anglican Church, and loyalty both to it and to Christianity in general must involve some degree of tension. For some passionately loyal Anglican souls the tension was more than they could bear; and feeling acutely uncomfortable, they lashed out at the nearest and handiest target. It was inconceivable that they should criticize our Lord, and they did not care (or dare?) to criticize the twentieth century. It is no doubt always true that there is a horrible contrast between the splendour of Jesus and the actual behaviour of the Body of Christ on earth, but to make the abuse of his Body the Church testify to the reality of one's loyalty to our Lord was to disqualify oneself from understanding wherein the greatness of the Church lies. They had all their knowledge about our Lord, about prayer, worship, and sacraments, at the hands of the Church they abused so wildly and incessantly: and the best of them acknowledged it.

In the generalization that the Church of England in the twentieth century is the spectacle of an essentially mature Church struggling to shepherd and to redeem the citizens and institutions of an essentially adolescent and raw era, we come near to baring the heart of the tension. It was a strain to be a citizen and a churchman. This strain was at its most intense between 1918 and 1939. Since then it has eased in various subtle ways, and the phenomenon called Anglicanism has steadily asserted itself as having, under God, the first claim on the loyalty of churchpeople. They had to learn that the Anglican Church claimed from them not derision and mockery but love and loyalty if they would serve her, and they were not accustomed so to express themselves. It was the reverse and the hard side of the truth that the Catholic Church in every part, and not least the Anglican part, is immortal with the eternity of the Body of Christ; and the leading achievement of the Anglican Church in this period is that it has steadily imposed this view of itself upon its members, and transcended every party view less wide than that of Anglicanism itself. This process was certainly necessary, but it was not without pains and tensions for many.

Here, again, was seen the enormous power to steady those temporarily uncertain of their moorings and assailed by bitterness of spirit possessed by a Church with a strongly marked pastoral tradition. It may be exemplified in the ecclesiastical odyssey of one of the greatest of her children, Evelyn Underhill, as her letters reveal it.

She did not care a straw about ecclesiastical statesmanship, and she repudiated most of its methods of expression,[1] but she had to make up her mind about Anglicanism and its value to herself. Her published letters show how the problem perplexed her, how her views on it changed and matured, and what the value of her membership of the Church of England was for her. In May 1907 she was, perhaps, just a little impatient with a correspondent who had raised the question of Anglicanism, and she summarily dismissed it as 'a slightly diluted Catholicism'.[2] In 1911 she had been sure for five years, and was still sure that the Roman Catholic Church 'was my ultimate home'. So strong was this conviction that 'to join any other communion is simply an impossible thought', and 'to have any personal dealings with Anglicanism seems for me a kind of treachery'.[3] But twenty years later, by 1931, her position had completely changed, and she explained it to a Roman Catholic correspondent thus:

> I feel I owe you an explanation of my 'position' which must seem to you a very inconsistent one. I have been for years now a practising Anglo-Catholic, and solidly believe in the Catholic status of the Anglican Church, as to orders and sacraments, little as I appreciate many of the things done among us. It seems to me a respectable suburb of the city of God—but all the same, part of 'greater London'. I appreciate the superior food, etc., to be had nearer the centre of things. But the *whole* point to me is in the fact that our Lord has put me *here*, keeps on giving me more and more jobs to do for souls here, and has never given me orders to move . . . Of course I know I might get other orders at any moment, but so far that is not so. After all He has lots of terribly hungry sheep in Wimbledon, and if it is my job to try and help with them a bit it is no use saying I should rather fancy a flat in Mayfair, is it?[4]

[1] See e.g. her letter of May 5, 1941: 'I never go to meetings nowadays nor, I fear, have I much belief in their usefulness. All this discussion about a "Christian Society", a "new Christian England" etc., seems so entirely on the surface, doesn't it? . . . The new life, when it comes, I think, will not be the result of discussions, plans and meetings, but will well up from the deepest sources of prayer.' *The Letters of Evelyn Underhill*, edited by Charles Williams (Longmans, Green), 1943, p. 307.
[2] *Ibid.*, p. 63.   [3] *Ibid.*, p. 125.   [4] *Ibid.*, pp. 195, 196.

Two years later, in March 1933, she was writing to another friend, and her position was still the same. Rome was attractive 'because it *does* understand and emphasize worship'. But she would obey her orders and stay where she was. 'We are here to feed His sheep where we find them, not to look for comfy quarters.'[1] It is a homely phrase but it exactly describes the great tradition of pastoral responsibility which in every generation carries the servants of the Anglican Church through their personal crises, through their moments of irritation with the Church, and keeps them within it as loyal members. Whatever happens, and though the very skies fall, there are still sheep to be tended. It is our office in the Church which gives us our charge to tend them. It is unthinkable that we should desert them, or let them down. For their sakes, therefore, we stay in our quarters, and discipline ourselves to talk less about our discomforts. Such thoughts as these must have rescued from ecclesiastical bitterness hundreds of churchpeople, and steadied them. The same thing is true of those moments of great perplexity when the pressure of trends, and tendencies, and events so enlarges opportunity and complicates duty that we can hardly discern between our right and left hands. It was so throughout the twenty years 1919 to 1939, and it is so still. But nothing that can ever happen in the world can absolve the Anglican Christian from fidelity to his pastoral charge, and this thought again steadies him for in the time of the breaking of nations there is always the anchor of clear knowledge of what the next pastoral job is.

III · *Giants and Heroes*

To read many of the documents by which the Church sought to stir and guide its witness during those twenty years, and to stretch memory backwards to recall the events of those years and the persons who shaped them, is to be left with two main impressions. These are that the Church was served by an unusually large number of men and women of the highest quality, a few of whom were giants; and that the events with which they had to deal were more than usually bewildering in their variety and complexity.

Certainly there were giants in the land. A single generation of the Church which saw on the throne of Augustine first Randall Davidson, then Cosmo Gordon Lang, and finally William Temple, could not be said to lack leadership of a very high order. As the years pass by one has less and less desire to quarrel with the judgement that Davidson was one of the two or three greatest of all the Archbishops of Canterbury. If towards the end of his years the firmness of his grasp faltered a little, as it seemed to do over the matter of the Revised Prayer Book, he had nevertheless raised his high office to a pinnacle of eminence and a height of authority which it had never before known. It provided the whole Anglican Communion with a

[1] *Ibid.*, p. 210.

badly needed centre of gravity, and through the influence of Lambeth when he reigned there the Church of England was held together and its unity was intensified. 'Certain it is that in Randall Davidson's tenure of the archiepiscopal see the office of Archbishop of Canterbury acquired a commanding position in the communions of Christendom unprecedented in the previous history of the Church.'[1] The judgement is not a word too strong.

This office he handed to his brother of York, Cosmo Gordon Lang, who might well have quailed as he contemplated the standard set. Probably he did quail for in his heart he was a humble man. To some he gave the impression of prelacy, but it was the impression of something set only skin deep in him, if indeed it was there at all. The true man was displayed when he spoke, as he sometimes did, of his unworthiness for the office he held, and when, near the end of his life, he said he must retire because he needed a few years to make his soul's peace. His courage was great, and it came out when he publicly rebuked the entourage of the Duke of Windsor just after the Abdication. It made him violently unpopular, as he knew it must, and it is difficult to think of another archbishop who would have dared to speak publicly in such a way and at such a moment. He was perhaps the most polished orator of his generation. On the occasion of the marriage of the Duke and Duchess of Kent, he gave an address which was a classic of its sort, and his lovely voice graced the beauty of the words he chose. He was an archbishop with whom people came first and public affairs second, and he had a wonderful discernment and patience. He was, for instance, Dick Sheppard's constant anchor, offering him a friendship which never wearied and never failed, and an understanding which that tormented soul could find nowhere else. In a very black moment of his life Basil Jellicoe, too, found great comfort and strength from the Archbishop. All who knew him well thanked God they did.

But if any one man can be said to have towered over all his contemporaries and to have dominated the Church of his day, that man was undoubtedly William Temple, successively Bishop of Manchester, Archbishop of York, and Archbishop of Canterbury. He would never admit that it was due primarily to himself that the Enabling Act was passed, and likely enough it would have been passed without him, but certainly not so quickly. He always used to say that the creating of the Life and Liberty Movement, and therefore the passing of the Enabling Act was due more to Dick Sheppard than to any other man. Indirectly, the Church Assembly, on this view, owes its existence to Sheppard, which is an ironical thought, seeing how constantly the Assembly infuriated him. But the two great conferences at Birmingham and Malvern, which did so much to gather together, to intensify, and to guide the Church's thinking on the relationship between religion and sociology, might never have been held without Temple's

[1] Bell, vol. II, p. 1153.

initiative or succeeded without his chairmanship. Without them, the witness
of the Church would have been sadly impoverished. But that is true of every
single thing which Temple ever did, and the list of his undertakings is staggering in its variety and its range. Other men besides him have done much
to establish the inevitability of the connection between Christian theology
and social order. He was not the only evangelistic apostle to the student
world of his day; and there were others besides himself who could give
retreat addresses and write devotional books of the highest spiritual order.
The Church had other philosophers, though not many. He was by no means
the only great diocesan bishop of his day, though no other has ever given
presidential addresses to his diocesan conferences of Temple's quality. But
if he was not absolutely unique in each and all of these fields, he was a
master of them all, and he was absolutely the only man who was. No one
but he, moreover, could have been quite so fully the architect of the
Ecumenical Movement. In his time he was the real leader of the whole of
Christendom lying outside the Roman obedience. He spoke with authority,
and everyone conceded that authority, in every one of these spheres of
Christian witness, and in others as well. We still stand too near to him to
attempt to decide the exact differences made to the witness of the Church
because Temple towered over it. But they are evidently very considerable.
The presence of William Temple was the greatest of all the assets the Church
possessed as she marched through a profoundly difficult era.

Nor was the Church without priests who by their preaching and living
had the power to quicken the hearts of vast masses of ordinary people—
men who were indeed popular preachers but who never became glib or
cheap. Such were Dick Sheppard of St Martin-in-the-Fields and Geoffrey
Studdert-Kennedy of the Industrial Christian Fellowship. These two were
not alone in this power but no one else had quite the same pre-eminence.
Of each it was true to say that the crowd would throng to suffocation any
church or hall in which they were billed to speak. Each of them was on fire
and burned up with the love of Jesus Christ, and each had a love for all his
children, most of all of the erring and luckless ones, that would never let
them rest. Yet they were very different men. Sheppard's genius was for
friendship. He could make a man or woman his friend for life after only
five minutes conversation, and it would be no surface friendship. It would
touch the depths of life. Kennedy, on the other hand, was not immediately
at ease with those who met him casually, and he could sit withdrawn and
silent for hours together. But his preaching of the Gospel was possibly the
finest, the most memorable and moving, of any heard so far in English pulpits in this century. It was sometimes slangy, but it also often contained
passages of such beauty that one could hardly tell whether they were poetry
or prose. It was not always in 'language understanded of the people' and
yet they always understood it and listened with breathless eagerness. Behind
all he said there was a profound and coherent system of philosophy. His

sermons went well into a book, as Sheppard's could not have done. To Sheppard on the other hand the Church owes much of the grand chance it has always had to proclaim the Gospel by broadcasting. His services were among the first to be broadcast and he himself had a great flair for broadcasting, a medium which Kennedy could probably not have used successfully. Both were men who carried about with them the visible stigmata of suffering, their own, but far, far more of other people's. Each had developed to a remarkable degree the power of inspiring trust in others, and wherever they went there were those who took one look at them and murmured, 'That man I know would understand my trouble.' Thus each carried on his shoulders an unimaginable, crushing burden of the woes of others. They both died what were, to human seeming, untimely deaths; and yet both had reached the point where they simply could not have gone on any more, dragging their weary bodies round the country. The wealth they gave in the Church to the cause of Christ cannot be estimated, but it was very great.

Besides its leaders and its prophets a Church must have its theologians, and of these the Church was not starved. Perhaps the most influential of them all was Clement Hoskyns—a judgement presently to be defended. Besides him there was Oliver Quick, a master of analytical theology, whose forte it was to disentangle the different threads of truth in a dogma and then weave them together in a new synthesis. His two great books, *The Christian Sacraments* and *Doctrines of the Creed*, quickly became classics of the art of theological integration. Father Lionel Thornton, of the Community of the Resurrection, reached far fewer people than did Quick, for he wrote for the pure scholar. But his book *The Incarnate Lord* was one of which other theologians speak reverentially, and most competent judges regard it as one of the two or three outstanding theological works of the period. It went far towards cutting a new road through a jungle down which scientists and theologians could walk hand in hand. In a far more popular way the same task was assayed by B. H. Streeter, both in his lectures at Oxford, and in his best known book, *Reality*. It had a very wide circulation, and did much to commend the Faith effectively to educated agnostics.

The theologians were matched by men and women upon whom another vocation was laid. It might be called the vocation of keeping alive the social conscience of Christians. There was a long roll of those who worthily bore that charge to the Church's good. Basil Jellicoe and Conrad Noel, James Adderley, Robbins and Jenkinson of Leeds, and William Temple were but a few of them; and among those who are alive still there are Maurice Reckitt, and Canon V. A. Demant. The same period saw the veritable prince of all principals of theological colleges, B. K. Cunningham of Westcott House, Cambridge, at the very height of his power. Among the many other vocations of which the modern Church stands in need that of the professed religious life of monastery and convent is conspicuous. In this field too there was uncommon distinction. A generation which saw Frere and Talbot at Mirfield, Kelly at Kelham, and Mother Maribel at Wantage could not regard itself as starved of monastic and conventual superiors of a high order.

But perhaps the outstanding feature of the leadership given to and within the Church during those twenty years was the rising prominence of laymen. No clerical author taught the Church half so much about mysticism as Evelyn Underhill: few taught us so much about worship. It is quite possible, too, that in her work as a director of souls and a retreat conductor she brought fully as many souls to God as any clergyman; and she spoke with an authority to which the whole Church, clergymen and lay people alike, listened with profound respect. In her most difficult art she trained successors who are with us still.

An uncountable number of lay people, and indeed clergy too, learned much of their theology at lay hands, and the Church was blessed by a host of lay theologians who had the art of effectively using new mediums for the popularizing of theology. How many people have had their theology at the hands of C. S. Lewis, and how many have been forced to think again and yet again about our Lord by Dorothy Sayers, through her broadcast plays, *The Man Born to be King*, and her admirable newspaper articles on the Creed? Side by side with them stood T. S. Eliot, perhaps the most considerable poet of our time. As a poet no one could ignore him, and the fact that he was content to be a loyal member of the Church of England must have made many an intellectual agnostic wonder if the Church was as dead and as despicable as he had assumed. The power of Charles Williams, a 'romantic theologian, i.e. one who is theological about romance,' was very great upon those who understood him. He was a towering figure as a poet, a critic, and a writer of celestial romances; and as a person his quality was such that when he died C. S. Lewis said of him, 'No event has so corroborated my faith in the next world as Williams did simply by dying. When the idea of death and the idea of Williams thus met in my mind, it was the idea of death that was changed.' For Williams was 'a masculine angel, a spirit burning with intelligence and charity'.[1]

The events, problems, and issues with which these people and the whole Church had to deal were both numerous and varied. These twenty years were very crowded. The Church Assembly had been born, and with it there had been set up an army of subordinate councils and conferences for every diocese, rural deanery, and parish, the total effect of which was to influence and to modify the life of the Church at a thousand points. Because the Assembly existed a mass of legislation was made possible—measures changing, inaugurating, or controlling such matters as Clergy Pensions, Dilapidations, Patronage and a score of others. A further consequence was the

[1] *Essays Presented to Charles Williams*, with a Preface by C. S. Lewis (Oxford University Press), 1947, pp. xiv and ix.

new method of governing the Church through central boards or committees. Throughout the period the sufficient supply of ordination candidates and their training remained a problem. There were many controversies. The Revised Prayer Book provided the most celebrated of them, and to that must be added the controversies caused by the Modernist Conference of 1919, by the public challenges of Bishop Barnes of Birmingham to the Archbishop of Canterbury over evolution, and by the Dean and Chapter's invitation to a Unitarian to preach in Liverpool Cathedral. The place of the Church in the educational world was always being debated, and so was the duty of the Church in matters social, political, and economic. The problem of reunion occupied at least as much time as any of these; and the problems of the Churches overseas in such matters as their relationship to government, to native marriage customs, and their maintenance, never ceased to be pressing. More and more attention was paid to the growing Ecumenical Movement; while at home the grave facts of the moral situation of the people of England, and the lamentable statistics of divorce, were always before the mind of the Church. Pressing upon it day and night were the secularist challenge, and the constant efforts the Church made in theology, in devotion, in renewal to meet it.

12

In the Sphere of Doctrine

I · The 'Liberal' Heresy

IN THE early nineteen-thirties Sir Arthur Quiller-Couch devoted one of his Cambridge lectures to the answering of Mr T. S. Eliot's abuse of Liberalism in his book, *After Strange Gods*. On one page of it Eliot had allowed himself to use the phrase, 'In a society like ours, worm-eaten with Liberalism,' and when Q's eyes fell upon these words they flashed with fire. He gathered his armour and advanced to give battle in the Arts School in Cambridge. What is this Liberalism which Gore distrusted, Karl Barth loathed, T. S. Eliot abused, Niebuhr denounced, and Hoskyns did so much to destroy? No one can hope to describe and gauge the temper and the effect of Anglican theology in the years after the first world war without first trying to find the answer to this question. The most superficial examination is enough to show that Q was justified in his bewilderment; for Liberalism is a spirit, a climate, an ethos, and it has to do with politics as well as with religion, and with literature as well as with politics, for its terms of reference are the ultimates of life and death.

The Liberalism with which the twentieth-century Anglican theologian had to do was in all essentials the same spirit which Cardinal Newman so detested a hundred years before. He denounced it, and its practitioners, almost as personal enemies. 'The men who had driven me from Oxford were distinctly the Liberals,' he wrote many years after the event; and the Liberalism with which they indoctrinated the eternal truth of religion was, he said, 'the half-way house to Atheism', potentially damnable because it preferred 'intellectual excellence to moral'.[1] But it was in Note A of his *Apologia* that he gave the most careful definition of what he meant by Liberalism.

[1] John Henry Cardinal Newman, *Apologia Pro Vita Sua* (Longmans, Green, 1865), from edition of 1904, p. 225.

Now by Liberalism I mean false liberty of thought, or the exercise of thought upon matters, in which, from the constitution of the human mind, thought cannot be brought to any successful issue, and therefore is out of place. Among such matters are first principles of whatever kind; and of these the most sacred and momentous are especially to be reckoned the truths of Revelation. Liberalism, then, is the mistake of subjecting to human judgment those revealed doctrines which are in their nature beyond and independent of it, and of claiming to determine on intrinsic grounds the truth and value of propositions which rest for their reception simply on the external authority of the Divine Word.

Thus Newman in 1865. But the intellectual climate of Europe has changed very greatly since Newman's day, and the liberal attitude which he described has added to itself the prestige of science and its technique, and the assumptions of democracy. Yet change the wording of Newman's definition but slightly, and we seem to be listening to the voice of the commissar. Schweitzer saw that when he declared that German criticism of the Gospels was inspired by German nationalism. Nevertheless the theologians have acquiesced too tamely in the name Liberalism. A darkening of counsel always attends the transfer to theology of a title valid in politics; and wherever in Europe Liberalism (in the political and cultural sense of the word) has been destroyed it has given place to a state of affairs which overthrows every Christian principle.

There is no beginning of the history of Liberalism on this side of the classics, and anybody who wants to dig down to its roots must go back at least as far as Plato, for ancient Greece is the true home of both the scientific spirit and of the highest ideals of man as great in his own right and perfectible by his own power, and it is the amalgam of these which makes theological Liberalism. In the history of the Jews in biblical times there is nothing of this, and from Genesis to Revelation the Bible continually asserts the exact opposite: the virtue of the world lies in its divine creation, history is the story of divine action in the world, and progress for humanity and perfectibility for man is a function of divine grace. Tension between views so diverse is inevitable and endemic, especially as both are noble, and in some sense both are true.

There is no need in such a work as this to attempt the task of tracing down the centuries the action and interaction of these contrasted ideas about the revelation of God, the nature of man, and the purpose of history. But the history of this process in England entered a new phase in 1859, the year of the publication of Charles Darwin's *Origin of Species*. Few people who speak of it as an intellectual landmark have ever actually read it. But its most important findings and conclusions were immediately popularized, and everybody knew that through Darwin science had given judgement that the method of progress was by evolution, that the mainspring of evolution was natural selection, that nature was a closed, coherent, and uniform system, and that evolutionary thinking had come to stay. The acceptable picture of man as harmless and innocent, as destined by the sheer power of automatic progress to create at last the civilization of his dreams, as perfectible by his own efforts, above all, as the centre of his own world, had been so powerfully reinforced as to become the only possible view of life to be entertained by anyone who cared to be thought intelligent. A God who created such a world might be acceptable, provided that one steered clear of the Genesis account of the process. But a God who disrupted the iron theory of the uniformity of nature by revelation, by miracle, or, worse, by acting within it at his own will and in ways utterly unpredictable could not be squared with the theory. The Bible believed that salvation came by faith; the liberal often doubted whether salvation was necessary, and if it was, he believed it came by man's own effort in righteousness. The Bible forbade trust in princes or any children of men, and held that our trust must be in God alone; the liberal placed his trust in the systems and codified techniques of knowledge in science, education, and politics to bring society to perfection and man to sanctity, or to complete him and make him every whit whole. Catholic and Protestant alike held with the Bible that the natural man is in opposition to God; the liberal believed that man is by his own nature made in the image of God and that Christ was divine through the perfection of his humanity. Once accept the religion of the Bible as true, and there is no escaping from the conclusion that Liberalism is justly described in the great anathema of the Commination Service in the Book of Common Prayer:[1] 'Cursed be he that putteth his trust in man, and taketh man for his defence, and in his heart goeth from the Lord.'

'Cursed' may seem to be an extravagant, an uncharitable, even a vicious epithet to apply to Liberalism, even though the rest of the anathema precisely describes its ethos, for it was a great tradition and it attracted and convinced the characteristically high-minded. The attitude towards life of men like Thomas Huxley and Lowes Dickinson, Professor Bury and Hastings Rashdall, Bishop Percival of Hereford and T. R. Glover was not likely to be ignoble. It might indeed be mistaken through excess of optimism, as the passage of time has proved it to be. But Liberalism's prestige was enormous, and in its heyday, the period of Asquith's administration, its optimism did not seem unreasonable. As a philosophy of life it had nevertheless parted company with the faith of the Bible, and had taken away from those whose thinking it influenced (probably the greater part of the nation) the armour which the Bible had given earlier generations. A faith over-optimistic about man, and deficient in every statement about man's need of God, could not guide humanity through the dreadful fires which were to come. As a consequence every noble cause in which Liberalism so passionately believed, the perfectibility of man by human resources,

---

[1] Incredibly, the service of Commination in the Revised Prayer Book of 1928 totally omitted this anathema.

man's necessary freedom as a glorious being, the free expression of knowledge, and the idea that natural man will normally choose the righteous course, lies today in ruins, and has to be rebuilt all over again.

It is very dangerous to become cynical about the idea of progress, and the nemesis of despair lurks in hiding for those who can only utter the word with a wry smile. The collapse of Liberalism as a theological conception had however created this very condition. Constant disappointment, and the inescapable evidence of the swift corruptibility of human beings, had dealt a deadly blow at all the assumptions on which the liberal belief in automatic progress had rested. After 1945 thoughtful men had little hope left. Ten years later they had less still. Yet in defiance of logic the fell process did stop short of the despair to which it ought in reason to have led.

Nemesis was somehow held at bay. It is still a mystery how this was done. The power of habit had much to do with it. Though they know the danger few people believe in their hearts that the world will actually collapse about their ears one fine morning, and that, if they survive at all, their lives will be utterly different from anything they have known. But more than this, it was as though reflective men such as had constituted the driving force of the now discredited Liberalism were waiting for some deliverance which they believed must surely come, though they knew not from where.

It came from a new prophet, a French Jesuit priest, Pierre Teilhard de Chardin by name, who combined in himself all the disciplines of a very great scientist with the training and devotion of a priest and theologian. In 1961 he burst upon the English-speaking world with his great and intensely difficult book, *The Phenomenon of Man*. It was very widely read, but few of its readers would ever have claimed that they understood it all. That did not matter because the book created an instinctive trust in its author, and any reader could and did gather from it what really mattered. It was that the idea of progress had been refounded on a new basis, and by an authority whose credentials could not be questioned. For it was scientific research which led de Chardin to accept evolution as the primary redemptive method of God, to argue from evolution back to the God whose will the whole process is, and forward to the ultimate perfectibility of man, and the certainty of the achievement of this goal of history. In other words, progress had been refounded and on a far surer basis than before.

This work of a scientist of the highest distinction has made a new foundation for hope, has made disbelief in progress a kind of heresy, and for a long time to come it will not be possible to argue about progress without reference to de Chardin. It is this Jesuit who has come to rescue the older generation of theological liberals from the debacle of their own making, and to set them on their feet in a larger room.

II · *The Decline and Fall of Modernism*

In 1925 Dr H. D. A. Major, Principal of Ripon Hall, Oxford, and Editor of *The Modern Churchman*, sailed for the United States of America to deliver the William Belden Noble Lectures in the University of Harvard. He had chosen as his subject the character, aims, and method of Modernism in England; and certainly if this phenomenon was to be explained, there could be nobody better equipped than Dr Major to explain it. For a cool, informed, and ample statement of what English Modernism stood for it would still be difficult to find anything more suitable than these lectures, where the modernist speaks for himself through the mouth of the acknowledged leader of his movement.

He was quite sure that it was proper to speak of English Modernism, and that there was in fact a Modernism of England which was both different and distinguishable from the Modernism of America or Rome. Their very enemies were different. The Roman modernist opposed mediaevalism, the American modernist opposed fundamentalism, while the English modernist had to take up arms against traditionalism. But what was it that English Modernism positively believed? His vital principle which underlay all he did, and from which everything that he believed hung suspended, Dr Major defined as fidelity to the 'operation in human history of the Spirit that was in Jesus Christ'; and immediately he added to those unexceptionable words the following expression of hostility which, by a curious association of images, the word 'Spirit' always provokes in the modernist mind, 'and the aim of the English Modernist is to set free that Spirit from those archaic dogmatic shackles and ecclesiastical burdens, great and grievous to be borne, which are hindering it from exerting its full and proper influence in the modern world'.[1] The English modernist, he was sure, was a separately recognizable identity; and he bore four positive marks of recognition. His Modernism is 'the outcome of an education which makes people acquainted with New Truth';[2] and this New Truth he must of necessity be resolved to use, thereby showing his faith in it. Yet because a man 'may know the New Truth and have faith in it, and be sure that it has a good use, he may not be a Modernist, he may be, and most often is, an Agnostic'.[3] To be a Modernist, he must believe that the New Truth serves religion, and that religion is absolutely necessary for all humanity. But not even this is enough, for in addition to it the modernist must 'love and value a Beloved Community—a community which enshrines our moral and spiritual ideals for humanity'. This community is the Church of Christ, and the Modernist is bound to be a churchman, and has no claim to the title if he is not.

[1] H. D. A. Major, *English Modernism: its Origin, Methods, Aims* (Harvard University Press), 1927, pp. 6, 7.
[2] *Ibid.*, p. 55.   [3] *Ibid.*, pp. 55, 56.

To be a Christian Modernist one must be convinced that our civilization needs not only the Christian Religion, but also the Christian Church. Probably the historic Christian Church seems to the Modernist to enshrine Christ's ideals very imperfectly. If so it will be his duty as a Modernist to strive to make it embody them more perfectly, but he may not sever himself from its membership, or believe that the Christian Religion can dispense with the Christian Church.[1]

On Modernist terms, loyal churchmanship is not only compatible with Modernism but essential to it, which no doubt is one reason why modernists in England have always opposed the disestablishment of the Church.

Dr Major then proceeded to furnish a list of the things which the Anglican modernist has cast away on coming over from Traditionalism to Modernism, and in which therefore he does not believe, and which he seeks to end. This list comprises seven doctrines. It is significantly longer than the list of what he does believe, for one of the ineradicable marks of the modernist is that he is always so much more conscious of what he does not than of what he does believe. The Modernist, then, refuses assent to the following propositions:

1. The conception of God the changeless despot who 'from a throne in the heavens governed the earth in accordance with certain inflexible principles'. In his stead the modernist asserts 'the God of emergent evolution, who is ever bringing new things to pass'.[2]
2. The doctrine of everlasting punishment, 'grotesque, absurd, incredible.'[3]
3. The doctrine of the propitiatory sacrifice of Christ. Here the words in the Prayer of Consecration in the Liturgy, 'who made there by his one oblation . . .' are called 'terrible'; and objection is made to the formulae 'for Jesus Christ's sake' and 'through the merits of Jesus Christ' at the end of prayers.[4]
4. The doctrine of original sin when interpreted as involving original guilt; and as a consequence he refuses assent to any doctrine of baptism which goes further than a statement of baptism as necessary to assert the protection of God and to admit to the Church.[5]
5. The eschatological doctrines of judgement and the second coming of Christ, but it is more the imagery under which these are traditionally asserted than the truths which these images assert which is repudiated.[6]
6. The belief in the infallibility of the Bible. It is not an infallible but an inspired Bible. 'The statement that the Bible is the Word of God is being replaced by the statement that it contains the Word of God,'[7] and we must now accept 'the assured results of criticism as to the origin, dates, composition, integrity, historicity, and scientific value' of the various books.[8]

[1] *Ibid.*, pp. 56, 57. [2] *Ibid.*, p. 102. [3] *Ibid.*, p. 106. [4] *Ibid.*, pp. 107, 108.
[5] *Ibid.*, pp. 110–12. [6] *Ibid.*, pp. 112–16. [7] *Ibid.*, p. 117. [8] *Ibid.*, p. 118.

7. The traditional view of divine revelation, which 'presented the knowledge of God as a unique system of truth miraculously communicated from heaven to earth'. In its place the Modernist would claim that 'revelation is implied in the very structure of the human mind, so that the process of thought, conscience, affection, truly understood, involve the recognition of the Infinite and Eternal. It is because we are what we are, and are becoming what we are becoming that God can and does unveil Himself to us, that is, *in* us. Hence the Modernist teaches that the divine method of revelation is internal—God speaking, not as Traditionalism teaches, in tones of thunder from the sky, but with a still, small voice in the human consciousness.'[1]

From that it is clear that there are many things of high spiritual importance which the Modernist believes, and which he has done much to safeguard. He believes in man, his greatness, his heroism, his high calling and destiny: he believes it is a most splendid thing to be human, and he believes it passionately. Over and over again Dr Major says that the Modernist continues to assert this or that Christian dogma because it supplies something which is necessary to human life. Thus the Modernist generally argued from the perfection of Christ's earthly life to his Godhead, not vice versa. Thus again Dr Major writes about the dogma of the Incarnation that Modernists think it precious because it 'conserves the highest values in life' and promises 'an augmentation of those values'. Its use to human beings is the criterion of its credibility.

The historic evidence upon which the Church believed the Incarnation was, much of it, false; its significance in many respects was misrepresented and misinterpreted: the Church held fast to the dogma, incredible and indefensible as it seemed in some respects. Why? Because it promised an augmentation of values in human life.[2]

Everything that the political liberal meant by his fine slogan, Trust the People, the Modernist meant also, and he supplied the liberal with theological grounds for his political and social faith.

He believed too in a God of energy who is eternally revealing himself in history through the Holy Spirit and in the human consciousness. The Modernist's God was emphatically a deity who was awake, alive, alert; and there has been no historic school of theology which has held a richer version of the doctrine of divine inspiration. And because this realm of spiritual realities was to him the richest, the nearest, the most verifiable fact of life, he believed that in his very iconoclasm he served a truly religious purpose, and he saw no presumption in his claim that in him a sage had at last arrived who had the right and the knowledge to judge between what was true and what was false in the whole body of traditional catholic

_____
[1] *Ibid.*, p. 119.   [2] *Ibid.*, p. 93.

theology. This rich scheme of the faith delivered to the saints, the 'Modernist claims freedom to investigate as a Christian right, and also freedom to reject what is false'.[1] So far as the doctrines of the Creed are concerned he was prepared to separate them into the categories of truth and error:

As editor of the *Modern Churchman* for thirty years I have no knowledge of Modern Churchmen who do not believe in 'the incarnation, the atonement, everlasting life, divine judgement', but I do know a great number of Modern Churchmen who do not believe in the virgin birth, in the resurrection of the physical body of Jesus Christ, in the descent of Jesus Christ into Hades between his death and resurrection, in his return at the end of the world to judge the quick and the dead at a great assize . . . These beliefs are all affirmed in the Apostles' Creed and have been held by orthodox Christians until recent times . . . If asked why Modern Churchmen do not believe these things, the reply is that modern biblical, historical, and scientific studies have made them incredible.[2]

Nor did this claim seem to him presumptuous. His right, even his duty to sit in judgement followed upon his doctrine of divine inspiration, and upon his belief that he had in his hands what his predecessors had lacked, the two instruments of biblical criticism and scientific method of investigation to guide him. Such was his faith in them that he never questioned their competence, and when their use seemed to bring out of the very Gospels themselves a divine authority for liberal humanism and even made of their hero the Liberal Christ, he rejoiced the more.

Many of the theologians and leaders of opinion in the Church, laymen like Lord Halifax and bishops like Gore, would if they could have had such Modernists as were clergymen indicted for heresy, and have taken away from them their licences as accredited teachers of the Church. This they could never do, partly because they could not take the whole body of the Church with them, and also because the whole process of trial for heresy and withdrawal of licence is made far more difficult in the Church of England than in any other Church in the world. The modernist priest, like any other who was intensely irritating to ecclesiastical authority, could take refuge behind the three barriers which Hensley Henson once approvingly described as the Church of England's 'inability to legislate secured by its subordination to the State, the relative moderation of its denominational confession, and the tradition of clerical independence distinctive of its legal system',[3] given legal form in the parson's freehold. So they were saved from any persecution and were able to say exactly what they liked with almost complete impunity.

On the other hand, if the main body of the clergy and laity were markedly unenthusiastic about any attempt to coerce the Modernists, they remained intensely suspicious, and they were never convinced by them. Very

[1] *Ibid.*, p. 94.
[2] Dr H. D. A. Major in a letter to *The Times* of September 4, 1945.
[3] Herbert Hensley Henson, *The Church of England*, p. 112.

few churchpeople were equipped to argue with Modernists, but they got the impression that the Modernists wanted to lead them into a theological land of haze and quicksand, where they would never know where they were, and from which every landmark and every patch of solid, firm ground had been carefully removed. Perhaps the teachers among them got hold of the Cambridge Biblical Commentaries, and read there, as Hensley Henson did on Good Friday 1934, their handling of the Passion narrative in St Luke's Gospel. The bishop read it, seized his diary, and wrote:

From the standpoint of the Humanitarians what special and perpetual significance can the Crucifixion of Jesus be said to possess? The critics have passed their rough desecrating hands over the evangelical narratives, and left little in them of all that has most touched the hearts of men. I read through the Cambridge Commentary on the Passion chapters in St Luke's Gospel and realized how spiritually desolating is the method of Bible study which it represents . . . '*A sublime touch, but probably not historic*' is the note on the words, 'the Lord turned and looked upon Peter'. The dramatic episode in which Barabbas is preferred to Jesus is '*somewhat unlikely*'. The whole account of Pilate's contact with the people is contained in a narrative which '*it is impossible to accept as history*'. The wailing of the women 'is probably unhistorical,' being made up of a number of Old Testament reminiscences. The words, 'Father, forgive them, for they know not what they do,' are marked as doubtful. 'But *whether the words are part of Luke or not, they are entirely characteristic of the spirit of Christianity, and of Jesus Himself; even if not historical, they are a supreme tribute to His memory.*' The mockery by the soldiers '*is unlikely*'. The touching record of the two robbers '*seems to move rather in the realm of legend than of history*'. It is difficult to make devotional use of a sacred scripture which is thus to be regarded.[1]

What conclusion could the teacher draw, except that either scripture was completely untrustworthy, or that modernist criticism of it led him straight into Cloud Cuckoo Land?

Further, the ordinary Christian could see no justification for the Modernist's reiterated statements about the finality of modern thought, modern scientific knowledge, or modern methods of historical research. All of these criteria-not-to-be-questioned, these twentieth-century taboos, led to the enthroning of the men who used them in a position of infallible eminence, so that all the ages of the world must abide the question of modern cultivated man, who alone was free and uninhibited. People read their papers, looked at the world where they lived, inspected such modern cultivated men as they knew, lived and died and agonized in the wars they made, and knew that modern man was no angel to sit in judgement upon every century. The Modernists might be very learned, but they seemed to be talking very great nonsense. It is for these reasons that in writing or talking about Modernism today one instinctively uses the past tense.

[1] Herbert Hensley Henson, *Retrospect of an Unimportant Life* (Oxford University Press), vol. II, 1943, pp. 317–18.

III · *The Modern Churchmen's Conference at Cambridge, 1921*[1]

All these traits of Anglican Modernism were given the most public airing they ever enjoyed at the conference of Modern Churchmen, held in Girton College, Cambridge, in 1921. There has perhaps been no conference of churchpeople in modern times which created quite so much sound and fury. When it had ended and its proceedings were published, the secular no less than the ecclesiastical newspapers were filled for days with denunciations and defences of it. So far did one newspaper go in attacking Hastings Rashdall, that he accused it of libel and obtained damages out of court.[2] He probably gave them all away, for few men have been more generous than Rashdall. Protests poured into Lambeth Palace. There were angry debates in Convocation. The issue of *The Modern Churchman* which contained the conference papers sold more than 6,000 copies. It was a celebrated occasion, amply trumpeted by all the resources of publicity; yet out of it but little came. It did not wear well. The modern student who obtains a copy of the relevant number of *The Modern Churchman* and reads the papers in it will not find himself much stirred. He is unlikely to be greatly moved even by the editor's introduction, which, at the time, caused particular anger.

Nevertheless, this conference had a real significance for the twentieth-century Church, though it was other than its members or their opponents seem to have supposed.

The conference had been called to consider the question of 'Christ and the Creeds'; and on that question it had nothing of lasting significance to say. But again and again, as it were in a parenthesis or a bracket, the speakers showed themselves to be most concerned about another question, the glory of man. They were conscious of the need to find a new and a surer theological foundation for the Christian doctrine of man, though they did not discern that for the twentieth century this was to be the problem of problems, and they showed no awareness that even then it was specially under attack. But in 1921 they were not peculiar in this.

When the organizers of the conference announced what its theme was to be, even their friends were apprehensive. Hensley Henson, then Bishop of Durham, caused a cautionary note to be sent to them through a third party. He wanted them to take heed what they were about lest they might 'create another crisis in the matter of belief before we have well made good such liberty as we have'.[3] It was not the advertised list of speakers which made him utter the caution. It was obvious what nearly all of them would be certain to say on such a subject, for most of them had been saying it

---

[1] All quotations from the proceedings of the conference are identified by the numbers of the pages in which they occur, and these are given in brackets in the text. All these references are to *The Modern Churchman*, edited by Dr H. D. A. Major, vol. XI, No. 6, September 1921.

[2] *Theology*, March 1940, p. 153.　　　　[3] *Ibid.*, p. 152.

steadily for years. But Dr Kirsopp Lake, who had carried his own variety of Modernism to such lengths of negation that he had scandalized his own friends, had just published his theories on the subject in his *Landmarks of Early Christianity*, and they were very alarming. If the members of the conference should be carried away by the excitement of the occasion and give Kirsopp Lake their support, they would be compromising the whole movement and carrying it into a quicksand. But the organizers would not listen to the bishop's advice. Far from that, they added a paper by Dr Foakes Jackson to the published programme, and it was known that this paper was intended to represent the joint views of Lake and himself. This paper was duly read by its author at an early stage in the conference. The conference, he said, had

deliberately chosen to discuss the very fundamentals of the Christian faith, and to face and not to shirk that most pointed of all questions: 'What think ye of Christ?' The reason for this choice is, I have the vanity to suppose, republication of the first volume of *The Beginnings of Christianity*, which Professor Lake and I have edited. (229)

The conference did not dissent from this attribution of motive, but made it clear that it intended not to commend but to repudiate the book. Of Dr Lake's own book, the editor of the *Modern Churchman*, writing in the name of the whole conference, observed that it was to be condemned as giving a portrait of Christ

historically unjustifiable and psychologically inadequate. The Liberalism which Prof. Lake jettisons may be alleged to have stripped our Lord of His miraculous characteristics, but it left him his moral and spiritual supremacy. But Prof. Lake's conclusions seem to deprive Him of the latter as well as of the former. (194)

It was certainly no wonder that the modernists were much more alarmed than the traditionalists by Lake and Foakes Jackson, for the 'Liberal Christ' which the Modernists had been at such pains to create was the very Christ whom these two scholars supposed they had dethroned. Foakes Jackson, speaking with grim relish to the conference, made precisely this claim.

We have been most severely rebuked by the Liberals of our own Church, who have my sincere sympathy. They are fighting a hard fight. On the one hand they see they are losing the support of the public because there is little demand for a reasonable presentation of Christianity. There is a growing conviction not the less dangerous because it now rarely finds a voice that Christianity can be ignored.

Then he turned to rend the Modernist liberals of the type gathered in the lecture room at Girton:

They have lost the historical Christ and have not regained him by converting him into a social reformer, a moral legislator, a revealer of a new conception of

God. They are preaching an entirely new religion and concealing the fact even from themselves. (229–31)

By Lake and Foakes Jackson, as by Schweitzer before them, the Modernists were being mortally wounded in the house of their friends.

The conference, then, had been called to discuss the relationship of Christ to the creeds. But what Christ? The 'uninteresting' Christ of Lake and Foakes Jackson was offered to the conference, and flatly rejected.The rigidly eschatological and partially deluded Christ of Schweitzer's *The Quest of the Historical Jesus* had always been repudiated by English Modernists. To accept his arguments would be to undermine the infallibility of scientific New Testament criticism, and this was the cardinal dogma of the modernist creed. Their own predilection was for the 'Liberal' Christ; but the papers read at the conference demonstrated that for them such a title was misleading and inaccurate, even though they liked to think of themselves as theological liberals. The Christ of this conference was really the 'humanist' Christ; and the broad effect of most of the papers was to justify and to explain this title. That Christ was perfect man they all passionately believed. That he was God they believed no less; but they derived his divinity from the perfection of his manhood.

Having chosen to discuss the problem of our Lord's relationship to the creeds they could not help but struggle to find in it an answer to the vital questions about the nature of man. They were sure that within the mystery of Christ's nature the only satisfactory answer was to be found. But they thought they could find it there only if they began with the humanity of Christ and then fitted his divinity into what they believed to be true about his humanity. 'I would urge (the orthodox religious teachers) to make sure of the Humanity of Christ and the Divinity will make sure of itself' (307). In saying this Dr R. G. Parsons spoke for them all.

In that there is nothing to which the traditionalist could object. But most other speakers said the same thing so much more extremely. Canon M. G. Glazebrook approvingly quoted Professor Henry Jones:

The error (of Dr Denny) does not spring from maintaining the divinity of Jesus but from denying the divinity of man. Nor can it be corrected by maintaining that Jesus was a 'mere man': the implications of that phrase are themselves profoundly erroneous and unjust to man. (211)

Dr Major declared:

Jesus Himself did not claim to be the Son of God in a *physical* sense such as the narratives of the Virgin Birth affirm, nor did He claim to be the Son of God in a *metaphysical* sense, such as is required by the Nicene Theology. He claimed to be God's Son in a *moral* sense, in the sense in which all human beings are sons of God. . . . I think historically today we must be strong to declare that the consciousness of Jesus was a full human consciousness, and that it was not supernatural and miraculous in any sense that cannot be attributed to a human personality. (276, 277)

Dr Hastings Rashdall perhaps caused more wrath than the reader of any other paper when he said:

> Jesus did not claim divinity for himself. . . . Never in any critically well-attested sayings is there anything which suggests that his conscious relation to God was other than that of a man towards God—the attitude which He wished that all men should adopt towards God. (278)

And again, from the same author:

> There is no more reason for supposing that Jesus of Nazareth knew more than his contemporaries about the scientific explanation of mental disease which current belief attributed to diabolic possession than that he knew more about the authorship of the Pentateuch or the Psalms. (281)

Now all that may well appear in equal degrees optimistic, credulous, and shocking to anyone who reads it today. But the courage of its faith in the perfectibility of man may well strike him as more remarkable still. This faith he based on the perfection of the humanity of Christ, not on the subsequent experience of the moral capacity of man in history. These men thus held a high standard of value of humanity, and they refused to be over-impressed by the depressing picture of man which had emerged from the war just ended. But when this was put as they put it, they involved themselves in heresy so deadly that all other more formal heresies paled beside it. This was the heresy of taking man and deducting God from him: it was to make God in the image of man. 'Orthodoxy, in beginning with God, began at the wrong end,' said Dr Bethune Baker (287). This was really shocking, for it was only another way of saying what Swinburne had said in his famous lines:

> Glory to Man in the highest! For Man is the master of things.
> But God, if God there be, is the substance of men, which is man.

This faith was at variance with the main delivery of biblical witness about the relationship between God and man, and it was therefore bound to be inconsistent with much of the orthodox creed. The credal doctrine immediately affected was that of the Incarnation, and on that the view taken by most of the readers of the papers was certainly defective. However, the Christology of the conference was often strikingly positive. C. W. Emmett spoke for many when he declared, 'I really want to show that the ordinary man may trust the general impression of the personality of Jesus which he gets from the Gospels' (214). Professor R. H. Lightfoot was passionately devotional and richly orthodox in his answer to the question, What do we know about Jesus? Professor Bethune Baker followed the invariable modernist dogma in refusing the miraculous element in the gospels:

> I can only regard this idea of the miraculous birth (of Jesus) as ætiological and honorific—in those days a natural and reasonable way of accounting for a great

personality and the experience of which Jesus was the cause and centre, as it would be unnatural and irrational today. (288, 289)

But apart from this he was not unorthodox, and did not think of himself so. Indeed he claimed that in many respects his thought about Jesus marched in step with that of Baron von Hügel (295). But it is not recorded that this great sage agreed.

The Modernist yielded to members of no other party in the Church in the absoluteness of his devotion and loyalty to our Lord, but the members of this conference answered the question of the relationship of Christ and the creeds by separating them at more than one crucial point, and this brought them into conflict with the whole body of the catholic minded, who at no time have believed that a personal devotion to our Lord, however absolute, is enough to make a man free of the whole Christian tradition. That they did make this separation between Christ and the creeds was recognized and admitted by their spokesmen. On the last night of the conference Dr E. W. Barnes, later Bishop of Birmingham, preached them a sermon in which he gently chided them for allowing their Modernist enthusiasms to take them too far, and for attempting to shuffle from under some of the vital doctrines of the Faith. He was, he said, an evangelical. As such, he was really disturbed that

one or two, in discussing subjects where language cannot adequately describe feeling, have seemed to doubt whether the Jesus of history was the unique Person in whom St Paul and St John saw the Only-begotten Son. I weigh, without prejudice, I trust, all that they have said. In the end I feel no hesitation in affirming that Jesus rose from the dead to become the living Christ, one with the Holy Spirit. (345)

And again, in the same sermon:

I imagine that our ignorance in this realm (the interaction of the human and the divine) has caused us to avoid questions concerning reconciliation, redemption, salvation. I regret the omission because such matters are central in Christian experience. (347)

When the conference was over, Dr Major printed in a special number of *The Modern Churchman* all the papers of the conference. To them he added a long and considered preface, in which he frankly admitted:

It would be idle to pretend that all the views expressed at Girton are in harmony with popular orthodoxy, or even with traditional orthodoxy. All that those who expressed them could hope is that they may be in harmony with progressive orthodoxy. . . . The Girton Conference speakers were more concerned to adjust their orthodoxy to the orthodoxy of the future than to harmonize it with the orthodoxy of the past. (193)

The whole idea of the 'Faith once for all delivered' was cast away by such an argument. Small wonder that this preface caused more trouble than all the conference papers put together. At the end of it he asked two questions of 'our traditionalist fellow-Churchmen and the whole Anglican Communion':

1. Will they accept the affirmation, 'God was in Christ', with the practical recognition in daily life that 'Jesus is Lord' as constituting the irreducible minimum for modernist membership in the Church and in the teaching and ministerial offices? If they will, then a Truce of God can be attained. But the question needs to be answered frankly and without delay.
2. Will they concede to modern Churchmen the right to modify the use of the Creeds, and to produce, if they will, alternative Creeds for use in parishes where they are desired by the parishioners, provided always that this be done in a wise, loving, and orderly fashion and with the authority of the Bishop? (200)

There was of course no hope of an affirmative answer to either question, and this Dr Major must have known very well. But in the mere asking of such questions there was nothing specially shocking or even novel. For years modernists—and not only they—had been struggling to find words and phrases for an acceptable, alternative creed. The whole of the preface suggests to the reader of today that neither its author, nor the members of the conference, were really prepared for the volume of the storm of wrath which followed.

The storm raged and its winds blew from many quarters. But there was a note of furious irritation in it for which the actual accusations made hardly accounted. It was partly due to the infuriating sense of superiority which Modernists blandly assumed; and this was expressed, for example, in a remark of Bethune-Baker's:

We ought perhaps to be content if most of our friends get on to the bridge (from the past to the future) and stay there safely, refusing to follow the more active among us who are exploring the country beyond. (292)

But their friends did not at all appreciate the suggestion. They did not like being regarded as timid sheep, bleating 'Safety First', and refusing to set foot on dangerous ground: and in any case they avoided the ground chiefly because it looked so very like Cloud Cuckoo Land.

As soon as the conference papers had been published, Hensley Henson publicly protested his repudiation of 'the extreme modernist opinions' expressed in some of them.[1] A. C. Headlam, then Regius Professor of Divinity at Oxford, reviewed the papers in the *Church Quarterly Review* of January 1922, and administered a very judicious castigation which fell upon authors and critics alike.[2] It was, however, in the Convocation of Canterbury that it was decided whether the occasion was to be regarded as a great crisis, or as an awkwardness which time would smooth if only people would refrain from exacerbating it. The question was raised first in the Bishops' House on May 22, 1922, in a very long debate, remarkable for

[1] *Retrospect*, vol. II, pp. 143, 144.　　[2] *Theology*, March 1940, pp. 193, 197.

the way in which each bishop who spoke showed depth of conviction matched by charity of judgement and real knowledge of the subject. The bishops were dealing with a petition (or a 'gravamen', to use the technical term for it) from some sixty Anglo-Catholic members of the Lower House, and with a counter-petition asking them to refuse assent to the petition. The one asked them to declare that the doctrines asserted at the conference were 'contrary to the teaching of the Bible and the Church'; the other stated that 'questions of essential truth can only be decided by the slow process of research', and demanded freedom of enquiry.[1] The bishops accepted neither. Instead they produced a resolution of their own:

> This House declares its conviction that adhesion to the teaching of the Catholic Church, as set forth in the Nicene Creed—and in particular concerning the eternal pre-existence of the Son of God, his true Godhead and his Incarnation—is essential to the life of the Church, and calls attention to the fact that the Church commissions as its ministers those who have solemnly expressed such adhesion.[2]

This resolution was the work of the Bishop of Gloucester (Dr E. C. S. Gibson); for he had joined with the Archbishop to persuade the bishops that to deal with the matter as the petition of the Lower House had suggested would be useful only if announcements of episcopal authority had power, and they had none. The Archbishop was careful to pour cooling streams of water on the idea that the conference had amounted to

> a great phalanx of heresiarchs set in battle array against the doctrine of the Church Catholic, and that we were called on to rally the Church in defence of the Christian Faith.[3]

He also said plainly that it had been the preface to the conference papers in *The Modern Churchman* which had caused most of the trouble:

> The papers were edited with a preface which attempts to speak in the name of everybody concerned. I realize that the word WE may be merely editorial, but it has all the appearance of meaning, 'We, the writers of the papers', and that seems to me gravely misleading and mischievous.[4]

On the same subject the Bishop of Gloucester had been still more crushing:

> It would be interesting to know whether any one of the members of the conference was consulted as to the Preface, or would be willing to take any responsibility whatever for the singularly ill-judged utterances of the writer of the Preface.[5]

It was, however, made very plain both in the Convocation debate and in the Archbishop of Canterbury's letter to Bishop Gore[6] that the Archbishop

---

[1] *Chronicles of Canterbury Convocation*, 1922, pp. 263, 314. (Cited hereafter as *C.C.C.*)
[2] *Ibid.*, pp. 325, 326.   [3] Bell, vol. II, p. 1140.   [4] *C.C.C.*, 1922, p. 354.
[5] *Ibid.*, p. 322.   [6] Bell, vol. II, pp. 1141–2.

had no intention at all of exercising discipline upon the members of the conference, and without him nobody else would be likely to move in the matter. So the storm blew itself out, and no Modernist was called upon to suffer even the mildest martyrdom. Perhaps it was the wisest course because as by instinct or inspiration the course of theology followed thereafter very different and much more suggestive paths, which, in time, were seen to be leading to a position of vital importance. Thereafter Modernism in the Anglican Church might remain as an organized party, and might also give birth to occasional aberrations, as in the Open Letters of the Bishop of Birmingham in 1927 to the Archbishop, but its contentions were seen to be side-issues and its characteristic language to be archaic jargon.

Nevertheless the Girton conference had one positive influence upon the development of doctrinal thought in the Church of England during this period. The storm it caused helped to change the Archbishop of Canterbury's mind; and whereas he had previously refused to appoint a Commission upon doctrine in the Church of England, he now acceded to the many requests that he should do so.

It was in 1920 that a group of young theologians, headed by Dr Burge, Bishop of Oxford, propounded to the Archbishop a scheme for a new report on doctrine, to be drawn up by an authoritatively appointed commission consisting of theologians from each of the recognized parties in the Church. Their purpose would be twofold: first to declare what the teaching of the Church of England is, and secondly to end doctrinal strife by the sheer weight of the fact that the declaration would be made by theologians of all parties. Over this work they were sure they ought to take many years. The Archbishop was very critical of this, and pointed out that only a commission with some kind of conciliar authority behind it could achieve what they desired, and this kind of authority he had no intention of giving. Would it not be far better to hold some kind of unofficial enquiry of the kind which had produced *Lux Mundi* in an earlier generation? To this Burge replied that *Lux Mundi* was the work of men of one school, whereas he had proposed a commission of men of all schools. There was deadlock, but the Girton conference broke it; and in 1922 the same proposal was made to the Archbishop by nine bishops, seventeen priests, and one layman. Davidson was again cautious. He harped on their youth in his reply, and feared lest they should try to produce a new criterion of orthodoxy. Burge sent an immediate disclaimer:

In reply to your Grace, we would wish to make clear that we do not contemplate, and have never contemplated, authority being given to a commission to frame either a statement of doctrine which would be binding on the Church or the clergy, or even a statement of doctrine which would *ipso facto* be held to be the official teaching of the Church.[1]

The Archbishop hesitated for six more months, but on December 28, 1922,

[1] Bell, vol. II, p. 1148.

he agreed to do what was asked, and, together with his brother of York, appointed the commission, with these terms of reference:

To consider the nature and grounds of Christian Doctrine with a view to demonstrating the extent of existing agreement within the Church of England, and with a view to investigating how far it is possible to remove or diminish differences.[1]

It seems likely that the commission on doctrine would not have had even this mild amount of authority behind it had not the Girton conference forced the pace. It did not make its report until 1938.

IV · *Sir Edwyn Hoskyns and the Eclipse of Liberalism*

To attempt to trace the movement of theological study and conviction through a period of a quarter of a century is to enter a maze, for no other field of knowledge attracts a greater volume of literature and eloquence. It is the common fate of the explorers of a maze to begin by following an attractive-looking path and then to find, after a few turns and twists, that it leads only to a dead end. Such had been the experience of those who had trusted the Modernists to guide them through the maze. After 1921 increasing numbers of these camp followers realized that they must go back to the beginning and start again; and this chronicle must follow them. But there is no hope of reaching the centre of the maze, no hope of our believing that theology during the last twenty-five years has moved in any identifiable direction, unless we can be provided with some thread of Ariadne to guide our steps. This thread, it has been suggested, is the steady growth of our consciousness of the Church as the Divine Society:

Indeed, one may say (declared the Regius Professor of Divinity at Oxford, Canon Leonard Hodgson) that the outstanding feature of the theological development of the last thirty years has been the recovery of the conviction that Christianity is essentially the religion of the Church, that is, of a society called into being by God to be the instrument of His work on earth. And bound up with this conviction, that the Head of the Church, the risen and ascended Lord Jesus Christ, is Himself God.[2]

Other threads might perhaps be chosen, but this one has a definite and identifiable starting-point, and it leads us clearly all the way until at last it leads us home to the centre of the maze. When we get there we shall find it is exactly the same place that we shall also reach when we follow the ramifications of the Christian social movement in the Anglican Church. Anglican theology today has come to the point where its strongest conviction is that the Eucharist, as the characteristic rite of the Divine Society, is the heart of the practice of Christianity and points symbolically to the only cure of a sick world. The Christian social movement is today convinced that in the Eucharist is dramatically enacted the moving picture of

[1] *Ibid.*, p. 1150.   [2] In *The Guardian* of August 18, 1944, p. 284.

the healthy social order. The two movements of thought and effort started from different ends of the world of Christian experience, and they have travelled by very different roads. But they come at last to one and the same centre of the maze, and thenceforward can travel onwards hand in hand through a future journey of limitless possibilities of blessing for the world. But to choose this particular thread to guide us through the maze inevitably involves the neglect of all the others. It means that we must spend all our time with the theologians who taught the theologians, rather than with the theologians who taught the non-specialist educated Christians.

With this thread to guide us we come quickly to the first landmark and have no difficulty in identifying it. In 1927 *Essays Catholic and Critical* was published. It was an important volume of essays by various Anglican theologians, all of broadly catholic convictions, and edited by Dr E. G. Selwyn, late Dean of Winchester. In his preface he claimed that the volume was in the succession as well as in the tradition of the *Lux Mundi* essays of 1888, and in fact it was the first volume of comparable importance in that field which had appeared since then. The purpose of Selwyn and his authors was to reckon fully with the great changes which had come over the theological scene since then, and to restate the catholic Faith in their light. They had been convinced of the need and the possibility of a synthesis between critical scholarship and catholic tradition ever since before the war of 1914; and the possibility of writing a book of essays to prove it was discussed between Selwyn and some of his contributors at a meeting they had at that time. The years had brought into play the high prestige of the critical movement in New Testament studies, which had triumphantly uncovered the origins and foundations of the Gospel. But they had also brought 'a keener discernment of the supernatural element in religion, and a renewed interest in the expressions of it which are seen in Catholic unity and authority, in whatever form these come'.[1] Their purpose was to weave these two new forces into a synthesis, and to use this synthesis for the reinterpretation of the historical basis of the Christian religion. This purpose and scope of the book was brilliantly expressed in its title. No one has seriously doubted that the authors did succeed in what they attempted, and their book at once became seminal, in the sense that it laid upon all subsequent theological study the necessity of reckoning with it.

Many fine things were in it. Perhaps there has never been a better short apologia for the necessity of religion as a whole than A. E. Taylor's *The Vindication of Religion*, a beautifully clear and wonderfully even-tempered essay of such quality that a single reading is a memory which time does not efface. *The Spirit and the Church in History*, by Eric Milner-White, late Dean of York, is a lyrical piece of writing from which one finds oneself quoting again and again. The editor's own contribution, *The Resurrection*, is still a classic example of the art of assembling complicated evidence,

---

[1] *Essays Catholic and Critical*, edited by E. G. Selwyn (S.P.C.K.), 1926, p.v.

clarifying and interpreting it in the briefest possible compass. There were other jewels as well, but the passage of time has left no serious doubt about which of these essays turned out in the end to be the most influential. It was Sir Edwyn Hoskyns' *The Christ of the Synoptic Gospels*, which has ever since exercised a profound effect upon Anglican theology. If there was ever to be a public competition in which one was asked to quote the most influential sentence in the field of theology written during the last thirty years, there would be many who would at once enter the first sentence of this essay, and they might well win the prize:

For the Catholic Christian, Quid vobis videtur de Ecclesia? What think ye of the Church? is not merely as pertinent a question as Quid vobis videtur de Christo? What think ye of Christ? it is but the same question differently formulated.[1]

The man who thus challengingly opened his essay, and in a single vivid sentence made plain its theme, was the Dean of Corpus Christi College, Cambridge. In 1926 he was known only to three very different circles of men; to the students of the Cambridge theological faculty, and to them he was a beloved master; to the men of the Lancashire territorial division he had served as chaplain during the war; and to the little company of academic New Testament scholars. Hoskyns mattered to fewer than did these others, but he exercised upon them, and on the students they taught in their turn, an influence profound, decisive, and lifelong. He had no remarkable gifts of leadership. His writing was not particularly attractive; it was indeed wrought out of a constant struggle, and so was often rough and obscure. His mind was essentially academic, though it was also catholic in the exact sense of that word. The catholicity of mind which made the *Farmer and Stockbreeder* a weekly treat led the devotee of exact, dispassionate scholarship to write on one occasion a splendid description of the academic mind as the layman sees it—'the innate tendency of the academic mind first to complicate what is obvious, and then to perform mental gymnastics as prodigious as they are unnecessary'.[2] This was never true of him, but it must often have seemed to be true to those who heard him for the first time; and even old students of his have said that in his later books he was apt to write after the manner of one who was always saying to himself, 'No, it can't be as simple as that: I must have overlooked some difficulty.'

The centre of his influence (wrote one of his pupils) lay in Cambridge; and for the past fifteen years it was true of him . . . that young ordinands gravitated to this University for the express purpose of studying theology under his direction. It is no dishonour to the Divinity Professor to record how men, and women, came to Cambridge for the sake of Hoskyns . . . In his hands theology became dynamic and creative. His lectures on the Theology and Ethics of the New Testament were exceptionally vivid, forceful, trenchant, and unexpected, and were

[1] *Ibid.*, p. 153.   [2] *Ibid.*, p. 160.

delivered with a sustained enthusiasm and excitement which it is impossible for anyone who heard them ever to forget: by contrast, his sermons, though equally emphatic seemed curiously restrained. It was through these lectures, and through his college teaching and his supervisions, that he left his abiding mark upon the Church of England: for through them he exerted an unrivalled influence upon the younger clergy, who remain to carry on the work from which God in His inscrutable wisdom has now recalled him.[1]

There are no overtones of personal loyalty in this testimony. Any enquiry among those whom Hoskyns taught at once draws similar expressions of gratitude.

The secret is in the fact that those whom he taught knew that they owed to him a great deliverance. Others before him had set themselves to remedy the mischief wrought by the application of the assumptions of liberalism to theology. Others, too, had realized, as Hoskyns did, just what this mischief was—a paralysing uncertainty about the Christian message, a haunting suspicion of the supposed intellectual inferiority of Christian theology when set over against current evolutionary thinking, a temptation to despair when all the promises of progress for humanity were one after another broken like straws. Both G. K. Chesterton and Charles Gore (to mention no other names) had in their different ways set themselves to perform just such a task. But Hoskyns was more radical than they; he went down to the roots of the mischief. These roots were embedded in the long reign of the negative criticism of the New Testament, which had ended by leaving the reader with only a 'tattered copy of St Mark's Gospel' in his hand, as Schweitzer had said, which had shrouded with mistiness the Christ of the Gospels, and had clothed with dubiety all the presuppositions which Jesus took for granted and the evangelists used as foundations. That was where so much of the contemporary despair among sensitive people had begun, where the refusal of freedom by so many of the young and ardent had started. That too was the point where the cure must begin. The same critical process which had been used to drive a wedge between Jesus and St Paul and to separate Christ from his Church must again be used—the same techniques, the identical methods—to destroy the conclusions to which it had seemed to lead. The theologian of the New Testament had compromised the present and only the theologian of the New Testament could restore the future. Remedies as well as judgements must begin with the scriptures read in the Church. It was with this conviction that Hoskyns began his essay in *Essays Catholic and Critical*, and when he had finished it he had so hoisted the modernist critics with their own petards that they have never again been able to hypnotize the Church. 'The Liberal Christ' still had his canvassers; of whom Dr Cadoux was the most famous. But fewer and fewer Christians hearkened to their charming. Hoskyns wrote

[1] Charles Smyth, Introduction to *Cambridge Sermons of Edwyn Clement Hoskyns* (S.P.C.K.), 1938, p. xix.

much else besides this essay, but perhaps it had a wider range of effectiveness on the theological sphere than anything else he wrote.

The essay is really its own summary, and any précis of it is bound to be arbitrary in its selection and relatively unjust. The problem was to discover the 'relation between the life and teaching of Jesus of Nazareth and the Christ of St Paul, of St John, and of Catholic piety', and further the relation 'between the little group of disciples called by Jesus from among the Galilean fishermen and the *Corpus Christi* of St Paul of the *Civitas Dei* of St Augustine'.[1] The Modernists, or Liberal Protestants, thought their studies had brought them to the point where they could say what these relations were. Hoskyns used five pages to state in summary form but with scrupulous fairness what their solution was. The spirit of it can be most conveniently shown by a quotation from Professor E. F. Scott's book, *The New Testament Today*, which Hoskyns himself copied for his essay, and put into a footnote.

Above all, the figure of Jesus stands out all the more grandly as the mists of theological speculation are blown away from him, and we come to discern him as he really sojourned on earth. It is not too much to say that by recovering for us the historical life of Jesus criticism has brought Christianity back to the true source of its power. The creeds, whatever may have been their value formerly, have broken down, but Jesus as we know him in his life, and all the more as his life is freed from the accretions of legend, still commands the world's reverence and devotion. The theology of the future, it is not rash to prophesy, will start from the interpretation of Jesus as a man in history.[2]

Now in that passage there are two main assumptions—that it is possible to blow the mists of theological speculation away from Jesus and that this has in fact been done, and that the historical life of Jesus which criticism uncovers shows him as standing aloof from the credal statements about himself, and separated from the content of super-nature of which the creeds are full. Such was the spirit of what Hoskyns called the 'Liberalism Protestant solution'. Its results had been to separate our Lord from the Church, from St Paul, to minimize the element of the supernatural in the Gospel, and not merely the element of miracle. Jesus, concluded the Liberal Protestant solution, 'did not claim to possess a divine nature',[3] did not found the Church, did not foresee a worldwide mission to preach his Name, and meant by the title 'Son of Man' 'his consciousness of the dignity of his essential humanity'.[4] What had been achieved by the use of the weapon of critical scholarship was a new sanction for 'modern idealistic humanitarianism', and, still more important,

A basis is now provided for a new reformation of the Christian religion, capable of ensuring its survival in the modern world. In the Gospel of Jesus is to be

---

[1] *Cambridge Sermons*, p. 153.   [2] *Ibid.*, p. 159.
[3] *Ibid.*, p. 156.   [4] *Ibid.*, p. 155.

found the pure religion of civilized and united humanity. Thus the assured results of liberal historical criticism form as necessary a prelude to the Christianity of the future as the preaching of John the Baptist did to the original proclamation.[1]

To the scriptures they had appealed, and to the scriptures Hoskyns determined to take them; and in the scriptures he took them more particularly to the synoptic Gospels from which they themselves had chiefly drawn their own Christological 'solution'. No one was more competent to do this than he, a New Testament scholar of European reputation, whom nobody would have dared for a moment to accuse of selecting evidence to prove a case. These Gospels were in fact the sacred writings of a living community, the primitive Church. The Epistles were the records connected with the processes of building the community. The only genuinely historical way of reading the Gospels was to read them in the light which the Epistles shed upon them. Nor could they be read at all in a patterned literary form unless the way of the Cross and the triumph of the Resurrection was the vital principle which bestowed shape upon the narratives. No one could possibly make sense of Good Friday and Easter Day who began by emptying that event, a single event, of its supernatural content. Furthermore, it was a first principle of objective historical criticism that Gospel stories in which the normal and the supernatural are inextricably mingled must not be read with the pre-conceived and fixed idea that 'what is supernatural has been superimposed by the irrational credulity of later enthusiastic believers'.[2] This is to reduce the Gospels to tales told, if not by idiots, at least by men who had no glimmerings whatever of literary craftsmanship, and the synoptic writers evidently had far more than glimmerings of it, whether it came to them by the inspiration of God, the light of nature, or (as possibly with St Luke) by literary training. Hoskyns went on to a long exposure of the fallacies in the 'Liberal Protestant Reconstruction'. It led to the demonstration that the only possible way of reading the basic documents, the synoptic Gospels, was to regard the supernatural element as being at least as primitive as the moral element; and that the 'exclusiveness, which is so obviously a characteristic of Catholic Christianity, may have its origin in the teaching of Jesus rather than in the theology of St Paul'.[3] Furthermore, he showed that the belief about modern life to which the 'Liberal Protestant' handling of the Gospels pointed was in fact completely at variance with the belief about life held by the synoptic writers, and derived by them from the teaching and practice of Jesus. 'The conception that the human order can be transformed into the kingdom of Heaven by a process of gradual evolution is completely foreign to the New Testament.'[4] He had in fact no doubt that the Gospel is ineradicably supernatural, and that the four written Gospels which contain it (the first three not less than the fourth) maintained at every stage of their growth

[1] *Ibid.*, p. 156.   [2] *Ibid.*, p. 165.   [3] *Ibid.*, p. 169.   [4] *Ibid.*, p. 171.

the balance between natural and supernatural in Christ. Thus the radical criticism of the Gospels had results quite other than had sometimes been supposed. It inseparably joined Christ to St Paul, and Christ to his Church, and formed a new and sure foundation for the catholic traditions of faith, life, and worship. Perhaps the heart of Hoskyns' work can best be summarized by a single quotation from the last section, the conclusion of his essay:

> From this reconstruction it will be seen at once that a whole series of contrasts underlies the Synoptic Tradition. . . . The contrast is not between the Jesus of history and the Christ of faith, but between the Christ humiliated and the Christ returning in glory. . . . The contrast is not between a reformed and an unreformed Judaism, but between Judaism and the new supernatural order by which it is at once destroyed and fulfilled: not between the disciples of a Jewish prophet and the members of an ecclesiastically ordered sacramental cultus, but between the disciples of Jesus, who, though translated into the sovereignty of God, are as yet ignorant both of His claims and of the significance of their own conversion, and the same disciples, initiated into the mystery of His person and of His life and death, leading the mission to the world, the patriarchs of the new Israel of God. The contrast is not between an ethical teaching and a dreamy eschatology, or between a generous humanitarianism and an emotional religious experience stimulated by mythological beliefs, but between a supernatural order characterized by a radical moral purification involving persistent moral conflict and the endurance of persecution, and a supernatural order in which there is no place either for moral conflict or for persecution.[1]

The high importance of what Hoskyns had done in this essay did not immediately disclose itself to all eyes. But little by little it came to be seen that theological Liberalism, having been attacked by a master hand wielding its own weapons, had been smitten in a mortal place. Since he wrote less and less has been heard of the 'Liberal Christ' and today that mythical figure appears no longer in works of theology.

Hoskyns had done much to deliver the parochial clergy from their mesmerized state. Much of the authority previously conceded to the modernists by the average parish priest had been due to their learning. Though they might seem to him to be all the time blowing pieces out of the rock of the Scriptures, and so destroying the basis of the Gospel he believed and was commissioned to proclaim, he had the discomforting feeling that they knew far more about the science of biblical criticism than did their opponents, and that they had been abused rather than discredited. But here, at last, was a new portent—a university professor, who knew at least as much and possibly far more about New Testament scholarship than any don who had spoken at the Girton Conference of Modern Churchmen, and whose standards of disinterested academic research could not be questioned. Hoskyns was an acknowledged oracle, and the oracle, having accepted the

[1] *Ibid.*, pp. 177, 178.

challenge to appeal to the work of the critics on the primitive evangelical writings, had done so and had given his judgement.

Hoskyns had destroyed an idol. He had shown that a particular treatment of the New Testament made nonsense of history. He had next to show that an application of the new knowledge to the Bible revealed the real faith of the Bible, and that this faith was worth the holding, because it was true, because it made history intelligible and consistent with ordinary human experience, because it was demonstrably the faith of the forlorn hope which conquers in the Spirit. He had to begin by exploding the Liberal Protestant fallacy, but his really basic and seminal work was to reanchor Anglican theology to the Scriptures, and to show that out of the Scriptures came the Church. Thus both Scriptures and the Church were equally given by God as parts of his very Word to man, and endorsed by Christ as such. The Scriptures as he expounded them became, so to say, more of a rock than ever, and became it precisely because of what the new methods of historical criticism had brought to their interpretation. They had brought into bolder relief than ever before the 'Scandal of Uniqueness' which is the distinguishing mark of the Faith of the Bible; and, as Hoskyns spoke or wrote of this 'scandal', he had the power to show clearly that as the God of the Scriptures was clothed with a rigid exclusiveness from all other imagined deities of man, so the demand of the Scriptures upon all who took them seriously was that because the mere holding of such a faith would be an offence, they too must accept the reproaches of exclusiveness. It was dangerous doctrine (the truth is nearly always dangerous) and liable to be misunderstood. But it was not tame and dull. It is small wonder that many students went to Cambridge simply to be taught by a man who spoke to them in accents like these. Hoskyns was no Barthian, though he understood Barth and greatly admired him. None the less, he became to Anglican theology the same kind of moving and disturbing force that Karl Barth was to European Protestantism.

13

The Results of Theological Principle in the Daily Life of the Church

I · *The Decline of Partisanship*

MANY PEOPLE are apt to think that theology is the splitting of hairs of academic theory and of the work of theologians as having no relevance to the practical problems of life. They are of course wrong, and the truth is the exact opposite of what they suppose. Nothing is so powerful in practice as a theological idea. As a matter of mere historical demonstration, notions about God and his purpose for the world do change history and alter continents, and they affect for good and ill the whole manner of man's life in the world and his relationship to his environment. Because Luther once insisted that justification before God is by faith alone all Europe was changed, and the getting and the spending of every peasant and every aristocrat altered its pattern and its rhythm. The power of theology is not less in a mechanical than in a pastoral age, and the work of Hoskyns and those who echoed and followed him, and developed still further the principles he had established, began to show itself in the daily life and worship of the parish churches within a very few years, and therefore to affect many thousands of people who had never heard his name or theirs.

He spoke the words for which so many were waiting and in accents which made them hear. His deepest conviction could be put in a phrase: the Faith of the Bible as the Word of God to be Practised in the Church of the Bible as the Body of Christ. That is exactly what Father A. G. Hebert, of the Society of the Sacred Mission at Kelham, had been steadily teaching for years. The mere recitation of the titles of his books shows it—*Liturgy and Society*, *The Throne of David*, *The Form of the Church*, *The Authority of the Old Testament*. The two great books of Father Lionel Thornton, of the Community of the Resurrection at Mirfield, exhibit exactly the same theological movement, for he followed *The Incarnate Lord* by *Common Life in the Body of Christ,* and the latter study is radically biblical throughout in a sense in which the former is not. The same assumptions also underlie the whole work of Father Hebert and many others on the Parish Communion, and the great liturgical study of Dom Gregory Dix of Nashdom Abbey, *The Shape of the Liturgy;* and they give form and shape also to a work so different from these as Dorothy Sayers' *The Man Born to be King.* Archbishop William Temple himself was moving fast towards it and away from the old emphases of liberal catholicism when he died. Soon after he was appointed to the Primacy he declared in the *Christian News Letter* that the Christian thought of all the world was steadily converging on some half-dozen affirmations, and the first of these he phrased as 'Decision for God who has spoken'.

The immediate 'practical' result of this movement of theological emphasis is that the strife of the historic parties in the Church has almost completely ceased, for once it was accepted the parties themselves were seen to be quite irrelevant to the situation created in the Church by this theology, and outside the Church by the strife of nations and the predicament of man. Partisanship on the century-old lines rapidly became out of date. For what was being taught was essentially a rediscovery and reassertion of the authority both of the Church and of the Bible—not the one by itself or the other, but both. Protestants and Catholics in the Church thus found much common ground. Protestants saw that many indubitably catholic theologians were laying more and more stress in their teaching on the Bible, while their own theologians were enthusiastically exploring the authority of churchmanship. In these changed circumstances High Church and Low Church rapidly became technical terms without meaning. It is very largely to this that we owe the blessed relief from the strife of tongues and pens between them. The last really discreditable outbreak of such sectarian strife was on the occasion of the debating of the Revised Prayer Book of 1928. It was most violent while it lasted, but it subsided with remarkable speed, and it is doubtful if we shall see any revival of it. When parties find that they have so much more in common than they once suspected, partisanship ceases to be.

II · *Baptism and Confirmation*

The new teaching about the Church is at once exciting and disturbing to those who hear it for the first time. The Church of our baptism is the Divine Society and the Body of Christ. It is the divinely given social mould within which alone it is possible to practise the Beatitudes of the Sermon on the Mount. Set, as it is, in the twentieth-century world, our own Church of England is again a missionary body offering redemption to a country needing reconversion and in a society which has now become sub-Christian. We are again the Church of the New Testament, living in biblical times reborn, and having a closer kinship with the Church of the first three centuries than could have been claimed by any generation of the Church in between.

The mere utterance of the word 'baptism' in this context at once brings one face to face with the first barrier which prevents the Church from becoming in practice what the theologians and the prophets have been declaring that it is in the mind of God. It is now generally acknowledged that the way in which infants are commonly presented for baptism comes near to being a denial of the true nature of the Church, and a mockery of the actual situation in which it finds itself. 'Indiscriminate Baptism' has been the practice of the Church for at least fifteen centuries, but it is only in the last twenty or thirty years that the clear knowledge has come that something is very wrong. Infant baptism, as we have been practising it for so many years, has now become a chronically sore place in the ecclesiastical conscience of the Church of England, and of other English Communions besides. The real trouble is that the spirit of baptism in the Early Church no longer applies, where, after the initiation, it followed the 'Easter Mass in the dawn, and first communion as the beginning of Christian life in the midst of the exultant Church'.[1] 'Exultant' is the ringing word in that sentence. We have made it almost impossible for members of the Church to 'exult' because a new member has been admitted. It is not nowadays a rare thing to hear priests who undoubtedly hold the full catholicity of the Church both in faith and in practice declare that baptism of an infant should be a privilege reserved for the infants of parents whose Christian profession cannot be doubted because it has been steadily asserted in the practising membership of the Church for years. They believe that the normal practice should be baptism only after full preparation, and therefore administered at the age of confirmation.

The whole theological problem has been carefully analysed by reference to the baptismal practice of the Early Church in the pamphlet from which quotation has just been made. Dom Gregory Dix finds the root of our trouble in our separation of baptism from confirmation and both from the first communion, whereas in the early days these three were all parts of one and the same rite. Diagnosis is not the same thing as remedy, and to suggest remedies was not Dix's purpose. But our practice of baptizing every baby presented to us regardless of whether there is the least likelihood or even possibility of its being trained to be a Christian not only makes nonsense of the whole doctrine of the Church as we have received it, but also (and precisely because it does so) it seriously hampers and embarrasses the whole witness and proclamation of the Church.

The most pressing aspect of the pastoral problem today lies precisely in those millions of English people of goodwill who sincerely regard themselves as practising Christians, who are baptized and insist on the Baptism of their children in

[1] Dom Gregory Dix, *The Theology of Confirmation in Relation to Baptism* (Dacre Press), 1946, p. 12.

infancy, but who regard the Christian life as something a man does for himself, individually and privately. . . . Of the Church as organic, as the Body of Christ, of the Divine life within it, of their own responsibility to it and for it, these people know and acknowledge little or nothing. . . . The existence of this vast amorphous mass of Pelagian goodwill, at least three or four times as large as the living Body of the Church which seeks to live by grace, is what muffles the whole impact of the Gospel, and the whole witness of the Church in England today. Deal with this problem, incorporate these people effectively into the life of the Church and you will have some prospect of making an impression on the equally large mass of sheer paganism behind. . . . The foundations of any long term policy lie in the field of right *teaching* about Baptism and Confirmation. A right change in this must in the end do something to dissipate this immense and disastrous misunderstanding.[1]

Anxiety had been expressed and agitation had been carried on in a desultory and sporadic way ever since 1898 when two Yorkshire rural deaneries, Dewsbury and Birstall, had delivered the burden of their consciences about it. But it was in 1920 that a strong joint committee of the Convocations of Canterbury and York made its report.[2] Dr Chase, then Bishop of Ely, had been its chairman, and six bishops had been among its members. The report was a very cautious document, and it betrayed itself, among other ways, by the weakness of its language about the sponsors which the Church requires in infant baptism. The primary difficulty first of finding suitable sponsors, and then of training them, was certainly mentioned; but the committee shied away from the suggestion that there might be certain babies whose baptism the Church ought to defer until there is a reasonable likelihood of its requirements being met. 'One caution is necessary. The command to make disciples of all nations . . . ought not to be restricted in such a way as to "forbid little children" to be brought to Christ because those who present them do not understand the blessings which Christ bestows in baptism, or the responsibilities which corporate fellowship with God involves.'[3]

That this committee of 1920 had solved nothing and satisfied nobody is shown by the fact that since then others have had continuously to put their hands to the work it had been charged to do. In 1937 the Social and Industrial Commission of the Church Assembly had produced a report on The Church and Youth, in which a great deal was said on the problems of baptism. The relevant part of this report was considered by the House of Bishops in the Convocation of Canterbury in a long debate. It brought out the useful fact that the remarks about baptism in the report had been the work not of clergy but of a body of young people. They had asserted that 'the present confusion seems to us to jeopardize the spiritual purpose of Holy Baptism'; and they had gone so far as to make certain practical sug-

---

[1] Dix, *op. cit.*, p. 34.　　[2] *Administration of Infant Baptism* (S.P.C.K.), 1920.
[3] *Ibid.*, p. 5.

gestions. They were that parents should be asked to attend preliminary instruction concerning the nature of baptism, that times of baptism should be much less frequent and much more should be made of the sacrament when these times came round, that sponsors should always be prepared, that the parents of a child should be asked to sign a solemn promise: 'We do solemnly promise, with God's help, that our child shall be brought up in the Christian Faith according to the teaching of the Church of England.'[1] These suggestions were sympathetically received by the bishops, who, one after another, testified to the universality of uneasiness. They were not, however, officially endorsed by them.

In January 1939 the Upper House of the Convocation of Canterbury turned again to the same problem. They produced most alarming statistics. In the last twenty-four years sixty-seven per cent of all the babies born in England had been baptized by the Church of England—that is, eleven and a half million babies had been baptized in our churches in that period. Yet the Easter communicants in 1937 had numbered only two and a quarter million.[2] There was agreement both among the bishops and the mass of the clergy that while there might be many remedies for that most disturbing fact, the reform of baptismal procedure was certainly one of of them. The bishops agreed that the priest of one parish ought not to baptize babies from another parish except by the consent of the other priest. But Dr C. S. Woodward, then Bishop of Bristol, in urging a resolution to this effect, regretted that it was advisory only, and said frankly: 'The difficulty is one which I confess I do not know how to deal with.'[3]

A further resolution that 'the clergy are justified in delaying the baptism of an infant on the ground that the parents are not ready to fulfil the Church's requirements concerning sponsors' was not carried. The Archbishop at the end made the blameless comment that we 'must make a sustained effort to see that the ideal, so far as possible, is realized'.[4] This was the report which caused the editor of *Theology* to write an article entitled *Baptismal Disgrace*.

III · *The Bible and the Bible Reading Fellowship*

'If the Church is the Household of grace, it is the Bible which anchors the Church to the true Word of God and which equips Christians for their warfare.' The words were those of the Archbishops of Canterbury and York in their message to the Bible Reading Fellowship on the occasion of its twenty-fifth birthday.[5]

Long ago, in that other world of 1911, the tercentenary of the Authorized Version of the Bible was celebrated. A flood of eulogistic literature

[1] *C.C.C.*, 1937, pp. 294–5.   [2] *C.C.C.*, 1939, p. 229.
[3] *Ibid.*, pp. 241–3.   [4] *Ibid.*, p. 245.
[5] *Twenty-Five Years: 1922–1947* (The Bible Reading Fellowship), p. 1.

poured from the presses. But it marked not the beginning but the end of an epoch in the history of the Bible. For three hundred years English Christianity had been Bible Christianity, and English literature had been moulded, nursed, and fed by the language of the Authorized Version. But for the next thirty-five years the influence of the Bible on the life of the nation, and even on the life of the Church, was to become steadily less, as the legend spread among the people that the Bible was no longer trustworthy. As Bible religion was the only religion the man-in-the-street knew, he ceased to practise any religion at all when he ceased to read the Bible, and to bother whether his children ever opened it or not. This is perhaps, the greatest religious change of this century, and it has been devastating.

Of all the agencies which have set themselves to remedy this disturbing, potentially disastrous state of affairs, the Bible Reading Fellowship has probably been one of the most successful. The story of the Fellowship is one of the romances of Anglican history in the twentieth century, and it constitutes an example of the true spiritual adventure, for it is throughout the story of God's action in power upon an enterprise begun and continued in fellowship, at every stage deliberately offered to God for his pleasure. Beginning in a single parish in Brixton in 1922, the Fellowship's leaflets of Bible readings and notes go today to thousands of readers every month in many parts of the world. They find queens and prisoners to read them, and every kind of person between these extremes; and when any priest of the Anglican Communion has a confirmation candidate who wants to read the Bible regularly but does not know how, it has become virtually an instinct to suggest first of all the use of the appropriate monthly leaflet of the Bible Reading Fellowship.

A chance conversation began it all. Or 'was it just chance?'[1] asked Canon L. G. Mannering twenty-five years later. Probably it was not. He was at the time vicar of St Matthew's, Brixton; and he was talking of the needs of the parish with his staff. What was needed in this typical and ordinary South London parish of 13,000 souls? They did not answer at once and off-hand; 'we talked and prayed about it.'[2] Then they knew. The need was not for more machinery, but for something basic and seminal, something to promote and spread and deepen the revolutionary simplicities of Christian living, prayer, the reading of the Bible, communion at the Eucharist, and all practised in conscious fellowship with others. The circumstances of the parish seemed to make necessary the monthly publication of a paper giving subjects for intercession and Bible passages for reading, with brief and simple notes. But it was not to be a purely private thing; those who took the papers must be in a conscious fellowship, with a weekly service for intercession and an exposition of the readings for that week, and a corporate communion each month. The papers were to be the badges of membership of a definite parochial society, the Fellowship of St Matthew. 'We will

[1] *Twenty-Five Years*, p. 15.   [2] *Ibid.*, p. 15.

make the venture,' wrote the vicar to his people, 'believing that God calls us to this.' This leaflet of a parochial fellowship in Brixton was the first publication of what was presently to be the Bible Reading Fellowship; and it soon begot a mighty progeny.

At first it grew slowly. When the first year ended 175 people were taking and using the leaflets in the fellowship, which was still parochial. Then three other parishes joined in the scheme; St Jude's, Brixton, St. John's, Eastbourne, and St Andrew's, Aysgarth, in Yorkshire. Between them they had brought the number to 500 at the end of the second year. Then Canon Tom Pym, at that time Canon Missioner in Southwark Diocese, took a hand, and gathered a number of South London clergy to tell them of what St Matthew's, Brixton, had been doing. Other parishes came in, and by the end of 1926 the circulation of the papers had risen to 1,500. There were now too many parishes to make it possible for a single leaflet of subjects for intercession to suit all their needs. Thus each one was bidden to makes its own list of intercessions, and the Fellowship's leaflet was confined to Bible readings and notes. It also changed its name to the Bible Reading Fellowship. Plainly it had outgrown the capacity of a single parish to deal with it, and that further and much wider growth was before it seemed clear. These things constituted not a crisis but one of those moments in the history of any movement which grows naturally from small beginnings when fresh decisions have to be made. Those in charge of the Fellowship's fortunes recognized this, but characteristically they would decide nothing until they had together sought to discover the decision of God:

> The Fellowship entered upon a new phase. There were indications that it might grow rapidly—all the more need therefore for prayer and guidance. What might be the purpose of God for this Fellowship? What line ought we to take? In May 1927, again under the leadership of Canon Pym, a group of us met for prayer and conference at the Diocesan Retreat House in Carshalton. It was unanimously agreed that the movement should be left to grow naturally and without publicity.[1]

A lame and impotent conclusion? At that moment it might perhaps have seemed so, for the only light they had was to carry on and not to force the pace. The decisive moment produced no new decision.

Yet in the next three years the circulation jumped from 600 to 20,000; and the papers were being read and used in many parts of the world. The original series of monthly leaflets had gradually to be multiplied into four or five different series. The leaflets were regularly published in a dozen different languages, and soon a special Braille edition was added. The work grew so fast that its direction had to be moved from Brixton in 1930 to an office in Westminster; and a full time secretary, Miss Margery Sykes, was engaged in 1930, and a full office staff to support her. Since then the office

---

[1] *Ibid.*, p. 28.

has had to be moved three times, as the work outgrew the accommodation. Through the years before the war the work went on; and during the war itself, though many of the Fellowship's members were cut off from their source of supply, there was still an increase of 98,000 new members. But what of those who had grown to rely on the Fellowship's leaflets for their Bible reading, and could no longer receive them? There were many, and one of them, in Haarlem, later told the story in words which constitute the best of all tributes to what the Fellowship had achieved.

When in May 1940 the Germans took possession of this country, a small group of members of the Church of England at Haarlem—mostly British wives of Dutch husbands—were left here without a padre, a church, or anything and by the end of the month those of us who were of the B.R.F., some six or seven, realized that no more leaflets would be coming either. We set to work and had a meeting every fortnight in turns at our houses, and put together all the old B.R.F. Notes we had (one of us even had them from 1933), and made a sort of 'circulating library' using the months of bygone years for our meetings and at home, e.g. my family always read them at family prayers. So we kept going, and thank God the Germans never discovered our meetings. By 1945 we were very much at the end of this circulating library, and when at the liberation the first Canadian Army Chaplain gave us a handful of the green 'For those on Service' B.R.F. leaflets we were very pleased, and now we can join again since January. Last year we still depended on friends getting them for us because we couldn't pay for them. So when you are together presently to give thanks for the many blessings of the B.R.F. our thanksgivings will be with you in the spirit, for a fellowship which meant so much in the hard time we had.

Facts and figures can etch no more than the dry bones of such a story. They cannot by themselves give any indication of what the story means in terms of the immensity of achievement, nor what the achievement means in terms of the lives it helps to mould, nor yet how it has come about that there is so remarkable a story to be told. There is no doubt about its grand scale. From 100 members to 351,000 in twenty-five years, and all done without publicity, without over-organization, without any use of the techniques of high-pressure salesmanship.

IV · *The Eucharist and the Parish Communion*

It is impossible to think of the Church without also thinking of the Eucharist, for it is the sacrament ordained by the Founder of the Church and the rite given to be used in the Church by which the Church's people are united to their Lord and to each other. The rediscovery of the phrase in the Creed, 'I believe in the Holy Catholic Church' by the Oxford Movement more than a hundred years ago led at once to a revaluation of the Holy Communion; and it is common knowledge that the great increase in every parish church of opportunities for people to receive their communion, and the steady growth in decency and solemnity when it is celebrated is due to the Oxford Movement.

The outward and visible sign of this prevailing view has come to be the Parish Communion, and the meaning of it was first set out at full length, in 1937, in a composite book of essays by various writers, called *The Parish Communion*, and edited by Father A. G. Hebert. The broad insight of all the writers is this: if you express your philosophy of the Church and the World by the phrase 'Let the Church be the Church', then you are led straight to the Parish Communion as the rite which most naturally expresses what you believe. The Parish Communion is the Eucharist at which all, or nearly all, the confirmed members of the parish make their communion together as the one family of God in that place. It is a joining of whole human families to offer the Great Sacrifice in order that they may be made into one supernatural family in the Church.

This conception of the place of the Eucharist in the life of the parish is a clear implementing of the conception of the Church rooted in the Bible and set over against the World. Those who believe in the Parish Communion do so because they believe these things about the Church.

The real aim (of the book, *The Parish Communion*, writes its editor) is to set forth a conception of the nature of the Church, which appears to compel the adoption of the Parish Communion as its necessary expression in liturgy. It is the idea of the Church that is primary.[1]

And what a theology 'compels', the facts of the modern situation of the Church encourages. The Church is so plainly face to face with a secularized world; all the more reason, then, that the chief service in the parish church on a Sunday morning 'should fully set forth the nature of the Church and that the members of the Church should fully know what the Church is'.[2] It is one with the Church of the Scriptures, and one with the primitive Church of the first three centuries, and as such should be conscious of its separation from the World and its position of privilege in the divine scheme of things.

Deep in the mind of the primitive Church, and colouring every strand of her belief, is the strong consciousness of the unique privilege with God of the 'Holy Church'. She is the new 'Israel of the Spirit' which has replaced the old 'Israel according to the flesh' in the Divine love and in the Divine plan for the universe.[3]

The Parish Communion, the authors believed, would help to inculcate this sense of privileged separation. The aggression of the modern world, moreover, makes this sense of separated privilege empirically necessary, and especially in the case of a national Church, like the Church of England, since the pressure of the state will always seek to persuade or compel the Church to accommodate her Gospel to 'the religion which the nation holds',

---

[1] *The Parish Communion*, edited by A. G. Hebert (S.P.C.K.), 1937, p. vii.
[2] *Ibid.*, p. 13.   [3] *Ibid.*, pp. 127, 128.

and as a speaker demanded in the debate on the Revised Prayer Book in 1928 'to bring the doctrines of the Church of England into accord with the doctrines of the people'.[1] Against this danger, too, the authors see the Parish Communion as a shield.

Whether the Parish Communion fulfils all these purposes or not, it is now the normal eucharistic practice in many parishes, and it is slowly changing and enriching the common understanding of churchmanship, its relevance and its value. One picture of it may stand for many. In the country parish of Temple Balsall in Warwickshire, it has been celebrated at 8.45 for thirty years or more. The service, which lasts an hour, is congregational throughout, and well interspersed with hymns, and the people come to it from all corners of the parish. For various reasons it is held 'in a room in the Almshouse court, known as the Parish Room, but originally the parish Boys' School, where many of the older men received their education, and with the schoolmaster's rostrum still *in situ*'.[2] There, in that room made holy, the Eucharist was offered in, for, and by the whole family of the faithful in the Household of Faith Sunday by Sunday. The people were their own choir. They sang Merbecke, and did not tire of him, and 'a very little musical talent went, by the blessing of God, a long way'. Everything was done to emphasize that this was the characteristic act of worship of a family. The notices and biddings were of simple homely things, causes, and persons— known to all and the concern of all. The people came in large numbers, and in families—the little children, parents, and grandparents all in church together; and the actual communion lasted long enough for three hymns to be sung during its course. All felt the service as their very own. A farmer milked his cows, delivered the milk, and then came two miles with his family on a motor cycle and side-car. A cowman rose at five o'clock to get his work done, another came with his wife who 'received the Blessed Sacrament with her baby in her arms and a little one of two years old by her side'. They all worshipped together in this way every Sunday. It taught them that they really were the Church, all alike in it and of it, an island of sanity and love in a frantic world; and that in the Church they walked with God for just so long as they walked together. When the service was over, they all had breakfast together, and

it was interesting to note how the congregation sorted themselves out at the breakfast. There were five tables in the room, one being appropriated to the children, who, for economical reasons were supplied with treacle instead of marmalade, and besmeared themselves accordingly: the boys and growing lads took possession of a smaller table. . . . On the other side of it were to be found the maidens of the congregation seated at a table specially claimed as their own— though they always welcomed the intrusion of guests of either sex. The middle-aged had a trestle table for themselves, while the clergy, church-wardens, and other leading members of the congregation, and visitors, occupied a central table

[1] Quoted in *ibid.*, p. 297 (note).   [2] *Ibid.*, p. 262.

in close proximity to the fire. Such is the courtesy of youth, and such the happy instinct for the fitness of things which prevailed in the little family which gathered there Sunday by Sunday after Holy Communion in church. Sometimes visitors would be present both in church and at breakfast. The unselfconscious and simple humility with which they would share the family meal, and the sensitive courtesy with which the village people welcomed them, were good to see.[1]

Such is the outline of Sunday morning family worship, which though still exceptional, is becoming the normal practice of an increasing number of parishes every year. It is a movement which seems bound to grow, and before very long it is likely that the exceptional parish churches will be those who still observe Sunday mornings as the Oxford Movement taught them, with an 8 o'clock Celebration for communion and either Matins or Choral Eucharist (or High Mass) at 11 for worship. It is idle to speculate just what effect this movement will have when it is the normal practice, but it is bound to work towards the integration of the members of the Church, and to do much to fulfil in worship and in life at least some of the promise lying hidden in the gradual unfolding of the dominant theological insight of Anglican history in the last thirty years. Its emphasis has been on Bible and Church, and it is leading us to a new focus on pulpit and altar.

[1] *Ibid.*, p. 263.

14

The Church of England and the Social Order

I · *The Work of the Pioneering Societies*

THE IDEA that because the Church is entrusted with the Gospel it has the positive duty of sitting in judgement upon the social and political institutions of the world, and the belief that the Gospel itself is maimed if it does not take society as well as individuals into its offer of redemption were the commonplaces of the Middle Ages. In 1850 they were strange archaic notions, and hardly anyone in England believed them. The few who did knew well that years of propaganda and teaching must pass before they could again be accepted by the Church as a whole. In retrospect there is far more success than failure. This story is punctuated and annotated by the work, almost incredible in the sheer volume of output, of the great men whose names are still alive, Ludlow, Kingsley, Maurice, Barnett and their peers. But they did not dominate the movement. They hardly even charted its course. They inspired it and they taught it. Most of the 'field' work was done by the little societies to which it gave birth. They had an influence out of all proportion to the smallness of their membership, and though they were sadly given to splitting into fragments and going off at wild tangents, which was their characteristic disease, their persistent devotion was profoundly influential. These little societies between them did most to bring us to where we now stand.

In 1877 was born the first of them. The Rector of Bethnal Green, Stewart Headlam, whose portrait Bernard Shaw is held to have painted in his *Candida*, founded the Guild of St Matthew. He was very much of a freak and an oddity—the sort of socialist who is no democrat, but who is at heart more deeply tinged with individualism than any believer in free competition and enterprise. But he had a superb courage, and an instinct for the telling dramatic gesture. When, for example, a young workman was killed in a socialist demonstration in London through being ridden down by the police horses, Headlam marched in front of his funeral procession from Bow Street, up the Strand to St Paul's and thence to Whitechapel cemetery. He forced the Guild into his own mould and painted it all over with his own colours. Its tone was catholic, its approach to social problems eucharistic. It held as its ideal the vision of a genuinely corporate Church within an omnicompetent state, at work in a society the citizens of which had undergone all the processes of economic levelling by means of socialist political action. Headlam and the Guild had so great an affection for the secularists they hoped to convert that they allowed the political affiliations of secularism too large a share in determining the policy of what was after all an avowedly Christian body. But though the Guild remained quite uninfluential in any political sense, for it never could boast more than 400 members, it has a niche in history, for it was the first corporate attempt to do something which had been badly needed since the Reformation and yet left undone.

In 1889 *Lux Mundi* was published. Those who have heard about but not actually read these essays are apt to suppose that they were all devoted to theology, and that their importance is due to their inclusion of Gore's first public avowal of the kenotic theory of the consciousness of Christ. *Lux Mundi* was indeed a landmark in the history of Anglican theology, but its editors had a sociological purpose as well, and two of the essays were purely social. There had been nothing of that sort in *Essays and Reviews*: between 1863 and 1889 theology had widened its borders. This greater width of interest testified to the catholicity of the book, and in the year of its publication its leading contributors, headed by Gore, founded the Christian Social Union. They had hoped that the Guild of St Matthew would serve the purpose they had in mind. But its colours were too bizarre and its politics too premature to suit their sagacious minds. Their purpose was to find out by the method of group research just what a Christian social order in the twentieth-century world ought to be. Until they had done this preliminary work they did not feel able to commit themselves to political socialism. As a group the Christian Social Union hardly succeeded in this main purpose of research, partly because it was never able to attach to itself enough of the economists and scholars without which it could hardly be done. But it 'taught its senators wisdom'. Idealists like Westcott and Gore became realists in matters of reform. It also did a fine work in a secondary sphere by pressing continually and effectively upon the conscience of the Church the evil of bad social conditions and it performed a great deal of the early education of Christian opinion, which was indispensable if Christians were ever to believe again that their very religion meant that they could not ignore the worlds of politics and industry. Here the fact that it had Scott Holland to write for it made a world of difference. But the Union was by no means content with its academic work. It struggled with the casualties as well as with the diagnosis of industrial disease. Gore, for instance, began his Oxford episcopate by publicly espousing the cause of the strikers in a Reading strike, subscribed to their funds, and

caused a thorough investigation to be made by social experts into the conditions of the working classes in Reading . . . showing that at least three thousand families in the borough had an income insufficient to maintain their members in efficiency.[1]

The Union was a larger and a less neurotic affair than the Guild of St Matthew. In 1910, its peak year, it had 6,000 members.

In 1906 the Parliamentary Labour Party was formed. Socialism had begun to stake its claim to a legitimate place in the constitution of Britain, and to make its bid for political power. Spurred by this significant event, another group of Anglican sociologists came together and decided that neither of the two societies already in the field met the needs they saw, and so founded another, the Christian Socialist League. This new Society was intended to be the infant Labour Party's soul. In politics therefore it was committed to socialism. In religion, however, it was much less uncompromising. It set out to be as 'comprehensive' as it supposed the Anglican Church was, and it refused to become partisan in its ecclesiastical sympathies. The particular contribution it sought to make to sociology was to be found in the emphasis it ceaselessly laid on guild socialism, and, negatively, in its steady denunciation of the whole idea of the omnicompetent state. It argued for the *communitas communitatum* as the ideal form of polity, and thus it approached catholicity by another road. To picture the body social as consisting of an endless series of various small and vocational communities, bound up in and held together by a single large community to which all alike owe loyalty, and which in turn has the duty of guaranteeing the freedom and autonomy of each is the federal approach to the ancient catholic idea of the state. The League had Father Neville Figgis as its fugleman who expounded its ideas tirelessly and brilliantly in lectures and books; and time has shown that it had a clearer idea of what were to be the really important social issues of the twentieth century than either of the senior societies in this field. But in 1910 it had only 1,200 members as opposed to the 6,000 of the Christian Social Union at the same date.

The mere fact that there were three separate societies all trying to do the same work had weakened the social witness of the Church as a whole. They were working in competition. Two of them had been founded to repudiate some of the ideas of the first, but they soon began to emphasize most of them afresh. Presently there was a fourth, for in 1918 the catholics in the Church Socialist League became uneasy about the lack of a definite catholicity in its basis. Conrad Noel broke away, taking a number of its members with him, to found the Catholic Crusade. The alarmed remnant

[1] G. L. Prestige, *Life of Charles Gore*, p. 335.

of the Church Socialist League promptly revised its constitution, now making it so rigidly catholic as to have the unhappy result of driving out the whole of its protestant wing. The Catholic Crusade, like most movements which start as a protest against a parent body, quickly became and remained more eccentric than creative. The results of thirty years of work by these societies in the field of social witness and awakening had not been outwardly impressive. Taken together, their membership did not total more than 8,000. But figures rarely tell the whole tale, and events showed that in many ways these societies had done more to awaken the Church than they could possibly have known; just as other events showed that they had done less than they supposed.

In 1908 came the first indication that these fifty years of propaganda had left a good many churchpeople with the impression that the socialist pattern of society was not incompatible with the Gospel. In the summer of that year the Pan-Anglican Congress was held in London, and was attended by delegates from every Church in the Anglican Communion. The second day of the Congress was devoted to the subject, 'The Church and Human Society'. This vast theme covered far more than socialism. Marriage and rural housing were among the many other matters debated on this day. But it was the meeting on 'Christianity and Socialism' which saw the greatest enthusiasm. The previously prepared papers agreed in affirming that nothing in Christian doctrine was incompatible with socialism, though Gore sounded a note of caution when he wrote in his paper, 'We have no socialistic State in existence, or near to coming into existence'.[1] But when he went on to say:

> This, then, is the first great claim we make upon the Church today: that it should make a tremendous act of penitence for having failed so long and on so wide a scale to behave as the champion of the oppressed and the weak: for having tolerated what it ought not to have tolerated: for having so often been on the wrong side. And the penitence must lead to reparation while there is yet time, ere the well-merited judgements of God take all the weapons of social influence out of our hands . . . we must identify ourselves with the great impeachment of our present industrial system. We must refuse to acquiesce in it. But more than this, we must identify ourselves, because we are Christians, with the positive ethical ideal of socialistic thought[2]

he found words for the frame of mind which most of his audience had made their own. The subsequent discussion clearly showed it. Speaker after speaker identified himself with Gore's judgement, and then went further than Gore had done and identified Christianity with socialism considered as a way of governing the state as well as with its ethical ideal. Two young priests, perhaps more far-sighted than some others, ventured to warn the congress that socialism, too, might become a tyranny. But they were heard

---

[1] *Report of the Pan-Anglican Congress* (S.P.C.K.), 1908, vol. II, Paper S.A. 6a, p. 3.
[2] *Ibid.*, p. 5.

heedlessly, and the gathering's true character was registered by the *Nunc Dimittis* of the veteran J. M. Ludlow, then 87 years of age, a friend of Maurice and Kingsley and one of the last surviving Christian socialists of 1848, the breathless year of socialism. 'In those early days,' he said, 'we could never have hoped to see such an audience gathered for such a purpose, and I believe that a true Christian socialism is the faith of all present.'[1]

The enthusiasm of a church meeting may perhaps not amount to much in terms of practical action; nor are the sort of people who can come from many parts of the world to attend a week's congress in London genuinely representative of the rank and file membership of the Church. It cannot be argued that the atmosphere of the Congress on that day reflected a corresponding atmosphere in all the dioceses and parish churches from which its members came. In 1908 there was still far to go before the Church as a whole could arrive at the position of accepting the social implications of the Gospel and of regarding the social order as well as the individual soul as a field of grace. But it was indeed much that by 1908 a congress geographically representative of the whole Anglican Communion had gone so far. It was also perhaps a little surprising. All this had come from what looked like such feeble instruments—a handful of small societies, one bizarre, one academic, and one politically socialist. They had the invigorating teaching of Maurice to hand down but they always looked like very earthen vessels to hold it. Nevertheless they had offered themselves, and unquestionably they had been used.

It would be a mistake, moreover, to give the impression that the only use which had been made of them was the prophetic one of judging and inspiring. Much other work had grown out of the movement, some of it practical and some academic. A fair sample of the former is the intervention of Bishop Westcott in the coal dispute in Durham in 1892. In 1891 the price of coal fell, and as a result in 1892 the coal owners of Durham resolved to reduce the miners' wages. The result was a famous strike. What gave it its fame was that it was settled by the personal efforts of the Bishop of Durham. From Auckland Castle Westcott anxiously watched events. He saw distress spread fast as the consequences of the strike were felt by every ancillary industry. Most households in the county were soon in debt. He decided that as a Christian bishop it was his proper business to act, and try to play the part of a mediator. He began by writing to the strikers' leaders, but 'had no encouragement whatsoever to attempt any service'.[2] Then he published an open letter to the Vicar of Bishop Auckland to suggest a conference between three coal-owners, three miners, and three business men from other trades. 'Would that I could do anything to further the

---

[1] *Ibid.*, p. 103.
[2] Arthur Westcott, *Life and Letters of Brooke Foss Westcott* (Macmillan), 1903, vol. II, p. 116.

meeting of such a conference as I have sketched. It would be truly a bishop's work.'[1] This also had no result. But the bishop refused to be rebuffed into silence and impotence. Three weeks later he wrote to both owners and miners to ask them to meet him together in his house at Bishop Auckland, and added that he would propose to both sides that, first, there should be an immediate reduction in wages of ten per cent (the owners were claiming 13½ per cent) and that the pits should at once be opened; and, secondly, that the question of any further reduction in wages should be referred to a wages board with power to decide on the claim. After some correspondence both sides accepted, and the bishop skilfully began the negotiations by providing a meal which he forced both sides to eat at the same table. Having thus prepared the ground, and created the only conditions which might make success possible, he sent them off into separate rooms, and himself went to and fro between them. This went on for five hours and all the time a huge crowd was gathered in the park outside, slowly waiting for news, and trying to guess how things were going by noting the movements of the heads of the different delegates in the windows. Eventually he had to make a very strong appeal in the name of humanity to the owners to persuade them to accept a ten per cent reduction in wages. But at last they did so, and the strike, or more properly the lock-out, was settled. It had been a great strain for Westcott. 'The last half-hour of waiting was terrible. I dare not think what failure would have meant.'[2] Afterwards he had to go out into the streets, and the crowds cheered him there.

It had been a very long time since an Anglican bishop was cheered in the streets. Less than a hundred years before an Archbishop of Canterbury had dead cats thrown at him through the windows of his carriage and a Bishop of Bristol had his house burned about his ears. But in only a few years to come another Archbishop of Canterbury, Randall Davidson, was to be cheered in the streets on the occasion of the general strike because he had intervened in such a way as to show sympathy for the claims of a proletariat in revolt, and his own independence of judgement in the face of the Very Important Persons. This tradition of episcopal peacemaking in industrial quarrels persisted. In the great coal strike of 1926 several bishops co-operated to seek ground of intervention, and were content to draw upon themselves the wrath of the government of the day.

Mr Baldwin, then Prime Minister, asked how the Bishops would like it if he referred to the Iron and Steel Federation the revision of the Athanasian Creed, and this was acclaimed a legitimate score.[3]

It is significant that on each occasion the bishops carried the general body of the Church with them and spoke in the name of Christian conscience;

---

[1] *Ibid.*, vol. II, p. 119.   [2] *Ibid.*, vol. II, p. 132.
[3] William Temple, *Christianity and Social Order* (Penguin Books), 1942, p. 7.

and this they could hardly have done had the work of the various ramifications of the Christian social movement in its early days been wholly uninfluential. To it we partly owe the fact that in England today we are not hampered as the Church in Europe is hampered by the terrible tradition that to be a socialist is automatically and necessarily to be an atheist.

Most of the credit was due to Methodism, but some part of it can justly be awarded to the early years of propaganda by the societies dedicated to the service of the Christian social movement. But there were large blocks of practising Christians upon whom their work had had little or no effect, and as an illustration of how hard it is to persuade the whole Church to hearken to the pleading of a self-evidently righteous cause when it involves the overturning of a tradition of long standing, it may be worth while to tell the story of the awakening of the Student Christian Movement to the challenge uttered to the Gospel by evil social conditions.

There never was a more alert, more imaginatively sympathetic, or a better directed movement than the S.C.M., nor one in which a higher proportion of the members genuinely meant business by their religion. Yet it was not until 1909, when it had been in existence for 17 years, that it dawned on its members that the Gospel had to do with society not less than with individual persons, and that a strong sense of responsibility for the Chinese coolie could not compensate for a failure to realize any corresponding responsibility for the English wage-slave. 'In the Student Movement the evils and disorders of society and their cause were never mentioned during the first seven or eight years of its history,'[1] wrote Canon Tissington Tatlow, its director; and he added, 'I knew nothing about social questions.' Nor had he so much as heard of the Fabian Society.[2] The record of the Movement in the fields of evangelism in the universities and in the sending out of men to work in the mission field was one of the glories of the Church in that generation, but Maurice and Kingsley might never have written a line and the various societies might not have existed for all the effect they had had on the leadership or the rank and file membership of the Student Movement.

Early in the century a few lone spirits in the S.C.M. had tried to remedy this neglect. As a result of their agitation the social problem was given a little space on the agenda of one or two S.C.M. conferences, and a few study groups came into being. But these tentative fumblings were dismissed by the annual report of the central committee in a single sentence.[3] Before the S.C.M. could awake out of its social sleep the wind had to blow upon it from without; and perhaps one of the most ultimate influential things the Movement's directorate ever did was to open the pages of its magazine to Dr J. H. Adriani of Holland in 1903. He used this invitation to deliver himself of many firm words on the subject of the social blindness

[1] Tissington Tatlow, *The Story of the Student Christian Movement*, p. 338.
[2] *Ibid.*, pp. 340, 338. [3] *Ibid.*, p. 341.

of the Movement. He accused it of not daring to face the real world of everyday secular experience:

Dare we know the world fully, and dare we feel how the world opposes itself to our faith? Our relations in life are based on commerce and industry. Ask the merchant. He will tell you that he approves of your going to Church and reading the Bible; he will offer you a gift for missions, but at the same time he will tell you that it would be ridiculous to apply the teachings of Christianity to commerce. Ask the manufacturer. His answer will be, 'I know many influences in my department, but those of Christianity are out of place there.' Ask the lawyer, 'Can you apply the laws of the Gospel in your profession?' He will look at you in amazement.[1]

Dr Adriani continued his catalogue, and made this acid comment:

When we study the literature of the World's Student Christian Federation and the different national Movements, we generally receive the impression that for us social and political life does not exist. . . . No one acquainted with the life of the Movement would think that its members did anything but attend Bible circles and conferences, read books on missions, and live in an entirely spiritual world.[2]

It was a bitter judgement, and it took some courage for the Movement to publish it in its own magazine. But it did what was needed. From that time onward the Movement slowly awoke. But in this matter also its directorate remained faithful to the S.C.M. tradition of gathering information first and acting afterwards, and Dr Adriani's article was followed by six years of social study circles, and occasional references to them in conferences.

In 1908 the Movement judged that the right moment had come for the whole of its work, in every department, to be tried and sifted by an impartial tribunal. Problems of great moment had arisen in every sphere of its life and they clamoured for solution. It seemed right therefore to submit the whole organization and life of the Movement to the independent scrutiny of fresh minds. A general Commission to 'wait upon God to know His will regarding the Movement'[3] was thus appointed. One of the features of the Movement's work which this commission found reason to criticize was the poorness of the response of the Christian student world to the social challenge, and it suggested this remedy:

The executive should arrange a meeting of four days' duration, and they should summon those who feel upon their hearts the burden of the problem of modern society, to come apart and intercede with God for guidance. While we recommend that addresses should be given to guide prayer, names of speakers should not be published, nor should any details of the programme be given which would tend to obscure the central issue—that of intercession for the guidance of the Movement in face of human suffering and alienation from God.[4]

The phrasing was significant and characteristic. It suggested the spirit of humble reliance upon the energy not less than the love of God which had

[1] *Ibid.*, pp. 341f.   [2] *Ibid.*, p. 341.   [3] *Ibid.*, p. 324.   [4] *Ibid.*, pp. 345f.

always been characteristic of S.C.M. and made it in so many ways one of the most fully seminal of all modern Christian movements. It was proved to be true on that occasion, as indeed on all others, that an assembly which meets in that spirit, and implements it by a programme expressing that the first and deepest of all its concerns is to learn God's will and to draw on his strength together will quite infallibly be used by him. Thus this Conference, which met at Matlock in the spring of 1909, became one of the memorable occasions in the history of the Christian social movement in England.

It was seminal, for its importance lay more in the stimulation and impetus it bestowed on the minds of the students present than in anything it said or did. Before the Matlock Conference it had been possible and even usual for Christian students to match their ardour for foreign missions by a curious lack of sensitive response to the godless social order at home. But after this conference the Christian student was generally socially conscious, and the missionary work of the Movement did not suffer. About a hundred people were at the conference, and it was the sort of conference at which the members really conferred, not the sort at which they provided an audience for speakers with famous names. There were, it is true, some who had been asked to introduce the subjects for discussion. Among them were William Temple, Kenneth Maclennan, and H. G. Wood, all of whom were later to become famous. But it was a gathering of equals, and not an audience for experts to dominate and lead. Thus the great occasion was a meeting which had no chairman and no set speeches, in which those hundred men and women simply waited on God in spontaneous and mostly silent prayer to see where the Holy Spirit would lead them.

There was no confusion. Some spoke to us, some led us in prayer, but it was felt that what everybody did was a real contribution to the gathering, and that in literal fact we realised what it was to be led as a body by the Spirit.[1]

After the conference ended a pamphlet was prepared and published called *Discipleship and the Social Problem*. Its purpose was to embody and express what it was believed that the Holy Spirit had impressed upon the conscience of the students who had thus waited upon him. This is a document of no slight importance in the history of the social movement in English Christendom. Its publication did not of course cause slums to fall down, unemployment to cease, and social security to be won. But it did register a new conviction of corporate sin and a new determination on the part of what is after all ultimately the most influential section of a civilized national community to pray and work and, if need be, fight for social righteousness as a vital part of the whole Christian Faith which these students had always held with vigorous conviction. The decisive things in it were two. First, it frankly recognized that the student world owed its whole privilege of higher education to the system which allowed so much

[1] *Ibid.*, p. 352.

social wretchedness for so many. 'The money which unlocks to him the glorious opportunities of a modern student would not come to him but for the labours of working men.'[1] It was much to have it publicly recognized in such quarters that all universities and colleges were ultimately carried on the backs of men and women in the series of mean and grimy streets in Manchester and Liverpool and elsewhere. This conviction that the corporate, anonymous but most real sin running through the whole social body was also personal sin was the second point of high importance in the pamphlet. It is we who are the social problem, admitted the students—we the privileged, not only the slum-dweller or the unemployed docker, we not less than the employer of sweated labour himself. Therefore 'from our hearts too must rise the generative force of good'.[2] The pamphlet ended with a noble definition of the vocation of the student who was called to be a moral person in an immoral social order:

> This discipleship must be a very costly thing, and day by day the price will be paid. . . . It will mean a slow and painful surrender of self-will and a daily attempt to walk in humility before God and men. Expenditure, pleasure, the choice of our life's work, and, above all, speech and thought as they touch those around us, must all be modified. . . . We are called to be meek. Since no quality is further from the practice and respect of our country, we shall do well to count the cost.[3]

Such words were not platitudes. They reflected a real determination.

III · *From Propaganda to Research*

Any movement which has as its purpose the bringing of the Church to realize both in theory and in practice the fact that the Gospel is the good news of redemption of society no less than of its individual members must always pass through two stages. First it must awaken the consciences of churchpeople to the social evils surrounding them, and try to bring them to the point where they are ready to say and to mean, *mea culpa, mea maxima culpa*. Then it must turn to showing to the awakened Church the practical steps which must be taken if the promised redemption is to be applied to the actual concrete situation of society so that it may be transformed into the likeness of the vision of God for it. The first stage is therefore one of persuasion or of propaganda. The instruments which the Christian social movement must use while in this first stage are such as will best stir up the sleeping consciences of Christians to the facts. The evils of an immoral social order are described as vividly as possible, and such descriptions are disseminated as widely as possible. Such is the function of a Kingsley, a Stewart Headlam, a Ludlow. At the same time desultory skirmishing takes place which pricks the hide of the immoral social order here and there, and serves the purpose of a double demonstration that at

---

[1] *Ibid.*, p. 349.   [2] *Ibid.*, p. 350.   [3] *Ibid.*, p. 351.

least some Christians are alert and on the march, and that secular reforming bodies, like the Parliamentary Labour Party and the Fabian Society, are not wholly without allies within the Church.

The blacklisting of shops which paid sweated wages and the refusal to trade with them was always a favourite form of this preliminary skirmishing. In this field one of the heroes had been J. E. Watts-Ditchfield, Vicar of St James-the-Less, Bethnal Green. In 1902 and 1904 he organized public exhibitions of sweated home work, such as matchboxes and pieces of tailoring. This led to the *Daily News* exhibition in the Queen's Hall in 1906, and paved the way for the Trades Boards Act. Another was voluntary ambulance work of every kind, and such ventures as the work of socially minded undergraduates in setting up and running boys' clubs in the grimmer districts of university cities. But this first stage has a beginning, a middle, and an end, for unless it wholly fails the day eventually comes when the Church as a whole begins to realize that precisely because it is a Christian body it has a social charge, and that corporate indifference to social evil is both corporate and individual sin. When the bench of bishops pronounces the principle that adequate wages are the first charge on industrial profits; when those who in the name of Christ attack slum landlords know that in this they have the mass of churchpeople behind them; and when the general body of the clergy and very many of the laity are no longer shocked by the statement that the Church has much to do with politics and economics, but rather take it as axiomatic—then the day has come when the Christian social movement has completed the first stage of its purpose and must be ready to pass over into the second and in many ways the more exacting stage. In so far as it is ever possible to do more than give the vaguest date, it may be said that by 1918 the first part of the journey was virtually completed.

The second stage is that of research. The awakened Church must be told what is wrong with society and how it may be put right, and in this the thinkers and academicians of the movement came into their own. These two stages naturally cannot be too neatly separated. Much of the work of the second stage was done in the early days of the first by F. D. Maurice, and the time will never come when ambulance work ceases to be an obligation upon Christians. Moreover, the office of persuasion has to be continued afresh in every generation, for Christians may at any time become inert and drowsy with original sin. Thus important work in Christian social research was being done long before 1918, and one of the charges made against the Christian Social Union by the more ardent spirits of the movement was that it was too academic, and not militant enough.

Charles Gore, for example, though no one felt more keenly than he the injustices of the social order, was always more active in the sphere of research. He was sure that the whole lamentable state of society was due to the Church's failure to find a satisfactory doctrine of the relationship of 'property' to 'personality'; and this conviction caused one vital piece of social research to be undertaken under his leadership in 1913, when he edited a composite book of high importance on the problem of property in a Christian society.[1] In 1912 Dr Vernon Bartlett, of Mansfield College, Oxford, addressed to the *British Weekly* a letter about 'Property and Christian Stewardship'. He then asked Gore to join him in issuing some popular literature to set out plainly what the biblical doctrine of property was. Gore replied that he could not so do. 'Before engaging in popular propaganda I needed to clear up the principle of property.'[2] He therefore edited a composite volume of essays, in which every contributor found that he had to go to the Old and New Testaments, and to the glosses of the early Fathers and the mediaeval writers, before he could find what he wanted. They all found that the Christian social pronouncements of the Reformation and after had nothing useful to say, and much that was so harmful that this alone did much to account for the fact that the social order had become 'the Acquisitive Society'. The contributors examined the problem from various points of view, and eventually they agreed upon five main principles which should govern the view that a Christian ought to take of his own property and of the function of property in a social order organized on Christian principles.

First of all they draw a distinction between the purposes for which the institution of private property exists. There is property which is used for power and property which is held for use. The former generally attacks freedom but the latter is necessary for freedom to exist. But if property exists for the sake of freedom and not for the sake of power, one needs to hold but little of it—'a very limited quantity on the whole'.[3]

But personality can only develop when man practises the art of living socially. No one can live a full social life unless he is a free being in a free society, and therefore it is the function of the state to foster and to guard the freedom of its citizens. The state therefore has a duty to curb the holding of property for the purposes of power, and this it can do only by levelling the amount of wealth citizens may hold. Those who possess too much property, more than is necessary to guarantee their freedom, must not complain about the levelling process.

It is, however, evident that unless such a process is to defeat its own ends it must be gradual, and in the meantime the need of charity will remain. But charity is justice. It is something to which the poor have a right in any Christian scheme of things. Here the argument makes use of a very striking quotation from Lucian, who was scoffing at Christian social ideas on exactly this ground, that property is for use and for freedom and not for power, and that the poor have a consequent right to charity, which is their due because it is not so much charity as justice:

---

[1] *Property*, edited by Charles Gore (Macmillan), 1913.
[2] *Ibid.*, p. ix.　　　　　　　[3] *Ibid.*, p. xi.

Their Leader, whom they adore, had persuaded them that they were all brethren. In compliance with his laws they looked with contempt on all worldly treasures and held everything in common. It is incredible with what alacrity these people defend and support their common interests—the interest of any of their number—and spare nothing to promote it.[1]

From all this it follows that the present laws of property are indefensible in Christian principle because they are so framed that the many are inevitably and legally sacrificed to the few.

But there will be no change which is a change for the better until people realize that the only authority they have for saying of anything, That is mine, rests on their readiness to say first, I am God's.

It is probable that very few people now read Gore's composite book on property and it is impossible to trace any effect it may have had on the progress of social reform. But nevertheless it was a real portent if a concealed one. It charted the course by which the Christian social movement was to go. From 1914 onwards the researchers more and more took charge of it, and the propagandists, while still having a vital work to do, as the post-war career of Studdert-Kennedy showed, became steadily less influential. In future the great names in the movement were to be of such men as Maurice Reckitt, its historian, Canon V. A. Demant, and W. G. Peck—all of them concerned primarily with social research and criticism.

But from the beginning the movement had had a deep evangelistic purpose. Its first affirmation had been that our Lord had come to save society as well as individuals, and that the Church's purpose was to offer God's redemption to man in man's contemporary world. There could be no separation between the individual and society because man is a social being. Therefore any movement which was trying to reclaim a social order in the name of Christ was working for the sake of the men and women who composed it; and the members of the movement always knew what secular reformers are apt to forget, that Christian principles and influence can only enter, say, the Lancashire cotton trade or the Stock Exchange by way of the people who are engaged in these spheres. Thus a Christian social movement is by necessity evangelistic. That was not overlaid by the new necessity to concentrate more and more on research. These two main preoccupations of the movement after 1918 were in fact to make it less of a 'movement' and to integrate it more and more fully both with the Church through its evangelism, and with society as a whole through its increasingly radical criticism of the whole basis of social living in a mechanized civilization.

The fact that it was to become more and more a movement of the whole Church, rather than of small groups of prophets within the Church who spent their time crying in what looked like a wilderness, did not mean that there was no longer need of a society to contain and express it. But it did

[1] *Ibid.*, p. xiii.

mean that the society would have to be one of a new kind—larger, with greater resources of money and organization, and more fully integrated with the official life of the Church. Thus at the end of the first world war, the old Navvy Mission, which had been the purely evangelistic and 'converting' instrument of the movement, amalgamated with the Christian Social Union, previously the chief instrument of social research and criticism, and together they gave birth to the Industrial Christian Fellowship. This quickly proved to be the sort of society which the movement needed to contain it and to guide the next steps of its growth. It was presided over by Prebendary P. T. R. Kirk, who rapidly showed his uncommon skill at holding in creative balance these two very different traditions. He was determined that the I.C.F. should be equally faithful to both of them, as indeed it has always been. More than that, he was determined that the two traditions should not be maintained in separation from each other, but that each should partake of the insights and methods of the other, and in this too, much the harder task, the I.C.F. has been markedly successful, so that it was from the beginning one society, not two relatively independent departments operating under a single name. We are so accustomed to the I.C.F. being a unity in itself that we are apt to forget how difficult it must have been to make it one.

The I.C.F. took the whole of Britain as its territory and divided it into vast districts. Over each of these it appointed a priest to direct the whole of its activities in the area and, if need be, to initiate new ones. Under the priest director worked a number of lay agents, and on these agents the real burden rested. They were the 'front line' of the I.C.F.'s battle to convert industrial Britain. Besides these, the I.C.F. organized a kind of flying squad of men and women of special abilities who were prepared to take its message by sermon and speech to any part of the country. The most celebrated of these was Geoffrey Studdert-Kennedy, whose every speech and sermon was a sustained spiritual effort of the most demanding kind, and who wore himself into an early grave by his incessant travelling and labour. At the headquarters of I.C.F. in Westminster the General Director reigned supreme, with a bishop (at first Dr Kempthorne of Lichfield) as the chairman of his executive committee, and to him fell the organizing of what quickly became the largest and most ambitious of all societies for the preaching of the Gospel to the industrial world of Britain. It was characteristic of a society which had to do this work in the new conditions of post-1918 society that one of the great features of the whole organization was the bureau of social research and the directorate of social and theological studies in London, which had the double office of compiling and publishing social and industrial surveys of a high quality, and of guiding and ensuring the study of the lay agents up and down the country, all of whom read under the direction of this office and had to submit for its correction regular papers on what they had read.

To be a lay agent of the Industrial Christian Fellowship was no easy task. He it was who week by week sustained the Christian cause in open-air speaking in such forums as Stevenson Square in Manchester or the Bull Ring in Birmingham, where a man had to stand upon his soapbox and gather an audience as best he might, attracting them from his multitudinous competitors by every art he could command. Then he would preach the Gospel to them, and declare its social principles. Sometimes he would have the help of some local priest, and on very great occasions the bishop of the diocese. But usually he must keep his pitch alone, or with the help of another agent if the district was big enough to justify two men working together. He nearly always did attract an audience, and though it was generally not so crowded an audience as those of the communist on one side of him and of the amusing crank or charlatan on the other, the I.C.F. audience once gathered was apt to stay until the end, which was always a prayer. This normally happened on a Sunday evening, and during the week the agent would probably speak at one or two dinner-hour meetings in factory canteens. In the years of heavy unemployment he would have much to do with the organization of the local occupation centre; and indeed where the local committee was vigorous and enterprising there was hardly an end to the number and the variety of the tasks which the I.C.F. agent would have to perform. Some of them had more specialized work to do. Two, for instance, were always travelling up and down the length of the pipe-line which carried the water from Thirlmere to Manchester, and acting as pastors to the navvies who kept it in repair. Two in Manchester persuaded the local committee to hire, decorate, and furnish a room in a slum street. This they made their headquarters, studying there during the mornings, and holding innumerable little gatherings of shop stewards or trade union officials or labourers of all kinds in the evenings, teaching the Faith by argument, and creating fellowship by cups of tea and patient listening.

These activities of the I.C.F. through clerical director, lay agent, and the central bureau for research and study went on all the time, day in and day out, summer and winter. Periodically the Fellowship would supplement these and draw them together by two types of venture with which its name became more and more associated as the years passed. They were the district mission and the great conference.

The district mission they called a Crusade. Periodically—perhaps every other year—the I.C.F. would gather together everyone on whom it could lay hands. Its lay agents were torn from their ordinary work. The special messengers, such as Studdert-Kennedy, were assembled. To them were added many of the local clergy. In all the crusading team might amount to a hundred people. For many weeks the ground had been prepared, and when the day came this evangelistic host would descend on a whole town or district, Birkenhead perhaps, or Barrow, or the Rhondda valley. There would be a long procession, and a great service in the parish church at which the crusaders were commissioned for the venture by the bishop of the diocese. Then for six nights or ten the crusaders would divide into little teams of three or four and speak on a pitch in the open air, and all would be brought to an end on the last night with a mass meeting in the market place or in some large hall. The crusaders met every morning for the Eucharist, for prayer, and to compare notes. The course of addresses they took was planned for them by the I.C.F., and the outlines were printed as a pamphlet, and all crusaders were expected not to deviate far from it. It was an exacting and exhausting adventure, and what did it all amount to? Were working men and women converted and brought into active membership of the Church? No doubt some were, perhaps many, but there is no knowing how many. The giant district mission, however carefully prepared and well organized, cannot help but be a gallant blundering in the mist. But lack of the possibility of verifying and analysing results is no argument against such adventures. There comes one picture drifting down the years of the atmosphere which an I.C.F. crusade not seldom created. Let it stand for all the others which cannot be known. It is a picture of Bishop Hough of Woolwich at a crusade in the Midlands. He laboured under many physical disadvantages, but he made such an impression on rough working men by the sheer power of his holiness that when he walked through the crowd after his meeting they were seen to touch the border of his garment.

IV · *William Temple and his Conferences*

Up to the present this narrative of the course of the Christian social movement in the Church of England has been like a length of rope. One end of the rope is so tightly woven that it is hard to distinguish the separate strands. The tightness of its weave is due to the fact that this end of the rope is held by Frederick Denison Maurice. The other end of the rope is just as tight. It is held by Archbishop William Temple. But between Maurice and Temple there is a distinct loosening of texture, and the different strands which make the rope can be separated and examined one by one. This is because no single hand was capable of grasping all the strands and holding them in synthesis. The various strands of the rope can be roughly sorted into four groups of threads. First, there is the cry, 'Have pity on the poor in the Name of Christ'. Second, there is the endeavour to make Christians admit that it is their vocation to pity the poor because they hold the doctrine of the Incarnation. Third, there is the realization that such a pity must involve economic and political thinking and proclamation, and that this is the Church's proper sphere because the Church is the Body of Christ. Fourth, there is the knowledge that these insights, which are brought into focus largely by propaganda and research, must lead also to an intensification of evangelism and of the office of the pastor because the socially disinherited are not, on the Christian view, a class or a group but so many individual persons, one at a time. We have seen each one of these strands vigorously plucked by the prophets and by the different guilds, unions, societies, and fellowships. Often more than one of them were taken up in a single hand, as, for example, by Gore or Studdert-Kennedy, or Scott Holland.

William Temple grasped them all, added another to them, and wove them into a new synthesis, so that the rope in his hands became a unity again—just a strong rope and not so many threads. This new thread is the characteristic ethos of Christian social thinking from the economic crisis of 1930 onwards. The heart of this ethos is a new realization of original sin as a social fact governing all other facts, and the experience of the claims of the totalitarian state upon the essential privacies, individualities, and freedoms of man. The terms of its discussion are the tensions between the ideas of the collective, the good citizen, the good man, and the Christian. The thread is a radical criticism not of a particular economic doctrine, not of any one political party, but of the whole basis of society. The whole corporate life of man in the world, the full range of his getting, spending, and associating, his relationship to the state and collective organizations of every kind, his dependence on nature, his tragic predicament in his world, in his family, and most of all within his own soul—nothing less than all of this became the proper terms of reference for the Christian social thinker, and his analysis became more and more radically critical under the pressure of world disasters of every kind, culminating at last in war.

Now all this was a vast field of learning for any man. But there have been those in our time who mastered it all, Canon V. A. Demant, for instance, on this side of the Atlantic, and Reinhold Niebuhr on the other. These, with Temple, gave the impression of moving at ease in these fields. But Temple had something which no other sociologist of his time possessed— an unrivalled power of clear and intelligible exposition, and also a great position in the Church. In the field of Christian sociology other voices were perhaps more authentically prophetic than his, but no other was the voice of leader and synthesist. And in his own genius for synthesis he was the cause of it in others. He had the power to draw from each member of a conference his own contribution, and then of weaving them all into a synthesis acceptable to everybody. So it was that the characteristic method of the Church's social learning and proclamation in his time came to be the kind of vast conference which was particularly associated with his name, of which the conferences at Birmingham in 1924 (COPEC) and at Malvern in 1941 were the most famous.

It would probably have been impossible to find anyone else but Temple who could have both conceived and carried through the two great conferences at Birmingham, and at Malvern. The conference at Birmingham called COPEC[1] took place in 1924, but it had of course been planned

---

[1] That is, Conference on Politics, Economics, and Citizenship.

years before that, and was intended to give focus to the characteristically Christian expression of the social idealism which was the mood of the nation for some years after the end of the first world war. There were many social evils which Christians should be fighting: COPEC was intended to provide them with a tactic, a strategy, and a goal. This purpose its secretary, Miss Lucy Gardner, described as the establishing of a 'norm of Christian thought and action for the further working out of a Christian order'.[1] The conference, which was of course inter-denominational, was heralded by a series of commissions which prepared for the conference studies of many aspects of the social problem as Christians saw it. The first of these, and also the ablest, was, however, theological: *The Nature of God and His purpose for the World*. It was symptomatic both of the temper of the conference and of the climate of sociological thinking of that time, that this report was never discussed. Perhaps it is also significant that the circulation of this volume was much larger than that of any of the others. It was presented by some of those who had prepared it, and when that had been done the conference passed on to the kind of subjects which in 1924 seemed to be its proper business. There was much vigorous criticism of the 'isms which at such a conference are always disliked—capitalism, imperialism, industrialism—and a good deal of bellicose denunciation of war. More than once Temple had to refuse to put a wildly idealistic or denunciatory resolution to the conference until its members had had time to bethink themselves that they might some day be held to their words. Under any other chairmanship, it was said by not a few of those present, the conference must have got out of hand, so bent were the majority of its members on lightheartedly promising new worlds for old at once and on the spot. All this was due to the fact that the conference was discussing sociological problems out of their theological context, and was therefore continually surrendering to the impulses of a transient mood of idealism. One of its most memorable moments was when Gore appeared on the platform in the city he had loved so well as its Father in God. He was received with tumultuous cheers, but replied to them by uttering forebodings:

This conference will be judged by its practical work, and for that I tremble. We need tremendous courage to ask ourselves frankly whether we are really prepared to accept these fundamental principles and to apply them whatever the effect upon our party politics.[2]

The event was to show that there were many churchpeople who were prepared for precisely that, and chief among them the chairman of the conference. Nor is it just to suppose that because one cannot precisely trace any direct influence of the proceedings of the conference upon the sociological development of the next twenty years that therefore there were no effects.

[1] Maurice B. Reckitt, *Maurice to Temple*, p. 172.
[2] *Ibid.*, p. 171.

Temple himself thought there had been, and at Malvern in 1941 he remarked:

It is said that gatherings of Christians have said similar things for a very long time, and nothing happens. My answer would be that a great deal happens. Of course much depends on the pace at which anyone expects human history to develop; some people want Utopia tomorrow, and of course they are disappointed. Between the two wars three great changes took place in England: the whole penal system was reformed in a wholly Christian direction; there was a vast extension of secondary education; and the proper housing of the people was at last undertaken on a great scale. I call that a good deal to happen in twenty years. It is true that no one can say just how much the Church or specifically Christian principles had to do with it. But the Church was solidly behind all these reforms.[1]

To this solidity COPEC had plainly contributed.

There was no other conference of this kind until the one held at Malvern in 1941. Temple was again its chairman, but in fact it was very different from its predecessor of seventeen years earlier. The pressure of lamentable national and international events had changed the world. At home, the general strike and the long miners' strike which followed it, the economic crisis with its aftermath of heavy mass unemployment and the challenge of the means test to the worker's standard of living and his sense of personal dignity and family integrity, left no one in England just where he had been in 1924. Experience was deep, bitter, and swift in those years, and many characters were changed. Add to that the steadily mounting horror of news from abroad, the perfidy and wickedness of the totalitarian state, wars in Abyssinia, in Spain, and in China, and finally the coming of a second world war, and all of these dire tidings delivering just the same challenge to the idea of human dignity. It was clear that a conference held in 1941 would have to go far deeper than the one held in 1924.

Nor had the Christian social movement in the Anglican Church stood still during those years. It had kept pace with the movement of events, and its prophetic thinking went deeper with every year, continually extending the area of its competence until it was dealing in every utterance with nothing less than the entire range of human social life and the whole nature of the human beings who lived it. Events, as they came, were spontaneously met and challenged by a Christian response from within the Church. The general strike was met by the famous intervention of Randall Davidson, still Archbishop of Canterbury. The miners' strike was responded to by the initiative of the bishops, headed by Temple and Dr Cyril Garbett, then Bishop of Southwark, who came within a hair's breadth of finding a basis for settlement, and were scolded by the Government for their pains. The economic crisis and the means test produced the famous letter from Temple to *The Times* asking the Chancellor of the Exchequer to use the budget

[1] *Malvern 1941: The Proceedings of the Archbishop of York's Conference* (Longmans, Green), 1941, p. 217.

surplus to restore the cuts in unemployment benefit rather than to lower the rate of income tax. The long years of heavy unemployment found the Church neither quiescent nor silent. In hundreds of parishes clergy and people undertook the heavy labour of providing and maintaining occupational centres, and of course responded fully to the sudden increase of the demands made for 'ambulance services' of every conceivable kind. The prophets and thinkers wrestled continuously to discover the causes of all this mounting woe, and to prescribe remedies which might be both Christian and effective. It was in this sphere and at this time that Canon V. A. Demant showed himself to be a prophet of uncommon power and deep perception; and he, perhaps more completely than anyone, has so married theology to sociology and economics and finance to both, that today no reputable Christian thinker seeks to separate them. From the point of view of total culture, T. S. Eliot entered the field with his very influential book, *The Idea of a Christian Society*, while the influence exerted from across the Atlantic by Reinhold Niebuhr, through his clarifying of the bearing of the original sin of man upon the tragic dilemma of his life in industrial society, was so wide that he influenced Christian thought in England as deeply or even more deeply than in America. The Christian social movement, had undoubtedly not failed to awaken the social conscience of the Church of England, nor to loose the strings of its tongue.

The movement, too, did not cease between 1924 and 1941 to dig new channels and weave new patterns for its self-expression, and in this it was true to its own traditions of a hundred years. The further awakening of the Anglo-Catholic wing of the Church to the inevitable connection between sacramentalism and sociology as a direct consequence of Bishop Weston of Zanzibar's electrifying appeal at the Anglo-Catholic Congress of 1923:

It is folly, it is madness to suppose that you can worship Jesus in the Sacrament and Jesus on the Throne of Glory when you are sweating Him in the bodies and souls of His children—

had led some of the older catholic stalwarts of the social movement to seize their chance to carry the fruits of his appeal onwards from works of mercy to the fields of sociology. Chief among them was Percy Widdrington, an old but an increasingly critical member of the Church Socialist League. He had gathered round him a group of thinkers, who had collaborated in 1922 to write *The Return of Christendom*, an influential Christian sociological treatise of the new kind, which insisted on going to the roots of all philosophy and theology in order to find a sociological synthesis. He added to his group men like Father Tribe of Kelham, and women like Ruth Kenyon, and they formed the Anglo-Catholic Summer School of Sociology, which met annually in Oxford for many years, and did remarkably able work. It was largely out of this enterprise that the famous Christendom Group sprang. To this men as various as the veteran Percy Widdrington,

Professor R. H. Tawney, and Canon V. A. Demant brought their insights and treasures, and 'the basis for a Catholic sociology was securely laid. A willing and energetic band of labourers set to work on the superstructure, and their activities, in what is now known as the Christendom Group, are not yet at an end.'[1]

The Christendom Group is the chief link which joins COPEC to Malvern; and it was this body of people which Temple entrusted with the preparation of the programme and the reading of many of the papers at the Malvern Conference. He himself emphasized it:

> I have been asked whether it is of deliberate design that most of those who have been asked to read the papers . . . are representatives of one school of thought and one angle of approach. That is quite deliberate. Our time is very limited, and there will be far more coherence in our thought if we enter on the consideration of each part of the subject from the same angle. . . . And as far as I know there is no single body of thought which is at once so extensive in its survey and coherent in its interpretation as that which these speakers represent—not without considerable differences, but with substantial unity of method.

Thus the pressure of events, the deepening tragedy of experience, and the widening in the terms of reference in sociological Christian thought as exemplified in the Christendom Group, all combined to make of the Malvern Conference something much less readily intelligible, less idealistic, but far more thorough and penetrating than its predecessor at Birmingham had been.

The conference consisted of about 240 bishops, clergy, and laity. The mere citing of the date when they met—1941—is enough to show that no such elaborate preparation preceded it as had been used to prepare for COPEC, and indeed the long studies of the sociological Summer School and the Christendom Group had in effect done what preparation was necessary. At the beginning the Archbishop stated clearly what the purpose of the conference was. It was to find the 'middle axioms' of Christian sociology; and his own words are the simplest explanation of this technical term:

> Theologians, and Christians who . . . have minds trained by education to appreciate the work of theologians should think out the general implications of fundamental Christian principles in relation to contemporary needs, so supplying what among the ancients were called 'middle axioms'—maxims for conduct which mediate between fundamental principles and the tangle of particular problems. This is the work we attempted at Malvern.[2]

From such a stem grew a bewildering profusion of branches—what is the attitude of the Church to the planned society? Do the formulas of the Church offer any guidance to family life? Is the Church's witness concerned with the possible end of civilized life? What is the relationship between

---

[1] *Maurice to Temple*, p. 178.   [2] *Malvern*, p. vii.

sociology and redemption?—these were but a few of the themes coming out of the main purpose of finding the 'middle axioms', and any one of them might well have had a full conference to itself. The value of the actual answers returned to them was probably less than the enthusiasts and certainly more than the denigrators supposed. The former view was represented by the title of a book written in America about the conference, to which its author gave the title *From Pentecost to Malvern*, while the latter was neatly expressed by the editor of *Crockford*, who surveyed the findings, reached for the works of Charles Dickens, hunted through *Martin Chuzzlewit*, and let Sairey Gamp express his mind with the immortal, 'Betsy, who deniges of it?' As the event showed, there were many who definitely 'deniged of it'.

It is, however, probably true that the chief value of the conference lay in the papers read and the discussion which followed them. They were difficult, for everybody was so obviously wrestling with immensities and imponderables, and struggling to move forward through tangles of jungle too tough for anything less than the co-operative efforts of the best minds of all mankind. It was inevitable, therefore, that at least some of the speakers were not really understood. But all this was a registration of actuality. Before all else the Malvern Conference was realistic, and not in the least optimistic, so that it had hope, and was able to convey it to others.

What did it all mean, and where lay its merit and its importance? Thinking over it all after it had been ended, the Archbishop found its significance partly in the stimulus it had given to the Church itself by 'gathering recent Christian thought on these matters into a focal expression and so setting it forward once more'. But, more important still, it had put 'the Church on the map again for many who had ceased to regard it as having any relevance for these problems'. This was in the tradition of the Christian social movement which made the conference, but not many realized that the Church had any relevance to their problems, and some of them were perhaps 'startled to learn what a body of churchpeople gathered for such a purpose was ready to say'.

15

The Church and Housing

I · *Accepting the Charge*

BOTH CHURCHES and governments suffer from the same characteristic temptation. It is to spin an endless web of theory, and to surround themselves with clouds of words; but to be coy and chary when theory should come to the point of begetting action. The Christian social movement for a hundred years had been chiefly occupied in propaganda, analysis and diagnosis. It had come to the point where it had done much to make good the Christian right to claim the whole social order as a proper field of redemptive grace. By the end of the 1914–1918 war it was time to do something tangible about it, to demonstrate that Christian social theory could by Christian social action take hold of enemy occupied territory and transform it.

Where there is social wretchedness the Church is, and has always been, actively at work, sweetening life at a thousand million points of strain and the only book which could record all this is the Book of Judgement. But there was one sphere of social action between the wars which was basic and seminal, not palliative, in which churchpeople and the accredited leaders of the Church played a leading and a conspicuously successful part. This was the sphere of slum clearance and new housing. This work more than any other was the Christian social movement on its practical side, crowning it with tangible things like human family life, bricks and mortar, investments and dividends, and the eloquence and thought of many generations of the prophets of the social movement. What churchpeople, acting under the inspiration of their faith, did to build flats and houses for the unfortunates condemned to dwell in slums is at once a thrilling, a copious, and a most diffused story. Merely to list the titles of the many public utility societies which Christians all over the country from Penzance to Tyneside set up, managed and financed in order to take people out of slums and give them decent dwellings at rents they could pay would occupy several pages of this book.

Memory goes back, for example, to Canon Thomas Shimwell of Manchester, passing all his days hand in hand with physical pain from a backbone injured in swimming at a camp for his Ancoats boys, and living contentedly year after year in his fantastically comfortless rectory with slums all round him, and having for company the railway horses in the stables across the road, with odours of dung all summer, and troops of rats all the year round. By devoted work for years he became the corner stone of an enterprise which took many families away from the Manchester slums, and built for them a housing estate in the suburbs. Or there was the persistent and gallant work of the Church in Penzance, starting with petitions from the Parochial Church Council of St Mary's church to the Town Council, and when the city fathers would take no action, the formation of a Rate Payers Association to sweep them from office in the annual election. In all this Canon Carr was the rector and moving spirit. He and Basil Jellicoe stood in the market place all day long to collect money to begin the scheme, and before all was done many families had been rehoused in Penzance. To take one more sample from a varied store, there was the action in the same sphere of the priest and people of St Nicholas, Guildford. When Guildford was certified as free from slums they looked round to see what they could do elsewhere to help the Church's housing ventures. Their gaze lighted upon the Bethnal Green Housing Association, and the parish raised the money to adopt and equip some of the flats they were building. They went further and formed a committee to establish friendly relations between themselves and the tenants. Others of these Bethnal Green flats were adopted by enthusiasts of the Christian social movement and named after its heroes, Gore, Maurice, Chesterton, Adderley, and others. The tenants all used to be told something of their own heroic patron, and liked to know it.

There is indeed a great story to tell of the Church's adventure in building houses and clearing slums, of how it blazed the trail which others, governments, and local authorities who could vote money and need not laboriously collect it, followed later. But only by rigid selection can it be made a manageable story, and one sample must represent a hundred. Let the story of Basil Jellicoe and the achievement of the St Pancras House Improvement Society Ltd in Somers Town, perhaps the most conspicuously successful and certainly the most romantic and picturesque of all these stories stand for all the others, and let the gaps which still remain be filled by token in the stories of what was done under Christian inspiration in Leeds, and in London by the Ecclesiastical Commissioners.

II · *Basil Jellicoe and the St Pancras House Improvement Society*

Out of all the thousands of people who come into Euston Station from the north every day, how many are there who realize that as they get out of their train at one of the arrival platforms they are within one or two hundred yards of the famous Church of St Mary's, Somers Town; out of which grew certainly the most famous and probably the most conspicuously successful of all the Church's feats in the field of housing? How many, indeed, realize that on their left lies what was until recently one of the most desperate slums in London, but now a slum no longer? Yet so it is. In nearby Eversholt Street is a plain, ordinary, not very beautiful, and unadorned church. There is absolutely nothing externally to distinguish it from a hundred others in just such districts as this. But it is a very famous church. From its altar came the vehement compassion, the drive, the resource which conceived a forlorn hope and thrust it onwards and onwards until that hope became accomplished fact, and the slums at that end of the Borough of St Pancras were only an evil memory. At this altar worshipped Father Basil Jellicoe, and from it he drew the strength and power to become the most famous missioner for decent housing which the Church has produced. Many others were in this venture beside him, and indeed it still goes on though he has long been dead, but no one doubts that but for him it would never have been a movement but only a dream.

Spontaneity is the word which comes at once to mind as one thinks of Basil Jellicoe. There was in him the basic element of freedom, the power to meet all experience with immediate response, ungrudging, spontaneous, unselfconscious. He could always make the experience of other people vividly his own, for he lived so fully in and for others that their hurts were his hurts, and their joys his own. He went to a place where almost everybody was deeply hurt by scandalous housing, and thus the very existence of slums anywhere was to him an affront and offence, a nagging pain in his mind. It gave him no rest by day or night, and so he was able to give no rest to himself. He was a flame of mingled suffering and joy. But the flame blazed so fiercely that it swiftly burnt itself out in death.

He was the most picturesque and, perhaps for that very reason, one of the most effective of all the priests who became notable warriors in the battle of the slums in town and country. Archbishop William Temple said of him, 'There are some with whom it seems to be a necessary quality that they should die young—Mozart among musicians; Keats and Shelley among poets; and among saints, with many another, Basil Jellicoe.'[1] The Archbishop had weighed his words. He deliberately placed Jellicoe in the company of the very greatest, and, judged by the standard of the immensity of personal achievement, he was worthy of that place. It is to compare the like with the unlike, but the fine blocks of flats hard by Euston Station and Keats' *Ode to a Nightingale* or Shelley's *Prometheus* are, considered as testimonies to the greatness of the human spirit, comparable. A saint is not a word to be lightly used, but Temple used it of him; and if to be a great

---

[1] In his preface to *Basil Jellicoe* by Kenneth Ingram (The Centenary Press), 1936, p. viii. I am heavily indebted to this biography throughout this section.

poet in the sphere of living is to be a saint there is no doubt about the rightness of claiming that title for Jellicoe. The Anglo-Catholic movement was
his inspiration and a wonderful home was his background. Between them,
they made him what he was. His field of competence was persuasion and
action: in the sphere of intellectualism he was always at a loss. He was the
type whose utter unselfconsciousness creates a deposit of story and legend
wherever life took him. Many pictures of Jellicoe come drifting down the
years. He would wander about Somers Town clad always in an elderly
cassock, and surrounded by hordes of clamorous children over whose heads
on wet days he would spread his cloak like a giant umbrella. He preached
on one occasion in Westminster Abbey on housing, rather startling the
congregation by his choice of a text, which was a Somers Town *obiter
dictum* of any wife with a recalcitrant husband, 'What! Me send for the
copper! 'E's my old man.' On that day he had picketed every door into
the Abbey with his Somers Town friends, who thrust leaflets about the
housing scheme into the hands of everybody who entered. He liked to go
to Chichester Theological College from time to time, and the students and
principal loved his every visit, even the visit when he brought a monkey
with him, a new pet he had impulsively bought on the way. His capacity
for sheer enjoyment was immense. Every year he made a point of going to
the annual fair at Bude, and would stroll round it, still in his cassock, and
go on all the roundabouts—alone if nobody offered to go with him—and
somehow gathering all the fair's workers round him in a cheerful talk, with
flashes of spiritual fire in it.

If any priest ever led a 'busy' life, he did; and yet seemed never pressed
for time, and always gave to everyone who sought him all the time that
might be necessary. He gave the impression always that the one to whom
he was talking was the one in all the world who mattered most to him.
His strength lay in his scale of values, and he knew that his real mission
was a pastoralia to individuals. His work for housing was always conceived
of as a direct consequence of his mission to individual persons. With him
it was human beings first and 'humanity' a long way afterwards—a scale
of values as creative as its opposite is deadly.

Somers Town is the district of the mission of Magdalen College, Oxford,
and it was as the college missioner that Jellicoe went there in 1921. He was
still a layman; his age was 22. In the next year he was ordained deacon,
and priest in 1923; and in that year Percy Maryon-Wilson joined him as
assistant missioner. He was thus only attached to the parish church of St
Mary, not its vicar; and the serious trouble was that the attachment between the mission and the parish church had become unhealthily loose.
The mission's clubs had thus become undisciplined and unruly. It is an
indication of the courage of this young man that his first action was publicly
to speak his mind to the offenders. 'I'm a very young man,' he told them,
'but I'm the new missioner. And you won't like me at all. You won't like

the things I'm going to do. I'm going to close down all this for a time. We've got to start again and start quite differently.'[1] How differently this was to be neither he nor his audience dreamed. The first difference was a re-tying of the knots which held the mission close to the parish church and its altar, for it was to be the veritable truth that the power house of the housing scheme was the altar of the parish church.

Somers Town, when he went to it, was not a creditable locality. For some reason great railway stations are often surrounded by slums, and in this Euston was worse than most others. Slums are only superficially alike. Each one has its own distinctive marks. The slum houses of Somers Town have gone to their own place, but photographs and pictures of them remain. From these it seems that bugs and the rotting, peeling plaster of bad stucco were their particular sign manual. There is one photograph of a large flat piece of wood. It is covered so thickly with dead bugs that hardly any wood can be seen. All those bugs came out of a single wardrobe. The houses were mostly tall and tenement-like. Each house found room for many families, and for all of them there was just one outside lavatory-cum-washhouse. The yards were haunted by rats, choked with debris, and covered with bricks fallen from the walls, which no one bothered to repair. Gruesome photographs exist of damp narrow death-trap staircases, with cracked walls and peeling paper; of a court's back entry at night, with pools of liquid, looking as though it might be made of blood and tears; of bent, broken and rusted railings guarding the approach to a portal of peeling stucco and a closed, paintless door, hiding horrors. There is overcrowding in every slum, but in this more than in most. The first seven houses the society bought had twenty-one families in them. One room, measuring ten feet by eight, housed a man and his wife and five children. There was a bed (the family kept all their clothes under that) three chairs, a table, some shelves and a kettle, but no oven. A final photographic record exists of a family group posed outside the door of their hovel—six adults, five children, the baby, and the cat. The cat was fat and well-liking. The baby and its white clothes were clean—and by what prodigies of sacrificial effort had that been achieved. The rest were clothed in what looks like sackcloth and tatters, and on the faces of the children is a terrible expression of puzzled desperation, and no hint or trace of gaiety.

The L.M.S. Railway had built some blocks of decent flats for its employees, but otherwise, said Jellicoe, Somers Town homes were

the Devil's holiday, a kind of perpetual festival of All Sinners. It has been produced by selfishness, stupidity, and sin, and only Love Incarnate can put it right. The slums produce something much more terrible than mere discomfort and discontent. They produce a kind of horrible excommunication; a fiendish plan on the part of the Powers of Evil to keep people from the happiness for which God made them, and from seeing the beauties of His world. . . . It is not more police-

[1] Ingram, *op. cit.*, pp. 20f.

men who are wanted in places like Battersea and Somers Town: it is God Incarnate in the hearts of loving human beings.[1]

In his daily visiting these were the scenes before Jellicoe's eyes; their human wreckage his hourly business. He saw them all, the child consumptive who might have lived, but not in Somers Town; the mother of children struggling to keep the family decent in conditions militating against the bare possibility of every decency; the husband and wife who got drunk most nights to drug despair; and the thief and criminal who found the railway station and its parcels office a good hunting-ground. But he saw them under the symbolic imagery of the Incarnate Lord of the Parable of Judgement and the Holy Sacrifice of the altar—Christ in people, Christ in his people, and so Christ in homes like these. The horror of this thought was the flame that burnt him, a flame rekindled every time he celebrated at the altar of St Mary's.

It was in 1924 that the four enthusiasts, Basil Jellicoe and Percy Maryon-Wilson, Miss Edith Neville and Miss I. N. Hill of the Charity Organization Society were joined by two old Magdalen men, Francis Hubbard and Kenneth Fraser, and became an unofficial committee sworn to do battle for decent houses for Somers Town. They had their determined enthusiasm. They even had an office. But that was all. The office was the dining-room table of the missioners with a battered tin box on it to hold the money and securities they hadn't got. The next thing they appear to have collected was an architect, Ian Hamilton, another Magdalen man, who had for some time been specializing in the sort of work they wanted done. They were all clear that they must form a public utility society and canvass for shareholders. It was not until July 1925 that they were ready to announce that the St Pancras House Improvement Society existed and was duly registered, and, still more important, that it had bought the freehold of eight slum houses, and now wanted £7,000 to buy them outright for reconditioning. This money was raised by subscription and in share capital in six months, but this might not have happened had not the appeal been noticed by Lord Cecil of Chelwood who used his name to give it public backing in the correspondence columns of *The Times*.

Lord Cecil's action was a portent, an evidence of things to come. For what distinguished the Somers Town scheme from so many others was the extraordinary skill of its promoters in gaining the support of public men of all kinds and their flair for the right sort of publicity. Priests of the Anglican Church generally have an instinctive dislike of publicity, and there is no reason to suppose that Jellicoe and Maryon-Wilson liked it any better than their brother clergy. But they had undertaken the kind of venture for which publicity was necessary. Very well then, publicity there should be, and plenty of it. But it was publicity always for the great plan to rehouse their

[1] Quoted Ingram, *op. cit.*, p. 36.

poor, never for themselves. They had visits from the Queen and the Prince of Wales, from archbishops and bishops of more Churches than their own, from admirals and famous authors. They gathered round them a great mass of sacrificial goodwill, and the spontaneous and timely help of Lord Cecil in the earliest days was repeated again and again by others as well placed as he to help in a crisis. They themselves refused no invitation to speak to meetings large and small about the scheme. When they spoke of it, whatever the audience, they did so in Christ's Name. They appealed always and to any and every kind of audience in the Name of the Lord, as the Old Testament prophets had done. There was nothing merely humanitarian about what they were determined to do, for they knew they did it as a vocation from the most High God to assert the sacredness of personality which Jesus had so constantly asserted, and against which the conditions of life in the slum were a blasphemy. Speaking in that Name, they were able to appeal far beyond the circle of Anglo-Catholic parishes (though it was to them they went first) to all who called themselves Christian.

Miss Edith Neville wrote down her recollections:

It is difficult quite to recapture the atmosphere of those early days—our boiling indignation and sense of frustration as we realized how little most people knew or cared that a family of 15 lived in two smoky little attics with the rain pouring in on them, that babies born healthy died after a few months of life in damp cellar rooms, that young men and women were starting new families in conditions which should have shamed our great-grandparents, the heart-breaking misery of it all, and yet at the same time all the excitement and joy of comradeship in a cause in which we passionately believed. We were hopeful, and could give hope to others. And then, it was frankly fun to confront absentee landlords with an exposure of the source of their incomes: to interview Cabinet Ministers and municipal officials and say to them 'We are going to rehouse slum dwellers whatever you have to say about it'; to shock complacent people with a faithful account of the habits and ravages of the bed bug. Fr Jellicoe sometimes talked about our work as a 'sanctified lark', and those who remember him will understand that original way of describing a hard and serious task. He moved others by his infectious gaiety and his deep sincerity—by his power of loving. He loved all sorts of people—outwardly very unattractive people as well as the people anyone could like—sour, cantankerous people, ugly and dirty people, as well as the gay and the brave, the quick-witted responsive people who made Somers Town so delightful. Fr Jellicoe was continually conscious that the Devil had made the slums. He never fell into the trap of thinking that 'these people' didn't suffer from such living conditions because 'they' were different: he knew that God did not mean people to live so and that it was no use just to be shocked—only to be shocked into action.[1]

In 1926 the society issued its first annual report. It showed a capital of

[1] *Housing Happenings*, edited by Irene T. Barclay (St Pancras House Improvement Society), No. 31, October 1946, p. 4.

£6,500; and announced that the first eight houses had been reconditioned, and families who had had to eat, sleep, be born, and die in a single verminous room, or even a cellar, now had self-contained flats, each one with its own bathroom. This had all been done not so much for the tenants as with them, for they had been consulted at every stage as to how the reconditioning could be done most conveniently to themselves. At the end of the first quarter of their occupation the total debt for rent was 12s. 9d.

Then came the first real crisis and challenge. One day early in 1926 the committee of management had a great shock. Three members burst into the room and told their colleagues that a chance opportunity of buying 69 houses and an open space of 10,000 square feet had come their way. They had seized it, agreed to purchase, committed the society, and please could they have a substantial sum for the immediate deposit and a further £25,000 in five months' time! The funds did not even run to the deposit, and as for £25,000 . . .! The committee could of course have repudiated them, and certainly nobody could have blamed it if it had. And yet, on the other hand, this property was geographically the key position of the parish: if they could get it they would have the chance to do far more than recondition old houses; they could build a whole block of flats. 'If we had funked it,' wrote Maryon-Wilson, 'there would soon have been a factory in Drummond Crescent, and St Mary's Flats—never.'[1] The Committee decided to accept the challenge.

The vital thing to do was to pray, and a day of continuous prayer before the Blessed Sacarament was arranged at Pusey House, Oxford. Then an old friend and a new one came to the rescue. Lord Cecil came to see for himself what was being done, and appealed again in *The Times*. This letter of his was publicly backed by Neville Chamberlain, then Minister of Health. A little later John Galsworthy spent a day being conducted round about the streets and homes of Somers Town. A year or two afterwards he was to make this visit the basis of the charmingly sympathetic chapters in his novel *Swan Song*, which describe the Church at work in a London slum. But his immediate reaction was to write for *The Observer* a full-length article on the slum problem in London, as exemplified in Somers Town, which extolled all that the society was doing, and pleaded for help. The paper sent him a cheque for his article, but he promptly wrote to Maryon-Wilson:

> This cheque has been sent to me by *The Observer* for the appeal I wrote for you. I didn't expect it, and I send it on to you for the St Pancras House Improvement Fund. I hope you are getting the money.[2]

Thanks very largely to him and Lord Cecil, they were; and within the time limit the whole sum they needed had flowed in, and the 69 houses and

---

[1] *Challenge*, a brochure issued by the St Pancras House Improvement Society, Ltd, 1933, pp. 47f.
[2] *Ibid.*, p. 48.

10,000 square feet of open space they needed was theirs. In 1928 the foundation stone of the new block of flats was laid by Admiral Lord Jellicoe and blessed by the Bishop of London; and the building of St Mary's Flats was begun. They were finished in fifteen months, and 52 more families had been provided with decent housing in the name of the Lord.

This event marked the end of the most difficult part of the journey the society had set itself to travel. Its members had not yet realized all their ambitions. Compared with what had still to be done, they had only just begun. But with the finishing and occupation of St Mary's Flats they had at last something tangible to show, and a feat actually accomplished, visible to any who care to come to look at it, always eases the path of those who must raise money or solicit investments. St Mary's Flats had been born out of a serious crisis, but those which were to follow had less painful births, though the purchase of the two-and-a-half-acre Sidney Street site was one which required faith and gave anxiety.

The rest of the 'bricks and mortar' part of the story can therefore be quickly summarized, and the dates flash past like milestones seen from a motor-car. 1930 was the year of the Solemn Dynamiting of the first of the old Sidney Street houses; in two months the first brick of the flats was laid by Admiral Jellicoe, and hardly had he done so when Queen Mary came to see what was being done. Next year came the turn of the other side of Sidney Street when General Sir Ian Hamilton came and did a Solemn Burning.

We had previously built a large bonfire, ten feet high, and on the top of this pyre had placed large models of a bug, a flea, a rat, and a louse, all stuffed with fireworks, and these were solemnly burnt.[1]

The year 1932 they called the Year of the Crossing of the Rubicon, but the space to be spanned was 'not a romantic stream of water by a drab and filthy street'. It was in fact Sidney Street, already partly laid low, but now to be for ever closed to allow another great block of flats to be built right across it. In the same year the society was offered another acre and a half fronting on Seymour Street, and had to find £38,000 in four months. Of this they had £12,000 in hand: the balance of £22,000 was subscribed within a month of the appeal for it being made. On that site lived 700 more people for whom new homes would be built. Thus, by 1933, the society which had started from nothing in 1925, owned six acres of land in Somers Town, had built 170 new flats and made others in the eight houses they had reconstructed. Truly, they found a desert and they made it a garden.

This narrative has now run far ahead of the personal story of Basil Jellicoe. Although it was his vision which created the whole adventure, and although it came to be tied more to his name than to any other, that

[1] *Ibid.*, p. 52.

was not of his choosing. From the beginning he had foreseen that if any part of the dream should come true it must be a permanent structure, the life of which would be reckoned in decades rather than in single years. Therefore others must be drawn in to share the responsibility from the beginning, and as the flats were built a permanent organization of management must be built alongside them. The original sextet was quickly multiplied, and an estate management committee set up. Even so, it was clear as early as 1927 that Jellicoe was doing far too much work, and he then took the first step of withdrawal in resigning his position as missioner while retaining the chairmanship of the society.

Henceforth his energy was to be given to the work of housing—but not in Somers Town alone. As public-spirited citizens in other places read what was gradually being achieved in Somers Town they cast eyes on their own slums, and said to themselves, 'If in St Pancras, then why not here?' But many, indeed most of them, realizing that the vital thing was to get a start, and that the right start was the kindling of faith and enthusiasm, believed that Jellicoe was the very man to do this for them. They rightly judged. To an altogether unusual degree he had the gift of communicating to others the creative pity and enthusiastic faith which flooded his own soul. In those years everybody who cared about housing said, Send for Jellicoe, and Jellicoe went to almost everybody. From Tyneside to Penzance, and from Cornwall to the Isle of Dogs and the Sussex Downs, and as far away as Canada he went to talk of slums and persuade people to combine to end them. It meant that he was less and less seen in Somers Town, and in 1932 the committee of the society believed it right to ask him to resign his chairmanship—a bitter parting for him, and a discipline most nobly borne, and saluted by the Archbishop of Canterbury when, at the last Somers Town function at which Jellicoe was present, he whispered to him, 'Well done'.

Jellicoe was a most successful persuader, but he was not made to be tied down in any one place, not even Somers Town, and in the end these perpetual journeys killed him. Outwardly he was all gaiety and friendliness. Every quality of an open, sunny nature seemed to be his, and by the infection of it he caused many others to share his own courage and faith. All these qualities and powers were really there; everyone he met felt them. He walked with God, and all knew it. But it may be perilous to walk with God, for one has then an intensified sense of the presence and the power of evil, and to Jellicoe evil was an omnipresent, malignant, personal force, always seeking a point of entry into his soul. The nearness of the devil, with all its horror, was hardly less real to him than the nearness of God. His intense sense of atmosphere, the very power which made him one of the most effective orators of his day, made him also terribly aware of anything hostile in it, and persuaded him that his own soul and body was a battleground in which spiritual powers of good and evil fought. It is so for all, but not all know it as vividly as he. But if his working life in the world was a strain—and few men have driven their bodies as ruthlessly—he could find peace in his spiritual life. Triumphantly he kept his soul, but it was too much for his body, which soon paid the inevitable price.

There is one picture of Jellicoe on tour which explains a good deal about him. He had come to a girls' school, and the headmistress wrote of his visit after he had gone.

I was a little apprehensive about the meeting because there was a small group of senior girls who were critical of and hostile to all religion and were certain to be scornful of what he was going to say. . . . He started off by talking about slum clearance, but he didn't seem to be able to talk at all easily. It was as if some hostile force were holding him up, deliberately working against him, thwarting him. He paced up and down the room, paused and hesitated, went to the stage curtains and tried to pull them apart, then sat down on the stage and got up again. At one moment I thought he was going to the back of the room to tell us he couldn't go on. However after a real struggle he got going and talked for an hour with magnificent fire and enthusiasm. He told the girls of the origin of the House Improvement Society, but he talked very little about slums or housing. He talked most of the time about the implications of our Catholic Faith: the heart of man as a slum until it had been touched and cleansed by the risen Christ. . . . At the end of the talk he seemed completely exhausted and very tired. Immediately when we had left the hall and were alone, he said with a challenging note in his voice: 'There is the devil in this place: there was a group of hostile people in the hall who were doing their best to make it impossible for me to talk.' He said he had almost decided to give up the effort and tell them that he couldn't talk that evening. . . . He then told me how he had felt the same hostile forces in Somers Town working to destroy all the Housing Society was attempting to do, and how only prayer and sacrifice could defeat the forces of the devil. As he talked there was unutterable suffering in his eyes and a strange radiance about his face: I have never seen such depths of spiritual suffering or such an ardent love of souls on the face of any man.[1]

It is on record that he knew both the mystical vision and the diabolical apparition. One day in 1930 he was expected home in Littlehampton, coming by road from London. But he did not arrive for some hours after his time, and then stumbled home, limp, excited, exhausted. A strange and terrifying thing had happened to him alone on the downs. 'He had seen a vision of goodness, he had seen into himself, he had been blinded.'[2] Six weeks' illness in a nursing home was the price to be paid. The next occasion, two years later, was also in Sussex; and again he had driven from Somers Town, this time in a lorry laden with mothers on an outing. His exhaustion was such that his friends with great difficulty persuaded him to cancel a preaching engagement and at last he obeyed and he lay for five days, sleeping little and eating hardly anything. The doctors tried to drug him, but

[1] Quoted by Ingram, *op. cit.*, pp. 56–8. [2] *Ibid.*, p. 107.

he wanted to be left alone on the threshold of a strange unseen world. All through this collapse there was interwoven a mystical strain. He spoke of a vision of the Holy Child which was almost about to be unveiled. He was disappointed, snatched back into the arms of sleep before that promise could take effect.[1]

This time the price demanded was five months in a nursing home. The third, three years later, in 1935, was the last. Once more he was in Sussex, nervous, restless, unhappy, struggling to work; and once more a nursing home was the only answer. It was his last resting place in this world, and for three weeks he lay there slowly dying. He talked little, but in the small hours of the last night of his life, he was heard to cry, 'Oh Lord, haven't I suffered enough! Oh Lord, let it be soon.' Soon it was: within a few hours the life ebbed away, and the soul of a great Christian was set free, carrying his sheaves to God who made him.

His monument is the great blocks of flats in Somers Town, the outward and visible sign of the service he gave to England. Many others share the glory of having given Somers Town health for disease, cleanness for filth, sunlight for foetid smelling darkness, of having put in the way of thousands denied it a new chance to live the creative life. But, humanly speaking, it could not have been done without the courage and the faith of Basil Jellicoe. His memorial is more than bricks and mortar; it is also a sacrament of families redeemed and saved.

III · *The Bishops Take Stock of the Housing Problem*

The cause Jellicoe and his friends had been serving so well in the limited sphere of Somers Town had all this time been steadily championed by the bishops of the Church of England, both individually in their dioceses and collectively in the Upper House of Convocation. Anyone who reads the debates of the bishops in the *Chronicles of the Convocation of Canterbury* during the period 1919 to 1939 would be cured of the popular delusion that bishops as a class took no interest in social welfare. Among the many social subjects raised in these debates housing stood easily first. It was a subject on which almost every bishop wished to speak and on which those who did speak quickly showed that they had gained an exact and deeply sympathetic knowledge of the facts, which only a personal knowledge of the lives of the underprivileged and a long, persistent study of the technicalities of the housing problem could have given them.

Of these debates, that which took place on February 13, 1930, was perhaps the most illuminating, concluding as it did by the bishops passing unanimously the strong resolution:

This House regards the overcrowded and insanitary conditions under which so many are compelled to live as a menace to the moral and physical welfare of

[1] *Ibid.*, p. 168.

the nation: it therefore calls upon all churchmen to do their utmost to remedy these evils in their own parishes and elsewhere, and it urges the Government to introduce as soon as possible legislation which will facilitate the abolition of the slums.[1]

(The legislation urged by the bishops was soon forthcoming in the Housing Act of 1930.) The debate was opened by Cyril Garbett, then Bishop of Southwark, who had made the subject of housing peculiarly his own. He had made careful enquiries, and they showed that by 1930 various schemes had been sanctioned which between them would clear away some 13,000 slum houses. Not all of them had then been carried out. In the meantime the position was still very bad, and the bishop produced many statistics to show how serious it was. In his own diocese the borough of Bermondsey was a typical example. Within it there were still 10,000 houses not really fit for human habitation, and 2,763 families were living in overcrowded conditions. Among London boroughs Bermondsey, Deptford, and Paddington tied for the first place in the table of infant mortality figures. In each of them 85 infants died out of every 1,000 born; and this was to be compared with Chelsea and Lewisham, with 48 and 52 deaths per thousand.

Other bishops eagerly joined in the debate, each giving examples of the state of housing in his own diocese, until, by the time the debate was ended a knowledgeable survey of the housing problem in most of England, as it stood in the winter of 1930, had been built up piece by piece. It showed, for example, that in Bristol there were still 25,000 people living under insanitary conditions, and that Leeds still had 72,000 back-to-back houses, while Birmingham had 40,000 and Bradford 33,000. But the chief value of this debate lay not so much in the statistical evidence produced as in the realistic evidence provided of the ratio between the achievements of the 'public utility' societies and the extent of the slum problem as a whole, seen all over the country.

The public utility societies were already numerous. Many of them were church societies in the sense that from the Church had come the impetus which started them and the lion's share of the work which maintained them. Of these the St Pancras House Improvement Society was the prototype. Practically all of them were Christian societies, in the sense that Christian people, acting directly under the inspiration of their Christianity, were the prime movers in them. To these every bishop gave high praise, and the work of many of them was mentioned by name, as for example, the Church Tenant Association in Bristol, which had been set up by the Bristol Council of Christian Churches, and had reconditioned many derelict houses in the slums of that city, turned them into flats, and let them at a cheap rent. There was the Fulham society, which had bought vermin-ridden houses in districts where there was only one water tap for a whole

---

[1] *C.C.C.*. 1930, p. 70.

street, and turned these houses into flats let at 8*s*. 6*d*. a week. In Birmingham, too, the COPEC Housing Scheme was at work in the same field of the reconditioning of slum property.[1] All these, and many more like them there were, and highly to be praised. But remember, said Garbett, that 'if there were thirty or forty times as many public utility societies at work they would only touch the fringe of the slum problem.' He then summoned his wide and detailed knowledge to strike a just balance between the achievement and the need.

In two test districts, one near Manchester and the other near London, private surveys have been carried out with a certain interval between them to see how far those slum districts had been affected by large building schemes carried out in or near the neighbourhood. Those surveys showed that the result had been practically negligible. Here and there undoubtedly there was an improvement, but taking the country as a whole slums and overcrowding were almost, if not quite as bad as they were some years ago. But whether things were as bad or worse there was agreement on every side that the conditions were extremely bad.[2]

In another episcopal debate in Convocation, in 1933, Garbett again took up the same point, and declared that out of 1,900,000 houses built since 1918, the public utility societies had built only 30,000.[3] These societies had blazed the trail, and done much to find an outlet in immediate and practical service for the convictions of the Christian social movement. But it was evident that the slums as a whole could not be ended by this kind of voluntary effort, and it was useful to have this authoritatively said by bishops who were not in the least likely to be unappreciative of what Basil Jellicoe and his peers had done.

IV · *Slum Clearance and Rehousing in Leeds*

There are more ways than one of creating and harnessing the Christian compassion through which slums are pulled down and their inhabitants less blasphemously housed. We have seen one way of doing it in the St Pancras House Improvement Society which formed a pattern for many other enterprises of the same kind in different parts of the country. This was the normal form of action for socially conscious churchpeople to take. But it was not the only possible form and it had certain necessary limitations. Where, as in Penzance, the slums were grievous in their condition but not enormous in their extent the method of the public utility society was feasible. But in places where the problem was so huge that the cost of dealing with it had to be reckoned not in thousands or tens of thousands but in millions of pounds no public utility society could be adequate to the need, for none had the financial resources and legal powers of a local authority, all of which would be needed to grapple with a problem on that scale. This was

---

[1] *Ibid.*, pp. 71–84. [2] *Ibid.*, p. 71. [3] *C.C.C.*, 1933, p. 349.

the position in Leeds, as indeed it was in other cities as well, but very specially so in Leeds. The slums there were so vast and the conditions of the people immured in them so dreadful that nothing less than the wholesale clearance of great areas with rehousing undertaken by the municipality could tackle the job as it needed to be tackled. The slums of Leeds had to be dealt with not piecemeal but all together and in bulk, and this was far beyond the power of any private enterprise of churchpeople, however devoted. There were, as a matter of fact, at least two public utility societies at work in Leeds, one of them working under the aegis of the Church Army, which had to their credit a token achievement.

Leeds provides social history with an outstanding example of municipal housing activity, and a living illustration of the practical consequences which followed in a great municipal housing enterprise when the policy pursued was derived principally from the mind of a Christian determined to apply the implication of the doctrine of the Incarnation in the sphere of housing.

The position that Leeds was in was summarized in 1921 in the Final Report of the Unhealthy Areas Committee, signed by its chairman Neville Chamberlain, and containing this paragraph:

The City of Leeds is perhaps confronted with the most difficult problem to be found in any of the provincial towns, owing to the enormous number of back-to-back houses, the building of which was continued to a comparatively recent date. There were altogether 72,000 of these houses in the city, not all, however, of the same type, but all characterized by the feature that they are arranged in close parallel rows. About 12,000 are of a fairly substantial character, with fifteen feet open space between the front of the house and the road, and with a separate W.C. entered from this space. Another 27,000 houses are built in blocks of eight, which open directly on to the streets and have their sanitary conveniences provided in an open space between each pair of blocks. These conveniences, therefore, can only be reached by passing along the street, and no garden or court of any kind is attached to the houses. The remaining 33,000 of these back-to-back houses are the oldest and worst, built in long continuous blocks opening directly on to the street; they are crammed together at the rate of 70 or 80 per acre, and it is difficult to suggest any method of dealing with them satisfactorily.

The problem was indeed a great one and one can only conclude that Leeds regarded itself as beaten by it. The 33,000 of the worst type of back-to-back houses, in which a quarter of the population lived, had all been built before 1872, and many before 1844. The 27,000 somewhat superior back-to-back houses, were built between 1872 and 1892. Only the remaining 12,000 back-to-backs were of later date and even these were built at the rate of 40 houses to the acre. But in spite of the social consequences of the continuing existence of such dwellings, little had been done in Leeds even to alleviate the situation. Between 1870 and 1930 only 4,500 demolitions took place. The largest demolition scheme which covered 2,790 houses, begun in 1895, was actually suspended before being completed, leaving 732 of the condemned houses still standing inhabited in 1930, with the Leeds Corporation as their owners and landlords. In relation to the size and gravity of the problem Leeds was markedly apathetic.

It was a grievous apathy. Buried in the files of the housing reports are many descriptions of what whole streets of such houses were like and what it meant to live in them. Structurally they were gaunt frames of decay held up by rotting black bricks. The walls bulged. Damp stained them and fungus decorated them. No damp courses had been provided and dry rot had spread like a flame. Workmen were always in and out, for only by incessant patching could these houses be persuaded to stand up for just a little longer. The oldest type, of which there were 33,000 or more in 1930, had just the two rooms, a living-room and bedroom. Under the living-room was a small coal-hole. Food had to be kept in a cupboard in the living-room, or on shelves on the stairway to the coal-hole. There was nowhere else to keep it. In the living-room the family sat and fed, cooked and washed, were born, ailed, died, and waited for burial. No hot water was laid on. There was just an earthenware sink with one cold tap. There was, to be sure, a fire—if one had any coal—and a kettle. In that one heated water to wash in, and one did what one could to keep clean. But it all had to be done in the one living-room. Baths took a deal of contriving. Many parents saw to it that their children were tubbed on Saturday nights. But even one bath meant much discomfort for the whole family, and the preparing of it was an exhausting business, so that often enough the parents themselves had no baths at all. The lavatory arrangements were particularly horrifying. No house boasted a lavatory of its own. Outside in the street there might be two built together to serve a whole block, and things were contrived so that there was a bedroom over them. But their only entrance was in the street so that every soul who wanted to go there must go out of doors first, and then, likely enough, find it occupied. Small children, and not they only, generally used the street. Pictures survive of one of the worst courts of such houses— dank, dark, sinister, a scene of decay and filth caused by greed. A little ragged girl poses before the camera and holds protectively a tiny sister, as though trying to shield her from the consequences of life in a place like that. That child has now been rescued. If she is living in Leeds today it is not in such a court as that nor in such a house. They have all been swept away, and in their place, on the very same ground, stand the Quarry Hill Flats, one of the finest communities of tenement flats anywhere in this country.

In the rescue of that child the Church, through one of its priests, played a very big part. That the old apathy disappeared, and that by 1935 Leeds had become, in the words of a later Minister of Town and Country Planning, 'the Mecca of all housing reformers' was largely due to the work of an Anglican priest, the Rev. Charles Jenkinson. He had been Vicar of St John's and St Barnabas's, Holbeck, Leeds, from 1927 to 1938, and at the same time had served on the Leeds City Council. He had now become an alderman, and when the Labour Party captured the City Council he became the Leader of the Council. For years an ardent advocate of slum clearance and good housing, he now had his chance to turn his dreams from a baseless fabric into bricks and mortar.

At first sight he presents something of a contrast to Jellicoe, except that he, too, clearly had the power to communicate his own enthusiasm to others. Jellicoe was closely associated with the Anglo-Catholic wing of the Church. Jenkinson had had no association with it, having been all his ordained life a member of the Modern Churchmen's Union. But had the two men met, which they never did—though Jenkinson was well acquainted with and had the highest admiration for Jellicoe's work—they would probably not have regarded their apparently divergent theological and ecclesiastical views as in fact fundamentally different. One has only to glance at the church at Belle Isle, Leeds, designed as Jenkinson wished it, with its noble 'English use' altar, its traditional vestments and ornaments, to appreciate that for him as for Jellicoe everything for which he tried to live was summed up in the Eucharist. His speeches at housing meetings were generally expositions of the two Gospel sacraments. 'How can we', he would ask, 'declare that in Baptism children are made members of Christ, children of God, and inheritors of the Kingdom of Heaven; or how protest at the Eucharist that we are in love, and in that disinterested and universal love which is charity, with our neighbours, and then tolerate such conditions for children and neighbours as exist in Leeds?' Then he would go on to relate the doctrine of both sacraments not merely to the general need for better housing but also the practical details of housing policy. Jellicoe could have made that speech. What is more, he often did.

It is indeed the details of what became known as 'The Leeds Housing Policy' which made that policy of worldwide interest. Slum clearance, and on a large scale, was being carried out in the middle 1930s in many places; but nowhere previously in any municipal scheme were the human aspects of the housing problem so fully appreciated or more practically met.

Jenkinson's activities in the housing field began in November 1930, when an opportunity occurred for him to become a member of the Leeds City Council. Already, and for over 20 years previously, a member of the Labour Party, party political action, when necessary, had no terrors for him: he had become increasingly convinced that nothing less than a strong political campaign could lead to Leeds housing being revolutionized in the ways he believed to be necessary. The weapon to be employed was to hand in the Slum Clearance Act, 1930, for which the then Minister of Health, Arthur Greenwood, had been responsible. But in Leeds, as elsewhere, the Act looked like becoming a dead letter: and Jenkinson was convinced that it ought to be—and determined it should be—operated to the fullest extent. Compelled under the terms of the Act to forward to Whitehall a five years' programme of slum clearance, the Leeds City Council forwarded one for the demolition of 2,000 houses in the five years, but accompanied it by a public statement that no guarantee was given that the programme would be carried out in the time. In fact, in the first two years, 1931 and 1932, a total of only 25 houses were 'represented' for demolition. This meagre programme was made by Jenkinson the commencement of his public agitation. In April 1931, he proposed, in the City Council, that a housing survey of the City should be made by the Medical Officer of Health. His resolution was defeated. At once Jenkinson published his speech, with additional matter as a pamphlet: and nearly 20,000 copies soon found their way all over the city. A press correspondence was opened up, and meetings were arranged; and within a month or two all responsible people in Leeds were aware that someone with considerable determination and no little knowledge of the subject was not going to let the matter of Leeds housing rest where it lay.

Jenkinson had sent his pamphlet to every clergyman and minister in the city; and in June 1931 the Leeds Chapter, the largest ruridecanal Chapter in the country, passed and published the following resolution:

In the opinion of this Chapter, housing conditions in considerable areas of this city call for urgent attention on moral as on other grounds. The Chapter therefore represents to the City Council that with a view to arousing the public conscience on this matter, it is highly desirable that a precise statement of the situation and possibilities under the Slum Clearance Act of 1930 should be prepared, and at least a summary of the facts published. The Chapter expresses the further opinion that the housing problem in Leeds should be removed from the sphere of party political controversy.

The last sentence Jenkinson heartily endorsed: and it was one of the greatest satisfactions of his life that, by unanimous resolution of the City Council, it was the agreed policy of the Council that not only the still remaining houses of the worst type of back-to-backs, but also the whole of the 27,000 somewhat superior ones, should be entirely demolished at the earliest moment.

Sufficient had now been accomplished to make Jenkinson's next and decisive move practicable. He tabled a special resolution that the City Council appoint a committee 'to enquire into, and report upon, the present position and future policy of housing' in the City. Shaken by the results of the publicity already given to the subject, this time the majority of the City Council gave way, and the committee was appointed. Working on Royal Commission lines, it took evidence, heard and cross-examined witnesses, and preserved a verbatim record of the proceedings. The Medical Officer of Health, the Churches—Anglican, Free Church, Roman Catholics and Society of Friends—day-school teachers, architects, property owners, estate agents, etc., gave evidence: and after over twelve months' work the committee reported. The Majority Report was a typed document of some thirty pages, the nature of it being sufficiently indicated by the central statement that 'no persons, however optimistic, can anticipate that we shall be able to cope with the problem' (of the 33,000 oldest type of back-to-back houses) 'satisfactorily inside the next twenty-five years'. The Minority Report, drafted by Jenkinson, was a printed document of ninety pages, including twenty-two appendices: and by its weight, arrangement and detailed statement of policy, at once occupied the field of public attention. Over twenty thousand copies of it were sold and the local Labour Party, after discussing and finally accepting the policy laid down in it, made it their principal plank in the ensuing municipal elections of 1933.

Jenkinson was lucky in the year 1933 in which elections were held. That year was noteworthy in housing history, for it was in March 1933 that Sir E. Hilton Young,[1] Minister of Health, declared in the House of Commons that the Government would stand no more trifling with the slum problem, and that he meant at once to call upon all local authorities to prepare a fresh survey of their areas and to follow it with programmes for the abolition of the slums, giving a definite date for the completion of their clearance, and with no governmental limit to the number of houses that might be dealt with. On the receipt of the ministry's circular all local authorities had to comply with its demands. The Leeds City Council, with the minority report in its hands, scrapped its earlier five-year programme and rejected the advice of the majority of its committee by forwarding a programme for dealing with the Leeds slums at the rate of 3,000 houses a year, but without defining any total to be dealt with. It was when matters had advanced thus far that the municipal election was held, in November 1933, by which the Labour Party, by a small majority, obtained control of the Leeds City Council.

Immediately after the election the policy was put into operation. Its principal features were: first, a Housing Committee of the City Council was set up—there had not hitherto been one—and Jenkinson was appointed its first chairman. Secondly, a Housing Department was established and staffed and a leading municipal housing architect brought in as Housing Director. Thirdly, the existing slum clearance programme was scrapped. The Minister of Health was informed that Leeds intended to 'represent' the whole of the worst type of back-to-back houses by the end of 1939—which would have meant the demolition of the last of them by 1942—with the first 8,000 'represented' in batches, before the end of 1935. Fourthly, the Housing Director was instructed to prepare estate layouts and housing plans on entirely new lines to provide for the placing of contracts for 8,000 new dwellings within the same period, to include a block of flats designed according to general instructions given; and also a hostel for homeless persons. Fifthly, an entirely new rent, and differential rent relief, policy was at once put into operation. It was the particular combination of ideas in

[1] Later created Lord Kennet.

this policy, even more than the magnitude of the programme, which at once put Leeds in the forefront of advanced housing authorities and brought to it housing pilgrimages from all over the world. The rate at which Jenkinson drove his committee and officials was deliberate and he has, since, often explained his reasons. He knew perfectly well that the ideas, which he and his committee were realizing, were far ahead of general Leeds opinion, but he believed they were right and necessary ideas. The difficulty was that what he and a few others could see clearly in their minds most other people would never see at all until the slum houses were going down in thousands, the new dwellings on the new estates going up in thousands and the rent policy actually operating over a wide field. He and his friends were therefore prepared for terrific opposition, much criticism and probable political defeat—and they received all : but he was convinced that in the two years for which his chairmanship was politically secure so much could be started and made certain that thereafter it would be impossible for anyone to depart seriously from the main lines laid down, that public opinion would inevitably endorse his views in the end, and that the political opposition itself, in face of the facts, would be forced to accept his general policy.

The demolition of practically all the slums of a great city and the rehousing of their inhabitants is naturally an intensely complicated business, and it is only possible to give here the barest description of some of the features of the Leeds policy in which the specifically Christian approach to the problem found expression.

First of all came the insistence that houses were to be built for people, and that to provide a mould for the proper development of family life the criterion of measurement of fitness must be in terms both of living and sleeping accommodation—not one and not the other but both. People, Jenkinson argued, need room to live as well as rooms. But because a sufficient number of bedrooms should be the basis of all housing accommodation, the policy of building nothing smaller than the two-bedroomed and nothing larger than the three-bedroomed house was plainly inadequate. Nowhere more than in Leeds was the question of bedrooms urgent. In the worst areas of the old back-to-back houses, there were 14,000 with one living- and one bedroom, and 18,000 with the one bedroom divided into two. The overcrowding in many such dwellings was of course fearful. Clearly, no mass provision of two- or three-bedroomed houses and nothing else could possibly meet the situation. It was therefore decided that on all new housing estates five different sizes of houses must be built, and planned on the basis that there must be enough bedrooms to separate boys and girls from the age of ten, and a limitation upon the number of persons in a bedroom, according to its size. For all ageing people special old people's flats were built, mixed in with the other houses, but having exactly the same amenities as the large family dwellings. Wherever a family had a member suffering from tuberculosis special provision was also made.

The second distinctive feature was the establishment of the principle that for every house demolished one new house must be built. Surprising as it may seem the law does not require this. It only requires the local authority to provide equivalent accommodation for the number of persons displaced, if the accommodation is not otherwise available. Under Jenkinson the Leeds Housing Committee went further than the law demanded. When 100 families were displaced 100 new dwellings of the sizes that the particular 100 families needed were provided. The result was that Leeds rehoused and kept on its estates 84·5 per cent of the total number of families of the cleared slum areas. This was an important achievement. It is comparatively easy to make a fair show in the flesh by wholesale demolition. The real test is what then happens to the people who are displaced. Only too often they gradually drift into nearby districts of poor but not yet officially condemned houses. It is not enough to take them to fine new corporation housing estates. The trouble is to keep them there. To have kept 84·5 per cent of them on the new estates is a much bigger achievement than at first sight it looks.

The Leeds scheme of rent relief, instituted by Jenkinson, and a matter of special satisfaction to him, was probably more responsible than anything else for this achievement. It was invented to implement the profoundly Christian principle that no housing or slum clearance policy can be regarded as humane or successful unless it actually enables families to live without hardship in the size of dwelling they need. It is common knowledge that nearly all municipal houses are subsidized out of the national exchequer and the local rates. The easiest way to distribute these subsidies is to divide the money equally over all the houses. But the larger the house, the greater the cost, and therefore the higher the rent. Even if the rent of every house is reduced by an equal amount it is still true that the largest houses are the dearest to live in. But often enough the families which need the largest houses are by no means those who are capable of paying the highest rents. If therefore this rule-of-thumb policy is pursued, many families either cannot afford the accommodation they need, or will only be able to occupy it at the cost of much hardship. Jenkinson's remedy was simple. All municipal rents were fixed at roughly the amount needed to make ends meet, and calculated as though there were no subsidies at all. Those who could pay that rent did so. The subsidies were placed in a separate pool and every family not in a position to pay the stated rent could apply for rent relief wherever the relief was needed, for the amount needed from time to time, for so long as it was needed, but for no longer. The rent relief scheme operated over all municipal tenancies in Leeds, and relief was given down to a minimum rent of sixpence a week for any size of dwelling. It was this rent scheme which more than anything else enabled Jenkinson to see his dream come true—that the families most in need should be properly housed and then be able to live permanently in the new houses.

The majority of the people rehoused preferred to live on the estates in separate cottage dwellings. But there were some, as there were bound to be, whose circumstances forced them to go on living in the centre of the city, and for them it was necessary to provide flats. Therefore 26 acres of slum cleared land in the heart of the city, almost opposite Leeds Parish Church, were selected as the site on which to build what was once one of the most famous blocks of 'working class' flats in the world. In their planning Jenkinson's distinctive views are evident. There are 938 of them, varying from ageing persons' one-bedroomed flats up to five-bedroomed dwellings. Only 15 per cent of the area is covered by buildings, and thus there is ample space, light, and air. Every flat has a private recessed balcony, but the commonest form of access to flats of this type by communal balconies was absolutely barred. Jenkinson would have no front doors on a common thoroughfare with consequent lack of privacy. Every flat opens on a landing serving only two flats, and is reached by one of the 88 automatic passenger lifts. There is a communal laundry, a community centre, spaces and equipment for games, and stores for prams and bicycles.

Finally, the needs of the perennially homeless were not forgotten. In the slum areas there were some common lodging-houses which had to be demolished along with the back-to-backs. For their inhabitants Shaftesbury House was built, and it was probably the finest hostel for the homeless in this country, taking 516 lodgers in self-contained sections for men and women.

All this work set a problem to the Diocese of Ripon, which rose to it by creating six new parishes and building six new churches for the Leeds estates between 1930 and 1939.

Thus within six years Leeds had been transformed. In 1933 it was still notoriously one of the most slum-ridden cities in England. In 1939 there were hardly any slum houses left. Instead the city had won for itself a tremendous reputation for having provided the best workers' flats in the country, one of the best hostels for the homeless, vast new housing estates, and a system of differential rent relief which is unique and which time has shown to be the instrument which can permanently give the chance of happiness and family decency to those who need it most. And for it all a priest of the Church of England was primarily responsible.

V · *The Ecclesiastical Commission*

There are still too many to whom the appearance of the Ecclesiastical Commissioners in a chapter devoted to the work of the Church for good housing would seem incongruous and even astonishing. Old legends die hard: and the legend that the Church, through the Commissioners, owns slum property and refuses to improve it, is one which has been exploded again and again; and yet people continue to repeat it and even to believe it. The even more wicked lie that the Commissioners own brothels and draw their profits has been nailed down many times—and is still told. When Dr Lang was Archbishop of Canterbury he once said publicly (and, no doubt, many times privately) that to assert that the Commissioners owned slum property was to utter falsehood, and 'I do not think I need qualify the word.'[1]

The facts about the estate in Paddington have been many times explained. The property, when the Commissioners were forced to take it over, was leased on a perpetually renewable lease, and the estate is held from the Commissioners by their head-lessees for 2,000 years. These had let again to sub-lessees, also on perpetually renewable leases; and thus neither the Commissioners, nor their head-lessees, have legal power to act. The power by which they might have acted they applied for in 1840. But when they asked Parliament for the power to end leases in order to secure control, there was a great outcry, and they were refused. Thus today no ground landlord, whether the Commissioners, or a municipality, or a private person can do anything to prevent a house, built on his ground but let on perpetually renewable lease, from being used as a brothel, as some of the houses in the Paddington estate have been.

It goes without saying that the Commissioners derive no profit whatever from the misuse of the houses. They receive merely the ground rent and they have in fact spent on preventive and remedial measures far more than any negligible sum of ground rent (less than a tithe of one per cent of the income of the estate) which could be related in any way to the property so misused.[2]

The only measure which would really be remedial is the disappearance of prostitution. The power to exercise any control over the use of property built by others on ground they have come to own by very ancient bequest is denied to the Commissioners by law. And yet they must suffer in repute for what is done in some of these houses. It seems hardly fair.

The other charge, constantly made and as constantly denied, that the Commissioners are slum landlords is even more unfair, and has even less substance than the libel of financial complicity in Paddington brothels. This charge is frankly a lie, though the secretary of the Commissioners puts it more politely:

The implication is entirely mistaken. The expert knows its untruth. The instructed Churchman can discredit it, because archbishops and bishops and leading laymen direct the Commissioners' policy. The student of politics rejects it, because he knows the Commissioners to be a public body under statute, with a representative in the House of Commons who can be questioned at any time by

---

[1] *C.C.C.*, 1933, p. 361.
[2] James Raitt Brown, *Number One Millbank: The Story of the Ecclesiastical Commissioners* (S.P.C.K.), 1944, p. 44.

any M.P. about any single house in any constituency. But there are others—and they are many—who are content to repeat what they have heard until it is controverted.[1]

The record of the Commissioners in the sphere of housing, both as landlords and builders, is a fine one. In 1884 they became the owners of a working-class housing estate at Walworth in South London. Hearing of the pioneer work that Miss Octavia Hill had already been doing in housing management, they invited her to manage their Walworth estate. She gave much of the rest of her life to managing the Commissioners' estates, and was employed by them until she retired in 1912. The work of the Commissioners was therefore the base from which the famous Octavia Hill system of management went out to bless the country.

It was under her persuasion that the Commissioners became builders as well as landlords. This happened in 1893 when the leases of some worn-out property in Southwark and Westminster fell in, and the Commissioners thus gained control. They decided that the houses were too old to stand repair, and must be pulled down. Until then their custom had been to give a building lease to a housing society, but Octavia Hill persuaded them that only if they built themselves could unity of planning over the whole area be gained, since it was too large for any single housing society to undertake by itself. They agreed, and thus created the tradition that the Commissioners are builders of houses as well as the 'exceptionally good landlords' which an independent housing enquiry in 1936 declared them to be.[2] The tradition set up in 1893 was extended ten years later to Walworth where they built a model estate of cottages in accordance with Octavia Hill's ideas. Since then, their building operations have extended to Lambeth, Southwark, Stoke Newington, and Paddington.

The Commissioners are in fact a very big concern, but as landlords they successfully avoid the trap of the great corporation in that they are never impersonal, soulless, and machine-like in dealing with their tenants. The perfect colophon of their long story of social beneficence is a little incident which happened during the last war. Their housing estate in Walworth was badly damaged in an air raid one night, and very early next morning, when it was only just light, their housing manager was there to see what had happened and what could be done for the tenants whose houses had been destroyed or damaged. She found the agent and the builder there already, discussing repair. There was a little group of tenants gazing ruefully at what had a few hours ago been their homes. One of them immediately sympathized—with her. 'Isn't it awful, Miss, for you?' Another, thinking of the future, asked the question which evidently mattered most to them. 'It doesn't mean we shall be sent off the Commissioners, does it?'

[1] *Number One Millbank*, p. 49.
[2] Report of a survey of the Commissioners' London property made by Miss Marion Fitzgerald in 1936. Quoted in *Number One Millbank*, p. 52.

All through the ages the Church has been a most notable worker in stone and brick and mortar, and in every century this work of hers has been poured into dwellings almost as fully as into cathedrals and churches. These three instances of what the Church did for housing in St Pancras, in Leeds, and in many parts of London by the Ecclesiastical Commissioners, are only samples of a socially beneficent story, too vast and various to be written.

16

The Parochial Clergy

I · *Ordination Candidates and Curates*

AN 'ABUNDANT SHOWER' of curates, Charlotte Brontë noted in the famous first sentence of *Shirley*, fell in 'affluent rain' upon the hills of Yorkshire in the later forties of the nineteenth century. Every parish had 'one or more of them', and, she remarked sardonically, 'They are young enough to be very active and ought to be doing a great deal of good.' This must be one of the very few occasions in the history of the Church when the word 'curate' is not coupled with the word 'scarcity'. Since that time almost everybody who has had anything to say about curates has begun by complaining how hard they were to procure, and few discussions of candidates for ordination have admitted that there were enough of them. Charlotte Brontë herself went on to say that this prodigality was a new thing. It had not always been so, and particularly it was not so in the days of the Luddite riots, the period of her novel. 'Curates were scarce then. . . . Yet even in those days of scarcity there were curates: the precious plant was rare, but it might be found. A certain favoured district in the West Riding of Yorkshire could boast three rods of Aaron blossoming within a circuit of twenty miles.'

At hardly any time, it would seem, has the supply of candidates for ordination kept pace with the demands of the Church and the growth of the population. But during the years between 1919 and 1930 the complaints of a serious shortage of ordination candidates were more widespread than ever before. There were reasons enough, for the situation was very alarming. During the years of the war the flow of ordinations had naturally dried to a thin trickle. By the end of 1918 the Church was very short-staffed, and the situation was steadily getting worse, and must do so for at least two years more, until the candidates for ordination from the army could complete their training. But even after 1920 the position did not seem to be much easier, and for some years, until 1930 at the least, this vital problem caused much anxiety, and almost incessant stocktaking.

A shortage of clergy is the fact which more than any other immediately touches and affects the whole life of the Church. Thus of all the many post-war problems of the Church this was the most widely discussed. But no one did more than the anonymous editor of *Crockford's Clerical Directory* to keep it in the forefront of the Church's notice. His annual preface to the fat black volume in which he surveyed with astringent wit and sardonic humour the events of the Church's life in the previous year became famous in this period. Whenever *Crockford* came out there was a rush to read what barbs the editor had hurled and to note with appreciation the wonderful neatness of their phrasing. But he deserved well of the Church for the pertinacity with which he kept attention focused upon awkward problems, and chief among these in his judgement was undoubtedly the shortage of ordination candidates and the consequent scarcity of curates. Almost every year he returned to it, and nearly always he contrived to record the alarm he felt in words which successfully communicated it to his readers. As it was exactly the same alarm every time it was no slight literary feat to be always finding new words and phrases to record it. In 1924, for instance, he wrote, 'In most parishes the Assistant Curate is already one of the rarer migrants, and he promises to become before long as scarce as the bittern or the bustard.'[1] In 1927 things were no better so he used stronger language :

It is not too much to say that if the history of the last ten years is continued for another ten the effective maintenance of the parochial system will have become impossible in all but a few favoured localities. Anything which can fairly be called *The Church of England* will have ceased to exist, and its place will have been taken by the sporadic activities of a denomination.[2]

In 1931, 'the situation is still going from bad to worse, and a crisis of the first magnitude draws nearer every year'.[3] Furthermore, when the editor commented in 1932 upon the 1930 report of the Church Assembly's Commission on the Staffing of Parishes he was sure that the figures given in that document, though certainly alarming, were not alarming enough. The report said that 1,168 additional clergy were needed to supply the deficiency, and that an annual average of 588 deacons would suffice. A few weeks after the report was issued its authors raised those two figures to 1,583 and 630. The editor was sure that even this correction was not drastic enough, and that no fewer than 1,830 new clergy were required at once.[4]

How far were the annual cries of alarm in *Crockford* justified? The gloomy predictions have not been fulfilled. The curate is not yet as rare as the bittern. The parochial system is still with us. The work of the Church is not yet reduced to the 'sporadic activities of a denomination'. In spite of the fact that the stream of new ordinations was dried up a second time by the last war, it cannot be said that the 'crisis of the first magnitude' which in 1931 'draws nearer every year' has yet arrived.

---

[1] *Crockford Prefaces: 1921–1944* (Oxford University Press), 1947, p. 33.
[2] *Ibid.*, p. 62.   [3] *Ibid.*, p. 105.   [4] *Ibid.*, p. 118.

When a great war begins it does not need exceptional prophetic abilities to see that very soon the Church is bound to be short of clergy, that every year the war lasts the position will get worse, and that no remedy can begin to be effective until several years after the war has ended. It was early in 1916 that the two archbishops began seriously to provide for the difficult situation which would occur when the war had ended. Already there were men serving in the armed forces of the Crown who had said they hoped to be ordained when they were demobilized. Every year their numbers grew. In the spring of 1916, therefore, the Archbishops of Canterbury and York gave a public pledge in the name of the Church that no soldier fit for ordination should be denied it merely because he could not pay for his training. This promise eventually involved the raising of £378,000, and it paid for the training of 1,039 service candidates. But for the training of most of them the ordinary theological colleges were not numerous enough, nor was their curriculum what was necessary for a man coming straight out of the army. To meet this special and temporary need the old prison at Knutsford was taken over and became the place where ex-servicemen intending to take Orders might receive their pre-university training. Altogether 675 such men were sent there, and of these 435 were eventually ordained. It must be the only theological college on record which was housed in a gaol, and perhaps it is the only gaol which its inmates have ever learned to love. Knutsford was a venture of faith and a magnificent one. There is no doubt that it saved the Church from serious disaster, especially in the years 1921 to 1924. Of the men ordained during the period more then 40 per cent were ex-servicemen, the vast majority of whom had had much of their training at Knutsford.

The Church had thus done its duty by the ex-service ordination candidate. But there were not enough such candidates to fill up the ever-increasing gaps in the ordained ministry of the Church. The average annual wastage from death and retirement was estimated at 550. Thus the same number of fresh deacons were needed every year merely to keep the number of working clergy constant, but it was not until 1932 that this number was reached. In 1921 and 1922 the numbers were 346 and 392. The next year it rose to 463 ; and this, though considerably better was 70 less than the lowest figure in the ten years before the war, and half of what was deplored as inadequate in pre-war years. In 1924 and the two following years the figures fell again to 436, 370, and 363. It was not until 1932 that the annual wastage figure of 550 was passed, and after that it rose steadily until in 1939 590 men were ordained. This recovery looks better than it really was, for all the time the population was increasing. Had it not been for the successful Sponsor Scheme by which generous individuals made themselves responsible, each for the financial needs of one candidate, the situation must have been worse still. By this scheme some 680 men were helped forward to ordination, which was a noble achievement.

This meant that up to 1932 curates were desperately short, and after that very short. When provision was made in the Patronage Measure for one representative in Convocation from the curates of a diocese if they numbered one-third of its total clergy only the dioceses of London, Southwark, and Liverpool qualified.[1] What all this meant for the pastoral work of the Church can be suggested in another way. In 1905 there had been 19,053 clergy in active work. In 1914 the figure had dropped to 18,180. In 1922 it was 17,162. In 1930 it was 16,745. Thus in the twenty-five years from 1905 to 1930 the number of clergy at work had dropped by 2,308; and in the same period the population had increased by 3,000,000. No wonder that from all over the country complaints were coming in of parishes with populations of 20,000 and more which were being worked by one priest alone.

The young men who thus approached by devious routes to the calling of the sacred ministry of the Church were markedly unlike Charlotte Brontë's curates in *Shirley*, and they were hardly less different from the average run of their own predecessors in the pre-war era. The new men were so much more experienced in life, and they tended more and more to come from a class of society different from what had been normal in the past. Many of them had seen an abundance of horror and violent death and had walked with danger for years on end, and they could not suddenly be as though these experiences had never come their way. Less and less of them came to a theological college by the old traditional journey of a sheltered background of economic security, a good public school, and one of the two senior universities. Their background tended to be one of much economic insecurity, and their personal and family financial resources to be few or none. The candidate who did not need help from some fund during his training became the exception. The young man who has never known economic security and an assured and unquestioned place in society cannot help but be different from one who has enjoyed these blessings from the day of his birth. It became therefore the business of the post-war theological colleges to make desperate efforts in heroic equalization, to take both types and make them members one of another, and to train all alike to be good priests and pastors. This was very difficult but it was often successfully done.

Not the least of the great blessings of the Church in the years between the wars was the unusual profusion of principals of theological colleges who could admirably do that very thing. Particularly was this true of the decade of peculiar difficulty, 1920 to 1930. During those years B. K. Cunningham reigned at Westcott House, Cambridge. J. B. Seaton, later to become one of the most loved diocesan bishops the Church has known, was at Cuddesdon. Leslie Owen, who eventually died as Bishop of Lincoln, ruled gently but firmly over the Bishop's Hostel at Lincoln. F. R. Barry, later Bishop

[1] *C.C.C.*, 1930, p. 571.

of Southwell, was first at Knutsford, and then at King's College London. There were others besides these, but if none had been of their quality, it would still be true that the Church was unusually blessed in this vital department of its life.

The situation of the post-war ordination candidate was often more difficult after he had left his theological college than while he was still a student there. Before he could be ordained he had to find, or be found, a vicar to employ him and a parish to serve. Without this title he could not be ordained. One would naturally suppose that in days when there were more curacies to fill than curates to fill them this would cause no difficulty to the curates since they would be able to pick and choose. For a few years after the end of the war this was indeed so, but not for long. The increasing economic strain of the nation which culminated in the economic crisis and the long years of mass unemployment seriously altered the curate's position. While there continued to be more curacies than there were curates the number of parishes, especially in the industrial districts, which could afford to find the £100 to £150 a year—the average amount that had to be locally raised to make up the sum received from grants to a bare living wage—steadily decreased. The time came, in the middle thirties, when the bishops had to be very cautious in accepting even very suitable men who offered themselves for ordination, because they knew well that it might happen that no parish could be found which could afford to employ them. In those years most of the dioceses which were worst hit by unemployment had three or four men who were in the cruel position of having exhausted their resources on their training, and who could not be ordained because no parish could be found which could afford to take them. The period during which they were unable to earn their living was thus unexpectedly extended for three months or more, and this was a very serious matter for them.

The financial stringency in parishes in industrial areas operated to the harm of curates in another way. It is of incalculable importance to the whole future of a clergyman that he should serve the first years of his ministry under the right vicar. If he goes to the wrong one his lot is wretched and lasting damage may be done to him. But with the best will in the world the scarcity of money made it very difficult to pick and choose the parishes to which a bishop would allow deacons to go. Only too often they had to go to the vicars of those parishes which could find them salaries, irrespective of whether they were the right vicars for them. Sometimes the misfits had results which were hardly short of tragic. If this was bad for the curate, it was also bad for the Church, which was unable to see to it that parishes and districts which most needed help got the help they needed. As individual curates had often to go to those parishes which could pay their stipends, so areas wealthier than others had advantages disproportionate to their real needs. The dioceses on which the real brunt of unemployment fell were those in which the numbers of curates at work also fell. At the ordinations at Michaelmas 1933, for example, all the three Lancashire dioceses put together had 67 men ordained. The dioceses of London and Southwark had 91. Yet at that time the poverty, strain, and distress of Lancashire was greater by far than anything London knew; and both the population and the extent of Lancashire was also far larger than that of the dioceses in London. This of course was precisely the reason why so many fewer men went to the dioceses of Manchester, Blackburn, and Liverpool than to the dioceses of London and Southwark. It was not the men's fault, nor the bishops'. It was simply that the Church had not seriously faced, much less solved the problem of the sensible management of its finances.

II · *The Trials of the Incumbent*

The 'povre persoun of a toun' in Chaucer's *Canterbury Tales* was a 'shepherde and noght a mercenarie'. A shepherd his successor of the twentieth century certainly was, and no less than his immortal prototype 'riche he was of hooly thoght and werk'. But he was more of a mercenary if 'mercenary' means one who must give an undue proportion of his attention to matters of pounds, shillings, and pence. This he could hardly help being. Even if his own income was, exceptionally, not a doleful anxiety to him and his wife, he could not hope to escape from giving nearly half his time and about two-thirds of the space in every number of his parish magazine to the soliciting and collection of money for the diocesan quota or the parish funds. It was singularly little use his protesting that he was not ordained to be even this sort of mercenary. He certainly did protest, but it made no difference.

Exceedingly little of the wealth of nations ever came the way of the Anglican incumbent, who after 1919 became even poorer than he had been before, and that is saying something. His plight did not go unremarked. Nor had it been unremarked by Chaucer and his successors all down the ages. But though clerical poverty has been one of the constant themes of English literature for 600 years, singularly little had been done to tend the parson's financial need.

It is true that between 1919 and 1939 more was done to raise the stipends of the clergy than had been done in the previous 400 years. But it was never enough, for the cost of living rose faster than the pay of the clergy. It was not until the decade of the 'fifties that, during the primacy of Geoffrey Fisher, the amount paid to the parochial clergy (and the methods of calculating and paying it) were brought into line with modern conditions. Today the lowest paid incumbent is unlikely to get less than £930 a year; the national average is about £960; and many parish priests receive more than this.

The first world war was barely over before the Archbishop of Canterbury opened fire on the age-long scandal. He chose the occasion of the presidential address to the Convocation of Canterbury to declare his indignation over

the present intolerable pressure upon the incomes of the clergy. It is a fact that at present in our country's life by far the severest pressure lies upon those who have small fixed incomes, and there are none upon whom the pressure falls more heavily than it does upon the clergy. I am often ashamed at seeing letters from rich men and women saying, 'We wish that you would help us in regard to getting an incumbent for this parish. We want a man of the highest possible qualifications' (that is the usual request) 'but the income is only £180 a year and we find it difficult to get the right man.'[1]

The Bishop of Salisbury suggested in the debate that 'the bishops might well for a time cancel some of their routine engagements and leave their innumerable committees to others in order to gather their people and put before them strongly and authoritatively the spiritual aspect of this pressing problem of clerical poverty'.[2] This some of them did, and there was a campaign in 1920 to bring the facts before the people. Some new money was raised and some benefices augmented. But something much more radical was needed.

The facts were disturbing and apparently intractable. There was not enough money in the assured annual income of the Church to give all its clergy a proper salary, and what there was was so inequitably distributed as to be a scandal and a rather bitter farce. Between 1919 and 1939 various efforts were made to raise the value of the poorest livings, and to make the distribution of income slightly less absurdly inequitable. But in 1939, out of 12,719 incumbencies 3,631 had an endowment income of less than £300, and 5,000 had less than £400. As for the inequalities, the average stipend of incumbents in 1921 was £426, of cathedral dignitaries £850–£900, and of bishops over £4,000. In 1927 a commission appointed to examine the financial position of the clergy found that the augmentation of benefices had by no means kept pace with the rise in the cost of living, and that the average benefice was worth 16 per cent less in actual purchasing power than it had been in 1914. Further, during this period the Church relinquished all income from coal-mining royalties and tithe, and the loss on tithe alone was £50,000 a year.

It would be quite untrue to suggest that the Church as a whole remained unmoved by this state of things, and much was done to remedy it between 1919 and 1939. The long-term financial position of the clergy was undoubtedly improved by the Clergy Pensions Measure and the Dilapidations Measure, but the gains from these helped the benefice more than the particular incumbent of it, while in the short run it embarrassed still further the incumbent during his working years for he had to pay his pensions premium and, more often than not, the dilapidations premium on his vicarage.

[1] *C.C.C.*, 1920, p. 44.　　　　[2] *Ibid.*, p. 50.

A start, however, was made on one difficult aspect of the whole problem, the unwieldy parsonage house and garden. In all dioceses a number of new vicarages of sensible size and construction were built. In the diocese of Winchester, for instance, some fifteen incumbents were provided with new houses by 1939, and their old vicarages sold or let. The war interrupted the process, but since then it has gone on slowly and steadily, and this particular part of the problem of clergy poverty is now well on the way to solution.

In 1935 a group of clergy and laity came into existence under the leadership of Dr Leslie Hunter, Archdeacon of Northumberland, and later Bishop of Sheffield. It came to be known as the Men, Money, and the Ministry Group from the title of the first pamphlet it put out in 1937. This was a plea for economic reform in the Church, and it started from the two agreed points of conviction that a Church which was really the Household of Faith must order its finances more equitably, and that nothing short of a really drastic remedy could do it. The remedy they proposed was that the whole of the parochial, cathedral, and diocesan endowments of the Church should be swept into a central pool, and then redistributed according to need and to the job to be done. Two years later the same group greatly elaborated this proposal in its second publication, *Putting our House in Order*, and enumerated at the end ten propositions for reform, which received wide support. By these propositions the whole of the Church's endowment income would be pooled. Then the same basic salary, rising to an agreed maximum by automatic annual increments, would be paid to the whole body of the clergy from the Archbishop of Canterbury to the youngest deacon. To this basic salary would be added family and educational allowances according to need, and an allowance designed to cover the necessary expenses of the jobs to be done. The parson's freehold would of necessity be modified, but there would be respect for life interests, and the need to raise considerable sums of new money was also recognized.

It was certainly a revolutionary scheme, and it is academically interesting to speculate whether there would have been any real chance to carry it into effect had not the war intervened. The proposers knew very well, and always acknowledged, that it could be done only by free consent of the Church; and up to the present the Church has steadily refused its consent to any serious modification of the parson's freehold. This group did, however, achieve one other thing, and that was not unimportant. Once and for all it disproved Anthony Trollope's cynicism. In *Framley Parsonage* he had discoursed on the tangled web of tithe and the 'remuneration of our parish clergymen', and had remarked

One cannot conceive that any approximation could have been made even in those old mediaeval days, towards a fair proportioning of the pay to the work. At any rate it is clear that there is no such approximation now. And what a screech would there not be among the clergy of the Church, even in these reforming days, if any over-bold reformer were to suggest that such an approximation should be attempted.

In *Putting our House in Order* just such a suggestion was made. There was no screech: quite the contrary. These suggestions were signed by twenty-five diocesan bishops, by many deans and archdeacons, by some forty residentiary canons and senior parochial clergy, all of whom were the very people who stood to lose most if they were adopted.

III · *The Church Assembly and the Clergy*

The Church Assembly was bound to affect the life and work of the clergy, for it was after all brought into being with that very end in view. Between 1888 and 1913, 217 bills dealing with ecclesiastical affairs were introduced into the House of Commons: of these only 33, that is 15 per cent, ever became law; the rest were dropped owing to lack of parliamentary time. This was the sort of situation which the Church Assembly was created to remedy, and which it certainly did remedy. The clergy were, moreover, amply represented upon it. It may be true, as is often asserted, that too many senior clergy—as for example practically the whole body of the archdeacons—were automatically members without having to submit to the processes of election. But even granting that, it remains true that the representatives of the general body of the parochial clergy out-numbered the ex-officio members, and therefore to every act of the Assembly which affected the lives of the parochial clergy the consent of their own representatives was necessary.

The first work of the Assembly was the clearing up of the long arrears of administrative reform, which the old system could not compass. Some of the measures which were introduced and passed to do this did undoubtedly bear hard on the clergy, from whom compulsory premiums for pensions and dilapidations were extracted. By a Church Assembly Measure, passed into law in 1931, any parish may, by resolution of the Parochial Church Council, choose to place itself under its protection when a new incumbent has to be appointed. If it does so, the patron may not make a definite offer to any candidate until he has notified the churchwardens, and they have seen and talked with the man and have had a chance to submit their views on the candidate in writing to the patron. The Measure gives the church-wardens no right of veto, but it is in practice almost impossible for the patron to appoint anyone to whom they are opposed.

In many spheres the Church Assembly's actions have on balance been beneficent. There can be hardly anyone who can seriously wish the Assembly had never been created, or who could view with equanimity the prospect of its sudden disappearance now. It has done much that it was essential to do, and which could not have been done without it.

It is not only or even chiefly in matters of financial reform or of discipline that it has most affected the life and work of the clergy. It is not even the facilitating of the passage into law of measures affecting the organization of the Church, as, for instance, the division of large dioceses and the creation of new ones, which has made the real difference. The really significant change which the Assembly made was the creation of machinery which forced the clergy to consult the laity throughout the whole range of the Church's life, and established the principle that the witness of the Church was not the affair of the clergy alone. In most dioceses and parishes this had, of course, been done before, but it had been a matter of grace and courtesy and prudence. After 1918 it became a matter of obligation. The Enabling Act provided for statutory councils on which the laity were to be fully represented at every level of the Church's life. Through Church Assembly, Diocesan Conferences, Ruridecanal Conferences, and Parochial Church Councils, all of which were forced by law to meet at regular intervals, every geographical area and district of spiritual competence was provided with its representative, responsible body which must be consulted, and on which lay people were fully represented by democratic election. They were given wide powers and responsibilities. So far from weakening, it greatly strengthened the hands of the clergy by putting them in a far stronger position to request and even require the help of their lay people. Co-operation made legally inevitable was practically inescapable, and became so settled a habit that today it is everywhere regarded as the normal state of affairs. But in the long perspectives of the life of the Church it is an unremarked novelty, and it has worked almost wholly for good.

Thus a vast reservoir of power has been tapped, and new sources of help are now open to the clergy to use. It is true that these sources were there before, and true that they were often used. But it has made a wealth of difference that the groundwork of statutory co-operation has been created.

In another way, too, the Church Assembly has been of positive benefit to the Church and its clergy. It established in every diocese the system by which both the diocese and the Assembly itself are financed by a regular, systematic, and graduated toll on every parish, through the quota payments. The collection of this quota has certainly added to the burden of work the clergy must do, for in many parishes it is still left to the vicar to see that the necessary money is collected, whereas it should be—and by now in most parishes it probably is—the responsibility of the Parochial Church Council. But the system is itself a great boon for it allows the diocese to budget properly, and through it the parishes are helped in a score of ways. There are grants for curates, and for candidates for ordination; and through this quota payment the diocese is provided with much paid and expert help in such spheres of work as moral welfare and voluntary religious education. All of this directly quickens and alleviates the work of the clergy, and for most of it the series of reforms made possible by the Enabling Act is responsible.

IV · *The Way of Renewal*

Whenever an appeal was made to the clergy as pastors and priests by their own bishops, the appeal was heard and response was made. Of all such appeals the most famous and the most influential was that made in July 1929 by the two new Archbishops of Canterbury (Cosmo Gordon Lang) and York (William Temple). They had just assumed their great offices, and, as they afterwards explained to the House of Bishops in Convocation, they conceived it to be their first duty to discover what at that moment the Church most needed. They had no doubt that it was the spiritual renewal of the clergy, undertaken in fellowship one with another.

Let any of your Lordships, said the Archbishop of Canterbury, put himself in my position, or in the position of the Archbishop of York, at the beginning of the exercise of the responsibilities entrusted to us. We were bound, as any honest leader is bound, to look round and see what it is the Church that we are called upon to rule most needs. It was a most searching question, and I ask you to believe, so far as I am concerned, that the answer was not lightly given. I did think, and I do think, and every experience of the last year increases my conviction that what the Church does need most is fresh study of and prayer around the Faith which we are commissioned to teach.[1]

With that conviction in mind they issued to the Church a joint pastoral letter, which they required to be read aloud in church to the people on the Sunday morning next after it had been received. The letter is here quoted in full:

PASTORAL LETTER TO THE CHURCH OF ENGLAND
From the Archbishops of Canterbury and York

Brethren in the Lord,

In this first year of our office we are moved to speak to the clergy and people about some of those things which are nearest to our hearts. Can we fail to have the hope that at this new stage in the story of the Church there may come some renewal of its life and power? Such a renewal will not come by mere appeals to the emotions, still less by new organizations. We are convinced that under the guidance of the Holy Spirit it may come if the whole Church will set its thought and prayer towards gaining a deeper and fuller appreciation of God, of His self-revelation in Christ, and the wonder and glory of the eternal gospel of His love and grace.

This gospel has been given. It is for the Church to proclaim it. The great body of truth about God and man which lies behind it has been given. It is for the Church to bear witness to it. But what has thus been given must be ever newly grasped—made real in life, interpreted and expressed to meet the needs of each successive age.

Is there not at this present time a manifest need of thus renewing the hold and unfolding the truth of the Gospel? Consider some signs of this need.

[1] *C.C.C.*, 1930, p. 29.

We are enclosed by a material civilization great in its achievements, confident in its self-sufficiency, in which no place is found for God or even for the spiritual life of man. The Church of Christ is called to give witness to the reality and claims of the things unseen and eternal. How can it give witness to these things unless they are manifestly real and powerful in the lives of its members?

Among our own people, not least among the young, there are many who are perplexed by difficulties or haunted by the fear that new knowledge is shaking the foundations of their Faith. To them the Church owes a two-fold duty. It must give them in fuller measure chances of learning what the Christian Faith really is. It must show them that through new light thrown upon the Bible and new discoveries of science rightly understood we are reaching a new knowledge of God and of His ways of revealing Himself. The Holy Spirit of God is worshipped and glorified when men are willing to be guided by Him into all truth.

Within the Church there are, we must thankfully acknowledge, many signs of zeal in the cause of our holy religion. Yet sometimes this zeal is narrow in range and in effect. It tends to be given to sections and parties rather than to the whole body of the Church. And aspects of truth and experience, when they are isolated, become onesided and exaggerated. It is only through the study of the whole Gospel of God that each aspect finds its place in the proportion of the one Faith.

Here may we speak a word about the difficulties in the ordering of our Common Prayer which recent events have brought about. It shall be only a word, for our eager hope is that the Church may rise above them to a higher ground and an ampler air. Suffice it then to say that the true way of solving these difficulties is that men of different outlook and traditions should not only tolerate but learn from one another, should come together, study together, so that all may bring whatever truth or experience they severally prize as an offering for the enrichment of the whole Church.

Once again, must it not be confessed that in many of our congregations there is a dullness of spirit, a languor of worship, a reluctance to make fresh adventures for the cause of God's Kingdom at home and overseas, strangely out of accord with the splendour of the Faith which they profess? Is not one reason this—that people so often take that Faith for granted, make or use no opportunities to grow in the knowledge of its length and breadth and height and depth? If by thus learning what the Faith really is and means they could gain some vision of the Love of God ever 'coming down from Heaven' in Christ to their own lives and their own parishes, drawing them into union with Himself and with one another in the fellowship of His body, speaking to them through His Word, giving His Life to them through His Sacraments, calling them to work with Him in the fulfilment of His Kingdom, would there not come to them new joy and zeal and power—'the garment of praise for the spirit of heaviness'?

It is difficult and indeed impossible for us within the limits of this Letter to say fully and clearly all that is in our minds. But our aim is very definite. It is to ask all members of the Church, clergy and laity alike, to make some continuous study of the Gospel of God's revelation of Himself in Christ, of the Bible and the Creeds wherein that Gospel is set forth, part of the corporate life and work of every parish throughout the land.

We make our Appeal first to the clergy. We know well the difficulties which beset them, the incessant demands which are made upon them. Our heart goes out to them in sympathy and understanding. But this call will not add to their burdens; rather will it relieve them. If they are encouraged and helped by authority to join frequently and regularly with their brethren in their deanery or district in a fellowship of study and prayer, they will find a real refreshment in their labours. They will be inspired to fulfil with new hope and zeal their office as the teachers of the people.

We make our Appeal also to the laity. Let them be willing to set their clergy free for more undistracted devotion to the Ministry of Word and of Prayer. Let them be ready themselves to use whatever opportunities for common study may be offered in due course in their own parishes. Let every parish be a school of sacred learning, wherein groups of men and women, old and young, many or few, may together steadily and prayerfully think out the meaining of the Christian Faith.

We write this Letter with the knowledge and goodwill of our brother bishops. We trust that when the Church's working year begins in the Autumn some steps may be taken in each diocese, in accordance with its own special conditions, to enable first the clergy and then the laity to respond to the Appeal which we have now made to the Church.

May the Divine Teacher, the Holy Spirit Himself, further our endeavour with His continual help. May He take of the things of Christ and show them anew to His Church in England now.

Finally, brethren, pray for us on whom so great a responsibility has been laid that God may frustrate all our Plans which are not His and so guide us by His Holy Spirit that we may serve His Church according to His Will.

Commending all who read or hear these words to the Blessing of Almighty God,

We are your servants in Christ Jesus,

Cosmo Cantuar:
William Ebor:

July 1929

It was a remarkable and a heartening message. It faced the facts of the Church's difficulties in modern society, but without scolding, and in such a way as to give real encouragement and to renew hope. The appeal came from those who had an undoubted right and a plain duty to make it, and it was accepted by the whole body of the clergy as a charge involving an inescapable obligation of obedience.

The phrase 'Way of Renewal' does not occur in the letter, but the whole movement it set in motion quickly became known by that title. In every diocese action was at once taken. The bishop of London, for example, chose 120 from the general body of his clergy to accompany him to High Leigh Conference House for a school of prayer. But the unit of response soon became the ruridecanal chapter, and the clergy of these chapters began to meet regularly together for study and prayer. Sometimes it happened that a chapter was content to meet in a schoolroom and listen to a paper read by its most learned member. When this was the pattern of response it did not last long because the proceedings were apt to be dominated by the naturally talkative, and constituted no more than just another meeting. But the pattern of the average Way of Renewal Group was mercifully very different. The clergy would meet once a month, always in the home of one or another of their members. A celebration of Holy Communion would be followed by breakfast, and this by a period of silent corporate prayer. Then the study would begin—perhaps a chapter of the Bible or of some agreed book. Somebody briefly introduced it, and the discussion which followed was so managed as to give every member his full chance to contribute to it. Then there would be a sandwich lunch, and the party would disperse in the early afternoon. A body of clergy who did this sort of thing every month for some years could hardly help but become a gathering of intimate friends before long, and whether these Way of Renewal Groups taught them much in the academic sense or not, they undoubtedly gave them a new sense and experience of what membership one of another really means. Co-operation became a habit, and even a tradition, and mutual trust displaced suspicion. The sense of solidarity among the clergy was greatly enhanced and the sense of ecclesiastical partisanship was steadily diminished by these exercises in fellowship and prayer; and there is no doubt at all that the Way of Renewal gave to the clergy what they urgently needed, and gave it to them not as medicine but as joy. Many of these Way of Renewal Groups continued in regular fellowship until the beginning of the second world war, and a few of them continue still. For not a few clergy these meetings are among the pleasantest of their memories; and not the least of the services which Archbishops Lang and Temple together gave to the Church was their first, the issuing of their pastoral letter.

17

Ministries Ancient and Modern

I · *In the Countryside*

THE GREATER part of the articulate thinking of the Church about its whole ministry to the people has been directed towards the better discharging of its work in the towns. But one of the features of the period between the wars was that a far more persistent and searching diagnosis was offered of the disease and health of the countryside than for many generations before. A considerable library of books and pamphlets was written and many committees and commissions investigated the problem between 1919 and 1939. The total flavour of all this oratory and writing was undeniably gloomy. The general ministration of the Church and the wholeness of its impact upon country life and work shared in this pertinacity of examination. One of the common features of this more ecclesiastical research was the invariable testimony to the truth of two opposites, the basic sameness but also the swift and widespread change of social conditions in rural places; and one of the commonest complaints was that the organization of the Church had not kept pace with this change. Perhaps the most distinguished of these examinations by the Church of its rural problems was the report of a committee appointed by Cyril Garbett, then Bishop of Winchester. This committee consisted of country clergy and lay people, and its chairman was the later Bishop of Truro, Edmund Morgan, who at that time was Archdeacon of Winchester, and also the rector of Old Alresford, a typical Hampshire country parish. They called their report *The Church in the Country Parishes*.[1] It is one of the indispensable documents for any consideration of the health of the Church in the country in this period. In his foreword Garbett vividly sketched the background against which it was written by his insistence that the 'unchanging, immemorial' countryside was in fact changing very fast indeed:

[1] Published by S.P.C.K., 1940. Cited hereafter as *Report*.

In the last twenty-five years changes have come with a rush and the transformation of the village has been rapid. With the break-up of the large estates, and the occupation of the manor houses by new-comers from the town, many of the old traditions have gone: the motor, the popular press, the wireless and the cinema have destroyed the isolation of the village: and the dispersal of the children for educational purposes is hastening the decay of its corporate life. Many of these changes are for the better, but they mean that the old village of English history is rapidly vanishing.[1]

The history of the Church in the village during these twenty years is therefore the history of how the Church struggled to cope with these changes.

The literature about the Church in the village from 1919 onwards is not on the whole flattering, and the indictments it draws are often severe. Let us take the indictment in its severest form. In 1925 a book was published[2] called *England's Green and Pleasant Land*. It consisted of a series of articles about the sadder side of life in the country, and it attracted much comment. The book was published anonymously, and the author's name has not been attached to any subsequent edition. In this book there is very much about the Church and its clergy, and this is a testimony to the fact that it is still impossible to think of an English village without its parish church and parson. But almost every reference stings, so that the testimony is inverted and backhanded. The sum of the author's complaint is as follows:

> In the fireside judgement of the mass of agricultural labouring families, the average parson is witless and lazy, a self-satisfied drone, who, by the advantage of his social position, has secured a soft job, to which he hangs on, although he knows, or ought to know, that much of what he keeps on saying about the gravest matters that can engross the human mind is untrue.[3]

There follows a great deal more to much the same effect; and then a passage in which the author admits that he does not believe the truth of the Christian interpretation of life, and himself goes to church occasionally in order to set an example. 'My complete absence would be an excuse for the non-attendance of others who are probably better at church than lying abed or dragging about the roads.'[4]

This abusive judgement would not be worth quoting were it not for the fact that its author tries to justify it by giving character sketches of a dozen country clergy whom he says he knows. He lists them alphabetically.

A.B.—red-faced and hearty, with 'a loud voice and a big belly'. He reads no books, and preaches 'poor stuff'. But he is most charitable and pastorally faithful, and a 'first-class neighbour'. 'There is not a kinder, more generous, or pluckier fellow. When there was an epidemic, he was fearless.'

C.D. reads no book and preaches drivel, but he has a 'high narrow sense of duty'.

---

[1] *Report*, p. ix.   [2] By Jonathan Cape.
[3] *England's Green and Pleasant Land*, pp. 90, 91.   [4] *Ibid.*, p. 92.

E.F. is a theologian, and preaches with conviction, though his congregation does not understand him. He gives much service to his village by immersing himself in local government.

G.H. is an amateur poultry farmer, reads no book, and is given to unseemly quarrels with choir and churchwardens.

I.J. is a sincere priest and a fine classical scholar. He plays football with the village boys. But his sincerity 'does not prevent him from being a blithering idiot'. 'After his death it was discovered that he was the anonymous donor of £300 which set the ball rolling for the cottage hospital, and that this was most of his bachelor priest's savings.'

K.L. is a scholar who assured a stranger that 'nothing whatever is needed in this parish' and so gave it nothing beyond the statutory services.

M.N. is a 'genial and generous old hunting man' who preaches for never longer than seven minutes, but he is charitable and kindly.

O.P. 'has lately been sent to a lunatic asylum.'

R.S. is dear, dutiful, and old, and has done a great deal for the social life of his village. He is an evangelical and an expert on the culture of sweet peas.

T.U. likes to be called 'Father', and is in fact the father of nine children. He is generally in trouble with his bishop because of his High Church practices, but he is faithful—'a most assiduous priest'.

V.W. needs a wash and brush-up, and he reads 'little of anything'. But what he does believe he believes with sincere intensity.

X.Y.Z. has no real vocation for the priesthood but is determined to serve his parish with his full powers. He is a zealous and outspoken champion of the poor and in their interests he defies the powerful. 'He asks the right questions at the wrong meetings.'[1]

Thus, very much after the manner of 'Characters of the First Eleven' in the school magazine, a far from sympathetic writer describes in 1925 the country clergy whom he knew. If so hostile a witness could find so much to praise, it is a reasonable inference that the Church was not ill but well served in the 'twenties by its country clergy. Of his dozen specimens, only one was utterly unattractive. Some of the others were oddities, and one or two of them were freaks, but that is not to say that they were faithless and incompetent clergy. The broad impression left by the catalogue is that the country parson could be counted on for pastoral faithfulness, for great personal generosity, for the service of the rural community, and for the championing of the under-privileged. Two out of the twelve were continuing the tradition that the country parsonage is a home of scholarship. The one valid and (apart from these two) consistent charge which the author brought against his regiment of parsons is that they did not read as they should have done—and this, if true, was a valid ground of complaint for by his ordination vows every priest is pledged to a life of study. But there

[1] *Ibid.*, pp. 82–6.

might well be excuses even for that neglect—loneliness, for instance, and sheer poverty so that the necessary books could not be bought; and of these continuous goads of the country parson's life the author showed no awareness whatever. The country clergy of the 'twenties, in fact, emerged with much credit from the exceedingly rough handling they got in this bitter book.

Such was the country parson as a very hostile critic of the 'twenties saw him. Side by side with that we may set the country parson and the situation in which he lived, and which he struggled to redeem, as his peers saw him in the late 'thirties. The best evidence here is the Report of the Bishop of Winchester's Commission of 1939, the composite work of eight country clergy and five laymen and women. The commission was appointed in order to

consider the work of the Church in country parishes under present day conditions, and to report what changes, if any, should be made in methods of work and organization to strengthen the work of the Church in rural areas.[1]

This report is as authoritative and experienced a picture as we are likely to get of the mission of the Church to the countryside and the people who live and work there. The fact that it was written by men and women who were themselves both country-dwellers and pledged to forward the mission of the Church in the country makes it all the more worthy of credence.

On the immemorial association between the Church and the land the report declines to build too much. The mystical exaltation of land as such, which occurred as a leading theme in one popular farming book after another, preaches a very superficial and uncritical nature-mysticism, which takes little or no account of nature's own need of redemption, and is difficult indeed to square with the Christian theological doctrine of creation. The report is clear that this identification is full of danger theologically, and that, if persisted in, it puts the country parson in a false position because the point of unity between the Church and the land as the practical farmer has seen it has for centuries been the tax called tithe.

We regard the Church's association with the land as out of date. The parson is no longer a landed proprietor or a farmer. Tithe was superseded by Tithe Rent Charge, and the Tithe Act of 1936 has almost completed the process of cutting the Church adrift from the land; and in spite of the financial loss suffered, we are glad that a fruitful source of friction between parson and people has been done away.[2]

Other writers, moreover, have in this same period given their testimony that a romantic devotion to the land is seldom found in the breasts of those who actually work upon it all the year round. There is, for example, the point of view of the tractor driver whom Mr C. S. Orwin has reported as

[1] *Report*, p. xi. [2] *Ibid.*, p. 8.

thinking aloud thus, as he drives his tractor, 'I looks at the bloody earth, and I says, "Blast it".'[1]

The Commission thus began by establishing clearly its own realism of view. The mission of the twentieth-century country parson could not be identified or refounded by attempts to couple the Church to any kind of nature mysticism, however up to date. The heart of his mission, on the other hand, is still friendship and prayer—and prayer comes first.

A country priesthood bravely shouldering the burden of intercession can be the instrument in God's hand for the revival of the whole body (of country life). Miracles would happen if every country parson used to the full the opportunities for prayer and study which God gives him.[2]

In the country, the Commission believed, the Church's mission was very difficult. The rural character made it so. The village community had a bad name for being inert.

There is a lack of zest in village life which shows itself in a childish ingenuity in making excuses, a knowledge of the right thing to do ... with too much indolence to get it done, and the defeatism which gives a new venture 'three years'. There is a sad element of truth in the epigram that 'Nothing succeeds like failure in the countryside'.[3]

Besides this, there was the resentment of class distinctions which nevertheless went hand in hand with a dour determination precisely by those who most resented them to perpetuate them in such unlikely fields as attendance at Holy Communion. The superstition that the Blessed Sacrament is for the gentry dies very hard in the country village; and what breaks the parson's heart most often is the spectacle of farmers' and labourers' sons and daughters who were prepared by him for confirmation, were then confirmed, made their first communion, and then never came to their communion again except perhaps on Easter Day. Many of the other diseases of country life, scandalmongering, and the dislike of seeing a bright boy or girl 'get on', were to be found just as readily in the life of the town. But in the tiny community of the village they loomed larger and were more socially and spiritually devastating. During the years between the wars agriculture was under a cloud, the countryside was being depopulated, and the improved social conditions of the town, higher wages, better houses, more entertainment, were not to be found in the country. The consequence was a still deeper and less easily eradicable lethargy. It needed a fine priest to work well in the country, and the villages needed the best parsons. The country vicar had in many ways a harder time of it than his brother in the town. A very experienced priest who has known both town and country from within has testified to the truth of this:

[1] C. S. Orwin, *Problems of the Countryside* (Cambridge University Press), 1945, p. 88.
[2] *Report*, p. 19.   [3] *Ibid.*, p. 3.

Like so many town parsons I was guilty of a slightly patronizing attitude to-wards country work. I thought I was in for a soft job. But my nine years at Winchfield provided the toughest job of my whole ministry, and proved to me that it is ten times easier to be a town parson than a country parson.[1]

Loneliness was the hardest and the commonest cross the country parson had to bear. If one compares the accounts of the country parson's life given by the clerical diarists of the eighteenth century, by men like Wood-ford, Skinner, or Cole, with what has been written and what one knows for oneself about the lives of their descendants of the twentieth century, one has the impression that the loneliness has intensified. Improved transport communications seem to have done less to cure it than might have been supposed. When St Clair Donaldson came from the diocese of Brisbane to be Bishop of Salisbury he was shocked to find how isolated and lonely many of the village clergy of Wiltshire and Dorset were. 'The spiritual isola-tion of many of our country parishes is as great as that of the most lonely I have known in Queensland.'[2] The Bishop of Winchester's Commission drew a distinction between social and spiritual loneliness. The bus, the car, and the telephone, they thought, should dispose of the complaint of social loneliness. But there were still plenty of country parsons who could afford no car and had no telephone, and one or two in their own diocese were living still in hamlets through which passed only a single bus in a whole week. Nor did the car and the bus cure the malaise of spiritual loneliness, which, with hopelessness, 'remain as besetting temptations'.[3] It did some-times happen that the country parson caught the disease of 'Nobody Loves Me', and the conditions of his life made it an insidious disease which it was hard to avoid. It was very easy for him to suppose that the diocesan authori-ties were not very interested in him, and that the village did not really want him and saw no particular purpose in the things his parish church stood for.

All these things conspire to tempt a man to lose faith in the worthwhileness of his job. He can easily become a decent-living and sober-minded office-holder who has lost hope in his own efficacy and faith in God's power to convert his people.[4]

There were however two other circumstances of his life which laid siege to his integrity as a priest. The first was his constant poverty, which was under-lined by the size of the house in which he had to live, and the broadness of the acres in which it was placed. From a score of sources, national and diocesan, the incomes of the poorest country livings were constantly aug-mented during the period, but these increments, welcome though they were, did not keep pace with the rising cost of living. A chronic shortage of money is a spiritual as well as a material affliction. It led in one parish after another to the second malign circumstance of the country parson's life—

---

[1] Arthur Hopkinson, *Parson's Progress* (Joseph), 1942, p. 107.
[2] C. T. Dimont and F. de Witt Batty, *St Clair Donaldson* (Faber and Faber), 1939, p. 111.
[3] *Report*, p. 13.   [4] *Ibid.*, p. 15.

the ever increasing amount of time he had to give to doing all the manual labour which men like Woodford and Cole seem to have enjoyed a sufficiency of cooks, housemaids, gardeners, and sextons to do for them. The parsonage with any domestic servants became a great rarity. The gardener, if there was one, was usually a man of seventy who came for a few hours each week. The sexton, if any, dug the graves, and no more. Everything else the parson and his wife usually did. On her fell the cooking and the cleaning, and on him the washing-up, most of the garden work (for the quickest way for the parson to lose the village's esteem is to have a badly neglected garden), and, not seldom the care of the churchyard, the lighting and stoking of the church boiler, and the daily pumping and carrying of water for the rectory in those villages where all water came from wells or a stream and not through the tap. A man who had to do all these daily chores (and many country parsons did) might remind himself that if he offered them to God they would turn into blessings for his people and himself, but it is not easy to do that with sincerity every day, and the pressure of their sheer and ceaseless inevitability made the life of prayer and study desperately difficult to maintain.

The test of whether or not a country priest is seriously trying to maintain it is whether or not he is scrupulous in discharging his obligation to recite the offices of Matins and Evensong every day, and to do this publicly in his church unless he is 'reasonably let or hindered'. It was twenty times harder for a country than for a town parson to do this. Before breakfast he had the chores to do. Afterwards he was apt to get immersed in a mass of duties. The church was bitterly cold on weekdays in winter, for no country church can afford to keep its boiler burning all the week, and even if it could there would be nobody but the parson to stoke it. There would probably be no congregation—at any rate, not for years—and it is hard indeed for most men to be both alone and 'real' in their daily recitation of the services. Yet where these difficulties were faced and the obligation was faithfully discharged the dangers of spiritual loneliness were met and beaten. So it was, for example, in the tiny village of Winchfield in Hampshire, where the rector, Arthur Hopkinson

day by day, for nine years, each morning walked across the fields from our lovely Queen Anne rectory to the lovely Norman church, unlocked it, rang the bell, and said Matins. In the evening I rang the bell again, and said Evensong. For years it was lonely worship; but gradually others joined me. I knew, too, that the men in the fields and the women in their homes liked to hear the bell and to know that someone was praying for them. . . . For me, this routine meant habits of discipline. . . . for it had not taken me long to discover how particularly difficult it is to maintain discipline *alone* in the country.[1]

The twenty years between the wars did not pass without any alleviation of these things being attempted. The ruridecanal conferences brought into

---

[1] Hopkinson, *op. cit.*, p. 114.

existence by the Enabling Act did something to break down the isolation between one village church and another, while the diocesan conferences did much to bring the parson, his wife, and some of his lay people into touch with others all over the diocese, and gave him the pleasant illusion of being, in part, the arbiter of its policies. The Way of Renewal movement of Lang and Temple, when fully used, did more still for the renewing of the springs of his spiritual life in the regularly gathered community of his peers and neighbours. Nor were these alleviations limited to the spiritual or democratic spheres of his life. It was in these twenty years that the Church began seriously to tackle the problem of the vast, unwieldy, and expensive country rectory. Many of them were sold, and new rectories of reasonable size and inexpensive to run were built instead.

Such were the weaknesses of the country parson's position. But they were matched by strengths; and first among these the Commission put the fact that he was resident, independent, and leisured at least in the sense that he was the arbiter of his own time-table. He was resident, and so could really be a pastor especially in times of family crisis; and he was available to take the lead in all kinds of village affairs. He was independent, and in a largely feudal atmosphere, he was often the only champion the poor and underprivileged could trust, and whose battles he often fought. He was leisured, and leisure is over and over again the condition of faithful pastoral work because it is an activity which needs time and cannot be hurried.

The country parson has plenty of time. While others are driven from pillar to post, hurrying about to classes, to committees, to meetings, scarcely able to fit their engagements into the crowded pages of their diaries . . . he has the priceless advantage of leisure. He has time to think and replenish his stores; he need not act without due deliberation. . . . He should never be idle but he need never be in a hurry. And that is one of the outward marks of sanctity . . . the saints are never in a hurry.[1]

As a consequence of this time to think, which the pressure of domestic chores does not destroy since they are largely mechanical, he could deliberately choose how best to serve his people and the Church. There was of course the inner life of prayer and study, and the round of services, and these were fixed marks. Being an Anglican priest there was also the demand of personal relationships to be met, and these 'still count for more than anything else in a village'.[2] But on these primary foundations the country priest could choose his own way of ministry. It was often the scholar's life, and oftener still the life of public service on the local government board or the hospital committee. If a census could be made of the many different types of service which the country vicarage rendered to Church and state between the wars, the list would be as impressive as it always has been, and the conditions were probably harder than for many years before.

[1] Charles Bigg, *The Spirit of Christ in Common Life*, p. 79. Quoted in *Report*, p. 10.
[2] *Report*, p. 11.

But the greatest single change that came over the position of the Church in the countryside was certainly the uniting of country benefices. As the value of money sank, and the depredations of the Tithe Act began to operate, it became more and more difficult to provide each country parish with its own parson. Men simply could not be found who could afford to accept the livings. On paper the obvious solution of the dilemma was to add the vacant parish to the charge of the nearest vicar and to add part, if not all of the stipend to his own. Not only was this the best solution on paper: it was often the only solution in sight. It had solid advantages:

If through a union of benefices (the vicar) is enabled to receive a stipend which will free him from anxiety and an excessive share of 'chores', the chances are that he will do better pastoral work. . . . But apart from economic considerations, a variety of opinions has been expressed, some clergy saying that it is an advantage to their ministerial life to have the wider scope afforded by union; others saying that it makes no difference either way; others again claiming that an incumbent does his best work in one parish with one church, and that a country parson has a whole time job even with quite a small population.

It was certainly true that very few of the villages affected liked it. When it came to the point each one always wanted the exclusive possession of its own parish priest. But none had a practical alternative to offer. The Winchester Commission made a rough calculation that 63 per cent of the united benefices had become content, that 28 per cent had resisted the suggestion but had become resigned to the accomplished fact, and that the rest were discontented. Often the parson sought to allay this discontent by providing each of the parishes with its full quota of services on Sundays, and by keeping going the organizations of each parish separately. Where he did this he had a truly dreadful Sunday, with perhaps three or four Celebrations, two morning and two evening services, and at least four sermons in the day. Sometimes it happened that one luckless vicar had three places of worship to serve; and by 1939 the number of country clergy with only one church was rapidly diminishing.

II · *In the Town*

To describe the work of the Church in the cities and towns is an impossible task, so many and so various are they. It seems best, therefore, to proceed by the method of taking samples, and letting them speak for the whole mission of the Church to urban England. Here then are two such samples, the one of Tyneside, and the other of the smaller unit of the country town, Alton in Hampshire.

NEWCASTLE UPON TYNE

In a vast modern industrial city which numbers its inhabitants by hundreds of thousands, religion is always at an initial disadvantage. Its people are too far from the sights of nature to be able easily to comprehend the realm of supernature and its relevance to their lives and concerns. Their crowd is too inchoate, too enormous for the sense of community, which is at the heart of the practice of Christianity, to be instinctive and unremarked.

The history of the Church in any great city would illustrate this fact, but it is seen more clearly in medium-sized cities like Newcastle or Bristol, with their own cherished traditions and clearly marked individualities, than in the enormous cities like London or Manchester which are altogether too vast to possess any particular character of their own. A full picture of the life of the Church in urban England would require the telling of its story in each city in turn, which is an impossible task. But it maybe illustrated in broad outline by trying to describe its witness in the period after 1919 in only one city, Newcastle upon Tyne.

Everyone who belongs to Newcastle claims that it is a city with a strongly marked character and individuality of its own. Those who write about it concede the claim. Geography has made it so, for throughout its history Newcastle has been more fully separated from the rest of England than any other city of like size. Scotland, it is true, is distant from it by only the length of a county, but beyond the border one is in a very different country. The Pennines cut it off from Cumberland and the Lancashire towns. South of it lay miles of moorland for generations, and though in the last hundred years the moors have been tamed and cut by macadamized highways and by railways, it is still true that Newcastle is widely separated from the West Riding of Yorkshire. For many centuries Newcastle had to provide for itself all it needed in religion, in culture, in learning, and in medicine; and it provided all of them with vigour. Its trade, too, was markedly individual. Only Glasgow shared the particular bounty of nature which brought coal and a navigable river together in such a way as to make the building of large ships the specialized domestic occupation. All these circumstances, operating unchecked over centuries and still potent, have made Newcastle and Tyneside as a whole perhaps the most independent, most fiercely patriotic, and most isolated industrial area in England. Its special character was described by an acute and trained social observer, Dr Henry Mess, in 1928, in these words:

There is a curious abruptness of manner which is very disconcerting until one has got used to it. The general temper of the area is individualistic, and hard to move along new lines. ... There is a great love of outdoor sport; an unusual knowledge of wild life; a great deal of interest in local history and antiquarianism. ... Tyneside is—we will not say militarist—exceptionally interested in all that concerns armies and navies. It is easily understood when one looks at its history. There is first of all the Border tradition; for centuries there was watchfulness against the Scot, and the great leaders of Northumberland were, above all, leaders in war. In the second place, Newcastle and Tynemouth are barracks towns, and the former is a great recruiting depot. . . . And in the third place, Tyneside grew and thrived on the race in armaments. Battleships and big guns meant wealth to the captains of industry, work to the rank and file, and dividends to thousands of local investors. Men love what they create and the Tynesider followed the fortunes of his craftsmanship all over the world.[1]

Such a city may have many black spots, but at least it is vital, it has a colour of its own, and it has in its bones all that is needed to create a sense of community. It has, in its very situation, that is to say, all the raw materials of the corporate Christian life. It is therefore one of the happiest places for a priest to work, for local history gives him a chance. It is noticeable that a priest who has once worked in Newcastle for a time and then left it to go elsewhere, often likes to get back there if he can.

The quotation given above is from Henry Mess's social survey called *Industrial Tyneside*, and an account of the genesis and purpose of this authoritative document may well serve as a starting-point of a description of the life of the Church in Newcastle[2] after 1919, since it was the initiative of Christians in Newcastle which caused the survey to be made and the book to be written. The great Conference on Politics, Economics, and Citizenship (COPEC) which was held in Birmingham in 1924 was followed by many local conferences of the same kind, and among them one in Newcastle. The Newcastle COPEC stirred those who came to it to consult together in order to see what they might do to apply Christian principles to the whole life of Tyneside. They decided that the first service they could offer was to discover and set out in intelligible form the actual facts of social life on the banks of the Tyne in the post-war age. Until the facts were known, and so assembled that they could be seen clearly and be easily weighed against each other, Christian social action must remain a form of fumbling in the dark. In 1925 these men and women set up a survey committee. It had Sir Theodore Morison, Principal of Armstrong College, as its chairman, and its membership consisted of industrialists, social workers, trade union officials, professors, and clergy. They decided to set up a social services bureau, and to appoint Henry Mess to be its director. The survey, *Industrial Tyneside*, was the first consequence of this action. It is a measured, dispassionate, and astonishingly full account of what it was like to live on Tyneside at that time. Crammed with facts and figures, it is nevertheless written so that they are clear; they are left to speak for themselves, and no commentary underlines them. It was this cool and lucid presentation of the facts which gained the admiration of so difficult a critic as Hensley Henson, who came from Durham to meet the clergy of Newcastle and Gateshead to commend it to them in measured terms of praise. It

[1] Henry A. Mess, *Industrial Tyneside* (Ernest Benn), 1928, pp. 25–6.
[2] In this account 'Newcastle' means primarily the city, and secondarily Tyneside as a whole. It does not mean the diocese of Newcastle, which takes in the whole of the county of Northumberland, which consists mostly of rural parishes.

poured on the social life of Tyneside, he said, 'maximum light with minimum heat'. William Temple, then Archbishop of York, also gave it the highest praise when he came to Newcastle Cathedral to preach at the service at which this survey was solemnly received at the hands of its author by the Church and offered at the altar. In all this the vigorous co-operation of the Free Churches played a big and perhaps a decisive part, and the salary of Mess was provided by the munificence of a Congregationalist layman.

The facts of social life on Tyneside in 1928, as the survey revealed them, were certainly disturbing; and they pointed to a poverty in the quality of family life of the majority of people which no Christian who believed the creed could tolerate with equanimity, for by it the doctrine of man implicit in the Incarnation was derided. By the building of ships and the hewing of coal Tyneside chiefly lived, and unemployment in both these basic industries was alarming indeed. In the shipbuilding and ship repairing industries between July 1923 and October 1926 the percentage of workers unemployed had varied from 30·6 to 61·3. At the beginning of this period the figure had stood at 59·4. Then it had gradually dropped to 30·6 in July 1924. From that date until October 1926 there had been a steep and steady rise to the horrible figure of 61·3. 'A bitter record,' commented the survey(55).[1] The situation in the collieries was no better. Miners working at the coal face could rarely earn £3 a week, and for that they were 'working longer hours than at any time during the last sixty years' (71). Most of the Tyneside coal, being hard steam coal, was exported. The general strike and the long coal strike which followed it had therefore been specially disastrous to Tyneside. Unemployment was heavy, but the poverty among those in full employment was scarcely less severe than among the unemployed, for at that date the unemployment insurance was not subject to the heavy depredations of the means test. Of all industries on Tyneside coal-mining seemed the most hopeless, and those belonging to it, both management and workers, had largely lost their faith in its future; and this failure of faith had been not allayed but rather exacerbated by the innumerable state commissions and reports which had been consistently unregarded. In coal-mining

the present situation is deplorable. Many collieries have closed down; the majority of others are working at a loss. Those men who have employment are working longer hours and earning less than for many years past. Many are unemployed, and there can be no doubt that there is considerable distress among them (74).

In housing the Tyneside situation was also menacing. The slums were as extensive as in most other industrial areas. The overcrowding was worse. In Newcastle itself, in 1921, 11·5 per cent of all the families were living in one room, and 25·3 per cent in two rooms; and in Jarrow and Gateshead

[1] The figures given in brackets in the text refer to the relevant pages in the survey.

the figures were still worse. In England and Wales as a whole those two figures were 3·6 and 10·5. It meant that 33·6 per cent of the families of Tyneside, or over 250,000 persons, were living in what by the official standards of the Ministry of Health were overcrowded conditions. This was a statistical distinction which Tyneside shared with Finsbury and Shoreditch in the County of London, but with nowhere else in England and Wales (79, 80).

The statistical consequences of Tyneside slums and overcrowding are set out in the tables of figures relating to infant mortality and the incidence of tuberculosis. As regards infant mortality the figures for the whole area of Tyneside were very high, but for Newcastle itself they had dropped between 1911 and 1925 from 120 to 96 per 1,000 live births, though this was 13 higher than the average of county boroughs in England and Wales (104). But the figures for tuberculosis on Tyneside were black indeed. Some of its towns ranked among the worst in the whole country.

The survey covered nearly all the aspects of communal life in the area, and came at last to conclude that in spite of much that made the social life on Tyneside a hopeful experience the whole picture was 'very dark' (165). Mess had been forced to present the picture in terms of many rows of figures and statistical tables.

But its real subject is the lives of men and women and of their children. . . . The overcrowding figures bring to mind homes so tiny and so crammed that they almost seem to protrude bedsteads as one passes along the street. . . . The health figures speak tragically to anyone who has sensibilities; they tell of house after house where there is some tuberculous member of the family, a child with swollen glands, a father in a sanatorium, or a daughter dying slowly in one of the two rooms which constitute a home. That violently fluctuating curve of unemployment (in the graph) corresponds to many hundreds of housewives who are trying to meet the ends of their households, with no assurance as to what money will be forthcoming on the morrow, or whether there will be any money at all (165).

And to set against all this in the opposite scale, Mess found but little. The voluntary social services, indeed, existed, and 'the great majority of social workers are members of Christian Churches' (142), but they were ill-organized, and there were many aspects of need they did not cover. Of the schools, he declared, 'One cannot believe that Newcastle will be content for ever to have its elementary schools so much worse staffed than those of Bradford and Nottingham, towns which it reckons as its peers' (167).

Such was the social situation in 1928. Bad as it was, it was presently to become even worse, for the world economic crisis was not yet in full swing, nor was the means test operating among the unemployed. But it was quite bad enough to be an intolerable burden to those on whom its weight fell, and an affront to the social conscience by which all Christians who really believe their religion are bound to be burdened. If therefore the people looked to the Churches for help and hope they looked to the place from which these graces ought to come. Mess's survey was a highly important part of the Christian response to that unspoken cry. But it was inevitably the work of a very few highly gifted Christians. If the Churches were to work towards the remedying of the state of affairs which the survey revealed, they must themselves be strong. What, in 1928, was their strength?

The survey has a chapter on this, but its author began it by remarking that it was bound to be an unsatisfactory account. One cannot compute the health of Churches by counting heads, and yet this was the only way open to the author to use. Moreover it was not a scientifically satisfactory way in itself. Different Churches kept their statistics according to different methods, and none kept them fully or exactly. Even if the ecclesiastical statisticians had taken lessons from the Board of Trade and compiled their tables after the manner of Whitehall, nobody could possibly determine what the figures would signify in terms of spiritual energy. None the less the survey did gather a number of interesting figures about the life and work of the Tyneside Churches. All of them relate to the year 1925.

The Anglican Church was baptizing 70 per cent and the Roman Catholic Church 18 per cent of all the babies born. In the Sunday schools of the Anglican Church were 19·5 per cent of the children, as opposed to 4 per cent for the Presbyterians and 8·4 per cent for the Wesleyans. 16 per cent of the children in the elementary schools were Roman Catholics. For Confirmations, Easter Communions, and Membership of the Electoral Rolls only the Anglican figures are given. They show that 3,519 adolescents were confirmed—about 20 per cent of all who might have been; that 31,540 people made their communion on Easter Day and 2,016 during Easter week; and that there were 46,658 names on the electoral rolls, or 9 per cent of the population over eighteen. The only comment the survey makes on these figures is that it is impossible to measure whether the Anglican Church had been losing or gaining ground in the previous twenty years. On the other hand the survey had no doubt that the Roman Catholics had gained ground, and that very quickly, until in 1925 they constituted one-eighth of the population.

In addition to compiling these statistics the organizers of the survey called in volunteers and took two counts of people going to church on an average Sunday first in Wallsend and then in South Shields. The Wallsend census was taken on a first Sunday in February 1928. Only adults and adolescents over fourteen were counted, and the count was taken at every service in every church of whatever denomination. The total population over 14 years of age in Wallsend was 33,000. Of these, 7,698 went to church that day—that is, about one-fifth. Fifteen per cent went to Anglican churches, 42 per cent to Roman Catholic churches, and 43 per cent to all the Free Churches put together. The census showed also that adolescents of every Church attended twice as well as adults.

The census in South Shields, which of course is in the diocese of Durham and ten miles from Newcastle, was taken on a dull and cold May Sunday in the same year. Here the Church of England had 30 per cent of the attendances, the Roman Catholics 22 per cent, and the Free Churches 48 per cent. The attendances amounted to about an eighth of the population, and again adolescents attended better than adults.

The figures are certainly less depressing than one might expect. In these two sample townships there was no question of 'less than a tenth of the population having any connection with institutional religion'. But if one mentions this census to those who know Tyneside well, one is apt to be told that Wallsend is exceptional and that church life there has always been very strong. The local people would say that the South Shields figures would be nearer the average for all Tyneside. Suppose then that these South Shields figures be taken as representing Tyneside as a whole, it would mean that on an ordinary Sunday in May 1928, one-eighth of the whole population went to church and could be classed as habitual churchgoers. That would give a total of roughly 102,300 churchgoers on Tyneside, since the population at the 1921 census was 818,422. Of these 102,300 (and working still on the South Shields standards) the Church of England claimed 30 per cent, that is 30,690. Judging the city of Newcastle itself on the same standards the position would be that out of a population of 275,000, 34,375 were churchgoers, and of these 10,410 belonged to the Church of England. These figures are so rough and approximate that they would make a trained statistician blush, and the mere citing of them may cause the spiritual purist to utter his warning that spiritual strength must not be estimated by counting heads. But allowing for both these cautions, and allowing also for the further unknown factor that no one knows or can ever know what proportion of churchgoers are spiritual passengers, it remains true that the Church on Tyneside and in Newcastle could number its adherents in tens of thousands, and that among them there was sufficient force and to spare to make a great deal of difference to the quality of social life on Tyneside if it could be effectively harnessed and set in motion. It is also a significant indication of the health of the Church that throughout this period of great industrial depression and then of war the standard of missionary giving in the diocese remained relatively stable. Annual contributions to S.P.G. rose from £2,828 to £3,477 between 1919 and 1920, then fell slowly to £2,095 in 1935, and then gradually rose to £3,589 in 1944.

On Tyneside between the wars a number of men were serving who were quite capable of doing this marshalling of spiritual power, and were determined that it should be done. Canon Oliver Quick, one of the two or three most considerable theologians of his generation, was at the cathedral. Among his colleagues there was Archdeacon Leslie Hunter, later Bishop of Sheffield, a man who has always had more numerous contacts with more varied spheres of life than it seems possible for one man to sustain, and who has a genius for finding exactly the right man for a particular job and persuading him to do it. There was Ronald Hall at St Luke's, Newcastle, and his curate William Greer, deep friends between whom life later put half a world since the one became Bishop of Hong Kong and the other of Manchester. These two would be bound to make anything move that they touched. At St John's, Newcastle, there was Dr Noel Hudson, later Bishop of the diocese, with a large and devoted congregation to form much of the backbone of any enterprise they espoused. At Gateshead, and later at Sunderland, Leonard Wilson reigned, and was heart and soul in the social movement. At Wallsend there was Canon Osborne, a disciple of Dolling, an erudite theologian, and a socialist. Behind all they did lay the work of Canon Newsom, Vicar of Newcastle, who had a perfect genius for friendship and for creating fellowship. These worked very closely together in those years. They secured the co-operation of the Free Churches, and were able to build in all sorts of ways the necessary bridges between the Churches, the agencies for social welfare, the trade union world, and the university.

Without this co-operation the whole effort must have been heavily handicapped, for the Free Churches were very strong. Much of the drive for social reform came from their ranks. The work done in this field by the Congregational Church of St James was of a specially high order, and the Central Methodist Church seemed to supply a considerable part of the Town Council. For over thirty years one of the leading social workers of Newcastle was Miss Theresa Merz, a member of the Society of Friends, but she eventually made her pilgrimage into the Anglican Church. The support of the trade unionists was also very important, for the trade union leaders counted for much on Tyneside, and many of them were fine Christian men. They did not officially co-operate very much in the work of the Tyneside Council of Social Service, but unofficially they gave it both sympathy and much effective help. From the Anglican side there was a tradition of social consciousness which had been slowly built before and during the war by such men as Bishop Lloyd, Cyril Hepher of St John's, Mole of St Philip's, and others. All these were thoroughly in touch with the life of the Newcastle community as a whole, and their work helped to build the basis on which the Tyneside Council of Social Service could rest secure.

Certainly there were giants in the Church on Tyneside. But these giants were not only to be found among the clergy. Many laymen of all kinds supported all they did, and some did far more than support. And here again, as so often elsewhere in this book, one sample must stand for a host. It is safe to say that much that was done for our Lord on Tyneside in those years would not have been done, or would have been done differently, had James Andrew Halliday not been living. He had left school at the age of fourteen and given his working life to the municipal gasworks, where he eventually became a senior clerk. He was also a Plymouth Brother who became a Quaker, and a Quaker who became an Anglican, being drawn to take this last step, as are so many Free Churchmen, by his need of sacramental worship. A politician (in the Liberal interest) and a lifelong pacifist, he was also a man who valued and combined in a fruitful synthesis the things of mind and spirit. He was a very exact man, the born secretary of any organization, tireless and persistent, and completely devoted to any cause he made his own. Perhaps the core of his insight was his belief that 'truth and light are best sought in the company of friends'.[1] All his life was given to the creation of that kind of friendship, and though he was an austere man, whose austerity was felt, he 'probably started more societies and study-groups than any other man in Newcastle'.[2] They ranged from the Economic Society to the Theological Society; and although not every society he began was successful, a high proportion were, and taken together they did much to demonstrate to the Tynesider that things are done best by friends, and that between men of very different tradition friendship is perfectly possible if sought against a spiritual background. In any society which he started 'his ambition was to do the heavy work of planning, organizing, and executing, and to leave for others the prestige of more honoured positions'.[3] Of such as he democracy is made, and when the Hallidays all die and are not replaced democracy will die with them.

Intellectually his three loves were political science, economics, and theology, and it was his interest in and deep knowledge of theology, eagerly encouraged by Oliver Quick, which brought him at last into the Church of England, where he became a sidesman in the cathedral. But more important by far than this was his starting of the Theological Society, ultimately the most influential of all his ventures. The Christian social work on Tyneside in those years rested on two pillars. One was the Tyneside Council of Social Service, which was Dr Mess's Survey Committee continued under another name. The other was the Theological Society which Halliday founded.

It was not to be just a lecture society, still less one for debate, least of all one for superficial interdenominational fraternities. It was to be a society for the study of truth in the sincere and peaceable atmosphere of spiritual fellowship.[4]

The last sentence has the typical Halliday hallmark. Quick was its first chairman, and Canon Osborne succeeded him. Halliday was its indispensable and indefatigable secretary. The 'Theological' quickly became one of the best societies of its kind in the country. In some ways it was unique. It had a membership of over two hundred, and it was the heart and centre of inter-denominational fellowship on Tyneside, teaching Christians of different Churches to be together at the levels of prayer and thought, and providing the best possible basis for their fruitful co-operation in social work.

[1] *James Andrew Halliday*, A Memorial Lecture by Leslie S. Hunter, Bishop of Sheffield (privately printed), 1932, p. 7.
[2] *Ibid.*, p. 16.　　　[3] *Ibid.*, p. 16.　　　[4] *Ibid.*, p. 12.

The survey had noted that for most of the social service which was being done at all Christians were responsible. The new Tyneside Council of Social Service provided the leadership and organization and the Theological Society provided the experience of inter-denominational friendship and co-operation by which this social service was informed, augmented, and made more effective than it had ever been. The Churches therefore set to work with a will to do what they could to help in the remedying of the social evils which the survey had disclosed, and to demonstrate that a Christian Church must always care as profoundly for the material as for the spiritual sufferings of people. This charge they bore in a great variety of ways, of which these three perhaps remain most vividly in memory after the passage of the years.

It was on Christmas Day, 1927, that the first steps were taken which led to the foundation of the Newcastle Housing Improvement Trust. A few days before, Ronald Hall, then vicar of St Luke's, had been handed the literature of the St Pancras housing effort by a friend who remarked 'I have a little money in this,' and he knew that 'a little' was all she could have! On Christmas Day he preached on the subject of Homes, using the St Pancras papers as examples. After the service a man said to him, 'Something must be done about this.' Something was, and that man eventually became Chairman of the Trust. Backing for the scheme came from many other churches and chapels, particularly from the parish of St John, and the first share was bought by a missionary in China. This Trust reconditioned some sixty houses in the centre of the city, and turned them into model workers' flats, and the enterprise was copied by other Christian citizens in some other parts of Tyneside.

The blight of mass unemployment smote Tyneside with special severity, and the suffering here, as everywhere else in Britain, was made far worse than it need have been by the means test. To meet this challenge the Christians of Tyneside found they had to do just what other Christians from other 'distressed areas' were also doing, that is, feeding the undernourished and providing occupations for the enforced leisure of so many thousands. The feeding of the hungry was done in many different ways in different parishes, but nowhere more memorably than in St Luke's.

The vicar and his curate found that it was on Wednesdays and Thursdays that people were hungriest, for by then the pitifully meagre benefit paid out on Fridays was often completely exhausted. At first they started a communal kitchen, but found that Tynesiders were too proudly independent to come to it. So they collected a cart, loaded it with soup, minced meat, and rice pudding, and the vicar pushed it round the parish while the curate walked in front ringing a bell. As they passed down the streets people came to their doors, paid the nominal sum of twopence so that it was not 'charity', and were given heaped plates full of the hot, nourishing food. This piece of work opened the way to another which was far more difficult, the building of a bridge between the communists and the Christian congregation. The curate got into touch with the chairman of the local communists and asked for his co-operation in the planning of recreation for the unemployed. But the communist kept on insisting that it was food and not recreation that the unemployed people wanted. He hit his belt and said, 'It's here we need it.' The soup and minced meat cart proved to him that the Church too realized this need, and that it was actually doing what it could to supply the need. Thus when he was asked to come to the Saturday night group meetings of the congregation he felt unable to refuse, and agreed to come, 'if I'm not in gaol'.

The Christian citizens of Tyneside also at that time flung themselves into the task of providing occupational centres in many places for the unemployed, and this enterprise, started at first independently in a handful of parishes, was taken over by the Tyneside Council of Social Service, and greatly expanded and developed by that body, which was in effect the Christian Churches in social action. This sort of work was being done all over the country, wherever the presence of many unemployed workers made it necessary, and nearly always it was Christians, acting under the inspiration of their Christianity who did the bulk of it.

When, in 1939, the war began it was not long before the normal ways in which Christians express their sense of social responsibility were made impossible to follow. The building of houses and the succouring of physical and spiritual distress, these are the obvious paths for ordinary Christians to follow who believe that their Christianity must embrace the whole of life. Between 1919 and 1939 the feats of Christian social work which can be described in a narrative were nearly always to build houses and to help the unemployed. What Christians have done for hospitals, though probably greater in range and extent, cannot well be written because a work that is a matter of routine, performed steadily for generations, rarely affords any particular story to tell.

ALTON, HAMPSHIRE

No one who visits Alton today would guess from its buildings that it is an ancient place with a long history, which is mostly placid but has at least one moment of high dramatic excitement. But it had its moment—a moment of high but strange and terrible dramatic excitement. This came to Alton, as to so many towns like it, in the Civil War. There is a brass in Winchester Cathedral which tells the outline of that story—how the royalist colonel Richard Boles defended Alton against the Cromwellians in 1643, and the last stand in the church itself:

his last Action, to omitt all Others was at Alton in this County of Southampton, was sirprised by five or six Thousand of the Rebells, which caused him there Quartered, to fly to the Church with neare Fourscore of his men who there Fought them six or seven Houers, and then the Rebell Breaking in upon him he

Slew with his Sword six or seven of them and then was Slayne himself, with sixty of his men aboute him. His Gratious Soveraigne hearing of his Death gave him his high Commendation in this pationate Expression, Bring me a Moorning Scarffe, I have Lost one of the best Comanders in this Kingdome.

It was a desperate day and a forlorn hope. Waller had 6,000 trained soldiers, and Boles 500 undisciplined recruits from the wilds of Ireland and the Welsh mountains. They were slowly pressed back to the church hill, then into the churchyard, and then into the church itself. They locked and barricaded the doors, but

hand-grenades were thrown through the windows, bullets spit, split and scattered on to the grey walls, and riddled the stout oak door . . . The hinges gave and the angry troopers fought their way through into the church where the Cavaliers piled their dead horses in the aisles for breast-works. 'Charles! Charles!' rang the loyal battle-cry through the Norman arches under the belfry as man by man the defenders fell. 'No surrender!' and the Colonel swore his sword should slay any who cried for mercy. But his men, untrained, borne back by sheer weight of numbers, gave way, dropped their weapons, and yielded. Boles, fighting to the last, was slain.[1]

Those were the first, and up to the present the last desperate doings in Alton, which thereafter relapsed once more into a decent and seemly obscurity. The church was a charnel house, but they cleansed it and repaired the breaches of it, carefully preserving the marks of bullets on the walls, which remain to this day.

Alton may have made no further stir in the history books, but in some ways it has been remarkable, and chiefly for the uncommon variety of the work of the Church there. On the edge of the town stand the fine buildings of the Lord Mayor Treloar's Hospital. It was originally built by the Absent Minded Beggar Fund as a National Memorial Hospital, but was transferred by Parliament to Sir W. P. Treloar for his hospital for crippled children, and became one of the most famous orthopaedic hospitals in the country. To staff and children the Anglican clergy of the town regularly ministered. Up the hill beyond the great breweries is one of the houses of the Community of St Mary the Virgin at Wantage, where the nuns look after some forty homeless and feeble-minded girls. The sisters came to Alton in 1911. At first their only chapel was a room in the house, but by 1913 they had built on to it one of the loveliest domestic chapels in the country; and here too the clergy of Alton minister to the sisters. Near to it is Morland Hall, a well-known clinic for the curing of tubercular complaints of bone and skin. There are two or three private boarding schools, a large infirmary, and a cottage hospital. To complete the list of the non-parochial institutions of Alton, there is Alton Abbey, inhabited by a small Order of Anglican monks and lay brethren, whose work in the world is

[1] D. H. Moutray Read, *Highways and Byways in Hampshire* (Macmillan), 1932, p. 399.

that of ministering to the bodily and spiritual needs of retired merchant seamen.

This work of pastoral ministry is borne by the clergy and people of the two parish churches of the town in addition to their normal round of parochial work. There is the church of St Lawrence, the ancient parish church of the town, the same church which was once turned into a charnel house by the Parliament army. The second parish church, All Saints, stands on the main road at the western end of the town, and it has become the 'high' church of the two. But it was not so when it was first built 'principally for the Working Classes' in 1873. Just before the consecration a lady offered to present the new church with surplices for the choir, but the building committee refused to accept them, solemnly minuting that

considering the extreme sensitiveness of the majority of the population for whom the church is principally intended, it might prove prejudicial in debarring some of them from attending the Church, therefore it would be more likely to induce Peace and Goodwill to let the Choir attend in their usual dress.

It is often easiest to describe the essential character of a place by contrasting it with some other place which is its direct opposite. What, then, is the direct opposite of an ancient country town like Alton? There is no doubt of the answer. It is the recently built, ultra-modern, district or satellite township of a great city like London. There are some twenty thousand people living in housing estates, small detached villas, or large houses all built on an area of land which twenty years ago was all fields, heath and woodlands. Everything is very hygienic, and all has been planned to emphasize the family's privacy, and does in fact emphasize its separation from other families. We may perhaps call it Sleepers' Hill, and anyone who knows Surrey will recognize it, for Surrey has many Sleepers' Hills.

In Sleepers' Hill nobody knows anybody; there is no pride of place; all are strangers. No sense of community exists. As a consequence there is much more unhappiness in Sleepers' Hill than in Bethnal Green or Lambeth. If one is ill in a slum, the fact is at once known and the neighbours are interested and try to do what they can to help. In Sleepers' Hill one could break one's leg and nobody would know. Disasters have to be shouldered alone. People would care if they knew, but life is patternless, and they are very unlikely to know.

Now Alton is in every way the precise opposite of Sleepers' Hill. In mentality it is fifty years behind it, and the pace of its life is far, far slower. But its enormous strength is that it is genuinely a community; and every man, woman and child has an authentic sense of belonging, and mattering. It is like a vast picture of a crowd, and everyone knows that if he looks he will find his own face somewhere on the canvas. If the butcher breaks his leg or the sweep has an unfortunate quarrel with a chimney and breaks his brushes, everybody knows about it and everybody is interested. In Alton

it is not possible to have purely private joys or sorrows, blessings or disasters; and if it is not completely and universally true that the joy of one is
the joy of all, and the hurt of one the hurt of all, at least these things are to
a wide extent shared. In Alton, as in other towns of the same kind, people
have a sense of security, for they live in a patterned life. They have their
own place in it; and they know where it is, and how it fits into the whole
picture.

Community of this power is dynamic, and dynamics, as Dean Bennett of
Chester was fond of saying, are ambivalent. They tend to produce disconcerting, as well as splendid results. One of the inherent weaknesses of the
Alton type of community is well known to anyone who has himself been
the citizen of such a place. It is the sense of rivalry between the smaller
communities within the larger. If a small town with strong traditions and a
strong sense of community has two parish churches, and these churches
are themselves strong communities, it is virtually certain that they will tend
to measure themselves against each other and will find it harder to co-
operate than they would if they were in two different towns. Similarly, there
is likely to be some rivalry between the different denominations in the
town.

The task of the Church in a town like Alton is therefore always the same,
and always twofold. There is first the common pastoral and evangelistic
task of all Churches everywhere, which in Alton is particularly exacting
because of the unusual variety of institutions which the Church must serve.
But beyond this lies the task of taking the community which exists as it
were by the light of nature into the realm of the supernatural, that it may
be purged of the distortions and excesses of internal rivalry. The history
of the Church in Alton during the years 1919 to 1939 is primarily the history
of its discharging of these two tasks.

First of all it had to be tackled and achieved as between the two parish
churches. Both were and are strong Christian communities. Both churches
are always full, and both have enjoyed a long succession of exceptionally
devoted men as their vicars. But All Saints, in spite of its refusal of surplices for the choir in its earliest days, quickly became a catholic strong-
hold, while St Lawrence remained what it had always been, broadly
evangelical in its traditions. For many years the two communities had little
to do with each other, and there was one famous occasion when the vicar
of the parish church was invited to preach in the daughter church and began his sermon by saying earnestly, 'I stand before you in fear and trembling.' It was an urgent work of the Church to lay this suspicion to rest,
and to put in its place a spirit of co-operation and fellowship. But to do
this, some work had to be found in which both congregations could share,
and big enough to tax the resources of each. This was found in the laying
to rest of the other characteristic aberration of community, the isolation
of the different Christian denominations from each other. This was tackled

and achieved in two ways. First, all the clergy of the town were brought and held together in a fraternal; and though it was very difficult at first this fraternal gradually became true to its name. They found their common field of work in the town's Council of Social Service, which for some years operated with imagination and fruitfulness, and shouldered a multitude of burdens.

But side by side with it the ordinary work of evangelistic and pastoral ministry and of worship went steadily forward in both parishes. It was exacting and exhausting, more so in Alton than in many other places. There are few towns indeed where the pastoral demand is so incessant, and none where it has been more splendidly met by all clergy over a long period of years. But although all the clergy have been devoted men, one has been completely outstanding; and his life was so fully the sacrament of the whole Christian proclamation and witness in Alton that it must be briefly told.

The spiritual history of Alton during the first thirty years of the twentieth century is a story which revolves round a hero, for what Father Wainright was to London Docks that, and more besides, Charlie Bond was to Alton. He was born in the place, and he lived and served and died in it: in all his life he only left it for the three or four years while he was preparing for ordination. He was, and yet he was not, the typical parish priest—the sort of parish priest that all good men want to be and so few of us actually become. He was typical in the sense that he perfectly exemplified the characteristic virtue of the Anglican parish priest in every age, for he was before all else the faithful pastor who knew all his sheep and loved them, and was loved by them in turn, and who was wise and tireless in his care for them since he loved them in Christ, being a man of intense spirituality and humility. It is not for every Anglican priest that all this can be claimed, but it is the type of priestly excellence that every Anglican Christian best understands and most reveres, for our saints are always the pastors and George Herbert was the very type and image of Anglicanism at its best. His qualities reappear in every generation, and in the twentieth century not the least exemplar of them was Charlie Bond, vicar of All Saints, Alton.

His history was romantic indeed. He first appeared on the stage of memory in 1890, when he was a butcher's errand boy of fourteen years old. One day he was wandering up the High Street when a traction engine, towing two truck-loads of bricks, came in sight and drew near. Charlie could not resist it. He ran and leaped for the bar attaching the engine to the truck. He caught it, swung his leg over it, and slipped and fell, and the wheels of the truck of bricks passed over his leg. It happened exactly outside All Saints Church to which he was to give all his life. He was at once taken to Alton hospital, his leg was amputated, and he lay there hovering between life and death for a long time. It was when this boy of fourteen was most gravely ill in the hospital that he had a strange and vivid experience.

He was in the dream state of semi-consciousness when two doctors, thinking him unconscious, were standing by his bed and discussing his case. 'Of course he can't possibly live,' he heard one of them say. And then he heard another Voice, 'Yes, you *will* live, and then you shall work for me in this town.' Now Alton hospital in the 'nineties was a remarkable place with a remarkable matron. She was Miss Clark, a fine matron of gently commanding presence, who had a deep hold on the things of the spirit. She interpreted her office as giving her a responsibility for her patients' souls as well as a charge over their bodies. There was a chapel in the hospital and the matron saw to it that it was used. Twice a day she gathered there all patients who could be moved and staff who could be spared, and she and they said together their morning and their evening prayers. Among them was young Bond, and everybody who knew him agreed that his time in Alton hospital was the turning point of his life.

But in the meantime there he was, short of one leg and no longer able to be an errand boy. Then it was that someone gave him a boy's set of carpenter's tools, and thereby solved the immediate problem and also gave him a joy which lasted his whole life. He was never so happy as when he was making things with bits of wood. It was his unfailing recreation, and he liked to think of himself as a carpenter-priest. For the present, however, it had to be his profession; and he started work again as a carpenter's apprentice. Soon he became a highly skilled craftsman, and when his artificial leg failed to give satisfaction he made himself another.

His hours of work at his new trade were very long, 6 a.m. to 5.30 p.m., and on Saturdays 6 a.m. to 4 p.m., and he was only fifteen years old. But while in the hospital he had been taken with a summons, a divine call, and his time was no longer his own. In the evenings he promptly started what came to be known as the Wash House Club. At the bottom of his mother's garden there was a little hut where she washed the family's clothes. There he gathered his friends, boys of his own age. They came together first as the expression of a piece of corporate hero worship for the men of the Alton Fire Brigade, which was famous throughout the county of Hampshire. The boys too were determined to have a fire brigade all of their own and emulate their elders, and under Bond they did it. But that was a summer game. When the long evenings began to darken early the boys still went regularly to the Bonds' washhouse, and there by the light of a few candles they held discussions on every problem under the visiting moon, they did some serious study, and Bond taught them to pray. After a year or two the Wash House Club outgrew the tiny hut, and the members transferred themselves to All Saints School, where Bond turned the club into a weeknight Bible class. He took it for years; and there are still people living who were in the Wash House Club and speak of it with great pride of belonging.

Thereafter his life followed the sequences which lead from carpentry to the priesthood. He became the Staff Sergeant of a huge Church Lads' Brigade, with a Bible class on his hands; then Sunday School Superintendent; then Lay Reader, with great men's services on Sunday afternoons and discussions of religion in the public houses at night; and all the time working at the bench for eleven hours a day. But that could not go on, and with a pang he withdrew from the carpentry and left Alton for the only time in his life to spend three years in Bournemouth performing prodigies of heroic study to get his A.K.C. degree, the condition of ordination. In 1914 he succeeded, and was ordained in Winchester Cathedral to serve the curacy of his beloved All Saints, Alton. He never left the town again.

He had at last come to the haven where he would be, and characteristically he spent the whole night before his ordination as priest in a vigil of prayer; and immediately after it, in a little room in the Royal Hotel in Winchester, he gave his first priestly blessing to his wife, who herself was a pearl among women and was always the sort of wife any priest might pray for. His vicar, Father Carter, had also many qualities of the giant, but not in stature for he was a tiny man, while Bond was vast in every way. So they were called the Little Father and the Big Father. He was a bulky man who walked awkwardly. His amputation had not been completely a success, except that it had saved his life, for the stump gave him constant trouble and the pad which carried the weight of his heavy body on to his wooden leg chafed abominably no matter how often it was renewed and changed. His whole life was a life of pain, and he was never wholly free from it. Nevertheless one impression he left upon all who knew him was of a man who was always laughing. He laughed with the whole of his great frame, every part of him joining in, till he shook and quivered all over with merriment. Perhaps the best indication of the impression his appearance made was the spontaneous comment of a gipsy woman whose baby he was once baptizing. As long as his mother held him the young Christian wept copiously, but when Bond took him his wailing was at once stilled as though by miracle. 'Ah,' commented the gipsy, not inaudibly, 'That be because you be fat and warrm.'

It was gipsy language for something more than a bulky frame and kindly face; and it pierced through to that quality of reassurance, of a bestowed sense of security, which flowed from him, and drew to him all conditions of men, women, and children to seek it. He seemed to them to carry about with him a sense of the Presence of God, an aura of bedrock spiritual reality; and it is of this that they still speak first when his name is mentioned. One felt safe with him, because he felt so safe with God. The unseen world was peopled for him, and was all about him. 'Do you know,' he said to a friend one day, 'that when I am at the Altar I am so thronged with the invisible host that I feel no thicker than a piece of paper.' Some years after Carter's death, when Bond was the Vicar, it was to him as though he was still in tutelage, for when he passed the pulpit 'he always saw the Little

Father looking at the Crucifix as he used to do when he was alive'. Once a worshipper

was right at the back of the church on my knees. I had been there some time and was just getting up to go out when I saw an angel over the two men who were by the Altar Rail. I did not know till then that Charlie was hearing a confession. I looked at it again and it was still there, so I knelt down again. When I told Charlie what I had seen some days later he never doubted it but thought it was quite natural.

He had the inevitable difficulties of his position to overcome, for he was a man of the people, and though absolutely classless and fundamentally cultured, his education had been extremely sketchy, and everybody had known him as Charlie from the day of his birth. To become a Lay Reader was one thing, but to be raised to the priesthood and set to minister in Alton itself was quite another. At first it was difficult. There was, for instance, an old hot-gospeller, salvationist friend of his, who said bewilderingly, 'What I can never understand is Mr Bond: he really was a converted man—everybody said so. He was saved and yet in spite of that he *still* stayed in the Church.' But what might easily have defeated a less spiritually-minded man and a less Christian community was overcome by Bond and his people quickly and creatively. Thus when Father Carter died, and his successor, the Rev. K. McMaster, had retired, the parish petitioned the Bishop of Winchester for the appointment of Bond, and the Bishop had no doubt that it would be right to break his otherwise unbreakable rule, and appoint the curate to be vicar of the parish where he was serving his curacy. It is worth adding that before he made his decision the wise bishop interviewed Mrs Bond—and had no more doubts. So Bond became vicar of All Saints in 1921, and life could hold no higher glory for him than that. He was of the same breed as the Curé d'Ars.

His incumbency of All Saints, Alton, is already a saga and will one day be a legend. It was fundamentally and tirelessly pastoral, for he was in the succession of traditional Anglican sanctity, which puts the pastoral ministry first and the prophetic a long way behind. The history of Charlie Bond's ministry will never be written. It had few high lights since it was simply a steady, persistent faithfulness which never flagged till death took him, worn out, at the early age of fifty-five. But there are momentary pictures of it which survive and have found their way into various kinds of written records, and they are the sacramental symbols of it all. They show him trudging rather painfully up the hill to St Mary's Home, where the Wantage Sisters live, carrying to them the reserved Host, and the brewery men taking off their hats as he passed because they knew what he carried. There is the picture of him at the local hop-pickers' mission each year, driving out in a wagonette into the field at Selbourne and standing in it to preach to the hoppers, and after dark pinning a white sheet to a couple of trees for a lantern service. Or there is Charlie Bond as Chairman of the Board of Guardians, doing a great pastoral work in the Institution, where, after a meeting or many visits, 'he used to get thirsty and would go into the kitchen for a drink of water, and he liked it out of a jug'. And beside the parish priest there was the missioner, much in demand for children's missions; and the almoner who, with his wife, refused to sit down to their own Christmas dinner until they knew for certain that no single home in his parish would be without one. And then, finally, there was the confessor, to whom people came from near and far to open their grief and to find in him an epitome of wise understanding and kindly courage.

Such was the evangelical-catholic, as he called himself, and the carpenter priest. When he died he was buried in a coffin made by his own tools; and his body was robed in vestments, a chalice and paten in his hands, and his old set of carpenter's tools by his side. His funeral was a great triumph. Every shop was shut, and every soul in Alton, and many far away, mourned for him, yet rejoicing over the spirit of a brave and just man, made as near perfection as this world ever lets us come.

III · *The Non-Parochial Ministries*

In the early 'twenties B. K. Cunningham complained that the Church of England had been too slow to welcome 'diversities of ministries' into its priesthood, and suggested that a greater flexibility might save us from the sort of priest who makes religion his God and not God his religion.[1] His words were prophetic, for one of the most striking features of the life of the Church during this period was the rapid development and the wide variety of the non-parochial ministries. For years past the student world had enjoyed chaplaincies of its own. They were provided by the deans and chaplains of the colleges in the universities, and by the innumerable ramifications of the Student Christian Movement. In Oxford, for example, the Oxford Pastorate, an evangelical organization for the shepherding of undergraduates quickly resumed its great work after 1918 under Christopher Chavasse, later Bishop of Rochester. Its centre became the church of St Aldate, and the work was steadily and imaginatively done by a number of very able and devoted clergy. This was matched on the Anglo-Catholic side by the pastoral work flowing from Pusey House.

After 1918 the number of the clergy who were engaged in other non-parochial ministrations, or who became specialists in some single branch of the total ministry of the Church to the people steadily increased.[2] The central boards and committees of the Church Assembly claimed a good many of them. Various works of healing—psychiatry, moral welfare, and

---

[1] Writing in *The Future of the Church of England*, edited by Sir James Marchant (Longmans, Green), 1926, p. 84.
[2] This theme is developed later in this book on pp. 551–558, as it was after 1945.

spiritual healing—occupied others. The more research there was into the problem of how the Church might be made more effective the more clearly it was seen that though the work of the Church rested on the parochial system there were many people and many fields of life which the resources of the parish church could not be expected to do more than touch lightly in passing. The urban industrial proletariat as a class was showing itself more and more immune to the traditional methods of evangelism which the parish church could compass.

The need had been diagnosed years before, and the application of the remedy after 1919 was less of a novelty than it sounds. The scale on which it was then done was new, but not the enterprise in itself. The need had been foreseen by the old Guild of St Matthew under Stewart Headlam, and it was one of his friends and disciples who appears to have done much of the pioneering. This was C. E. Escreet, a lifelong socialist priest, successively curate of Battersea, Vicar of St Andrew's, Stockwell, Rector of Woolwich, and Archdeacon of Lewisham. Many of the enterprises which are commonplace now were already being done at Stockwell and at Woolwich under Escreet at the beginning of the century. His life was a saga, and his genius lay in awakening an enthusiasm for social work among very large numbers of men and women in his congregation. At Stockwell in 1889 he formed a parochial church council, the rules and constitution of which almost exactly foreshadowed those of every parochial church council today. At Woolwich he had more than a hundred people on the roll of his lay workers, and most of them were men. His clergy were voluntary factory chaplains and his people assisted them. There were regular meetings for prayer, worship, and religious teaching in a large drapery shop, in a dressmaker's workshop, and in a factory for the mass-production of pyjamas and shirts. All this naturally led to a great deal of welfare work; and as it all developed, the Free Churches joined in, and the whole enterprise was beautifully poised so as to lead from an undenominational basis to active membership of one or other of the churches taking part. Archdeacon Escreet is today largely forgotten, but he and his people, acting in perfect partnership, did much of the pioneering at Woolwich from 1900 onwards, and he has claims to be regarded as one of the patron saints of the whole modern enterprise of taking the Church into the factory.

The need for specialized full-time factory chaplains was plain, and between the wars the Church began to provide them. The work of such a chaplain is largely undenominational. He recruits the congregations of all the local churches, not merely his own. By meetings, by private talks, by group discussions he teaches the Faith, and he breaks down the opposition between Church and factory. He makes all kinds of personal contacts, and he follows them through all the stages of welfare and remedial work. He restores, if he can, to modern industry the friendship that used to exist between the village church and the village craftsman, whether blacksmith or thatcher. His is a real ministry of reconciliation, and it is desperately difficult.

The great need to bridge the gulf between the Church and the industrial worker carried a few priests into forms of ministry much stranger than that of the factory chaplain. In the Church of England Hugh Lister was perhaps the foremost example of these, just as his contemporary, the Abbé Godin, was in France. For men like these it was not enough to become chaplains in factories. They were driven by an inner compulsion so strong that it was nothing less than a divine vocation to become one in every sense with the men of the industrial world whom they wished to win for Christ. They must speak their language, think their thoughts, share their lives in every detail, fight in their battles, live by their standards of comfort, and in nothing be separated from them. Their ministry was characteristic of their tormented age, and their heroism deathless.

Hugh Lister, born in 1901, was a graduate of Trinity College, Cambridge, with a pleasing passion for railways which carried him into the service of the Great Western Railway. But the experience of living in railwaymen's dormitories in Cardiff awoke in him a tremendous sense of compassion for the industrial worker, and made him clear that he must express it not as a railwayman but in the ordained ministry of the Church. At Cuddesdon he set himself to learn the strength of asceticism in the ordering of the devotional life, and he was ordained to serve a Poplar curacy. From there he went to become one of the secretaries of the Student Christian Movement, and he set himself to live and work on the standards allowed by unemployment insurance. This experience temporarily broke his health and permanently deepened his compassion. He was ill for two years, and on his recovery he became a member of the staff of the Eton Mission at Hackney Wick. He was then 34.

The church at Hackney Wick was flourishing but there seemed to be few working men in the congregation—a fact which challenged Lister. He determined that one way or another he would get hold of them. He had no doubt of the path he must tread. It was the conditions which he saw in Hackney which, he believed, did more than anything to foster secularism in working people; and it was the Church's business, and his own as a priest of the Church, to change the conditions. But he felt he could only work for this from within the conditions to be changed; and he must use the only possible instrument for change, the trades union movement.

One of the most unusual things about him was his passion for trade unions. He once wrote a letter to the employees of a factory in Hackney which had no union:

You and your mates have not got your rights as workers till you have a say in the wages and conditions under which you work. And you have no say whatever till you are organized in your Trade Union. An employer may be good: he may be bad. That is not the point. The point is that as long as he can deal with his employees one by one, as single individuals, he has all the say and they have none. And that is wrong. Is it not high time that you followed the example of your fellow-workers recently in other factories in and around the Wick and helped to make a Trades Union firm?[1]

When he knew what he must do, he did it with a single-minded and thorough directness which made him extraordinarily effective.

He went with humility to working men who he knew cared that conditions in Hackney were what they were. He set himself to be taught by them, and he identified himself with them in every way, living as they lived, and spending on himself no more than they spent. At first they looked on him with tolerant amusement, and one told him he was too 'pansy'. But soon he had built up a team of a dozen working men determined to make Hackney a trade union centre, and they saw nothing amiss in accepting his leadership. Together they founded branches of the appropriate union in one factory after another, and when this involved the calling and running of a strike neither Lister nor his friends shirked it. Between 1936 and 1939 Lister organized at least three strikes to win recognition for the union and to get better conditions for employees. It did not make him popular with the local employers, at least one of whom pointedly withdrew his firm's subscription to the Eton Mission. But it was before this that Lister himself had resigned from its whole time and salaried service, and had used his savings to buy a house to serve as his own home and a centre for his trade union companions. He continued to take services in the church all Sundays, and early every morning he was there to worship at the Eucharist, himself celebrating in his turn.

All this he accomplished in three years, for when September 1939 came he joined the Welsh Guards, rose to become a major, and was killed in France in 1944. He joined the army because he was clear, as he had always been clear, the fascism had to be fought, and he must take his chance with his mates in the firing line. In some ways the most considerable of all his feats was to win his friends to his views on conscription, and to issue jointly with them a manifesto commending it to the trade union world.

While doing the work of a trade union organizer Lister never forgot that he was a priest. He would have said that this was the way in which he was called to work out his priesthood. His habits of prayer and receiving of sacraments, in fact his whole rule of life, was maintained in Hackney at the same level of austere intensity as they had reached at Cuddesdon, where his asceticism had caused anxiety to the college authorities. Nor did he ever forget that he was a fisher of men for Christ and his Church. But he would force religion on no man, nor would he make church membership any kind of condition of his friendship. Some of those most closely associated with him went to church with him, and others did not. But he was the

[1] Alice Cameron, *In Pursuit of Justice: The Story of Hugh Lister and his Friends* (SCM Press), 1946, p. 81.

devoted comrade of all alike and all equally. He used to hold weekly meetings for prayer and Bible study in the house, and between ten and thirty men usually came to them.

His experience led him to exactly the same conclusion that the Abbé Godin in Paris was to reach independently, that the way of evangelism among factory workers was *par excellence* the small dedicated group, and that it had this primacy by reason of the intensity of fellowship which its small numbers made possible. 'I find the value of that in my own (trade union) branch, where we have a little knot of men and boys who do pray together and preach at each other once a week. . . . What we have to attend to in the Church is community, not morals. Have a community which prays to Christ and morals can look after themselves.'

Lister, then, had something to do with the initiation and development of another feature of the evangelistic ministry of the Church of his day, the small group or cell. Its history is long and honourable and stretches back at least to the reign of Henry VIII. It had in a sense been given a fresh birth by Sidney Ruscoe, the vicar of a London suburban parish, West Norwood, who took very seriously to heart the promise of our Lord, 'Wherever two or three are gathered together in my Name there am I in the midst of them.' He persuaded many of his lay people to organize themselves into little groups of not more than nine in number, who met regularly for prayer, study, and waiting upon God in each other's houses. Out of this shared experience there grew a very strong bond of fellowship, which is always the soil in which evangelism grows best. But at the same time many others were independently feeling their way towards the same idea, and among them was Hugh Lister.

Thus the growth of these groups or cells was quite unorganized and spontaneous, and therefore it was untidy and ragged. All the more was this so because the motives which brought many different people independently to the judgement that the small dedicated and committed group of Christians was the best way of advance were very different. Some, like Lister, came to it gradually out of their own experience. Others saw in it the twentieth-century equivalent of the essential evangelistic method of the Early Church. There were some who saw that by their cellular expansion the communists had spread their doctrine over the world, and believed that Christians should imitate them. The motive of yet others was that of impatient revolt against the ever increasing weight of organization in the Church, and these saw in the essentially unorganized cell movement something which inspired them with fresh hope. Others again approached the matter more theologically, asked what was the basic pattern of spiritual energy in the Bible, and answered their own question by pointing to the small, disciplined group, corporately and expectantly waiting upon God. So it was that as the fatal year of 1939 drew near the idea of cellular expansion began to spread very rapidly, and cells came into existence in many parishes, and in some factories. Not until the war came did the great expansion of cellular work take place, for the conditions of war favoured its growth. In those years the method was developed into the different series of such cells or companies linked together in a living whole, such as the series which worked under the titles of 'The Nails', and 'The Servants of Christ the King'. It was a new way of evangelism, radically biblical, and providing a body to implement the truth which pioneers like Lister had been teaching the Church, that the way of evangelizing in secular spheres of life must be the winning of the larger community by the infection of the small community within itself; and that the heart of infection was fellowship. This whole movement is intensely alive today, and much of the hope of the future depends upon its development.

The same idea of unleashing the power of the laity, and persuading them to accept their charge of responsibility in Christ's name for all the work of the Church, lay behind another development of lay evangelism. This became known as the Parish Meeting; and it was an attempt to do for the whole congregation what the cell did for a section of it. The heart of this enterprise was the periodical gathering together of the whole congregation (or as many as could or would come) in order that the whole body might talk over its problems and plan its witness and work together. It was in fact an effort to make it become in practice what it already was potentially, the Body of Christ in and for the area of its competence. Much of the pioneering of this work was done in a Sheffield parish, and though the Parish Meeting is much easier to start than to maintain, it has spread to many other parishes, and there seems no limit to the power it may one day become.

The common denominator of all these inter-war developments of specialized ministry is the emphasis they all laid on the laity. These ministries were not something done for the laity by the clergy. They were enterprises done by clergy and laity acting together for the sake of other laymen and women who remained untouched by religion; and their essence was the belief that the key to all modern evangelism is lay power. It was this emphasis which specially distinguished this from earlier periods in the history of the Church of England.

IV · *The Ministry of Architectural Suggestion*

If one of our Anglican ancestors of two hundred years ago came back from the grave to examine the modern Church, the most obvious change that he might remark is the great care now given to the cleanliness and decency of our parish churches and their decorations and furnishings. These changes, he would be bound to agree, are wholly for good since they constitute a perpetual ministry of suggestion. Most of them are to be placed to the credit of the Church of the last half-century. Whatever modern

Anglicans may have failed to learn, at least they have learned that labour or devotion given to the upkeep and seemliness of parish churches is never wasted. This labour they give, even if it is only in the matter—the exacting and expensive matter—of the altar flowers. Our churches are nearly always clean and obviously cared for, and their decorations and fittings increasingly betray an informed taste.

The care of churches has been the subject of much informed regulation. One of the innumerable consequences of the Enabling Act was the setting up of Diocesan Advisory Committees before whom the authorities of every parish must justify any structural alterations, or any additions to fabric or to decorations they may be contemplating. Until the Advisory Committee is satisfied that the proposed scheme will enhance the beauty of the church, or at the least will do nothing to harm it, they do not advise the Chancellor of the diocese to issue the necessary faculty for the work. Gone are the days of irresponsible and ignorant alterations of churches, and no one may now choose ornaments or stained-glass windows by the simple criterion of his own fancy. This is no slight advance, as will be realized by anybody who recalls the ruination to the look of churches caused by the aesthetically ignorant zeal for renovation shown by so many of our forefathers.

But this regulation, and curbing of excessive local individualism, might have been burdensome if it had not come hand in hand with greatly improved artistic standards, and with an enhanced sense of responsibility to posterity for the maintenance of the beauty of the churches we inherit. Besides this, there has also grown up among us in the last thirty years a strong distaste for unseemliness in church. It has become a rare event to find altar linen which is less than scrupulously clean or altar books which are mouldering or torn, or flowers which are withered and dropping. Most churches have some sort of guild of those whose business it is to keep the chancel and the sanctuary clean and fresh. When renewals are needed, or some scheme of decoration has to be put in hand, it is now easy to get expert advice. Societies like the Warham Guild have done an impressive work all over the country in preparing schemes of decoration, or lighting, or rearrangement of furniture, in which experienced knowledge and impeccable taste have been gladly placed at the disposal of parish churches, so that they may make the very best of the resources they have.

The Church of Christ has always been the greatest of builders, and in the years between the wars the Church of England built a large number of new churches. But many, perhaps most of them, were built in an entirely new way and in accordance with a novel idiom; and at last there was a strong movement away from medieval and Victorian Gothic. Most of these modern churches were built naturally enough to serve the new housing estates springing up all over the country. Among those designed as no churches in England had ever been designed before were St Nicholas, Burnage, Manchester; St Gabriel's, Blackburn; Testwood, in the diocese of Winchester; St Saviour's, Eltham; John Keble Church, Mill Hill; and there were many others besides these. Externally they were various indeed. Some seemed at first to be merely bizarre, and bitter complaints were made that they looked more like factories than churches. Others, like St Nicholas, Burnage, which somehow gave the impression by its curves and absence of angles of an immense ship, were immediately satisfying. But all were original, and none merely copied another of the same type. Their interiors, too, were novel—or they seemed it; and this novelty was immediately impressive and won almost universal admiration. The novelty lay not so much in the unusual placing of side chapels and lady chapels as in the sense of space and light. There was an unbroken vista with no pillars or screens to spoil it, and there was a glad welcome to all the light of heaven and no dark stained glass to dim it.

It was as though the architects and the builders of the Church had woken one day in the nineteen-twenties and determined to revolt against all the ecclesiastical conventions of church-building; and at the same time so to build as to enable the type of worship and the characteristic way of evange-lism suggested by the Book of Common Prayer to come alive in the modern age. Church architects like N. F. Cachemaille-Day and his fellows had first of all to revolt if they were to do this successfully. Their revolt was against medieval and nineteenth-century Gothic, and not against the square box churches of the eighteenth century, for these set out to do what the Gothic churches deliberately avoided, the designing of churches in which every part could be seen from every other, and priest and people be so placed that in worship they were members one of another, a community.

It is the Prayer Book ideal of worship. But the Gothic churches had been precisely designed to make it as difficult as possible. As Dean G. W. O. Addleshaw and Mr Frederick Etchells have demonstrated in their exhaus-tive *Architectural Setting of Anglican Worship*,[1] the medieval builders exalted the principle of the numinous over the principle of community, and believed England would be converted by a renewal of the sense of awe. To renew this sense, the architect must enhance the mystery of what was done in church by clothing it in 'dim religious light,' and by removing the priest at the altar far from the body of worshippers, who must only glimpse and never see him plainly. Hence the multiplication of pillars and rood screens, expressly designed to make the view of the altar fitful. Whatever may be said for this conception, and it is not the function of this book to argue the matter, it is certainly not the conception of the Prayer Book which undoubtedly expects that the dynamic force behind the processes of the conversion of England will be the strength and the outward-going of the community of worshippers.

The fourteenth-century architects thought thus and their eighteenth-century successors thought otherwise. But the nineteenth century reversed

[1] Faber and Faber, 1948.

the insight of the eighteenth and returned to Gothic. That it did so was the work of the early tractarians, largely expressed through the Cambridge Camden Society.

Few undergraduate societies have exercised such an influence as the Cambridge Camden Society (founded in 1839). By 1843 it had as its patrons two archbishops, sixteen bishops, thirty-one peers and members of Parliament, and a membership of no less than seven hundred. The society revolutionized the whole arrangement and appearance of our churches; and there is hardly a building in any part of the world, belonging to the Anglican communion, which does not betray the influences of its ideals. . . . The ecclesiologists started with the belief that there is a specifically Christian style of church architecture in which every church must be built. The architecture was that of the Middle Ages, and its most perfect expression the Gothic of the fourteenth century. . . . They believed that a perfect plan of a church was at hand; that it had been worked out in the fourteenth century; and that one had only to adopt the plan to restore the splendour of mediaeval worship. In designing a church it was all important to adopt this plan, and only then to think about the convenience of the congregation.[1]

Hence the font in the corner, where no one can see the baptism; and hence the altar far removed from the people, and pillars and screens to hide it from them.

The very uniformity with which this conception was applied to church-building for nearly a hundred years, and the rigidity of the plan spelt tyranny, and this tyranny hid from the worshipper the splendour of Prayer Book communal ideals. It has been in our time that the Church's architects have revolted against it, and almost every new church built in England has repudiated it. If we are now learning again that the Prayer Book is right in its belief that the strength of the Church is the strength of its community, and that this community is engendered by a particular way of worshipping God, it is to the ministry of suggestion in the architecture and arrangement of the modern housing estate churches that we largely owe it.

[1] Addleshaw and Etchells, *op. cit.*, pp. 203–5.

18

The Witness of the Cathedrals

I · *Cathedrals Used and Abused*

IT IS chiefly because the parish churches find they cannot do without them that the cathedrals still stand. They are virtually the only mediaeval buildings in the country which remain not as ruins but as glorious houses of God, not merely still in daily use, but more fully used and by more people than they have ever been before. To keep them standing, roofed, warmed, and equipped for worship through the centuries has cost enormous sums of money; and every cathedral has swallowed in repairs and maintenance an amount of money many times greater than the sum needed to build it in the first place. On Lincoln Cathedral alone £139,000[1] had to be spent between 1919 and 1939; and in the same period many thousands of pounds were spent on Chester and St Paul's, and no doubt on other cathedrals as well. In the same period Liverpool Cathedral was steadily building and Guildford Cathedral had been begun. This money has mostly come directly or indirectly from the parishes, and if the parish priests had really disliked the cathedrals as much as in many generations they said they did, they could easily have prevented the money being found, and the cathedrals today would either be like Fountains Abbey or in the rather chilly custody of the Ministry of Works.

But cathedrals have been disliked as often as they have been loved. When Bishop Paget of Chester preached his farewell sermon in the cathedral he recalled how one day he had come across a large party of workingmen visitors from Sheffield standing before the rood and singing with reverence and devotion the hymn, 'When I survey the wondrous cross'. 'Such a thing as that', he remarked, 'would have been absolutely incredible —the cathedral authorities would have made it quite impossible—fifty years ago.' His comment revealed one of the characteristic charges which have so often been made against cathedrals, a fussy archaic dignity which

[1] *Crockford Prefaces*, pp. 140, 168.

nursed only decay. Another charge was that they were the homes of exceedingly well-paid idleness; a third, that they were remote from ordinary people. The evidence for these charges was strong from Benson's day until our own; and the fact that of few if of any English cathedrals could such charges reasonably be brought today is evidence of the reality of the renaissance we have seen in the last fifty years. But they have had to travel a long way to lose their bad name. We are apt to forget how bad it was. Most people could quote Bishop Blomfield's angry comment about St Paul's, but it was comfortably long ago (in 1836) that he said it. An anthology of similar remarks could, however, be easily continued well into modern times. No one believed more heartily in cathedrals than Archbishop Benson, yet he himself said of them in 1877:

Thirty years ago cathedral bodies were in the very depth of unpopularity. Nothing but some Heaven-born instinct in the English people then prevented their extinction. . . . The most far-reaching, the most effectively and beautifully constituted, the but-lately most influential Christian institutions of the country had been enervated, paralysed, devitalized until the basest appointments to their honours could injure them no further.

When Hensley Henson went to be Dean of Durham in 1913 he succeeded to the charge of a cathedral in which in quite recent times one dean

baffled by the Chapter in some effort of nepotism, sulked in such wise that he would no more attend the daily services in the cathedral. Annoyed by the ill behaviour of some students, he shut them out of the cathedral as a body.[1]

Again, when Dr Lang, as Archbishop of York, went officially to visit Chester in 1925 and preached in the cathedral, he praised Dean Bennett's great work there by describing the low standards of cathedral life and worship which made that work so necessary:

Little more than fifty years ago (our English cathedrals) might have been described as the lost heritage of the Church of England. The glory of the former houses had passed away, and to the latter houses no glory had yet come. Their bodies, so to say, remained beautiful and imperishable, but the soul seemed to have gone. A strange blight seemed to fill their great spaces, and a smell as of death seemed often to pervade them.

And though much had been done to bring back their life, much more still remained to be done:

The cathedral, though once again the House of God, has still to win its place as the mother, the central church of the whole diocese to which the tribes of the Lord, the people from its towns and villages, go up with gladness. In many dioceses and in many parishes the cathedral is still a place remote and strange. Individuals may enter it sometimes, but it has little place of its own in the corporate life of the Church.

[1] *Retrospect*, vol. I, p. 151.

The purpose of Lang's sermon was to say how untrue this judgement was of Chester; yet by 1925 there were many other cathedrals of which it was becoming just as untrue, and there were probably none where the cathedral as an institution or the dean and chapter as a corporate body could have sat for their portraits to Hugh Walpole in his devastating novel, *The Cathedral*. Yet it was from an amalgam of that novel and their memories of Trollope's Barchester that many people drew their ideas of what the daily life of a cathedral was like.

Today nobody who knows anything about them supposes that they, or the people who worship in them, are truly portrayed either by the satire of the novelists or by the strictures of the preachers of a generation ago. Their renaissance has been remarkable. 'The ancient cathedrals,' said the anonymous Editor of Crockford in 1943, 'are objects of more widespread interest than at any previous period. It is sometimes said that the present day is the Cathedral Age.'[1] Fourteen years before, he was saying the same thing still more strongly, 'There is hardly anything more noticeable in the life of the Church than the resurrection—that is not too strong a word to use—of Cathedral Churches.'[2] This anonymous writer is notoriously not given to bestowing praise lightly. The cathedral renaissance has indeed been one of the most striking features in the life of the Church, and a great deal of it has taken place before the eyes of those who are still living. But it is a story with two quite distinct phases. First the cathedrals had to be made useful. Then they had to be made lovable. The first phase has Archbishop Benson for its hero; the second revolves round the name of Bennett of Chester.

II · *Cathedrals Made Usable*

Benson was a man who thought on the grand scale, after the manner of the great Victorians. He had a vision which he held tenaciously throughout his life. It was that the Church of England was charged by the pressure of events with nothing less than the whole world's Christianity. This he wrote in a private letter to a friend, while he was still Canon and Chancellor of Lincoln Cathedral, and the rest of his life at Truro and at Lambeth showed that he meant exactly what he said. He believed also that the English cathedrals were the instruments of this dream, the divinely given institutions through which it could best be realized. If the Church of England was to lead the world's Christianity, the first thing to be done was to reform the cathedral system. 'With us,' he wrote, 'there are most important works not done now at all, nowhere likely to be done, nowhere capable of being done, unless cathedrals undertake them.' These 'important works' were five in number—the training of the clergy of the diocese in 'scientific theology and pastoral care, the inspection of religious education, the whole work of evangelism, the preparation and supervision of a new Order of Lay Readers,

[1] *Crockford Papers*, p. 275. [2] *Ibid.*, p. 83.

and the oversight of all the Sunday Schools', which he believed were 'The catechetical institutions of the English Church'. He therefore wanted in his ideal cathedral a dean and at least five canons.

At Truro he was never able to achieve all these aims, though he went far towards them. But he did contrive to become the dean of his own cathedral. It was on principle that he did it, for he was certain, and in his book he said it over and over again that 'the breaking up of the cathedral system really took the form of the drawing apart of chapter and bishop'. This unification of the two offices has, it may be added, been vigorously opposed by all the deans, and few, if any, of the bishops have desired it. Benson did great things for Truro, and through Truro for other cathedrals. He was the pioneer of the effort to think out again the question of what a cathedral is for in the modern world; and his reforms were copied elsewhere. When Bickersteth, for example, became Bishop of Exeter he had unusual luck in that all four canonries in the cathedral became vacant in the same year, so he had the chance to do completely what Benson could only do partially. He made one canon the diocesan missioner, a second had charge of all foreign missionary work, the third supervised the whole range of religious education, and the fourth he called his pastoral canon whom he appointed to look after the younger clergy. The only idea of Benson's he did not adopt was the identification of the offices of bishop and dean; the statutes of Exeter did not allow of it.

Benson's influence shaped the course of the English cathedrals for years. He had addressed himself to an ancient dilemma which goes back at least to the days of Charlemagne. The first purpose of a cathedral is to provide what is excellent in worship, beauty and music. This has never been doubted. Since the bishop has his throne there it must also be the mother church of the diocese, and must maintain a steady relationship with its clergy, people, and parishes. If that is all, Benson's conception is indisputable, and the purpose for which residentiary canons exist is to provide the diocese with the suffragan bishops and archdeacons, and heads of the various diocesan departments. That is what Charlemagne thought. Canons were appointed to cathedrals, he said, to provide teachers in the schools, historians, and diocesan servants. He saw to it that this was done. Both he and Benson, and all others who, having grappled with the problem, have come down on the diocesan side of the dilemma, were nevertheless insistent that, though the first purpose of a canon was to be a diocesan servant, he was also a member of the cathedral chapter, and so must take his full share in maintaining the essentially corporate side of the cathedral's life.

But there is indeed a dilemma. A canon who is first of all a suffragan bishop or a diocesan director of education, and only secondarily the servant of the cathedral where he holds his stall, does in practice find himself involved in a constant conflict of loyalties. He is appointed to be a diocesan servant whose salary is provided by his tenure of a cathedral canonry. On these terms the claim of the diocese must come first with him, and since Benson's day the diocese has become an ever more omnivorous master. It demands, and it can swallow, all the time which its servants have; and they spend their lives in ceaseless alternation between committee meeting and incessant travelling round the parishes of the diocese.

What then becomes of the cathedral's own ministry? Beyond its steady provision of the daily round of the worship of the Prayer Book, and the maintenance of its standards of music, and of the building itself in all its beauty, has it any ministry of its own? It is certain that Benson's conception of a cathedral produces a great bewilderment of deans. Only a few years ago a good and godly man was appointed to the deanery of an English cathedral, and within a week he used a university sermon to confess that he had very little idea of what a dean should try to do. He was not to be blamed, for on Benson's principles a dean must become something of a decorative official without much function, and it is not surprising that Benson wished all diocesan bishops to be deans of their own cathedrals. The great merit of Benson's ideas is that canons of the cathedral cannot be idle, and are guarded from the sin of sloth. Before his vigorous broom swept these great temples, it had for centuries been a reasonable charge against them that they had become the homes of dignified, easeful and affluent idleness. Thus their reputation of being also the beautiful centres of envy, malice and intrigue had waxed and grown strong, and it was not wholly libellous. Trollope's Barchester was more than just a satirical caricature. It held an uncomfortable amount of truth. From all this Benson rescued the English cathedral. When his influence grew to its full height, and all cathedrals were staffed by canons of bustling diocesan activity, then at least cathedrals became useful again, and the old charge of beautiful decadence could no longer be levelled against them.

But it was all done at the cost of the other and older tradition that a cathedral must have a ministry of its own, and that a large part of its ministry should be the activity of corporate prayer, and the provision of a centre of sacred study and scholarship. Before becoming Dean of Durham, Hensley Henson had given much thought to this problem. He was a steady and deep admirer of Benson, and in most of his writings he was apt to quote him with reverential affection as though he regarded him as an unquestioned arbiter in all that affected the life of the Church. But when he became a dean he found himself critical of and in opposition to all Benson's ideas of the true purpose of a cathedral, and he wrote his thought in his diary.

Mostly my mind runs to the older (though too rarely accepted) ideal of the learned and studious dean, standing outside the practical work of the ecclesiastical administration. This ideal is now generally disregarded, and, in some powerful quarters, repudiated. It has been replaced by the *diocesan* conception, which Benson formulated and pressed forward. I observe in the reports of Westcott's two visitations of this foundation how he was dominated by the notion that Deans and Chapters must find their justification in their *diocesan* service, whereas I apprehend that their true function in the system of a National Church is to correct the local influences and localizing tendencies of the diocesan and parochial organizations. . . . Deans and Canons should remember that the interests specifically allotted to them, the maintenance of liturgical standards, and the pursuit of sacred studies—are not local but national in the loftiest sense. The attachment of canonries to diocesan services . . . means the appointment of canons with a view to such services, and this must sooner or later destroy the *raison d'être* of these foundations.[1]

If he had written this passage some years later he would no doubt have used some other word than 'National', but never, to the end of his long life, would he have changed his verdict.

There is no doubt that in essentials he was right, though at that time he was bidding the wind to cease from blowing. The service of the diocese had become almost the alpha and the omega of the ministry of the cathedral. He had moreover no suggestions to make as to how the human frailty of canons, like all other men, to lapse into idleness when they have no specific and identifiable duty to perform, could be combated. Nor did he show any consciousness of the idea that a cathedral might have a very fruitful ministry to the many thousands of people who visit it every year. By 1920 Benson's victory was complete, and almost all English cathedrals were working according to the pattern he had laid down. He had made them efficient and useful in the service of purposes not strictly theirs, but it seems never to have occurred to him that cathedrals have their own distinctive part to play in the whole witnessing life of the Church.

For all this a price has had to be paid. Cathedrals are not now renowned as centres of sacred learning. The canons rarely have the leisure to become real scholars. Striking and also amusing evidence that deep learning and diocesan usefulness can very rarely coexist in the same residentiary canon was given in a debate in the Convocation of Canterbury in 1925 on the motion 'That a Committee of this House be appointed to consider what practical steps can be taken to encourage the efficiency of Cathedral Chapters regarded as seats of learning.' This debate, like most others, had no observable consequences for the institutions discussed, but it drew from the Dean of Lincoln a sardonic description of what happened when the canons of a cathedral were appointed with a view to their diocesan usefulness:

The members of the Chapter of Lincoln go about as much as ever they can when they are asked. They are also put on every committee in the diocese. As a consequence they hardly ever have any time left in which to open a book.

This provoked Canon T. A. Lacey of Worcester, a very eminent scholar himself, to add his testimony:

[1] *Retrospect*, vol. I, pp. 151, 152.

It is no use talking about making cathedral chapters centres of learning. The members of chapters are far too busy. It is impossible and undesirable to make cathedral chapters centres of learning. Other places ought to be made centres of learning. Cathedrals are not the places for it.[1]

He did not say which places he would choose to be made centres of learning, but subsequent history suggests that it is to the monasteries that we must look. A very large part of the most original and influential work of scholarship during the last twenty years has come out of the Anglican monasteries. Lacey was not a man whom anyone could accuse of caring too little for scholarship, but he was a realist and he rightly diagnosed the results of the modern development of cathedral life. A cathedral can uphold its high standards of worship, its chapter can be a genuine community of prayer, and neither of these is incompatible with the fulfilling of a great number of diocesan charges. But no chapter can add to all this the most exacting function of being a school of sacred learning and the producing of original work.

The Church cannot have it both ways. It must choose what kind of cathedral it wants. The trouble was that up to 1920 the Church had knowledge of only one kind of cathedral, the sort which had built its life on fidelity to Benson's ideas. Having seen no other, it could not choose, and before there could be a choice there had to be a demonstration of what a cathedral could do to create a fresh ministry of its own. That had to wait for the appointment of a dean of high genius who brought a fresh and original mind to the problems of a cathedral's purpose, and who, forgetting Benson, thought it out for himself. In other words, the Church had to wait for the day when Frank Bennett became Dean of Chester.

III · *Cathedrals Fulfilled*

When Frank Selwyn Macaulay Bennett was made Dean of Chester in 1920 one of the first facts he discovered gave him a shock, but it also helped to chart his course. It was that there were quite a number of people who had lived their whole lives under the very shadow of Chester Cathedral but had never once been inside it. The same lamentable fact would have been true of most other cathedrals, and it is still true of some. Those who live under the shadow of a cathedral are generally of two very distinct kinds. There are the dwellers in the close or the precincts, and there are those in the little tangles of dark and insanitary cottages which are so often to be found just round the corner within a few hundred yards of the cathedral walls. These are the people who are so apt to think that the cathedral is not for such as them. They do not become sightseers because they live so close to it that they take it for granted. They do not become worshippers because they suppose that everything inside it is all pomp and solemnity, a ritual of class-

[1] *C.C.C*, February 1925, pp. 29, 32.

consciousness, in which they can have no part and which offers no place for them. In this they are mistaken, but they do not come inside to be convinced of their error.

It takes a very long time to get rid of a general sense impression. It lives on long after the facts which once justified it have changed and been reversed. For years, even for centuries, English cathedrals did give the impression of a beautiful but a cold remoteness, and many members of their congregations felt that they were there on sufferance, and for fear of feeling it far more people never went inside. There was indeed an occasion even as recently as 1940 when the dean of an English cathedral informed the members of the congregation in his Christmas Day sermon that they were allowed to worship in the choir only by the grace of the dean and chapter, who could at any time turn them out and keep them out.

In the nineteen-twenties a whole series of cathedral reforms were undertaken in order to reverse the facts which had given rise to this sad general impression. Time had shown that to make a cathedral a centre of diocesan usefulness did very little to make it the spiritual home of the people: to be useful was not the same thing as to be lovable. In this second reforming movement, Chester cathedral became the inspiration and the criterion for all the rest. It was not alone in its pioneering work, but far more than any other at that time it gained the public reputation of being determined to make itself a spiritual home for all manner of people, and of giving the warmest possible welcome to every soul that entered its doors. Its brilliant success in this enterprise was due to the vision and the personality of its dean, F. S. M. Bennett, who, more than any other single figure, became the hero and the linchpin of the whole effort, going on simultaneously in many cathedrals, to get a cathedral to be used by all because everybody who came into it was made at once to feel himself a welcome guest in his own home, and God's.

Bennett was a genius. But his genius is capable of analysis, and the different threads which, woven together in synthesis, went to form the unity which made him the greatest dean of his generation, can be separated and identified. First and foremost he was a pastor, and the Church of England has always known how to appreciate that. He was interested in people, in all people just because they were people. He liked all kinds of people, and he had no sense of class-consciousness anywhere about him. Thus he had the power of inspiring their confidence. The cathedral he loved because people came to it, and he undertook all his heavy work of renovation and reform in order to make them want to come to it. When he had done it and the cathedral was always full, he was always inside it. His pastoral opportunities came to him in the cathedral, so he stayed in it and sought no work outside it. He loved crowds not more and not less than he loved the separate individuals composing them. Where he saw people in the mass or singly he was equally interested in them for he was a natural psychologist, to whom no crowd was an ordinary crowd and no person an ordinary person. All alike became to him an adventure in perception and understanding. Thus he came to have a most penetrating knowledge of how people's minds work; and he gave full recognition to the vast potency of the general impression that a place, or a political party, or a movement stamps upon the imagination. He knew that it takes a vast amount of reasoning to destroy a false sense impression, and that suggestion is many times more powerful than argument or exhortation. More than that, he knew exactly how to create the general impression he wanted, and that in cathedrals, as he once remarked, 'the great thing is to arouse interest, and stately nothings won't do it'. He was certainly no enemy of stateliness in the right place: no dean ever took a more minute care than he over the marshalling of a procession, over getting every detail of a Sung Eucharist exactly right. The eye, the ear, and the nose, he believed, were the organs through which one received one's impressions—and particularly the nose, for he once said, 'The best preparation for a great crowd in a cathedral is to burn some incense.'

He had, moreover, a strong sense of humour, a tremendous zest for life, for everything which breathed and lived, and a corresponding distaste for inertia, decay, and death. It gave him the power to quicken sloth into urgency, to take the inert and give it motion. The outburst of King Hezekiah might well have been his motto, 'The living, the living, he shall praise thee as I do this day'; and when he looked upon ancient buildings, he instinctively echoed the same monarch's earlier remark, 'The grave cannot praise thee, death cannot celebrate thee.'[1] Things that were dead he contemplated with no pleasure at all, especially when they were cathedrals, and about the sort of decay he found in parts of the building at Chester he once wrote, 'Some may think that ruins are pretty. This is a perverted taste. The ruin of a soul and the ruin of man's handiwork are both horrid. The only ruin that is nice is the ruin of something that was horrid to begin with, like a dungeon.' These quotations have made clear another of his native strengths, an eye for the effective choice and arrangement of words. In his book, *The Nature of a Cathedral*, there are any amount of unusually vivid phrases which catch the eye and linger in the memory—as, for example, this, 'Beauty is just the veil of thinnest lawn through which the pure in heart may see God.' A man who could talk and write like that was bound to attract attention towards whatever he was undertaking, and one of the reasons for the phenomenal speed of his success at Chester was his flair for the right kind of publicity. He could not possibly help making other people aware of his dreams and convincing them that they ought to be pursued until they became living facts. Nor did he find much difficulty in persuading them to help, which was important because every dream of his depended on the previous raising of a very large sum of money. In Bennett,

[1] Isa. 38.18, 19.

in fact, the man, the need, and the opportunity all met, and the work done in and for Chester cathedral in his time became one of the great episodes and influences in the life of the Church in modern times.

To him a cathedral was no museum; museums are full of dead things, so he disliked them. He had very little of the archaeologist's interest. The cathedral he dreamed of was a lovely living thing, and the life in it—living people, living worship—was for him nine-tenths of the loveliness. A great church was a place provided by God to be a home of peace and beauty, of release and joy, a bit of Heaven lent to the earth. There, more than anywhere, he thought, the work of Heaven could be done on earth, for within a cathedral Heaven should be able to communicate its own blessed spirit.

During the summer (he once wrote) extraordinarily good people organize missions on the sands of Blackpool and elsewhere; but all the sea shore sands of England are not a patch on the opportunity of its cathedrals on Bank Holidays and summer Saturday afternoons.

But before anything like that could happen, people must be made to want to come. The cathedral must be made interesting, and its interest must be made known. When the people came, it must seem to them as a home; so it must be obviously welcoming, both in atmosphere and in appearance. It could only have a welcoming atmosphere if all who worked there, dean, canons, vergers, choir, and cleaners, were themselves a family, happy in the home. The abolition of all tips to vergers was only a part, though an essential part, of this process. In the welding of various grades of workers and differing individualities into a team of single-minded enthusiasts Bennett showed himself greatly skilled. If the cathedral was to be welcoming in appearance, there must be no fees of any sort, no forbidding or minatory notices, free access everywhere and nothing locked but the safe.

I do not think myself that a Cathedral can even begin to do its proper work until it has replaced visitors' fees by pilgrims' offerings. This being my rooted conviction, I should have urged the abolition of fees in our Cathedral at Chester, and should have stuck to the policy of a free Cathedral, even if we had lost money by the change. As a matter of fact we have increased our receipts five-fold and each year they go on increasing.

The people who were to find it a home were broadly of three kinds, the casual visitors, the people who came on some diocesan occasion, and members of various vocational groups, as for example soldiers from the Cheshire Regiment. The need of the first required a priest to be generally on duty, if only to be available for those moved by the beauty of the place to open their grief. One of the reforms Bennett advocated but did not achieve was the reduction of the residentiary canons to two, but these two were to be full-time cathedral men. Moreover, he would have the full staff of cathedral clergy present at the Eucharist every morning, and at Compline every night. Those who came on a diocesan occasion would find it all the more a home if they could be fed and hold their meetings on the premises.

By a real cathedral (he wrote) I mean a great central, family house of God, through which, and through its many essential chapels, the diocese can express its manifold corporate life, under the shadow and in the inspiration of which it can do its rapidly increasing business, and in which or near which it can find refreshment for soul and body. At Chester we have just decided to move our diocesan offices into a house adjacent to our refectory and cloister, where we shall enjoy hereafter, and all under the same roof, a spaciousness and convenience that many a city might covet for its municipal buildings.[1]

Visitors who came as members of some vocational group would feel the cathedral was their home if they could say of one of its small chapels, 'This is ours.' Bennett was a great believer in making a full use of the chapels, and he once wrote:

A cathedral without chapels is like a gaunt, unfurnished house; a cathedral with chapels furnished, but used for no particular living purpose, is like a great house occupied by someone who does not know what to do with it.[2]

Such a man, tenaciously holding to just such visions, was Bennett when, one day in 1920, he surveyed Chester cathedral with the eyes and from the point of view of its new dean. There would, he saw, have to be many changes before any of his dreams could bear their fruit. Internally, it was far from welcoming; externally, parts of it were in bad disrepair. Two generations before Dean Howson had collected, chiefly in America, £100,000 for its repair. This money had kept the cathedral standing erect. His successor, Dean Darby, had also done much to furnish the chapels, and had erected a rood over the entrance to the choir. Bennett therefore, as he himself was always saying, did not enter upon a wholly neglected heritage. Nevertheless there was much structural work left for him to do. The north wall of the nave was unsound, the tower was shaky, the refectory was ruinous, the roof of the north transept needed overhauling, and the north-west corner of the building was 'mouldy and tottering'. All this meant that he must first immerse himself in the raising of the £25,000 which would be needed for repairs. In the meantime he could make a start on the inside; and very soon every forbidding notice was taken down, fees and tips were abolished, and the cathedral was free and open for every hour of daylight on every day in the week. Chapels were gradually cleaned and furnished and then dedicated to the honouring of this society or that, of the Cheshire Regiment, of the Mothers' Union. Forty helpers were quickly enlisted and trained to show visitors round. The dean himself was almost always to be found there, a tall figure in a cassock, with a welcoming manner, and an astonishing knack of making people want to talk with him, and, if need be, of piercing at once to the heart of their trouble. The fame of it quickly travelled, and the news spread far that at Chester something unusual and exciting in the life of cathedrals was happening. People came to see what

[1] *The Times*, August 5, 1924.   [2] *Ibid.*, August 5, 1924.

it was, and went away to tell enthusiastically of what they had seen. Through this spreading process came much of the finance needed to save the building structurally, to rebuild its refectory, and to make its cloisters again usable and beautiful. The speed with which all was done can be illustrated by the dates of the rebuilding of the refectory. In 1920 it was a ruin, with neither windows nor roof. In 1922 it had been re-roofed, but inside it was still 'full of mess and out of gear'. In 1923 it was ready for use. It had four long tables and a high table, each with clean cloths and gleaming silver; and its high west window made the great room gloriously light. Pilgrims could be fed; and the diocese could and did use cathedral and refectory for a three-day convention of a hundred priests, who could find all they needed, beds alone excepted, without once leaving the precincts of the cathedral.

The impression which all this made was great and wide, and in due course it reached the London press. The accounts of it there published are perhaps the best of all the testimonies to the work Bennett did. First, there is *The Times*, of July 28, 1924.

A CATHEDRAL IN USE
New Methods at Chester

No traveller can enter Chester Cathedral today without feeling at once that it is different from other cathedrals. There seem to be a great many people in it; and they are all moving about, or sitting quiet, or unpretentiously on their knees, just as if they were very much at home there. If he is used to the ways of English cathedrals, he may even feel a little ill at ease when he can find no notices forbidding him to do this or that, no locked gates, and not a single official demanding 6d. He begins by wondering whether he has had the bad luck to be an intruder upon a specially invited party, and whether he ought not apologetically to slip out. A very little perseverance will show him that he, too, has been specially invited, and that all day and every day throughout the year the whole cathedral is open and free and his.

That is the first and most easily apprehended aspect of the great, the revolutionary change effected by Dean Bennett in his four years at Chester Cathedral.

... The ancient refectory of the monks, till very lately a ruin, is now a refectory once more, roofed, glazed, inviting, set with tables, and having a kitchen of its own (though it is no more than the passage way to the great kitchen of the monks), from which food, both cheap and good, is passed through the old buttery hatch, whether to the Chapter when it takes a meal there together in brotherhood, or to choir-treats, school-treats, parties of Cheshire soldiers, mothers' meetings, from any place in the diocese.

... and on the east side of this there are four chapels. One of them is specially devoted to the Church Lads' Brigade, the Boy Scouts, and boys in general. Another, the chapel of St George, is the chapel of the Cheshire Regiment and its war memorial. Another is for the Church of England Men's Society and men in general; and in the fourth, which is for missions, stands a big globe so that you may find the very place where this or that missionary is working and say a prayer for him. There is also a chapel for the Navy (Chester Cathedral has the colours of H.M.S. Chester which flew at the battle of Jutland); the Lady Chapel is the women's chapel; there is a chapel for girls, and at the west-end, near the font, is the cheerful place where children come to look at pictures and books, and leave their little offerings of flowers and paintings, and say their prayers, and sometimes begin to play until they are gently shepherded into places fitter for play.

   ... One could multiply detail; but only a visit to Chester Cathedral can properly convey the unusual impression of a Cathedral that is in use and alive from end to end, a place where everyone is made to feel at home and where religion is made to seem quite natural. It is no small thing that this confidence in the public's honour and care has not once been abused; and it is interesting to learn that, since all fees were abolished, the receipts from visitors have been quadrupled.

Two years later, E. V. Knox, of *Punch* visited the cathedral, and wrote in the *Punch* of August 4, 1926, in his own charming style of what he found.

   ... Earlier in the summer, I was moved (also in Mr Punch's pages) to criticize the authorities of a Midland Cathedral for their grudging policy of opening that building to visitors for only a brief hour-and-a-half each Sunday; and the time restrictions and sixpenny fees to be contended with in many other cathedrals have long been a source of provocative grief to this too feeble but persistent pen. Well, let me say roundly that Chester is a model. It is the most friendly and welcoming English cathedral that I have ever entered. Not a closed door; not a verger in sight; everything explained and made interesting by placards; picture-postcards on sale everywhere at twopence each, but no one to collect the two-pences—you are put on your honour to drop them in a slot; and, more perhaps than all, there are garden seats *on which you may sit* around the fish-pond and fountains and among the flower-beds of the cloisters. I was never more pleased, more surprised.

   At first it had seemed incredible. I stepped warily, at every turn wondering more and more what could have happened, why I was being given such latitude, why I was unmolested. In God's most beautiful and spacious houses we get so accustomed to importunity and warnings. Was there a vergers' strike? Had there been a massacre of vergers? And then, at the entrance to the slype, I found one of the notices explaining the position. 'Free access to the whole cathedral,' it runs, 'both on Sundays and weekdays, is given to visitors, in the confidence that they will in return—' and then follow the expectations, which are briefly, that they will behave themselves and remember that cathedrals are expensive to maintain.[1]

Today, there is no cathedral in England where Knox would be 'molested', as he calls it—none in which he need pay one penny which he does not gladly choose to give. This is one measure of the place Bennett has in the story of the twentieth-century Church.

But there is still another standard of measurement. One day a middle-aged woman was shopping in Chester. She had long been ill, and was facing much other trouble, and, being tired, thought she would go into the cathe-

---

[1] Reprinted by kind permission of the proprietors of *Punch*.

dral to rest for a little. She entered the nave and sat still and quiet, when suddenly a tall man in a cassock came and sat down beside her. She had never seen him before and had no idea that he was the dean. He smiled at her and said, 'You've had a lot of trouble in your life, haven't you?' 'Yes, but how did you know that?' Then he talked for five minutes, and left her. She never saw him again, but the memory and inspiration of that five-minute encounter remained with her all the rest of her life, and strengthened her at the moment of death. So it was for one woman, and for how many more? He had found cathedrals useful, and he made his own, and through his own so many others, lovable as well.

IV · *Cathedral Pilgrimage 1934*

If a cathedral is to claim in action its title of the Mother Church of a diocese, it must somehow make itself a place where the mass of Christian people are spiritually at home, and to do this it must show a concern for the strains and problems which help to determine the shape of life for the people it desires to welcome. In 1934 Britain was in the thick of the years of mass unemployment, and the agonies of it formed the first of all concerns in all minds, not only in those who were immediately its victims. At first sight it might seem that the grandeur and magnificence of cathedrals made one world and the anxious insecurity of the millions of unemployed workers made another, but nobody who had any vision of the cathedral as a mother of churches and people could be content with this separation. Thus when the suggestion came from a group of experienced social workers who were searching to find an answer to the chronic problem of the contradiction of widespread want in a world of plenty, that some good might come of mass pilgrimage to British cathedrals by people who would be pilgrims within the purposive context of the unemployment crisis, the idea was at once welcomed, first by the Dean of Canterbury, and then by all the other cathedral bodies in the British Isles. It would give them a chance to show once more that the Church cared deeply for the privations and anxieties of the millions who were out of work, and that the cathedrals, popularly supposed to be so remote from the cares of ordinary people, so superbly secure that they could not come alongside the minds of the insecure, were as concerned as the little parish church in the back street which had all its parishioners on the means test, and so could never escape from the problem by day or night.

Between July 1 and 14, 1934, this vast but scattered pilgrimage of Christian folk of all kinds took place. It was headed by the King and Queen who themselves became pilgrims to Westminster Abbey, joining in the opening pilgrimage service there, and wearing the pilgrimage badge. Everyone was asked to go on pilgrimage to at least one cathedral during the fortnight, and to pay the sum of half a crown for doing so, or if not half a crown then a shilling, and if even a shilling could not be afforded, then just a penny or two. The whole of the money offered was to be used for the good of the unemployed in those parts of the country where the burden was heaviest to be borne.

It was one of those spontaneous gestures which touched the chords of public imagination. The long pain of mass unemployment had left hardly any citizen untroubled in mind. But it was not in mind only that he was disturbed. His conscience also was affronted, and although no one could say just what effect upon the challenge of unemployment a great cathedral pilgrimage would have, and no one supposed that this would have power to put men back into work again, yet he dimly remembered that there was an ancient tradition that to go on pilgrimage was one of the classic ways of expiation. The ordinary citizen could not say *mea culpa, mea maxima culpa*, but it was in his conscience that unemployment most affronted him, and he could not divest himself of his own share in the guilt of it, so that the suggestion of a pilgrimage of expiation and sympathy was welcomed with an eagerness which those who first made it had hardly expected. The whole press fostered it, and in an article in the *Yorkshire Post* on July 7, 1934, Harold Nicolson spoke aptly for Church, press, and people when he praised the plan, because its originators had

shown much psychological ingenuity. The whole world is tired of impersonal travel, and this scheme provides the desired touch of romance, of individual service, of purpose. The pilgrim will have before him on every journey a sense of destination. He will enter the cathedral feeling that he has come from afar to perform this service.

The pilgrims were numbered in scores of thousands. They came by foot and by car, by water and by air. Some, as at Durham, were too poor to afford even a sixpenny badge, yet they thronged the great cathedral and offered their mites, and at the end *The Times*, on July 13, 1934, gravely commented on such as these, 'The pilgrimage has confirmed the popular saying, "It's the poor that helps the poor".' Travellers in Britain of many nationalities joined in; at Canterbury the pilgrims included Finns, Swedes, Hungarians, Indians, Africans, and many others. There were not a few who promptly improvised their own cheerful variations on the common theme. Two Cambridge undergraduates, for example, collected an elderly two-seater car and made pilgrimage to each one of the fifty-four cathedrals from Truro to Aberdeen; a number of people tramped the ancient Pilgrim's Way from Winchester to Canterbury; at Portsmouth, where the pilgrims were gathered each day on the Grand Parade to be led in procession by the the bishop to the Cathedral, the long file was headed by two young men who had dressed themselves in the pilgrims' garb of the Middle Ages. All these with their judicious mixture of gaiety and purposefulness were in the pure Chaucer tradition, and afford an interesting example of how a tradition may linger for centuries unforgotten in the subconscious imagination of a nation, until an occasion comes which recalls it to memory.

In every cathedral there was a great pilgrimage on the Sunday, and every weekday pilgrims were met by the dean or provost, were conducted by him round the cathedral, and a service held for them. As the whole enterprise was connected with unemployment challenge, this prayer was normally used at pilgrimage services:

O God of all wisdom and might by whose Spirit of truth man gains control of nature and makes her yield abundance of good things; give us, we pray thee, skill to speed our ploughs, to set our engines working, to pursue the path of science, to quicken enterprise and stimulate invention, and so to solve the problems of exchange and distribution that we be no longer tempted to destroy, or to restrict, or to withhold the things men lack, nor suffer needless want in a world where thy plenty abounds.

Apart from the services, each cathedral offered the pilgrims some special attraction of its own. At Derby the cathedral was decked with special banners and pictures. Durham opened its famous library and exhibited its historic manuscripts. At Manchester, true to the Lancashire tradition, they performed selections from *The Messiah*. At Winchester an historical play, *The Marriage of Henry IV*, was performed thrice daily in the Close, and at Evensong 'the finest works of Wesley and other Winchester composers' were sung. At Exeter rest-rooms and meals were provided. In fact every cathedral did all it could, and nearly all found that they were crowded by pilgrims every day in the week.

It accomplished the raising of a large sum of money for the help of the unemployed, but something more than this, something intangible, indefinable, but real had been achieved. The cathedrals had taken one more step out of their old, fabled position of majestic aloofness from ordinary life and common folk; and the old tradition of Christendom that a pilgrimage was an event charged with spiritual potency had reasserted itself. It was left for an American observer to find the apt phrase of summary: 'Its dignity, purpose, and gentleness made a beautiful demonstration of a nation's sympathy for the unemployed, and its abiding interest in the leadership of the Church.'[1]

V · *The Resolution of the Dilemma*

Bennett's work at Chester was done by 1937, and he died in 1947. Was he right about the use and purpose of cathedrals, or was Benson? The two pictures had been fairly and vividly presented, and though they overlapped at many points, anyone could see that they were very different. It was now for the Church to judge. In its half-conscious and ruminative manner the

[1] *The Cathedral Age*, Washington, Autumn 1934.

Church brooded gently on its choice for nearly twenty years. During this time most residentiary canons were still appointed to be diocesan servants first and cathedral canons second, and episcopal letters of appointment were still apt to underline in heavy black type this priority of function. But the cathedrals themselves could not go on as though Bennett had never existed to show them a new and better way. One after another they struggled to make themselves copies of Chester. They abolished fees and tips. They took pains to see that the ever increasing streams of casual visitors and parties of pilgrims were properly welcomed, helped and shepherded. They gladly provided at least most of the surprisingly large numbers of big special services asked for by various church societies, and different 'secular' organizations. They raised and spent steadily mounting sums of money on the fabric, on beautifying the buildings, and on their choirs and music.

But all this had to be carried by the Benson type of cathedral organization of staffing, which meant that three canons out of the customary four had most of their hearts out in the diocese, and had perforce to give most of their time to diocesan work. The strain was heavy, and the machinery of the system creaked. By 1950 it was clear that the burden was becoming too heavy for the shape of the system as it then existed to carry, and that, unless cathedrals were to be allowed to grind to a halt, something must be done to relieve them. The only possible relief was a quite revolutionary change in the system under which they worked, and that the obvious revolution was the abandonment of Benson's ideas of the purpose of cathedrals, and the adoption of Bennett's. Cathedrals are immemorially the magnets of grievances aired and accusations hurled by the parish churches. But when it came to the point, nobody was prepared to see them abandoned to the impersonal custody of the Ministry of Works, and therefore everybody was ready to provide the necessary finance. The Church had judged between the two pictures, and had come down on Bennett's side.

The story of how this came to be done belongs chronologically to a later chapter in this book, for it was not until 1958 that a Commission of the Church Assembly resolved the dilemma with a precise finality which, since it has become the law of the land, is likely to last for several generations. Its decision was that cathedrals are indeed the mother churches of their several dioceses, but that also they are churches with their own separate and distinctive ministries. This principle was written into the law, and not only into the Commission's report, by the Church Commissioners' acceptance of responsibility for the payment of the Dean and two of the residentiary canons on condition that these three men were whole-time cathedral clergy, and not part-time diocesan officials. The report of this Commission still remains to be discussed in its proper context in a later chapter and in more detail. But what it means is that the battle between Benson and Bennett raged until 1958, and then Bennett won it.

19

The Search for Christian Unity

I · *The Lambeth Appeal of 1920*

NO CHURCH passes through total war without being soiled in the process. It lives and works in all the warring nations, and on both sides of the barrier. It cannot stand apart from the miseries and glories of the nation in which it is set to witness, and it cannot avoid being itself compromised by every shift to which a nation fighting for its life is driven. Nor is a Church in any position to throw stones at the curse of nationalistic separations, for disunity is the immemorial occupational disease of every religion, and the Christian religion not less than others. Nevertheless great worldwide Churches do more easily think internationally than secular governments. Their faith and the inner springs of their being are cosmic in range. The diseases of separatism, though chronic, are for Churches also aberrations; and it is easier for Churches than for nations when a war has ended to come back again to their true course of seeking the unity of peoples and civilizations in a common loyalty to the King and Lord of all. Because both these characteristics lie deep in the situation of Churches, it is right and seemly, because it is good both for Church and state, that as soon as possible after a totalitarian war is ended a great international Church should gather its representative rulers from all over the world. Such a gathering reminds the world that in spite of all that has happened humanity is one and indivisible; and it offers to churchpeople an opportunity to express their sense of corporate repentance, and a chance to take up again their true mission of co-operation in creative fellowship in the proclamation of the Gospel in the changed world which a total war always makes.

It was this instinct which caused the Archbishop of Canterbury to determine to summon all the Anglican bishops to come together at the earliest possible moment after the war had ended for another Lambeth Conference, which was held in 1920. But those who looked only at the passing moment of history in 1919 and 1920 may well have doubted, as some did doubt, whether the time was ripe for it. Could the bishops do anything whatever to influence the calamitous course of political and economic fact? But they might even by the mere fact of their assembling, and apart from any wisdom which might come out of it, do something in the field of suggestion which would have the effect of changing the meaning and allaying the bitterness of the facts. The background of the Conference could hardly have been more gloomy. Of the peacemaking at Versailles, J. M. Keynes had already delivered his judgement in *The Economic Consequences of the Peace*, a work of that highest journalism which is bound to be read, and which so describes facts and makes prophecies as to create universal moods. Half a dozen little wars were still being ferociously fought. Greeks and Turks were at each other's throats. All the Russias were a sea of totalitarian cruelty. The infant League of Nations had already been virtually sabotaged by the refusal of the United States Congress to ratify the pledges of participation given by Woodrow Wilson. All content and all sense of great achievement had fled from the world, which oscillated feverishly between a false prosperity and a miserable destitution. Every democratic assembly of government was so behaving itself as to make a mock of democratic principle.

This lamentable catalogue had forced many people to realize that to build again upon spiritual foundations offered the only hope. A conference of bishops, truly international in character and dedicated to just such an enterprise, might itself be an occasion of that hope, and therefore it was welcome. But all the more it was necessary that it should speak words with real meaning and deliver a message quick with spiritual power. To deliberate for weeks, and then to produce an encyclical letter and a crop of resolutions piously hopeful and platitudinously uninspired—if this were to be all, it would almost be better that the bishops should never be brought to Lambeth at all. Small wonder that the bishops came there heavy with responsibility. They knew better than anyone that the subjects which such a conference at such a time must consider were precisely those which most provoked platitudinous utterances. Some of them pressed their doubts on the Archbishop, Randall Davidson, who was indeed singularly well aware of them himself. But having taken full account of every possible danger, and having done his cautious utmost to be armoured against it, the sum of his judgement agreed with that of the hopeful, that the Conference ought to be held, and at that particular time, and that the holding of it would, in the providence of God, be a signpost for the tormented world pointing the way to the land of peace.

The members of the Conference themselves held very varied opinions about the range of its influence. On the one hand there was Bishop Lawrence from America, who said, 'I doubt if there are a hundred persons in the United States who attach the smallest importance to its decisions.'[1]

[1] Hensley Henson, *Retrospect*, vol. II, p. 17.

On the other, there were the Bishops of Peterborough, Hereford, and Zanzibar who joined forces to write a brief impression of the Conference and who were sure that 'whole churches and congregations were on the *qui vive*, watching in tense expectancy for any signal which might be hoisted at Lambeth'. The truth no doubt lay midway between these judgements. No conference is ever as important as its enthusiasts or as uninfluential as its pessimists suppose; and this Lambeth Conference, as things turned out, was one of the most influential of the whole series. What made it so was the work done by its committee on reunion, for the Lambeth Appeal for Unity which the committee drafted and the Conference issued was certainly not the least important of the documents in the long history of Christendom. Its influence lay in the catholicity of experience of the bishops who issued it, in the circumstances of the moment in history when it was proclaimed, and in the actual phrasing and arrangement of its contents. The year 1920 was certainly a landmark in Christian history, and the bishops whose work made it so have been described in the published diary of one of their number, Henson of Durham, who was certainly no uncritical admirer either of them or of the Conference, in words which are well worth quoting:

The bishops themselves impressed me as a body of men intensely earnest, not (with few exceptions) either learned or men of marked intellectual powers, but devoted to their work. It is no exaggeration to say that the Conference had something of the range and largeness of a truly Catholic assembly. Some of the missionary bishops are ecclesiastical statesmen of no mean quality. Several men struck me as genuinely apostles, e.g. Brent, now Bishop of Western New York. The prevailing spirit of the Conference was neo-Tractarian, though there were a good many bishops who would call themselves Evangelical. . . . There is a real desire for union with non-episcopalians, but no adequate perception of the difficulty.[1]

Thus even Henson, who also wrote, 'I count the days till this precious Conference is over',[2] paid testimony to the universal faithfulness of the Anglican episcopate; and because they brought that quality to Lambeth with them the Conference was undoubtedly used by God.

The Conference gave its mind to many subjects but it lives in history for its handling of only one of them, and that by far the thorniest, the reunion of the Churches of Christendom. On the night in which he was betrayed, our Lord had prayed again and again that all his followers should always be held together and form one indissoluble body.[3] But this had never been so. To end this scandal was the dream of all the bishops who came to Lambeth. But the history of the efforts to give unity for division had not been encouraging, and reunion is always an alarming subject to discuss. It is so easy to utter vague platitudes of aspiration which have no life in them, but in avoiding the platitudinous it is even easier to exacerbate the

---

[1] *Ibid.*, pp. 22, 23.   [2] *Ibid.*, p. 15.   [3] John 17.20, 23.

divisions, and even to add new schisms to old ones. In hardly any field of human thought and action is it harder to avoid doing more harm than good. That is true of reunion generally and always. But it was, so to speak, even truer than usual in the circumstances of 1918. Every great war is an example of the judgement which overtakes disunity in the political sphere; and the end of each one causes a deep longing for international unity among all ordinary folk. So it was in 1918. But by 1920 it was already clear that the ordinary instruments of state diplomacy could not bring it. Here at Lambeth were the bishops of a great supra-national Communion of Churches, meeting in the name of Christ and praying for the inspiration of the Holy Spirit. The erring statesmen had claimed no such authority and offered no such credentials. Might it not be possible for such a body of men at such a moment of history to show a new road to the unity of mankind by taking the unity of Christendom many steps towards realization? If it was impossible to give unity to people who worshipped the same God and recited the same creeds and read the same scriptures, how could it be possible ever to unite all mankind politically in fruitful co-operation? So many pondered and watched, and the bishops who were appointed to serve on the reunion committee of the Conference knew it. It made them solemn with burdens.

When Gore wrote apprehensively in January 1920 to the Archbishop:

I hope that Divine Providence intends the Church of England to exist over the next year or two without a schism which would separate off the Catholic section, but I dread the Lambeth Conference and its consequences.

he was thinking of the modernist and the reunion issues, and the latter he judged especially dangerous because reunionists were people 'who yield themselves to their amiable impulses and do no clear thinking'.[1] But he wrote before he knew the composition of the reunion committee. It contained no doubt some men justly described in Gore's words. But those who carried most weight in it were famous for being awkwardly honest, for being *difficile*, not for any sort of amiable muddle-headedness. These were such men as Henson of Durham, Weston of Zanzibar, Gibson of Gloucester, and the Archbishop of Rupertsland, ready to pounce upon and correct any tendency to put sentimentality before principle: and it had the Archbishop of York (Lang) for its chairman, who led and guided the committee with a skill, a tact, and a vision which was quite incomparable. His chairmanship of it was perhaps the most perfect single piece of work he ever did. The amiability which is impatient with principle and tends to breed schism is, moreover, a fruit of too much optimisim in the approach to a task. But there was very little anterior optimism among the bishops who composed the committee. Rather they laboured under a sense of foreboding and even dread.

I had some conversation (noted Henson) with the Archbishop of Rupertsland

[1] Bell, *Randall Davidson*, vol. II, p. 1004.

on the prospect of 'Reunion' in the Conference. He said he was not hopeful: for he found a change for the worse in the feeling of the bishops. He said that the Archbishop of Melbourne (Dr Lowther Clarke) was as depressed at the prospect as himself. I had a few words with D'Arcy, now Archbishop of Armagh, and he also seemed rather disheartened.[1]

These men, in their several ways, were all on the side of those who put first reunion with non-episcopal Churches of the English-speaking peoples. The strongest among them, Henson, was especially determined to bring about union between Anglicans and Presbyterians. In his diary of the Conference he wrote almost as if only the Presbyterians mattered to him. 'I drew a distinction between Presbyterians and other non-Episcopalians. . . . My demand was that we should acknowledge frankly the validity of Presbyterian Orders and Sacraments.'[2] But other bishops, like Weston, who would naturally see everything from a strictly catholic point of view, were themselves just as apprehensive. After the Conference was over Weston joined with Woods of Peterborough and Linton-Smith of Hereford in the writing of an account of the Conference,[3] which reveals clearly how at first the difficulties were much more clear to them than the opportunities.

Every account of the proceedings of the committee lays emphasis on the sense of frustration and stalemate which made the first half of its course a weary, apprehensive business. Every time Weston of Zanzibar rose to speak—and he was pertinaciously eloquent—the other bishops, having memories of Kikuyu, eyed him warily. They had to listen to a good deal of denigration of the Conference from him, and to acidly humorous suggestions that the bishops would do better to go and live in the slums and ask to dinner the people they found there. In the first days of the committee he sketched an outline of the shape which he believed the great united Church of the future would take, and suggested that the way to it might well be through federated groupings of Churches, in which the non-episcopal denominations might well form one such group. But this suggestion seemed to get nowhere, and for day after day the committee sat in uncreative perplexity. Especially was this true of that part of the committee charged with the relations with non-episcopal Churches. It reached deadlock, and came near to breaking up; and Henson noted that 'there is a bad spirit among many members'. The context makes it clear that the stand made by some bishops against any approach to non-episcopalians was what provoked his charge.[4]

This frustration was due to the continuous effort of the bishops to move along paths which at that time could lead nowhere, and which were littered with the corpses of earlier optimistic travellers. They wanted to produce

---

[1] *Retrospect*, vol. II, p. 3.   [2] *Ibid.*, pp. 4, 5.
[3] The Bishops of Peterborough, Zanzibar and Hereford, *Lambeth and Reunion* (S.P.C.K.), 1921.
[4] *Retrospect*, vol. II, p. 10.

a scheme for reunion, a sketch of a united Church, a plan for definite action. But all the time they knew in their hearts that the great mass of worshippers of all Churches had even still but little realization of the evils of disunity, and less desire to end them. It was when they faced the fact that the first thing they had to do to promote reunion was to convert their constituents to desire it that they began at last to make progress. Their earlier discussions, their interviews with nonconformist leaders, and the reviews they had made of previous reunion movements provided them with a mass of useful material. The question was how it might best be used. Then, on Sunday, July 18, the answer was given to a little group of the bishops sitting on the lawn of Lambeth Palace. The Archbishop of York was there, and the Bishop of Peterborough (Theodore Woods), and two American bishops, Rhinelander and Brent. The Archbishop of Canterbury joined them, and for an hour or more they went through the material they had collected, and the various resolutions they had suggested. The trouble was that it all left them cold, and would be bound to leave others cold. Conference resolutions are invariably chilly, and have no power to warm; and what was wanted was something the mere reading of which would set the blood moving and quicken the desire. To which bishop it was that the inspiration came history does not say, but the suggestion that all the material should be used to inform the theme of a great appeal made history. The party on the lawn considered and approved it, and little by little the rest of the committee were brought to the point where they could say of the project, 'It seemed good to the Holy Ghost and to us.' Bishop Palmer of Bombay, a master of good English, wrote most of it; and eventually the whole Conference accepted it and sang the Doxology over it. Thus the document known to history as the Lambeth Appeal was born. It proved to be the act which gave that Lambeth Conference its fame, and the issuing of the Appeal was a landmark in the history of reunion.

We, Archbishops, Bishops Metropolitan, and other Bishops of the Holy Catholic Church in full communion with the Church of England . . . make this appeal to all Christian people. We acknowledge all those who believe in our Lord Jesus Christ, and have been baptized into the name of the Holy Trinity, as sharing with us membership of the universal Church of Christ, which is His Body. We believe that the Holy Spirit has called us in a very solemn and special manner to associate ourselves in penitence and prayer with all those who deplore the divisions of Christian people, and are inspired by the vision and hope of a visible unity of the whole Church.

Thus the Appeal began, stressing the fact of fellowship and striking the note of penitence. It was deliberately made, be it noted, to people, not to Churches, recognizing that the only power which can give us back our unity is the passionate desire of the ordinary people of Christendom for it. The letter was an appeal, and appeals must always be addressed to the heart and conscience; but it was also a realistic document, which asked people to face the facts and to think about them in the light of quickened emotion and an awakened conscience. First of all it was necessary to define the Church into which all Christians should be able to come. It is a sacrament of God's general will for fellowship.

We believe that it is God's purpose to manifest this fellowship, so far as this world is concerned in an outward, visible and united society, holding one faith, having its own recognized officers, using God-given means of grace, and inspiring all its members to the world-wide service of the Kingdom of God. That is what we mean by the Catholic Church.

This Catholic Church can be built only on the 'whole-hearted acceptance of' the points of the old Lambeth Quadrilateral, the Scriptures, Creeds, Sacraments, and 'a ministry acknowledged by every part of the Church as possessing not only the inward call of the Spirit, but also the commission of Christ and the authority of the whole Body'. The last of these points had always been the difficulty and would continue to be so. But the Appeal bracketed the statement it was bound to make of the Anglican principle of the ministry with a prior acknowledgment of the Anglican share in the sin of which this difficulty was the consequence, and with an anterior offer of a concession which went further than the Church had ever gone before. The first arm of the bracket was drawn in these words:

We acknowledge the condition of broken fellowship to be contrary to God's will, and we desire frankly to confess our share in the guilt of thus crippling the Body of Christ and hindering the activity of His Spirit.

Because the Appeal had said that, it could go on to say the more creatively that the Lambeth Quadrilateral was still a basic condition of union. But even this irreducible minimum was more qualified than it had ever been, and in such a way as not to weaken any principle in it:

We, who send forth this appeal would say that if the authorities of other Communions should so desire, we are persuaded that, terms of union having been otherwise satisfactorily adjusted, Bishops and clergy of our Communion would willingly accept from these authorities a form of commission or recognition which would commend our ministry to their congregation, as having its place in the one family life. We can only say that we offer it in all sincerity as a token of our longing that all ministries of grace, theirs and ours, shall be available for the service of our Lord in a united Church.

That was a big step forward. It offered to non-episcopal Churches that Anglican priests would accept, say, a Methodist commission if Methodist clergy would accept an Anglican commission by episcopal ordination. It asked nobody to repudiate his previous ministry.

God forbid that any man should repudiate a past experience rich in spiritual blessings for himself and others. Nor would any of us be dishonouring the Holy Spirit of God, whose call led us to our several ministries, and whose power enabled us to perform them. We shall be publicly and formally seeking additional recognition of a new call to wider service in a reunited Church.

The Anglican Church thus made it clear once and for all that it neither expected nor desired reunion by piecemeal submission.

The Appeal was made to all Christendom by the Church most fitted to make it; and this act, just because it was done in this particular way, made the Lambeth Conference of 1920 the most important of the whole series.

II · *Report of Progress*

The bishops ended the Conference by solemnly and spontaneously singing the Doxology when the Appeal was accepted. The Bishop of Durham remarked in his diary, 'Everybody was delighted at having reached the end of the Conference, but whether the effort has been worth while may be questioned.'[1] The Archbishop of Canterbury knew that what had been done was profoundly right and of historic importance, but he was not carried away by it, and he forgot none of the difficulties ahead.

He knew that the non-episcopalians would urge that, important as episcopacy might be for future ordinations, it was not important enough to render it necessary for Anglicans to ask those who were already Ministers to receive episcopal ordination: and that the non-episcopalians would almost certainly propose that Anglicans should simply recognize their ministry as it is.[2]

This he knew would cost a grave and deep schism in the Church and make confusion worse confounded.

The Appeal was sent to the heads of all the Churches, and each of them returned courteous and encouraging replies. The bishops at the Conference were asked to do all they could to bring it to the notice of people of all denominations in their own dioceses, and to do all they could to encourage discussions between representatives of the different Churches. In a very short time discussions and negotiations of every kind, both official and private, were proceeding in many parts of the world. The years between 1920 and 1930 are the delight of the reunionist and the embarrassment of the historian, for every month that passed added to the variety and complication of the story he would one day have to tell. Not only were these discussions proceeding between dozens of different Churches, but the pattern was made still more complicated and involved by the several world conferences of Churches under the aegis of the Ecumenical Movement, each of which, directly or indirectly, contributed its own quota to the mass of reunion material which the Lambeth Appeal created. G. K. A. Bell's *Documents on Christian Unity* deals only with the first consequences of the Lambeth Appeal during the years 1920–1924, and it includes only the more important of the available documents. There are ninety of them, printed in

[1] *Retrospect*, vol. II, p. 21.   [2] Bell, *op. cit.*, vol. II, pp. 1014, 1015.

a book of 382 pages, and there are few parts of the world, from Hungary to New Zealand and the West Indies, which did not contribute at least one document to Bell's collection.

The bewilderment of the modern student who is looking for the wood and cannot find it because of the trees was, however, not shared by Randall Davidson who kept his finger on all these discussions in a masterly way, and knew at any given moment just how far each discussion had gone, where it stood, and whither it was tending. At Christmas 1923 he sent out a pastoral letter to all the bishops of the Anglican Communion to give them a picture of the whole reunion scene as he saw it a little more than three years after the issuing of the Appeal. This letter shows that the Appeal really did have the effect intended. It was meant to provide a fresh start and to set things in motion, and this it certainly did. 'That Appeal has in all cases formed the background to what has been done and said.'

'Done and said'—inevitably there had been far more saying than doing, but then the saying, the discussions and negotiations, must naturally come first. Nevertheless talk and the composition and exchange of learned documents had in fact brought about solid and impressive practical results so far as the Orthodox Church of the East was concerned. The Patriarchates of Constantinople and Jerusalem had recognized the validity of Anglican Orders, and the Church of Cyprus had followed their example; and a measure of guarded intercommunion was in fair prospect. The conversations at Malines between Roman Catholics and Anglicans, with which the next section of this chapter deals, were in full swing. A whole series of discussions between Anglicans and the non-episcopal Churches in many parts of the world had been begun and were proceeding in an atmosphere of cordiality and friendship. It looked at that moment as though they might really lead at last and in time to the healing of that breach, and the Archbishop, never at any time given to extravagant optimism, wrote of them:

It seems to me that we have a right, with thankfulness to Almighty God, to regard the position in Great Britain itself as fraught with hope. There can be no question that the leaders upon all sides, and through them the officers, clerical and lay, of the respective Churches are disposed in quite a novel degree to appreciate one another's position and to look forward to a yet nearer approach.[1]

Of three years' work this was indeed an impressive balance sheet, and in every case the Anglican Church, having issued the Appeal, had maintained the initiative in asking for the discussions.

Nevertheless these high hopes were not maintained as the years went by. By the next Lambeth Conference in 1930, there was but little more progress to report than the Archbishop's letter of 1923 had registered. The difficult mountain of episcopal and non-episcopal orders had resisted every attempt to scale it. The Appeal had undoubtedly done much to produce friendly

[1] Woods, Weston, Smith, *op. cit.*, p. 340.

relations between the Churches, and had been worth the issuing for that alone. But actual reunion seemed no nearer than it had been, except for the Orthodox Church. The difficulties are vaster by far than most people realize, and as an illustration of them this account turns now to describe three typical sets of reunion discussions, with the Roman Catholics, the Orthodox, and the non-episcopal Churches. These three form a fair sample of the course of many others.

III · *Malines*

The largest branch of the Church is of the Roman obedience, and in thinking of reunion it is impossible to ignore Rome for long. To do so is to indulge in unrealistic dreaming. It is particularly true of the Anglican Church that she may not forget Rome, for she claims to be catholic in history and in temper, and she has maintained intact all the visible insignia of catholicism. But it is also true that the Anglican Church claims to be reformed, and has ties of loyalty and debts of gratitude to the Reformation. She can therefore no more forget her duty to the several protestant Churches of the world than she can forget Rome. This uniquely central position in Christendom may offer Anglicanism special opportunities in the work of Christian unity, and it was this position which made it apt and meet for the bishops of the Anglican Communion to address to the whole of Christendom an appeal for unity. But this centrality means that any effort to seek for unity made by the Anglican Church must be difficult and complicated beyond the ordinary because it is impossible for her to move so far in one direction as to lose touch with other Churches. It is inevitable that the Anglican course in matters of reunion is always specially tortuous and involved, and that its history should always take on the air of highly complicated diplomacy. This initial difficulty of having to face two ways at the same time makes discussions and negotiations with any one Church far more delicate and exacting than they would otherwise be, but it is part of the *data* of Anglicanism and it has to be accepted.

From the time of the Reformation until 1920 there had been few negotiations with other Churches, but among them was one serious approach to the Roman Catholics. The conversations conducted by Lord Halifax and others in 1894 and 1895 may have been unofficial but they were serious. But they ended discouragingly with a slamming of the door by the Pope with his promulgation of the papal bull *Apostolicae Curae* in 1896 which declared Anglican Orders invalid. This wrecking of all hopes had been in part engineered by the English Roman Catholics; and it was greeted by Cardinal Vaughan with public acclamations of joy, and remarks to the effect that the 'Erastian and Protestant Church of England rejects all idea of a sacrificing priesthood,' and finds itself 'shivering in insular isolation'. To this he added his considered opinion that the dream of the reunion of the Churches was 'a snare of the Evil One'.[1] The ground of scholarship in these polemics was cut from under the feet of the Roman Catholic controversialists by the devastating reply to the bull *Apostolicae Curae* which the Archbishops of Canterbury and York composed and despatched. But the polemics continued for a time.

As long as the papal bull *Apostolicae Curae* remained the unalterable policy of the Holy See not even the limitless optimism of Lord Halifax could suppose that discussions between the two Churches could lead anywhere. Thus from 1896 to 1920 no attempts to resume them were made. But the Lambeth Appeal for unity was sent to Cardinal Mercier of Malines, and produced from him a most friendly reply. Here at any rate was a cardinal who did not think that Satan prompted all talk of reunion. The Lambeth Appeal, moreover, contained an offer so worded as to suggest a possible way round the impasse of the papal declaration on the validity of Anglican Orders, for it declared the readiness of Anglican bishops and clergy to accept from other Churches 'a form of commission or recognition which would commend our ministry to their congregations, as having its place in the one family life'.[2] This phrasing seemed both to Halifax and to the Abbé Portal, the survivors of the earlier discussions, to offer fresh hope, and they resolved to seize it. They went to see Cardinal Mercier, Halifax carrying with him letters of introduction from the Archbishops of Canterbury and York, and finding Mercier more than agreeable to the opening of a fresh series of discussions under his own chairmanship if Halifax would bring two Anglican friends with him, the first of the Malines conversations was arranged. Halifax was to take Walter Frere, superior of the Mirfield Community and Armitage Robinson, Dean of Wells, with him—a choice not made by Randall Davidson, Archbishop of Canterbury, but pleasing to him because the absolute self-control of the one and the deep scholarship of the other would do much to keep the exuberance of Halifax in check, while his enthusiasm would act as a goad to their caution.

There have been many accounts of the series of conversations at Malines which began on December 6, 1921, and continued intermittently until October 12, 1926. These accounts are chiefly concerned with the matter of the discussions, and the effect they had upon ecclesiastical politics at Lambeth and at Rome. But they all make it clear that the story of Malines is a drama of personalities. Had the men who met at Malines been other than the particular individuals who took the matter in hand, the talks would certainly have taken a different course and probably dealt with different subjects. They might indeed never have been held at all, and must have ended far sooner than they did. They constituted an heroic effort of a handful of individuals to find a basis upon which it might some day be possible for Rome and Lambeth to talk on terms of equality with an honest and good intent to find the way to end the centuries of separation. All who took

[1] J. G. Lockhart, *Viscount Halifax* (Bles), 1936, vol. II, p. 79.   [2] *Ibid.*, vol. II, p. 267.

part in them were painfully conscious that although they had the blessing of the highest authority on both sides, they were not delegates, they could commit nobody, and whatever conclusions they might come to might very well be at once repudiated by the two Churches. Thus it was that all of them were perpetually struggling to persuade the ecclesiastical authorities to give them more authority by publicly appointing them to do this work, while both Pope and Archbishop were determined not to be drawn into any committal which would make difficult the loyalty of the Christian souls for whom they spoke.

The whole episode turned upon the personality of Cardinal Mercier, and when he died the talks died with him. He was a fearless saint, a great ruler, and man of heroic humility. During the first world war the faith of the Belgians and their capacity for resistance under foreign occupation was symbolized in the eyes of the outside world by two men. One was King Albert and the other was Cardinal Mercier, Archbishop of Malines. His outspoken courage in resisting and denouncing the evil the Germans were wreaking was one of the beacons of Europe in the darkness of those years, and when the war ended he had a prestige throughout the continent which no other ecclesiastic enjoyed. If one wanted an example to show that the common phrase, a Prince of the Church, is not necessarily in contrast with the spirit of the Head of the Church as shown in the Gospels, then Cardinal Mercier would be as good an example as history can offer. If there was to be any hope that the conversations would lead anywhere, Mercier was not only the best man that could be found to represent the Roman side, he was also the only man of all those who took part who could possibly have maintained the part of chairman. He had a passion for reunion, and, rare among Roman Catholics, sufficient understanding of the Church of England to know that it could not come either by individual conversions or by absorption. He preached union with, not absorption in or submission to the Roman Church. How near union was to his heart is shown by the spirit of the pastoral letter he wrote to her clergy to reprove such of them as had questioned his welcome to the conversations:

A great nation was, for more than eight centuries, our beloved sister; this nation gave the Church a phalanx of saints whom to this day we honour in our liturgy; it has preserved astonishing resources of Christian life within its vast empire; from it numberless missions have gone out; but a gaping wound is in its side. We Catholics, kept safe, by the grace of God in the whole truth, we lament the criminal sundering which tore it away, four centuries ago, from the Church our Mother; and there are Catholics who, like the Levite and the Priest of the old Law, reproved by our divine Saviour in the parable of the Samaritan, would have a Catholic bishop pass by, proudly indifferent, refusing to pour a drop of oil in this gaping wound, to tend it, and try to lead the sick man to God's house whither God's mercy calls him. I should have judged myself guilty, if I had been so cowardly.[1]

[1] Lockhart, vol. II, p. 309.

Roman Catholics who can so honour from their hearts another Church are the right people to take the initial steps which might lead some day to a restored unity. At the same time there was a sense in which Mercier was the most thorough-going of all Romans. He held the full doctrine of the papal supremacy with a deep conviction from which he never wavered, and never could have done. More than this, he went even further in his devotion to the Blessed Virgin than his co-religionists would have been ready to go. He wanted the Church to bestow upon her a new title—Mediatrix; and he worked and prayed for the day when the Church would lay it down as an article of dogmatic faith that divine grace came to men and women only through her intercession. With that doctrine no Anglican could have had anything to do. But it seems that none of the Anglicans who took part in the conversations knew at the time that Mercier had this in his mind.

The three men on the Anglican side who took part in the first three of the five series of conversations were Lord Halifax, Father Walter Frere, and Armitage Robinson. For the last two conversations the Archbishop of Canterbury officially delegated Bishop Gore and Dr Kidd, Warden of Keble College, Oxford, to join the original trio. In his diary, Hensley Henson put his finger on the real weakness of the position:

> Can anyone who knows the men and knows the Churches pretend to think that Anglicanism is fairly represented by a distinguished mediaevalist (Armitage Robinson) and four Anglo-Catholic leaders?[1]

And what he had written privately, he soon said publicly in a letter to *The Times*:

> In these conferences the English delegates are not the men whom English Churchmen would naturally regard as champions of the 'historical Anglican position and claims'. . . . All of them, with one doubtful exception, are prominent Anglo-Catholics, and one of them, Lord Halifax, is so Roman that the Archbishop has thought it necessary to repudiate his opinions in a special note.[2]

The 'one doubtful exception' was presumably Gore. But having found a handy label which fitted them all, Henson tied it round their necks much too summarily, forgetting that no trio or quintet of men is disposed of or sufficiently docketed by being called Anglo-Catholics or protestants and left at that. They were in fact as fully different men as could be found in the Church. No one ever believed more sincerely in the catholicity of the Anglican Church than Gore or Frere, but they did not believe it in the same way, and they expressed it very differently. Halifax refused to include Gore in the original party, thinking that for this he would be 'impossible'. Armitage Robinson, the most learned theologian among them, seems to have played but a little part. It consisted mostly of mislaying important papers at the moment when they were most needed. When he arrived at Lambeth to report to Davidson, he found he was once more without the

[1] *Retrospect*, vol. II, p. 146. [2] *Ibid.*, p. 147.

papers he needed, a circumstance which did nothing to inspire a thoroughly uneasy archbishop with confidence in the negotiators.

Just as Mercier was essential to the whole enterprise and the only possible chairman of it, so on the English side everything hinged on Lord Halifax, without whom there would have been no conversations. It was his second chance to further the dream of his life, and as he was now a very old man it was bound to be his last. He was an extremist in all he did, and these facts set in violent motion the whole of his latent capacity for single-minded enthusiasm. No one was ever more selfless, and yet, unconsciously, he saw this effort dramatically as a personal challenge, a chance to vindicate the cause he had ever made his own, and his own life with it, since his cause and his life were to him one and the same. He had neither reserve nor detachment. His faith so burned within him that it created in him a credulity at which others marvelled or blasphemed, and made him impatient with relevant facts. When, for instance, the Roman Catholics so insisted that the papal primacy was given by the very appointment of Christ himself as to shock all the other Anglicans, Halifax was not shocked at all, and was quite prepared to accept it as the price to be paid for keeping the talks in being, magnificently disregarding the vital fact that no Anglicans could possibly accept it. Knowing his Halifax very well (and loving him dearly) the Archbishop had expressly to warn him:

Don't detract from the importance of the XXXIX Articles. Don't budge an inch as to the necessity of carrying the East with us in ultimate Reunion steps. Bear constantly in mind that in any admission made as to what Roman leadership or 'primacy' may mean, we have to make quite clear too that which it must not mean.[1]

The warning was certainly necessary. But the intensity of faith which Halifax brought to the task held him firmly cleaving to his purpose, and no amount of delays, set-backs, and extreme caution from authority proved able to deter him. They bewildered him for the moment, but they were quite powerless to dim even for a moment the light he saw. The last years of his life were strenuous indeed, and by all medical rules he should have collapsed and died under the strain, but his faith gave him these extra years, and his inflexible determination carried him through them to the last bitter moment when Mercier died, and the Roman authorities ordered the talks to end.

On December 5, 1921, the Anglican travellers, Halifax, Frere, Armitage Robinson, arrived at Malines, and their hope was reinforced by the courtesy of Cardinal Mercier who sent his secretary to meet them at the station. In the great drawing-room of the Cardinal's palace Mercier, a tall and grave figure who was always the very flower of courtesy, welcomed his guests. The next morning the conversations began. They nearly always

[1] Bell, *op. cit.*, vol. II, pp. 1260f.

followed much the same course. There was Mass in the domestic chapel at seven. Coffee, rolls, and butter were served at nine; and at ten o'clock the Abbé Portal took the Anglican party into the drawing-room, and the vicar-general, Monsignor van Roey, and the Cardinal entered. They all sat round a small circular table. Mercier invoked the blessing of the Holy Spirit upon them, and they began. The talk went on till lunch-time, and after that there was a break until four, when they met again and continued the discussion until dinner at seven. At nine o'clock the guests were expected to go to their own rooms, where they read or wrote until bedtime. The talks generally lasted for two days, so the programme did not seem to be exhausting; and although disagreements must perforce be expressed and explained most of the time, Mercier's personal charm made it easy to speak the truth as one sees it in love. When, at a later stage, Gore came, he thought it his duty to speak of Anglican convictions with all his own ruggedness, but such was the atmosphere of loving kindness which Mercier had created among them that he knew well he might do so without giving any offence. When Gore went back to London, and thought again over what had passed, it was Mercier's goodness which was uppermost in his mind; and he took pen and paper and wrote to his host:

I can hardly express, because it is almost inexpressible, the sense of your goodness towards we Anglicans at Malines. It is not only that you have been so generous a host, but also that you have succeeded in making we heretics feel so completely at home in your house that we felt able to speak with perfect freedom even about the most disagreeable topics. I was touched to the quick by your most persevering tolerance, and I ask your forgiveness if I have said one single word more than was necessary to make clear our position.[1]

But whereas Gore found that in his host, others, and notably Frere, found something else to add to it. This was so ingrained and insuperable a failure to understand the Anglican position that it might be called a blind spot:

The largeness of his heart embraced us all but his head did not seem to take in our position. . . . Naughty children we were, but we must be treated with the utmost patience and generosity.[2]

That may be true of his attitude during the first part of the conversations. But as they proceeded the Anglicans found that it gradually became less true, and before the end they saw him tentatively grasping for a position where he at last began to think of the Anglican Church as an inexorably corporate body, and to see that the hope of reunion turned on Rome being willing to treat with her as a partner in Christendom, and to talk of incorporation rather than submission. Even while Frere sensed that the Cardinal's patience and generosity were qualities deliberately willed in him, he knew well the contrast between Mercier and the English Roman Catholics,

---

[1] Prestige, *Life of Charles Gore*, p. 483.
[2] Frere. Quoted in Lockhart, vol. II, pp. 305f.

who would have individual submission or nothing, and realized that never have conversations between Anglicans and Roman Catholics been carried on in so thoroughly Christian an atmosphere.

There were five sets of talks in all, but the last was concerned only with producing an agreed record of the results of the first four—an attempt to tidy up an episode which all knew could go no further. The first discussion began in October 1921 and the last in October 1926. They had all agreed to begin with a point-by-point comparison of the Thirty-Nine Articles with the formularies of the Council of Trent. Pusey had said once of these two documents that they seemed to him potentially reconcilable. But the comparison of the formularies led them very quickly into a discussion of the processes by which a truth becomes a matter of faith in the Roman Church, and from there it was not a long step to a consideration of all the really vital questions at issue between the two Churches. This first series of talks was not more than a trial run or a preliminary skirmish, but all the major points which were to come up again and again were produced and given a preliminary airing. Of these, two haunted them all the time. They were the position of the Papacy in Roman theology and in a fully reunited Christendom, and the relationship of the Anglican Communion to Rome if full communion were restored between them. Under these two main heads of fundamental disagreement all other sources of division, the Roman additions to scriptural doctrine and the validity of Anglican Orders, could be comprehended. Once settle the difficulties of the Roman doctrine of the Papacy and the terms on which the tradition and self-respect of a local Church could be kept inviolate even when that Church was united to Rome and all the other difficulties would very quickly settle themselves.

It was the primacy of the Pope over the whole of Christendom rather than his infallibility when he speaks *ex cathedra* on matters of faith and morals that formed the staple of the Malines conversations. On this matter Mercier was completely unyielding. It was for him not a logical necessity but a dogma full of emotional power. When, in the course of the conversations, a new Pope, Pius XI, was elected, Mercier at once wrote to his diocese that three hundred million people paid their homage to the new Holy Father.

In the intimacy of their conscience and in their full personal independence they paid him the complete homage of their faith, and the submission of their intellect, will, and filial affection, ready to accept death if need be, rather than to infringe, I do not say one of his commands, but the least of his wishes.[1]

To his extravagance of language even Halifax demurred, specially as Mercier had thoughtfully provided an English translation that it might be read here. 'I am afraid it won't do us much good. Let us only hope it won't do harm. Foreigners never can understand the English mind.'[2] From the beginning to the end of the talks the Romans never yielded one inch on

[1] Bell, *op. cit.*, vol. II, p. 1261.   [2] Lockhart, vol. II, p. 280.

the necessary supremacy of the Pope. All Christians whatsoever owed him allegiance and unquestioning obedience. He was not among other bishops *primus inter pares*, but supreme and unique in his own right, and all forms of ministry were derived from Christ and through the Pope, and the Pope alone. This the Romans would state as often as might be required. They did not tire of it. They might vary the words they chose to state it, and the tone of voice in which they uttered them. But the doctrinal position never changed in the least. The only real discussion they would permit about it was over the question of whether the Pope had this position by the ordering of the Church or by the divine and direct appointment of God in Christ. The Romans were sure that it was by divine appointment, and so was Halifax who held it our Anglican duty 'to recognize a Primacy not merely *jure ecclesiastico* but *jure divino*'.[1] None of the other Anglicans would follow him thus far, but the Romans, perceiving that Halifax was willing, and overestimating his influence on the Church of England, were prepared to listen to Frere, Gore, and Armitage Robinson while they argued learnedly and at length on the real meaning of the scriptural text, 'Thou art Peter and upon this rock I will build my Church.' They found the Romans both naïve and uninformed about the ordinary processes of biblical criticism. Frere also commented, 'One of the texts concerning St Peter had hypnotized the Roman Catholics in their outlook, to the exclusion of the scriptural description of the Church itself.'[2] Their attitude on this vital dogmatic issue was well summarized by Gore in a letter to Halifax, 'The R.C.'s showed themselves quite unrelenting on the dogmatic issue. . . . They did even more—they made the discussion on the grounds of Scripture and antiquity more hopeless than ever.'[3]

The shadow of this doctrinal impasse was seen in the first of the conversations. In the hope of preventing the shadow from becoming the too solid flesh in other conversations the Anglicans suggested that the doctrinal issue should be dropped, and instead that they should talk of the methods whereby the Anglican Communion might one day be brought into union with the Holy See. When they heard of this request the Archbishop of Canterbury was doubtful of its wisdom and the Cardinal was surprised. Nevertheless he agreed. The event showed that Halifax was wiser than either of them at this juncture. As long as the conversations were held to this one point they did achieve something. It was not union: it could never be that as long as there was a fundamental cleavage on doctrine. But the Romans showed themselves ready to make, and even themselves to suggest real concessions. In the future it may prove really important to have it recorded on paper that a group of responsible Roman Catholic clergy were prepared to make suggestions as to how the Anglican Communion could be reunited to Rome by methods other than individual submission, and on terms neither humiliating to Anglicans nor at variance with their whole tradition.

[1] *Ibid.*, p. 292.   [2] *Ibid.*, p. 319.   [3] *Ibid.*, p. 302.

Two main points were involved here. The first was that in the Papal Bull *Apostolicae Curae* Rome had pronounced Anglican Orders invalid. Was there any way round or over that? The wording of one of the clauses of the Lambeth Appeal for Unity suggested to the Abbé Portal that there might be. The Anglican bishops had written:

We are persuaded that, terms of union having been otherwise satisfactorily adjusted, Bishops and clergy of our Communion would willingly accept from these authorities a form of commission or recognition which would commend our ministry to their congregations, as having its place in the one family life.

Portal said that in this clause the Anglican bishops had set a great example of Christian humility. But Mercier, reading it aloud, was then silent a moment and spoke with hesitation, saying that even so some form of supplementary ordination would probably still be required.

The second point also involved the validity of Anglican Orders, but more indirectly because it was concerned with the attempt to persuade Rome to agree that the only way to treat with the Anglican Church was to treat with her as an equal. In the time of Queen Elizabeth, Anglicanism was established only in a miniature isolated outpost of Christendom, in the provinces of Canterbury and York. But now the Anglican Communion was a world-wide family of Churches, and constantly growing, second in size and in political importance only to Rome herself. On this point Mercier and his friends were far more conciliatory. They were prepared to recognize the special position which the Anglican Communion must occupy in a united Christendom, and provided her bishops would agree that their authority was derived from the Pope, they could agree to the continuance of particular Anglican traditions, such as use of the Book of Common Prayer and the marriage of the clergy. At a later stage Mercier himself said the Roman Church must not attempt to absorb the Anglican. They must work, on the other hand, for a union of the Churches. He then quoted with approval the opinion of a canonist whom he had consulted, and who had said that there should be a new patriarchate of Canterbury, with its own liturgy and canon law, and that when this had been done the Roman Catholic sees in England should be suppressed. This canonist, though highly respected for his learning, was naturally speaking for himself, but Mercier would not have quoted him to the gathering had he not himself approved his opinion.

This concessiveness was naturally academic, but it was still concessiveness. It led nowhere: it could not, for it was based upon the supposition that the doctrinal issues were solved. Halifax was delighted, but both the Archbishop and Gore were perturbed lest the Anglicans should be conceding too much, and Gore wrote:

The concessiveness of our delegation to Malines, apparently at the first Conference and certainly at the second, seems to me more disastrous and perilous the more I think of it. It astonishes me to hear from the Dean (Armitage Robinson) what he was prepared to admit as to Roman supremacy.[1]

The Archbishop, though expressing himself less forcefully, was just as disturbed, especially over the suggestion that Anglican bishops should accept the *Pallium* from the Pope. He wrote to Mercier, as well as to Halifax and his friends, to insist that it was useless to discuss administrative terms of union while the doctrinal issues were still unsettled.

These were the points with which the five conversations were chiefly concerned. But running through the conversations like a single thread may run through a complicated pattern of weaving and yet be always noticeable was the search by both sides for official authorization. Without this the talks must remain no more than academic discussions which could not lead to where all alike wished to go, and which might even lie under the condemnation of wasting the time of busy men. Mercier's hopes were raised by the election of a new Pope (Pius XI) in 1922, for he was known to have reunion much at heart. Soon afterwards Mercier was assured 'by an authorized but confidential voice'[2] that papal authority looked favourably on their enterprise and hoped it would continue. He reported this to the Archbishop himself, and wrote to Halifax to say how he hoped that 'the Anglicans with whom we should be conversing next time would be "Anglicans named by the Archbishop of Canterbury in order to consider etc." '[3]

But the Archbishop of Canterbury was in a most difficult position. Having sponsored the Lambeth Appeal he could not, even had he wished, withhold some form of recognition from the Malines conversations. But at the same time he could not forget the negotiations even then in progress with the Orthodox Churches, the Old Catholics, and various protestant Churches, and could take no step towards the Roman Catholics which would be likely to make such negotiations more difficult for they were after all so much more promising. Nor could he go further officially than his fellow churchmen were prepared to follow him, and it was obvious that hardly any of them were ready to submit to any form of reordination or to admit the doctrine of the supremacy of the papacy if it meant conceding that the whole priesthood of the Church derived its validity from the Pope. Besides, he was himself completely loyal in his own heart to the Anglican position, and he wrote his considered judgement upon the conversations in these words:

> It ought to be made clear on the Anglican side, beyond possibility of doubt, that the great principles upon which the Reformation turned are our principles still. . . . It would be unfair to our Roman Catholic friends to leave them in any doubt as to our adherence, on large questions of controversy, to the main principles for which men like Hooker or Andrewes or Cosin contended. . . . What those men stood for we stand for still.[4]

[1] Bell, *op. cit.*, vol. II, p. 1267.   [2] Lockhart, vol. II, p. 281.
[3] *Ibid.*   [4] *Ibid.*, p. 299.

He well understood the many Anglicans who were not prepared to go one inch of the journey towards reunion with Rome on any terms; and these were not powerless by any means. While the Malines conversations were going on the chief preoccupation of the Archbishop was the revision of the Prayer Book, and every passing day made it more evident that he could not hope it would be easy to pilot it through the Church Assembly, the Convocations and Parliament. If the protestants were to be made more suspicious than they already were it might well be impossible, and the bishops, to whom Davidson early reported what was going on, were emphatic in their warnings of trouble ahead. Moreover, while he, like everyone else, held Halifax in love and and veneration, he did not trust his judgement and he almost dreaded his exuberance. Nor did he think that either Armitage Robinson or Frere could be a sufficient brake on any car which Halifax was driving.

Accordingly he was inflexible in maintaining the distinction between recognition and authorization. He would openly and officially recognize that the conversations were proceeding with his knowledge and approval. This he did by including some account of them in his pastoral to the bishops on the progress of all reunion negotiations; and also by officially appointing Gore and Kidd to join the original team. He also maintained a close connection between Mercier and himself by correspondence. But beyond that he would never go, for indeed he could not.

Gradually it became apparent that the conversations were not to have anything more than this by way of official recognition on either side, and that the majority of Anglican churchmen profoundly distrusted them. It was clear, too, that at least some continental Roman Catholics were also hostile to them, for Mercier had publicly to rebuke them for their lack of charity. This knowledge became the signal for the English Roman Catholics, who one and all disliked them intensely, to go openly into action against them.

Halifax remembered only too clearly the fate of the earlier series of discussions, and so he had begun this time by going to see the Cardinal Archbishop of Westminster and asking for his 'good services to help in every possible way to bring about such conferences as Leo XIII discussed in 1894'. Cardinal Bourne received him graciously:

Ah! Cardinal Mercier! (he said) I know him well and have a great regard for him; we were at Louvain together. He is a great man, a most distinguished personality with a strong influence. I am *very glad* that you have seen him.

'My visit', added Halifax, 'was a great success.'[1] Was it? Even at that early date Bourne had not gone one inch beyond a courteous sympathy. Before the course of the conversations was half run Father Woodlock was writing in the Anglican papers to express his hostility, and his belief that nothing could come of them because

---

[1] Lockhart, p. 273.

With us the infallibility and supremacy of the Pope is a dogma which rests exactly on the same authority as does that of the Godhead of Christ.[1]

Later still, when it was clear that the conversations were not to be in any way official, he went much further and wrote continuously to the newspapers in the most intransigently Roman style, in which he was fully supported by the English Roman Catholic press. In the midst of this controversial activity of his he was firmly rebuked by Mercier for misrepresenting Halifax and misquoting Portal, but more than that, because he was

Attacking the Conversations and making it a grievance that his own experience and advice had not been sought. Mercier rejected assistance from such a quarter and dissociated himself from such methods of controversy. He and his Catholic colleagues were as familiar as was Fr Woodlock with the doctrine of the Church and had no intention of betraying it. He ended by charging Fr Woodlock with ignoring the plainly expressed wishes of the Pope himself.[2]

Mercier asked Halifax to have this letter published in *The Times* but Bourne managed to prevent it, and then himself publicly attacked the Church of England at York. By then Mercier was dead, and Rome sent word to his successor that the talks must cease, and the report about them must not be published. The *coup de grâce* was given on January 6, 1928, when the Pope issued the encyclical *Mortalium Animos*. The doctrine of the Papal Supremacy was restated in the extremest language, and certain unidentified movements towards reunion were condemned. A fortnight later the *Osservatore Romano* announced that the Malines Conversations were ended, and would not be resumed.

The English Romans had once more triumphed. But what gave them the victory was the death of Mercier. As he had been in life so he was in death. The doctors told him he had incurable cancer. 'Tonight I have something to offer to the Holy Virgin. It is something quite out of the ordinary,' he replied. Halifax realized at once that this would be the end of his dream. He heard that Mercier would like to see him, and, a very old man though he was, he at once made the journey to Malines. There he saw once more the great prince of the Church who had become his friend. Mercier was very weak and his life was fast flowing away. But he found strength to beg Halifax to persevere with the talks, and he dictated a last message to the Archbishop of Canterbury:

Ut unum Sint: it is the supreme wish of Christ, the wish of the Sovereign Pontiff: it is mine, it is yours. May it be realized in its fulness.[3]

Then he took from his finger the ring he always wore, his gold episcopal ring which his family had given him at his consecration, and he insisted on giving it to Halifax, and then he blessed him and let him go.

[1] *Ibid.*, p. 294.   [2] *Ibid.*, p. 321.   [3] *Ibid.*, p. 327.

The end of the story concerns this ring. Halifax wore it on a chain round his neck until he died. Then it was welded to a chalice, above its base, which the present Lord Halifax presented to York Minster. In that great church this chalice, with Mercier's episcopal ring set in it, has been used ever since on three occasions in the year, on St Peter's Day, and on the anniversaries of the deaths of Mercier and Halifax.

IV · Kikuyu

Kikuyu, in East Africa, is a name which matters in Anglican history, for it was in successive conferences held there that one of the most persevering attempts to find a basis for union between Anglican and Nonconformist Churches was made. This effort was spread over eighteen years. It began in 1908—but at Maseno, not Kikuyu—and it continued at intervals until 1926 when the third and last Kikuyu conference ended and it was lamentably clear that nothing could be gained by calling another. Efforts were still made, however, to stave off the confession of failure. It was not until 1937 that it became finally clear that one more effort to find the way to a union of separated Churches had failed and no one could deny it.

In 1908 representatives of most of the reformed Churches at work in the area met at Maseno in order to reach sufficient agreement to form a federation of missionary Churches in East Africa. The Anglican dioceses of Mombasa and Uganda, the Church of Scotland, the Methodist Church, and the interdenominational Africa Inland Mission all took part. But in 1911 this effort ended in deadlock. Then in 1913 they tried again at the first Kikuyu conference, and this time they did produce a basis of federation. They agreed to assign to each mission its own geographical sphere of influence, and to a system whereby a convert who moved from one area to another would be welcomed and shepherded wherever he went. A limited degree of safeguarded intercommunion was established, and an interchange of pulpits between ministers of the different Churches was agreed. On the vital question of ordinations the conference decided that all candidates should be trained according to an approved system, and then 'be duly set apart by lawful authority, and by the laying on of hands'.[1] It was at the end of this conference that the united Holy Communion was celebrated by the Bishop of Mombasa in the Presbyterian church at Kikuyu which brought the Bishop of Zanzibar into the field in tempestuous denunciation and involved the whole Anglican Communion in bitter controversy, which only the opening of the first world war stilled.[2]

That made two failures, of which the second had been sensational. The persistence with which they decided in 1918 to try yet again is therefore

[1] Rt Rev. J. J. Willis and Rev. J. W. Arthur, *Towards a United Church, 1913–1947*, Part I, *Kikuyu and After* (Edinburgh House Press), 1947, p. 31.
[2] *Op. cit.*

especially praiseworthy, particularly as Frank Weston, whose intervention and charges of heresy had wrecked all the hopes of 1913, was still Bishop of Zanzibar. He was a formidable figure to have in any reunion discussions, but there could be none without him. It was the sincerity of their missionary zeal which made them try yet once more, for the transference of European sources and causes of division to East Africa, where the Moslems were so strong, was doing great damage to the native converts and seriously weakening the influence of Christians with the colonial government in matters of education.

The third conference at Kikuyu met in July 1918, and was composed of members of the four Churches which had suggested federation in 1913. Again the dioceses of Mombasa and Uganda were represented by their bishops. But on this occasion Dr Frank Weston and a priest from the Universities' Mission to Central Africa were present as guests. Whether guest or member he was bound to dominate the conference, and this nettle was at once grasped. Before any discussions about terms of union were even begun, the delegates asked Weston to tell them where he stood. He had definite proposals to make, and he outlined them in a speech the whole tone of which showed how absolutely he was with them all in longing for unity. His proposals were nine in number, and of these only three were controversial, for they involved a declaration about episcopacy. He asked acceptance of the facts about episcopacy, that it has always existed and that it ruled the greater part of Christendom. But he said, too, that it need not be a monarchical or even a diocesan institution, and he advocated the democratic election of bishops. 'Nor', he added, 'is it essential that we hold any one view of episcopacy on the doctrinal side provided the fact of its existence and continuance be admitted.' But he did demand that all the Churches must 'consent to some episcopal consecration and ordination' without which it would not be possible for members of non-episcopal Churches to minister in Anglican churches. But if they would do that, he himself would 'gladly come before any of their congregations, and accept any form of popular recognition'. By these proposals the delegates were surprised, which is strange, for they were the utmost that a bishop holding Weston's views could offer. After a period of reflection the Free Church missions rejected them giving various reasons, of which this weighed most:

We feel that no basis which places the Church above the Word of God, no ritual which would take the place of personal communion, and no ecclesiastical control which limits personal liberty in vital things, or fails to honour authority conferred by our own Churches, is possible.[1]

It was therefore evident that the diocese of Zanzibar could not be a partner in the federation. But there were other Anglican dioceses in the area, Mombasa and Uganda; and these were prepared to go further than

[1] *Op. cit.*, pp. 56–8.

Zanzibar. The conference therefore proceeded to write a constitution for what is called 'The Alliance of Missionary Societies (Protestant) in British East Africa', in which it was first of all made plain that this was a federation of missionary societies and not of the Churches through which the Societies worked. A united Church they hoped one day to see. Their immediate purpose was an alliance of missions. This constitution was signed and endorsed by the two Anglican bishops, and it was eventually ratified by the home authorities of all the missions concerned in it.

Although this Alliance was based on a common acceptance of Bible, Creeds, and the dominical Sacraments, it was at first limited in its range to matters of organization and administration, and it left the thorny questions of intercommunion and ordination alone. If it worked satisfactorily in these easier fields, these questions were bound to be raised sooner or later, but they could be left until they clamoured for solution. In the meantime there was exceedingly important work the Alliance could do in that field which was becoming more significant for missionary expansion than any other, the relationship of missions to government. All the missions in the area could now speak to the government with a single voice through the Alliance, and this they did. They took up with the government every question which affected the welfare of the natives, and they dealt with the educational and medical government departments with a new and enhanced effectiveness. The power of their new administrative unity was such that no government could ignore them, and missionaries became members of various legislative and executive committees of the government. It was a notable example of how greatly the power of Christians over the organization of society is increased if there is unity and co-operation between them.

The full conference of the missions which had formed this Alliance met once more at Kikuyu in 1922. Since the previous conference of 1918, the Lambeth Conference had met and had placed its famous appeal for union before the whole of Christendom. The bishops at Lambeth had, however, expressly declared against intercommunion and exchange of pulpits. The new Kikuyu conference warmly welcomed the Lambeth appeal, but, moved by their own experience of harmonious co-operation and by the bewilderment of African natives over the ecclesiastical divisions of the Churches of Europe, they demanded more than the bishops at Lambeth had been prepared to grant. The missions in the Alliance resolved to ask the home Churches to which they owed obedience for the following concessions:

1. That at all future ordinations of African ministers the various Churches accepting the basis of the Alliance should be represented by those authorized to ordain in the various Churches, who should participate in the actual ordination so that all African ministers so ordained would be freely recognized as ministers in all the Churches concerned.
2. That all fresh missionaries be ordained in the same way.

3. That ordained foreign missionaries already at work in the country should at once be given the power of mutual recognition.
4. That eventually communicants of any branch of the Church become communicants of all the others without the requirement of a special religious ceremony.

The last request meant that the alliance was now prepared to go further than it had gone before, and to remove the idea of a United African Church from the status of a dream to that of an immediate object of policy. The Church of England could not of course grant their requests, but it was sympathetic towards their formulation. The Church of Scotland called their proposals exceedingly attractive.

The Alliance then set up a Committee on Reunion in order to prepare the way for the United African Church, which it believed to be so nearly a matter of practical politics that in its documents it always referred to it by its initials, U.A.C. The Committee defined the aim as an autonomously governed united Church, regulating its acts 'by the necessity of maintaining fellowship with the Church universal', and that after union all members of the uniting Churches would be equally full members of the U.A.C. But all this was dependent upon agreement between the Churches in the difficult matter of the ministry, and the sacraments which depended upon it. This could no longer be shirked, and it is remarkable that the committee found itself agreed on these proposals:

1. That all ministers of the uniting Churches ordained before union be fully recognized as ministers in the United African Church.
2. That all future ordinations to the Presbyterate (Ministry) be performed by the laying-on of hands of at least one Bishop and two Presbyters (Ministers).
3. That without accepting any theory as to its reasons the ancient practice of presenting Bishops Elect to three Bishops for consecration be agreed to.

But before any man can be ordained in any Church he must be trained, and to ask for a unified, universal ministry in a single limited Africa Church must be to ask also for a single theological school for the whole Alliance in which the African priests of the future might be trained. The committee proposed therefore to set up an Alliance Theological College in which all ordination candidates should be required to reside for at least the final part of their training. But this college never came into being.

On paper it might well have seemed to the committee that this last part of their plan might have been the easier to carry into effect. It was logical that a single theological college should precede the unification of the ministry. Moreover the Alliance had by now become experienced and successful in the building and management of schools. Their Alliance High School at Kikuyu quickly became the most famous institution for the higher education of Africans in East Africa.

A result of the third Kikuyu Conference, held in 1926, was that

Communion services, at which all communicants partook were regularly held and conducted by ministers from the various Churches; and in 1935 an *Order of Service for Holy Communion*, approved by the Churches of the Alliance, came into use.[1]

Moreover, the Representative Council of the Alliance agreed in 1929 that visitors from any Church in the Alliance to a district where another Church was in possession of the field, should be freely admitted to communion in that Church without having to conform to its special discipline.

But in 1929 eight Africans of the Kikuyu people were ordained to the Church of Scotland, three at Kikuyu and five at Tumutumu. At Kikuyu a Baptist, a Methodist, and an Anglican priest took part in the laying on of hands; and at Tumutumu two Anglicans joined with the ministers of the Church of Scotland in the act of ordaining. For this action the Anglicans had no episcopal authority. They had not sought it. It was a spontaneous act on their part. Nine years later, in 1935, an Anglican bishop (Dr Heywood of Mombasa) and three Anglican priests were present when three more Africans were ordained in the Church of Scotland, but though the bishop gave the address, the Anglicans took no part in the actual ordination. Between those two dates, various Africans were ordained in the Anglican Church, but the ministers of the other Churches were not invited to take part in it, for the decisions of the Lambeth Conference had made it impossible to give such invitations.

V · *The Fellowship of St Alban and St Sergius*

In the negotiations at Malines and at Kikuyu we have seen the failure of the direct effort to find a basis for reunion between Anglicans and Roman Catholics on the one hand and Free Churchmen on the other. What we have now to witness is a different approach to the same problem, this time involving a part of the Orthodox Church, in which Anglican and Orthodox Christians came together to pursue fellowship and mutual study and understanding, and at a later stage unexpectedly found themselves face to face with a problem of reunion, which both sides felt they must grapple with and pursue.

The expulsion and exile of many Russian priests by the Bolshevists had had at least one effect which had benefited Christendom as a whole. These priests had established themselves in Paris, and had there set up a thriving theological academy, where they prepared for ordination an average of forty students a year, and from which a great deal of first-rate and original theological work came and was available to all the Churches of the Western world. Nikolai Berdyaev was one of these exiles, and all his greatest work was done in Paris. He became one of the unofficial theological tutors of every Church in Christendom, a man whose books one had to read because

[1] *Op. cit.*, p. 71.

of the immense distinction of his mind and the depth of his learning. Writing in exile he had a far wider range of influence than would ever have been his had he not suffered the deep pain of exile from his beloved Russia. With him at the Paris Academy were men of the stature of Bulgakov, Bezobraxov and Florovsky, and many others.

In this Russian Academy in Paris the Student Christian Movement was soon at work, and it was under its auspices that the Fellowship of St Alban and St Sergius was begun. Its purpose was to provide a mould in which Anglican and Russian Orthodox clergy and students could seize the chance of this proximity and come together regularly. As with most things the Student Christian Movement undertook, so with this: 'let there be a conference, and then see what would come of it.' The first conference took place at St Albans in 1927; and this was so successful that a second was held a year later, and the decision to create the Fellowship of St Alban and St Sergius was taken.

It consisted of Anglican and Orthodox members, clergy, laity, and students, and there were a few Free Churchmen, who were associates rather than members, and who held a sort of watching brief. The members had to accept the declared aims of the Fellowship, must observe the rule of regular prayer for the reunion of Christendom, and 'must have the experience of eucharistic worship in the Orthodox and Anglican Church'. The society was one for prayer and spiritual intimacy; it was not, as its members said again and again, any kind of negotiating body between the two Churches.

Its valuable work was for the most part done by the annual conferences. The quality of fellowship achieved was of a high and impressive order, and these conferences gave hundreds of Anglicans a new understanding of the Orthodox liturgy and methods of worship. There was a regular interchange of liturgies at the daily Eucharist; one morning it was celebrated according to the Orthodox use, and the next according to the Anglican use. Members of each Church attended every day, but they made their communions only on those days when their own liturgy celebrated by their own priesthood was in use. The same alternative order was followed every evening when the Anglican Compline alternated with the Russian Vespers. During the day the members prayed, ate and studied together; and it was arranged that the two sides should have an equal share, again in strict alternation, in the reading of the papers to be discussed. It is impossible for sincere men and women to share thus in all the springs of devotion without in the process gaining a vast amount of understanding of each other, or that they can fail to carry fellowship and comrades over the bridge which divides both from community. There were many who learned at these conferences at St Albans and, later, at High Leigh, what the Russian word *sobornost* or catholicity really means, and they learned it in the only way they could, that is by actually living in the context of these conferences. Those who were regularly present found that the Russian liturgy spoke to the deepest things in them, and drew from them a haunting sense of unity with their Russian friends.

This was a remarkable achievement for there were real difficulties to be overcome. They were mostly due to the inherent difference between the two nationalities, and between men who were exiles and others who were at home and free. The Anglicans found the Russian habit of taking as long as possible over everything both trying and exhausting. Russian services seemed very protracted, and their speeches interminable, and often unintelligible. Once Russian speakers were fairly launched, nothing on earth, certainly not the dinner gong or the signal for morning coffee, would stop them. They would start with some fairly clear and obvious statements, and then delve steadily deeper and deeper, uncovering one fundamental basis after another, with an ever increasing air of being in the sorest travail. Soon they had left their Anglican listeners far behind, and the chairman—not a coveted post—had to decide whether to stop the Russians in mid-course and seem rude, or whether to ignore the refreshment bell and let everyone's lunch or coffee get cold. There is a real truth in P. G. Wodehouse's casual remark about Russian fiction: 'A Russian novel is one in which nothing whatever happens until page 394 when the moujik decides to commit suicide,' and there is a sense in which it applies also to Russian theology. Then the Russians, in their turn, found themselves both bewildered and shocked by the Anglican habit of assuming as beyond argument the agreed results of biblical criticism. Even the book of Genesis they refused to regard as allegory, as the Anglicans did, but always spoke of it as 'metaphysically true in what they called the realm of meta-history',[1] a phrase which did not notably lighten counsel. This in turn brought out the Anglican sense of superiority, and it was a Russian member who wrote:

When the very possibility of critical research in connection with the Scriptures was denied, when beforehand there was prejudiced rejection of the last results of criticism, which was sometimes shown by some of the Orthodox members of the Conference, then the English seemed troubled, and often, on seeing such an attitude, became deaf to our arguments, and affirmed that we were simply scientifically behind them, and not therefore competent in these questions.[2]

When Bishop Gore, taking for granted the Christian social attitude, insisted on the translation, 'The Kingdom of God is *among* you,' the Russians were distressed when he would not change it to '*within* you,' since it seemed to them to undervalue the mystical interpretation of the Faith. Again, 'a phrase used by the Bishop, "Christianity is a life to be lived before it is a doctrine to be believed" puzzled at least one group.'[3] Moreover it was found that the 'Western ethical emphasis' was apt to clash with the 'Eastern eschatological expectation' even over such unexpected matters as the value

[1] *Report of the Second Anglo-Russian Student Conference* (SCM Press), 1928, p. 8.
[2] *Ibid.*, p. 11.   [3] *Ibid.*, p. 22.

of the conversion of Constantine.[1] Finally, it was discovered that the word 'truth' did not mean the same things to the two groups, which is not to say that the Russians valued it less highly than the Anglicans. One who was present at all the conferences defined the difference thus, 'We must remember that two conceptions of Truth are at stake. To the Orthodox Truth practically equals unanimity. In the Western tradition Truth is something outside and beyond the Church : there is an element of exclusiveness about it.' These differences were never overcome in the sense of being charmed out of existence. But they were made to seem unimportant when set beside the reality and depth of the communion of spirit enjoyed by the two sides of the Fellowship.

From 1927 to 1933 the Fellowship placidly followed the course it had charted. Every day at successive conferences the Orthodox and the Anglican members prayed together, became friends, and tried to understand each other more and more. Each shared in the other's liturgy and the daily eucharist, but they did not attempt to communicate together. But to one of the Russian members, Father Sergius Bulgakov, this seemed an intolerable deprivation. They had done so much together for so long that they had become a unity. Why, then, must they stop short at the sharing of the sacrament of unity? Was it not spiritually dangerous to continue for too long in a mere discussion of differences? Was it to be for ever true that discussion in prayer and fellowship lead only to more discussion? But he was too much of a realist and had too strong a sense of church order to suggest that they should simply defy it by communicating together forthwith. These things he had long been pondering, and at last, at the conference at High Leigh in June 1933, he thought he saw a possible compromise, and he suddenly laid it before the Fellowship. It was that the Fellowship should take what he called 'molecular action', and proceed with a plan of intercommunion for its own members, without waiting for the two Churches as a whole to act officially. But in order to safeguard the principle of church order, he asked that the first communion together should be inaugurated by a special sacramental blessing to be bestowed upon the Anglicans by an Orthodox hierarch, and that the Anglicans should submit to it and accept it as 'an act of sacrifice'.

The great difficulties of reuniting two Churches which have once been separated, even though they have a common dogmatic basis of belief, are illustrated by the long negotiations which followed this proposal and the tensions to which they exposed the Fellowship. If it had not been worthy of its title, they would have broken it to pieces. Here was a body of men the reality of whose devotion to the cause of reunion could not be questioned, men who had spent seven years in learning to test, to know, and to trust each other, men who interpreted their membership of the Fellowship as involving a charge to set forward the union of their Churches. If reunion

[1] *Ibid.*, p. 23.

were the easy thing which the unwary think it, such men as they could have accepted Bulgakov's proposal at once. They could not do that, and Bulgakov had not supposed they could. But being what they were, they could not summarily reject it. Inevitably there had to be much discussion, examination, definition, and negotiation; not less inevitably the long process smothered the germ of the idea, and to read the papers which tell the story is to wrestle with what has every air of a peculiarly involved and tortuous piece of international diplomacy, in which complication silenced simplicity, and all the actors knew perfectly well that it was doing so, and yet were helpless to stop it.

The executive of the Fellowship devoted its next meeting to Bulgakov's proposal. Its chairman, the Bishop of Truro, Frere, was cautiously welcoming, and said that the remoteness of full sacramental union was not so great as was sometimes supposed, but he was also very technical and full of words like 'Economy', of distinctions between praying and negotiating bodies, and of questions about how far such a Fellowship as theirs could be regarded as a canonical body. This meeting set in motion a series of negotiations of great complexity and length, which need only the briefest description here. In November 1933 Bulgakov and the Bishop of Truro met. Frere was still welcoming in manner, but in substance was even more cautious than he had been before. He counselled 'careful discussion proceeding over a period of years', to which Bulgakov replied rather pathetically, 'The plan of the Bishop of Truro is to go on discussing it at five or six conferences, and I myself (as well as the Bishop of Truro I imagine) cannot be at all sure that we shall both be in this world for these five or six conferences.' These conversations were reported to another meeting of the executive in February 1934. Bulgakov showed himself increasingly apprehensive over the unexpected opposition of many Russians to his idea, and yet persisted with it because, he said, 'I am sure that a reunion of the Churches by the official and diplomatic way will never be achieved.' However, the Fellowship as a whole was sure that the conversations must still go on, and at the conference in June 1934 the Bishop of Truro, as chairman, consented to their continuance on three conditions. They were that the corporate thinking must be clear and accurate, that any action taken must be disciplined and unhasty, and that the Fellowship must definitely state its readiness to make this task its own. This decision was taken privately to William Temple, who approved of it but added:

With regard to the proposals of Bulgakov you will remember that the recent decisions of both Convocations would approve inter-communion at gatherings of the Fellowship in a case of this sort. I confess I do not think that the Convocations will go further and specify certain Fellowships or Societies as those which may most reasonably avail themselves of the permission then given in general terms.

But by the end of the year (1934) it was clear to most of the members that there was really no chance of a unanimous acceptance of the sacramental blessing, nor of the intercommunion which it was designed to inaugurate. For on December 16, A. F. Dobbie-Bateman, a layman who was the convener of the executive, wrote a note in sad terms:

The first question is: is the proposal for Intercommunion between the Orthodox and Anglicans still alive? I do not mean: is it still on the agenda? but has it within itself any further power to move and inspire our thought? My own impression, for what it is worth, is that, at any rate in its present form, this proposal cannot now be considered alive. . . . The plain fact is that the proposal has scarcely moved one step forward during the discussion of the past year.

He gave a summary of the reasons for this deadlock, and then added, 'I certainly must admit a considerable degree of disillusionment,' and asked pertinently, 'If the Fellowship is actively to pursue the cause of reunion, what kinds of activity are open to us? But he did not attempt to answer his own question. He had accurately sensed the hitherto unspoken judgement of his fellow-members. They had given the proposal every chance, and it was clear that it could not work. In May 1935 Bulgakov made a last desperate attempt to keep it alive, but vainly, and after that it slowly petered out.

Instead of nurturing Bulgakov's proposal the discussions had smothered it. Yet they were carried on by men of goodwill, who were friends, and who had known each other at the deep levels in Christ. If these men failed, no others in the same circumstances could have succeeded. The blame, if blame there be, falls on the circumstances, not on the men. At the time when Bulgakov made his proposal the circumstances which made it impossible from the beginning of course existed, but they were not then seen clearly. Nor could they have been, for only by the kind of discussion which followed could they be displayed in a clear light.

VI · *Estimate of Progress*

The stories of Malines, Kikuyu, and the Fellowship of St Alban and St Sergius are all disappointing. Yet to the high hopes with which each began the Lambeth Appeal contributed much. That was the great merit of the Appeal: it did quicken hopes which before it were rather moribund, and it did cause all sorts of people in every Church to take fresh heart and a deep breath, and to start out once more to tread the old and weary road. But the journey became weary again as it always had done before. The fault of this was certainly not in the Appeal. It aroused hope. It even offered a way round the old Hill Difficulty of different conceptions of the ministry, by which no Church was asked to surrender anything but only to add to what it already possessed. It set things moving which had previously run down into a dejected quiescence. It succeeded in what it set out to do. The consequences were indeed disappointing, but the fault was not in the Appeal. Where, then, was it?

The three examples of reunion activities inspired by the Lambeth Appeal suggest some part of the answer. Malines showed that reunion is never possible where the parties disagree on vital doctrine, where one party demands surrender as the price, and where the negotiators have no real backing from their Churches in the shape of a widely felt desire to be reunited. Kikuyu shows that nothing permanent is to be had from attempts simply to by-pass the crucial difficulty of Orders and impatiently to treat it as the idiosyncracy of a few theological pedants. The Fellowship of St Alban and St Sergius shows that intercommunion is the fruit of reunion and not a means to it, and that when it is treated as a means it does the aim of reunion no good, and comes near to breaking what measure of unity in the spirit has already been achieved. These three examples, taken together with the other discussions and negotiations which the Lambeth Appeal set in motion, suggest also that a clear line of demarcation must be drawn between the action of small, private and unofficial groups within the Churches, and that of the action of Churches as a whole through their officially appointed leaders who negotiate in the name of the whole body. Both kinds of action are necessary. Each is essential to the other. The function of the small unofficial group of members of two separated Churches, such as the Fellowship of St Alban and St Sergius, is to create a desire for unity and the spiritual atmosphere of friendship, understanding, and trust in which it can be pursued. If it goes beyond that, it jeopardizes the good it has done and runs the risk of creating positive harm, and for small groups to run independently ahead of the Churches to which they belong hinders the cause. Negotiation is the function of Churches as a whole, carried on by their appointed officials. The solid achievements in the field of reunion between 1920 and today have always been the fruit of officially conducted negotiations between Churches. They include the recognition of the validity of Anglican Orders by most of the various Patriarchates of the Orthodox Church, the achievement of full communion between the Old Catholic Church in Europe and ourselves, and the setting up of the united Church of South India.

20

Missions and Christian Community

I · *'One of the Greatest Eras'*

THIS TITLE is in inverted commas because it is a quotation: but what gives this fact significance is the source from which the quotation comes. It is from the seventh and last volume of Professor Kenneth Scott Latourette's, *A History of the Expansion of Christianity*[1]—a work fully as authoritative as it is monumental. This last volume covers the thirty years 1914–1944, which, at first sight, most people would promptly classify as one of the most discouraging eras the Church of Christ has ever experienced. But Professor Latourette does not think so. Over and over again he calls these thirty years 'one of the greatest eras of Christianity'.[2] However grievously Christianity suffered in some lands, its gains over the whole field were greater than its losses, and in 1944 it was exercising a more potent influence over the world than in 1914.

When the last volume of Professor Latourette's work was published in 1945 some reviewers in secular journals rubbed their eyes over the author's optimism, as though it was somehow a sin for a Christian writer to display the unfashionable but Christian virtue of hope. But the really significant fact about this judgement that this was one of the greatest of all the eras of Christian expansion is that it was made, and reiterated again and again, by the man who quite probably knew more of the detail of missionary work than anybody else in the whole world. As he surveyed the world, region by region and country by country, he gave ample documentation for his estimate. At last no serious doubt was left in the reader's mind because the Professor had forced him to keep his eye on the big maps.

In 1944 there were more Christians than in 1914; they counted for more in world politics, and they were more evenly spread over the world. No one could reasonably hope to say which of the various Churches of the

[1] Published by Eyre and Spottiswoode, vol. VII, 1945.
[2] E.g., pp. 3, 65, 410.

world had done most to make this era great, but the Professor states emphatically that it was due more to the non-Roman than to the Roman Catholic Church.[1] In any case ecclesiastical competitiveness in Christian expansion is both unseemly in itself and foreign to the modern spirit of co-operation between nearly all non-Roman Churches, which has done more than anything to make the expansion possible.

The movement towards co-operation between the Churches and the missionary cause have been in our time inextricably intertwined, and everything which has happened in the missionary sphere since the Edinburgh Interdenominational Missionary Conference of 1910 proves that it really was the portent which at the time it seemed to be. 'Hang on to co-operation like grim death,' ran the cable from the Chinese Christians to the new International Missionary Committee set up after the Edinburgh Conference. The Churches have done so, and the expansion was made possible. There is therefore no separating for the purposes of literary convenience the cause of Christian unity from that of worldwide evangelism, and the two stories must be told together. Far from separating them, there is yet another to be added. This is the story of how the Churches perceived with steadily growing vividness that their evangelistic task was the bringing of the saving power of the Gospel not only to separate individuals all over the world but also to the total culture, the social order, the systems of getting and spending of these individuals. This is the story of the Churches' growing sense of responsibility for the life and work of people as much as for the people themselves.

This width of co-operation forms what is known as the Ecumenical Movement; and this in turn is like a rope woven out of three strands. They are the movement towards unity, which came to be called Faith and Order; the movement towards the re-creation of the systems which support society as well as of the people who compose it, called Life and Work; and the whole world cause of missions. But the Ecumenical Movement, though made out of the plaiting of these threads, is nevertheless more than their sum. It has been a steady drawing together of non-Roman Christendom, joined in these last few years by the Roman Catholic Church itself. This movement has reversed in our own time the universal trend of Christendom for more than fifteen hundred years towards the ever wider separation of the Christian bodies. By AD 500 nearly all Christians were united in a single Church. From then until our own time the spirit of independent separatism had triumphed over the spirit of unity. But from 1910 onwards, and especially after 1918, the spirit of unity began to triumph over the spirit of separation, and that at a time when the pressures of secularism were driving the nations of the world further apart than ever before. Moreover, the new unity of co-operation is not, as the unity of AD 500 was, the triumph of any one Church over its rivals. It is a unity of spirit, not of absorption. Its aim

[1] *Op. cit.*, pp. 16. 17,

precludes any possibility of unity by absorption, for it is a drawing together of Christians of different ecclesiastical loyalties who bring precisely their differences as well as their points of agreement into the larger fellowship, and who welcome each other in Christ's name as bringing different experiences of church life, which by their differences enhance the richness of the common pool of experience to be explored and shared.

Thus while 'Faith and Order' was concerned with reunion, and missions with evangelism, the Ecumenical Movement has been concerned with both but not exclusively with either. It hopes indeed to pave the way to reunion, but 'it is wholly to misread the history of the ecumenical movement to suppose that it is simply concerned with reunion'.[1] It is indeed concerned with evangelism, for it grew out of an evangelistic and missionary soil and has always been rooted in the soil which nourishes it. But all the great conferences of the movement have laid their stress on the renewal of the Church, and therefore the movement has been thus defined, 'Essentially the ecumenical movement stands for the recognition that evangelism, unity and responsibility for society, entwined under the Cross, are the indispensable marks of a Church which would be renewed into the likeness of its Lord.'[2]

The movement began in a conference—Edinburgh 1910—and during the years between the wars it marked its growth by periodic conferences—Stockholm 1925, Lausanne 1927, Jerusalem 1928, Oxford 1937, Edinburgh 1937, Utrecht 1937, Madras 1938. and Amsterdam 1939. It was indeed an era of great interdenominational conferences. But until 1937 each of them was organized under the aegis of one of the supporting movements out of which the Ecumenical Movement was made. Thus Lausanne and Edinburgh were concerned with Faith and Order, Stockholm and Oxford with Life and Work, Jerusalem and Madras with missions. The title made a real difference, but the membership of these conferences seemed to be often much the same, as did the technique of organization. The same great figures of the Ecumenical Movement were to be seen at most of them, whatever their theme, 'not simply (or even partly) because they liked conferences but because they realized that the conferences were ultimately all about the same thing'[3]—the renewal of the Church. They found, too, that they were all about the same thing in another sense. However complex the world scene, and however multitudinous and various the problems of Christendom laid before the conferences by the delegates, it was realized that every speech was talking of the same war. From the Arctic to the Falkland Islands and from California westwards round the globe to Formosa it was one war—Christianity versus Secularism, or God versus Mammon. It is undoubtedly true that in this period the several Churches did very much to renew their life by a full use of the conference as an instrument;

---

[1] Oliver Tomkins, 'Reunion from Above or Below?', *Theology*, 1948, p. 284.
[2] *Ibid.*, p. 285.   [3] *Ibid.*

and this tendency seems certain to continue. The interdenominational and international Christian conference has been doing for modern times much that the General Council of the Church did in ancient times. It is the invention of twentieth-century Christendom, and the primary instrument of whatever community it has achieved.

II · *The Great Conferences*

There seems in retrospect to be no doubt at all of the great power for righteousness which the long succession of conferences exercised. Nor is there any doubt that they were always exacting and exhausting. It took months of work to organize them, and the achievements of one in the series had to be tied to the hope for the next by the labours of continuation committees. While they were in being every account which has been written of them agrees that they laid the delegates under heavy strains of more than one kind. These strains bore most heavily on those who had the leadership. There was, to begin with, the inevitability of physical fatigue. The long sessions of the conference must be attended, and the still longer sessions of its subordinate committees. At these every speech, every interjection must be hearkened to with sympathy and concentration. Without this it would be impossible to draft the reports and messages, and other documents by which alone every conference clarifies its own collective mind, and makes the world outside aware of its judgement. Every conference therefore had an enormous amount of paper work to be done against time, during its course. It could only be done by working far into the night. At Edinburgh, for instance, Archbishop Temple wrote home, 'I was writing till 1.15 last night; I wrote continuously for $4\frac{1}{2}$ hours, and so finished a draft of the Message.'[1] It was quite a commonplace sentence for him to write during any of these conferences—and he was present at most of them. On another occasion, at Jerusalem, he sat all morning in his committee, and then

after lunch I attended a small Committee because I am to be joint-chairman on the Christian Message in relation to other religions. . . . We shall have two mornings on that subject in full conference, and two afternoons on it in groups— Hinduism, Buddhism, Islam, Confucianism, Secularism. Then a committee made of the chairmen and secretaries of those groups with Speer and myself, will settle down to draft 'findings', to report to the full conference, and go on till we have done.[2]

Nor was it only Temple who was thus driven. Everybody who bore office in such conferences, and had a share in the interminable drafting of documents which had to be done, was bound to emerge at the end a very tired man.

[1] F. A. Iremonger, *William Temple: His Life and Letters* (Oxford University Press), 1948, p. 410.
[2] *Ibid.*, p. 395.

Sometimes, too, the physical conditions under which the delegates lived were not such as to ease the burden. At Jerusalem, the only way Temple could get a bath was to walk over to the Bishop of Jerusalem's house and get one there. Where he was put to live no such luxury existed. It was a hut in a long building

> with a corridor right through the middle, and doors along it into compartments five yards long and three yards wide. The furniture is a small but comfortable bedstead, and a table carrying basin, jug, etc. There is no sort of cupboard or drawer. We are partitioned to the roof on the corridor side but only as high as the angle of the outside wall and roof between the compartments. The whole thing is made of board and sounds travel. Consequently I knew all about the unfortunate man in the same row who had violent sick attacks at 1.0, 3.0, and 5.0 A.M.!! ... There is a draught in the hut this evening for some reason so my own candle is hopeless on the table. I have had to put it on the floor and write lying on the boards on my tummy.[1]

But perhaps the most exhausting thing of all was the struggle for understanding between delegates of so many different nations and races, and such widely differing church traditions. This naturally came out most clearly at the conferences on Faith and Order. At Edinburgh it proved alarmingly difficult to combine in any agreed statement the protestant anxiety for intercommunion before formal unity, and as a means to it, and the Anglican insistence that unity must be achieved first and intercommunion would then crown it. In fact, the two views were not reconciled: it was hard enough for each party to understand the other's point of view. At Lausanne, on a rather more doctrinal level, the discovery that while the Lutherans and the Orthodox both demanded a statement that the Church is both visible and invisible they put precisely opposite interpretations on the terms they both used, caused a real increase in the strain all the delegates were bearing. Nevertheless there was hardly a soul at these conferences who hesitated to say that the strain of attending them was much more than worth while, and history certainly supports them. A new thing, the 'great new fact of our time', was being born, and it was not likely to be without travail.

This 'new thing' was of such a nature that though it was conceived in the matrix of faithfulness to the missionary cause, it could only be brought to birth in the setting of the great international conference. If one looks at the actual achievements of these conferences in the particular spheres they set themselves to occupy, it is easy to be despondent about them. Lausanne and Edinburgh were exploring the path which might lead to the formal union of the Churches. They revealed a surprisingly large element of agreement among them. Stockholm and Oxford were concerned with the processes by which the 'kingdoms of this world', the actual social order in which all Churches are set, become the kingdoms of our Lord. A terrific amount of work went into them and a whole series of volumes of analysis

[1] *Ibid.*, pp. 394, 396.

came out of them, but to all appearances the twentieth century plunged unimpressed along the road to perdition. A cynic might easily say that the time and the energy of many good men, and the money of the faithful, were wasted because they did not produce immediately solutions to all the problems considered. But the giants who inspired the conferences, Bishop Brent of the Episcopal Church of America, whose episcopate of the Philippines was one of the special glories of the Anglican Communion, Archbishop Sederblom of Upsala, and, in the next generation, Archbishop William Temple, all of them busier and far more realistically minded than any cynic, did not judge their time wasted, and never doubted the value of what was being done.

The value was in the meeting, in the fact that at Edinburgh, for example, in 1937, 414 delegates from 122 Christian Churches in 43 different countries prayed, lived, and worked together, speaking in love the truth as they saw it precisely about matters of high sensitiveness, which were life and death to all of them, and by which they were divided almost as often as they were united, and yet went away not only friends for life, but with an awareness of unity stronger by far than any awareness of separation. This they did in different contexts again and again in those twenty years in centres as far apart as Madras, Jerusalem, and Stockholm. At last the ground was prepared to give this new-found unity of friends in Christ a more formal and permanent shape, and in the summer of 1937, at Utrecht, the three strands—missions, Life and Work, and Faith and Order—were ready to be woven into a single rope, and the constitution of the World Council of Churches was worked out by the delegates of more than 70 Churches, under the chairmanship of Temple. Even in the war of 1939 that rope did not break, and in 1948 the World Council of Churches had its first conference at Amsterdam. Much had in fact been done by these conferences which without them could not have been done at all for the reunion of Christendom, for the Christianizing of twentieth-century social and international order, for the whole missionary cause. But if nothing whatever had been done to further any of them, the whole series of conferences would still have been amply worth while, for through them nation and Church did speak peace to nation and Church. While governments split into fragments, dragging their hapless citizens with them, the unity in joy and co-operation in love of the Christian Churches remained a strong and enduring fact, on which, and as it seems on which alone, the nations of mankind in their search for peace can count.

III · The Missionary Seed Bed

The separate endeavours and accomplishments of all these conferences have been estimated a dozen times, and stand on record in the voluminous reports which their committees published. There is already a considerable literature about the formative years of the Ecumenical Movement and any worth-while addition to it would require not less than the space of a whole book. No attempt need therefore be made here to enumerate what each conference did. We turn instead to a broad outline of the general development of the missionary adventure during the period, in which the Church of England played a part of hardly less importance, and shouldered a burden quite as heavy, as she had done in the half century before.

Before 1918 it was becoming evident that the days of missionary pioneering pure and simple were over. Geographically speaking, the Gospel had been taken to the whole world. Just as there were no more large tracts of land left for explorers to discover for the first time, so there was no considerable part of the world where some kind of an organized Christian Church did not exist. There could be no new Columbus and no new Livingstone. This does not mean that the need for Christian expansion had passed. But in future the expansion would have to be spiritual rather than geographical, and the new ground would have to be won not by isolated Christian adventurers, however heroic, but through the work and prayer of organized Churches. The missionary's would have to be a controlled activity, for wherever in the whole mission field he might work he would be in some diocese, with a bishop set over him and some kind of diocesan organization, however rudimentary, behind him. The nineteenth-century pioneers had done their work for they had planted the visible Church in every land; and the conversion of souls, as of the forms of civilization which nourished these souls, had become, as it always must, the function of the organized Church.

Now all these missionary Churches had been founded by one or other of the older Churches in the British Empire or in the United States. They had sent them their missionaries, their bishops and clergy, and provided much of their finance. These Younger Churches as they came to be called, were thus tied by many cords to the older Churches at home. This state of affairs plainly could not and should not continue for very long, more particularly in view of the increasingly passionate political nationalism of the countries of the East. It was therefore inevitable that the universal theme of missionary discussion after 1918 should be the way in which these cords could best be severed, or at least slackened, and the Church in Africa or in China become genuinely and authentically African or Chinese while yet remaining Anglican. To use the technical term, how could a young Church become indigenous, a Church completely native in soil of its own national and racial culture?

To this problem the missionary conference at Jerusalem returned again and again. No one doubted that the Church of Christ in any land must become native to that land, but how was it to be done? The stage of growth reached in 1928 was that practically every Anglican Church had become what the members of the conference called autonomous. They were all Churches, that is, in the words of one of the delegates, whose growth has resulted 'in the transfer to these national Churches of ecclesiastical government, and the independent control by themselves of all their own ecclesiastical affairs. The adoption of credal statements, the ordination of their clergy, the admission and discipline of their members, the question of union with other Churches are wholly within the governing authority of these Churches.'[1] To have got so far from the leading strings of ecclesiastical paternalism was no slight feat. But still it was not enough to be autonomous in the sense defined above: a Church must advance towards becoming indigenous, just as the Church of England centuries ago had to advance to the fully indigenous state in which it now is. Two years before, the famous missionary statesman, John R. Mott, had suggested a definition of what the word 'indigenous' should mean. An indigenous Church, he said, was one which fulfilled these four conditions:

1. It must be natural, homelike, and belonging to the country.
2. The 'Church edifice must be planted right in the heart of the people wherever they are.'
3. Its architecture and every art it uses in worship must be native architecture and native art.
4. It must be self-supporting, self-governing, and self-propagating.[2]

But the conference was sure that 'there is not today in any mission field in the world a national Church which is either completely self-supporting or adequately self-propagating.'[3] That indeed was true, for all alike had to receive considerable grants in money from one or another of the missionary societies at home. Eventually the conference adopted this formal statement of what an indigenous Church is:

The Secret of a Living Indigenous Church

A Church, deeply rooted in God through Jesus Christ, an integral part of the Church Universal, may be said to be living and indigenous when

1. Its interpretation of Christ and its expression in worship and service, in custom, art, and architecture incorporate the worthy characteristics of the people, while conserving at the same time the heritage of the Church in all lands and in all ages.
2. When through it the Spirit of Jesus Christ influences all phases of life, bringing to His service the potentialities of both men and women.
3. When it actively shares its life with the nation in which it finds itself.
4. When it is alert to the problems of the times and as a spiritual force in the community it courageously and sympathetically makes its contribution to their solution.
5. When it is kindled with missionary ardour and the pioneering spirit.[4]

[1] *Record of Jerusalem Meeting of the International Missionary Council* (Oxford University Press), 1928, vol. III, p. 78.
[2] *Ibid.*, p. 46.   [3] *Ibid.*, p. 44.   [4] *Ibid.*, pp. 208f.

This definition, though in some ways still vague, does point clearly to the two essential marks of an indigenous Church. These are that if in Africa it must become as authentically African as the Church of England is English, and to that end must work towards the day when it can provide the whole of its ministry from among its own people.

It required action on many lines. One step was the asserting of equality of status as between older and younger Churches. Here the actual composition of the delegates to the great missionary conferences, which became steadily less and less dominated by Europeans, helped impalpably but enormously. At Edinburgh in 1910 the coloured Christians were little more than twenty out of some 1,200 members of the conference. At Jerusalem in 1928 more than a third, and at Madras in 1936 more than half the delegates came from the younger Churches. On a lesser scale the same thing had been true in China. In 1907 the centenary celebrations of the beginning of the mission to China were not graced by a Chinese speaker, and not a single Chinese sat on the platform. In 1913 the Shanghai conference of missions in China was nearly dominated by the Chinese. In 1921 the President and the Chairman of the Business Committee of the National Christian Conference of China were Chinese, as also were more than half of the members of the National Christian Council which the conference set up.

The road to the independence of the Anglican Church in China was greatly smoothed by the vision and perspicacity of Archbishop Randall Davidson. When the first Chinese national was appointed a bishop in 1917 it was Davidson who insisted that he should make his oath of canonical obedience to the Anglican Church in China, the Chung Hua Sheng Kung Hui, and not, as hitherto the English bishops in China had done, to the diocesan authorities at home. Furthermore, when in 1928 Bishop Molony of Chekiang wished to resign, Davidson not only made him offer his resignation to the Presiding Bishop of the Chung Hua Sheng Kung Hui, but he saw to it that Bishop Molony's successor was chosen by the Chinese House of Bishops, and consecrated in China, not in England.

They chose an Englishman, Bishop Curtis. A few years later they would probably have chosen a Chinese. For the road towards the status of becoming an indigenous Church has its outward and visible milestones, and these are reached when the young Church not only chooses its own bishops, but begins to choose its own nationals to be bishops. Before 1939 this had begun to happen in China, Japan, India, and Africa; and their record in the desperate years to come showed their fitness for rule and responsibility.

The growth to indigenous maturity of the younger Churches was also aided by the immemorial instinct of the pioneer missionaries of all Churches to add works of healing and education to their directly evangelistic work. In unbroken succession from Pentecost onwards the Church has always regarded the healing of the body as of hardly less importance than the healing of the soul, and one of the very first acts of all missions had been to provide hospitals, doctors, and nurses. This work went on steadily, and it was harder than it otherwise would have been for even the most embittered nationalist agitator to gain credence for his charge that a European mission, which thus served the people at the point of their acutest need, was secretly determined to exploit them in the interests of European spiritual domination. Another form of the same realization that European missionaries were in Africa or China in order to build up an authentically African or Chinese Anglican Church, and not just a new province of the Church of England, was the new missionary policy to bring into the Church whole families or villages, and to make them the unit of conversion, rather than individual converts one at a time. The great developments in missionary educational policy whereby for the first time there was close co-operation in many lands between mission and government in the whole range of public education, of which the college at Achimota is perhaps the most celebrated of many such symbols, all told the same tale. To look at the work of Anglican missions as a whole in the years 1919 to 1939 is to be convinced that the whole adventure was governed by the clear aim to lead the younger Churches as quickly as possible to the stage of development in which they could be rightly left free of all kinds of tutelage, and so become fully indigenous.

The home base in England of all this missionary activity was as alert and as energetic as it had ever been in the past. The great societies, S.P.G., C.M.S., and the others, were served by men of particular distinction and ability. They carried most of the routine burden of maintaining financially the various missions which they had founded years before, and they worked in almost perfect co-operation with each other. Behind them was the International Missionary Council, in which was concentrated a great deal of the necessary work of missionary research, and which was served by men of the calibre of J. H. Oldham and William Paton—names which stand high on the long roll of missionary heroes. There was, however, one new feature of the landscape of the home base of Anglican missions, the Missionary Council of the Church Assembly. This body was not quite the novelty which to many people it seemed to be, and it had quite a long pedigree. In 1884 two provincial Boards of Missions were set up for Canterbury and York, and within a few years these Boards sat together instead of separately. In 1908 they became the Central Board of Missions. Nevertheless the Missionary Council, which began in 1921, though a lineal successor of these, had a much more official existence because it was a Council of the Church Assembly, and therefore an organ of a statutory body. Archbishop St Clair Donaldson of Brisbane was brought back to England as Bishop of Salisbury with the intent that he should also become the first chairman of the Missionary Council, and, while neither supplanting nor attempting to supplant the traditional missionary societies, under him it became a body of great importance. Before he died he had made it an essential part of the missionary organization of the Church. Its purpose, as its first chairman saw it, was to 'cement the relationship of the Missionary Societies to each other and to the Church at large',[1] and also to be the organ of the missionary education of the Church at home. The second purpose has been splendidly achieved, but the first has caused, and still causes, a certain amount of tension.

The heart of the difficulty came over the slogan which the devotees of the Missionary Council were fond of using—the Church is its own Missionary Society. But in days gone by the societies had done the work of the Church because the Church, as a corporate body, was content to leave it to the voluntary societies. These reflected the different ecclesiastical traditions of the Church's history, and in the passage of time had attracted a great mass of loyalty to themselves through the fellowship in missionary and evangelistic work which they had provided. They had also contracted all kinds of financial obligations of the most sacred kind, and they doubted, probably with justice, whether the Missionary Council would be able to command even a quarter of the financial support which they enjoyed. Their policy throughout has been to aid the advance of ecclesiastical independence through the growth of a proper church structure of the missions they had founded, and they all took ceaseless pains to ensure that the relationship between them would be one of co-operation and not of competition. The Missionary Council in its turn has never claimed that it ought to supersede the societies, but has from time to time claimed through its annual reports that missionary Churches ought to be able to speak direct to the Church of England, as one Church to another, but that in fact they have to speak as 'Church with Missionary Society'.[2] This in turn is denied by the societies. The heart of the tension has been most neatly laid bare by the then secretary of C.M.S., Canon Max Warren, in his pamphlet *Iona and Rome*, which he begins by pointing out that

the terms 'Iona' and 'Rome' are used to symbolize two creative and contrasting ideas as to how the missionary task of the Church in the world can be fulfilled. . . . The one lays stress on inspired spontaneity working through voluntary associations, believing this method best calculated to break new ground. The other emphasizes the need for centralized direction.[3]

This tension has never, however, developed into anything which could be called a quarrel; and the record of missionary work suggests that it is the sort of tension which gives health to the whole body which contains it. Certainly the Missionary Council is here to stay, for it has done so many necessary things which could not have been done without it. Just as certainly, the voluntary societies, affectionately known by their initials, are permanently an essential part of the missionary picture of England.

[1] C. T. Dimont and F. de Witt Batty, *St Clair Donaldson*, p. 143.
[2] Quoted in *Iona and Rome*, p. 10.   [3] *Iona and Rome*, p. 2.

In the fulfilling of the Missionary Council's educational charge the name of St Clair Donaldson, Bishop of Salisbury, is of the greatest importance. When he came back from Australia he was very concerned at the fact that far too many churchpeople at home took no interest in missions and had no knowledge of them. The burden was being borne by the few, and the many were too engrossed by the affairs of the Church at home to have any attention left to spare for the Church overseas. But this, he believed, was due to ignorance, not to a fundamental weakening of imaginative sympathy. He was therefore sure that the first work of the Missionary Council must be to present the facts to the whole body of churchpeople in such a way that only the blindly insensitive could fail to hearken. He therefore persuaded the Missionary Council to set in simultaneous motion two enterprises whereby prayer might be so fruitfully wedded to knowledge as to ensure response.

The first part of the task was the creation of the Jerusalem Chamber Fellowship of Prayer. In 1925 Donaldson gathered a group of men and women round him in the Jerusalem Chamber at Westminster Abbey. They asked why the Church seemed to be relatively unimpressed by the fact of the greatest Christian opportunity in history, and they decided that it was due to poverty of prayer as well as to poverty of knowledge. They decided therefore to begin a circle of intercession to pray systematically for the extension of Christ's kingdom. Such circles have been started many times, but this, the Jerusalem Chamber Fellowship of Prayer, was unusual in that, without advertisement or publicity it quickly numbered its members by thousands in many parts of the world. They issued to their members suggestions for intercession, and rules of sacrificial self-discipline in prayer—and these were of a conspicuously high spiritual quality. Few more moving or searching acts of prayer and praise have been written than the set of prayers based on the seven objectives of the Jerusalem Fellowship, which are printed as an appendix to Donaldson's biography. The effect of all this widespread work of prayer, which amounted to something not far short of a prayer revival in the Church, was of course incalculable—hid with Christ in God. But occasional pieces of evidence cropped up to show a little of the power for righteousness set loose by this great enterprise. There were, for example, the undergraduates, who, inspired by their prayer through the Jerusalem Fellowship, persuaded their friends to join them in giving up the whole of a summer vacation to touring the dioceses in order to spread knowledge of the missionary situation. They offered themselves to the Missionary Council, who prepared them, sent them out in groups around the country, with quite remarkable results. This was only one of the tangible results of this Fellowship of prayer, and there must be hundreds of others of which no record exists.

The other enterprise of the Missionary Council under Donaldson's chairmanship arose out of his resolve to 'provide the Church with a considered policy for its work overseas'.[1] This was the World Call to the Church. The mission field was divided into six great sections, the Far East, Africa, India, the Moslem World, the Jews, and our own people overseas. The first four volumes were published in 1925, and the last two in 1928. They were prepared and written by commissions of people who had knowledge of the facts of each area. But an unusual feature was that churchpeople in each diocese were asked to take a hand in the necessary preliminary study. Donaldson's own diocese of Salisbury was asked to study the needs of India, and study groups met regularly in many parts of the diocese. Their reports were highly knowledgeable and expert documents, and their publication formed a new chapter in missionary history. The editor of Crockford, than whom no one was ever less given to uncritical enthusiasm, noted of them:

It may be doubted whether any Church has ever possessed so complete a summary of its foreign work and opportunities. The collection of the necessary statistics alone must have been a very laborious undertaking. Yet no one could possibly call any of the reports dull. The first impression they produce on the reader's mind is not far removed from bewilderment at the kaleidoscopic changes which are taking place in every part of the world, not least in what have been for centuries the three great citadels of immutable conservatism, India, China, and the House of Islam. The second, astonishment (if it is not profane to use the word in this connexion) that so much has been accomplished with such slender resources.[2]

To write and publish a series of reports so comprehensive and authoritative would have been impossible without making heavy draughts upon the specialized funds of knowledge which only the missionary societies possessed. The societies enthusiastically took their full share in preparing them, so that the most notable piece of missionary enterprise in England after 1919 was the result of willing, fruitful co-operation between the old societies and the new Missionary Council.

By 1925 the first four reports of the World Call were ready, and it remained to present them to the Church as a whole. Donaldson was quite prepared for either success or failure, and he explicitly said so in his preface. 'It may be that the facts when known will themselves act with awakening power upon the Church.... On the other hand it may be that the Church will turn a deaf ear, that the seductive influences of comfort, and the zest of domestic controversy may have paralysed her spirit.' In the event, the more hopeful guess turned out to be the true one, and the World Call was certainly heeded. But this was due not only to the informed excellence of the reports. Even more the response was due to the fact that the reports constituted a call, the World Call, and the trumpet uttering the call was sounded loudly and skilfully. Few bishops have shrunk from publicity more than Donaldson, and few could use it more fully and pertinaciously

[1] Dimont, *op. cit.*, p. 148.   [2] *Crockford Prefaces*, p. 61.

when it was necessary. The sounding of the call was admirably managed. The first blast of the trumpet was sounded at the opening conference in London in January 1925 in the ears of three thousand delegates, representing every diocese in England, every kind of churchmanship, and every missionary society. One after another the call to the home Church from its daughter Churches in China, Japan, Africa, India, and the Near East was brought home to those present. It was clinched in one of the most eloquent speeches that even Dr Lang, then Archbishop of York, ever made, who was always at his best—and *what* a best that was!—on a missionary occasion. The peroration was the theme, Now or Never:

> It may be, for all I know, a real crisis, when the Church will stand at God's bar, and the issue will be whether at this moment in the world's history it accepts or shirks its primary trust. Read these Reports quickly and you will hear behind you all the time a voice sounding like a bell, with most impressive persistency—Now or Never. The chance is here, it may be seized, or lost for ever.[1]

In the dioceses there were similar scenes, and everywhere crowds of church-people were gathered to hear the reports interpreted. One immediate result was a large and swift increase in the membership of the Jerusalem Fellowship of Prayer. Other results were seen in the increase of volunteers for missionary work and in augmented giving of money.

It may perhaps be also laid, at least partly, to the credit of the World Call that throughout the period there was a steady increase in the attractiveness of missionary literature which ranged from the twopenny pamphlet to the long and serious book, such as J. H. Oldham's *Christianity and the Race Problem*, which is one of the classics of missionary scholarship. The Church was blessed in those years by the possession of an unusual number of men and women who could write of missions with great vividness, and force the ordinary reader to see both the immensity of the issues at stake, and also how missions really were making history in changing the face of large portions of the earth. There was Basil Mathews, whose book *The Clash of Colour* was one of the most widely circulated of all missionary books; and later his mantle was donned by Canon McLeod Campbell, who, in successive annual surveys of the total missionary scene, has enriched the Church by presenting his wide and scholarly knowledge in language no less vivid and forceful. Churchpeople in these two decades had less excuse than ever before if they paid no heed to the missionary challenge.

Out in the mission field itself, which was so vast that it stretched over half the world and took in whole continents, conditions were so varied that but little experience was common to every part of it. Nevertheless there was some common ground. The missionaries in places so far apart as West Africa, Korea, India, or China did find that some of their experiences and

[1] Dimont, *op. cit.*, p. 151.

problems, however differently dressed, were basically the same. The militantly secular conception of life, with its concomitant doctrine of individual man as the slave of the collective state, was the universal and ubiquitous enemy which all had to fight. The English missionary everywhere found that his special work was more institutional than pioneering. For the most part he was wanted to man the schools, the hospitals, or the theological colleges. He had to learn to be something of an administrator as well as a pastor, and it was but seldom that he could depart into the blue to villages and settlements where they had never heard the name of Christ. The great days of the individualistic adventures in evangelism were inexorably past.

Dom Bernard Clements may serve as an example. Few priests have ever been more evangelistically minded than he. But when his abbey at Pershore (the Benedictine community of monks now at Nashdom) sent him to take charge of their work at Kumasi in West Africa, he found that he had first of all to become a mixture of architect, diplomatist, and contractor, and that success in his real business of teaching absolutely depended on his first achieving some measure of success in these other and, to him, rather alien fields.

New college buildings had to be started, endless 'contracts' achieved, some kind of domestic economy established, means of transport found. . . . In January 1928 the new buildings were started. The gathering in of the necessary funds must have been an excruciating business, even though Dom Bernard excelled in the art of begging for the needs of the church. 'This is the ninth day of building', he wrote to his mother, 'and the walls of the chapel are two feet above the ground, and the foundations of the lecture-room block are in.'[1]

By April the college was ready to be ceremonially opened; but the work was not finished. In May the builders were still busy, shouting so loud to each other that Dom Bernard's lectures on moral theology could not be given because no one could possibly hear his voice above the din. Then a tornado came, and the college was flooded, and carpeted all over with warm mud. When that had laboriously been cleaned, the planting of the garden had to be carefully planned and carried through. Thereafter he would have to

spend an arduous morning, struggling with accounts and incomprehensible balance sheets, and be defeated in the struggle. Then dry-minded business men came out to Kumasi and tried to argue with him, and on some occasions he lost his temper, retorting that he was a priest and not a bank clerk, and then turn to quick and hot repentance, and once again wage war on the demoniac ranks of figures which seemed to him so stubborn, incomprehensible, and idiotic.[2]

Such were the external conditions in which one of the greatest missionaries of the day, and thousands of others, had to labour. Success or failure in these things governed the possibility of their being able to do the real work

[1] E. M. Almedingen, *Dom Bernard Clements* (John Lane), 1945, p. 73.
[2] *Ibid.*, p. 75.

for which they had been sent out. Nor, on the other hand, could a man hope to do the one job only. Bernard Clements was sent to be the head of the Kumasi Theological College—much more than a whole-time occupation in itself. But he was also responsible for the work of the Church in the town of Kumasi, and in an area as large as Wales, with sixteen outstations. Much time, therefore, had to be spent in travelling; and often enough there were no roads. So it was with most missions. The letter from the bishop in the mission's periodical which circulated at home among its supporters was often composed chiefly of vivid accounts of his journeys, and their difficulties.

Anglican Churches overseas were educators, healers, builders, and evangelists. They received, taught, and cared for vast mass movements of converts, as in South India and the Philippine Islands, with resources of men and money quite ludicrously insufficient. But it was perhaps in their attitude to quite another institution, the institution of the colour bar, that Anglican missions in this period became most famous. The constant and outspoken condemnation of the general attitude of white settlers and of governments in South Africa towards the African nationals by all the South African bishops was most courageous. It did not make them very popular with governmental authority, but the Church in South Africa became known as meaning exactly what it said when it spoke of the equality of all human beings in Christ, and in it the coloured peoples knew they had a champion and a friend. Much the same story was repeated farther north, in Zanzibar and in Kenya, where Archdeacon Owen, among others, wrote a grand page of missionary history. So it was, too, on the other side of the continent with Bernard Clements who refused to allow the accidents of colour to make even the least difference to his relationships, and heartily rebuked such white people as did. 'May I tell you', one African wrote to his mother, 'that we Africans love your son very much. In fact there is nothing adequate to say about him except "a black man born white".'[1]

All this may seem a catalogue of comparative trivialities when set against the immensity of the storm of evil so soon to rage over the world. But in that storm the work was tested, and in the test it was shown that it was good. Of the heroes and heroines of the mission field during the second world war, and particularly in those parts of the world occupied by the Japanese, this is not the place to speak. That great story of martyred Papuan and Karen nurses, of the discovery that Christian missions could turn cannibals into saints in two generations, of the bravery, faithfulness, and privations of missionaries of every kind, has now been told many times—and these men and women have become at once our pride and our accusation. To read it is to live again in the magic of the language of Heb. 11.35: they 'were tortured not accepting deliverance'. One single indication of the proven greatness of the work when tested shall suffice. No one has ever yet

[1] *Ibid.*, p. 79.

put the essential spirit of missions more grandly than Bishop Strong of New Guinea in his now classical broadcast to his people while the Japanese were landing in their islands.

I have from the first felt that we must endeavour to carry on our work in all circumstances, no matter what the cost may ultimately be to any of us individually. God expects this of us. The Universal Church expects it. The tradition and history of missions requires it of us. Missionaries who have been faithful to the uttermost and are now at rest are surely expecting it of us. The people whom we serve expect it of us. Our own consciences expect it of us. We could never hold up our faces again if, for our own safety, we all forsook Him and fled when the shadows of the Passion began to gather round Him in His Spiritual and Mystical Body, the Church in Papua. Our life in the future would be burdened with shame and we could not come back here and face our people again; and we would be conscious always of rejected opportunities. The history of the Church tells us that missionaries do not think of themselves in the hour of danger and crisis, but of the Master who called them to give their all, and of the people whom He trusts them to serve and to love to the uttermost, even as He has served and loved to the uttermost. . . .

No! my brothers and sisters, fellow workers in Christ, whatever others may do, we cannot leave. We shall not leave. We shall stay by our trust. We shall stand by our vocation. We do not know what it may mean to us. Many already think us fools and mad. What does that matter? If we are fools, 'We are fools for Christ's sake.' I cannot foretell the future. I cannot guarantee that all will be well—that we shall all come through unscathed. One thing only I can guarantee is that if we do not forsake Christ here in Papua in His Body, the Church, He will not forsake us. He will uphold us; He will sustain us; He will strengthen us, and He will guide and keep us through the days that lie ahead. If we all left, it would take years for the Church here to recover from our betrayal of our trust. If we remain—and even if the worst came to the worst and we all were to perish in remaining—the Church will not perish, for there would have been no breach of trust in its walls, but its foundation and structure would have received added strength for the future building by our faithfulness unto death.'[1]

By this missionary faithfulness history was made. But even this was not an isolated instance of faithfulness. It was, in a sense, a dramatic climax, a sacrament of many generations of faithfulness on the part of thousands of entirely obscure and unknown men and women of the Anglican Church, who knew that they must take the Gospel to the ends of the world, and continue to serve their people to the ends of time. They have created far more than they could ever have dreamed. The existence of the Anglican Communion can be credited to them. The Ecumenical Movement was embedded in their work. The hope of millions of the underprivileged in all parts of the world was and is built of their fidelity.

[1] Ruth Henrich, *South Sea Epic* (S.P.G.), 1944, pp. 22, 23.

PART THREE

1939–1965

21

The Nondescript Years

THERE ARE just a few epochs in history which, unlike John Donne's island, are entire of themselves, each one with its own beginning, middle, and end. Though they are of course always parts of the ceaseless flux of history, yet there is a sense in which they are separable from it, and distinct in their own right. In the history both of this nation and of its Church, one such episode is the period of the thirty-one dark years which began in August 1914 and ended in August 1945. War is their theme, a ceaseless war carried on first in one way, then in another, and then in the first way again, a long fight to dominate or to defend the soul of man and its freedom. Once before there was a Thirty Years War in European history. That was the first, and one might possibly call 1914 to 1945 the Second Thirty Years War.

On August 4, 1914, the war began. History, reeling from the shock of it, shook herself out of her antique paths and began to move on a quite new course. That day has been called, in the title of a book describing all that happened in it, 'The Last Day of the Old World', and indeed it was. It was the day of that world's suicide. That war was a blunder: it is just possible that it might never have happened. The war of 1939 was planned, and there never was much chance of avoiding it. The planning was done in the interval of twenty years, partly by fighting but mostly by intrigue. Those years never were anything more creative than a continuation by other means of the same titanic struggle for the freedom of the human soul. In September 1939 the old war flared into open and unconcealed life again, like a volcano erupting once more after a period of shaking and grumbling. But it was the same volcano. In August 1945 it blew itself out at last, and on that day the history of England, of Europe, and indeed of most of the world, passed into an entirely new phase. Ever since then we have been grappling with a total novelty, not least the novelty of knowledge that any future world war must be the last, for it could destroy all life on this planet.

The twenty-one years' interval between the two parts of the same war must either be read in some such way as this, or founder into meaninglessness under the weight of its disappointment, even its shame. Only if these years are regarded as an integral part of a Second Thirty Years War will they escape in the long run from the historians' epitaph of total insignificance.

What is true of the nation in this period is true of the Church as well. Though there are subtle differences between them, they cannot be disentangled. All through history Church and nation share their glories and their shames; and the shame of both was then the terrible contrast between an honest and steady desire to do what was right and creative, and an almost absolute failure to achieve either. The nation, or the state, longed for peace, tried to work for it, and for its pains got in the end the war its very fear had helped to make certain. The Church longed to take its Gospel to all the people, that through their Christian discipleship they might find the things belonging to their peace. In this it worked desperately and valiantly. But what it actually achieved was a wider gulf between the Church and the mass of the people than ever before, and the idea of the Christian society as coterminous with the English nation was further from achievement in 1939 than in 1914.

Of the record of the Church of England in the 1914 war some account has already been written in earlier pages of this book, and the many efforts made by the Church from 1918 to 1939 were described. The snap but inevitable judgement on them must be that they were hapless. Not often has such a sustained wealth of effort produced so microscopic a result. The sphere of the Church's work in providing decent homes for people living in slums was, as we have already seen, an exception to this depressing record of effort unfulfilled. After all, a house is a concrete thing and a lasting achievement. Where it is built, there for a long time it stands, and someone lives in it. Nor is there any doubt that the tireless propagandist work of the prophets of the Christian social movement, led by William Temple, was really effective. It undoubtedly prepared the ground for a better understanding by the Church of the social revolution which came after 1945, and a clear discernible line joins this long effort of persuasion to the Beveridge Report on Social Insurance, and to the revolutionary social legislation of the post-war Labour Government which this report did so much to shape.

No doubt some would judge that this effort or that deserved a better epitaph than anyone can now write for it, and an age in which men of the calibre of Lang, Temple, Henson and Garbett sat on the bench of bishops was not starved of leadership of a high quality. But they were very exceptional even in their own mitred company, and, except for J. H. Oldham, the period of lay leadership had not yet come. There were those who wrought valiantly through all those years, and the efforts they launched were many. But taken all together they produced little lasting change for good, and it is probable that success was impossible from the start. The whole nation, and the Church with it, was crippled by the terrible loss in the trenches of a whole generation of the very best young male life of England. The intellectual climate of English life became steadily more and more hostile to the Christian religion itself, to all its moral values and their restraints, and especially to the Church which was generally understood, by a sense impression as invincible as it was unarguable, to be the visible embodiment of everything the people as a whole were hot to repudiate. Through all those twenty years it was never possible for the Church to do much more than keep its machinery oiled, its wheels turning round, and to maintain itself in being. That it contrived to do just this through so many years of mediocrity and indistinction was a testimony to its unfailing sense of pastoral responsibility. Heroic success in Church or state was just not on the maps of the day.

The resumption of the open war in 1939 provided many different circumstances from the first round of the conflict in 1914. It was always more possible to regard the war of 1939 as a crusade because spiritual wickedness in high places reached such a pitch of sheer diablerie that it spread with the velocity of a forest fire, and none could pretend that it was other than it seemed to be. The slaughter, though grave indeed, was, so to speak, more discriminating. Air raids took the place of trench warfare, and actual battles were periodic and limited in space and time rather than incessant. There were many days, perhaps most days, rather than just a few, when one could say that 'all was quiet' on every front. Thus the slaughter was by no means confined to one class only, all the world's young men, but ran through whole societies, picking victims of every kind here and there. The actual suffering was probably more terrible, but also far less irreparable, and the wastage was quickly made good. It is hard to think of any good thing, except victory, which came out of the 1914 war, and easy to think of many good things coming out of the 1939 war.

Of the reaction of the Church of England to the war of 1939 there seem to be few dramatic tales to tell. Insofar as the clergy represent the Church, they were in a position, because of the kind of war it was, to take a much fuller share in the general suffering of the people, whether in uniform or out of it. Large numbers of them immediately became service chaplains, leaving their parishes at home for years on end to the care of curates appointed by the bishop, which, as we shall see, was later to become a source of unexpected embarrassment to all concerned. The chaplains were in no way at all sheltered or feather-bedded. They faced all the dangers of the fighting men, and, often enough, suffered and died with them. They became prisoners of war, dragging out the boredom of the weary years in prisoner-of-war camps in Poland, and at the end of the war performing prodigies of contrivance bringing out their men through all the obstructive confusion of Soviet Russia; or they accepted long spells of suffering, sickness, sometimes torture, and often death on the Burma Railway or in the prisons of Malaya. At home they shared with their people the weariness and the danger of the air raids, and, with hardly an exception, they stood fast and took whatever came, and they faithfully tended their stricken people at the moment of their greatest need. It is on record how the Provost of Coventry (Richard Howard), looking sadly at the total ruin of his cathedral, was inspired to see beyond the material catastrophe and find hope in the symbolism of the event. The destruction stood for the eternal experience of the Cross, but for Christians this presupposes a resurrection; and one day, he vowed, the Easter garden of a great new cathedral should stand in all this desolation, and through it peace and reconciliation be preached to the nations. It was his sure hope, and he lived to see the fullness of his desperate dream. Most of the dramatically heroic stories of the Church in the war came from the younger missionary Churches in Malaya, New Guinea, the South Sea islands, and other lands occupied by the Japanese; and a sample of these heartening stories has already been given in this book.

It may, or may not, be coincidence, but it is certainly fact that in those years lay apologetics of a quite new, even an original, kind began to appear from the press, and did much to redress the scandal of the mass apostasy of the intellectual world from the Christianity which had served all their forefathers. It was during that war that Charles Williams, exiled to Oxford with the University Press he served, began to lecture there and became well known. Most of his 'spiritual thrillers', which expounded the Faith in a new way, were first published in the years immediately before 1939,while his directly theological works, *The Descent of the Dove* and *He came Down from Heaven*, and all his explorations of the symbolism of Dante and his exposition of the Arthurian corpus of legend, were published while the war still raged. But it was by his Oxford lectures, by his genius as the spiritual confidant and adviser of the young men and women still in the university, and by his persistent and ceaseless stream of journalism, that he became so widely known and deeply admired and won a large audience for his earlier books. He died very young, in the summer of 1945, but he had already risen to the eminence of one of the foremost expositors of Christian truth of his day, and his reputation is still bright.

The power and originality of both C. S. Lewis and Dorothy Sayers, and, for that matter, of Charles Williams as well, has been estimated in an earlier passage, but it was during the war that an acknowledged authority as Christian spokesmen came to them all. And on this wide throne they were joined by T. S. Eliot, whose *Four Quartets* was published in 1944, and also by Robert Bridges, the Poet Laureate, whose long epic, *The Testament of Beauty*, though first published in 1929, was read widely throughout the war as the number of editions it went through in those years shows. All of these found new and challenging ways of presenting the truths of the Gospel, and the philosophy underlying the Christian Faith. What these and other writers did was to make Christian theology exciting again, and to do much to restore to the Church, which had for long years lost it, the reputation of intellectual respectability.

To use Coleridge's word for the interpreting class, the clerisy of 1918 and onwards to at least 1930 had mocked, fumed, and sneered, and had used their high literary skill to destroy much of the spiritual and moral armour of men's trust, while creating little, or nothing at all. The clerisy of 1939 were men who had a creative spiritual purpose, and their eyes were bright with it. Their steadfast and original service of the Kingdom of God by their pens did much to ensure that the Church was able to enter the new world of 1945, and to be sure of a fair hearing from educated people when she tried to interpret its novelties in the light of Christ.

When in 1944 the war was clearly seen to be drawing to its close it was already plain to many that a new epoch of history would come quickly to life when the fighting ended. What the new promised land would be like none could then know, and few even guess. That it must be very different from the waste land in which for thirty years men had stumbled vaguely in search of their identities and their souls was both the universal determination, and implicit in the scheme of things, in the shape which they had taken. There was then one man, and one man alone, whom the Church was trusting to lead it over the chasm of divide; a man who, though undeniably belonging to the old world, and exemplifying it at its best, was known to have the prophetic part of his sight trained on the new world he undoubtedly knew we must enter.

This man, William Temple, who had for many years carried a heavier burden than any man should, was therefore preparing to shoulder in addition the weight of the Church in the unknown future. The Church was thrusting it on him because there was simply no one else who could carry it; and though an exclusive reliance on any one man, however gifted, is always bad for any Church, there was at that time no help for it. The miracle of Temple was that he carried so much for so long, and the whole Church was content that he should. For he was a portent the like of which none had seen before and few would see again, and he attracted a tribute of sheer admiration which did not fall far short of the attitudes proper to worship.

> But as for Caesar,
> Kneel down, kneel down, and wonder,

said Enobarbus in tones of awe though he was still Antony's man. The words only just stop short of idolatry, but they do capture the feelings which Temple kindled, albeit unconsciously, in very many of the clergy and laity, and more particularly of the young men he ordained himself.

It would be difficult to exaggerate the shock of dismay which stunned the Church when he died so suddenly on October 26, 1944. It was entirely unexpected. He did not expect it himself. His last letters show that he had no idea at all that he lay in danger of death. It was well known that he was ill, but it was supposed that his malady was no more than a very obstinate attack of the gout which had periodically laid him low all through his life. When he died of a sudden thrombosis the news struck numb with dismay all who had come to rely on him, and almost on him alone, to lead the Church into a better future. All of a sudden their world seemed to be emptied of comfort.

Upon the immensity of his achievement the curtain of an unanswerable finality had fallen. He whose powers were so phenomenal had gone. Through all the years of his life they had been steadily concentrated upon the service of the Kingdom of God, and so the multiplicity of his talents had been held together and intensified. No storm shook him. Through all the dark days of war he stood still in the order of his service. He suffered, as in modern war all men must, but he remained serene, and he gave steadfastness to a thousand weaker spirits. In his last years a new gravity came over him, and the vast laughter which had for so long characterized him had gone from him. The reserve and the mystery which always had underlain his immediacy of response to relationships came nearer to the surface of his personality. Those who knew him only in the last years of his life could hardly have echoed the epitaph of the Cumberland dalesman, 'He was a very jolly man', with which F. A. Iremonger winds up his biography.[1] He had been once but was not now, and this new gravity perhaps suggested a wholly unconscious perception—for there is no evidence of it in any of his later letters—that he was nearing the end of his journey through this world. But this only added to the sense of strength which flowed from him.

It was no wonder that when he died there were some who were unable to understand how God could have allowed it. But it may be that God was to be praised and thanked. The passage of time enables us to see now what could hardly be seen then, that in fact the train of his powers had already run into its natural terminus. He had already come to the very edge of all possibility. For more than twenty years the history of the Church had revolved round him, and a weight of trust had been placed on him which no other man of his time could share. When these are the facts the death of the hero is a shock which makes all his followers reel, but the blow may sometimes turn out in the end to be a healing surgery.

Was it not also the crowning mercy bestowed upon the hero himself? At the time it was a man who had admired him but constantly criticized him who almost alone saw that clearly. In a letter to Cyril Alington, then Dean of Durham, written on November 12, 1944, Hensley Henson said:

I think he is *felix opportunitate mortis*, for he has passed away while the streams of opinion in Church and State, of which he had become the outstanding symbol and exponent, were at flood, and escaped the experience of their inevitable ebb.[2]

[1] F. A. Iremonger, *William Temple*, p. 631.
[2] *Letters of Herbert Hensley Henson*, edited by E. F. Braley (S.P.C.K.), 1950, p. 159.

There is no doubt that Henson judged rightly. Even during his last year at Canterbury there were, as we can now see, signs of a just turned tide, the faint beginnings of a slow retreat. Those who have read the collection of his letters written towards the end of his life can hardly have missed the evident signs of recession. Had he gone on longer he must have repeated himself, and soon the Church would have noted the repetition and been disappointed. Moreover, most of the enterprises with which he had been so long associated, theological, social, ecumenical, had, by reason of the war, been put into cold storage. Could this very tired man have breathed fresh life into them when the day of the possible reanimation dawned? It seems very doubtful. His work had been done, and there was now no more that he could do. It was perhaps the last of God's many mercies to him that he was allowed to pass without pain and at peace into the world of permanence and complete fulfilment. He was spared the experience of that desolating sense of failure which, however unreasonably, so often darkens the last days of the best.

Among those who came to his funeral in Canterbury Cathedral on the last day of October there were probably few who realized how fully he had lain 'under the Mercy' when he died. Their minds were filled with grief, and not less with triumph, and perhaps also with their need to grapple with a future looking momentarily empty. The day was grey and drizzling and the setting sombre. A dank wind sent clusters of dead brown leaves scurrying round the feet of the people waiting to enter the cathedral, and when they came in they found but little natural light. The service breathed a quiet and restrained solemnity of triumph for a very great life. Poignant and stately it moved through the liturgical rhythms of death and resurrection, and came to the last hymn:

> The strife is o'er, the battle done;
> Now is the victor's triumph won.

While it was being sung the domestic chaplain, Ian White-Thompson, took Temple's pastoral staff from the lid of the coffin, and placed it on the altar in token that the office it symbolized had been taken away from one archbishop and must soon devolve on another. The coffin was hoisted on to the shoulders of the bearers, all of them sergeants of the East Kent Regiment. While they slowly carried it out the choir sang the centuries-old prayer:

> God be in my head, and in my understanding;
> God be in my eyes, and in my looking;
> God be in my mouth, and in my speaking;
> God be in my heart, and in my thinking;
> God be at my end, and at my departing.

It was what had happened, a statement of accomplished fact. God had always had free course in every part of his life, and his enormous wealth of natural powers and talents had from the beginning been divinely directed.

Of all the innumerable company of Christian people who had sat at his feet, or had been privileged to know him, none could doubt that God the Lord, to whom alone belong the issues of death, had been with him at his departing no less than through all his life. Elegies of grief and anthems of gratitude saluted him as he went forth now on his last journey in this world, and an epoch of history went with him.

This epoch had indeed come to its irreversible end. Temple's life marked the final end of Victorian Christianity seen at its best, and he, more than any other churchman, had summarized and crowned all that was best in it. In all essentials he had himself been among the most eminent of the Victorians. Almost all of his attitudes to the deep problems of human life in God's world he inherited from his illustrious father, Archbishop Frederick Temple. Though the ways in which these attitudes were expressed changed in his hands, growing much more temperate, their essential nature remained the same. Exactly the same theological and moral certitudes were to be seen in the son as in the father, but also the same eagerness of welcome to new knowledge, the same unshakable conviction that at the last love must conquer all, the same essentially paternal attitude of Church to people. Both were very forward-looking men, and, largely through his long leadership of the Christian social movement and the Ecumenical movement, William Temple built a bridge across the deep chasm which yawned between the last decades of the Victorian world and the very different world of the mid-twentieth century. Across this bridge the Church advanced to claim for Christ the bewildering promise of the new world of revolutionary turmoil. But, like Moses, he was not himself allowed to enter it. Some future historian may well judge that Temple's summary of the best of the Victorian epoch, and his greatest service to what has succeeded it, lay in the welcome he bespoke from the Church to the social revolution which he prepared for but did not live to see.

22

A New Archbishop in a New World

I · *The Appointment of Geoffrey Fisher*

TEMPLE WAS buried on October 31, 1944, but it was not until January 2, 1945, that Geoffrey Fisher, Bishop of London, was officially invited to succeed him. It was a moment in history when the Prime Minister might reasonably have felt dazed by the amount of business which crowded daily upon him, though he showed no sign of it. It was not Churchill's way to delegate to others any appointment which belonged, through the Crown, to his office; but it was his way to procrastinate longer than most of his predecessors with ecclesiastical appointments, and this was in part due to the fact that he knew little about the Church of England. Even so, the delay was absurdly protracted and has never been satisfactorily explained. Cyril Garbett, Archbishop of York, fumed about it and called it a scandal: 'We are like a Government without a Prime Minister.'[1] Much business was held up until the appointment was at last made, but it was not chiefly for this reason that the delay was of some importance. It probably matters even to the Kingdom of God that the right man should be made Archbishop of Canterbury. For an archbishop above all men it is necessary that there is no suspicion of intrigue or bargaining, of using the appointment to reward political friends or of withholding it to show disapproval of old critics. An untoward delay therefore does matter in the economics of the Kingdom, and once the reasonable limits of waiting have been reached, each further day sets rumour free to fertilize suspicion.

Fisher's appointment was made public just too late to keep rumour dumb. Speculation about what really happened behind the scenes has gone on ever since, and it has never been either satisfied or quelled. Enquiry has come to centre round one question: if George Bell, Bishop of Chichester, had not made speeches criticizing obliteration bombing by either side in the war, would he rather than Fisher have been offered the appointment?

[1] Charles Smythe, *Cyril Forster Garbett* (Hodder and Stoughton), 1959, p. 296.

Since evidently he was not offered it, was he passed over as a punishment for his outspokenness, or had he never been on the list of those who were possible? The Crown keeps close counsel and the questions have never been answered. It follows that the suspicion remains strong still. There were then and there are now some, perhaps more than is known, who would have greatly preferred the appointment of Bell, and Professor D. M. Mackinnon spoke for them in the March 1963 number of *Theology* in an article on 'Justice'. He was urging how necessary publicity is to the doing of justice, and suggesting by implication that the benevolent dictatorship of the head-mastership of an English public school is not a good apprenticeship for an Archbishop of Canterbury. He then added this footnote:

The historians of the Church of England may yet recognize that the worst mis-fortune to befall its leadership in the end of the war was less the premature death of William Temple than his succession by Fisher of London, and not by Bell of Chichester.

The root of the objection which this speculation crystallizes is the suspicion that Bell would have been more evidently a modern man of the modern world, and less of an aristocrat benevolently ordering a paternalistic world for its own good. There may be some truth in this, for in Fisher there always was the slight touch of the eighteenth century, while every instinct Bell had and every impression he made was of the twentieth century alone. But Bell too was essentially a Victorian struggling to be modern. It is true also that Fisher disdained, while Bell valued, much of what the modern world appears to enjoy and even to heed. Fisher's scorn of the press was not only a weakness, but a serious mistake. Bell might have been equally disdainful (it is so often hard not to be), but he would not have shown it so openly, and therefore would not have earned himself so bad a press. But as to whether the modern world would have gained by the appointment of a more contemporary-minded archbishop than Fisher was, and so be less distant from the Church than it is, is no more than a speculation, and certainly it does not follow. Experiment is always important, but then so is continuity, and Fisher gave equal weight to both sides of the equation.

It does not look as if at the time any other name was seriously considered. Garbett of York, his biographer tells us, was tentatively sounded, and replied at once that it was out of the question because of his age.[1] Mervyn Haigh, Bishop of Winchester, was spoken of by some, but his already failing health made the choice impossible. Garbett's judgement at the time was that Fisher was the only possible choice, and he added prophetically that though he was a man too little known outside the Church his sheer good-ness and ability would carry him along his difficult road.

Thus there succeeded to the throne of St Augustine one of the least

[1] Smythe, *op. cit.*, p. 296.

known archbishops for many years. But he was not quite an enigma, and what was generally known about him was significant. He was known to combine the firmness of a disciplinarian with the kindness and charm of a man who really cared for people, and found a point of contact with every person he met. His mind was both subtle and far-seeing. This enabled him to come quickly to the heart of each problem brought to him, so that he could reduce it to its simplest form and so deal with it. He was a skilled administrator, who enjoyed administration and was as much at home with financial statistics as the good manager of a bank. He had the untroubled health of a strong man, always one of the first qualities of a successful archbishop, and could bear long strain. His immense powers of concentrated industry made astonishingly few drafts upon the resources of his nervous system. By these qualities he had reduced the undisciplined chaos of the diocese of London to pattern and order, and that without losing a friend or making an enemy.

All this was known. The list of qualities so far is one which would sit well on the shoulders of any good civil servant. It is impossible to say that he was more or less a man of God than other bishops. He had his spiritual reticences; he observed them and expected others to observe them in return. The most inward springs of his life were not on view, but that they truly nourished him none who had knowledge of him doubted. A deep and real humility was his most obvious spiritual quality, and only those who are stayed on God can be truly humble. Garbett, who saw deeply into most men, perceived it, and prophesied that, yoked with his unusual ability, it would give him the power to grow into the measurement of his new charge.[1] His faults, the occasional bursts of asperity and the sudden assumptions of the authoritarian attitudes of the headmaster of a public school, lay no deeper than the surface of his life. He irritated with them but he never hurt. Humility seasoned all. Twenty years later it was to enable him to lay down his great office without any fuss, with no pangs because he was no longer at the centre of things, with none of the backward-looking regrets such as most of his predecessors had voiced. He laid himself quietly on the shelf of dispensability, and became the cheerful assistant curate of a west country village. His tenure of office was memorable; the manner of his leaving of it was unforgettable. If he was not one of the most spectacular he was certainly one of the better archbishops of modern history. The Church took little hurt from his hands, and gained much from his leadership.

II · *The New Pilot Takes Over*

The new Archbishop of Canterbury was enthroned on April 19, 1945. He assumed his great office with characteristic quietness. He made no large gestures of speech but simply promised to do the best that he could. In one way he went into Lambeth Palace at a moment fortunate for himself. The

[1] *Ibid.*, p. 297.

war in Europe had one more month and the war in the Far East four more
to run, and even after the fighting had ended the preliminary sorting out
of the chaos all over Europe must take a long time. One consequence would
be that the normal pressure of daily work on Lambeth (which Lang had
called incredible, indefensible, and inevitable) must be lessened. Other
archbishops had been flung into the frenzy immediately after enthronement,
and without so much as a single day's breathing space. Fisher was luckier.
His first year in Lambeth Palace was probably the easiest of all, and he had
time to think and pray. The temporary slackening of the Lambeth business
and of the archbishop's public engagements also gave him a chance to take
the measure of the tendency of the Lambeth organization to smother an
archbishop under the incessant pressure of the work it provides for him.
Fisher was the first archbishop for a very long time who actually succeeded
in taming the machine's well-meant efficiency and found a way to avoid
being daily drowned by waves of paper. But even for him that might not
have been possible if the machine had been running at full stretch on the
day of his enthronement.

Every Archbishop of Canterbury knows well that he must be faithful to
all the duties of his daunting office, and therefore that he must spend most
of his time in doing exactly what every other archbishop has done. This
can easily take up the whole of his time and energy, and if he allows this to
happen he will never make any personal mark on the history of his Church.
But Fisher, most properly, meant to bestow upon its life some contribution
which should be all his own, and, providentially, he had this fallow period
of nearly twelve months to think what it should be.

His actions thereafter left no doubt of his decisions. He had resolved to
devote himself and all the resources of the position he held to the achievement of two primary purposes. The first was the reform of the administrative procedure of the Church, without which it must continue to be impossible to pay the clergy adequately; to set administration free to fulfil its true
purpose, the enabling of the pastoral ministry; and to restore to the Church
the spectacle of an obedient clergy within an orderly society. The second
aim or purpose was infinitely more important. It was to make it his special
business, even his vocation, to further and to deepen the togetherness of
Christian people everywhere, both inside and outside the Churches of the
Anglican Communion.

The facts of his primacy can be read in no other way, and throughout the
whole of it, but especially in its early years, no purpose could have spoken
with the direct immediacy this had to the condition of the generality of
people everywhere. For he had to operate for long years in a jaded, frightened and uneasy world in which the years of terrible suffering had spent all
passions but one, the desperate search for some unity of man to establish
real peace, and in which each person might at last find some answer to the
perplexing riddles of his own identity. The frightening sense of the insecur-

ity of the human position was in England contrasted with the reality of the social revolution set in breakneck motion by the legislation of the new Labour government of 1945. It produced an affluent society, poverty at last banished, with lots of money for all, but not much to eat, and a flourishing black market, with modern Nyms, Pistols, and Bardolphs disgracefully dominating the social scene. From the Church's point of view there were too few giants of the calibre of Fisher himself, George Hubback, Metropolitan of India, and Geoffrey Clayton, Archbishop of Capetown, available to deal with it. The impression of a serious lack of distinction would fade, but for a long time to come most Christians must be weary and their world unsettled and too flat. Moreover this post-war world showed by every aspiration to which it gave voice that it was out for nothing less than the unity of all mankind everywhere and without exception. In international politics this mastering desire was to be voiced by the contradictory ideals of a world organized around the insights of Karl Marx, the United Nations, or smaller groupings of peoples like the North Atlantic Treaty Organization, or the Community of Europe, or such federations as the United Arab Republic and the Indonesian Republic. In commerce the whole trend was towards fewer and far larger units of trading, groups of companies, common markets, and take-over bids. There was everywhere a disapproval of competitiveness, an exploration of the many roads which might give to men a unity instead of a separation in all that belonged to the needs of their common life, politics and culture. And all the time this undefined, inchoate, but most real desire was mocked by the constant triumph of every old force, like all the new nationalisms, which embedded the separation of man from man ever more deeply.

In a world of maddening frustrations like this the new archbishop had to work, and he framed his primary policy to swim with rather than against the tide. To the idea of world unity through politics, trade, or culture Fisher could have nothing influential to say. To the idea of ecclesiastical unity between hitherto separated Churches of Christ he could have much to say which would be profoundly influential, and he determined to say it. In so far as he could have any success at all, it would reinforce and encourage all the forces working for unity on still larger stages. An achieved unity of Churches could have an influential effect on the progress towards political and commercial unities, and indirectly but truly work for the world's peace. There Fisher determined to put all his weight. When at last the history comes to be written of how the Churches of the world at last found the way to their own unity as one holy catholic Church of Christ, the name of Geoffrey Fisher will have an honoured place of a creative pioneer.

It was in November 1945 that Fisher took the first step towards the fulfilment of his purpose. Since one of the great difficulties in the way of promoting the unity of separated Churches is the wide difference between the catholic and the protestant temperaments, and the deadlock it often causes, he thought that to have this deadlock examined by a group of catholic theologians might help to clear the air. He invited Dom Gregory Dix, a monk of Nashdom Abbey and an historian whose big book *The Shape of the Liturgy* had made him famous, to convene a group of catholic-minded theologians 'to examine the causes of the deadlock which occurs in discussion between Catholics and Protestants, and to consider whether any synthesis between Catholicism and Protestantism is possible'. This group, which had T. S. Eliot as one of its members and met under the chairmanship of Michael Ramsey, the present Archbishop of Canterbury, went to work in a most leisurely way and did not publish its quite short report until the summer of 1947. It had some valuable things in it and particularly an exposition of the function of catholicism within Anglicanism, But its members appeared to see no ground, other than their own vituperative hostility to what they called liberalism, on which catholics and protestants could stand together. The group met for the last time in January 1947, and sent the typescript of their report to the archbishop. He thanked them kindly, and drily commented on the disparity between excessive analysis and meagre synthesis. They had worked too slowly. Long before Fisher had even read their work it had been made irrelevant to the cause it was supposed to serve by the quick passage of events. Weary of waiting longer, the archbishop had acted on his own.

His quiet thought had taken him to the point where he knew he had something new to say about reunion, and a fresh proposal to make. Meanwhile he had been invited to preach the University Sermon at Cambridge on November 23, 1946, and this, he thought, would be the right pulpit and the right occasion for what he had to say. He would seize and use it to declare his full mind. The sermon, 'A Step Forward in Church Relations', was, judged by the practical results it had, one of the most influential of our time.

The archbishop began in the classical manner with an exposition of his biblical text, but soon moved forward to a declaration of his purpose. 'It is of the unity of the Church that I want to speak.' The real problem now was how to get inter-Church discussions started again, and to find competent theologians and historians who were willing to give any more time to them. In the past they had always come to deadlock, and unless there was a fair chance to get beyond the old boundaries nobody was anxious to begin such talks all over again. Deadlock had produced a kind of paralysis of the negotiating will.

I sense (declared the archbishop) a certain reluctance to begin at all. A distinguished theologian has recently expressed the opinion that all schemes of reunion should be postponed until further study, theological thinking and prayer in all Christian communions have led them to a recovered apprehension of the integrity and balance of Christian Truth, alike in the sphere of Faith and in that of Order, based on a renewed understanding of the Scriptures of the Old and New Testament and of the witness of Christian antiquity. This is to suggest that nothing should be done until the theologians have begun all over again and reached agreed conclusions: the past does not suggest that such theological unanimity will come in any foreseeable future.

The whole process was urgent. It could not be allowed to await the dilatory pleasure of academic theologians with their cautious distinctions, their laboured definitions of the indefinable, their petty splitting of hairs. Reunion negotiations were like a hopeless tangle of traffic at a road junction. Nothing could move until the jam had been cleared. The archbishop did not trust the theologians to clear it for him.

Nor did he have much hope of the dynamite of what he called the constitutional method. It had been tried time and again and always it had failed to get anywhere. For the Church of England it was the least promising of all methods of searching for unity. It would at once call into question the status of the Church 'as by law established'. Worse still, it might compromise the identity of the Church of England as the matrix of the whole Anglican Communion.

Its position in the Anglican Communion requires that the Church of England should not confuse its own identity. It is the nodal point of that Communion. It is one thing for four dioceses in South India to go out of the Anglican Communion into a province with a constitution of its own and a position within the Catholic Church still to win. But for the Church of England to go out of the Anglican Communion would disrupt that Communion itself by depriving it of its nodal point.

This was to say that discussions between Churches about their constitutional positions, or about their differences over their principles of ministry and sacraments, led nowhere. Yet it was vital that reunion discussions should begin again, since for some years now it had been stuck motionless at a dead end, with no road forward or backward.

The archbishop, therefore, in a phrase destined to become famous for at least two decades, suggested in the pulpit of Great St Mary's that the Free Churches might consider 'taking episcopacy into their own systems'. Before he came to his actual proposal by which he hoped the processes of reunion would be set moving again, the archbishop produced his credentials and outlined his motives:

There is a suggestion which I should like in all humility to make to my brethren of other denominations. We do not desire a federation: that does not restore the circulation. As I have suggested, the road is not yet open, we are not yet ready for organic or constitutional union. But there can be a process of assimilation, of growing alike. What we need is that while the folds remain distinct, there should be a movement towards a free and unfettered exchange of life in worship and sacrament between them as there is already of prayer and thought and Christian fellowship. . . . My longing is not yet that we should be *united* with other Churches in this country, but that we should grow to *full communion* with them. As I have said and as negotiations have shown, no insuperable barrier to that remains until we come to questions of the ministry and government of the Church. Full communion between Churches means not that they are identical in all ways, but that there is no barrier to the exchange of their ministers and ministries.

The archbishop then made and defined his new proposal:

The non-episcopal Churches have accepted the principle that episcopacy must exist along with other elements in a reunited Church. For reasons obvious enough in church history they fear what may be made of episcopacy. But they accept the fact of it. If they do so for a reunited Church, why not also and earlier for the process of assimilation, as a step towards full communion? It may be said that in a reunited Church they could guard themselves in the constitution against abuses of episcopacy. But they could do so far more effectively by taking it into their own system. The Church of England has not yet found the finally satisfying use of episcopacy in practice; nor certainly has the Church of Rome. If non-episcopal Churches agree that it must come into the picture, could they not take it and try it out on their own ground first?

After this the archbishop soon left the pulpit. He had launched his ship. He had made it clear that he meant to steer his course by the star of the service of the cause of reunion, and he had staked much on the new proposals he had made to start the whole process moving again.

He had been very successful. Together with the Lambeth Appeal of 1920, his Cambridge Sermon constitutes one of the red-letter days of the whole movement. For a long time the sermon achieved only its immediate purpose of getting the discussions started again. In 1951 the editor of Crockford summarized five documents and reports of such discussions, and acidly remarked that they were studded with all the usual and discouraging words like 'formidable barriers', 'unresolved tensions', and the like. 'Other familiar phrases of this weary company reveal the long journey ahead and the probability of its ending at its starting point.' The Crockford Prefaces have never been remarkable for their blithe spirit or even for their faith, but in 1951 it was true that the situation was still discouraging. No one could then foresee the distance we have all travelled since then. Today, as we shall see later in this book, the rawness has all been charmed out of the air, and in the field of reunion things are now happening which even as recently as 1960 would have been utterly inconceivable. How much is owed to the Cambridge sermon preached in 1946 it is hardly possible even to guess, but it did take the movement out of the deep freeze and got inter-Church discussions started again. There is surely a connection between the sermon and the new proposals for communion and finally organic unity between the Methodist Church and the Church of England. It had been one of the most effective of modern sermons.

Fisher knew well that the Church of England could not any longer serve the great cause of Christian unity merely by reiterating the somewhat stale shibboleths about being a bridge Church between protestant and catholic

Churches. The service would have to be given through her membership of the whole Anglican Communion in which, as he pointed out in his Cambridge Sermon, she held a key position. But again, the service of the Anglican Communion could only be given fully if this great federation of Churches was at peace and unity in itself, achieving a high degree of spiritual togetherness, which, in turn, was possible only if the Anglican Communion was deeply conscious of itself as an identity in Christendom with a deliberately pondered mission all its own. He therefore made the fostering of this self-conscious unity the secondary integrating concern of his own archiepiscopal ministry.

In one way and another he laboured at this through all his years. The Lambeth Conference was the first instrument of this purpose (though not the only one), and in 1945 it was obvious that the first thing to be done was to summon the next Lambeth Conference as soon as possible. The last had met in 1930, so that the next was already five years overdue. But memories of the 1930 conference were not happy. In more ways than one it had been the least successful of the whole series, and the whole body of the American bishops, and some of the Canadian ones as well, had not found it a very happy experience because it seemed to them to be managed too exclusively by the English episcopate. With this experience, and the inability in wartime to give much heed to the tending of the bands which bind the Churches of the Anglican Communion together, the knots had become dangerously loose. There was no question of the American bishops refusing to come to another conference, but it would be no good if they did not come gladly and willingly, and with a full expectation that it would be an experience which they enjoyed.

In 1946 therefore Fisher made the first of his many journeys abroad. He went to the United States and to Canada with the purpose of using his gifts of diplomacy to the full. He visited many of the American and Canadian bishops and charmed them. It was a most successful pilgrimage, though, on the surface, a very simple one, and it passed with but little notice at the time. But in the event it had a considerable importance. Had he failed the Lambeth Conference of 1948 would still have been held, but it might easily have been the last. If it is true that this first post-war conference had an integral part in the gradual refounding of the Anglican Communion's consciousness of itself and its mission, then the archbishop's first overseas pilgrimage played an important part in the process.

It also established the healthy precedent that an Archbishop of Canterbury in the modern world must be a constant traveller. Garbett of York had been doing this for some time in the past, and would continue for an astonishing number of years in the future. But York is not Canterbury, and Fisher was the first Archbishop of Canterbury to be constantly on the move around the different centres of the Anglican Communion. To this he owed what was one of his great strengths, that what happened in

Kenya or Nigeria was to him every bit as important, and just as real and immediate, as what happened in Westminster. He had put away from him the slightly parochial view of his office which his predecessors for many years seemed to have held.

The other primary purpose which Fisher set himself to fulfil was to bring the organization and the administration of the Church out of the eighteenth century in which it was still lingering and into the twentieth. It meant, as this kind of reform always does, a great strengthening of the hands of the central bureaux of administration, and it carried a number of disadvantages. The Central Board of Finance in Westminster, and its subsidiaries, the several diocesan Boards of Finance, in being given freedom from the hampering of many archaic regulations, were necessarily given powers to exercise this freedom which seemed to many parishes to be as dictatorial as they were expensive. The power of the purse was held by central committees of various kinds, and though their strings were unloosed and they poured golden largesse in the shape of grants of every kind, it did, and does, often seem to the parishes as though the Church has become rather like an ecclesiastical civil service, governed not by its bishops but by a string of committees against whose decisions no appeal lies. On the other hand the steady increase of the stipends of the clergy, which was one of the main purposes Fisher always had, would never have been possible if the Church Commissioners had not been given the freedom to invest their money freely, like any other commercial concern, in whatever stocks or real property promised a better return than the old restricted investments could ever do. The price to be paid for skipping a century and a half and bringing the Church's administration suddenly into line with modern requirements was heavy, but the cost of failure to do it would have been heavier still.

III · *Three Reports: Evangelism and Atomic Power*

As the war drew slowly towards its end many in the Church began to wonder what its special work must be in the next phase of its life, when the strains of the moment had lessened, and there was time to pray and think again. At the end of any tremendous ordeal a people who have survived it must, if they are not wholly insensitive or eaten up by the *hubris* which the Greek gods always avenged, wonder for what purpose they have been saved. To this question the Church of England, just because it is the established Church of the realm in the sense in which others are not, could return but one answer. Its purpose at all times in general, and in 1945 in particular, was and is the same purpose—to lead the nation in preparing the way of the Kingdom of God. The Church is evangelistic or it is nothing. It lives by its search for the Kingdom of God or it dies. It seeks for converts or it rots. It tries to bring all the institutions of the nation under the obedience of Christ or it withers. Ultimately it has no purpose other than and beyond this. All its worship, all its scholarship, its every sacrament, all its pastoral work must contribute to this overmastering preoccupation with the Kingdom, or they are words and rites operating feebly in a void.

In the same way, just as an established Church must be evangelistic in spirit, so it must be prophetic in speech. The conception of the Church as the embodied conscience of the nation has often been contested, but it is certainly true that the Church is expected to deliver some judgement on every moral crisis which arises. In 1945 one of the supreme crises of all history suddenly burst upon a totally unprepared nation. The Japanese war was ended summarily by the dropping of two atomic bombs on Hiroshima and Nagasaki. None but the few knew that weapons so dreadful existed, but when the news of what they had done and could still do was given to the people, all knew instinctively that a new and a terribly dangerous era of history had been born. The demand at once made that the Church of England should declare its mind on weapons such as these was perfectly reasonable. There are some moments when an established Church has no right to be dumb and this was one.

The Church, then, remembering that there never was a moment when evangelism was more plainly necessary, and conceding the reasonableness of the demand for some guidance on the frightful problems of atomic power, entered the post-war phase of history with the reports of three special commissions in its hands, the first on evangelism, and the other two on the moral issues of the atomic age. She had at least been very prompt in producing them.

The report of the Evangelistic Commission, pretentiously entitled *Towards the Conversion of England*, was in many ways an ill-starred document. The Commission, appointed in 1943 by William Temple, was potentially a very strong one. It contained many people of high distinction, who were gathered from all walks of life save one. The whole working-class area of life was left unrepresented. Its chairman was Christopher Chavasse, the then Bishop of Rochester, the most charming but also the most obstinate of bishops. He would, and he did, fight almost to the death for every detail that he personally wanted to see in it. Much time was wasted in trying to make sure that what other members of the Commission wanted to see in their report actually appeared in it when it was published. The Commission worked hard and fast, and in the end produced a report which at least most of them could conscientiously sign, though at one time this looked as though it must be impossible. The report had a sub-title, 'A Plan dedicated to the Memory of Archbishop William Temple'. The latter sentiment was vindicated by the inclusion of quotations from his various works as sub-headings to the different chapters. But a plan is what it never was.

To those who felt profoundly uncomfortable because they saw no answer to the question of what the Church of England could do to show by her evangelism her gratitude for the salvation of the nation, the report had little comfort. No one really needed it to tell him that he lived as a member of a national society in serious danger of ceasing to be Christian in any recognizable sense. The analytical part of the report made that point clearly enough. It was by far the best part, but it only put clearly and vividly what almost everybody who thought at all already knew so well. The remedial part of it consisted of little more than suggestions that this or that experiment might be tried. There was no recognition at all of the fact that a great theological crisis was developing, and of writings like those of Bonhoeffer the report showed no awareness. Yet already his were the points destined to be pregnant for twenty years or more ahead. Thus in spite of the high authority of the names of the men and women who signed it, in spite of the fact that it was read and debated in every rural deanery of the land and in most parishes, it remained a very damp squib which has had no identifiable result of any kind, except for one, namely that it does seem to have done something to inspire the Mission to London, of which some account is given on a later page. For the rest it was a long and heavy piece of work which was without visible result, and a contribution to the sad ministry of frustration.

The two reports which the Church produced on the challenge of the newly discovered atomic power spoke far more immediately to what the whole nation knew to be its real condition. As soon as the war was over it was to this issue that the Church at once addressed itself. To those who asked then, and have so constantly asked since, Why doesn't the Church say something about the atomic bomb?, the answer is that it did say something, and that with urgent promptness, and that what it said was well pondered, very responsible, and went straight to the roots of the problem. It is doubtful whether anyone having authority heeded the guidance of moral theology in the use and abuse of atomic power, but at least no one could fairly complain that none had been provided. The work was done with great speed. There were two commissions, and they were connected in the sense that the report of the first was the subject matter of the deliberations of the second, and the cause of its ever having been appointed at all.

At the end of 1945 the British Council of Churches appointed a commission under the chairmanship of Dr J. H. Oldham, 'to consider the problems created by the discovery of atomic energy'. Its report, *The Era of Atomic Power*, was written and published in less than a year, which must be nearly a record. Published by the SCM Press, it could be bought in the shops in May 1946. The Church Assembly immediately debated it and was not wholly satisfied with it, for it passed a resolution requesting the Archbishops of Canterbury and York to appoint a second commission to consider the work of the first. Gordon Selwyn, Dean of Winchester, was the chairman of this second commission, and its report, *The Church and the*

Atom, was published by the Press and Publications Board of the Church
Assembly in 1948.

Each of these reports was impressive, and rightly releases the springs of
admiration in those who read them today. But they impressed for very
different reasons. *The Era of Atomic Power* was very much the product of
the Ecumenical Movement and bore all its characteristic insignia in the
style and method of its writing. It was rather vague and diffuse in speech.
It lacked the scholarly precision of its successor, and it was full of words
like 'dialogue' and 'involvement' which had already become the jargon of
the movement, and which some years later drew wrathful comments from
Professor Gordon Rupp when, in an article in *The Guardian*, he called the
Ecumenical Movement 'the First Murderer of the Queen's English'. All the
same, it was a solid piece of reasoning. It was emphatic on the terrible
dangers to the world which had been unloosed by the exploding of the first
two atomic bombs; but the members could reach no unanimity among
themselves as to whether the new bomb, and its still more terrible successors, might rightly be used in another war:

We have no solution of the dilemma to offer. If the final test were to come in
another war, the members of the Commission would almost certainly find themselves divided in their choice; and this division is only a reflection of the present
divided mind of the Church.

That is a non sequitur. The dilemma reflected the division in the mind of
the nation, even of civilization itself, rather than merely of the Church.
Men were divided as citizens, not as churchpeople.

What is chiefly interesting about this report today is, first, the evidence
it gives that the Churches were so quickly awake to the realities of the
problem, and realized their duty to give what help they could; and, second,
that the diagnosis of the spiritual weakness of the time was so surprisingly
forward-looking. It is, for instance, in this report of 1946 that we find described for the first time since the eighteenth century the contemporary disbelief in the idea of progress, and a cynical attitude of mind and speech
towards the mere possibility of it. Due and very necessary warnings were
given of the danger of a widespread decay of the once common assumption
that progress really happened and was written implicitly into the very
scheme of things. It was a prophetic piece of wisdom.

It is also interesting to find in this report what must be one of the earliest
summonses to Christians to seek for what Oldham and his fellow commissioners clumsily called Otherworldly Worldliness, and today we call Holy
Worldliness:

To say that what the world needs today above all else is an other-worldly worldliness is an easy intellectual assertion. It can only be given life if each individual
man is prepared fearlessly to search for and lay bare in his own heart and mind
the existence of this conflict and the urgent temptations that arise from it.

It will be seen that this report raised, perhaps for the first time in a Christian context, many of the desperate problems we have been thinking about ever since. But it could indicate no solutions and hardly so much as a clear statement of the principles on which, one day, a solution might be found. But the British Council of Churches served the day well in promoting it, for it put the real issues clearly before all who read it, and it provoked and prepared the way for a far better report on the same subject.

But its total effect was not held to be satisfactory by the Church Assembly, and the reason for this is shown by this passage in the second report, *The Church and the Atom*:

Unanimity and moral certainty are notoriously hard to come by whenever circumstances shaped by sin drive conscience to a choice of evils. As will appear, there are points at which we too disagree. We are therefore too painfully conscious of the glass about us to think of throwing stones at our predecessors. But we cannot, like them, make a virtue of necessity and claim that to 'live with the dilemma' and 'endure its torment' is a beneficial discipline. We believe that the soul seeks peace and certitude, not tension and paradox, as the condition of its sanctification; and, at the risk of labouring the obvious, we would point out that, where we have expressed two conflicting opinions, they may both be 'probable' (that is, supported by solid reasons) but they cannot both be right.

That is delicately but incisively put. The conflict among the members of this second commission did not arise over the morality of having used, or intending in the future to use, atomic weapons of war, for all were sure that the use of the bomb was in any case wrong, some thought relatively and others absolutely wrong. But the wrongness was asserted and the rightness denied by a unanimous judgement:

A majority of the members of this Commission is unconvinced by the plea that the object of the use of atomic bombs against Hiroshima and Nagasaki was not destruction, but the administration of a 'psychological shock' which would end—and in fact did end—the war immediately. The minority is impressed by this plea, but is not prepared to defend the details of what was done.

It was at the very point of the report's originality and strength that this division among the members of the commission was confessed. This was the exposition of the centuries-old teaching of the Church on the conditions of the Just War, and the debate on whether these conditions ought still to have force. Was it true that the whole conception of war as 'just' if those who waged it abided by the canonists' rules and restraints, and unjust if they broke even the least of them, had become so theoretical as to be absurd? It might well be so, but then so much the worse for the world.

To read *The Church and the Atom* today is to be struck by its depth, its originality, and also by the evidently wide learning of the distinguished moral theologians who wrote it. They took their time over the task laid on them, and so were able to produce a profound examination of war when seen as the catastrophic consequence of human sin. While sin continues to exist, war must always be possible. Therefore while the long-term purpose of the Church has always been to serve under God in the conquering of sin, and so to abolish war altogether, the short-term function of the moral theologian has been to work to keep the practice of war within clearly drawn bounds, to make clear where these boundaries of morality in war ought to lie, and thus to mitigate the suffering of the innocent. This the Church has done by its theory of the Just War. The best chapter in the report is the one in which the whole body of the Church's thinking on what makes a war just or unjust is summarized. From this the commission constructed a theory of the rules of morality in modern war, and applied it to the events of the particular war which had so recently ended.

The commission was thus led unhesitatingly to denounce the obliteration bombing of whole cities which both sides had practised in the war just ended. What had happened in Cologne was no more and no less wicked than what happened in Coventry. It denounced firmly all the pretensions of unlimited national sovereignty. 'Christians cannot admit unlimited rights of any kind, and must therefore resist all claims that a sovereign state is entitled to do what it pleases.' It was also emphatic and outspoken in its condemnation of the demand for unconditional surrender, which, on the principles of the Just War worked out in the Middle Ages, it is immoral for a victor to impose upon the vanquished, since it turns him into nothing better than a victim. On the other hand the commission held that these same principles enabled them to pronounce as moral the retention of the atomic bomb in a nation's armoury, on the ground that it is a government's duty to prevent as much as it is to resist aggression, and the existence of atomic weapons can be (and in fact has been) a deterrent.

This sober and scholarly investigation by moral theologians was so excellently done that few modern readers could fail to admire it. But it built a large edifice on the careful principles of the Just War which the mediaeval canonists had worked out. These principles were, and in theory still are, part of the canon law of Christendom, and it was surprising to see how firmly they stood when applied to the very different circumstances of the war just ended. They provided a perfectly adequate ground for the great independence of moral judgement about different features of the war which the commissioners had shown. But was it after all an academic debate, and were the commissioners living in cloud-cuckoo-land? What chance was there, the cynic might reasonably ask, that any nation engaged in a war for survival would pay any heed to a set of mediaeval canonical rules to govern the waging of war?

Gordon Selwyn and his fellow authors were well aware of that. But it is the business of moral theologians to speak the truth as they see it on the issue under their judgement. The fact that people may not listen does not absolve them from this duty. Once launched, an atomic war can be restrained by no principles at all since it must at once destroy the whole power of the very civilization which ought to restrain it. But this is not necessarily true of a conventional war, and most wars are still of that type. Even today there are enough Christians among the nations to persuade their governments to keep the violence of acts of war within the limits of what Christendom has laid down as constituting a just war. But that is on condition that they know what these principles are and why they exist. In setting them out so clearly, this commission served well both Church and state at the time, and might one day do so again.

As moral theologians whose view of life is embedded in the scriptures as well as in the tradition of the Church, the members of the commission were well aware of all the difficulties the realist would see, and did not forget the mockery the cynic would indulge in. So long as sin exists insecurity must exist alongside it, and war remain a constant danger. Its chairman, Gordon Selwyn, spoke for them all in a striking passage in the foreword he personally wrote:

Nations live under a more fearful and urgent menace than has ever faced mankind before. Insecurity of this kind produces certain well-known reactions: the Epicurean's 'Let us eat and drink for tomorrow we die' is one of the commonest. Another is fatalism and the apathy that so often accompanies it; yet another the simple paralysis of fear. Christianity has its own reaction to conditions of this kind. Recognizing that fear and the consciousness of menace have disastrous spiritual fruits, it translates the object of the fear from the outer to the inner world, declares the insecurity of life to be one of its fundamental assumptions, and claims that not pain and physical death but sin and the 'second death' are the only true objects of fear.

The second of these atomic reports was in fact one of the ablest and most thorough documents of its kind which the Church has produced in the last twenty years. It offered no facile solution to the most perplexing of modern problems, no easily optimistic comfort to the fearful, or the tormented in conscience. It did not offer these things because it could not. What it gave the Church was a survey of the problem when seen from a Christian point of view. But it faced the facts. It put them in the context of the immemorial moral theology of the Church, and it showed to all who heeded it the path which led to the only sure peace which this world can properly offer.

Thus the Church quickly made attempts to grapple with the bleak world of peace at the point of its deepest intransigence. By the end of 1946 who could fail to see how sombre this world was? It was a world of hardening separations. It was the world of the Cold War and the Iron Curtain; the world of the young self-conscious nationalisms in India, Indonesia, and most of Africa; a world in which the very instrument of chiefest hope, the United Nations, was hamstrung by the veto; a world growing more 'secular' in organization and spirit; a world more mobile than ever before, and yet increasingly a neighbourhood, in which people remained steady and settled in their habitations in proportion as they remained primitive in their way of life; a world teeming with millions of displaced unfortunates and separated families, cold and hungry and hopeless; a world to which the Church must find new ways of ministering or fade away, slowly and ignominously, into the mists of history. The three reports were all part of the ministry of frustration; but this may sometimes be creative and potent in the end.

23

A Year of Anglican Stocktaking

I · *Inventory*

THE FIRST four years of Dr Fisher's primacy form a distinct and a definable period in the last two decades of Anglican history. In so far as this history forms a story which can be written chronologically, the year 1948 is the first stopping-point. Since 1945 the Church of England had necessarily been sorting itself out after the long disturbance and chaos of war, and struggling to find the best pattern on which to rebuild its life amid all the new circumstances. By the end of the year the new archbishop's policies were all in full view, and the first two major events of the period, the first post-war Lambeth Conference and the First Assembly of the World Council of Churches at Amsterdam, had both taken place. The life of the Church of England and the whole Anglican Communion in 1945 was like a great commercial concern in a state of confusion because no one had been able to make a proper inventory. By 1948 the inventory was almost complete. The themes dominating Anglican history through the years to come were listed plain to be seen. The page was turned, the new chapter of history ready for action and study.

In 1947 the royal assent was given to the instrument by which India and Pakistan were made independent sovereign nations. The event was at once greeted by a terrible butchery as the two new states confusedly jostled for position. It was most severe but it did not last long. Thereafter the Church in that vast part of Asia had to reconnoitre to find its new function, and it was clear that a new page in the history book of Christian missions had been turned. Much of the work of the Church would go on and much would end, and the spirit in which all had been done would be made anew. None could then assess the coming change but none could fail to recognize its signs.

Also in 1947 the King and Queen, with the two princesses, paid their state visit to South Africa; but the general election of the next year ended the long reign of Field-Marshal Smuts and replaced him by Dr Malan, heading his triumphant and, for many years, invincible nationalist party. One consequence was the proclamation of a republic, and thereafter South Africa's repudiation of her membership of the British Commonwealth. The repressive attitude of the nationalists towards all the black and coloured peoples of the land was well known, and did not fail to be implemented. Thus another great nation into which the Church of England had lavishly and for years poured her resources of men and women, buildings and money, became, like India, a missionary question mark. South Africa was indelibly marked on the map of Anglican consciousness by a stain, which would remain there for years.

In 1947 William Ernest Barnes, Bishop of Birmingham, published his notorious book, *The Rise of Christianity*, which by its wild negations of so much of the Gospel narrative and its unscholarly procedures and unscientific assumptions made many wonder how he could conscientiously remain a bishop, and earned him a formal reproof from the House of Bishops in Convocation. Its inadequacies of scholarship minimized its influence, and in fact it marked a theological dead end. But it was one call of the warning trumpet that the day of major theological restatement was coming, and with this task the Church has been occupied ever since. Perhaps too it served the necessary purpose of reminding the Church that reforms in administration could not easily be separated from changes in theology. For in that same year the administrative reforms had begun. Negotiations were in train between the Ecclesiastical Commissioners and Queen Anne's Bounty to find the way to achieve a union whereby one duplication of administrative machinery could be simplified. The agreement was signed in 1948, and the two organizations became one with the new title, the Church Commissioners.

Much thought was also being poured into the effort to find better and stronger bonds of cohesion between the Churches of the Anglican Communion. This exploration was reaching forward already to the larger purposes of defining for Anglicanism its function within Christendom as a whole, and of defining the relationship of the Anglican Communion to the World Council of Churches. In 1948 all this had been crystallized by Bishop William Wand of London who then published his composite book of essays by various writers called *The Anglican Communion*.[1] Much of its importance came from its timing, for it was an attempt to explain just at the right moment what the phenomenon called Anglicanism really is.

By 1948 therefore it was evident that anyone who studies the Church of England in the most recent phases of its life is not grappling with any narrowly parochial theme. His mind must be in Capetown and Delhi almost as constantly as in Canterbury and York. Nor is there a way of telling the story of the Church of England and her fortunes in the last twenty years in isolation from all the other Churches belonging to the

[1] Oxford University Press, 1948.

Anglican Communion from Greenland to Peru and from Washington to Tokyo, of which the two provinces of Canterbury and York, geographically so tiny, are still the nodal point. The history of any Church is always what it does with its theology, and theological study knows no frontiers of Church or state. There, every Church learns from every other, and has a concern with every other. The concern becomes yet more intimate in the tracing out of the desire for church unity, and, in a period when this is the chief of all the leading themes, it is impossible even to think about the Church of England without also thinking of, say, the Methodists, the Presbyterians, and, still more since the Second Vatican Council, the Roman Catholics.

The history of the Church of England has very seldom been purely insular and, ever since Victorian times, it has become international. The chief form this internationalism takes in this period is to make the history of the Church of England the story of othernesses struggling to be fused into togetherness, always with her assistance, sometimes under her protection. No boundaries of race or colour apply. And the Anglican struggle fits into and complements the struggle of all the world in the same period to find unity and to escape division. It has been tragically unsuccessful so far because the forces of separation are strong, and there is incessant conflict between the centres of power around which the othernesses might cohere. The Church of England is only one of the forces trying to find ways to serve this larger unity. But in the last twenty years all her efforts have been consistently directed to the search for the wide unity of the world itself approached through the unity of the world's Churches.

II · *The Church of England After the War*

All these hopes of ecclesiastical leadership depended, as always they must, upon the spiritual health of the mass of the clergy and their people. But immediately after a major war no Church can be filled with creative vigour. Before even the wind of God can blow right through it, there must be a preliminary period of reconstruction to correct the consequences of so giant a disturbance, and a time of convalescent repose to heal bruised spirits. The four years which end with the Lambeth Conference in the summer of 1948 form a prologue to the drama of the Church's story in the first twenty years of the uncomfortable peace. As they passed, almost every major problem with which the Church had to grapple between 1945 and 1965 became visible and took identifiable shape. With nearly all of them we are grappling still.

When the war ended the Church of England was in no condition to undertake the exacting service of any new cause. Aerial bombing had destroyed many of its churches and schools, but this kind of damage was not serious in any decisive sense. Church buildings could always be replaced and in a few years most of them were. What was much more serious was the dispersion of so many members of most of its congregations as the result of the kind of war it had been. Few parish churches ended the war with more than a fraction of the regular worshippers they had when it began. For a Church still parochially organized a chronically mobile population is a very serious matter. Since 1939 the constant changes of the place where one lived as well as in the circumstances of living had been on so vast a scale that restlessness had become a habit, and had bred the loss of the old desire to settle down in a home with the intention of staying there till death. But this kind of settled stability is exactly what the Book of Common Prayer presupposes. It compresses between its covers the ethos of a Church ministering through many parishes to settled communities of God, composed of people and families who normally are born, live out their lives, and die in the same place. For very many years this had not been true of English life as a whole, but after 1939 it became most exceptional, and it is unlikely to be true again for further ahead than we can see. But rootless people are seldom contented. So it was that after 1945 the Church had to minister parochially as best she might to a people suffering from the malaise of a deep discontent. It made the dialectic of love very difficult to maintain, and many of the presuppositions of the Book of Common Prayer exceedingly irrelevant. The people as a whole had become psychologically and socially difficult for a parochially organized Church to serve, and even to reach; and the parochial system had become too irrelevant to too many lives for it to be possible to work it at more than half strength.

In addition to all this, the Church was bound to be relatively crippled by the shortage of its clergy for several years to come. For five years very few men had been ordained, while the normal loss by death and retirement had not ceased. This situation had naturally been foreseen, and some of the service chaplains had been charged to search for and encourage likely young men in uniform who might become the ordination candidates of the future. They found many and kept in touch with them. They sometimes set up impromptu pre-theological schools for them. On demobilization most of these men passed into special schools or theological colleges, but at best at least two years after the war were bound to pass before any could be ordained, and even then the difficult manpower situation of the Church would be little relieved for at least two years longer still. By 1945 many parishes were without vicars. Some had been deliberately kept vacant by the bishops in order that when the war ended there might be parishes to offer to service chaplains returning to civil life. Many other parishes were held by men too old and too tired who in normal times would have retired long ago but had gallantly continued to hold the fort which no one else could man.

This situation was made yet more embarrassing by a decision which seemed to be plainly right when it was made, but which nevertheless worked badly as time went on. In 1939 it was made a principle of national policy that every man who left his job to serve in the armed forces of the crown should, as a matter of right, be reinstated in that same job when demobilized. This was done in order to avoid the grim spectacle of officers and men who had fought for their country having no work to go to when the war was over. This had been a major scandal in the aftermath of the 1914 war, as indeed the unwanted ex-soldier had been the mocking consequence of almost every war in history. For the layman the transition of war to peace, aided by a carefully thought-out and fair demobilization system, worked more smoothly in 1945 than ever before. The ex-soldier no longer presented an unmanageable problem.

The same principle was applied by the Church to the clergy who became service chaplains. To those already incumbents of parishes it was promised that when the war was over they should return to the parish they had left if they so wished. For five years therefore such men, and they were many, had been vicars in absence, and their parishes were looked after either by their curates or by some priest whom the bishop appointed. The system worked ill. It made much bad blood. The curate-in-charge often had to find rooms because the vicarage continued to be occupied by the vicar's wife and family. There was sometimes trouble over what proportion of the benefice income should be paid to the curate-in-charge and how much remained the property of the absent vicar, who was in any case drawing the full salary of a chaplain. In addition it happened very often that the people who had been served for five years by the curate came to think of him as their vicar, and sometimes preferred him.

When general demobilization began this well-meant plan became very embarrassing. Chaplains who had been away on active service for five years were naturally eager to get home again and resume their normal lives and work. In this desire they found an unexpected sympathizer in Hensley Henson, at one time Bishop of Durham, and then living in retirement in a Suffolk village of which he himself was acting as curate-in-charge. In December 1944 he wrote in his diary:

I cannot think it wise to ignore the 'claims' of the army chaplains who will have been withdrawn from pastoral work in England for at least six years. They may find the positions which normally would have been assigned to them occupied by men whose principal claim to appointment was their presence in England, and the urgency which forced patrons to fill the parishes without delay.[1]

The words were prophetic. In May 1945 Japan was still undefeated and no one could then guess that her surrender was only three months away. On the defeat of Germany some chaplains were inclined to demand their immediate demobilization, and to argue that for the rest of the Japanese war their places should be taken by a new and different set of priests. They

---

[1] *Retrospect of an Unimportant Life* (Oxford University Press), vol. III, 1950, p. 282.

were, moreover, far from satisfied with the announced demobilization procedures as they applied to them. This situation became so awkward that the Archbishop of Canterbury asked Mervyn Haigh, Bishop of Winchester, to go out to Germany and the Low Countries and to investigate the grievances of the chaplains, and to suggest remedies which both they and the chaplains' department of the War Office could accept. Haigh was a fine ecclesiastical diplomatist. He had the gift of friendly sympathy untainted by any sentimentality, and could cut his way quickly to the heart of any situation, however complicated its trappings might be. He succeeded in his mission, and after his visit no more was heard of the complaints of the disgruntled chaplains, nearly all of whom were quickly released and allowed to go back to their parishes at home.

This episode—it was no more—was an instance of how history may resemble and yet differ from its precedents. In 1918 the service chaplains disturbed the Church by their impatient eagerness to get their reforming hands on the ecclesiastical machine. Their desire then was to have a share in making it the kind of Church more fit to welcome returning heroes, and better able to build swiftly the City of God. In 1945 neither the chaplains nor their men had much belief in visionary dreams. They were as urgent as their predecessors in their demands for release, but it was simply because they thought, very naturally, they had been on active service long enough, and they wanted to come home. But for the disturbance to so many parishes caused by so long an absence of their rightful vicars, and for the sadness and disillusion of the curates who had been so long in charge of them, and had done so well, there was no easy remedy. These things worked themselves out in the end but it took a long time.

III · *'Lord, What is Man?'*

The first Labour government with unassailable power was returned by the general election of 1945, and at once it proceeded to build the social revolution. By controls of every kind, by state planning on the widest scale, by nationalization of many industries, by the taming of the power of finance, and by the national health service the whole outward shape of English life was changed. It did not make a comfortable society, and many hard-won liberties were cavalierly treated. On the other hand the centuries-old curse of economic insecurity, of grinding poverty, of the power of class privilege, had been banished once and for all. A whole national society, reasonably to be called affluent, had been brought into being. The achievement was astonishing. At no point in all this process did the Church of England, or any responsible body within it, try to halt it, nor yet to impede it by undue nostalgic criticism. For years past the Christian social movement had been pleading in advance for the Church's glad welcome to some such event, and all this torrent of persuasive words had not been without effect. The Church was as eager as the people to build Jerusalem on this material earth, and saw the enterprise as part of the Gospel itself.

Only by state enterprise and parliamentary legislation on the widest scale could such a goal be pursued; there was no other conceivable way. For this the Catholic social movement had for years been pleading, and trying to persuade the Church that there was no necessary contradiction between state action and Christian social doctrine. Most of this prophetic work had been done in France and Germany, but their voices did reach these shores and helped to save the Church from the negative criticism that state action accorded ill with evangelical freedom. The thing was to build Jerusalem at top speed, and if this could only be done by the action of the state, then so be it. No criticism could therefore reasonably lie against the Church for being too lukewarm, or even hostile, to the general trend of the revolution in the first few years after the war. On the other hand most of her members were benevolent beholders rather than active partisans. Though it had tried very hard, the Christian social movement had not succeeded in seriously modifying the old tradition that Churches must have as little as possible to do with politics.

The nation had been made secure but not contented, and the chief criticism lying against the Church in those years was its failure to see where the discontent lay, and to try to find some remedy for it. State action which necessarily interferes with many privacies may produce some mighty good which could never have been achieved in a less drastic way. But of necessity it is bound to diminish private as well as public freedoms, and to produce in all kinds of people the frustrating sense that as against the state or any of its instruments they are utterly powerless. So questions were bitterly asked about whether the individual person had not been reduced to a cypher, to an impotent cog in a machine. No feeling is so quick to breed discontent even among those who were sure that even this price of the revolution was worth the paying.

There is no need to labour this point, for it is obvious and has been endlessly written about. What the Church at that moment appears not to have discerned is that all such ephemeral questions raise an eternal one about the personal identity of a human being, and that this was very much her concern as being part and parcel of the Gospel itself. What is man? How in modern circumstances can a citizen claim the rights of individual personality, and what are those rights? How can a man be content unless he knows and cherishes his own personal identity, and how is this identity different from all others? What right grounds are there for him to make any such claim, and by what practical steps is the claim urged? Such questions as these may have been very dimly perceived by so many who felt themselves wounded because there appeared to be no answers, but the wounds were real and they hurt. Of this vital matter the Church of England in those years showed little awareness, and yet it was indeed its concern, for this was to be its vital battlefield in years to come. Some prophets were indeed addressing themselves to it, the existentialists and writers like Martin Buber, for example. But such voices were little heard in this country, and it is a probable judgement that one root cause of whatever ineffectiveness the Church of England may have shown in the twenty years since the war is due to her failure to perceive in time the point on which the whole weight of her thought, prayer, and witness should have been brought to bear.

At the time there was a man in France who saw more clearly. Teilhard de Chardin, a priest of the Jesuit Order and one of the foremost scientists of the day, was not then well known in England, though in France and many parts of Asia his was already a familiar name. In 1949 he read a paper to a learned society at Les Moulins in which he addressed himself to precisely this, the major human problem of the post-war world. He called it, significantly, 'The Heart of the Problem'. He began by reckoning with the fact that all his hopes of progress turned on the solution of the religious problem, but of this he could see no hope at present, though he was sure that he knew what the solution must be.

Among the most disquieting aspects of the modern world is its general and growing state of dissatisfaction in religious matters. Except in a humanitarian form there is no present sign anywhere of Faith that is expanding: there are only, here and there, creeds that at the best are holding their own, where they are not positively retrogressing. This is not because the world is growing colder: never has it generated more psychic warmth! Nor is it because Christianity has lost anything of its power to attract: on the contrary, everything I am about to say goes to prove its extraordinary power of adaptability and mastery. But the fact remains that for some obscure reason something has gone wrong between Man and God *as in these days He is represented to Man.* Man would seem to have no clear picture of the God he longs to worship. Hence the impression one gets from everything taking place around us is of an irresistible growth of atheism—or more exactly, a mounting and irresistible de-Christianization.[1]

He was sure that the trouble lay in an unrealized but deep conflict between the aspirations of the modern world to move forward, unaided by God, to a glorious future for man in this world, and the aspirations of the Church to carry man upwards to the union of himself with God in some world other than this. He was naturally thinking of his own Church when he wrote these sentences:

By definition and principle it is the specific function of the Church to Christianize all that is human in Man. But what is likely to happen (indeed, is happening already) if at the very moment when an added component begins to arise in the *anima naturaliter christiana,* and one so compelling as the awareness of a terrestrial 'ultra-humanity', ecclesiastical authority ignores, disdains, and even condemns this new aspiration without seeking to understand it? This authority, which is no more nor less than Christianity, will lose, to the extent that it fails

[1] Pierre Teilhard de Chardin, *The Future of Man* (Collins), 1964, p. 260.

to embrace as it should *everything that is human on earth*, the keen edge of its vitality and its full power to attract. Being for the time *incompletely human* it will no longer fully satisfy even its own disciples.[1]

But what he said was as true of all Churches as it was of his own: and his remedy, the divinization of matter, or the putting of an equal effort into the building of God's Kingdom on this earth as into the preparation of souls for heaven, applies all round. For there his trust was placed. Churches must go forward with the world as well as upward beyond the world.

Let there be revealed to us the possibility of believing *at the same time and wholly* in God *and* the World, the one through the other; let this belief burst forth, as it is ineluctably in process of doing under the pressure of these seemingly opposed forces, and then, we may be sure of it, a great flame will illumine all things: for a Faith will have been born (or re-born) containing and embracing all others— and, inevitably, it is the strongest Faith which sooner or later must possess the earth.[2]

These were tones not heard in England until several years later, and then in the form of discussions about such matters as the real meaning of the word 'secular', whether it was a term of abuse or whether to be a secular man was a title Christians should gladly claim. Our contemporary debate is almost confined to the ground where theology, sociology, and psychology join hands to discover and to assert the vital truths about modern man, his neighbour, and his God. But by the Church of England, as by the Roman Catholic and other Churches, this truth of strategy was hardly perceived for another ten years or more, though it is understood now. But in 1948 this, perhaps the most important theme of all, was still lying hidden under the level of consciousness.

IV · Amsterdam and Lambeth

When William Temple was enthroned as archbishop in Canterbury Cathedral in 1942 he spoke in his sermon about the Ecumenical Movement, and, in a phrase which at once became famous, he called it 'the great new fact of our time'. Before the war it already existed in germ form, and much preparatory work to make it possible had already been done by such bodies as the Faith and Order Movement and the International Missionary Council. This work had been so persistent and successful that by 1939 the seed had grown into an identifiable body, and although during the years of war the whole movement had to be put into cold storage, it was deemed possible to call a giant conference of all the non-Roman Catholic Churches of the world, with which the Orthodox Churches of the East associated themselves. Thus the First Assembly of the World Council of Churches met in Amsterdam in 1948, and a new chapter of ecclesiastical history was begun.

[1] *Op. cit.*, p. 265.   [2] *Op. cit.*, p. 268.

From the very beginning of the Council ten years before, the Anglican Communion had steadfastly supported it. Many Anglicans went to Amsterdam. They had to find their right place in an assembly dominated financially by the Americans, and theologically by the famous protestant divines of continental Europe, such as Karl Barth, Hendrik Kraemer of the Netherlands, and the Czech communist Josef Hromadka. The Anglican delegation could offer no names of comparable prestige, and the chief contribution they made by their presence was the shielding of the movement from the reproaches often levelled against it, that it was no better than a pan-protestant movement on a large scale. The Anglicans were known to be heart and soul in it because they believed that it would work towards the knitting together of the Body of Christ by helping to create the conditions of an organic union between all Churches.

This was not the conscious purpose of the Amsterdam Assembly, which did not set out to provide ambitious schemes of reunion all round. It claimed that the World Council really existed first of all for the discussion of affairs of common concern to all Churches, and to provide them with an instrument through which they could speak with a single voice on international affairs. But it is a possible judgement that it was within the most difficult of all fields of reunion that the World Council of Amsterdam was in the end the most influential. There seems to have been a direct link between the meeting of the World Council at Amsterdam and the softening of the relationships which Rome held towards other Christian Churches, and it has been stated that the World Council's meeting was one factor which contributed to the decision of Pope John XXIII to call the Second Vatican Council. The Italian journalist Carlo Falconi kept a diary of the events of the Second Vatican Council, and rewrote its entries in book form under the title, *Pope John and his Council*. He shows himself very much aware of the World Council of Churches, mentioning it six times in his index, and in the course of the book he offers this estimate of the influence of the Amsterdam Assembly on the policies of the Papal Curia:

We must not forget the other ecumenical movement of Protestant origin later reinforced by the Orthodox Church. Throughout the Pontificate of Pius XI this movement seemed to be well-intentioned and it merely aroused his disparaging irony. But after the first assembly of the world Council of Churches in Amsterdam in 1948 it quickly became so powerful as to threaten to isolate the Roman Church unless the latter hastened to establish relations with it.

Then he adds a brief account of how the various Roman officials tried to reassess their problems of which this was only one, and ends with these two sentences offering a judgement of high importance to his own Church and to all others struggling to assert the relevance of Christ to the modern world:

The first condition for making history is to enter into it; and the first way to do that is to open the mind to an understanding of the times. The rest follows of itself.[1]

That, in other words, was precisely what de Chardin had been trying to say in his own way in 1949.

But there is still more evidence to support the same point, and from a more authoritative source. Hans Kung, the German catholic theologian, whose words carry great weight in his Church and also among Christians outside it, mentions the World Council of Churches many times in his book about the Second Vatican Council, *The Council and Reunion*, and finally makes this estimate of its ecumenical importance:

It is indeed especially important during the time of preparation to listen to the voice of non-Catholic communions: Orthodox, Anglican, and Protestant. We Catholics cannot, in this connection, overlook the fact that almost all non-Catholic Christian communions are included in the World Council of Churches. We cannot overlook the fact that in the World Council, in spite of all the differences in principle that there are, a great work has already been done for unity. This work has not been done *against* us but—understood aright—*for* us.[2]

There could be no better or more disinterested evidence of the great importance of the Amsterdam Assembly, and of how influential it was to become. The mere fact that all the non-Roman Churches met together there in 1948, quite apart from anything they attempted or achieved, had begun to propel the Roman mind towards the search for a new basis of the unity of the separated Churches with the great Church of Rome.

In the summer of 1948 the Lambeth Conference met for the first time for eighteen years and faced an utterly changed world from that of 1930. The completeness of its representation was a token of the hope which animated its members. In his visit to America in 1946 the archbishop had charmed into quiescence the suspicions of some of the transatlantic bishops, and they all came. There was just one uneasy moment during the course of the conference when the incautious speech of an English bishop was taken by some of the American bishops to mean that they were about to be treated as second-class citizens, and the archbishop had to act hurriedly to reassure them. This he did without too much difficulty, and the hope which began the conference stayed with it to the end.

Every Lambeth Conference is heralded by the same cautionary chorus. The faithful are told that though it is held at Lambeth and the Archbishop of Canterbury presides over it, he has no constitutional authority over the other bishops, and is their chairman only because they choose that he should be. Nor, the chorus sings, has the conference any power to bind or loose any of the participating Churches. All this is common form. It is no

---

[1] *Op. cit.* (Weidenfeld and Nicolson), 1964, p. 45.
[2] *Op. cit.* (Sheed and Ward), 1961, pp. 277f.

doubt necessary to say these things each time, and the repetition is perfectly harmless because, after all, nobody takes the least notice of it.

The Lambeth Conference is nevertheless better understood by the Church than most other forms of ecclesiastical assembly. Its meeting is eagerly anticipated, its proceedings are the cause of much public curiosity, and its findings, when published, immediately become news. No enthusiasm by churchpeople needs to be laboriously besought; it is there to begin with. There is no need to beseech the newspapers to take some notice of the conference; they do that automatically. Large numbers of people really do want to know what the Anglican bishops' opinions on matters of the day are. Perhaps this is just because they are bishops. Bishops, as a race, are frequently unpopular but seldom uninteresting. The decennial Lambeth Conference undoubtedly kindles more interest than most other kinds of ecclesiastical assembly can command; and this fact suggests that, in spite of the cautious disclaimers of its spokesmen, it has an authority all its own which is no less real for being undefined and indefinable.

Why is this? In part, no doubt, it is due to the shallowly romantic spectacle of crowds of bishops of all colours in their rochets and lawn sleeves crowding into St Paul's or Westminster Abbey for the opening or closing service. Episcopacy in uniform is very photogenic. At a deeper level this wide interest is due to the reflection that here, gathered into one place, are the bishops of all the Anglican Churches, men of every colour, brought from most parts of the world, bringing with them all their years of experience, all their stores of wisdom, and coming, each one, with the authority of the people of his diocese behind him, whose problems, whose troubles, and whose strains he knows well. Surrounded by prayer and sustained by sacraments they deliberate for six weeks about all the major issues in Church and state which have arisen during the years since they last met, and eventually they will pass their judgement upon them. To all but the insensitive the thought kindles imagination.

Moreover, they are wise enough to meet in private so that each one can speak his mind without fear of publicity, or indeed the temptation to angle for it. There is a mystery about a Lambeth Conference which keeps people guessing, and enhances their curiosity to find out what the bishops think. At last the report is published and people can read it. It is known to be anonymous and corporate in the sense that nothing is written in it which tells the reader a word about the processes which led to its being what it is. No one knows which bishops espoused or which opposed any part of it. What is eventually published is known to be, and actually is, the corporate judgement of the whole Anglican episcopate upon the issues debated. So much wisdom, so much experience of so many different fields of life, is contained in such a conference, that the opinions it expresses must always be worth considering, and may often be valuable, and even make history.

To read the findings and reports of the conference of 1948 at this distance of time is to receive the impression of a body of very hopeful and some-times rather optimistic bishops who were trying to be realists, but were all the time misconceiving the nature of their own world. In this they were not alone. There were then very few indeed in any walk of life who per-ceived much of what was still hidden in the womb of the future. Today, for example, it seems an astonishing piece of wishful thinking that the encycli-cal letter of the bishops could declare, 'For those who have eyes to see, there are signs that the tide of faith is beginning to come in.' What, one wonders, were those signs? Many of the declarations or findings, too, were sufficiently misconceived for it to be necessary to reverse them in the Lambeth Conference of 1958.

But all this is wisdom after the event, written from a maddeningly olympian hindsight. At the time, the published results of the conference show clearly how the bishops of that day regarded their world, their Church, and the charge they bore in both. This responsibility they defined in the opening encyclical letter, which they required to be read aloud in every church on the same day. It was a noble piece of writing, and it is now widely known that for the most part it was the work of Mervyn Haigh, Bishop of Winchester and secretary to the conference. Its keynote was a deep com-passion for all human suffering everywhere, but also an inexorableness of demand on all from whom these bishops had the right to ask it, together with a constant reminder that the comfort of the Holy Ghost was on offer to all, and there to be had. The whole Church was summoned to a special evangelistic effort:

> The supreme task of the Church today is to win the nations of Christendom back to the knowledge of God . . . and to take the good news to those who have not yet heard it. We call upon our people to engage in this campaign and to put themselves into training for it. God, in His mercy, has given to us in our Con-ference a clearer vision of His will and purpose for His Church and of its mission in the world. To these we bid you dedicate yourselves.[1]

But the bishops knew how much they asked, how difficult life was for so many from whom they asked it. This compassionate knowledge they ex-pressed in two very beautifully written paragraphs, which carry Mervyn Haigh's unmistakable style at its best. They breathe charity and hope, successfully communicating both, and deserve to be rescued from the dust now lying so thick upon them in the files of the libraries.

> We know well how hard it is for many of you to live as Christians in the pre-sent age. Some of you have to meet opposition in non-Christian homes; some are a small minority of Christians in non-Christian lands. Many of you are trying to bear your witness in face of contempt and ridicule, in the places where you work day by day. All at times are tempted to lose heart and to wonder whether, under such conditions, Christian living is possible, or whether, if possible, it is

[1] *Lambeth Conference 1948* (S.P.C.K.), p. 17.

worth while. We are certain that it is possible, and worth everything, and we write this letter to tell you why.

Whatever man may do, God is undefeated. God reigns. The world belongs to Him, and in it He is working out that purpose which He has revealed to us in Jesus Christ. He uses imperfect and sinful men to be its servants. Christians may not always be better than their neighbours, but we serve a better Master. His is the cause that has life and hope in it.[1]

Men who can summon their people in language like that have earned the right to be followed.

The bishops began with the Christian doctrine of man, and addressed themselves to the question of what rights the Church must claim for him in the circumstances of the modern world; which is to say that they began in the right place. They believed that the two major threats to these human rights lay in the current tyrannies of contemporary state despotisms, and in the forms of organization leaving God out of account on which so many modern states were relying for economic recovery. They were ruthless and were bound by no recognition of moral law. But all these lamentable trends were subsumed together under a title which now dates the document: 'Against all these forms of secularism the Church must proclaim that man is a being created by God and is under His sovereignty.' Today no assembly of bishops could write quite like that, but would be bound to insert at that point a lengthy dissection of the meaning of the word 'secular'.

On one serious weakness of the Church as she faced this challenge the bishops were outspoken. It was a very serious omission in the Church's armoury that she had not formulated a satisfactory doctrine of work. For lack of such a doctrine there was too little to set against the threat to the Christian rights of man made by nothing more dramatic than our sheer human idleness. The report delved deep into the dilemma between the sheer necessity of mass production and the maintenance of good craftsmanship, and a man's pride in the work of his own hands. It did not resolve the dilemma, for it could not. Today automation and redundancy, words hardly known to the bishops of 1948, have made the dilemma yet more insoluble. Moreover, no satisfactory gospel of work has yet been produced by the Church.

The conference gave much attention to the Church's discipline of marriage, which constituted then, as still it does, a social problem as difficult as it was urgent. On the problem of birth control the bishops had no single word to say. On the indissolubility of Christian marriage they were unyielding, and they reinforced the custom of using the Blessed Sacrament as a means of discipline, even punishment, for those who, by contracting fresh marriages while one partner to the previous marriage still lived, had broken the Church's rule. But all this rigour was most reluctant, and the salve of a deep compassion drew its sting.

[1] *Ibid.*, p. 16.

The point to which the conference gave the largest part of the space of its report was the issue of church unity. Here the birth of the united Church of South India naturally held the centre of the stage. The conference's welcome was sincere but cautious. It could hardly be other because, while most of the bishops were eager to accept the bishops, priests, and deacons of the South India Church as the equals in every way of their counterparts in every Anglican Church, a substantial minority were still conscientiously unable to accord them this degree of recognition. A phrase of escape had to be concocted, and it registered regret 'that it is not yet possible to pass any definite judgement upon the precise status of such bishops, presbyters, and deacons, or to recommend that they be accepted in the Anglican Communion as bishops, presbyters, and deacons'. The Church of South India had still some distance to travel, and so, for that matter, had the Anglican episcopate, before the day of its complete recognition dawned.

Apart from South India, this section of the report is chiefly interesting today as giving some indication of where the whole reunion movement was actually standing in 1948, and some means of gauging the effect of Archbishop Fisher's Cambridge Sermon two years after its delivery. More progress seemed to have been made overseas than at home. Schemes for the unity of many separated Churches were in active preparation in North India, Ceylon, Nigeria, and Iran; and the Anglican Church was involved in them all. On the other hand the hopes for reunion with the Free Churches in Britain were still encased in the deep freeze where the war had deposited them, and we were in the stage of rather laborious preparations to take them out of it. Talks with the Church of Scotland had been suspended in 1934 and had not yet been renewed, though there was a promise that they would be. Similarly, the approaches made to the Free Church Council after the Lambeth Appeal of 1920 had also broken down. They were to be begun again, but in what form the report did not say. In 1948 therefore the prospects of reunion in Britain did not seem very bright. But the bishops registered their determination to do all they could to get the whole process in motion again, and in their report so many references were made to Dr Fisher's Cambridge Sermon that there is no doubt that it had been singularly effective.

The problems of baptism and confirmation were also discussed at some length, and there was a very good section on the Anglican Communion, its nature, its place within Christendom, and its future strategy. The germ of the later Pan-Anglican Conference at Toronto was first quickened to life in this Lambeth Conference; and the new Anglican Staff College at St Augustine's College, Canterbury, was the identifiable fruit of its work.

All in all, the place of this Lambeth Conference in the long series is not difficult to determine. It listed problems but it did not solve them; and it wound up the three post-war years of Anglican stocktaking. It was an end and a beginning. It was necessary that the most august of all assemblies of

Anglican bishops should be held, and held just at that time. When all the bishops left Lambeth for their dioceses all over the world they knew that the Church was the stronger for their coming together, and they were clear in what directions they must try to lead the Church in the next ten years. The stage was set and they had endorsed what had been done to arrange it. The cohesion of the Anglican Communion must be still further strengthened. It must work loyally within and in good relationships with the World Council of Churches. Through thick and thin, and at almost any cost, it must pursue the greater goal towards which these things led—the organic union of the still separated Churches of the world. It must somehow weave its life into the actual shapes of the life people had to live, and reinforce in this way the Christian doctrine of Man. One note only was lacking from the report: there was no reference to the coming struggle of Church and state in South Africa, and this was indeed a surprising omission, for in 1948 the first serious clash with the government was imminent.

24

The Church in South Africa

I · Geoffrey Clayton, Archbishop of Capetown

AMONG THE 329 bishops who had spent the summer of 1948 at Lambeth
Palace, there was one who went home to face a destiny of which he could
have little idea when he landed in England. He was a very large man, heavy
with flesh, yet of most abstemious personal habits, who moved painfully
on a stiff leg. He was unmarried, and remained so gruffly shy to the end of
his life that it took a long time to get to know him. His personal discipline
was austere, and his powers of sustained work impressive. Geoffrey
Clayton left this island to travel home to Johannesburg still an almost
unknown man, an anonymous face in a crowd of bishops. Quickly appointed to one of the two or three key positions of the whole Anglican
Communion of that day, he won great renown as a man of just judgement,
a brave champion of the Church and all its people, and he became one of
its foremost heroes. In less than ten years he was dead.

What waited for him in South Africa was the archbishopric of Capetown, and through that the rule of the whole Church of the province, and
this in a time of nationalist intransigence and deep tragedy. His former
metropolitan, Russell Darbishire, died without presage or warning in
England before the Lambeth Conference began. A breathing space of a
few months gave Clayton time to think out the position in his Church
which the archbishop's death had created, and he knew it was possible
that he would be elected to succeed him. This duly happened, and Clayton,
assuming resolutely what it was already certain must be the most difficult,
the most inexorably testing, position in all the Churches of the Anglican
Communion at that moment of history, entered upon the last stage of his
surprising career, the enigma of an unknown man sitting in a chair of
fame.

His life had been full of surprises. Nothing in his previous career suggested that in this quiet, withdrawn man lay buried the makings of a

remarkable overseas bishop, and the ruler of the most difficult of all Anglican provinces who succeeded gloriously through what looked like the the unrelieved frustration of an absolute failure. He did not dispel South Africa's tragedy. He never came within miles of it, for no man could. His ministry at Capetown was the perfect example of the classic Christian insight that the right endurance of an unbroken frustration may often be the gateway to conspicuous success. Born in 1884, he was the son of a Bishop of Leicester, and was educated at Rugby and at Pembroke College, Cambridge, where he graduated with a first in theology and a first in classics. For years he lived the academic life of a university town. Within a year of his ordination as deacon he became a Fellow of Peterhouse, and two years later he was made Dean of the College, having the responsibility for the maintenance of college discipline. This office he held for ten years, and for the last two of them he combined it with being the vicar of the small church of St Mary's the Less. In 1924 he turned his back on the life of a bachelor don in college, and accepted the appointment of vicar of Chesterfield.

Much can be deduced from this curt epitome of a career; for example, that he belonged to the catholic wing of the Church, and was not dismayed by the prospect of surprising change, but there is nothing in it to suggest that such a priest would be likely to become an outstanding bishop in modern South Africa. Those who appointed him to be Bishop of Johannesburg to succeed the ebullient and impulsive Arthur Karney, who never weighed a word, had some of the recklessness of authentic inspiration. They took their risk in faith, and it was justified in the event. They had found a man cautious in wisdom, who spoke in public only after he had mastered all the facts of the issue concerned, who measured the effect of his words with scrupulous care, and who left nothing to chance. But they also found one who was steady as a rock and staunch in courage once he knew where he must stand and his mind was formed and settled.

He was called to be the archbishop of a new country where, in things ecclesiastical as well as things political, the very air of the place seems to breed an intransigent extremism. One Christian Church is passionate in its advocacy of racial apartheid, while another tends to be tempestuous in the language with which its hatred of all forms of racial inequality is expressed. Both draw their inspiration from the same set of scriptures and from the same Redeemer. In South Africa it seems to be most difficult not to be an extremist on one side or the other of this great divide. It was one of the great characteristics of Geoffrey Clayton that he could never be an enthusiast for anything other or less than the Christian faith. He had neither blindness nor prejudice. When he became archbishop he almost bent over backwards to be fair to the South African government. He pleaded incessantly for an unprejudiced examination of its case, and for a responsible temperateness of criticism. When at last the ineluctable facts drove him into open opposition, the condemnations of his wisdom were profoundly effective. He did not save the African from tyranny. No one could. But he held his Church together, and he made it stand firm.

Thus it was that the bishops of the province had no doubt where they must look for a successor to Darbishire. Clayton came to Capetown in 1949, and both his clergy and people found that they had an archbishop who was determined to be their kind but exacting Father-in-God, who knew every one of them, and demanded from them all every last ounce of effort and saw that he got it. They knew that what he asked he gave himself. His life was disciplined, his powers of sustained work phenomenal. He got out of bed at six o'clock, and before seven was always in his chapel where he said matins, celebrated the Eucharist, and went through his daily meditation. Thereafter he worked steadily, doing his letters, keeping his engagements, working on his speeches or charges, until, often enough, two o'clock in the morning. He lived with pain. Something was wrong with one leg, and he limped through the house, which almost shook under his great weight. When he sat down it was on a sofa with one leg up and straight. He had a terrific voice and a great laugh which was famous, but he had very little small talk. To his clergy he was most welcoming provided they were doing their work as well as they possibly could—and he always knew. He was also immensely generous, but thoughtful with his generosity. For himself he lived a sparing and a frugal life. His greatest gift was his skill at coupling in a fruitful synthesis the immemorial certitudes of the classical theology with the problems of the moment, and he drew from his classical training an unusual degree of skill in speaking his mind in simple language and with short words, so that no one could doubt what he meant. In public his speech was as clear as it was temperate. He judged all men, whether friends or foes, by the lights of the Gospel and by the standards of charity. To despise any human being was for him the worst sin of all. To ridicule or to humiliate a man of any colour roused in him a searing anger. He often said that he tried to be a bishop without any sense of colour, and this delivered him from too swift a condemnation of those in authority until at last their own actions left him with no choice. Then his stand was impressive and his protests formidable. He was perhaps the wisest and the farthest-seeing man in the South Africa of his day.

It is as the Christian statesman that he will be remembered by the world, but it was as their true Father-in-God that his clergy first thought of him. It was, for instance, no slight undertaking for an elderly, a very stout, and a lame archbishop to contrive the means of travelling to the island of Tristan da Cunha, his remotest parish, whose isolation is a legend. He did this in 1955, taking passage in a naval frigate, being hoisted down the ship's side in a chair, then lashed firm in a rudimentary canvas-bottomed boat, and paddled perilously ashore. But it was an adventure the islanders and their chaplain never forgot. A year later he wrote to this same chaplain :

I am afraid that it is not likely that a confirmation will be possible next year. I doubt whether I could manage another trip to Tristan. You might well reply that if I can't do my job I ought to resign. That is my own view, and I told my fellow bishops so. But they asked me to withdraw my resignation and to carry on till after Lambeth, and I have promised that if I am well enough I will do so.

Such was his humility. Four months later he died.

Into the Church of the Province of South Africa the Church of England had for many years poured many different resources, thus redeeming the shameful neglect of its earliest years. But now it had long been realized that South Africa was a mission field of crucial responsibility, in that what happened there was likely to be decisive for the whole continent, and even for many lands far beyond it. It had been treated as though, in missionary work, no other part of the world mattered quite so much. Thus, most of the religious orders of the Church of England, both for men and women, had long maintained well-staffed stations there, particularly in Johannesburg and the Transvaal, and their record of service was indeed spectacular. What the work and witness of the Mirfield Fathers had meant to the Bantu who lived in the city's slums has been vividly told in Trevor Huddleston's *Naught for your Comfort*; and what the native African priest, trained by such men, could be like at his best anyone who has read Alan Paton's *Cry, the Beloved Country*, and rejoiced and almost wept over his wonderful portrait of the saintly old Zulu priest, knows well. However shrill in their defiance some of the prophets might be driven into becoming, a Church staffed by such men and women was rich in promise, and no one dare yet judge whether it was wealthy or poor in performance. Martyrs always look like failures for a time, but in the long run they are apt to win.

The Church was rich in schools, in hospitals, in settlements, and clubs of every kind. So far as the equipment of this world is concerned, few, if any, overseas Churches were so amply furnished, or their needs so well provided. To all outward appearance Clayton seemed to inherit an externally affluent Church, well stocked with buildings, and well staffed with clergy, monks, and nuns, of the highest quality which England could provide. But he knew that the reality was far different. In 1948 Field-Marshal Smuts had been defeated in the South African general election, and the nationalist leader Dr D. F. Malan had succeeded to power. When Clayton was enthroned in Capetown Cathedral a year later, it was clear that an entirely new situation had been created, which, to all human seeming, held out no promise at all. Though long preparing, the crisis which was brought to a head by Malan's electoral victory would last through the years to the present day, and still be as dangerously far from a solution as ever. But it was one of God's crowning mercies to the Church that it was Geoffrey Clayton who was called to struggle with the terrible problem in its early stages, and to lead his Church through its steadily growing fires for the eight years of life which remained to him.

II · *Clayton's Powerful Language*

Almost any sincere priest who was suddenly called to be the Archbishop of the Province of South Africa at a moment of deepening clash between Church and state would no doubt have dealt with the situation in much the same way as Clayton did. Indeed, he said all the obvious things, and yet added to them a touch of distinction which made him so impressive as a person, and enhanced their value. This touch was all his own. Nothing is more impressive about him than the unexpectedness, the suddenness with which the crisis drew out of him the fullness of his stature, and set free in him an interior greatness which before had only been guessed at. He had not previously moved in the sort of circles from which archishops are normally drawn. One looks in vain for his name in the indexes of any of the standard archiepiscopal biographies of the time. Cosmo Gordon Lang, William Temple, Cyril Garbett: so far as one can tell from their biographies, not one of them had had any dealings with him at all. At most he was to all of them just one more overseas bishop. Once enthroned as archbishop he proved at once his real greatness; and one who served with him and under him through all those years—C. T. Wood, the Archdeacon of Cape Town—has written the just epitaph of his public career:

Archbishop Clayton was the man chosen by divine providence to match the hour. Many felt that he came too late to his high office. He was aware of this himself. Yet those extra years of waiting and discipline bore their fruit in the maturity of his judgement and the clarity of his thought. The deceptive simplicity in analysis and pronouncement which marks his style is the result of those years of painful wrestling with the complexities of the material before the summons came.

That passage occurs in the archdeacon's introduction to the edition of Clayton's archiepiscopal charges which Wood edited in 1960, and the Oxford University Press published under the title *Where We Stand*.

These charges, delivered to diocesan and provincial synods from 1949 to 1956, are models of what such things should be, and very seldom are. They are rooted in a profound theological belief about God and life to which every succeeding event on the temporal political plane can be related, and in which everything that happens finds its real meaning and its true value. All events and all people are seen *sub specie aeternitatis*, and thus they have their own significance and their own dignity. The political facts arranged themselves in his mind in a beautiful order, and are free from complication in the interpretation he gave them. It is perfectly possible to annotate the successive hammer blows of deepening challenge which the South African government hurled at the Church from the temperate but devastating commentary upon them which these charges of Clayton's provide. It is in fact the easiest way of telling this part of the story. But more than this, these charges always held notes of an extra distinction of their own which stamped them as the work of a Father-in-God, who knew just how to speak the passage which would get them remembered, and the touches of exhortation which give strength to the hearer at the moment when he most needs it.

Clayton's charges made the annual synods the great occasions of church life in the diocese. They were events which no one would willingly miss. The diocese assembled in the cathedral. Holy Communion was celebrated early in the morning, and then, after breakfast, the stillness of intense surmise held sway over the vast congregation as Clayton limped into the pulpit, and began to deliver his charge. He could make skilled play with his voice, and vary its pitch and pace and timbre to suit and underline the meaning of any particular passage. Those who heard him say that there was an unconscious touch of Sir Winston Churchill's manner in his great wartime speeches—the same deliberateness, the same slight huskiness, above all the same delight in the hammer blows of short words, and the determination to make clear beyond all possible doubt the full meaning of his mind.

Here, in 1949, he was laying down the principle of the sanctity of human personality which, throughout the crisis, was to be the yardstick of all his judgement:

> So far as God has revealed to us, there is nothing else, except the individual person, that is of eternal value. Heaven and earth shall pass away. But you will not pass away. When Shakespeare made Prospero say, 'The cloud-capp'd towers, the gorgeous palaces, the solemn temples, the great globe itself, yea, all which it inherit, shall dissolve, and, like this insubstantial pageant faded, leave not a wrack behind,' he was right about everything else, but wrong about 'all which it inherit'. Man's works, man's environment, yes, and God's works, pass away. But man remains. That is why the Christian faith is the charter of man's greatness, the ground of his importance. That is why the rejection of the Christian faith carries with it a debasement of the human currency, a devaluation of man. For man's importance depends on his relationship to God. He matters to God and he matters for ever.[1]

After that it is not surprising to find him denouncing apartheid on the next page. But first he had provided his scales of measurement, and had drawn them so clearly that none could mistake what they were. Or here, in 1953, at a black moment when the Bantu Education Act had become law and Christians were tempted to embitterment and despair, is the Father-in-God speaking to his clergy:

> My brethren of the clergy. You set out with high ideals. You have often been disappointed. The things you wanted have not happened. Well, there was no promise that they would. There are two great commandments, the love of God and the love of neighbour. Don't try to live on the love of neighbour. It is because you can't do that that you need retreats and such things. It is only the love of

[1] *Op. cit.*, p. 4.

God that will save you from growing sour and cynical, or content with secular compensations. You can't live on the love of neighbour. You can live on the love of God.[1]

Today those words have an unmodern ring, but a bishop who can speak to his hard-pressed clergy like that is loved and followed.

III · *The Collision of Church and State*

The Enthronement of Geoffrey Clayton in Capetown Cathedral and the assumption of power by Dr D. F. Malan's Nationalist government were very nearly simultaneous events. For fourteen years at Johannesburg Clayton had been watching and waiting. He could have little doubt what would happen. The one hope was that the Cape wing of the party might put the brake on the extremism and violence of the Transvaal wing, for Malan was a Cape man and not a Transvaaler. Malan, as a person, he probably found appealing. He was a cultured man, who had won his doctorate at a Dutch university with a thesis on the philosophy of Bishop Berkeley, and had gained his political prestige by his championship of the Afrikaans language. But he was as determined as the most violent extremist to secure for the Nationalists absolute, unchecked power; and he was the first apostle of apartheid, for this Afrikaans word first became popular in the election of 1948 which brought him to power, and was intended to replace its English equivalent, 'separateness'. The Bantu were destined to become a race apart and a race servile. The only question was how long it would take to achieve it, and the real difference between Malan and his Transvaal allies was that he had some regard for public opinion in other countries while they had none at all.

The arrival of even so personally attractive a man as Dr Malan to sit in the seat of power, which he lost no time in making unassailable, was therefore alarming. In his very first charge to his diocese Clayton sounded still cautious notes of warning. He began with domestic affairs, the need of the diocese for more priests. This he followed by his striking passages already quoted, about the sanctity of human personality. Then he turned to the problem of the Coloured people, of which his own diocese was so full, and said:

With the best will in the world to understand and appreciate the policy of apartheid, I cannot see that there is anything in it for coloured people. Where is the land that they shall 'develop on their own lines'?—and what are those lines?

And then he went on to speak his own mind on apartheid itself:

But there is something else which certainly affects human personality. The present petty attempts to carry out apartheid produce a sense of humiliation. This is made quite inevitable by the way in which some of those responsible for the

[1] *Ibid.*, pp. 30f.

policy have allowed themselves to speak publicly in insulting terms of the non-Europeans. It is difficult to exaggerate the harm that that has done. . . . If there is anything made quite clear in the gospels it is that contempt for other people is wicked. And that is because the people you despise happen to be the people whom God loves.[1]

Petty attempts? But soon they became far from petty. In 1953 it was Dr Malan's own government which forced through the South African parliament the two enactments which left the issue beyond all doubt for Christians. They were the Bantu Education Act, and the Criminal Law Amendment Act, which between them turned South Africa into a police state. The purpose of the first act was stated to be to adapt Bantu education to the subservient role which the Bantu could expect to play in a white community state. To bring this about the act provided that every school for Africans must be under the control of the government, that all schools which were independently maintained by Churches or private bodies of any kind must be registered with the Department of Education, that the Minister of Education could at any time cancel the registration and thus close the school, that the syllabus must provide for much more Afrikaans and much less English to be taught, and that all teachers must refrain from commenting adversely on government policy. The insistence on the teaching of the Afrikaans language betrayed the influence of Dr Malan himself; and a speech made by the minister chiefly concerned, which was printed and circulated as official, left no doubt as to the meaning and purpose of the act. It was to remove Bantu education from the influence of the Churches, and to train the Bantu for the subordinate, the permanently subordinate place in the state which the government thought he ought to have. The speech said much about the 'civilized community of South Africa', and explicitly defined that phrase as meaning the Europeans. The Bantu predominately, but also the Coloured people and the Indians, were not Europeans, and therefore made between them the uncivilized community in South Africa.

The Criminal Law Amendment Act brought in the police state, and carried South Africa into line with the totalitarian dictatorships of Europe. It prescribed very severe punishment, including flogging, for inciting anyone to break the law by way of making even peaceful protests against it. It also gave the Governor General power to proclaim at will a state of emergency in any part of the Union. Wherever a state of emergency had been proclaimed then all laws except those regulating the functioning of parliament and the elections to it were suspended, and the government could legislate by decree. Naturally the Governor General could do no such thing by his own will or judgement, nor yet refrain from doing it. His public actions, like those of any constitutional monarchy, could proceed only from the advice of the cabinet. The electoral law was exempted from

[1] *Ibid.*, p. 7.

this draconian act because the government had previously so amended and 'rigged' it as to make the position of itself and its supporting Nationalist party unassailable by any known democratic means.

In his address to his diocese in 1953, with its significant title, 'Hag-ridden by Fear', Clayton reacted to these acts with his characteristic caution. He fastened first upon the extension of apartheid, and then upon the dangers involved in giving a minister of state 'the power to pass judgement on an individual or an institution without recourse to the courts'. He then uttered the following and most characteristic sentences, which are so carefully worded that one can almost smell still the midnight oil burnt over them:

> I want to say a few words about the Bantu Education Act, and the anxiety which has been caused to very many of us by the appointment of a Cape Province Coloured Education Commission. The Bantu Education Act puts Bantu education in the hands of a Native Affairs Department, and like other recent legislation it puts dangerously wide powers in the hands of an individual minister. It makes it possible for him so to use his power as to make Bantu education the kind of education which will only fit people for a permanently inferior position. There is something peculiarly offensive in educating people to fit them only for an inferior position and then to withhold from them more responsible positions on the ground that they are not fit for them. There is a very widespread fear that this is the intention. What I want to say is that while I regret that so much power is put into the hands of a particular minister, we have no knowledge that he will use his power with that intention. I don't think we must assume that that will be so. Similarly we have no knowledge what the Commission on Coloured Education in this Province is going to report. I deprecate the assumption that the worst is bound to happen. It may happen. But do not let us make ourselves miserable before it is necessary. I think myself that to expect the worst is to make the worst more likely to occur.[1]

It was entirely characteristic of Clayton to refuse to believe the worst before he must, and to decline to criticize publicly anyone in a responsible position until the evidence accumulated which left him with no other course. But the worst duly occurred; Clayton must have known that it would. Within a year we find him saying to his diocesan synod:

> Last year, in speaking to you about the Bantu Education Act, I said that it put dangerously wide powers into the hands of an individual minister, but that we had no knowledge of how he would use those powers. Unfortunately we now have that knowledge as he has outlined his policy in a speech to the Senate which has been printed and circulated as official. The purpose of his policy is to remove the influence of Christian missions from the control of Bantu education—what he calls the changeover from mission to community schools—and to train African Natives for such positions as in the view of the present Government ought to be open to them. . . . Light is thrown upon the Minister's policy by his criticism of the existing system because it makes people believe that they have a

[1] *Ibid.*, p. 27.

place among the civilized community of South Africa. He explicitly defines the civilized community of South Africa as the Europeans. 'Bantu education' is apparently a form of training which is to fit people to take their place in an uncivilized community in South Africa. . . . All this is of course most deplorable.[1]

He had no choice left but to declare and commit himself, and this he did with grave and responsible emphasis. The Church must take no part in this 'fantastic' Bantu education, for if it does, it will have to be bound by a 'syllabus of which it cannot approve'.

But whatever the political and racial situation, however black and lowering the sky, always and in all circumstances the work of the Church has to go on. It was one of the features of Clayton's synodical addresses that, in spite of the frightening anxieties of the present, he never forgot this or allowed his hearers to forget it. The address of 1945 must have been one of the most anxious he was ever called to give, but he ended it with the strengthening words of the bishop who, before all else, was a true Father-in-God:

So we shall go back from this Synod to our work. To the clergy I would say 'Don't be discouraged'. Don't think you would be much more effective if you were, somewhere different from where you are. Ask God to help you love your people and to save you from the grievous sin of despising them. As you love them better you will serve them better. And my brothers of the laity, remember that you too are soldiers in Christ's army, and that you cannot contract out of His war. Don't be too critical of your clergy. It is unlikely that your rector will have all the gifts of all the Apostles. When you speak of the Church, remember that the Church is you; that it is your witness even more than that of your priests that is effective in your parish, and that you are called to nothing less than so to live that men may trace the lineaments of Jesus Christ in your life.[2]

The two legal enactments which had finally convinced Clayton that the South African government was inexorably bent on courses which the Church could not approve, and was bound sooner or later to resist, constituted the turning-point. After that the dismal story of apartheid administered by a police state which departed further and further from any pretence of legality or fair play of any kind unfolded itself with all the inevitableness of a tragic drama. There was no way of staying it.

Malan resigned in 1954, and was succeeded by J. G. Strydom, a fanatical Transvaal republican, who was the sworn enemy of all non-Europeans, all English people, the British Crown, and the Commonwealth. Events followed fast: in 1955 there were forcible removals of non-Europeans from Sophiatown, in the next year the arrest of 156 people of all races and the launching of an almost interminable Treason Trial, which was to falter on for years, and in 1957 the passing of a clause in an apartheid bill which gave the government powers to exclude Africans from attending any church situated in a white area.

[1] *Ibid.*, pp. 32, 33.　　　　　　[2] *Ibid.*, p. 40.

That there must be a struggle was evident; that it must be a long one was not less evident. In all his reactions to these lamentable events Clayton always took the long view. He must protest, as he did, but he must not increase thereby the sum total of hatred or fear; he must oppose and criticize, but he must not hold up any man to contempt or ridicule. He must remember that by what he publicly said the power of love to reconcile in the end would be a little increased or decreased. All this responsibility he bore with a steady consistency which did not waver. He followed the course of his deliberate choice, and he carried his Church with him.

The world watched. It had little choice but to watch, for it was certainly not left unaware of what was happening. The long crisis had already produced a considerable body of literature, much of which was of very high artistic merit. *Cry, the Beloved Country*, by Alan Paton, had been published in 1946, and it was read throughout the world. It was an exposure of the evils of breaking up the old tribal system while putting nothing in its place. His next novel, *Too Late, the Phalarope*, which appeared in 1953, was not less powerful and yet more sad; it dealt with the racial segregation laws on their sex relations side. The Sophiatown evictions were described by an eye-witness of them, Father Trevor Huddleston, in *Naught For Your Comfort* in 1956. The book immediately became famous, and it deserved its fame for it was a beautifully written piece of work, and it communicated the despair and agony both of its author and of the luckless non-Europeans who were being treated as sub-human chattels, and had no redress. The fact that the publication of the book coincided with the decision of the Community of the Resurrection to withdraw Father Huddleston from South Africa naturally increased its circulation. This withdrawal would seem to have been the only thing that saved him from deportation as an 'undesirable alien', which was presently to happen to the Bishop of Johannesburg and, much more surprisingly, to the calm and gentle Hannah Stanton, who, unlike both the Bishop and Father Huddleston, had nothing of the stormy petrel anywhere in her. Side by side with all this, the press of the world continued to thunder, and the intolerable cruelty of the working out of apartheid was trumpeted regularly in the sessions of the United Nations. Has any government anywhere, excepting only the Nazi government of Germany, had so consistently bad a press as the government of South Africa? And has any government heeded it so little?

In his charges Clayton himself showed no awareness of the writings of his more tempestuous lieutenants, and never referred to the heavy criticism of the world's press. Naturally he knew it all, but, as he said himself, 'I have done my best to make clear to fellow Anglicans in England and elsewhere how complex the situation in this country is, and to discourage pronouncements on points of detail and condemnation of particular persons. And that I shall continue to do.' His instinct was always to act through the Church, and therefore he saw in the very vehemence of the protests flowing in from different parts of the Anglican Church a means of cementing further the fellowship between the several Anglican Churches. It was entirely characteristic. Out of this welter of fear and repression some good could be made to come, and the life of the Anglican Communion was the point where he hoped to find it, and intended to promote it:

> I should like to say what a tremendous strength and encouragement it is to receive the kind of letters that I have been receiving from the leaders of the Anglican Church in its various provinces throughout the world; not only from Canterbury and York, Ireland, Scotland and Wales, but from the Presiding Bishop of the Anglican Church in the United States, from Canada, from the Archbishop of Sydney, who is Primate of Australia, all writing on behalf of their Churches, come letters assuring us of sympathy and support, asking, is there anything we can do to help you? The answer, of course, is Yes. We want and need your prayers; and here is something to pray about. The Anglican Communion has become a family in a sense in which it has never been one before; a family in which the truth of St Paul's great saying has become recognized: 'When one member suffers all the members suffer with it', and where there is a real desire to bear one another's burdens. All this is a matter of the deepest thankfulness. God forbid that anything should be done which can weaken the sense of unity of the Anglican Communion throughout the world.[1]

Then (and as one reads it one can almost see the man gathering his strength for it, and those who listened rising to it) he came to his moving peroration:

> And yet it remains true that each must bear his own burden. And we have got to fight our own battles. We alone know the details. We alone can estimate the practical difficulties. Perhaps also we alone know the strength there is in the positions which in spite of that strength we believe to be mistaken. It is we who are in the firing line. May God give us grace to be worthy of the trust that He has placed in us. May we never through cowardice and fear of consequences fail to bear our witness. But let us be as sure as we can that our witness is true. The truth is not usually popular. But it is not our business to be popular with any section or any racial group. It is our business to be faithful. . . . May I add one personal word. I am conscious that I have a very heavy load of responsibility to carry. I did not seek it. And I know my own inadequacy. I ask your prayers, and the prayers of the Diocese, that I may have a right judgement in all things, and may care only for God's glory and the true welfare of His children.[2]

That charge was given in 1954, the year after the passing of the Bantu Education Act.

The pace of the tragedy quickly gathered momentum as repression, protest, outrage, and retaliation followed on each other's heels in a dreary sequence. But Geoffrey Clayton's own part in the story was nearly done, and he had not long now to wait for his reward and his peace. In 1957, immediately after the departure from the country of Trevor Huddleston, the publication of his book, and the beginning of the famous Treason Trial,

---

[1] *Ibid.*, pp. 38f.   [2] *Ibid.*, p. 39.

the government uttered the fateful challenge to the Christian Churches working in South Africa, to which there could be but one answer. It was the very thing that Clayton had always dreaded, and had used every power he had to avoid. But it came and now he must face it. In 1957 the government produced another of its long succession of Apartheid Acts, and in this one there was a clause giving the appropriate minister power to exclude African Christians from entering any church situated in an area reserved for Europeans. By governmental command the colour bar was to apply to the buildings of the Church, which hit at the basic principle of the Incarnation itself. It is true that the execution of it waited upon the decision of the minister; true also that he had not yet applied it. But Clayton knew he could wait no more. He called the bishops together. None had any doubt of what must be done. In their names he then wrote this, his last, letter:

Dear Mr Prime Minister,

We, Bishops of the Church of the Province of South Africa, are approaching you rather than the Minister of Native Affairs because we believe that the issues raised in clause 29(c) of the Native Laws Amendment Bill cannot be regarded merely as Native affairs. It appears to us that as far as the Anglican Church is concerned, Churches and congregations in every urban area within the Union, even those mainly attended by Europeans, will be affected by this clause. Further, it is our belief that the Clause raises the issue of religious freedom and more particularly that of freedom of worship, and we venture to submit that this is a wider issue than that of Native Affairs only.

We desire to state that we regard the above-mentioned clause as an infringement of religious freedom in that it makes conditional on the permission of the Minister of Native Affairs

(a) the continuance in existence of any church or parish constituted after 1 January 1938 in an urban area except in a location which does not exclude Native Africans from public worship;

(b) the holding of any service in any church in an urban area except in a location to which a Native African would be admitted if he presented himself;

(c) the attendance of any Native African at any synod or church assembly held in an urban area outside a location.

The Church cannot recognize the right of an official of the secular government to determine whether or where a member of the Church of any race (who is not serving a sentence which restricts his freedom of movement) shall discharge his religious duty of participation in public worship or to give instructions to the minister of any congregation as to whom he shall admit to membership of that congregation.

Further, the Constitution of the Church of the Province of South Africa provides for the synodical government of the Church. In such synods, bishops, priests, and laymen are represented without distinction of race or colour. Clause 29(c) makes the holding of any such synods dependent upon the permission of the Minister of Native Affairs.

We recognize the great gravity of disobedience to the law of the land. We believe that obedience to secular authority, even in matters about which we differ in opinion, is a command laid upon us by God. But we are commanded to render unto Caesar the things which be Caesar's, and to God the things that are God's. There are therefore some matters which are God's and not Caesar's, and we believe that the matters dealt with in clause 29(c) are among them.

It is because we believe this that we feel bound to state that if the Bill were to become law in its present form, we should ourselves be unable to obey it or to counsel our clergy and people to do so.

We therefore appeal to you, Sir, not to put us in a position in which we have to choose between obeying our conscience and obeying the law of the land. We have the honour to remain, Sir,

Yours faithfully,
(signed on behalf of the Bishops of the Church
of the Province of South Africa)

GEOFFREY CAPETOWN
(Archbishop and Metropolitan)

The signing of this letter was Clayton's last act in this life. Late at night his chaplain brought the typed copy into his study, laid it on his desk for correction and signature, and went out of the room while the archbishop read through it. A few minutes later the chaplain came back to the study and knocked. There was no answer. He went in. The letter had been signed and lay open on the desk. The archbishop lay dead on the floor.

Though worse, much worse, was still to happen to his dear African and Coloured people, he had led them and all the people of his diocese and province through the most bitter years of their history. By his wisdom he had held them all together and kept them true to their Christian Faith and their Anglican heritage. It was God's final mercy to him that he passed so quickly to his fulfilment and his reward. But when he died no word of condolence came from the South African government and no minister of state attended his funeral, or was represented at it.

IV · *The Third Act of the Drama*

'I would maintain', wrote Archdeacon C. T. Wood, one of the most experienced priests in South Africa, in a letter to the author, 'that the climax of our witness in South Africa was in 1960, and that since then our influence has steadily declined.' It is a depressing judgement, but it is recorded by one who knows of what he speaks. Later in the same letter he mitigates it a little:

While it is perfectly true that we have the longest and best record of any Christian body in this country in our stand against Racialism, it is also true that we do not carry all our people with us. . . . All this of course gives great opportunity to the enemy to blaspheme. Yet I would myself hold that the fact that we have set our face in the right direction is of the greatest importance and value, even if the record of our witness is stronger than its practice.

The judgement can be tested by a recitation of the facts in their chronological order.

Geoffrey Clayton died on March 6, 1957. The letter quoted in full above, which he signed just before he died, immediately caused the Dean of Capetown to erect a notice outside the west door of his cathedral, and in the largest possible print, which ran thus:

THIS CATHEDRAL IS OPEN TO WELCOME MEN AND WOMEN
OF
ALL RACES
TO
ALL SERVICES
AT
ALL TIMES.

The official letter to the government was incorporated in a pastoral letter from all the bishops to the Church, which, by their orders, was read aloud in July of that year on one Sunday in the month at every service held that day, and in every Anglican church in the Union. In this the bishops called their people to disobey the segregation clause in the regulation about public worship, and publicly pledged themselves to a like disobedience. The Church in fact was openly courting persecution, and, if necessary, offering martyrs. But the government was too wily to oblige it, at any rate on that issue. Up to the moment of writing there have been no prosecutions on the charge of disobedience to clause 29 (c) of the Native Laws Amendment Bill. Few things are more dispiriting than the hurling of a brave and potentially costly show of defiance in the face of powers and potentates which continue blandly to ignore it.

It may be that the government judged that the weaker brethren in the Church would do its work for it. For it is again the judgement of the Archdeacon of Capetown that

we do not carry all our people with us. There are parishes in the Province who do not in fact admit non-Europeans, and there are parishes who have separate services not always due to language difficulties. Our Church Schools (so-called, but it is difficult to define what exactly constitutes a Church School) are not integrated, although there are more non-Europeans in them than the public realize, but no Africans.

It is probably true that no Church, whatever it did or said, has ever had the least chance of influencing the South African government. But in the long run it is Christian influence upon the mass of the African and the Coloured population which counts, and upon which the building of the Kingdom of God depends. In that sphere the tacit application of the principles of apartheid to the public worship of a Church, and in heedless or stealthy defiance of the bishops' instructions, fatally weakens the witness of the Church, and accounts for much of what decline of its influence there may have been.

Meanwhile a successor to Clayton had to be found and the bishops of the Church in South Africa looked to the English episcopate for him. Their choice, which seemed to many as inspired as it was surprising, fell upon Dr Joost de Blank, who, first as a parish priest in the east end of London, and then as the suffragan Bishop of Stepney, had by his imaginative ministry built up a great reputation. He was tireless, charming, slow to make up his mind and adamant when it had been formed, and had the power to attract and make permanent friends of all kinds of people. He was also vehement and volatile; in almost every way the exact contrast to Clayton. But his repute was deservedly very high, and when the appointment was announced no one doubted that the right successor had been found. He left England supported by the hopes and prayers of very many of his fellow Christians, and if a malign fate had given him time, his might well have been one of the great primacies of the day. But time was what he was not allowed to have. After a reign of only four years, he was stricken by an illness so serious that he had no choice but to resign and come home.

He was enthroned in Capetown Cathedral on October 25, 1957. It had been supposed by those who did not know him that the Dutch element in his ancestry would make him more acceptable to the South African nationalists than Clayton had been. No hope was ever more vain. Though ever a fighter, he came, as he said in his first charge, 'determined to follow the example of the Buddha and to maintain "a noble silence" until constrained to raise my voice'. Then he visited some of the worst slums in Capetown, where he witnessed the effect of the Native Laws Amendment Act, 'as man and wife and parent and children were pitilessly separated'. He protested, and then began 'the calumny and contumely to which I have been subjected since coming to this country. . . . I was vilified and abused on all hands.'

It was indeed true, and it continued to be true. In his charges he did give a like emphasis to the ministry of reconciliation, but that part of them was, so to say, less audible than the tempestuous denunciations. The nationalists found their suspicions underlined, and regarded him as the head and tail of their enemies. It is hard to see how he, or any other man, could ever have succeeded where Clayton had failed. Where in fact he did succeed was in his efforts to attract more priests to serve in the Church in South Africa. In the end, his sudden and grave illness forced his resignation only four years after he had assumed his great office.

In August 1958 Dr Strydom, the Prime Minister, became mortally ill and resigned. His place was taken by Dr H. F. Verwoerd. Although a man of great personal charm, he was also the most ruthless and uncompromising of all the Nationalist leaders, and more than any other had been the brain behind the apartheid system. From him it was unlikely that there would be any accommodation, or any desire for reconciliation, and in fact none has come.

The new Prime Minister got quickly into his stride. The apartheid regulations became steadily more and more onerous. The forcible evictions from Sophiatown were ruthlessly continued until what had been a model township and a garden became a ruined wilderness of broken bricks and mortar. The laws which required every native to carry his pass were enforced with a steady increase of severity. But it was not until 1960 that the real climax came with a series of events which meant that nothing in South Africa could ever be the same again, and that things must become much worse before ever they could become better. In the early months of that year Mr Harold Macmillan, the English Prime Minister, toured Africa, and made in Capetown his famous 'wind of change' speech, in which he gave warning to the nationalists of South Africa that the British Government could not countenance, much less endorse, their policy towards the native population.

The speech was bitterly resented, but it is improbable that there was any chain of cause and effect to join his words to the outrages which so quickly followed. In Cato Manor in Natal the police were trying to stop illicit whisky distilling when a crowd of natives suddenly attacked them, and nine of them were bludgeoned to death. That was bad enough, but what followed was worse by far. For on March 21 the Sharpeville massacre took place, when, in a dispute about the hated passes, the police suddenly opened fire upon a crowd of natives near the police station, killing 67 Africans and wounding 186 more. The firing went on for 40 seconds, and 750 rounds were fired. Many of the victims were young people, women, and elderly men; and the wounded were taunted by the police as they lay in helpless pain. In the House of Commons Sir Winston Churchill sombrely quoted Macaulay, 'And then was seen what we believe to be the most frightful of all spectacles, the strength of civilization without its mercy.' That happened in the Diocese of Johannesburg, and its immediate consequences were the arrest of Hannah Stanton, an obviously innocent victim of governmental panic, and her deportation after long imprisonment. This action was soon followed by the deportation of the Bishop of Johannesburg himself.

The fatal year, however, provided yet one more chance of redemption and reconciliation, but it was, humanly speaking, the last chance. Immediately after Sharpeville the archbishop and the bishops of the province sent the Archdeacon of Capetown to Geneva to appeal to the World Council of Churches in session there to try to arrange for a meeting of all the Churches in South Africa, with the purpose of securing a united front against the evils of apartheid. These Churches met at Cottesloe in the Witwatersrand University in the second week of December 1960, and they included the three Dutch Reformed Churches. The conference produced many valuable findings, and emphatically condemned the principle of apartheid, as well as its actual workings. At first the representatives of the very powerful Dutch Reformed Church of the Cape and the Transvaal gave general assent to the findings. The less influential and strongly fundamentalist Nederduitsch Hervormde Kerk refused their assent, as it was always known they would. But the tragedy was that when the agreement of the delegates of the Dutch Reformed Church went before the synod for endorsement, the synod refused its consent, not once but twice. Both these Dutch Churches then withdrew from the World Council of Churches. Thus Cottesloe failed, and with it the last chance had gone.

Thereafter there seemed no ascertainable grounds for hope, no way left which led to a place where the Church could stand and offer reconciliation to the African and his government. Protests had been made in plenty. They would continue to be made. They were and they are without any avail. The Church continues to serve the people. It is honouring the promise of Archbishop Clayton that wherever the people are made to go, there the Church will follow them. How much influence on the souls and lives of the African people this faithfulness may have no one can say. The larger hope is always there. The short-term future seems black.

25

The English Parish
and the Kingdom of God

I · *The Parish in Decline*

THE ANGLICAN bishops at Lambeth in 1948 had used language of high
solemnity to call the whole Church to a great evangelistic effort. Anglicans
everywhere were summoned, by those who had every right to make such
demands of them, to 'win the nations of Christendom back to the knowledge of God, and to take the good news to those who have not yet heard
it'. They must put themselves into training, as though for a campaign, and
dedicate themselves to it. The summons, and the words of comfort and hope
surrounding them, were read aloud to every congregation and from every
pulpit. Anglicans thus had their marching orders and they could not mistake them.

In the Church of England this meant a fresh and costly demand upon
the parish churches, since for centuries in a parochially organized Church
the parish had been its obvious, and often its only, executive instrument.
Whatever view might be held of the ministry of the laity, and however this
concept was defined, it remained true that the parish could not operate
either pastorally or evangelistically without its clergy, nor move far in any
direction apart from their leadership. If the bishops were depending on the
parishes to do the greater part of the work for the growth of the Kingdom
of God at that moment of history, then everything turned on the consent
of the vicar and on his ability to undertake the extra work involved.

In 1948, however, and for at least another five years, the parochial
clergy were ill placed to respond to new demands. They might and they did
wish to respond. They knew as well as anyone the importance of what was
asked. But the fact remained that there were still too few of them to do
more than hold the position as it was. For ten years there had been few
ordinations. In 1947, for example, Dr William Wand, Bishop of London,

instituted Articles of Enquiry among all his clergy, and by way of comment on the answers he received:

Over and over again I have had to notice that those answers reveal a bitter disappointment that our manpower is at the moment so weak, and that it shows so little sign of speedy replenishment. I am afraid that the facts are there, and there is little we can do at the moment to improve them. Two world wars have reduced the number of the clergy, and it will be a considerable time before their ranks can be filled. We have been ordaining two or three men—not many more— at our Ordination services in the last few years. There are signs of an improvement, and already we have eleven candidates for the ensuing Ordination. But it will be a long time before we go back to the fifty or sixty at each Ordination which used to be a characteristic of this diocese.[1]

Three deacons at a time when fifty or more were customary—a bleak prospect! And if this was true of London, which, by long tradition, had been the most potent of all diocesan magnets for ordination candidates, other dioceses were likely to be in a still worse position.

They were, and particularly if they were north-country dioceses. This statistical table of the fall in the number of curates in the industrial centres of the province of York between 1938 and 1949 makes the ominous facts plain. During those eleven years the number of curates at work in Manchester had dropped from 141 to 54. In Liverpool the comparable figures were 158 and 58; in Sheffield, 106 and 43; in York, 122 and 54. In Birmingham the position was yet more catastrophic, for there the figures were 178 and 38.[2] Another table published in the same article in *Theology* tells the lamentable story in different statistical language. In 1949, 14,972 parochial clergy were at work in England. Of these, only 3,974 were working in the province of York, which thus had at its disposal only 24·54 per cent of the total clerical force but had to minister to rather more than one third of the whole population of the country. It meant that in Middlesbrough, for example, there was one priest to 6,330 people, and in Hull one to 5,600. That was bad enough, but there were plenty of industrial parishes where one vicar was trying to minister to 15,000 or even 20,000 people, and with no hope at all of a curate to help him. If he was a good man, he broke his heart or his health, or both. If an average man, he came at last to terms with his impossible situation. He held his statutory services and he was the pastor of the faithful. Just occasionally, he even managed to get a short holiday. But gradually he came to accept the fact that there was little else that he could do. The clergy do not make the Church, but it is hard for it to exist without them. A simple sum showed that unless the annual number of ordinations was increased several times over, a Church without clergy must be the logical end of the process.

---

[1] *Our Day of Opportunity* (S.P.C.K.), 1945, p. 5.
[2] Compiled by G. F. Townley, Archdeacon of York, later Bishop of Hull; and published in *Theology*, December 1948.

It was bound to be several years before this sombre picture could have light and hope painted into it. To some extent this has since happened by means of events which nobody in 1948 could have supposed likely, notably by a surprisingly large number of older men, often holding important positions in the world, offering themselves for ordination. But for several years after 1948, to those who took mathematics seriously, it looked as if it might be necessary for the Church to postpone the attempt to be a militantly evangelistic body if the parish was to carry on its shoulders the heat and strain of the battle.

But another and ultimately a more serious malaise was already afflicting the parochial system. From time to time in the past the Church of England has seemed to decide that its pioneering and evangelistic work must be entrusted to other than parochial hands. The last years of the seventeenth and the early years of the eighteenth centuries constituted such a moment. They formed the era of the founding of the great societies, the Society for the Propagation of the Gospel and the Society for Promoting Christian Knowledge, whose history has been so long and so distinguished. It was as though there had been a definite decision that the works they were founded to do were no longer within the competence of the parishes, and must be done for them. The parish had lost status. The evangelistic initiative returned to the parish churches in due course, and throughout the Victorian era they held the power of the Church in their hands. But for many years they lost it. In 1948 only the very far-seeing could discern that the situation of 1700 was repeating itself, and that the parish was beginning to move into one of those historic moments when its importance in the divine economy would temporarily diminish. Ten years later the fact was plain. The parishes of England by themselves were no longer capable of presenting the Gospel to the English people.

In the early chapters of this book the central importance of the parish in the economy of the Church of England was often asserted. In the last resort, it was said, Anglican history was made in the parish; and when the parish failed to be true to its own destiny, no amount of success elsewhere could compensate for it. The parish church was the centre of gravity of Christian power, the vicar and his faithful inner ring of people the arbiter of its fortunes.[1] All these judgements were true, or believed to be true, when they were written. But that was in 1943. Five years later the Church was working in a very different world, the lineaments of which could not at that time be foreseen. By then the parochial system, as understood by so many centuries, was beginning to lose its force. Another period in which the parish was to move into a state of temporary eclipse was beginning. In 1948 the signs of this movement were few; in 1950 they were unmistakable.

Long before the diagnosticians of the Church's ills had decided where

[1] See, e.g. pp. 22, 23.

the disease of the parish church lay, but after it had been recognized that something was amiss, reforms of many kinds were put in hand. Some of them will be described in following pages. But the principal sum of many changes has been that the old independency of the parish church and its vicar has been slowly drained away. This process has much further still to go, but it has already gone so far that no one can see how the self-sufficient independence of each separate parish can be restored. Today we have come to the point when it has recently been seriously proposed that we should abandon the parochial system altogether, close most of the parish churches, concentrate our resources on a small number of strategically placed centres of worship, and send the parochial clergy to earn their living in various kinds of welfare jobs in the world. In 1943 anybody who put forward a suggestion like this would have been thought to be out of his mind.

For these reasons the parishes in 1948 were not well placed to respond to evangelistic appeals. That they did respond as best they could, even heroically, the following pages will show. But such large areas of modern life had moved out of their ken and their reach, and their work had to be supplemented by an ever increasing number and variety of non-parochial ministries. Every year which passed made more plain the really acid fact that in every industrial centre, whatever the parish church did, whatever experiment it tried, however heroic the sacrifices of its people, the mass of the 'working class' would quite certainly and depressingly fail to respond in any significant way.

II · *The Mission to London*

Seen from this point of view, the outlook seemed bleak. But it did not daunt William Wand, the Bishop of London; nothing could ever do that. If human calculation showed no way forward, it was all the more necessary to demonstrate that dark though the day might be a highway did exist. Wand never denied the facts, but he was determined to wrench out of them an adventure of advance, and that on the largest possible scale. The mammoth Mission to London of 1949 was his answer.

Bishop Wand was a very exceptional person. He was a scholar who had made his own way in the world by hard work and a good brain. Starting from unpromising social beginnings, he had won his entry to Oxford, where he became a Fellow of Oriel College. His scholarship remained fresh in him always. As the long list of his books shows, he had never allowed the cares of administration in which he was immersed most of his life to smother his scholarly interests. He was also, and from the beginning, a notable personality, eminent in his own right. After he had served his turn as a parish priest, he was elected Archbishop of Brisbane, and worked there until brought back to England during the war to become Bishop of Bath and Wells. Somerset did not keep him long, for in 1944 he was appointed to succeed the new archbishop in the see of London. Blessed by almost perfect physical health and the optimism which so often accompanies it, he had trained himself in habits of apparently tireless industry, and he had always lived the devotionally disciplined life. Whatever the pressures of his public duty he continued to read and to write every day. His sense of style, thus fed and trained, showed itself in the fact that he never spoke in public without having something real to say, and what he said fell always into its perfectly constructed paragraphs and sentences. Neither in writing nor in speech was he ever loose or slipshod. A very remarkable man, with the gifts of a prophet and a power to inspire the loyalty and the affection of those who served under him, he gave all his powers to the leadership of the most onerous diocese in the country, and yet never allowed himself to be made dull by its cares.

The war was barely over before his plans were made. He saw the danger of allowing the gloomier facts of the Church's situation to prevent the diocese of London from making some forward move. He realized that the spectacle of the most terribly battered of English cities refusing to accept defeat, and, in spite of all the difficulties, marching boldly and publicly to claim its kingdom, must have some effect of encouragement upon the evangelistic witness of the Church in the rest of the country. The difficulties were very real. As we have seen, three new deacons were being ordained at a time where sixty had long been customary. Out of 700 churches only seventy had escaped damage in the air raids and seventy had been totally destroyed.

We recognized that the greater part of the cost of replacing and restoring buildings wrecked by bombs would be borne by the government's War Damage Fund. But to supplement those payments and to meet the needs for which we could get no outside help we reckoned that we should need at least threequarters of a million pounds. We had to set ourselves to the task of raising that amount.[1]

But though the days were dark and the prospects alarming, they seemed to Wand to be the Day of Opportunity—a phrase which he never allowed his diocese to forget. Men's bad days often make God's opportunity, but you need a great leader to believe it himself and get it believed by others.

He therefore conceived a plan of immediate, corporate adventure for the Kingdom of God, which, on the heels of the war, he put into practice at once. The plan had three parts. The diocese must accept a widespread and thorough reconstruction of every field of its life, and for this a large sum of money must be raised. There must then be a forward evangelistic movement on a very large scale. It must grow out of, and be seen to follow from, the reconstruction and the finding of the money to finance it, and thus it would save reconstruction from becoming an end in itself. It must lead towards the Kingdom of God. The Mission to London was the forward

---

[1] William Wand, *Changeful Page* (Hodder and Stoughton), 1965, p. 184.

movement, and from the beginning it was to be the whole point of the plan and the peg on which every part of it hung.

The bishop therefore began by sending Articles of Enquiry to each parish, and when he had considered their replies he built upon them the addresses of his Visitation Charge, which he delivered in eleven parts at eleven different centres. At the same time at each centre he formally received the gifts the people had collected to meet the expenses of the reconstruction of the diocese. They amounted to the sum of £36,370.

The Visitation Charge he firmly called *Our Day of Opportunity* and the S.P.C.K. published it in 1948. Though when read now the little book seems inevitably dated, it is still impressive for the fortifying note of confident hope which the bishop put into every part of it, the very wide range of the Church's witness which it covered, and the distinction of the prose in which it was written. Whatever the difficulties of the moment, he had no doubt that the Church in London could immediately move forward to lay seige to its kingdom, and he successfully inspired those who heard him to share to the full the confidence which animated him. This passage on the Blessed Sacrament with which he ended the address at Enfield was entirely characteristic of the charge as a whole:

We must make the whole environment in which we live capable of expressing the beauty and splendour of Almighty God. I believe that in the parishes where that effort is consciously made there is a beauty, a power, and a splendour that comes out from the Church, flowing from the altar, penetrating every home, and kindling a fire on every domestic hearth. The greatest gain we have made in the religious sphere in the last century has been the renewed grasp of the sacramental principle and the endeavour to work it out in every detail of our daily lives. If we in these days can reinforce that lesson and adapt our teaching of it to the needs of our generation, then I believe we shall be able to give to the men and women of our day something which they very sorely need. We have the answer to our questions in the Gospel of the Kingdom. That is the Gospel we must preach, and today is our day of opportunity.[1]

Speech like that has the power of fire in it. Heard in the difficult and unpromising days of 1947, it strengthened many feeble knees and it set many tired feet marching again.

The goal of this treading was an evangelistic mission to the whole of the diocese of London to be conducted as a single, vast, and imaginative enterprise. The calculations of the realists had for years warned the optimists that the day when adventures on this scale could be expected to produce the results hoped for had long since passed away, and that persistence in them was a defiance of actuality. The bishop and his advisers refused credence to the jeremiads. They judged that the case for making a great public gesture of faith all over London at that moment was overwhelming. The Church must be seen to be defying fell circumstance

[1] *Our Day of Opportunity*, p. 66.

precisely because it was also seen to be battered by the disasters of war, and afflicted by wounds not yet healed. But what was proposed constituted a tremendous undertaking for any diocese at any time. The mission was organized in district centres rather than in each separate parish, but to staff it involved the finding of no less than 155 missioners. The work of preparation followed courses normal and abnormal, traditional and inventive. What was notable, and to a large extent fresh, was the large part the laity played, especially the men among them, and their fertility of resource in providing a steady stream of publicity of every kind. Another feature of the preparation as impressive and memorable as it was unusual was the strong support the bishop had from the national press. The bishop himself has described it:

> The main difficulty was to be sure that the news of our doings did reach the man in the street. In London you have to make an awful lot of noise if you are to be heard above the din. What we did was to go in for an expensive advertising campaign. We received a good deal of help from various public bodies; and the Londoner, as the time drew near, became familiar with our poster of a man looking across London at the cross on the dome of St Paul's, and with our slogan, 'Recovery Starts Within'.
>
> One of the finest gestures was made by the Editor of the *Evening News*, who invited me to write his leaders for a whole week, and announced in advance what his paper was doing for the sake of the Mission. At least one of his subscribers wrote that he would never buy a copy of the paper again, but the Editor went on quite unperturbed, and I am sure we benefited greatly—not from my articles which were amateurish enough, but from the fact that a leading London daily should be known to be thus helping us.
>
> A further opportunity of excellent publicity was furnished for us by Lord Rothermere and the *Daily Mail*, when they invited us to hold a service, led by the massed choirs of the parishes around Olympia and accompanied by the Royal Marines' band, on the final evening of the Ideal Home Exhibition. The press as a whole and the B.B.C. were consistently helpful.[1]

The Mission began in the late spring of 1949 with a great service in St Paul's Cathedral for the commissioning of the 155 missioners who came from every part of the country. Four long processions converged on Ludgate Circus, climbed the short and famous hill, and entered the cathedral in one long, long line, where they filled every seat, stood in rows along every aisle, and the remainder, for whom no place inside could be found, stood in a vast crowd on the space on top of the steps and followed the service relayed to them by loudspeakers.

Announced by posters in all the underground stations, and heralded in each of the 122 centres by brass bands, processions with banners, and even, in one place, by a Heath Robinson-looking mobile bell unit, and otherwise supported by every device to catch the eye and assault the ear which a highly resourceful laity could invent or provide, each of these centres had a very large congregation night after night, with overflow meetings outside.

[1] *Changeful Page*, pp. 192f.

When all was over an inquest was held, and a summary of achievement
was printed and published in a pamphlet called *Recovery Starts Within*.
To read it today is to get the impression that, with one significant exception,
the results were much what one would expect. The already faithful members
of the Church were fortified and enheartened. On the general mass of the
unconverted, living contentedly without God in the world, the Mission had
very little effect. The significant exception was the surprisingly large number
of people who, before the Mission, had stood poised delicately on the
shores of the lake of the worshipping life of the Church, and who then
plunged into the waters of salvation and have been swimming in them
ever since. Superficially it sounds like a recitation of a rather chilling success, a tale which has sadly to be told so often at the end of most modern
attempts to revive the once effective methods and formulas of the old-
fashioned parochial mission. But that is not how the bishop saw it; and
as the whole conception was his, it is right that he himself should provide
the final judgement in his own words written sixteen years later:

> We had no cause to complain of lack of interest or of numbers. From all
> quarters came news of big and increasing audiences. It was less easy to be sure
> that we were attracting quite the people we wanted. The bulk of them were our
> own faithful, who had done all they could to prepare for the Mission and were
> now enjoying the fruits of their efforts. We were aware also of a considerable
> number of lapsed church-goers, who were being won back to the practice of their
> religion. We should have liked to hear of more of the unconverted being drawn in.
> There were indeed a certain number and some of them benefited permanently
> by the experience; but we can unfortunately claim no greater success than
> others in making contact with the genuine man in the street—or on the assembly
> line.[1]

Nevertheless, in the calmly judicious perspectives of history, the Mission
to London of 1949 was of great and real importance. Its timing gave it its
significance. For too long the Church had supped the diet of failure and
accepted the definitions of impotence. Here was a demonstration, staged in
the battered capital city of the country, that churchpeople had faith in the
Gospel, and in their mission to proclaim it, and that they did not intend to
sit down tamely before the reproaches of paralysis. They could still organize a giant undertaking and carry it through. But above all it was a testimony to the faith, the courage, and the powers of leadership of a great
bishop, who was also a scholar and a prophet.

III · *The New Housing Areas*

London, however, was not England. By 1949 the real parochial field of
battle for the Kingdom was moving away from the downtown parish in
Stepney, or Ancoats in Manchester, at one time, but no longer, the Mecca

[1] *Ibid.*, p. 193.

for the young Anglo-Catholic curate with the fire of the Gospel in his heart and the love of the poor in his bones. The Christianity of England began to be decided in the new towns, like Stevenage, or the housing estates which were already growing up on the fringes of all the cities where the young married couples of the country with their broods of children were being concentrated. There, if anywhere, was the youth of the land, living in great concentrations of immaturity, with every box-like house entered by the family on the day the last window was filled with glass. All the streets swarmed with playing children. In most housing estates, and in almost all new towns, there was for a long time little else besides row after row of new houses, their gardens still all brickbats and builders' rubble, the muddied or dusty unmade roads, and the tired and irritable young mothers plagued even more by loneliness than by the all-pervading dirt. The vanished fathers had gone far away to work before eight o'clock and were seldom home before seven. These new conurbations could be wells of loneliness and airy prisons of frustration. The new house was often apt to be a dwelling rather than a home, the estate a district rather than a neighbourhood. The desire of too many hearts beating in such places was to get back on all possible occasions to the old haunts whence they had been withdrawn, and where they knew old friends and were known by them.

When the Church, in the shape of the young priest-in-charge, came down the rutted road knocking at the doors, there was nearly always a welcome and a warm one, but too often that was as far as it went. He probably had no church other than a galvanized tin tabernacle, or sometimes nothing roomier than a builders' hut, to offer them on Sundays. There he ministered almost alone, and of these people he was charged to make a community of God. To give him a real chance to do it, the policy was to get the priest on to the estate before the bulk of the new tenants arrived, that is, while the estate was still in the early stages of building. The local authority would normally reserve for him one of its first houses. He thus had somewhere to live, but for a long time he had little else. The other necessities of his calling —a church, a hall, and the equipment for both—he had somehow to provide for himself as he went along. It was seldom that he thought he had an enviable job. The stories which come from the young clergy of the new housing estates and the new towns in the first ten years of their lives have a note of grim dourness about them.

And yet, on the face of it, the priest on the housing estate, and still more his slightly older brother who was chosen to be the first vicar of a brand new town still in the building, had a very enviable job. The romance of it was plain. Under his hand, in his pastoral care, he had the youth of England, and the young married people who were making a new start in their lives. The Church could offer no man a job of greater importance, or even of quite the same urgency. He was a pioneer enjoying an astonishing freedom for his age. Everything around him was growing, and nothing was static. He need be hampered by no traditions, for he inherited no other man's work. He could, and in fact he must, start from scratch. But, like all other pioneers, he must be able to stand up to loneliness, for loneliness was all round him, charging the air he breathed every day. This vocational disease of the new housing area laid siege to his own spirit as well as or even more than, his people's. His own calling worked out in such a milieu was bound to emphasize his sense of separation because, for a very long time, he must offer them the things that truly belonged to their peace, and for which most of them had, both literally and metaphorically, very little time.

It is true that the Church of England, acting through its bishops, its diocesan Boards of Finance, and the Church Commissioners, did from the beginning recognize to the full the tremendous importance of all these fresh conglomerations of housing, and put the problems they set in the front row of all competing priorities. Neither in encouragement and interest, nor in the providing of much of the necessary money, did the Church fail the young priest-in-charge or his people. But yet it is true that, in spite of the obvious romance and the adventure of it all, the success stories of the Church in the new housing area are exceedingly rare.

In those days an article in a newspaper describing the romance, the adventure, the excitement, and the tremendous importance of the work of the Church in such a field would normally kindle a sheaf of sad and despondent letters from the men actually at work in it. Something was clearly wrong, and analysis of such correspondence made clear what it was. Three complaints occurred over and over again. The first was loneliness. The people were lonely and the parson was lonely. Probably working single-handed, it was too seldom that he seemed able to cure their loneliness, or his own. The few among them who were churchpeople were apt to form the habit of going back to their old parish churches on Sundays, or to fail to form the habit of worshipping in whatever kind of building it was that served them for a church in the new parish. Many others went back to the streets, the public houses, and the cinemas they had known familiarly for years. Few among them all had any particular desire for a new church of their own, and fewer still were prepared to accept any responsibility for building it. But if they did stay at home on Sundays they liked to have their children out of the way, and it may be that they did accept a certain sense of spiritual responsibility for them which they had repudiated for themselves, so that the Sunday School or the Children's Church was often the most outwardly successful part of the priest's work.

The second common complaint follows from the first. The priest had everything to do himself which in most parishes elsewhere would be done for him. He had to be his own collector of subscriptions, his own accountant, his own Sunday School superintendent, even at times his own organist and choir trainer. To this he must add the pastoral care of all the people, thousands of them, who, if he were there in the early stages of the building of the estate, poured in faster by far than he could possibly hope to keep pace with. This heterogeneous collection of strangers he must turn into friends, these families into a congregation, and all into a community of God. It was the only cure for their loneliness, but he knew well that though this was what they needed, what he had been commissioned and sent to give them, it was the last thing in the world they consciously wanted. This was the third common complaint, and the three made a daunting list which in fact daunted many.

The first vicars of the completely new towns were also liable to suffer many disappointments. Many of these towns were built on an area of land belonging to as many as half a dozen country parishes round about, and it often took complicated and seemingly interminable negotiations to extract their wholeness from the care of six pairs of clerical hands and place them firmly in one pair. When at last the new vicar's charge was indubitably his own, he had the task of giving to the new town a character and a soul of its own, and of expressing this sacramentally by the stone and brick of a really worthy new church and a fine church hall. The charge was so interesting to the rest of the Church and to the public generally that, more than most clergy, these vicars and their curates (for in new towns there were always curates) felt themselves working always under the arc-lights of publicity. It was necessary that they should, but they were apt to find the glare wearing. They carried—and they knew it—a terribly heavy burden of responsibility, and sometimes they were so incessantly conscious of it that it seemed almost to overwhelm them, and to enfeeble their initiative. They too dwelt in the mist of loneliness, for in the new towns the sense of isolation and rootlessness was for a long time very strong. By hard and incessant work they made full proof of their ministry, and they did all they could to serve and teach their people, and to give them a sense of belonging to a new community with all its life to build. But it was intensely difficult, and could only be fulfilled by the work of several generations of pastoral fidelity. The first vicars of new towns were seldom able to continue in a longer stay than was necessary to build the new church. The pace of their life was too hot for any man to sustain for long.

Although there were exceptions, the Church plainly found the new town, the housing estate, and the vast block of flats a field of ministry of peculiar and unexpected difficulty. The devotion was there. The great importance of what was being attempted was fully recognized, and money was poured into them. But it is still exceptional to find people who really liked living in any new area of housing, and common to hear incessant complaints of loneliness. The clergy working in such places always felt that they should not be left there too long. They too could not escape from the common malaise that they were too often a congeries of individual families who fight shy of more than the most casual of relationships with their neighbours. That is to say that one of the first conditions of evangelistic power of the Gospel, and of the instinctive way of ministry of the Church of England, was commonly absent from most of the new housing areas, and the undoubted devotion of multitudes of the younger clergy could not put it there. Thus it has come about that the impact of the Church upon the people in the myriads of council houses or flats built since the war is tragically less than might have been hoped.

IV · *The Church in the City*

At the other end of the scale was the old single-parish-church town like Rugby; and the larger towns like Bury in Lancashire, or Halifax in the West Riding of Yorkshire, or, on a larger scale, Leeds, where there were many separate and independent parishes but one undoubted and un-challenged parish church of the whole town, the vicar of which has always held a special position of civic eminence in the town and pastoral priority among the clergy. Almost all of these have to tell sad stories of retrench-ment in the last twenty years, and the sum of these reports is the gradually lessening impact of the Church on the people of the industrial town. St Mary's, Portsea, one of the most famous of English parishes, is typical, with its melancholy recital of mission churches closed and the number of curates halved.

But Rugby is the most convenient example of the industrial town with one vicar, one parish church, and many curates ministering under the vicar in the several mission churches. The history of the Church in Rugby since 1910 has recently been the theme of an exact and laborious piece of research by Mr David Clark, once a student at the William Temple College in Rugby, and now a Methodist minister in Yorkshire. His work has not yet been published, but it tells, and annotates with copious statistics, the discouraging story of the downward curve of the graph of church atten-dance, and of the influence of the Church on the life of the town from 1910 to 1960. His survey involved him in pertinacious enquiry into the affairs of every church in the town, whether Anglican, Roman, Free Churches, or the various sectarian conventicles. All of them seemed to be ready to answer his questions. The history of each one was the history of them all. Everywhere church attendance has slumped continuously and disastrously. In its industrial, social, and civic life the town had removed itself further and ever further from the influence of any Church. It is true, but not com-forting, that in Rugby the same story would have to be told of the influence on town and people of active trade unionism, of all political parties, and of all other forms of social organization which live and have their purpose in the desire to serve others. There are many causes of this sad state of affairs, which would be just as true of most industrial centres in England, and they have been analysed again and again. Mr Clark in his turn contributes to this library of analysis, but he also does something far

more constructive. He sees a possible remedy and he works it out in some
detail.

First of all, good Methodist though he is, he is convinced that the Church
of England must supply the leadership in any effort to regain the lost
ground. No other existing Church can do so. Rugby, and indeed England,
cannot be saved without the English Church, though never by that Church
alone. But in Rugby, as in other towns of roughly the same kind, the
Anglican vicar is the town's vicar and the parish church is the town's
church. Centuries of tradition lay the task squarely on Anglican shoulders,
and if we fail to give this leadership no other Church can supply it. But the
Church of England cannot do it alone, and it would be madness to try.
The first condition of its being done at all is the steady and full co-operation
of every kind of Christian Church in the town, and consistently followed
over very long periods. This means something like a permanent mission
of teaching and pastoral service; and in this every Church must take part,
and be seen to take part. This they are unlikely to do unless they all have
a full, responsible share in the planning of whatever is to be done. The
Church in Rugby, says Mr Clark, has lost its sense of mission. It must
recover it or fail completely, and this is its only choice. But the mission
must be both long-term and modern.

It must work along the lines of present-day social and cultural patterns and not
across them. To think in terms of campaigns and occasional house-to-house
visitation schemes is like trying to halt an express train with a shotgun.

Where Mr Clark is most interesting is in his insistence that his remedy
cannot work at all unless the Anglican clergy, and particularly the vicar,
stay in their posts for much longer than is nowadays usual. He attributes
no small share of Rugby's troubles to the failure of its vicars to stay there
long enough for their influence to tell, and to the too rapid promotion of
its curates to benefices of their own. What Rugby needs, he often says, is
a vicar who stays there many years, and makes the service of the Church
in this single town the chief work of all his life. He singles out Baillie and
Blagden for special praise because each of them stayed there for many
years. They were both pre-war vicars, and it was since their time that the
troubles his graphs show began to be so obvious and so ominous. Their
successors, he says, though all of them very remarkable men, stayed in
Rugby too short a time. They never had the chance to reach the moment
when they could be genuinely influential. Most were too quickly promoted
to bishoprics. The rest found the physical and mental strain of being vicar
of Rugby too much for their health to sustain for long, so hot was the pace
of their lives.

The dilemma is most formidable. On the one hand there is no doubt
that Mr Clark is right in diagnosing a situation which only a permanent
mission lasting for years can relieve, and again right in claiming that its

first condition is that the clergy should stay at their posts for a long period of years. On the other hand, the calibre of men likely to be appointed to such posts as the vicarage of Rugby is so high that most of them are almost certain to be offered bishoprics, and an almost irresistible pressure will be put on them to accept them. The others are unlikely to be able to stand for very long the undoubtedly increasing strain of such positions. It resolves itself into a question of what the Church really wants. If it wants the permanent mission in a town like Rugby, and regards the rewinning of the lost ground in such places as being of vital importance to the Kingdom of God, it must allow a promising young vicar to give all his best years to it, and refrain from using him too early to recruit the episcopate. It must encourage him to re-plan the day-to-day conditions of his incumbency in such a way that his energies are not continually drained by matters of small importance to that Kingdom, and must stand firmly behind him when he is criticized for withdrawing himself from them. At the same time—a point which Mr Clark never mentions—if a vicar is appointed to fulfil such a charge as this, and on the understanding that he stays at his post for a long time, what is to happen if the choice proves to have been mistaken? It would then be essential to find some just and unhurtful way of removing him from this post and placing him in another. The permanent mission to a whole town and the full maintenance of the parson's freehold cannot always be compatible, and if the lost ground is to be recovered, the former is the more important.

The complaint of the ineffectiveness of the Church working through its parishes in the large town and in the new housing estate was, as we have seen, sufficiently constant to be ominous. What it portended was the realization that the parish alone could not effectively minister to these vast, but different, conurbations of population. Some way of supplementing the parochial system would have to be found. But what of the financial and commercial centre? No such centre is of comparable importance with the City of London, and there, thanks to the imaginative ingenuity of Bishop Wand and his advisers, very notably Oswin Gibbs-Smith, at the time Archdeacon of London and now Dean of Winchester, a notable experiment was conceived which showed a new way forward.

This was the conception of the guild church. Essentially it was an adaptation of the old idea of the territorial parish to the new conditions of the neighbourhood. The hope was that it would be possible for the people crowding into the City every day to be better served, and for the Church to make a deeper mark on them and on the whole of the corporate life of London which they represented, than could ever have been done without considerable changes in the old parochial system in the area. This hope was fulfilled. The guild church did much to save the situation in the City. This it did by a quite sparing degree of change, but it was such that it struck yet another blow at the old independence of the parish and its territorial unassailability; and it compromised, but without wholly destroying, the parson's freehold of the vicar. What has been done in the City of London could also be done, with modifications, in the heart of Manchester, Liverpool, Birmingham, and elsewhere, and particularly in the heavily over-churched centres of many of the cathedral cities.

The problem set by the City of London was the problem of the centre of Manchester or Liverpool writ large, but with accompanying circumstances all its own. In 1950, 5,627 people slept within the City in their own homes, while nearly 500,000 people travelled into it every day to work, and then travelled back again over long distances to their own homes in the suburbs. To serve these people there were 46 parish churches. Some had been destroyed in the war. Many needed to be repaired before they could be used again. Almost all of them were architectural treasures, many being Wren's churches. The traditions and affections which had gathered round them during the centuries were so thickly encrusted that their very names were a legend. The City without St Mary Woolnooth, St Lawrence Jewry, St Helen's Bishopgate, or St Bartholomew's the Great! It was unthinkable! But if the unthinkable was to become the practicable, much thinking would have to be done to find their right use in the post-war world. What was plainly impossible was to repair and maintain 46 parish churches, and their clergy, for the service of no more than 5,627 resident people.

The obvious answer was to add pastoral responsibility for the 500,000 people who worked every day in the City, but who had their homes elsewhere. But these were not and, as the law stood, could not be the parishioners of the City parish churches. For many hundreds of years in this country the cure of souls has been bound up with the territorial jurisdiction of the parish church. Neither the law nor the Church officially recognized a vocational jurisdiction. Each one of these 500,000 people was the responsibility of some vicar outside the City. The City vicars were legally responsible for the 5,627 residents, and for these alone. No man could legally be the concern of two vicars at once unless the law was changed. But the only possible change would mean that the Church must officially admit that parish churches as such can no longer serve the needs of people at work, and they are the chaplaincies of private family life. The problem could not be solved by the 46 parishes themselves, but only by some authority higher than their own. It sounds obvious, but it involved the quite revolutionary idea that even in its own area there can be a higher authority than that of the parish church.

Ancient history provided the germ of the idea of what might be done. For many centuries the City of London Livery Companies had maintained their old links with particular City churches. St Lawrence Jewry, for example, was regarded as particularly the church of the Lord Mayor and the Corporation of the City. This ancient fact was seized and developed by the quick imagination of the responsible authorities into a dream of parish churches of a completely new kind, the old idea of the guild church ministering to the merchants of a trade, and of making them responsible pastorally for the 500,000 daily workers but not responsible for the tiny resident population. This vision was accepted in principle by the Church Assembly, and the legal draughtsmen set to work to clothe the dream with a body of law. For before anything could be done at all, a number of parish churches would have to be unchurched, that is, deprived of their territorial status, and, as the law then stood, it was illegal. The legislation, once prepared, went quite quickly through all its parliamentary stages, and the City of London (Guild Churches) Act, as it was called, became part of the law of the land in the summer of 1952.

The Act created a new picture of the ministry of the Church in the City. By uniting two or three neighbouring parishes under a single vicar the 46 parish churches of the City were reduced to 24. Where there were such amalgamations one of the churches became the new parish church; the others became redundant chapels of ease. Of these, sixteen were chosen to become guild churches. The minister in charge of a guild church is a titular vicar but he is not an incumbent. He does not possess the parson's freehold, and his status is not territorial. He is appointed for five years, with the possibility at the end of that time of an extension of not more than three years, and the extension can be renewed indefinitely at intervals of three years, or else not renewed at all. A guild church vicar has a weekday ministry to the City workers and to others which he may exercise just as he thinks fit. He has no statutory obligation to hold services in his church on Sundays. But he is expected to have some specialist qualification through which he and his church can serve the Church as a whole at that point of its need. To take just one example, the guild church of St Katherine Cree has become the centre of the whole Church's mission to industry, and its vicar has always been the director of the Industrial Christian Fellowship, and his church its headquarters and its worshipping home.

The old links of many of these new guild churches with one or another of the City Livery Companies have been carefully preserved, and any one of them may become the church of some aldermanic ward as well as a guild church. If this happens, an alderman and two common councillors of the ward become *exofficio* members of the parochial church council. The guild church of St Lawrence Jewry was confirmed as the church of the Corporation of the City, and the Corporation appoints its vicar. Thus the vicar of a guild church may find himself fulfilling four functions. He must do what he can to minister to the daily City workers and in any way which seems good to him and to them. He may well have a responsibility to one of the City Livery Companies, and perhaps to his aldermanic ward as well. He must use to the full, and through his church, his specialized knowledge for the benefit of the Church as a whole. The then Bishop of London, Dr Wand, justly summarized the whole conception in these words:

The City may become a great laboratory in which new methods of ministry, new spiritual expedients, and new pastoral techniques may be tried out for the benefit of the Church as a whole.

It constitutes a real advance, and what is possible in the City of London should not be impossible to adapt elsewhere.

V · *The Church in the Country*

The village churches of the country in post-war conditions were ripe for much variableness and many shadows of change, and it was not possible for them to escape the attentions of the architects of ecclesiastical reconstruction. The problem they posed can be adumbrated by the quotation of a single figure. In 1939 sixty-five per cent of the parishes of England were still so rural that their populations did not exceed five hundred. This figure had been broken down a little in one of the most authoritative small books ever written about modern rural life, Professor C. S. Orwin's *The Problems of the Countryside*, and there he had written:

> It may come as a surprise to some to learn how small are the majority of village communities. In the four counties of Devon, Berkshire, Huntingdon, and Westmorland ... there are about 772 parishes with populations of not exceeding 2,000. Of these only ten per cent exceed 1,000, while 45 per cent, nearly one half of them, have only 300 people or fewer. The great problem of the countryside is how to make life more abundant for the rank and file of dwellers in these little places.

In the country it was true, as it still is, that life cannot be abundant without the many services, both spiritual and social, which the parish church provides. In a village the church can still matter profoundly, and it is round the vicarage that much of its common life revolves. But the shortage of ordination candidates, for which in 1945 no one could see a remedy, meant that it was not possible for each country parish to be provided with its own separate vicar. Nor was it right to send any man, except perhaps some scholar who needed peace to serve the Church by his scholarship and at the same time to undertake a small pastoral charge of his own, to a task which could not possibly occupy enough of his time, or call out the fullness of the powers he had to offer. Nor would it be easy to find the right men who were willing to do it. Even today, when rural reconstruction has gone very far, the duty of finding the right incumbent for a remote country parish is the nightmare of patrons. When Mervyn Haigh was Bishop of Winchester he once remarked that it took him an average of thirty letters and three interviews to find a vicar for a country living, and at any given moment he would have not less than five vacant. In the diocese of Norwich the problem was still more serious, for there it was almost common form for a country parish to be without a vicar for a year or more, so difficult was it to fill the vacancy. The intractability of the problem, bedevilled as it always was by financial difficulties, varied from one diocese to another, but everywhere it became so serious that it was not possible for the system to remain unmodified.

To meet this situation, after strenuous debate in the Church Assembly, the Pastoral Reorganization Measure became law in 1949. By this measure every diocese was required to carry out a survey of its own diocesan needs in the light of the manpower and the money available, in order to provide for the better cure of souls in the parishes. Town parishes were not of course exempted from the operation of the measure, but it was first of all for the good of the country parishes that it had been framed and passed. What actually happened was that the diocese formed a reorganization committee charged with the duty of surveying a neighbourhood, and suggesting ways and means by which two or more adjacent country parishes could be amalgamated when one or other of them next fell vacant. The theory was that where this kind of arrangement was made one vicar could do the work of two or more, thus providing a necessary economy of manpower, and giving to the vicar a more nearly full-time job than the recitation of the number of his population might suggest that he had.

In practice it was not so simple nor so obvious. The number of the parishioners has never been a just criterion of the demand that a country parish makes upon its vicar, who, more often than not, must do for himself and by himself everything which his brother in a town parish would expect to be done for him. He was very often his own churchyard mower, his own boilerman, his own cleaner and bellringer, and sometimes the drawer of water from the well for his own house. If he took a holiday or fell ill, he or his wife must undertake all the business of finding a substitute. His life was apt to be hard and lonely, and the number of his people made little difference to the weight of the pressure of these chores.

The system of union actually adopted meant, moreover, that though two parishes were amalgamated their parochial institutions remained separate. There were two parochial church councils, two branches of the Mothers' Union, two Sunday Schools, two sets of accounts. The vicar under the measure was not legally required to provide the full Sunday services for each church. But many tried to do so, with the inevitable consequence that Sunday was a day to be dreaded, which often ended in a wretchedness of physical and spiritual exhaustion. It is true, however, that as the period wore on, this position was gradually made more tolerable by the wide extension of the system of lay readers.

The question of the vicarages also caused much complication and some heartburning. The parish in which the vicar lived seemed to have an advantage over the others in the union; and though the vicar did all he could to treat each of his parishes with equality and fairness, there is no doubt that a vicar living round the corner is a much better proposition than one living in the village two miles away. Often a new vicarage had to be built, and the money received from the sale of even two old ones rarely covered the cost of the new. Thus the Church had to raise very large sums of money for the diocesan Dilapidations Boards to spend each year, and this was in addition to the money required to keep the existing vicarages in architectural seemliness and order. All in all, it was a device which nobody liked, but it was known to be essential, and no one was able to suggest a better.

On this measure the Editor of Crockford made comments in the preface to the issue of 1955–56 which were less than generous:

> We recognize the regrettable necessity which has caused many of these schemes, but they seem to us to have become an unholy passion with some bishops and archdeacons, who roam the countryside seeking what parishes they may devour. Some of these schemes have resulted in an unwelcome increase in episcopal patronage, most of them do violence to local sentiment, and inevitably weaken the life of the Church in the countryside.

Of these various statements only the first was indubitably true, the second was false, and the rest dubious. But the passage is worth quoting because it did lead the able but acidulous anonymous editor into a good tentative definition of the Group Ministry, which was the other and the more excellent way of ministering economically to small rural parishes. He would prefer, he said, to see this kind of amalgamation done in the towns rather than in the country, remarking that it would first be necessary so to improve the pay and the status of curates that men would be content to stay longer in their curacies, and to use their individual gifts in a wider area than that of a single parish.

The editor, however, was rather behind the times. What he asked for in 1955 had already existed since 1949, but, in full form, only in one area. This famous experiment in group ministry began in that year in as rural an area as could be found in England, centring upon the village of South Ormsby in the Lincolnshire wolds. The Rev. A. C. Smith, the first vicar of all the parishes involved, was indeed a pioneer, and he wrote a book, *The South Ormsby Experiment*, which S.P.C.K. published, to describe what was done.

The Lincoln Diocesan Reorganization Committee made a very thorough survey of the whole diocese, and published its findings in a pamphlet significantly called *No Secret Plan*. It strongly recommended that in the heart of the Wolds a new experiment should be made whereby no less than fifteen small country parishes with twelve churches might be grouped together into a single unit, served by one vicar, with a number of curates to help him. The area was 72 square miles, and the total population of it was just over 1,100 souls. If, therefore, this new kind of ministry could gain the consent of the people and be made to work well, then this pioneer experiment would make history, and become very significant for the future of the Church's ministry in country districts.

The first thing to do was to win the consent of the people. A public meeting was called and the bishop went to it. He carefully explained the plan and said that among other *desiderata* was the attraction of younger clergy to his diocese, and the provision of a proper rural training ground for them such as only this kind of group ministry could provide. The agreement of all concerned was won, and the following delightfully named parishes agreed to unite to form a single new parish of this kind—South Ormsby, round which the union was centred, Ketsby, Calceby, Driby, Harrington, Brinkhill, Somersby, Bag Enderby, Telford, Salmonby, Oxcombe, Ruckland, Farforth, Maidenwell, and Worlaby. Before the union these parishes had been served by six elderly and independent incumbents. Not all of them were vacant in 1949, and a start was made with eight, which at first were served by a vicar and a newly ordained deacon. As other parishes fell vacant, it became possible to attract more curates and lay workers. But not until several years had passed did the last parishes become vacant and come into the union.

The whole of this scheme centred upon the parish of South Ormsby, the vicar of which, the Rev. A. C. Smith, now Archdeacon of Lincoln, had already been resident there for a year or two. Because this was a piece of pioneering work he had everything to learn and there was nobody to teach him, no previous experience to serve him for a guide. It was therefore all-important that he should be the right man and be prepared to stay at this new post at least until the shape of this new ministry had become firmly established. No one who has read his book can doubt that he was the ideal priest to accept this new charge. But he himself was most uncertain about it. He has himself told with great frankness the story of how he rebelled against the duty the bishop was laying upon him, and has quoted fully from two letters the bishop wrote him when he was trying to make up his mind whether, after all, he ought to go back to being a town parson again. The bishop's letters, so kindly, so understanding, and yet so firm, are a model of what such things ought to be, and yet so seldom are:

As far as I can dissect the matter you are not happy in the country and you feel that you made a mistake in going to South Ormsby and are therefore restless. As against this, the position was, you accepted South Ormsby and thereby committed yourself to do your best, which you have done. You are all the time hankering after a town job which may or may not come your way. No man can do his work with one eye on it, and the other on something else turning up.

If you decide to take on the grouping experiment it must be with the clear determination that this is the job to be carried through and that you will not be able to consider yourself free to look at anything else for at least six years, by which time you will see how the work has turned out. I tried to put before you as clearly as I could how anxious I am that this first experiment should be successful. I believed, and still do believe you could make a success of it if you can fully throw yourself into it. But if you are to be shaken by doubts every time an offer is made to you, now is the time to withdraw and we shall know where we are.

In these matters I studiously avoid bringing any sort of pressure to bear. A man must decide these things on his knees, and with his own conscience. All I need is to be sure that if you put your hand to this plough there will be no turning back. So the answer to your question at the end of your letter, Do I still wish you to carry on? is 'Yes. I know you can make a job of it if your eye is single.'[1]

Who could resist such a letter from his bishop? The recipient made his decision at last, and firmly; he would accept the charge and pioneer the experiment.

He began with the eight parishes which between them presented him with six churches to serve; for the first six months he had not even a deacon to help him. 'Sundays', he drily remarked, 'were always hectic.' That must be the prince of understatements.

I notice from my old service lists that I used to cater for every church and spent my time rushing from one small church to another, always taking seven services and travelling 70 to 80 miles on Sunday. Six months of this was certainly more than enough for a man in his late thirties, and would have taxed the energies and patience of a younger man, but it was known that an assistant was on the way.[2]

But one vicar and one deacon do not constitute a group ministry, and the time drew near when all the other churches would be added to the sum. His first task therefore was the recruiting of a proper staff, his second the making of the repairs to a number of the little churches that would fit them for worship, his third the welding of so many tiny and scattered congregations into a single parochial community, his fourth to overcome the transport difficulty by collecting the money for, and then personally driving and maintaining, a parish bus.

It took two years to recruit the staff which eventually came to consist of the vicar, two curates, and a deaconess. The curates came and left, as curates always do, but nearly all of them were married men with families who had promised to stay for at least three years.

The curates have come from varying backgrounds. One was from Sweden, another a retired schoolmaster, one an agricultural worker, one from New Zealand, another from the Royal Air Force, one had been a land agent, another a solicitor, and yet another a director of a firm of builders.[3]

The group had retained three of the vicarages and sold the rest. The vicar lived in one, the curates in the other two. From the outset of their ministry the curates thus became priests-in-charge of their own districts, and responsible for them. But they were also members of a team. They planned their work together, sharing it out among them all, but living under the vicar's direction. But what makes individual priests into a team is the acceptance of a common devotional life and spiritual training. Upon that every group

---

[1] *The South Ormsby Experiment* (S.P.C.K.), 1960, pp. 48f.
[2] *Ibid.*, p. 25.   [3] *Ibid.*, p. 53.

ministry worthy of the name must be founded. In nothing was their experiment more successful than in the emphasis it put from the beginning on the corporate devotional life of the team, and the thorough way this discipline was provided.

The training may best be described by outlining the life we lead together. The first point of importance is that we are always a team. The curates receive their title to the Mother Church of South Ormsby though they live and move and have their being in the parishes in which they reside. We meet together at South Ormsby for Matins, Holy Communion, and Meditation on Mondays, and this is followed by breakfast together. Then comes teaching in the two village schools, followed by the staff meeting, when reports are presented on the work of the previous week and progress of the Sunday work, together with planning for the future. . . . The same routine is observed on Wednesdays and Fridays when we meet to worship at the parish churches where the curates function and we again have breakfast together. On Saints' Days the staff meet for worship at other churches in the Group in turn, but do not have breakfast together afterwards.[1]

Devotional discipline for rural clergy could hardly be more regular and thorough, and either a man rebels under it or else he is drawn into genuine community with his fellows, and this in the right proportions of independency and corporate reliance, each on all. It is the heart of the group ministry idea. Where it is done successfully the winning of the loyalty of the people to the larger unity of the Kingdom is, in time, almost certain. In South Ormsby it took time, but in the end it was done, and the Christians in the area worshipped as happily in one church as in another. Archdeacon Smith very properly goes into much detail about parish magazines, schemes of teaching, finance, and the like, to show just how it was all done. There we need not follow him. But the South Ormsby group ministry constitutes a genuine success story, and the archdeacon is its hero. He pioneered an experiment and it succeeded.

It has already been copied in various places, North Suffolk, Norfolk, and, in a very different milieu, among the downtown parishes around Miles Platting in Manchester. Clearly the group ministry is an idea with a big future.

VI · *Christian Stewardship*

It was however in the middle fifties that some of the more persistent perplexities of the English parish began to find relief by the adoption of a movement called Christian Stewardship. This had begun its life ten years earlier in either New Zealand or the United States of America. The claim of being the birthplace of the movement has been made by both widely separated nations but to which of them it rightly belongs seems never to have been decided. Nor does Christian Stewardship point to the name of any particular man as its founder. Few beneficent movements in the

---

[1] *Ibid.*, pp. 53f.

Church have been so anonymous, and since its beneficence is so amply attested it does not seem extravagant to credit it to the operation of the Holy Ghost.

At first it was a particularly thoroughgoing application of the principles of the Parable of the Talents to the almost chronic impoverishment of the parish church. God gives to his people all they have and all they are. To him they are responsible, and to him they must one day account for their use of his gifts. They are in fact his stewards. Therefore the parish which was invariably short of money to do the will of God was almost certainly suffering from some little realized but deep-seated spiritual disease. For God would not ask for a work to be done for him if he knew it was financially impossible to do it. He had already provided for what he wanted to be done.

This the Stewardship Movement realized, but its originality lay in the steps it took to deal with the situation thus diagnosed. A stewardship campaign in any parish rested on two simple principles. The work of the Kingdom of God in the parish was the charge laid on the whole people of God, and not only on a few of them. Therefore all the people must decide together what was needed, how much it must cost, and how this money was to be provided. This meant careful surveys of the work of the parish by clergy and laity acting together, and still more careful budgeting. The whole congregation must know what was needed, why it was needed, what it would cost, and, after full consultation, must agree together about it. Then the necessary sum of money must be found, and would be found if all of them, and of the others in the parish, gave really sacrificially of what God had bestowed on them. For this to be possible at all the faithful, armed with all their new knowledge of the needs of the parish church if it was to do its job, must visit the indifferent, put their case, and ask for their pledges.

Such were the bare bones of the method adopted by hundreds of English parish churches from 1954 onwards. A stewardship campaign was therefore much more than an elaborate effort to raise money. It was the church becoming the Church first in the sacramental field of finance, and then in the sphere of evangelism. Many parishes found that by a good stewardship campaign, done on the right lines, the whole corporate and spiritual life of the church was quickened, and that the campaign had all the evangelistic effects of the one-time parochial mission. It was a great power of conversion.

VII · *The Liturgical Movement*

Of all the experiments tried, and the attempts made to inject fresh life into the blood stream of the English parish in recent years, the Liturgical Movement has been the most successful, if success can be estimated by the speed of its spread, and the ubiquity of the parishes where its fruits are now to be found. The heart of the movement's conviction and message could be put, with absurd brevity, like this: what every parish church always does is to gather a congregation for the worship of God, and this worship is offered in the due form and order of the Prayer Book. If the Church exists to provide for the worship of the people, then it may be precisely through this worship, and its various implications, that the Gospel can be persuasively presented to the people whose lives it does not yet touch. But this is on condition that the congregations, and the individual people who form them, are themselves transformed by their habitual worship into what Christ would have them become. 'Let the Church become the Church' was the slogan constantly used; and another supplemented it—it is the business of the Church to turn the families into a congregation and the congregation into a family. The type of worship by which this could be done was plainly the Holy Communion. The purpose of the Liturgical Movement therefore was to make the Eucharist the chief service of the week, and so to celebrate it that it was *the* service for the whole family of God, from oldest to youngest, in which each one had his part to play. The implications of this sacrament, done regularly week by week in this way, would result, it was hoped, in the congregation coming to think of itself as an evangelistic force, ready and eager for corporate action to serve the Kingdom of God.

The movement has roots which, as we have seen on earlier pages, stretch far back into the period between the wars. They were partly French and partly English. In France, the Liturgical Movement became the contribution of the parish church to the effort of the whole Church to make a Christian impact on the industrial worker. Father Michonneau's book, *Revolution in a City Parish*, which described how the Liturgical Movement has transformed the life of the parish of Colombes in Paris, was very widely read in England, while Colombes became a centre of pilgrimage for many Anglican clergy. Since the war the enquiring pilgrims have tended to go to the parish of S. Severin, across the river from Notre Dame Cathedral. Everything the Liturgical Movement means at its best can be seen there. The whole life of the very large congregation is an expression of mission founded upon Eucharist to the entire neighbourhood, and in every field of its life. The impression one always has of it is that of an intense and happy vigour, and an astonishing fertility of social experiment through which all the children of God come to be loved wherever and whoever they are. Twelve priests work together there as a group ministry, and the parish could easily use as many more.

In England the movement was embedded in two books, and in a number of preliminary experiments in different parishes. In 1935 Father Gabriel Hebert of the Society of the Sacred Mission at Kelham published his well-known book, *Liturgy and Society*. It examined the whole movement of contemporary society away from God, and it showed how the Eucharist, rightly done, was the source of the power by which the social order might one day be redeemed. This was a seminal book which had real authority behind it. In 1945 it was reinforced by another, by Dom Gregory Dix of the Nashdom Benedictine Community, *The Shape of the Liturgy*, which, though a very scholarly history of the development of the liturgical forms of the Eucharist in the course of history, breathed everywhere the power of making religion exhilarating, and demonstrated the influence of the Eucharist over the forms of social order. Dix's book was very much the complement of Hebert's. Both were religious; both examinations of the social power of religious formulae and ritual action; but Hebert's book was primarily sociological, while Dix's had far more to say about the power of the Eucharist over the individual worshipper to turn him into what he called 'Eucharistic Man', and thus to make him into a fit member of the redeeming and redeemed social order.

The parochial experiments were many, and those made by the parish of St John's, Newcastle-on-Tyne, as well as in the cathedral of that city, have been fully described on earlier pages of this book. One of the few success stories coming from new housing areas was the building of the new parish church of John Keble on the Mill Hill housing estate of the London County Council, which was done in an astonishingly short time, and where the priest responsible for it, Oswin Gibbs-Smith, now Dean of Winchester, built the whole of that ministry on the Family Communion as the Liturgical Movement then—in 1938—understood it.

A new movement called *Parish and People* was founded in 1950 to espouse the fortunes of the liturgical renewal. After all these years it still exists, and by adopting the varied concerns of the radicals it appears to be able constantly to renew its first life and vigour. In England as well as in France the movement has exerted an authority and shown itself possessed of a steady permanence which none of the forms of specialized mission to the industrial world has ever fully shared. For both in France and in England the parish is an historic idea, or a shape of ministry, which is well understood and thoroughly familiar. The work of the movement is not yet done. In many ways it is still only at the begininng of its life. But parochial fidelity to its ideas has transformed the situation in many English parishes, and has been the fact which, more than any other, has done something to raise the status of the parish in a period when all else combined to depress it. The fruit of the Liturgical Movement is real even if it is not easy to define. On the one hand, it has not yet converted the nation; on the other hand, it has promoted and strengthened the fellowship of Christians, which the Fourth Gospel regards as lying near the heart of Christian effectiveness. It has helped to emancipate the laity by finding so many of them things to do in church, which is one step towards their discovery of their function in the service of Christ's Kingdom in the world.

26

The Reconciling Church

I · *The Needs of the Nineteen-Sixties*

ARCHBISHOP FISHER'S second Lambeth Conference met in July 1958. It was very different from his first, and much more significant. In 1948 the Lambeth Conference had summoned the Church to the work of evangelism, and this had been the theme which held the different parts of its report together. Little had come of it. After great wars the Kingdom of God stands still for a time, and it does not at such moments of exhaustion come in all of a rush. In 1958 the bishops set the Church a more modest task. They claimed from it during the next ten years an act of multiple reconciliation, and they struck this note at the beginning of their Encyclical Letter:

At the heart of the Christian gospel is that thought of reconciliation which has been the keynote of our Conference. At the heart of the world's confusion is the failure of men to understand and accept the way God offers by which they may be reconciled to him. In such situations it is the urgent duty of the Church to be the channel of Christ's reconciling power. We have tried to see all problems of reconciliation, for the solution of which the spirit of renunciation and self-sacrifice is an essential condition.

This contrast between the evangelistic purpose of 1948 and the reconciliatory purpose of 1958 is a good and handy summary of the change of climate which the past decade had brought to the world. Though by training and profession bishops view passing events *sub specie aeternitatis*, this makes these perspicacious men see them more steadily, and their judgement of the broad meaning of these events is the more likely to be just. A ministry adjusted to the true and universal needs of men in 1958 and for some years afterwards must be broadly reconciliatory. This purpose would be flexible enough to cover everything the Church might try to do, and because it is the kind of ministry in which neither failure nor success can be even guessed at the time, it is not subject to the discouragements which attend the more definite and short-term plans of evangelism, or the ill-starred efforts of Churches to persuade national states to alter their policies. Reconciliation is a purpose lying at the heart of the Gospel itself, and to engage in it in whatever way might be possible was the summons which the bishops at Lambeth issued to the Anglican Communion of Churches.

Between 1948 and 1958 the world had advanced to a point of divisive suspicion and strife which gave the idea of reconciliation an immediate relevance. The universal atomic war so dreaded in 1948 had not happened. Instead there had been a series of nasty small wars and armed nationalistic revolts, which were particularly cruel and seemed interminable, and which were far more deadly for the dream of human fellowship. In 1948, however, with the exception of South Africa and Malaya, the trouble spots which could be foreseen did not lie in Anglican dioceses. But time had made game of the forecasts, and long before 1958 the Anglican Church was involved to the full in the consequences of fighting in Cyprus, Kenya, Korea; and, it was plain, must soon be further involved in the coming nationalistic struggles of the whole of Central Africa. In the world of national politics there was going to be plenty of room for Christian reconciliation.

Plenty of room too for reconciliation's frequent price! In St Paul's Cathedral there is now a scroll of modern Anglican martyrs who have given their lives for their faith. It goes back to 1851 and there are at present 206 names on it. When whole families were put to death for Christ's sake, as had happened during the war in areas occupied by the Japanese and after it in Kenya, only one name is inscribed for each family. The number 206 is therefore only a minimum figure. Of these names, 88 are those of Kikuyu tribesmen who stood firm for Christ and were horribly killed by the Mau Mau. How much of what degree of reconciliation there has been in Kenya has been due to the suffering of these brave men and women? But Christian martyrdom has not ceased in the modern world, and the Anglican Church has its own roll of honour.

But Christian reconciliation through the strange power of martyrdom has been exceptional, and the situations to be reconciled have usually been caused by sheer confusion and infirmity of statesmanlike purpose. The settlement at the end of the war in Korea is an example. Korea formed an Anglican diocese, and the civil war there began in 1950. The United Nations intervened; the United States and Great Britain were at once involved. China came in on the other side. The fighting lasted for four years and the patched peace of 1950 left the country much as it had been before, divided into two parts, each of them foreign to the other, with a terrible legacy of hatred, fear, and suspicion to be reconciled. Organized Christianity had been banished from North Korea since 1939. No Church was left there to function in any way, so that when the peace of 1953 came at last there was nothing left in the northern half of the country on which to rebuild it.

In the south the Church recovered fast. Christians multiplied quickly. Today they number about seven per cent of the population, which is exceptionally high for an Asiatic country. By 1958 the bishops at Lambeth could look at the diocese of South Korea with a sober hope. The work of reconciliation would have to go on there for years before the scars of civil war could be healed, but at least there seemed a reasonable hope that it could be begun.

It was indeed plain that for years to come and in many parts of the world political fears and ambitions would breed fratricidal hatreds which nothing but the slow processes of reconciliation could heal, and they only against the barriers of terrible impediments. As reconciliation was a multiple process so also it must be a slow one. But there was room and more than room for it in the universal Church, within the Anglican Communion, in the family and the home, in the whole structure of modern industrial society.

Reconciliation applies all round and to every corner of the map of the world which a spiritually minded geographer would draw. It was essential to the whole purpose of uniting separated Churches. In 1958, though reunion was writ large on this map, the only positive achievement since 1948 was the union of most of the Churches of South India into a single united Church, and the recognition of its ministry by the English Convocations. Anglicanism as a single self-conscious motive force within Christendom was on this map. But there were still wide oceans of misunderstanding, and some narrow seas of bitterness, between one Anglican Church and another. To Africa, to China, to India the missionaries had brought so much else besides the Gospel, the patronage of colonialism for instance, that as these nations became newly independent many even among their Christians were showing resentment of spirit, and exhibiting it in bitterness of speech and writing. In this context the salve of reconciliation might take many forms, and did, as we shall see, take two forms in particular, the establishment of a staff college for the whole Anglican Communion at St Augustine's College, Canterbury, and the appointment of Bishop Stephen Bayne of the United States as the first executive officer of all the Anglican Churches. So wide is the concept of reconciliation in Christ.

The Anglican episcopate, which is the one and the only body able to speak with accepted authority to all the Anglican Churches of the world, had charted the course which the whole Church must follow for at least the decade in which we still stand, and it was no more, and no less, than the message of good news which constitutes the Gospel. From all creation God was in the world reconciling it to himself, and its members to one another. This is the one theme which holds together the otherwise scattered parts which remain to be written in this meditation upon an historical theme, and it is sufficient to unite them in a single pattern. There was thus no extravagance in believing that the word 'reconciliation' was what the Holy Spirit was saying then to the Churches, and still he says it.

Not many encyclical letters have been as impelling and as practical as this one. From the Report of the Lambeth Conference of 1958 the air of oracular analysis and optimistic summons, of which the Report of 1948 had been so distressingly full, had been banished. Since then the bishops had learned that brave words from the Church are of no avail in situations over which the Church can have little control. For the Church to preach peace to angry national governments bent on aggression is usually an exercise in futility. To summon the Church to work for reconciliation is more sober and more realistic, for the Church is then given something which it can do. For the reconciler takes the strained racial or political or social situation as he finds it, and then works within it, performing what acts of reconciliation he can. Gradually, almost always imperceptibly, the rawness creeps out of the air, tempers abate, strain loosens. At last the ground is cleared for men of goodwill who have the power to act to make changes of policy. The reconciling Church can set free the men of responsibility to make creative decisions, but it does not presume to say what these decisions ought to be. For all these reasons a Church bent on reconciliation is not embarking on a ministry of frustration.

II · *The Source and the Means of Reconciling Power*

When it was clear that reconciliation must be the theme of the Lambeth Conference, the subsidiary studies of its committees almost decided themselves. That all must begin with a call to the study of the Bible was plain because it is within its pages that the divine message of reconciliation is contained. The committee appointed to report on *The Holy Bible: Its Authority and Message* was a very strong one. Its chairman was Dr Michael Ramsey, now Archbishop of Canterbury; its vice-chairman Dr Philip Carrington, Archbishop of Quebec; and among its members was Dr A. T. P. Williams, then Bishop of Winchester, who had for ten years been heavily involved in the preparation of the *New English Bible*. These three names alone were sufficient to guarantee the scholarly soundness of whatever might be said. They resisted any temptation to strain after novelty and so, in one sense, said nothing that was new. But they showed themselves very well aware of the perplexities which both the form and the traditional language of the Bible must raise in the minds of many modern men who had had all their training under other and very different scholastic disciplines. The report really was an appeal to such men as these, and the committee's findings were at one point prophetic:

The Conference believes that the presentation of the message of the Bible to the world requires great sensitiveness to the outlook of the people of today, and urges that imaginative use be made of all the resources of literature, art, music, and drama, and of new techniques appealing to eye as well as to ear.

This recommendation was much expanded in the relevant part of the report:

In presenting the message to those who are outside the Christian tradition, the Church has to face the needs and difficulties which are sometimes discussed under the word 'communication'. The message has to be given with awareness of the setting of the lives of those who hear it and of the ways in which their mental outlook is formed.

The contrast is great between the traditional language of the Christian faith and the modes of thought of a scientific culture. This question needs much study within the Church, and it has no easy solution. While there is theological language which calls for constant paraphrase into contemporary idioms, there is also theological language which is difficult for many, not because it is old, but because it is poetical, and awareness of this can assist the work of Christian teaching. So can the use of good modern translations of the Bible.

This need of modern translations is referred to in other places in the committee's report, is mentioned as though it were a *fait accompli* in the resolutions, and is hailed with gratitude in the Encyclical Letter as 'opening up the Scriptures to new generations'. It was therefore clear to the bishops that the enterprise of translating the Bible into modern language would not only commend its study to those who were defeated by the archaic language of tradition, but also be a vital preliminary function of the use of the Bible in reconciliation.

In asking for an outstandingly good translation of the Bible into contemporary English, the bishops were not clamouring for the moon. In 1958 it was already more nearly an achievement than an aim, for it was well known that at least two translations of the New Testament were well under way, and one of them was within a year of fulfilment.

It was a priest of the Church of England, Prebendary J. B. Phillips, who had already done much to make Bible reading popular again. His work is one of the modern romances of publishing. During the war he was the vicar of a parish in South-East London. He had a youth club there and he found that those who came to it, try as they might, could make no sense at all of the New Testament Epistles. His expositions helped little because the stately but archaic language of the Authorized Version lay outside all possibility of their understanding it. He therefore began to make for them his own translation. He first tried his hand on Colossians, and sent the text to C. S. Lewis, who warmly encouraged him. By 1947 he had completed all the Epistles. At the suggestion of C. S. Lewis, who also contributed a laudatory preface, he called the book *Letters to Young Churches*. It took an absurdly long time to find a publisher, and Phillips had to face many disappointments. But eventually it was accepted by Geoffrey Bles, and a highly profitable association between author and publisher was begun.

Letters to Young Churches, published in 1947, was immediately successful and circulated widely. Thus encouraged, Phillips went on to translate the whole of the New Testament, and, under the title *The New Testament in Modern English*, this was published in 1959. Up to that moment Phillips had therefore given twelve years of his life to the specialized work of biblical translation, and, having now embarked upon the Old Testament, he is still continuing in his chosen course. Very few men have spent so many years more creatively, and better served the proclamation of the Gospel to the world.

His translations are careful, linguistically faithful, but so polished that they show no outward trace of the depth of learning or the immensity of hard work put into them. They use, but always with tact, all the resources of modern typesetting, paragraphing, chapter heading and cross heading. He and his publisher have made the books fair to see, a pleasure to handle, and more immediately inviting to a general reader than any of their predecessors. But all this, though most important, would have availed little had not the actual translation been both authentically contemporary and in fact exciting to read. It would be wrong to judge his work from the standards of literary criticism alone, even though in fact it does stand up to such a test, for it would mask the immensity of the achievement. The point was to produce an accurate translation in modern language which all kinds of ordinary people would want to read and enjoy reading. The fact that up to the present no less than four and a half million copies of Phillips' translations have been sold in different parts of the world is the evidence that he has wonderfully succeeded in what he undertook. How many people there may be who became interested in the New Testament, and found pleasure, and more than pleasure, in reading it in the new translation, it is impossible to do more than guess. But out of four and a half million copies sold, the number of such readers cannot be small. Phillips in fact has done much to remove the reproach that in England the Bible was fast becoming an unread book; and had he served the Kingdom of God in no other way, he has yet served it magnificently, and at one of its points of great need.

His success has not been lonely, and he does not stand on an isolated peak of eminence. In 1946, at the moment when, far away in South London, Phillips was just finishing his translation of the Epistles, the Presbytery of Stirling and Dunblane in the Church of Scotland made an approach to the General Assembly of the Church and asked that a translation of the Bible in modern language should be undertaken. It cannot often have happened in history that a comparatively isolated body of ministers of any Church has passed a resolution of such momentous importance. The Assembly immediately welcomed it, and being sure that a work like this must be done ecumenically—by all the Churches and for them all—a conference of delegates from the Church of England, the Church of Scotland, and the Methodist, Baptist, and Congregational Churches was summoned to meet in the October of the same year. This body accepted the charge, and later added to its number representatives of the Presbyterian Church of England, the Society of Friends, the Churches in Ireland and Wales, and the Bible Societies of England and Scotland. It was therefore to be a work of all the reformed Churches of the British Isles.

The committee elected J. W. Hunkin, then Bishop of Truro, as its chairman, and began its work in 1948. Hunkin died suddenly in 1950, and his place was taken by Dr A. T. P. Williams, at the time Bishop of Durham and later of Winchester, and now living in retirement, who has been the chairman ever since. The direction of the translating work was entrusted to Dr C. H. Dodd, one of the greatest of living New Testament scholars. Up to the present, only the New Testament part of what has been called the *New English Bible* has been published, and this was done in 1961. The introduction has described the method of procedure, which is as different as anything well could be from the way in which Prebendary Phillips tackled the same task:

The Joint Committee appointed a panel of scholars . . . whom they believed to be representative of competent biblical scholarship in this country at the present time. The procedure was for one member of the panel to be invited to submit a draft translation of a particular book or group of books. The draft was circulated in typescript to members of the panel for their consideration. They then met together and discussed the draft round a table, verse by verse, sentence by sentence. Each member brought his view about the meaning of the original to the judgement of his fellows, and discussion was continued until they had reached a common mind. . . . There is no member of the panel who has not found himself compelled to give up, perhaps with lingering regret, a cherished view about the meaning of this or that difficult or doubtful passage. But each learned much from the others, and from the discipline of working towards a common mind. In the end we accept collective responsibility for the interpretation set forth in the text of our translation.

There are, it seems, a few things which a committee can do as well as a private person working in solitariness, and biblical translation is one of them. The *New English Bible* is something of a masterpiece of the same order and rank as the Authorized Version, which itself was the corporate work of a committee.

It is a translation into contemporary idiomatic speech, having behind it the authority of the best biblical scholarship which was to be had, and which guarantees its meticulous accuracy. Whether it is invariably successful when judged from a literary point of view is a matter of taste and opinion. Test it on passages so universally known and loved as I Corinthians 13, or the Magnificat, and this translation seems to add lustre even to them. The Magnificat in particular is a most beautiful piece of writing. In church it reads aloud very well, and a lesson read from the *New English Bible* takes no longer in the reading than the same passage read from the

Authorized Version. These translators in fact have shown rare skill in making an archaically phrased sentence intelligible as well as accurate without adding to its length.

In its first five years, the New Testament sold five million copies in the new version. Some of the books in it were published separately in pamphlet form, and gramophone records made. Though these figures are very impressive, this work is only at the beginning of its publishing journey. It has still to be completed by the addition of the books of the Old Testament, and when the whole Bible is published in one volume there will be an immediate and still further outreach of its circulation. It is of course 'official' in a sense not true of most immediately preceding translations, and this has given to it a field of its own of semi-automatic circulation. There can be few churches which have failed to provide themselves with one or more copies, and few clerical studies in which it is not to be seen. But when full allowance has been made for this kind of automatic sale, it remains the fact that hundreds of thousands of copies have been absorbed by the reading public. It is true also that the success of the *New English Bible* has not compromised the continuing success of *The New Testament in Modern English*. The two works continue on their journey in partnership and not in competition. Between them they have made their way into at least six million pairs of hands; and to this must be added what sales the other modern translations, such as those of Dr E. V. Rieu and Ronald Knox, may have had. It is a most significant fact, and it is hard to believe that it adds up to anything less than a resurgence of Bible reading among a people who were in danger of losing the art, and losing with it the reconciling messages of God. No one can even begin to guess what effect on the growth of the Kingdom of God this biblical translating may have had, and will certainly continue to enjoy, but clearly it cannot be slight.

III · *The Freedom of Husband and Wife*

The more one studies the Lambeth Conference of 1958 from a later vantage point, the more pregnant and creative it seems to have been. The only subject the bishops touched without letting fresh light into it was 'The Reconciling of Conflicts between and within Nations', and this report was inevitably a rather lightweight affair. It had to utter the kind of optimistic generalities of which it was obvious from the beginning that the statesmen who alone had the power to change situations would take no notice at all, as in fact they did not. But apart from this the bishops allowed themselves only sober and practical dreams. They confined themselves to the situational problems in which their own work had made them expert, and in which their pondered words would carry weight. They passed from the Bible to the problems of church unity, and what they had to say made an undoubted landmark in the long history of reunion. They helped to make possible the dramatic quickening of the process since then. Similarly, when they pronounced on missionary strategy and progress within the Anglican Communion, they were moving within a country where they had the authority and the knowledge to make tactical plans, and, as we shall see in a later chapter, the policies they framed and the practical provisions they made to implement them bore a heavy crop of fruit. If it is the task of a Lambeth Conference to analyse the situations bearing upon the Church at the time of its meetings, and then to set up for the whole Church its targets for the next ten years, the conference of 1958 was one of the most significant of the whole series. As for the remainder of this book we shall be dealing with its direct and indirect fruits, there is no need here and now to adhere slavishly to the expounding of the findings of its various committees.

But the committee which considered 'The Family in Contemporary Society', of which Bishop Stephen Bayne of Olympia in the United States was the chairman, broke fresh ground in a field more urgently needing all the arts of reconciliation than most others. The steady rise in the proportion of marriages which end in the divorce court, and the consequent threat to the stability of family life, is a matter on which both Church and state are bound to be very sensitive, but also one where there is great conflict between the two on how it should be dealt with. For many years the problem had grown steadily more ominous, and the Church's position less and less intelligible to those who stood outside it. In 1955 the Archbishop of Canterbury had given his famous lecture to 'A Group of City Men' on *The Problems of Marriage and Divorce* and there he quoted statistics to illustrate the scale of the problem:

> In 1871 there were 190,112 marriages and 171 divorces.
> In 1910 there were 267,712 marriages and 596 divorces.
> In 1920 there were 379,982 marriages and 3,090 divorces.
> In 1933 there were 318,191 marriages and 4,042 divorces.
> In 1953 there were 344,488 marriages and 30,326 divorces.[1]

Those figures are catastrophic. Small wonder that the theme of marriage and family has been the hardy decennial of Lambeth Conferences from the beginning of the series. No social problem is more urgent or, it seems, less soluble, and the deadweight of sheer wretchedness which such figures as these measure is beyond the power of imagination to compass. Every bishop has letters every day reporting to him new and pitiful matrimonial casualties. They ask his advice, they invite his judgement, they plead for his compassionate understanding. The problem is in the air of every land all the time, and there is none in which the bishops have a more obvious competence. The primary difficulty from the Church's point of view has always been the same, how to get into creative relationship the need to

[1] *Op. cit.*, (S.P.C.K.), 1955, p. 16.

protect the Christian view of marriage, to provide children with their right to a stable home, to strengthen the basic social institution of the family, and to show Christian compassion to those who suffer so endlessly by matrimonial failure.

The Lambeth Conference of 1948 had produced a report on this subject, with the title 'The Church's Discipline in Marriage'. The conference of 1958 produced another report on the same subject, but it had a different title, 'The Family in Contemporary Society'. There is a world of difference between the titles and also between the reports. Both were deeply and equally compassionate towards those unhappy souls who, in marrying again after divorce while the previous husband or wife still lived, were breaking the rule of the Church. Bishops, after all, are very seldom unmerciful men. But both were equally insistent on the maintenance of the disciplines the Church had evolved to deal with the problem. The 1958 report went almost out of its way to endorse the judgements of its predecessors that no divorced person can be married in church, and that the admittance to Communion of anyone who had a previous husband or wife still living, and had married again, must always depend on the consent of the diocesan bishop concerned. The bishops of 1958 did not weaken in the least, and were careful to state that they still stood by the old disciplines. The mingled rigour and compassion of all Lambeth Conferences is understandable, and probably inevitable. But the Church's disciplines had manifestly failed to supply any ground for marital reconciliation, and had done nothing to halt the rising tide of marriage breakdown. Nor did the words of the bishops in 1958 make any difference to the Church's handling of the people whose marriages had failed, though it is perfectly possible that they may have saved many marriages in danger of failing.

For the report broke fresh ground and brought a great liberating force into the tangled field of sex relations within marriage. The failure to manage these aright had always been a cause of marital failure, and one reason for this failure, where it existed, was the uncertainty of what was right from a Christian point of view in the field of sex, coupled with an instinctive repudiation of most that the Church had said about it in the past. What the conference had to say about this took the Church right out of the cloud-cuckoo-land of the past and into the new world of the mid-twentieth century.

It was the first time that a Lambeth Conference had squarely faced the idea that sexuality, because it is an instinct implanted in man by God, must have a theology behind it, and that, if it does, sexual intercourse must be a joy to be sought by Christians within the terms of this theology, and not a discreditable necessity to be ashamed of. The theology makes it clear that while the procreation of children is one purpose of sexuality, it is by no means the only purpose:

Neither the Bible nor human experience supports such a view. Where it has been held, the reason generally lay in a fear of the misuse of the sexual relationship or in a false sense that there is, in any sexual relationship, an intrinsic evil. Neither fear nor a false sense of what is 'evil' is a helpful guide for humanity, in this or any other matter.[1]

But in fact the Church had for many centuries been riddled by this fear of sex, and by the deep belief that there is something discreditable about it; and this puritan superstition—it is no less—had done great damage to many marriages which otherwise might have been perfectly happy. Lambeth Conferences had usually tackled the problem in the context of the use of contraceptives, and as recently as 1920 the bishops unanimously rejected every kind of contraceptive appliance as being intrinsically immoral.

> We utter an emphatic warning against the unnatural means for the avoidance of conception, together with the grave dangers—physical, moral, and religious— thereby incurred, and against the evils with which the extension of such use threatens the race. In opposition to the teaching which, under the name of science and religion, encourages married people in the deliberate cultivation of sexual union as an end in itself, we steadfastly uphold what must always be regarded as the governing considerations of Christian marriage. One is the primary purpose for which marriage exists, namely the continuance of the race through the gift and heritage of children; the other is the paramount importance in married life of deliberate and thoughtful self-control.

The damage done by such sweeping statements as this was hardly to be measured, and yet hitherto it had been all that the Church could say. But in 1958 the bishops at last shook themselves free of all these cold and unhelpful negatives, and offered to their people for the first time a view of sexuality as the gift of God, given for the joy of men and women, necessary for their completion as persons, and offering them more love to love God with. The bishops in 1958 flatly contradicted their predecessors of 1920:

> The procreation of children is not the only purpose of marriage. Husbands and wives owe to each other and to the depth and stability of their families the duty to express in sexual intercourse the love which they bear to each other. Sexual intercourse is not by any means the only language of earthly love but it is, in its full and right use, the most intimate and the most revealing; it has the depth of communication signified by the biblical word so often used for it, 'knowledge'; it is a giving and receiving in the unity of two free spirits which is in itself good (within the marriage bond) and mediates good to those who share it. Therefore it is utterly wrong to urge that, unless children are specifically desired, sexual intercourse is of the nature of sin. It is also wrong to say that such intercourse ought not to be engaged in except with the willing intention to procreate children.[2]

To this firm and clear statement which pronounces a long, disastrous tradition of the Church to have been mistaken and void, the whole committee of 38 bishops put their hands. The report of a committee does not bind the whole conference, and the relevant resolution, which states the

---

[1] *Report* (S.P.C.K.), pp. 144f.   [2] *Ibid.*, p. 147.

opinion of the entire Anglican episcopate, was more coldly worded, but it did not contradict what the committee had written, and therefore the view of sexual relations in marriage quoted above is to be regarded as the decision of the Lambeth Conference. It was a tremendous step forward and to thousands of men and women an enormous relief.

The pronouncement put a welcome end to the long, unseemly, and unreal debate among bishops and casuists as to whether contraceptives were sinful or allowable. For the decision that sexual intercourse was right in and for itself, and apart from the intention to create children, was automatically a decision for family planning, and therefore for the means which make it possible.

Family planning ought to be the result of thoughtful and prayerful Christian decision. Where it is, Christian husbands and wives need feel no hesitation in offering their decision humbly to God and following it with a clear conscience.[1]

On the clinical methods of family planning the bishops said only that, subject to the requirement that they are admissible to the Christian conscience, they are matters of private choice. They ruled out abortion, artificial insemination, and interrupted coition; while of voluntary sterilization they declared that it was admissible only in the most exceptional circumstances. For the rest, husband and wife who wish to find through sexuality 'a gate to a new depth and joy in personal relationship', while at the same time limiting the number of their children, may use all other means which science lays before them.

The bishops put all this liberating thought about the deep problems of the modern Christian family into a very wide context. There was, for instance, a long section about the threat of the swift increase of the world's population; another about the unhealthy pressure of industrialized society upon the family; and another about the embarrassment of trying to enforce Christian monogamy upon an anciently polygamous society, and here the committee found itself unable to come to any definite conclusion, which is not surprising. But all in all this was one of the most liberating pronouncements about the family and marriage to come from the Church for many years, and if the Lambeth Conference of 1958 had said only this, it had deserved to be remembered and honoured in church history.

[1] *Ibid.*

27

The New Specialized Ministries

I · *Reconciliation and the English Parish*

WHEN THE bishops at Lambeth called the whole Church to an urgent effort of reconciliation it was plain that in England the lion's share of the charge must be carried by the English parish churches. But from 1958 onwards to the present day they found it very difficult to bear. In twentieth-century terms Christian reconciliation means healing the feuds of person with person, family with family, one Christian with another, the Church with the outside world and the Church with the state, and all this in the name and by the power of God. The parish church was in touch with personal and family relationships, though hardly ever with all of them, but with few of the rest of these equations of reconciliation. Its chances of winning for Christ the loyalty of the factory, the trade union, the great youth organization, existed indirectly, if at all. It was this impotence of the parish church to attempt at all what mattered most in the reconciliation of the secular world of England to God which slowed down the reconciling process in England, and which caused the disillusion of so many of the younger clergy with the worth of the parochial system as they had experienced it. In large numbers after 1958 they betook themselves to minister in other spheres.

The swift growth of specialized and non-parochial ministries therefore became one of the major changes in the clerical economy of the Church of England in recent years. Most of these ministries act independently of the parishes, and even in isolation from the normal diocesan system, except in so far as the clergy involved in them may be licensed to officiate in the churches of the dioceses in which they happen to live. To which diocesan bishop, for instance, was such a functionary as the clerical secretary of the Church's Council on Foreign Relations responsible? All of these ministries are in some sense in competition with the parochial ministry for they drain away from the service of the parishes an increasing number of the younger clergy, while at the same time they turn to the parishes to find the money to sustain them. These new ministries foster an image of themselves as the modern evangelistic pioneers who try to occupy many fields of modern life which lie beyond the reach of the parish churches. Therefore there is tension between the parish priest and the specialist priest, and few features of the life of the modern Church would be as likely to cause the bewilderment and excite the disapproval of our forefathers if they could return from the grave to see it.

Changes in the Church do not always follow the patterns of change in the world, but they are often subtly connected with them. In the world the specialist has become king. The specialist clergyman in the Church, while not aspiring to so exalted a position, is certainly demanding an ever widening scope for the exercise of his own talent. But the process is embarrassing and demands large drafts of charity from all concerned. It has not been easy for the parish priest and his people, upon whom the history of English Christianity has depended for so many centuries, to accept gladly the fact that the gulf between the Church and the secular organizations of modern society is one which they are quite unable to bridge. Yet so it is. The field of the unchurched multitude cannot now be won by the parish churches alone. They are equipped to provide for the worship of the faithful, and to become the universal chaplaincy to the family in its home. But whereas it was once true that the home was the centre from which all life was influenced, it is true no longer. The home is only one centre of power among many, and most are out of the reach of the parish church. The development is uncomfortable but it is not likely to be halted. Few enterprises are now more urgent than the discovery of a creative relationship between the parochial and the specialized ministries.

As long as the non-parochial ministries were few no difficulty arose. The parish churches have never grudged their toll of priests to the university, hospital, and prison chaplaincies, the armed services, to such societies as the Student Christian Movement and the Missions to Seamen. Still less have they resented the volunteering of their younger clergy for missionary work abroad.

But the specialized ministries have drawn the clergy away into many new fields—many into the service of the B.B.C. and Independent Television, others into youth organizations, into different kinds of industrial mission, and into the work done by the various boards and commissions set up by the Church Assembly. Along such broad streams as these many of the younger clergy are being drained away from the service of the parish in which their forefathers would have spent the whole of their ministerial lives. The different ministries to which they go are all necessary, and no priest is to be blamed who takes his service to one or another of them. But together they make up a strongly flowing river of loss from the service of the parish. It is not surprising that some prophets are suggesting that the

Church ought to work towards many fewer and much stronger parochial centres of work and worship; and in time it may well become difficult to staff more than these few.

But there would not be this increasing exodus from the parochial ministry if the clergy as a whole were satisfied by it. They are not. Something daunts them. It is not the curate's position of subordination to the vicar which so disturbs them. If they are not better priests than their fathers were, they are as good. It is that they believe their lives could be better given to the service of the Kingdom of God in some non-parochial sphere, and there is an increasing plenty to choose from. They are judging that the parochial system is now such that the Gospel cannot be communicated by the parishes to the many, but only to the few. And so, after a year or two, they go, gladly taking the risks of their exodus, and showing a praiseworthy scorn of the automatic security of the parson's freehold which, in a few years, must automatically become theirs if they stay in parochial service. But in large numbers they forsake it, without a backward glance.

The general nature of their discontents they reveal in their letters to the church newspapers. They range from the supposed neglect of their bishops to the high stone wall of the indifference of their parishioners. Such complaints as these are perennial, and perhaps not more true today than in the past. But underlying them all is the reiterated charge that to serve as a priest in a parish is to spend far too much of one's time grappling with trivialities of many kinds, all of which, when taken together, are incapable of influencing seriously the course of the Church's present struggle to win for Christ the love, the worship, and the service of the world of infidelity. Whether they are right so to think is beside the point; what matters is that so many do. As against all this, and as part of the same correspondence, there stands the brave testimony of a Cambridgeshire vicar, who, having felt all these goads in his own flesh, knew he must stay where he was and make of his own frustration a creative ministry of reconciliation:

We come to the fundamental problem. I do not believe that the battle for Britain's soul is to be won with paper and ink, nor yet with the ablest possible use of mass media, and I believe the reason for this to be profoundly theological. From the doctrine of the Trinity downwards, the Christian faith seems to be concerned with persons-in-relationship. It seems to follow that the extension of the faith is only possible in so far as its exponents, clerical and lay, allow themselves to be involved in personal two-way traffic.

Can we clergy hope to lead people into the freedom of Christ-relatedness unless we are prepared to expose our own selves to the ignorance, the distrust, the defensive superficiality and the plain rejection which are the religious 'facts of life' for the majority of people who live in some parish? One knows these facts statistically, but the existential encounter with them and the further fact that one can do so little to alter them is admittedly shattering.[1]

[1] *Church Times.*, August 6, 1965.

This may be the highest courage of all, to hope without hope, to stand firm in a desolation. It is possible to criticize the declaration of course, and most of those who move into the new non-parochial ministries do not contract out of this person-to-person relationship. Only a few become administrators, or talk only with their own kind. What the vicar wrote temperately most youth chaplains must be tempted to utter despairingly. It is no soft option into which these young men move when they decide that the parochial ministry is no longer for them. But the disillusion, the sadness, the revolt, the resignation to frustration as one's daily bread, are all of them evidence of a deeper malaise of the Church. It is that the communication of Christianity has long been failing.

II · *The Instruments of Communication*

A communication between any two people or sets of people means the entering into a relationship in order that, by a good understanding between them, a fruitful dialogue may result. But in that sentence two technical terms occur—'communication' and 'dialogue'—which have become prominent in Christian writing precisely in proportion as it has been realized that the presentation of the Gospel by the Church to the people is heard by fewer and fewer ears, so that neither a right relationship nor a good understanding is created and no true dialogue can result. It is this fact of the Church's situation today which is causing the defection of so many clergy from the parochial ministry because they do not believe that the parish is now able to perform the acts of communication itself. One purpose of their going into the new ministries is to take what they hope will be a more effective share in the communication of the Gospel to the people, and to get into the position where they can take a fuller part in the consequent dialogue.

Throughout the centuries the Church has relied on speech, presence, example, writing, art, and music to present the Gospel to the people. Of these the first three are effective but not measurable. Sermons, teaching, and study groups are essential and potent, but none can know the power they have. The presence of a Christian with a non-Christian often communicates the faith with magnificent effectiveness: how many have forsaken unbelief because 'So-and-so was different' no one can guess, but all know that they are many. The tacit example of the Christian hero also makes the faith credible, but it cannot be measured. Of writing, art and music the Church has always made a full and a ceaseless use. To these instruments of persuasion and suggestion the fact that there is any Christianity in the world today is due.

In the last forty years the possibilities of these immemorially ancient media have all expanded both in form and in the extent of the audience to be reached, and this has imposed upon the Church's spokesmen in any of these fields of communication the duty of learning to use many new techniques. There is nothing new in presenting the Faith through books, but the writing today of the kind of religious books which reach the people outside the Church involves many novelties, because the straightforward argument which appeals to reason, which is the classic form of theology, now reaches fewer and fewer readers, and those it does reach are almost always the already convinced. By authors who can write religious books of a new kind the Church has been very well served in the last forty years, as the mere recitation of names such as Charles Williams, Dorothy Sayers, and C. S. Lewis shows, and of course there are many others as well.

Newspaper journalism is a more difficult field but it is also well occupied. For years past many newspapers have provided a regular religious feature article. *The Times* characteristically provides each week the Saturday sermon. For very many years Manchester's *Guardian* has carried a weekly religious article. They were first written by Canon E. L. Hicks; then Canon Peter Green succeeded him, and, calling himself Artifex, wrote them for many years. He in turn was succeeded by the present author who wrote them for ten years or more. The *Daily Telegraph* also gives regular weekly space, as does the *Sunday Times*, to a religious feature. It would be possible to extend this list to cover weekly as well as daily papers, but almost all of them are newspapers written for an educated public. It is probable that the newspapers who count their circulations in millions would be just as welcoming, but the journalists, whether clerical or lay, who can present religion in that 'admass' style of vivid but jerky writing are exceedingly few. Christian persuasion in print has always required ample space to spread itself. If its modern persuaders want to communicate the Faith to the multitude they will have to learn these new techniques, and few tasks could be more difficult.

Christian teaching through the visual arts goes on as healthily as ever, as all the decorations of Coventry Cathedral and many in Chichester Cathedral testify. The Church owes a heavy debt to artists like Stanley Spencer, Graham Sutherland, and John Piper. The long tradition of English church music has been splendidly reinforced in our own time, and who can say what the communicating power of a composer like Vaughan Williams has been, or deny that it has been great?

But one of the titanic changes which has come over the scene of Christian communication through the written or spoken word, the visual arts, and the musical score, has been brought about by broadcasting and television, for the microphone and the television screen take each of these media, weave them together into a unity, impose wholly new techniques of presentation upon them, and make of them a message which can reach into almost every home in the land.

In March 1923 Lord Reith, the first executive head of the B.B.C., invited Randall Davidson, Archbishop of Canterbury, to dinner, and to listen to the wireless for the first time. Davidson, 'entirely amazed', at once saw the tremendous importance of it, and summoned a meeting of church leaders the very next day. From this meeting grew the Central Religious Advisory Committee of the B.B.C. which still exists:

> Then, as now, its discussions proceeded from the premiss that there ought to be a religious element in broadcasting, to a consideration of the consequent question—'If so, what?' Then, as now, its members were chosen by the B.B.C. for the contribution they might severally make to the building-up of religious broadcasting. Then, as now, they were to be collectively representative of Christian opinion in this country—to be the bridge between the Churches and the B.B.C. Then, as now, the B.B.C. looked to the Committee for informed advice, prior to the exercise of its own final editorial responsibility.[1]

This council, consisting of distinguished representatives of all the major churches, and presided over for many years by Cyril Garbett, Bishop of Winchester, was the creation of Lord Reith and Randall Davidson. In the intervening years its membership has been enlarged, and there are subsidiary councils of the same kind in each of the B.B.C. regions. Though the responsibility for what is broadcast or televised, and how this is done, belongs to the B.B.C. alone, the council remains so important to the B.B.C. that, in the words of the Rev. Kenneth Lamb, the present Head of Religious Broadcasting, 'if it did not exist, it would be necessary to invent it.'

The Religious Broadcasting Department is served today by 27 clergymen and 6 laymen, each region having its own separate staff. The overriding purpose of the department is not merely, or even chiefly, to see that religion gets a fair share of programme time. More than that, it exists to serve the Corporation in what it has defined as its highest duty, 'the search for truth', and, for broadcasting purposes, this truth is that which 'a man or a society treats as being of ultimate value'. Therefore, because 'religion has many dimensions; to this extent all broadcasting is religious broadcasting.'[2] If this is true, then when the Corporation gives time on the air to the expression of opinions which are hostile to Christianity, as it must and should, this too is religious broadcasting.

From the beginning the Religious Department of the B.B.C. has had an onerous and a responsible job. As its head attests:

> Very roughly, 3 per cent of the B.B.C.'s whole output is originated by the Department. This includes nine hours' programme time each week on Home, Light, and Third taken together, three hours of network television, and another ten hours and three hours respectively for regional listening and viewing. It also comprises five hours weekly on the General Overseas Service. A total all told of some thirty hours' programme time weekly. Thirty-three of us in the Department are, in one way or another, directly responsible for producing programmes. Six of us are laymen, the other twenty-seven are parsons.[3]

[1] Kenneth Lamb, *Religious Broadcasting* (B.B.C.), 1965, p. 4.
[2] *Op. cit.*, p. 5.   [3] *Ibid.*, p. 6.

The programmes are of great variety. They range from services of all kinds to discussions and talks, from 'Meeting Point' to 'Postscript'; and they are placed in the most—not, as in many countries, in the least—advantageous times of the day. An infinity of care goes into the preparation of each one of them. A seven-minute epilogue on a Sunday night requires several hours of rehearsal time. A single televised service in church has at least two days of preparation. A very high standard of technical excellence is so constantly achieved that the very occasional falling below it is indeed conspicuous.

The producers of these programmes count their hearers and viewers in millions, and to this enormous audience the religious programmes of Independent Television, which adopts much the same standard of values, must be added. Over the air day by day and night by night the Christian Faith is being ceaselessly communicated and its importance to the whole life of man in the world is being asserted. Broadcasting has become the most influential means of communication which exists. Its effect is incalculable, for there is no way of measuring it. How can anybody estimate the influence of such superbly presented television programmes as the Coronation of Queen Elizabeth II or the funeral of Sir Winston Churchill, or in sound broadcasting, the play-sequence of Dorothy Sayers' *The Man Born to be King*? Its power to help particular groups of people, and particularly the sick, can be guessed with reasonable accuracy. If it has not as yet converted the nation, its power has become that without which a future conversion is hardly possible, and it has done more than any other instrument whatever to prepare the ground on which the Christian advance which all Christians long and pray for may one day become possible.

III · *The Integration of the Specialist Priest*

Meanwhile, the modern situation is dangerously separating the priest of the specialized ministry from the priest of the parish church, and it is the former, not the latter, who is in the lonely position of being 'out on a limb', exposed to the temptations of isolation. The life of the parish priest need not be lonely; his ministry is fitted into an old and well understood pattern of support through the organization of rural deanery, archdeaconry and diocese. He has his own regular altar and he can be supported every day by the worship of his own church. The work he does is in essentials the work of every other parish priest, and the problems which perplex, and sometimes torment him, are those of all his brethren. If he seeks the advice or the comfort of any of them, he speaks of what is known among them all, not of some specialized mystery of his own which no one but himself understands. He lives within a pattern of fellowship and help, and he need not suffer spiritual loneliness unless, as too often happens, he chooses it for himself.

With the priest of the new specialized ministries it is very different. All specialists everywhere are in a sense pioneers and the custodians of some mystery which none but they understand. By the nature of their calling they tend to walk alone. Of the specialized priest this is particularly true. Unless he can somehow contrive it, he has no altar of his own and no church which is his. A peripatetic, he has no worshipping community which sends him out, receives him back, and supports and strengthens him by his consciousness of belonging. He stands outside the organization of the Church. Though a member of it, he lives his life and does his work from what must be an uncomfortable position on its boundaries, on the periphery of its timeless ministry. His personal spiritual life he must tend and feed for himself and by himself. His pattern of specialized living is very different from what was held out to him in the sacrament of his ordination. The aim, the means, the goal—these are all the same; the context of these things is far different. He works from an office and not from a church, and that is the heart of his trouble.

The same reflections apply to the specialized ministries themselves in their own functions. However necessary the modern predicament has made them all—and of that there can be no serious doubt—they too stand perilously out on a limb, and are detached too far from the normal life of the Church. There is no way to keep them in touch, to keep competitiveness in bounds, and to avoid the waste of overlapping effort. No general oversight, no directing authority over them all exists. Between them and the parishes yawns a gap so wide that it is a barrier, and the parish cannot leap over it. Like the clergy immersed in them, the specialized ministries stand too near the very edge of the Anglican pastoral tradition. If they could be welded together and brought back into the accepted pattern of the Church's life it would be for their own good, and the good of the work they try to do for the Kingdom.

Since they are a mute protest against the inadequacy of the parish in modern life, it is only very exceptionally that the parish can lead them home to the heart of the Anglican tradition. But there are other instruments. One is a large extension of the new device of the guild church as it now exists in the City of London. The other, and far the better, is the cathedral, which, embedded more deeply than the parish itself in the long history of Christendom, is no unintelligible novelty but an institution loved and understood. It might have been created for such a task as this, and at least one cathedral is already richly fulfilling it.

28

The Ministry of the Cathedral

I · *The Cathedrals Commission of 1958*

IN THE autumn of 1958 the Church Assembly appointed a Commission 'to prepare, in consultation with the Church Commissioners, a Measure to supersede the Cathedrals Measures and to make such other alterations in the law relating to Cathedrals as may seem desirable to meet the needs of Cathedrals at the present time'. The language of these terms of reference is far from exciting, but in the event this Commission did far more for the cathedrals than any of its many predecessors. It was a strong Commission. The present Bishop of Leicester, the Right Rev. Ronald Williams, was its chairman. Four deans, two provosts, three residentiary canons, and six laymen and women formed its membership. It published its report, *Cathedrals in Modern Life*, in 1961.

This report will be remembered with gratitude by the English cathedrals for a long time to come on the strength of an opinion which it stated with great emphasis, and of a recommendation which implemented it, and which, in due course, became part of the law of the land. The opinion was that cathedrals have a proper and essential ministry of their own, and that in modern times this is more important than ever before in the evangelistic economy of the Church.

Owing to the mobility which the motor car has brought to modern life, Cathedrals both old and new become places of pilgrimage far in excess of anything previously known. Not only do tourists arrive in vast numbers at the Ancient Cathedrals, but also in modern Cathedrals parties from schools and societies arrive on pilgrimage. If they can be welcomed, shown round, and helped to see the spiritual purpose of a Cathedral, an evangelistic agency comes into play and this might be of considerable importance. With mobility has come the possibility of diocesan services and these take place in great numbers in all Cathedrals. More and more secular organizations seek the privilege of regular or occasional services, and it is to the Cathedral that they look as the most natural *venue*. Far from being outmoded, the Cathedral Churches of England have never before served as living centres of worship for such a wide variety of ordinary Church members.[1]

The statement is somewhat sparse. It limits itself to big services and to what is done for casual visitors. Nothing is said about the cathedral's role as a mediator and reconciler between the parish and its competitors, between the vicar and the clerical organizing secretary, between the traditionalist and the innovator, and this is indeed a role of cathedrals today and tomorrow. Much else is omitted. But at least it is made clear, and the Church Assembly accepted it, that the cathedrals are doing something of great importance for the Kingdom of God, and that none but they can do it.

Having thus attested their belief that cathedrals in the twentieth century have a function in the spheres of evangelism and the cure of souls which is, so to speak, native to the modern age, the members of the Commission had to go on to suggest ways and means of enabling the cathedrals to perform them. A great deal was said about their straitened finances and suggestions were made as to how their poverty might be relieved. But it was in the matter of their staffing that the Commission broke fresh ground:

> Our suggestion is that there should be in every Cathedral a Dean and two residentiary Canons holding no other benefice or demanding diocesan office but engaged solely in Cathedral work. We would include in the term 'Cathedral work' assistance to the Bishop in his cure of souls of the whole Diocese. For the Cathedral is the Bishop's Church and the Mother Church of the Diocese and its work should not be regarded as being confined to the Cathedral Close. This minimal constitution of a Dean and two Canons would enable the Cathedral to act as a collegiate body in which prayer was offered daily for the diocese, and to which the parishes were welcomed; and to be the centre from which aid of a pastoral or theological nature could be dispensed for diocesan needs. Canons might undertake such work as the direction of Ordination Candidates, and post-ordination training; or advise the Bishop and clergy on pastoral or sociological or industrial questions. We are quite clear that these two Canons ought not to be Suffragan Bishops, Assistant Bishops, or Archdeacons, or to be appointed to such substantial diocesan administrative work as Director of Education or Secretary of the Diocesan Board of Finance. We believe that in nearly every diocese two such Canons could be fully and usefully employed without waste of manpower.[2]

This suggestion was implemented in due course and became law in 1964. As a result of it, every cathedral must have a dean and two residentiary canons, who are called cathedral canons, who may not hold any of the offices mentioned above, or, in the language of the measure,

> be the holder of any office to which he was appointed by a person or body other than the administrative body of the cathedral church and for which a salary or stipend is normally paid.

[1] *Op. cit.* (Church Information Office), 1961, pp. 4f. [2] *Ibid.*, pp. 9f.

Every cathedral, from 1964 onwards, must have a dean and two canons each one of whom must regard himself as the servant of the cathedral, find all his ministry in it, and in so far as he reaches out to the diocese and the Church at large must do it through the cathedral, and not independently of it. The measure provided that each of these three was to be paid by the Church Commissioners, and not, as heretofore, by the cathedral itself; and this has naturally been an enormous, but still hardly a sufficient, relief to the heavy strain on the cathedral's purse. A cathedral may still have other residentiary canons beyond these, but if it does it must pay for them itself out of its own resources; and such other residentiary canons as it may choose to have are in no way restricted, as the two cathedral canons are, in the type of service they give.

Thus one of the oldest and most difficult tensions of cathedral life and ministry is at last in a fair way to being resolved. The old dilemma of whether residentiary canons exist to provide the diocese with its suffragan bishops, its archdeacons, and various other of its necessary clerical officials, or whether a canon appointed to a cathedral should give to it the whole of his service, goes back in history at least as far as Charlemagne. That titan solved it temporarily by roundly declaring that the first purpose of canonries was to provide schoolmasters, and because it was Charlemagne who said it, so at once it came to be. It is possible to trace back to this decision of his the development of the cathedral schools into the new twelfth-century universities, the greatest gift of the Middle Ages to the world.

From that time to this there has been a sporadic and yet a constant conflict between bishops who wished to use the canonries to which they had the right of appointment to provide salaries for diocesan officials, and deans who saw their dreams of the fuller ministries the cathedrals were capable of fulfilling constantly stultified by their canons being forced to give most of their time and service to the administrative needs of the diocese. The battle had swayed to and fro, and to the fact that it was always threatening or was actually being fought, the very bad days through which cathedrals have passed were partly due. At last, towards the middle of the nineteenth century, the conflict resolved itself into a general and more or less grudgingly accepted pattern by which a dean presided over a chapter of four canons. Of these only one was a full time cathedral servant, and he was usually the treasurer, and of him it was required that he must be in more or less perpetual 'residence', always on hand and available for consultation. It naturally meant in practice that the dean and the treasurer formed an unofficial but real executive committee within the chapter, and what those two decided was generally done. The other three canons were appointed to be diocesan officials of one kind or another, and were chosen by reason of their capacity for whatever office it might be, rather than for the service they might give to the cathedral. They had to keep their periods of 'residence' during which their mobility was just a little restricted like that of any other canon, but during the rest of the year they were expected to be out and about in the diocese, on Sundays as well as weekdays, and the cathedral was thus almost a minor sideline of their lives for three-quarters of the year. It is not surprising that against this pattern of cathedral life and ministry deans were apt to protest unceasingly.

As long as this was the accepted picture of a cathedral's dean and chapter, the cathedral was bound to be a rather conservative institution performing a traditional ministry very well and an experimental ministry not at all. The daily round of worship done excellently was possible enough in those conditions and the standard of music could be maintained at its high level. The old tradition that a cathedral must be the home of learning suffered because canons chosen to be either financial administrators of the cathedral or diocesan officials were most unlikely to be scholars as well. The idea that a dean and chapter must be a spiritual college of regular corporate prayer and worship, and beyond that a community at love and peace with each other, necessarily suffered. Too many canons were always away, and the customary pattern made for so much tension and friction that the maintenance of a true community life was particularly difficult.

Only when this long historical background of cathedral life is kept in mind can it be appreciated how revolutionary the findings of the Cathedrals Commission really have been. When they became law they solved at one stroke the old problem about the purposes of a cathedral and the staffing necessary to fulfil them. The old strain and tension is over and done with, because the Commission put to the Church the belief that modern circumstances laid upon cathedrals fresh and heavy ministerial responsibilities of their own. It has underlined their increasing importance in the evangelistic economy of the Church, and it has implied that there were things cathedrals could do for the Kingdom of God which could not be done by any other institution. All this it implemented by the new pattern of the constitution of deans and chapters which it laid down. The Church, acting through the Church Assembly, accepted the findings; and the Church Commissioners, by taking over the payment of the dean and the two cathedral canons, endorsed it financially. The sentences from the Report which were quoted above might well have been printed in scarlet type, for they heralded a red-letter day for the English cathedrals.

III · *The Cathedral's Modern Ministry*

The Commission was sure that cathedrals have such a ministry but vague indeed about what it is. The two instances of caring properly for the crowds of casual visitors, and the staging of big and special services for diocesan and other occasions, are both things which the cathedrals have been doing for years. There is nothing either novel or experimental in them, and they have long been part of every cathedral's traditional function. But the Commission was wise to refuse to particularize further because to the question, What can the cathedral do to minister more effectively to the twentieth century? each cathedral must give its own separate answer in terms of its own circumstances. Nevertheless the principles of a right answer are the same for them all, and the most urgent task for cathedrals today is to think out what these principles are.

At bottom they are the right dovetailing of experimental into traditional ministry. The cathedral has a very rich ministerial tradition which it has been discharging for centuries, and it is in the light of this tradition that cathedrals are known and valued. At bottom the tradition is built upon the excellent performance of daily and ceaseless worship, done with all possible care, and surrounded by a majestic and beautiful building, and by the regular performance of church music belonging to all the ages. To that is added a sense of responsibility to the arts, and the artists who live by them, whether sculptors, painters, composers, dramatists, or craftsmen of every kind. The frequent use of cathedrals today for orchestral concerts, for pictorial exhibitions, for dramatic performances of many kinds, is one way in which this traditional sense of aesthetic responsibility is worked out and expressed. Underneath all this is the tradition that a cathedral must be a true community of persons in Christ, and that the whole large and varied cathedral foundation, from the dean to the newest choir boy, must be a single-minded corporation made excellent and gracious in welcome by the love and trust, in Christ, which each one has for each and every other. Anthony Trollope sensed this. Barchester was praised for its musical and devotional fidelities, and when its clergy were performing those functions they were sympathetically drawn. But the heart of the plot was the attack from without upon such community as the cathedral had, and by their reaction to that the characters were judged. To fail to be a community is the point at which cathedrals have often been vulnerable, and sometimes still are. This failure, where it exists, is the more devastating in that it seriously detracts from the fulfilling of any other ministry.

All this is the basic foundation upon which every modern experiment a cathedral may try must be built. It would be quite impossible, and monstrously wrong, to attempt to detach any experimental ministry from this traditional ministry. The daily offering of the Eucharist and the unvarying recitation of the offices of Matins and Evensong are the fundamental conditions of every other kind of ministry to be accepted, and therefore they come first. But on top of all this there is the vision of the community of a great cathedral identifying, reaching out to, and reconciling the larger communities of the world around it, reconciling them with each other and with the Church. It was for this, whatever it may mean, that the Commission set the cathedrals free and equipped them anew.

A great deal of thinking needs to be done, and a tentative beginning has been made by the Provost of Coventry, the Very Rev. H. N. C. Williams, in his book, *Twentieth Century Cathedral.* He is sure that

Cathedrals can and must discover their role as personalizing and reconciling centres for the total community about them. The Church will never fulfil its duty to be the reconciling agency for the total community until it begins to see and to deal with the community as a 'whole' unit in the regional areas which are definable, and adopts a flexible organization to articulate this 'wholeness'.[1]

But this vision presupposes a period of sociological enquiry, for the communities concerned have all to be identified. It also presupposes the providing of some kind of 'reconciliation' between the various experimental ministries of the Church, who, between them, but in separation from each other, are doing this work of exploration now, and also between them and the traditional ministry of the Church as exercised in the parishes. All this, he believes, is something which cathedrals, and they alone, can do.

Areas of community which are obviously greater than a parish area of community need acknowledged centres from which work at this supra-parochial level can go out, and in which the new patterns of community can become conscious of themsleves as members of a greater community. If there were no other justification for the existence of cathedrals in the twentieth-century world, it would be sufficient that they dedicated themselves to be bases for the outgoing, exploratory work necessary to meet the needs of the great and ill-defined areas of community which three centuries of industrialization have produced.[2]

All this is no more than the preliminary exploration of a vision, but the idea of Christ reconciling to himself the kingdoms of the world must in the second half of the twentieth century mean something very like this.

What it all means has still to be decided, and every cathedral will have to work out the principles in terms of its own circumstances. But the reaching out of cathedrals to find such ministries must everywhere involve three difficult and delicate issues which must be faced and solved. The first of them is the relationship of the cathedral to the parish churches of its own diocese to which it is bound to be a mother of churches. This is difficult because the mother is necessarily in competition with her own daughters, and the competition is not on level terms. Unless a cathedral closes its doors altogether it is bound to gather to itself a congregation of its own, and to expect the neighbouring parish priests to like it is to ask too much of human nature. Thus a deep and real loyalty of daughter to mother churches is always shot through with an element of suspicion which can rise to the top at any moment, and because of this most cathedrals are very sensitive to the danger of even seeming to tread on parochial toes. In the present and the immediate future this tension is more likely to be exacerbated than healed. The parishes can hardly help but become more and more conscious of the fact of their falling status, and to be particularly jealous

[1] *Op. cit.* (Hodder and Stoughton), 1964, p. 42.   [2] *Ibid.*, p. 87.

for their honour. If the Cathedrals Commission on the one hand and the Provost of Coventry on the other are right, then cathedrals are likely to have more and more importance in the whole system of the Church. While the parishes are falling into the trough of a wave, cathedrals are mounting to its crest, as is shown, among other things, by the fact that ours is one of the great ages of cathedral building. Add to this the fact that the cathedrals are equipped, as the parish churches are not, to contain and express whatever is involved in this new ministry of community searching and reconciling, and we have all the materials out of which jealousy and suspicion are made. But the fact remains, as the Provost of Coventry has written in the same book, that

the parish cannot be the unit to minister effectively to a community as evidently supra-parochial as the industrial communities of our great cities. To divide, for instance, Southampton Docks into the parishes in which by the accident of swamp drainage and land reclamation it happens to fall is absurd. Unless such an integrated community is to be regarded as such and worked as such, either under a separate staff or by a team ministry of all the parish priests involved, no effective work is possible at all. Not less absurd is it to regard parochial boundaries as having any relevance in relation to the vast industrial areas of our big cities.[1]

It is perfectly true but the parishes cannot be expected to like it. What the cathedrals must not do is to refuse the new ministries opening up before them for fear of parochial susceptibilities. But some way will have to be found to allay the suspicions certain to arise.

The second issue is very different. The new grounds of ministry which the Provost of Coventry proposes to the cathedrals is already being tentatively but independently explored by a host of experimental ministries, working wastefully in independent isolation from one another. The priests concerned in them, as we have seen, themselves suffer from this isolation. A cathedral, and only a cathedral, is in a position to gather such clergy and the ministries on which they are engaged, under its welcoming roof, to provide them with the regular daily worship they need, to give them the chance to be members of a steady and regular community, and to hold all these ministries together under a single and unified control.

But this it can only do if the cathedral is itself a true community of Christ. This is the third issue to be borne in mind all the time, and the careful tending of this community is more than ever a part of the modern cathedral's ministry.

III · *Coventry Cathedral*

Both as places of pilgrimage and as the homes of imaginative ministries the prestige of cathedrals today has been much enhanced by the youngest and newest of them all. The success of Coventry has bestowed both an architectural and a ministerial new look upon the whole cathedral scene. Romance

[1] *Ibid.*, p. 36.

surrounded its building. Its consecration in the presence of the Queen was quickened and made immediate for millions by the brilliance of its televised publicity. Its success thereafter was phenomenal. Pilgrims came in vast numbers day after day for many months, and they still do. Their gifts cleared the building debt, and helped to give Coventry a degree of freedom from financial worry which most other cathedrals cannot enjoy. Coventry in fact is blessed by many advantages, and it uses them all to the full.

From the very beginning, from the day in 1950 when the decision to build again, to clothe the idea of promoting social and international reconciliation with the bricks and mortar of a great new church, was taken, thought about the spiritual and social purposes of the building went hand in hand with thought about its architectural design. In June of that year a competition to find the right architect was launched and to each candidate a full statement of the conditions of the competition was sent. This document carried a page with this message from the then bishop of the diocese, Neville Gorton, and the then provost, R. T. Howard:

> The Cathedral is to speak to us and to generations to come of the Majesty, the Eternity, and the Glory of God. God therefore direct you.
> It is a Cathedral of the Church of England. In terms of function what should such a Cathedral express? It stands as witness to the central dogmatic truths of the Christian Faith. Architecturally it should seize on these truths and thrust them upon the man who comes in from the street.
> The doctrine and worship of the Church of England is liturgically centred in the Eucharist. The Cathedral should be built to enshrine the altar. This should be the ideal of the architect, not to conceive a building and to place in it an altar, but to conceive an altar and to create a building.
> In the Anglican liturgy it is the people's altar; the altar should gather the people, it should offer access for worship and invitation to go to Communion.
> With the altar—in unity of worship—there is the preaching of the Gospel among our people of Coventry and the interpretation of the Word.
> The theology of the Cathedral we put before you to direct your thought. Prayer will be with you from the Cathedral crypt and from the Diocese of Coventry. May God be with you in this great matter.[1]

There followed a long and exact statement of the requirements and conditions, and among the latter was this:

> Provision should be made inside the new Cathedral (possibly round the outer walls) for, say, eight 'Hallowing Places', each one symbolizing the sacredness of one of the fields of activity which make up our daily human life, e.g. work, the arts, education, the home, commerce, healing, government, recreation.[2]

Then the competitors were told that they must find the right place for a well designed chapel of unity, and also for a Christian service centre of

---

[1] Basil Spence, *Phoenix at Coventry* (Geoffrey Bles), 1962, pp. 3f.
[2] *Ibid.*, pp. 110f.

ample size and adequate equipment. The design of Sir Basil Spence was the one accepted and he was chosen to be the architect.

The cathedral was consecrated on May 25, 1962, and the new provost, the Very Rev. H. C. N. Williams, and his staff began their adventurous but dangerous ministry. When Provost Howard retired, the new Bishop of Coventry, the Right Rev. Cuthbert Bardsley, had chosen Harold Williams to be the first provost of the new cathedral. When the appointment was made the walls of the cathedral stood only a few feet high above the ground. Williams therefore inherited the design and the outward shape, but over the rest of the whole conception he was the pioneer who had the tremendous task of supervising the building work, of deciding a great deal of its interior furnishings, and of planning the use to be made of the cathedral when it was finished.

No appointment could have been more happy and none more creative. Williams had always been a genius at pioneering new and difficult enterprises, and the Church of England probably had no other priest with comparable gifts. He came to Coventry from the vicarage of St Mary, Southampton, where he had rebuilt that large church, which, except for its spire, had been totally destroyed during the war. He made it one of the most imaginative churches in the south of England. Though it was large and stood in a pastorally unpromising situation, he filled it with worshippers, and he gave it a ministry of its own. At the same time he took the whole of Southampton Docks into his charge, and there among the dockers and stevedores, the officials of their unions, and the management of the docks he built up a most effective ministry. He was a man born to be a pioneer, and for this work he possessed two priceless gifts. He could hold and balance in his mind at the same time the carefully thought out vision of what he hoped to do, seeing the end of the process in the beginning, and every small detail contributing towards the wholeness of the great design. Though he laboured over detail of every kind he was never swamped by *minutiae* because he always saw every brick in relationship to the whole erection it was to serve. Nor was his head ever in the clouds, bemused by the splendour of the vision, because he never lost sight of the fact that dreams remain castles in Spain unless they are erected bit by bit on a basis of meticulous attention to the endless and small details involved in them at every stage. Such a man must always be something of a dictator who finds incomprehension hard to understand, and opposition, which pioneering genius must always create, hard to bear. He is like an artist making something all his own, who needs and welcomes all the help he can get, but it must be to forward his own conception, not someone else's. It is impossible for such a man, always and necessarily an individualist at bottom, to avoid occasionally making enemies of lesser minds. But Williams has shown that he has the gift, rare in a man of his kind to weld a great variety of distinguished colleagues into a community of loving co-operation, while holding them all ruthlessly and relentlessly to the service of his own conception of what a new cathedral should be, and this without ever putting their loyalty to too great a strain.

Such a man he was who came to undertake a great pioneering task which might have been made for him, which probably nobody but he could do, and to perform it with the wearying searchlights of publicity trained upon him all the time. It was an ordeal, for he is a man who, at heart, dislikes publicity, and, left to himself, would shrink contentedly from it. But publicity was a necessary element in the vision he had, and so he must learn to work in it.

Filled with an interior humility Williams faced his new and, in all probability, his greatest charge. In his own words, used not once or twice but many times, he was scared. 'I was terrified of the job—for all sorts of reasons I was terrified of it. I knew it was going to be just about the most vulnerable job in the Church of England for the next four years.' That he said in a television interview, and he then went on to define the broad picture he had of the new ministry he was creating. In essentials he has repeated the definition many times since then, but never more clearly:

A passion of mine has always been—and I could never have been ordained if I hadn't had this passion right from the beginning—that the Church makes sense only if the Church is the expression of the wholeness in the community. The Church is irrelevant to the community if it doesn't give the impression of being a coherent society within an incoherent community. The Church has not only got to be the pattern of the unity of society but it has also got to be the means of expressing that unity when it is discovered. This involves the Church mixing itself up with the community a great deal more than it does, involving itself in the tensions and cross-currents of society, understanding them, and meeting society on the vast area of common ground that exists between them.[1]

There his task was, and he and his colleagues must attempt it with half the world watching all the time to see if they stumbled and fell. These colleagues number many more than would be found on the staff of any of the older cathedrals. There is the provost and the two cathedral canons which are now standard in all cathedrals, a larger number of cathedral canons, some of whom hold other parochial appointments, and many laymen and lay women. One of the canons has the worship of the cathedral in his charge. The rest of the staff address themselves to the industries of the diocese, the civic and administrative life of the city, the ministry of healing, the care of the thousands of pilgrims, the music of the cathedral, dramatic work of all kinds, international youth work, education, and many other forms of modern ministry. They have their plant inside and underneath the cathedral and it is ample and most extensive. There is even a subterranean broadcasting studio which is in constant use and from which the news of the day is sometimes read.

[1] *Cathedral Reborn* (English Counties Periodicals), p. 40.

All these men and women who labour at so many different ministries have their own share in the daily worship of the cathedral, and are expected to come to the weekly chapter meetings, so that each one, while fulfilling his own function, has knowledge of and a concern for the work done by all the others; and all these people and their works are subject to the single, uniform direction or guidance of the provost and the chapter. All the ministries are subsumed within the cathedral ministry, and take their inspiration and their colour from it. All the priests and laymen who perform them are not working in vocational or spiritual isolation, but are part of a great team of the Lord and members one of another.

This strongly communal spirit of an outgoing cathedral is not left to chance, but from the beginning has been carefully tended, and the rhythm of chapter meetings, to which all the staff come, was devised with this end in view. In *Twentieth Century Cathedral* the provost has himself described it:

The fellowship of clergy and laity involved in these activities meets with unbroken regularity for a morning every week, a day every month, and a week every year. The weekly meeting begins with morning prayer, is followed by Bible study for an hour, and continues with discussions about the programme for the following week, the sharing of work, the undertaking of responsibility for specific tasks arising out of correspondence and the planning of long-term projects. By this means each knows broadly what everyone else is doing, and each may call on others for help.

The monthly meeting takes place out of Coventry in the village of one of the Cathedral chaplains who is also Diocesan Missioner, and therefore lives in 'the Diocese' rather than near the Cathedral. This day begins in the village church with morning prayer and Holy Communion, is followed by breakfast in the Vicarage, Bible study and business, and lunch in the Manor house where for years month by month a deep fellowship, capable of containing and absorbing the slightest friction, has been built.

The annual week's conference takes place, for the same reason, away from the Cathedral. It has been held on Iona, and at Faringdon in Berkshire, and in Sussex.

As nearly as possible once a month the senior staff of the team meets with the Bishop to discuss general policies and long term objectives.

Personal contact is essential to any warmth in such a fellowship. A central staff common room, as well as the concentration in one place of all administration, means that contact is never by correspondence or by the circulation of formal minutes and memoranda, but by regular and continuous personal meeting. The Cathedral Refectory adds the important value of being able to eat together.[1]

All this is held together and intensified by the cathedral Eucharist, which, beautifully and impressively done, is the chief Sunday service, and into which an endless care for every little detail has been poured.

Here indeed is a fertilization of otherwise competing ministries, and the

[1] *Op. cit.*, p. 79.

frame of a single unified pattern into which all can be fitted, and all work together. The means, a team of specialists in a community of co-operation, is exactly framed to serve the end, the expression of the wholeness of all community in Christ. For this Coventry cathedral was built. For this every part of it was framed and knit together by Sir Basil Spence and by Provost Williams. It can perform all this function because it is new, with no traditions to hamper it, no financial straitness to stultify it. It has an almost completely free hand. It can concentrate the whole of its resources on the work it tries to do.

No other cathedral, not even the new ones, is quite so free and so fortunate as this, though even Coventry's freedom had to be earned and deserved. But in degree, and each in its own way, other cathedrals can do, and some are doing, such of the same ministry as their circumstances will permit. If the chief purpose of the mid-twentieth-century Church of England is the salvation of the community of the nation through its own discovery of itself, the cathedrals have an indispensably important rôle to play, and none but they can play it. Coventry is showing them how.

29

One Mission to One World

I · *No Parochial Theme*

FOR A long time, in fact for the length of three chapters, we have stayed at home in England. It is time now to move out into the wider world of Missions, the Anglican Communion, and the Ecumenical Movement to look at the new patterns of organization which have been created to equip and to free the reconciling power of Christ to bring the world's Christians closer together in charitable understanding. We are to see how, since 1958, Anglicanism has become, in intention if not yet wholly in accomplishment, a single, united, self-conscious unity of its own with its own mission to its own world, how this springs out of the missionary expansion of the last 150 years, and how it leads us, through the Ecumenical Movement, towards the day when the several Churches of Christendom become the one holy, catholic and apostolic Church for which our Lord prayed on the night when he was betrayed.

These three broad streams of Christian outgoing—Foreign Missions, Pan-Anglicanism, and the Ecumenical Movement—all began their journeys long ago. But it was after 1958, and largely in the strength of the impulse provided by the Lambeth Conference of that year, that they came together to form a broad, swiftly flowing river, deep and navigable. As when a tributary brook first debouches into a larger stream, or a great river flows into the sea, its own water is for a time still distinguishable from the greater water into which it has flowed, so it is still possible to distinguish from each other these tributaries of the one mission of the whole Church. But just as the muddy water of the Nile very soon becomes one with the blue water of the Mediterranean and loses its separateness, so it will presently become impossible to separate Foreign Missions, Anglicanism, and Ecumenism. They should, if all goes well with them, become the single reaching out of the whole Church of Christ to the whole world of God, one reconciling operation of one Church to one world. This is indeed no parochial theme.

The interweaving of these strands is an enthralling but also a very complex and multiform process, and as chronology is half the secret of historical clarity, let us begin with the briefest recitation of the significant facts in their chronological order. Only then can we hopefully begin to separate the strands of the process and see how they were woven into a single cord.

First of all there is the list of new provinces of the Anglican Communion. This is always one test of the growth of the Church. Under the Anglican rules any four adjacent dioceses may become a new province. They then elect their own archbishop and diocesan bishops, may draw up their own constitution and make their own canons, and they may revise the Book of Common Prayer as they wish. They are not in any way subject to the control of the Archbishop of Canterbury. The new province has all the independence it wishes, though it knows that if it goes too far it may lose its place in the fellowship of the Anglican Communion. Since 1955, when the new province of Central Africa was formed, there have been three others: West Africa in 1956, East Africa in 1958, and Uganda in 1960. To these must be added the New Archbishopric of Jerusalem, which was formed in 1957. It is not strictly a province even though it has an archbishop, but it represents all the Anglican Churches of the Middle East.

When the Lambeth Conference assembled in 1958 it inherited the fruits of a number of diverse events which had occurred in the previous four years. In August 1954 a World Anglican Congress was held at Minneapolis. It was called together to consider the theme of 'The Call of God and the Mission of the Anglican Communion'. In the judgement of Dr Fisher what came out of it was the invitation to all the regional Churches to contribute their due and allocated share to the sustaining of the new Jerusalem Archbishopric, and the Anglican staff college at St Augustine's College, Canterbury. A little later in the same year the Second Assembly of the World Council of Churches was held at Evanston. It was a conference so enormous that intimacy was lost and proper debate was impossible. The Americans thought the practical results of so vast an effort were meagre, but it did something to carry the reunion movement a stage further by its exhibition of the difficulty of marrying the catholic to the protestant understanding of the common faith, and by making it clear how great must be the intellectual effort of theological scholarship if the ground was to be cleared for actual proposals of unity.

In 1957 the International Missionary Council met in Ghana and made a notable contribution to the equipping of theological education in the mission field of the world. It raised a large fund of four million dollars with which to start inter-Church theological colleges to train ordination candidates of every race, of which the first was set up in the Cameroons. But it did something still more important. It put forward proposals that the International Missionary Council should enter the World Council of

Churches as its Division of World Mission and Evangelism. This amalgamation duly came to pass at the Third Assembly of the World Council of Churches at New Delhi in 1961.

The Lambeth Conference met in 1958 and took due note of all these events. They were full of hope, but if the fruit of them was to be gathered the Conference judged that the time had come to create the new position of Executive Officer of the Anglican Communion of Churches. To this Bishop Stephen Bayne of the diocese of Olympia in the United States of America was appointed in 1959. In the next year, 1960, the Archbishop of Canterbury made his apostolic journey to Jerusalem, to Istanbul, and thence to Rome to be received in audience by Pope John XXIII. In 1963 the report of the long discussions between representatives of the Church of England and the Methodist Church was published under the title, *Conversations between the Church of England and the Methodist Church*, the result of which was to bring the unity of the two Churches to the very brink of achievement. Finally, the most recent and probably the most effective of all Anglican Congresses assembled at Toronto in the summer of 1963.

II · *The Missionary Development*

That foreign missions form the seedbed of the Ecumenical Movement is one of those statements which are made in all the books; but the frequency of its repetition does not prevent its being true. It is a mere matter of history that the first World Missionary Conference at Edinburgh in 1910 gave the signal for the international co-operation of missionaries and their societies which has never since ceased. From the co-operation of the missions in an area to the co-operation of the several Churches to which they belong is not a long step. Consequently it has more often than not been in mission fields that the early attempts to unite Churches have been made, prematurely and abortively at Kikuyu between 1908 and 1926,[1] successfully in South India in 1947, though it was not until 1955 that the convocations of Canterbury and York recognized the validity of the ordinations in the Church of South India.

Most foreign missions are founded, equipped, and conducted by organized Churches, or the missionary societies which act for them, and by the Anglican Communion among others. Their history is therefore so closely bound up with the development of Anglican Churches in the world as to be inseparable from it. Foreign missions caused that growth; apart from them, Anglicanism would be still a form of British Christianity and no more. This intimate closeness of relationship was recognized by the Lambeth Conference as long ago as its second meeting, in 1878. The Anglican bishops then formed two permanent committees, the first the Consultative Body of the Lambeth Conference, the purpose of which was

[1] See above, pp. 424–28.

to prepare for the next Lambeth Conference and to represent the different Anglican Churches to each other; the second, the Advisory Council on Missionary Strategy, which was formed, as its title suggests, to advise the bishops on missionary problems. In theory it was to consist of the Primates and Presiding Bishops of the Church, which made it most difficult for it to meet. In fact, though this body was created in 1878 and has been kept in theoretical existence ever since, it languished in cold storage until 1948, and even then did not leap into full life and vigour until 1958. But when, in the following years, the great awakening came, this body was there to be one of its instruments of expression.

Missions, then, being in a sense the only begetters both of Anglicanism and of the Ecumenical Movement, are just as closely bound to both of them as they are to each other, and the fortunes of all three rise or fall together. The history of the Church since 1958 is the story of the closer cementing of this togetherness, and its immediate goal has been to get rid of any distinction between foreign missions and the Church, considered as separate organizational bodies. To this end war has been declared on the term 'foreign missions' altogether, and the modern prophetic purpose is to rub it out of the dictionaries and even to expunge it from the consciousness and the vocabulary of Christian people. Instead we are being bidden to talk about Mission, and to think of that as the perpetual function of the Church at all times, in all places, and to all people. We are to look forward to the day when there is one Church conducting one mission to one world; and this day is prepared for by the increasing cohesion of the still separated Churches, Anglicanism among them. The whole outreaching of each of these Churches is called Mission, and this sense of mission is what cements them more firmly together.

Because all such hopes must remain unproven dreams unless the members of different Churches and traditions can meet together for fellowship, discussion and decision, the milestones of the latter part of the long journey have been vast world conferences. It was one such conference, Edinburgh 1910, that set the whole process in motion. Since then, in spite of the intervention of two world wars, the whole Church of God has held fast to its belief in the power of the great international conference, and its history cannot be written in isolation from the bewilderingly large number of such gatherings that have been held between then and now.

As always, the missions pioneered the process of searching for the Kingdom of God by means of the mammoth conference. They began with Edinburgh in 1910, and continued with Jerusalem in 1928, and Tambaram in 1938. These were all World Missionary Conferences. The Ecumenical Movement which has as its ultimate aim the organic union of all Churches naturally works within the same pattern. It has so far held three World Assemblies, the first at Amsterdam in 1948, the second at Evanston in 1954, the third at New Delhi in 1961. The Anglican Communion of

Churches has not merely followed the same lead. There is a sense in which it may be said to provide the leadership of the movement to provide internationally minded Churches with a voice to speak and a body to act. The Lambeth Conferences which began in 1868, though confined to bishops, were from the beginning a demonstration of the authority which an ecclesiastical conference representing many nations might have; and as long ago as 1908 the first Pan-Anglican Congress was held, and its fortunes were described in earlier pages of this book.[1] Two wars intervened before there was another on the same scale; then the second was held at Minneapolis in 1954, and the third and latest happened at Toronto in 1963.

Of necessity the world conferences are all very expensive affairs, and the cost to their leaders in gruelling hard work was suggested on an earlier page in the context of William Temple's leadership at Jerusalem.[2] They all produce a prodigious amount of eloquence of varying value, a mass of printed preparatory studies, and long reports of their proceedings. All of them are followed by a cloud of subordinate regional conferences and continuation committees. It is therefore difficult to sort them out in memory, and even to remember some of them at all after the passage of a few years. But if the whole Church of God is to advance from Foreign Missions to Mission, from many interpretations of the Gospel to the one Gospel of God, from many Churches and groups of Churches to one united catholic Church, it is difficult indeed to see how this could be done except by the use of the periodic world conference. Though naturally those mentioned above were of unequal value, every one of them provided some impetus of its own to carry the whole three-pronged movement a stage nearer to its goal. But among them all the last two have counted for most. At New Delhi the last shreds of distinction between Missions and Churches were blown away when the International Missionary Council died honourably and was reborn as the Division of World Mission and Evangelism of the World Council of Churches; while Toronto, as we shall presently see, provided a terminus for two centuries of Anglican development, gave a richer meaning to the word Anglicanism, and offered to the Anglican Communion of Churches what was little less than a new start and a fresh lease of life.

The missionary pioneers have done most of the necessary thinking, and the missionary in the field has carried the greater part of the burden. Into the amalgam of 'One Mission One Church' the missionaries of every Church have brought their treasures. Since 1958 they have been difficult to win. Statistically the post-war figures sound healthy. Professor Latourette's famous optimism, with his often quoted statement that the twentieth is one of the greatest centuries of Christian advance in the world, has any amount of statistical evidence to back it. There are a number of figures in Bishop Stephen Neill's *A History of Christian Missions*[3] which suggest

[1] See above, pp. 191–5.   [2] See above, pp. 438–9.   [3] Penguin Books, 1964.

abounding evangelistic health. The World Council of Churches can speak for no less than 300 million Christians, a third of all the Christians in the world. In 1958 there were 43,000 protestant missionaries at work, a fourfold increase since 1900, and of these 27,333 came from the United States. Everywhere the missions of the various Pentecostal congregations were strikingly successful. In Central Africa alone the converts of the Pentecostal Churches of Canada had grown from 55,000 in 1957 to 90,000 in 1961. In Sumatra there were 103,528 baptized Christians in 1911; by 1941 they had grown to 380,000. In India the Christian population rose by 32 per cent between 1921 and 1931. In Latin America there were 500,000 protestants in 1914, and 7 million in 1964. Even allowing for easy successes—and the often quick failures—of such Christian bodies as are not members of the World Council of Churches, it all sounds healthy enough; and it is at least evidence of the tremendous effort the Churches continue to put into their overseas work.

But figures say little about emotions, and the psychological climate of so many nations, once missionary territories but now raw and touchy with nationalism, has made the mission work of western Churches exceedingly delicate. It is true that from the missions of western Churches the young nations of Africa and elsewhere received most of their education, their chances of better health, and even much of their sense of their own dignity as human persons. In fact the Gospel was given to them. But the early missionaries brought them much else besides Christianity. In a very notable book, *The Missionary Movement from Britain in Modern History*,[1] Canon Max Warren has investigated the motives underlying the outreaching of the Church of England to undeveloped countries in the last 150 years. The first purpose was always and everywhere to bring the Gospel, and the deepest motive was sheer gratitude for the possession of the Gospel. But there was much else. The sense of paternalistic obligation to 'the heathen in his blindness', the belief that his own indigenous religion gave him a life 'nasty, brutish, solitary, and short': these have died very hard. And if the heathen must be saved from himself, trade would help and so would the just, competent government of a superior race from the other side of world. Imperialism itself has saved lives as well as destroyed and demeaned them. The missionaries were not immune—how could they be?—from the consciousness that they represented a superior race advancing to the rescue of an inferior one. All the resented attitudes of condescension, superiority, paternalism, even contempt, were found in missionaries far less frequently than in traders and administrators, but that is not to say that every missionary in every place and at all times kept himself and his activities free of these stains.

In the last ten years all such attitudes have been met by a violent resentment. Nothing is better documented than this revolt, and Canon Warren

[1] SCM Press, 1965.

summarizes a vast and universal body of evidence in a telling paragraph
at the end of his book:

> I have dwelt at some length on these psychological aspects of the revolt against
> the West because it is very important indeed for our subject that we realize that
> something of the same spirit of revolt and suspicion and distrust of the West is
> to be found among many Christians in Asia and Africa. In the religious sphere
> the revolt is not indeed against contempt. But it is a revolt against paternalism.
> In this respect the western missionary partook of the arrogance of the western
> mind. There was for long, and it still survives more often than we care to admit,
> a tacit assumption that the Church in Asia and Africa would need the supervision
> and guidance of the westerner for a very long time. Like Uzzah of old the western
> missionary tended, with the very best intentions, to keep his hand on the ark of
> God to prevent an accident. If only relatively rarely has he suffered the fate of
> Uzzah that has been due to the mercy of God, and to the patience of the Chris-
> tians in Asia and Africa.[1]

Thus the missionaries of the west have been driven out of China, their
activities have been heavily circumscribed in India, their once privileged
position in Ceylon has been taken away from them. Africa is now filled by
the spirit of pride in its own African history and achievement; and in the
spread of Christianity in Africa that achievement is great.

Over a very large part of Africa Africans first heard of the Christian Gospel
from other Africans. The first missionaries to the Eastern Congo, to the Southern
Sudan, to North-Western Kenya, to Tanganyika were in every case African.[2]

Africa is now looking after its own concerns and learning proudly its own
history, and these are not western concerns and not western history. It may
yet take its religion from the Christ of the Middle East and the shape of its
Church from Europe, but to both it demands to give its own African interpretation. We have to reckon, writes Canon Warren, with

the African's growing awareness that Africa has a history of its own quite independent of that history within which he has been subjected by European domination.

The other great emotional force which is driving him

is the very rapid growth of an awareness of what we may call 'Africanness', a
clumsy word to translate what the African statesman-poet, Leopold Senghor, has
defined as *negritude*. It is with these two positive sources of the African drive
towards recognition that the Christian Church has particularly to do. What it
does with them may well decide the form that will be taken by Christianity in the
Africa of tomorrow.[3]

The old paternalistic condescensions of the west are utterly incompatible
with this new spirit. They have already lost an empire, but they need not
lose a Church, for when the administrators and the traders have been
expelled from some newly independent country the Church which the early

---

[1] *Op. cit.*, p. 166.
[2] Max Warren, *Christianity in the New Africa* (Prism Pamphlet No. 8), 1965, pp. 7f.
[3] *Ibid.*, p. 2.

missionaries planted remains. But it must at once shed every trace of its old colonial spirit.

For a long time now all the statesmen of the Churches have realized this very well, and the old method of reacting to the protest was to build up the indigenousness of the young Churches as the first step towards the growth of their own independence. The breakneck speed with which new African provinces of the Anglican Communion have been founded in the last few years is one part of this process. The indigenous goal is reached when every African or Asian Church has its own national priests and bishops, its own theological colleges in which to train them, its own interpretation of Christian doctrine to teach them, and is in total and unchallenged control of its own affairs. This process has gone far but not far enough or fast enough; and with the Church as with the state it has been a case of giving too little too late.

It is for this reason that the marriage of Mission to Church provides the best hope of all. The idea has a long history, and the document which more than most brought it into the field of practical politics was written as long ago as 1925 by Dr S. C. Leung, the chairman of the Kwantung Divisional Council of the Church of Christ in China. He wrote it as a preliminary paper for the World Missionary Conference at Jerusalem in 1928, and naturally enough its proposals were couched in a Chinese setting:

> It seems to me that the time has now come when the missions and the missionaries might well consider the question of organizing themselves on a different basis, so that the missions and the Chinese Church will hereafter not appear as two parallel organizations, and that all activities initiated, maintained, and financed by the missions should be expressed only through the Chinese Church. This means the recognition of the Chinese Church as the chief centre of responsibility now attached by the missions to the Chinese Church, the willingness of the missions to function only through the Chinese Church, and the willingness of the individual missionaries to function as officers of the Church, and no longer as mere representatives of the mission boards, who are entirely beyond the control of the Chinese Church.[1]

Not many documents have been more pregnant, and these sentences traced the outlines of what has so recently come to pass. They achieved their first purpose when the Jerusalem Conference accepted them, their second purpose when the Ghana conference translated them into the proposal that the International Missionary Council should amalgamate with the World Council of Churches, and their third purpose when this proposal was accepted by both sides at the New Delhi Assembly of the World Council of Churches.

At least there is now the chance of a fresh start. On paper at any rate Mission has been wedded to Church, and Dr Leung's vision has become fact. 'If the Churches knew what they were doing at New Delhi they have

[1] Quoted in Stephen Neill, *A History of Christian Missions*, pp. 516f.

committed themselves to a revolution',[1] Bishop Neill comments at the end of his book. There is just a suspicion of sardonic questioning in that remark. But it is true that the record of the last of the great conferences, that of the Anglican Communion of Churches at Toronto in 1963, suggests that perhaps they did know. All the evidence is that the Churches of the west are penitent, and because of this they are also hopeful. This part of the story has now been brought up to date. Mission is now inseparable from Church, and the new creative pattern of Churches in many lands co-operating on a basis of complete equality is no longer an impossible dream because the organization to express it is now in being.

III · *The First Executive Officer of the Anglican Communion*

On April 19, 1959, Bishop Stephen Bayne, at the time Bishop of Olympia in the United States of America, was appointed to be the first Executive Officer of the Anglican Communion of Churches. The Lambeth Conference of 1958 created the new office by its series of resolutions on 'Progress in the Anglican Communion,' the 61st of which had a clause which ran:

The Archbishop of Canterbury with the approval of the Consultative Body shall appoint a secretary to serve under the direction of the Archbishop, who may, if the Advisory Council so agrees, be also the Secretary of that Council.

The committee's report gave briefly the background of the resolution:

In recent years it has become evident that this Communion, which has been characterized by a spontaneity of growth, is destined for greater and perhaps more dangerous responsibility. Despite the crises of nearly half a century it can bring to the modern world conflict a tempered wisdom and a spiritual stability which can reinforce the hopes and aspirations of the human race in its pilgrimage.

It is obvious, however, that it will not fulfil this task unless it takes cognizance of some of its weaknesses. Dispersed throughout the world and working under every conceivable condition, its growth tends to a fragmentation of its efforts and a failure to reap the full benefit of its resources. It needs to be reminded in all its parts that no one lives to himself, and that as a body with a common life the whole is always something greater than the sum of those parts. In the context of the modern world with its pressures, competing systems, rival philosophies, and expanding frontiers of knowledge, the need for consultation is of paramount importance.[2]

But for this they wanted a man rather than a committee, and they registered their awareness of the danger of setting up a bureaucratic department. The novelty was absolute, the step important, and the choice inspired.

Before the man could be searched for, it had to be decided whose servant he should be, and by whom his salary was to be paid. There were in existence, as we have seen, two permanent bodies of the Lambeth Conference, the Consultative Body and the Advisory Council on Missionary Strategy,

---

[1] *Ibid.*, p. 558.   [2] *Report*, p. 69.

and it was to the latter rather than the former that the committee appealed. But the Advisory Council, though theoretically set up by the Lambeth Conference of 1878, had in fact never met until after the Conference of 1948, whereas the former had been in existence all the time. In 1948 the Advisory Council was called out of its long deep freeze, and between then and 1958 had done useful work, but according to Bishop Bayne it had done nothing to implement the resolution of 1948 that each Church should appoint regional officers to care for liaison and communication between the different parts of the Anglican Communion. But in his historical note at the end of the correspondence relating to Bishop Bayne's appointment, Archbishop Fisher bridled a little at this charge, saying:

> It is not quite true. Canon McLeod Campbell was appointed secretary of the Advisory Council, and all the regional churches appointed their representatives to the Council. The machinery was there. But Canon Campbell was also full-time secretary to the Church Assembly Missionary Council, as it was then called. The Lambeth Conference gave him no money and no extra staff with which to fulfil his duties to the Advisory Council, and its members were scattered all over the world. So it inevitably led a very desultory existence.[1]

All the same the cause of the Kingdom was notably served by Canon McLeod Campbell through all those years, for year after year he wrote a series of outstandingly good reports on the missionary situation of the Church, which were published in book form.

In any case what the Advisory Council had been able to do between 1948 and 1958 was clearly not enough, and to the Lambeth Conference of 1958 it was clear that it never could be enough until some outstanding personality was appointed, and provided with a staff, an office and a salary, to be its secretary. It took from August 1958 until April 1959 to complete all the preliminary negotiations, but by then all was at last ready, and Bishop Bayne's appointment was announced by the Archbishop in the following terms:

Anglican Executive Officer

At the request of the Lambeth Conference, 1958, the Metropolitans of the Anglican Communion have appointed a new officer with the title of Anglican Executive Officer.

The chief duties are on the one hand to act as controller of the Anglican Advisory Council on Missionary Strategy, and on the other hand to exercise a general supervision on behalf of the Consultative Body of the Lambeth Conference on all matters affecting the Anglican Communion which call for attention between the decennial Conferences.

As the office is a new one it will be for the first holder of it to discover how best to fulfil these duties and to render his best service to the various Provinces of the Anglican Communion in their joint concerns.[2]

[1] Stephen F. Bayne, *An Anglican Turning Point* (Church Historical Society of Texas), 1964, p. 23.
[2] Bayne, *op. cit.*, p. 11.

In a personal letter dated March 13 the Archbishop expanded a little the terms of the official announcement still to be made:

> You mention your own strong feeling that there ought to be a certain degree of looseness in the new post making it clear that this is not an English invention, nor merely an extension of my office. With that I wholly agree. I might have been guilty of describing it as a kind of auxiliary office to me: I really never meant that, but I did realize that I should be unloading many things on to you to my own great relief which at present I carry almost entirely on my own shoulders. But, of course, in this office you are entirely your own master, responsible to the Anglican Advisory Council on Missionary Strategy for any tasks that you take on at their request, and responsible to the Consultative Body of the Lambeth Conference for any assignments you take on at their request (which means in effect at my request): so there we are.[1]

In all of the correspondence which Bishop Bayne uses in the Preliminary Note of his book, there is neither mention nor indication of how it came to be that the choice fell on him, or whether anyone except himself was ever considered. It looks as if the Archbishop and the two Councils knew from the beginning whom they wanted.

At any rate the choice was certainly inspired, and if the appointment really did constitute the Anglican turning-point of his book's title, it was Bishop Bayne himself who made it so. His personality was exactly suited to the task he had accepted. Pleasant and easy in manner, he was most likeable, and he had the gift of bestowing on all others the ease he had himself in all manner of conversations. There was depth and often profundity in his speeches and his writing; and he had to the full the good journalist's gift of winning and holding the attention of an audience for every utterance of his whether by voice or pen. His mission was of paramount importance to him, but he had too strong a sense of humour to be under any temptation to take himself too seriously, and so, as the French would put it, he never made the importance. How would it be possible not to warm to a bishop who thus began an article?

> One of my peculiar occupational hazards is that of being exposed to all our different Anglican Prayer Books, as I go to and fro in the earth. Being an American, the Prayer Book I know best is that of the Episcopal Church; and left to my own devices, I would simply command that every Anglican province adopt it forthwith, since it is probably used in heaven anyway. (Note: This remark is not intended to be taken with utter seriousness.)[2]

From that point he plunged into the depths of Prayer Book Revision; he safely could, for he had made sure of the unwavering attention of all his readers. Most of his speech and writing had that kind of compulsive note in it, as for instance when in a speech to the Toronto Congress he said of an American diocese he had once served in:

---

[1] *Ibid.*   [2] *Ibid.*, p. 192.

Many people in the diocese had the feeling that the Church was an association of people, a kind of memorial association for a deceased clergyman named Christ, whose ideals were important and who was an early supporter of the American way of life. To such people mission was something you did for somebody else. Mission was a way in which you kept God in business.[1]

He was indeed a man who had to go to and fro in the earth. The first of his annual reports to the Archbishop of Canterbury, and through him to 'the churches of our Anglican household', had a section called Communication, of which this was the first paragraph:

During 1960, since we left Seattle on New Year's Eve, 1959, I have travelled just under 130,000 miles. The first six weeks of the year Mrs Bayne and I and two of our children were en route from Seattle to London, coming by way of Honolulu, Japan, South East Asia, India, Jerusalem, and Rome. . . . During those six weeks, it was possible for me to learn something of our churches in Japan, the Philippines and Borneo, and make briefer calls in Hong Kong, Djakarta, Singapore, Calcutta and Jerusalem. Since our arrival in London I have made four trips to North America, two to South Africa, as well as a dozen briefer ones to the continent of Europe and elsewhere. In the course of all this journeying I have been able to make official visits to our churches in Scotland, the United States, Canada, South Africa, and Japan, and to the Philippine Independent Church. I do not anticipate any less travel than this in 1961.[2]

Such was his power and such his life. If the Anglican Communion today is more conscious of itself and its mission than once it was; if it wears this consciousness with humility and expresses that by its new knowledge of the interdependence of all its parts; if there is a new drive in its sense of mission; then it owes much of this sobering blessing to its first Executive Officer who fulfilled every hope set upon him and, more than any other single man, made the Toronto Congress of the Anglican Communion possible.

IV · *The Drive for Church Unity*

In the fields of political ideology, the patterns of commerce, international cultural co-operation, and in many others, the world, being now a neighbourhood, expresses its impatience with the old separations of man and feels after the unity of the whole human race. At the same time all these aspirations are mocked every day by the potent surges of nationalism and the bitter rivalry of the ideologies, even among and within themselves, which are building higher than ever before the walls of human separation. Future historians may well judge this to be the great paradox of the age. But it exists and in the heart of it is the numerically smaller but far less unsuccessful spectacle of the several Christian Churches of the world all struggling to find the way to their own unity. The more closely the Churches

[1] Quoted in Peter Whiteley, *Frontier Mission* (S.P.C.K.), 1963, p. 49.
[2] Bayne, *op. cit.*, p. 31.

can draw together the greater will be their power to draw all humanity together; and the search for the unity of Christendom is the characteristic contribution which the Churches have long been making towards the larger unity of human beings enfolded in a universal peace.

With this purpose the Ecumenical Movement began, and it brought into being the World Council of Churches to be the primary expression and instrument of its aims. It exists to give all the constituent Churches opportunities to express their common views on matters concerning them all, and also to work for the eventual organic unity of all the Churches. But the initiative of unity so far has been local, and has arisen out of the more national responses to the challenges and opportunities provided by events first in one neighbourhood and then in another. The World Council then takes cognizance of what has been attempted or achieved in some particular area, encourages it, and gives it real and important help to bear its full fruit. It is not yet a sovereign body over any Church, and perhaps it never will be.

The committee on 'Church Unity and the Church Universal' of the 1958 Lambeth Conference filled forty pages with its accounts of negotiations for different schemes of unity proceeding all over the Anglican world. Very few have yet borne the fruit which will one day reward their patience and faith, but the length of the list was evidence of the vitality and persistence of the effort, and also of its universality. But the two really dramatic events in this field which have filled all Christian minds with fresh hope have happened since 1958. The first, chronologically speaking, was the coming together of the Archbishop of Canterbury and Pope John XXIII in 1960, and the events of the Second Vatican Council which followed two years later. The second was the drawing together of the Church of England and the Methodist Church, and the production of the first definite plan to achieve the unity of the two Churches.

On October 26, 1961, very soon after he had resigned his archbishopric, Archbishop Lord Fisher of Lambeth went to Newcastle-upon-Tyne to speak to the diocesan conference. His theme was 'Church Unity and Ourselves', and in the course of his speech he said:

Up to and into the last war, and later too, there were very scanty relations between the Roman Catholic Church and the Church of England. In the time of Cardinal Hinsley there were some promising beginnings; but after his death they ceased, and attempts to revive them failed. Anyone behind the scenes knew how hostile the official attitude in the Roman Church here in England was. There has here been a quite remarkable change. Shall I say that the Iron Curtain has gone?

Less than a year later, on September 30, 1962, he preached in Grace Cathedral, San Francisco, and returned to the same broad theme. He thanked God for the Second Vatican Council, and for all that had already happened, 'so marvellous in our eyes':

For centuries the Churches have been hostile to one another, often bitterly and cruelly hostile. They have worked against each other, they have prayed against each other. . . . For 400 years all diplomatic relations between the Church of Rome and other Reformed Churches of the West have been completely broken off.

Could they really now pray with and for one another? The answer was already, Yes. A new fact in church relations had been created, a new hope born; and the archbishop who spoke so thankfully of it had himself been not the least among its architects.

The approach to Rome had been the crown of his whole career. He had put the unity of Christian people in the foreground of his prayer and work, and to this cause, more perhaps than any other, he had dedicated his priesthood. Such success as had been granted to him had come in the fields of relationships between the Reformed Churches, between the several Churches of the Anglican Communion, and between the different parties in the Church of England. But never until the very last years of his primacy, not before 1958 at the earliest, could he have dreamed that the chance would be given to him to grasp on behalf of his Church a hand of friendship held out by Rome herself.

There had, it would seem, been a moment as far back as 1948 when a dent had been made in the armour of Rome's age-long exclusiveness by the success of the First Assembly of the World Council of Churches at Amsterdam, and by the fact that for the first time the Orthodox Churches of the East sent official observers to it. The Curia had of course known all along about the ecumenical effort which the World Council of Churches represented, but had held aloof from it. But there are isolated pieces of evidence that Rome found Amsterdam both significant and disturbing. The well-known Roman theologian Hans Küng mentions it; and Carlo Falconi, the journalist who wrote in diary form an account of the Second Vatican Council, has this to say about it in his introduction:

Throughout the Pontificate of Pius XI this movement seemed to be well-intentioned and it merely aroused his disparaging irony. But after the First Assembly of the World Council of Churches in Amsterdam in 1948 it quickly became so powerful as to isolate the Roman Church, unless the latter hastened to establish relations with it.[1]

There was a further fact which Falconi also mentions. The statistics of world population, and the predictions to be drawn from them, were seeming to threaten, if not the survival, at least the predominance of Rome:

The terrifying and inexorable problem of Rome lies, quite simply, in the statistics which forecast that Catholics, today representing 20 per cent of the world's population, 5 per cent of whom are practising, will by A.D. 2000 be reduced to 9 per cent, 1.8 per cent of them practising. In other words the Church's struggle is

[1] Carlo Falconi, *Pope John and his Council*, p. 45.

a struggle for survival and not only of the Roman Church but of all Christian Churches. The significance of the ecumenical movement is, in fact, no different from that of the Council: both are born of the same urgent need to seek safety. For this reason they have come together, and the Christian world now strives to present a united front against what has been defined in religio-racial terms as the new barbarian invasion.[1]

But it is not by the power of such diplomatic and statistical calculations as these that the corporate repentance of Churches is born. The streak of incurable disinterestedness in man is too strong for that. And yet without some such act of corporate penitence friendship cannot be substituted for hostility, suspicion, and fear. The Curia did issue a document, signed by Cardinal Ottaviani, in reply to the hopes of Amsterdam, but it was a cold and dusty answer. The moment to move had not yet come.

Nor could it come for so long as Pius XII remained Pope. The climate of the twentieth century is one in which the intellectual patrician finds it hard to be at his ease, difficult to walk freely, and harder still to waken a response of heart and mind in the mass of the people to whom he must successfully appeal if he is fully to serve a great cause. Pius XII was the withdrawn aristocrat of deep but private piety, detached from all but his own kind. John XXIII was a man of the people, whose real and costly spiritual austerities were hidden, and around whom a great mass of genial legend naturally clustered. He had what his predecessor lacked, a freedom of uncalculated response to every situation. A book could easily be made of the stories of his spontaneous and heart-warming gestures, every one of which was a consequence of his percipience of the best that was concealed in the heart of every man or woman he met. His elevation to the Papacy never for one moment abated it. Over his election it is easy to believe that the Holy Spirit presided, for in the twentieth century it was just such a man as he was, and no other kind of man, who was capable of leading his own Church, and others as well, towards the things belonging to their peace and unity, and the Roman Church to a dramatically swift change of heart towards the rest of Christendom.

Born on November 25, 1881, Guiseppe Roncalli was elected Pope John XXIII on October 28, 1958, at the age of almost 77. He was crowned Pope on November 4, 1958, and he died on June 3, 1963, after a reign of four years and seven months. It cannot often have happened in history that a man so old achieved so much in a time so short. His tenure of the Holy See hearteningly illustrates in our own time the old truth that great changes in history may be prepared for by impersonal trends and tendencies, but are not brought to birth until the right human, individual person arrives to be the midwife.

The story of his pontificate has been written many times already, and will be told again and again in the future. Only the barest outline is necessary

[1] *Ibid.*, p. 42.

here. On January 25, 1959, within three months of his coronation, he announced the aims of his pontificate. They were to revive the diocesan synod in Rome, to bring up to date the code of canon law, and to hold an ecumenical council. The first session of this, the Second Vatican Council, began on October 11, 1962.

But almost two years earlier, on December 2, 1960, Geoffrey Fisher, Archbishop of Canterbury, had visited Rome and had been received officially in private audience by Pope John. Such visits as this do not happen spontaneously but take long in the preparing. Dr Fisher was sure that he must make an apostolic journey, carrying with him the whole authority of his office, to Jerusalem and Istanbul as well as Rome. If he was to see the Pope it was essential that he should see also, and in the same journey, the Ecumenical Patriarch. He had to be sure that he would be welcomed in Rome as Archbishop, not as a semi-private episcopal pilgrim; and because much publicity was bound to surround the gesture, he must also be sure that there was a good chance of the visit having some power to contribute towards a new and more friendly atmosphere between Rome and Canterbury. With Pius XII there could have been no such assurance, for to the day of his death he had believed that universal submission to Rome was the only path to Christian unity. But Pope John had publicly abandoned that idle dream. For him the way led first through the friendship of Christian people of every Church, and at last came to the great goal of the uniting of Churches, as whole entities, with the Roman Church. His part in the long journey was the taking of old enemies and the making of them into new friends. As far as the Anglican Communion was concerned, the first step towards this larger aim was to meet the Archbishop of Canterbury face to face as Pope to Archbishop but also as friend to friend. The second was to invite the Anglican Communion to be represented at the Vatican Council by their own appointed observers.

Towards the end of 1959 Dr Fisher made up his mind and set the machinery of preparation in motion. He spoke of what he wanted to do to several of his senior bishops and assured himself of their support. Then he made his own approaches privately to the Vatican. Pope John welcomed them warmly. The fact that he was going was made public on November 1, 1960, and, with very few exceptions, the forthcoming visit was gladly welcomed from the English side. On November 22 he set out on this pilgrimage. First he was to go to Jerusalem, then to Istanbul, and finally to Rome. He arrived there on December 1 and preached that day in the Anglican church of All Saints, Rome, when he said:

For the first time for four hundred years (and indeed longer) an Archbishop of Canterbury has come in his official capacity to Rome: and he has come neither to boast nor to complain, but only to greet His Holiness the Pope in the courtesy of Christian brotherhood. This could only happen, I could only have suggested my visit here, because the Pope on his side has made it clear that he would receive me in a similar spirit, in the courtesy of Christian brotherhood. Here is indeed a Day of the Lord, like many Days of the Lord, simple, unspectacular, hardly to be observed, a whisper of the still small voice of the Holy Spirit.[1]

The next day the Archbishop went to the Vatican, and with friendship and courtesy Pope John received him. What passed between them has never been divulged. If it was it would probably seem pedestrian and undramatic. It was always meant to be just a friendly talk and not a piece of indirect diplomacy. The purpose of their meeting was simply to create a spirit of trust in friendship between the highest authority of each Church, and this purpose was fulfilled indeed. It had always been Pope John's way to talk instead of discuss, to make friends rather than to negotiate. But as a result of the visit one new fact emerged. It was agreed that the Archbishop should have a personal representative at the Vatican, and Canon Bernard Pawley was appointed to be the first representative.

This was almost Fisher's last act as Archbishop. He had made his apostolic journey, as he said in his sermon at Jerusalem, 'late in my life, late in my experience of Christian faith and living'. But it crowned the most consistent endeavour of that long life. Always he had tried to find the way to serve well the cause of Christian unity. No one can say, and it would be impertinent to guess, just what was the effect of this famous meeting between these two kind, genial, but very different men. The Second Vatican Council might very well have taken just the same course as in fact it did if they had never met at all. And yet some of the virtue might have been lost to it. From the English side it kindled a respect, even an affection, for Rome which had not existed for centuries before.

What it had drawn from the Roman side the tortuous convolutions of the Council gradually disclosed. Fisher lived to see the first fruits but Pope John did not. It was on December 6, 1964, that the Roman Catholic Hierarchy of England and Wales issued their statement on what was in future to be permissible in relationships between the Roman and other Churches. It was made in response to the Pope's promulgation of the Council's Decree on Ecumenism. Other hierarchies acted rather earlier than the British and some were less conservative. But the result was a set of liberations which, even five years before, would have been judged by both sides to be impossible for centuries to come:

Elected representatives and public officials may in future attend services in non-Catholic churches in the course of their civic duties.

As friendship between Christians grows, invitations are increasingly extended to certain Catholics to attend non-Catholic churches on special occasions such as the induction of a new Vicar or Minister. These invitations may now be accepted.

Suitably qualified priests and laymen may, with the approval of the Bishop,

---

[1] *Feeling our Way: Three Sermons* (Church Information Office), 1960, p. 20.

accept invitations to speak in non-Catholic churches, provided that the address does not form part of the service.

There were six of these liberating clauses, and only the three most important are quoted here. They were embedded in a two-page document which, while still insisting on the great differences still remaining between the Roman Catholic and all other Churches, yet exhibited throughout the charity and friendship which, in our own time and before our eyes, have at last supplanted the hostile rivalry of many centuries between the Roman and all other Churches in England.

Though the drawing near of the Methodist Church and the Church of England has naturally caught the eye and held the imagination of the public less than the sudden change in our relationships with Rome, it is with the English Methodists that we are nearest to a formal unity. For the first time in all the English discussions and negotiations on unity between separated Churches, a definite plan for it has been produced, with a timetable, and even a draft of the service to be used for the inauguration of the first stage, the exchange of ministry between the two Churches.

The committee of the 1958 Lambeth Conference, reporting on the situation as it then stood, found little to say. Conversations between the theologians of both sides began anew in 1948, and for the next ten years explored the idea that Methodism might take episcopacy into its own system, and that if it did the way would be open to such mutual recognition of the two ministries as would make possible a real inter-communion between the two Churches. These proposals the negotiating committee published in July 1958, just in time for the Lambeth Conference, which welcomed them, but pointed out that organic union, not inter-communion, was the final goal. Beyond that the bishops said little because the document they were considering was no more than an interim statement (by which title it at once became known), and because they knew that the committee had not finished its work.

It was not until 1963 that the committee published their work in its final form, and this pamphlet, *Conversations Between the Church of England and the Methodist Church*, is one of the most important of all documents in the history of reunion. The committee proposed that both Churches should resolve to go forward to the achievement of full communion, and then, to make this definite, they added:

We see this as involving
  (a) The reconciliation of the two Churches in a service for which we suggest a form in chapter 6, and which involves the integration by reciprocal action of their respective ministries.
  (b) The acceptance by the Methodist Church of episcopacy in continuity with the historic episcopate, and the practice of episcopal ordination for its ministers in the future.

(c) The provision of means by which the Churches during the period of full communion could co-operate and grow together by consultation, common action and common devotion at all levels.[1]

To that the committee added a footnote to make even more explicit what they meant by the period of full communion:

This means, in particular, that the Church of England would agree to admit to communion baptized and communicant members of the Methodist Church in good standing and would officially authorize communicant members of the Church of England in good standing to receive the sacrament of Holy Communion at the hands of Methodist ministers, each Church undertaking to respect the pastoral discipline exercised by the other Church. Further, the ministers of each Church would be eligible to celebrate or preach in the other Church, at the invitation of their respective authorities,[2]

But this plan for full communion presupposes a high degree of reciprocity between the two ministries, each of which must be recognized as truly ministers by the other. The committee's draft of a Service of Reconciliation was intended to do that very thing:

The service has been constructed on the principle that there should be a formal reception of the members and ministers of each Church by accredited representatives of the other, performed in such a way as will enable each member to communicate and each bishop, priest and minister to officiate in either Church.

The service will be followed as soon as possible by the consecration of certain Methodist ministers to the episcopate and thereafter ordinations in the Methodist Church will be performed by bishops assisted by other ministers.[3]

The service then proceeds to the point of this mutual recognition. The Anglican Bishop lays his hands on the head of each Methodist minister, receives him 'into the fellowship of the ministry in the Church of England', and gives him authority to exercise the office of a priest. Correspondingly the presiding Methodist minister does the same, and with the same words, to each Anglican bishop and priest.

This solemn reciprocity would be necessary to inaugurate the first stage of the plan, the period, lasting some years, of full communion between the two Churches, during which they learn to live together and co-operate to the full, but nevertheless retain their distinct life and identity. But this would all be pointless unless it was intended to lead, and in fact did lead, to the goal of full, organic union whereby there would be one Church instead of two.

Thus the committee provided a definite plan, but also a time-table. The plan was published in 1963. In that year it was to be commended for study to the Convocations and to the Methodist Conference. By 1965, it was suggested, they should be ready to pronounce judgement on it. If then both

---

[1] *Op. cit.* (Epworth Press and C.I.O.), 1963, p. 9.
[2] *Ibid.*, p. 10.   [3] *Ibid.*, p. 37.

Churches accepted the proposals in principle, it would be for them to decide 'how they would wish to proceed to their practical implementation'. The timetable was kept. On the Anglican side the plan was laid before the ruri-decanal and diocesan conferences, which, without exception, accepted it, usually by large majorities. The Convocations accepted it in May, 1965, as enabling further negotiations to clear up the 'points of concern' which had come to light. On the Methodist side Conference approved the plan in principle on July 5, 1965, but also asked for further joint study. The position at this moment therefore is that both the Church of England and the Methodists have endorsed the proposals of the joint committee, that full organic union between the two Churches is both possible and desirable, and that it must be prepared for by a period of full communion. We have now therefore to wait and see what happens next, but it will be surprising if in the end these proposals, endorsed in principle by large majorities on both sides, come to nothing. There is no doubt at all that this report has more than justified all the labours of the distinguished Anglicans and Methodists who produced it, and that it is one of the most influential documents in the field of reunion which has ever been written.

V · *The Anglican Congress at Toronto*

The use of the international congress or council as a means of impelling the development of Anglicanism rose to a climax with the Toronto Congress, held in August 1963. Few who were there, and none who have since written about it, seem to have had any doubts of its immense potential importance, or that it wrote the title and decided the theme of an entirely new chapter in the history of Anglicanism. It is doubtful if another such congress will be held for a long time to come. But this is not because of its size, great though it was, for after all what a Church has done once it can do again. Its size however was considerable and daunting. Over 1,000 delegates came to it; they represented the 43 million Anglicans in the world, and belonged to 18 provinces and more than 340 dioceses. The organization of the meetings and the hospitality of the delegates, the one efficient and the other gracious and imaginative, fell on the Church in Canada, and particularly the diocese of Toronto. It could not have been better done.

But there is another reason why Toronto is unlikely to be repeated for some time to come. It is that it did something new in the history of giant congresses, which, by its nature, cannot be repeated to order, or indeed at all, until this new thing has had time to work itself out and to show what forms it is going to take. For Toronto afforded an example of something rare in history, a great communion of Churches in the throes of corporate and perfectly genuine repentance, an exhibition of creative humility, a resolve to do something practical as a result of it, and at least the outlines of a definite plan whereby this penitence could yield its proper fruit. All this the Toronto Congress did. There is nothing new about members of conferences standing in white sheets and confessing to the sins of those who sent them there. That kind of corporate narcissism is common form among Anglican gatherings of every kind, and it is usually most uncreative. But Toronto was quite different. The confessional was there, and so was the penitence, but the plan for better things was there too. Bishop Bayne, one of its chief architects, has himself provided, as is most fitting, the summary of the atmosphere of resolve which, at least for those who were present, made all things new, and caused them to stand dazzled in surmise:

No question or critical comment can dilute in the slightest degree the massive and unforgettable power of the Congress and its satellite meetings. There were those who feared that the summer would bring an increase of confessional self-consciousness, a renewal of Anglican narcissism, a symposium of like-minded denominational *aficionados*. This did not happen. The Congress was unmistakably a gathering of the Church of Christ within the Church of Christ, infected with the greatness of the Church and our calling, and moved to respond with an impulse as strong as any in our history. The questions for the Anglican Communion now are what response we are equipped to make, and what changes we need in our structure to make a more adequate response possible.[1]

The lessons taught by the previous conferences at Jerusalem and New Delhi had been accepted and learned, and Toronto applied them. The delegates all talked about Mission, and never about Missions or Missionaries. They all clamoured that Anglicanism was not an end in itself, that, like everything else in life, it must die to live, its death the immolation of itself in some greater and more nearly universal Church of the future. They endorsed in almost every speech the Archbishop of Canterbury's declaration, 'The Church that Lives to Itself will Die by Itself'. They said all these things and many others like them; and if that were all they said or did, this Congress would have perished like a baseless vision and left not a wrack behind. But they did far more. They produced a new resolve in the form of a document which they all solemnly endorsed, and on its developing implementation the fame of Toronto will rest, for it was a profoundly revolutionary document for any Church to accept.

To this document, the blueprint of a programme, they gave what must surely be one of the most cumbrous titles ever conceived. They called it *Mutual Responsibility and Interdependence in the Body of Christ*, which has inevitably been shortened for common speech into the dispiriting initials MRI. But it has survived, and more than survived, even this nomenclature. The document was a plan to implement a penitence. It passed through its early stages before the Congress saw it. Two weeks before the Congress began some fifty men of long missionary experience met together at Huron College, near London, Ontario. They came from all over the

[1] *An Anglican Turning Point*, p. 82.

world and they discussed the modern problems of mission, as they knew them, in freedom and equality. After a week they handed over their findings to the Advisory Council on Missionary Strategy, which consists of all the Primates and Metropolitans of the Anglican Churches, who were joined by some of the missionary statesmen of the earlier meeting. What they had to do was to take the fruits of this meeting and others, all of which were held to find a possible basis for world-wide thinking and planning of mission, and conflate them into a manifesto to present to the Congress. But they had to take note of all the uneasinesses and discontents which each of the preliminary gatherings had revealed. In every one of them, said Bishop Bayne, 'certain deep hopes, discontents, determinations, insights kept welling up to the surface'.

This was all part of the uncomfortable probing of conscience which always precedes any true penitence. The Churches which theoretically made up one Communion of free fellowship in Christ, had for years, in practice if not in intention, been separated into 'haves' and 'have nots', into rich and poor relations, into Churches which did good and others which were done good to. Eventually the Advisory Council sorted out all the material presented to them, and presented the result to the Congress in a six-page document. It is so short a statement of so revolutionary a theme as to be almost its own summary.

It began with a short prologue on the coming-of-age of the Anglican Communion:

The full communion in Christ which has been our traditional tie has suddenly taken on a totally new dimension. It is now irrelevant to talk of 'giving' and 'receiving' churches. The keynotes of our time are equality, interdependence, mutual responsibility. . . . The time has fully come when this unity and interdependence must find a completely new level of expression and corporate obedience.

To that end the document asked first for a comprehensive study of needs and resources throughout the whole Communion. Then it asked each Church to accept its share of an immediate commitment of fifteen million dollars over and above all existing budgets. This was not to be thought of as a once-in-a-lifetime appeal, but simply as a first step to meet immediate needs, not long-term needs. The first of these was the rescuing of the new provinces from 'the humiliation of beggary', and to set bishops free to 'be the spearheads of mission'. It asked also for an extension of 'the whole process of inter-Anglican consultation', and to make this more possible it asked the Congress to agree to the appointment of seven Regional Officers to do for the seven major areas of Anglicanism what Bishop Bayne had been doing for the whole of it. Finally it asked every Church to study radically the form of 'its own obedience to mission', and exhorted all to be ready to accept the give and take of true fellowship in the one Body of

Christ. It ended with this statement, printed in the document in heavy black type for emphasis:

We are aware that such a programme as we propose, if it is seen in its true size and accepted, will mean the death of much that is familiar about our Churches now. It will mean radical change in our priorities—even leading us to share with others at least as much as we spend on ourselves. It means the death of old isolations and inherited attitudes. It means a readiness to forgo many desirable things, in every Church.

In substance, what we are really asking for is the rebirth of the Anglican Communion, which means the death of many old things but—infinitely more—the birth of entirely new relationships. We regard this as the essential task before the Churches of the Anglican Communion now.

All this was put before the Congress, debated in public and worked over in the study groups. From this process three lines of criticism emerged. The first was that the Advisory Council (which in practice meant all the Primates and Metropolitans, wielding between them a corporate authority than which none could be higher) still seemed to be thinking in terms of Anglicanism alone, and that this giving and receiving should somehow and one day be extended to apply to other Churches than the Anglican, as a means of promoting the unity of them all in a single fold. The second criticism was that the proposal to create seven new Regional Officers might create the impression that a bigger and better organization was all that was needed for the rebirth of the Communion. The third criticism fell upon the request for an immediate and a named sum of money, for fear that the document might be read in the Churches as just an appeal for more money, and thus lose most of its point. What happened in the end was that the Advisory Council's document was accepted as it stood, but that it was supplemented and glossed by a much shorter Congress Message which was to be read aloud in all the churches, and which, while retaining everything essential in the original document, avoided the three matters of contention. Nevertheless, the document remains in its entirety as the findings of the Anglican Congress of Toronto.

In order to give force and point to these proposals, it was announced by the Archbishop of Canterbury that in future all the Primates and Metropolitans of the Anglican Communion would meet together every two years, and that these meetings of theirs might take place anywhere in the world, certainly not always at Lambeth.

So far the omens are propitious. It looks as though Anglican Churches everywhere are taking the proposals of Toronto seriously, and what may happen as a result of it is still hidden in the future. But the patterns of a new life, a new enterprise, a new idea of the mission of the Church to the world, have been laid down, and the organization to contain them has been built. The missionary movement has coalesced with the World Council of Churches, which is a cumbrous but necessary way of saying that mission, undifferentiated and undistinguished, is the primary function of all Churches everywhere. The Anglican Communion at Toronto has taught that all the Churches of Christ are equal, and on the same level both in giving and taking, and has provided the germs of an organization to express and make practical these otherwise vague aspirations. The Vatican Council has met and finally committed the Roman Catholic Church to its full share of ecumenism, with all its hopes and in some measure already its practical policies. The aim of complete union between Anglicanism and Methodism in England is far advanced. The organization to express all these aims is either complete or in the making. For the relatively few years since 1958 this is no contemptible record.

30

An Explosion of Doctrine

I · *The Stillness Before the Storm*

JERUSALEM AND New Delhi, Rome and Toronto—the international Christian conferences held in these places had, when added together, amounted to the hope of a revolution in Christendom in the field of church relationships and the organization of Churches for their common mission to the world. But their work, though astonishing in its scope and thoroughness, was still incomplete. They organized the possibility of mission, but they had very little to say about the actual message of this universal mission, and less still about how it could be hopefully presented in the modern world. All this effort of corporate penitence and resolve, though no less moving and no less sincere than the separate repentances of individual Christians must always be, nevertheless raised in many reflective and sympathetic minds the sad question of whether it was in time. For before there can be a mission there must necessarily be an evangelistic message, and the fact remained that large sections of the modern world had given notice that if this message was what they supposed it must be they would not be able to heed it.

For years past the failure of the Church of England, and every other Church, to win a wide response to the good news of the love of God had been notorious. The fact of this failure was universally admitted. The reasons for it were analysed again and again in what had become a bewilderingly vast body of literature. All these depressing analyses had provided a host of diagnoses but no cure. The fact remained that most of the traditional ways of presenting the Faith were proving themselves impotent to reach the minds of those who, on the standards of the Gospel, might be supposed to be the most 'valuable' of all to God. The ordinary teachings of what Christian behaviour was intended to be had done little more than engender scorn in intelligent non-Christians, and moral bewilderment among many of the best and most sincere of the convinced

Christians. In every Church many of the more intelligent younger Christians, while holding resolutely to the whole pattern of the practice of their Faith, were secretly fighting despair. They were rapidly becoming the disappointed Christians. They still believed that only the Gospel could save the world they knew, but they could not see any hope of its being able to take hold of the world in time.

All this was an unspoken criticism of traditional theology and morality. Ever since 1958 the Church had been penitently organizing itself for revolution. But however necessary that was, it was bound to be useless as long as its essential message remained conservatively entrenched behind all the frontiers of change. While the Church's organizers, its ecumenists, its leadership generally, had become steadily less hidebound and more adventurous, its theologians and its casuists had moved hardly an inch out of their old ivory towers. Within those walls they had worked assiduously and with careful scholarship. The years between 1945 and 1962 had been much enriched by the labours of the pure theologians, the ecclesiastical historians, and most of all by the work of the New Testament scholars. The contributions which all these devoted men had made were of great moment. But, speaking generally, such scholars as these had been working within a very conservative mould and using reactionary idioms and language. The result was that they had nothing to say to the ominously growing number of people who, either having no belief in God or being indifferently agnostic towards him, could not be expected to show any interest in their peripheral territories of theism. They had been doing their fighting on the wrong battlefields where in the nature of things no decision could lie, and in consequence they wrote their books for each other and not for the world. That both doctrinal and moral theology would have to begin all over again, using very different methods of research and communication, had occurred to very few theologians or casuists.

But it had occurred to some, such as Tillich in America, to Bonhoeffer and Bultmann in Germany, to R. Gregor Smith in Britain, as also to the students they had taught. These men, and others like them, had for many years seen that a new world was upon them and that new men were making it, and they had been struggling so to restate the central truths of the Gospel that these new men of a new world could grapple with them and make sense of them. The axiom from which they started was that modern man had quite suddenly become adult, and that he was new in the sense that none of the ages of history could show anything quite like him. That this new man, scientifically trained and believing that science could now solve every problem with which time might present it, was now in control of his world and stood in no need of God's assistance with its direction, was the focus of the challenge which they knew they must meet. The moralists among them knew that even if modern man was in control of his world, he could not control himself, but they knew also that the traditionally phrased morality, descending with little change from the early and the mediaeval Church, was powerless to halt the strong tide of moral disaster, or still the gnawing pain of moral perplexity. To the situation which faced them only the humanists could be heirs, and already, in the form of the philological philosophers, hot for the dignity of man, they were advancing to claim their kingdom. The astronomers and the cosmonauts were unfolding the coverings of the universe, and were pointing to hitherto unimaginable vast-nesses, which seemed to many to make man small and of no reputation. Just this was what the Gospel had always flatly denied, but what sense did the Gospel make of the sort of world which the astronomers were expand-ing, the technologists controlling, and the cosmonauts exploring?

The barriers between the modern man and the traditional theologians were tall and formidable, and in theology as they were teaching it there seemed no power to break them down or to climb them, since these theo-logians—the great majority—were quite conspicuously failing to take into account, and much less to grapple with, the essential novelty of this modern world. The few who had seen the point of this unprecedented novelty had, in spite of all their efforts, failed to gain the hearing, except in a purely academic sense, of even their fellow scholars in the Church, much less of the generality of churchpeople, and less still of those outside the Church whose loyalty they hoped to win with their innovations. At the same time the fact, well known to all and disputed by none, that the traditionally stated Gospel was failing to appeal to an ever larger proportion of human beings, con-stituted a desperate challenge to the Church, and up to 1962 there seemed no way to meet it. This dilemma must be resolved if New Delhi, Rome, and Toronto were not to be emotional dead letters. The Kingdom of God can-not be brought in to any age without the organization to contain it, but without the acceptable message of the Gospel there is no Kingdom.

Thus it is possible to read the history of the Church's theology from 1958 to 1962 as the ominous stillness of a gathering storm. The Church in these years was very occupied with its organization for rebirth, reunion, and mission. It was quite essential that it should be, and it did it well. But the development of its fundamental teaching had lagged far behind. It was now necessary that the Church should awaken theologically and begin to live in its own world. It had not yet done so, and therefore the storm was brewing.

II · *Beginning All Over Again*

The storm gathered in 1962 and broke in 1963. The book of theological essays called *Soundings*, published in 1962, provided the first ominous but still rather vague rumblings of it. In the next year the book *Honest to God* set all the fireworks and thunderings of the long-pent storm free to rage in fury. It shook the theological earth at the time, it has disturbed it ever since, and it will do so for a long time to come.

Soundings[1] was a collection of essays by nine Cambridge theologians (and one from another university) which was edited by Dr Alec Vidler, Dean of King's College. One of the most stimulating and original thinkers of the Church, who had made his reputation by his exploration of the borderland between theology and history, he had for many years been the editor of *Theology*. No man can hold that position as long and successfully as Vidler did unless he is interested in the theologians themselves as well as in the theology which they teach. Just as there are some historians whose chief interest is in historiography, the ways in which history gets written and the philosophies of history underlying them, so there are theologians whose concern is with the patterns of theological writing and the philosophies which they display. Alec Vidler was one, and probably the most distinguished of them, and he gathered round him these nine scholars who were of the same mind as himself, and shared every corner of his intense anxiety over the failure of the Gospel to make its way. They gave their book the sub-title *Essays Concerning Christian Understanding*, and the heart of their common approach was adumbrated in the title of the first essay by the Rev. Howard Root, *Beginning All Over Again*, and in this passage from Dr Vidler's introduction:

> The authors of this volume of essays cannot persuade themselves that the time is ripe for major works of theological construction or reconstruction. It is a time for ploughing, not reaping; or, to use the metaphor we have chosen for our title, it is a time for making soundings, not charts or maps. If this be so, we do not have to apologize for our inability to do what we hope will be possible in a future generation. We can best serve the cause of truth and of the Church by candidly confessing where our perplexities lie, and not by making claims which, so far as we can see, theologians are not at present in a position to justify.
>
> That is to say, we believe that there are very important questions which theologians are now being called upon to face, and which are not yet being faced with the necessary seriousness and determination. We do not profess yet to see our way through them: and we do not want to reproach ourselves with looking for a way round them. Our task is to try to see what the questions are that we ought to be facing in the nineteen-sixties. . . . We do not wish to evade the assessment of our work by our contemporaries—we shall welcome it; but we believe we are handling questions that are not likely to receive definite answers for a long time to come.[2]

In other words they were asserting that no theological map of the modern universe was now possible, and that though no doubt it would one day be possible again, because the Gospel remains the Gospel in every age, the time for its confident drawing was far distant. The world had already begun all over again; it was now for the theologians to follow suit. For the present all genuine theological work must be experimental, tentative, and

[1] Cambridge University Press, 1962. [2] *Soundings*, pp. ix, xi.

empirical. Those who demanded theological certainties could be given only dusty answers, but they would be honest answers. No such tones as these had been heard in theological utterances for a long time.

Except at one point *Soundings* produced a rather muffled explosion. It was a very scholarly work by a body of academic teachers, who wrote always with caution and restraint. But in every line it heralded a revolution. Few statements are more revolutionary than to say that theology is no longer capable of drawing a map of the world, that it must be content to ask the questions it cannot answer, and that it must begin its work afresh. As an implied criticism of traditional theology such statements were devastating. The true humility of its contributors which caused them to confess openly their theological bewilderments, and to eschew the making of any large claims, had itself become a revolutionary power. The high academic reputation of the writers cast an aura of respectability over their contributions and dulled the bang they caused. But unlike so many academics who live all their lives in a university, these knew thoroughly and accepted unquestioningly the world in which they had been set to live. They knew, for instance, that theology had much to learn about that world, and that they must take their teaching from the hands of those they wished to teach. They were ready to enter into a dialogue with them. But all these attitudes of mind are themselves approaches to creative revolution. It is unlikely that *Soundings* was read by many who were not already convinced Christians, and it was read by comparatively few among them. But there were not many of the more violent theological statements made in the storm which was coming which *Soundings* had not either made or implied in advance, and these writers, by the fact that they could never be accused of striking public attitudes of their own, helped to win for the utterances of the firebrands a fairer hearing than they would otherwise have had.

But *Soundings* may probably be remembered in history as providing the first really public airing of what has come to be called the New Morality. It is only for the sake of convenience that the New Morality is here treated separately from the New Theology. There was no such separation in the minds of those who were pleading the cause of theological revolution, and their criticism of tradition proceeded on both the moral and the doctrinal fronts at once. In *Soundings*, this trumpet was blown by the Rev. H. A. Williams, Dean of Trinity College, Cambridge, in the essay called 'Theology and Self-Awareness'. For the most part it was an examination of the relevance of Freudian psychology to Christian living, and from that it passed into an attempt to restate the biblical doctrine of justification by faith. When seen in this light, Mr Williams claimed that much traditional Christian morality is concealed cowardice. In the fields of murder and theft he had no difficulty in expounding his point in such a way that it could give no offence at all. But sex is not so safely academic, and when Mr Williams passed on to deal with that he wrote these sentences:

A great deal of what Christians call virtue, on closer inspection turns out to be cowardice of this kind—a refusal to give myself away because I am too frightened to do it. This is most obviously true in the sphere of sexual ethics, because here more than anywhere there seems to be an enormous amount of double-think. If I am to give myself away to another person, I cannot, in any circumstances, exploit her or him. To exploit is to withhold. It is totally incompatible with giving. But this is not at all the same thing as saying that in certain specifiable circumstances I must always be exploiting and never giving. Yet this is what the Church says about sexual intercourse outside marriage. Such intercourse may be often, perhaps almost always, an exploitation, unilateral or mutual. But there are cases where it need not be and isn't.[1]

He then instanced a couple of cinema films which many may think were not particularly to the point, and in any case did not prove it, and then he added:

Must not all of us have the courage of Jesus and address ourselves to his words —'It is written, but I say unto you'? The risk is admittedly appalling. But our Lord warned us continually that unless we are prepared to risk everything, we shall never find our lives.[2]

The author was in fact claiming that though adultery was wrong nine hundred and ninety-nine times out of a thousand, it might be right, or at least more right than wrong, the thousandth time; and he was taking the risk that most people tempted towards it would certainly regard their own case as the exceptional thousandth. Though this passage only occupied two out of a total of 39 pages of the essay there was something of an outcry because in fact Mr Williams was preaching from a different point of view the same contingent morality which used to be regarded as the sign manual of all infidelity.

The risks of this standard of morality were great, and this Mr Williams freely admitted: in fact he called them 'appalling'. The circumstances justifying the risks remain uncertain. So much depends on how these risks are viewed by the people concerned, and whether they think of them as risks at all. But it is the business of the historian rather to describe controversies than to pass judgement on them. There is no doubt that this tentative suggestion of Mr Williams gave birth to an important controversial progeny. Much pleading and much repudiation followed it, and so has been born what has come to be known as the New Morality. The prophets of this line of ethical teaching have accepted and endorsed it and the traditionalists have angrily repudiated it; so that it now stands waiting for the judgement of the Church, though it will be a long time before any verdict is given.

Both Mr Williams, and those who have since expounded his plea more fully, have attempted to speak to the true moral condition of the age, and therefore they have been heard. By an unscholarly selection from a mass of

[1] *Op. cit.*, p. 81.   [2] *Ibid.*, p. 82.

generalizations it would not be difficult to document the suggestion that this age is in a state of chaotic moral disaster. That would be tendentious pleading, and any picture painted in this way would be to a large extent false. But it is quite certain that in the field of morals all is far from well, and that the area of morals where the disasters mostly lie is the field of personal relationships. It is more often than not the misapplication of the strong and universal urge of sex that drives them astray. Therefore, though morals are always far more than sex relations, Mr Williams was justified in thus particularizing and instancing a general argument. That the element of sex in all personal relationships is being more than usually intractable is proved by, among other things, the dangerously high and growing divorce statistics. Then there is the dilemma of so many of the best and socially most valuable people, not the worst and the morally heedless, who so often find themselves in situations caused by some aberration of sex, and then honestly do not know what in the given circumstances is the right Christian course for them to follow. All who receive their confidence and have to try to give them advice know their plight well, and how pitiful it is. They also know that the circumstances of each case determine what the advice must be, and that nothing could be more hopeless than trying to insist on the same stock answer to the same kind of sin without regard to the circumstances. When these are taken into account, the adviser may well find himself giving contradictory answers to two sets of people who are caught in the net of exactly the same kind of sin. To his embarrassment, he finds himself dispensing in the study the contingent morality which he has probably denounced in the pulpit, only he calls it by some less compromising title. If he is reflective, he justifies his inconsistencies by the fact that this method of tentative approach gives divine grace room to move and time to work.

The extent to which modern England is involved in moral delinquency on the one hand and a sincere moral bewilderment on the other could be argued long and without arriving at any certainty. But it is perfectly clear that the one or the other is the plight of very large numbers of people; and clear also that the old rules and certitudes of the traditional Christian moralist cannot now stem either tide. To some they bring a sense of angry repudiation, to others bewilderment. It is not therefore surprising that the prophets of a supposedly new but still Christian morality find an eager hearing.

As a title the New Morality is a misnomer. There is in fact nothing new about it, for those who hold it are very eloquent about the tension of 'law' with 'charity' and the restatement of the doctrine of Justification by Faith, and both of these are written into every part of the New Testament. Far from being any novelty it is in fact as old as the Gospels themselves, and though the ethics built upon it are unsystematized they are neither more nor less than the moral teaching and ethical practice of Jesus himself, when seen fairly and in their proper balance. That this teaching has seemed to many a shocking novelty is a wry comment on the ethical teaching of the Church for many centuries, and the issue it raises is that of the Church's authority.

The heart of this new pleading is to find the way to put the idea of charity above the idea of law without destroying respect for law in the process, to make the sanctions of Christian behaviour more positive than negative, and to refound in twentieth-century terms the vital doctrine of justification by faith. It is therefore the revival of a very ancient controversy, for by no one has a legalistic morality been more bitterly or incessantly castigated than by both Jesus and Paul. Without faith in the grace of God no exemptions from the codes of law can be tolerated, and without charity there could be nothing but condemnation for them. But with grace and with charity it becomes possible to treat individual cases on their own varying merits. The new moralist would always prefer the question, What, in the circumstances of all the people involved, does charity demand? to the question, What does the Christian moral law say about this situation? He would add that the first question will always be more searching and more exacting than the second. The protagonists of the new ethic would further claim that this is the way in which our Lord actually worked, and dealt with the people who came to him to find their peace.

It is with the business of applying the principles of charity to the actual problems of living that the trouble has come. Once say that charity must predominate over law, and freedom over restriction, and the old principle of contingent morality is at once brought back into play. It wakens unfortunate memories and it creates prejudice. Yet it cannot be avoided if the new moralists claim the sanctions of the New Testament for their belief that morality is not a legalistic code but a charitable response to a set of personal circumstances. For if one admits that there may be exceptional circumstances in which it is better to kill a man than not to kill him, better to steal than not to steal, there is no way of denying that, most exceptionally, it may be better, or at least less harmful, to commit adultery than to refrain from committing it. But on these terms the cutting edge of the flat, unexceptionable negatives of three of the Ten Commandments is blunted, and much of their authority is lost. It is also true that all this pleading is terribly dangerous because all normal men and women who heed it must be tempted to think of their own case as so wholly exceptional that the normal prohibitions do not apply, and so, often enough, to become judges in their own case.

But if charity is to predominate over law none of these dangers can be avoided. Nor, on the very principles of charity, can its relationship to law be precisely defined, because the adoption of any unexceptional definition would bring back legalism through a new door. The dilemma is most real and most painful. Though by now this New Morality has been expounded for us in several books, it is true that so far we have had no more than a tentative outline of it. In three fields particularly much more careful research is needed which the prophets of it must undertake before their whole case can be fairly judged. The first is to ask how far it recapitulates in twentieth-century terms the moral insights and ethical practices of Jesus himself, and to answer the question, Is this New Morality in fact anything other than the application of the ethical insights of the Gospel? The second is to face the question whether what is being taught is anything more than the training of man to choose rightly between two evils in circumstances which rule out all possibility of a choice of the absolutely good. The third, and most important of all, is to define where the Cross, the supreme act of Christ, comes into all this. It is difficult to believe that there can be any resolving of the strain of tension between charity and law in a world much given to evil unless the principles of Calvary provide it. But what may be meant by such a statement as this the new moralists as yet seem hardly to have enquired.

In a work of history, such as this, there is no need to expound the New Morality more closely. Enough has been said to show how explosive it is. For years to come the Church must have much of her being in these dangerous fields, but this dwelling place can be creative if all who inhabit it apply to the inevitable controversy the principles of charity to which they are appealing.

III · *The Crisis of Belief*

'The book appears to have sold more quickly than any new book of serious theology in the history of the world.'[1] Thus its publisher, the Rev. David Edwards of the Student Christian Movement Press, writes of *Honest to God*, the short and difficult paperbacked book of Dr John Robinson, Bishop of Woolwich, which he published in 1963. Within three years almost a million copies were in print in various languages. A book of which such claims can be made becomes at once a significant fact in history, properly to be discussed in historical works both ecclesiastical and sociological, and its author makes for himself a name to be remembered for very many years.

The publication of this book was the event which loosed the long pent-up thunders of the gathering storm which exploded in a great and sudden roar, and the echoes of it have gone on reverberating round the hills of the world ever since. It immediately set in motion a tremendous public debate, and for a long time the air was full of violent charges and denunciations and the defences made against them. The former were as intemperate as they were noisy, and the defenders from time to time adopted a tone which was both injured and shrill. *Honest to God* in fact caused a great controversy. Just as no previous theological book had sold so quickly, so none had caused so much excitement or given rise to so much quarrelling. What other work

[1] *The Honest to God Debate*, edited by David L. Edwards (SCM Press), 1963, p. 7.

of academic theology has created so great a stir that within six months it was necessary to issue another book, just twice as long, to capture for historians the highlights of the controversy? This was done in *The Honest to God Debate*, which consisted of a preliminary account of the bubbling ferment in Christian belief, the citation of many private letters and reviews, and a brief postscript to the debate by the bishop himself.

An event so unusual, even so unique in academic history, formed a most significant portent. The historian of the future will have to account for it since this is a fact likely to be influential in the making of his world. The part scandalous, part comic impression of a bishop of the Church appearing to deny much that the Church teaches is not enough to account for a tenth part of the circulation. There is nothing new in that; the list of bishops who have earned that sort of notoriety is not short. It is not that the book was the work of an original thinker, or said things which had never been said before. It did say many of them in a new and very challenging way, but the ideas it propounded had all been suggested, either by direct statement or by implication, long ago by theologians such as Bonhoeffer, Bultmann, Tillich, or by some of the writers in *Soundings*. There was nothing new in the claim that mankind had suddenly become adult, that man's powers were now such as no previous generation could so much as have imagined, that he was learning to manage his world and live his life without God. No news could be more stale than the sad announcement that the modern Church had failed notoriously to offer to modern man a message about God which interested him and which he could accept. That fact had been proclaimed and accepted for years.

But *Honest to God* was a book which had tremendous power and vitality. It drew it in part from the resolute honesty of its author, who, convinced Christian though he was, was determined to take nothing whatever for granted, and refused to exempt any sacrosanct symbol, even any divine person, from the agnostic scrutinies of modern secular man—a title he accepted for himself. He, a trained and an eminent academic theological scholar, was doing for the theologically innocent modern technologist what he hoped the technologist would one day do for himself. The bishop accepted his habits of mind, adopted his fundamental assumptions and even many of his unexamined axioms, and then, cautiously and with much stumbling, he looked at the traditional faith of the Church through agnostic eyes which, for the purposes of the book, he had made his own. They were not reverent eyes. They belonged to a man who began by believing that most religious language is meaningless, that the supernatural scheme of things within which Christianity has been expounded is no longer credible, that religion, having in the past done more harm than good, has now become utterly uninfluential upon the courses of the world. These were eyes which had seen nothing from the inside of the Church, and misunderstood much of what they had seen from the outside. They were nevertheless the eyes of a man in revolt against most things traditional, and against any idea of revealed religion. They saw crudely, but they were the eyes of the man with whom the Church must have creative dialogue if, humanly speaking, she was to survive.

Honest to God was the overture of this dialogue. Cautiously, himself stumbling often, the bishop looked at the Faith through the eyes of the technologist, gave him his full say, and then, after the manner of all overtures, outlined for him some of the themes of a possible restatement of the Faith in his own language. But it was the overture of a still unwritten work because theology is not yet in a position to draw a new map of the world. But all this meant not only a repudiation of many sacrosanct words and phrases of traditional theology, but also, and more, a repudiation of much of the whole traditionalist way of looking at God and his world.

Small wonder that there was trouble. It might have been avoided if the bishop had written the book in the true form of a dialogue, and allowed the technologist, or whatever other lay figure he had in mind, to utter his own irreverences. But he chose a different pattern for it, no doubt because he was himself thinking aloud. The result was a very radical reinterpretation of Christian doctrine, but to those who are bewildered by it reinterpretation will always look like elimination. Some of the bishop's language about myth, about whether the world now had any place left for God, about whether there was any sense in which it could be asserted that God is a person capable of personal relationships, did indeed sound like a presumptuous repudiation of the entire treasury of Christian theology, and a harrowing of heaven. In particular, the only place he seemed able to find for God was as 'the ground of our being', and this cast doubt upon the idea of God as existing in any way independently of his own created world. This, in turn, compromised the old idea of God as transcendent as well as immanent; and it seemed to many to strike at the root of most personal devotional practices, perhaps because, on these terms, there was no particular and identifiable function left for God to perform.

Such were the negative impressions which a hasty reading of the book left, and they were very unfair both to the book and to the man who wrote it. His purpose was positive throughout—to find the way to present the Gospel to modern man. But he was blowing trumpets, not pondering strategies in the cool, ordered and safe lucidity of some cabinet war-room.

But somehow—no analysis could define how it was—he channelled the winds and gathered together the tides of all the contemporary disquiets about the health of Christianity, the relevance of the Church, and the hopes of the Kingdom of God which could be placed in both. The response he got was unprecedented, and much more of it was welcoming than abusive. To very many he offered new freedom, new hope.

The Bishop of Woolwich blew the trumpet that was heard, and started the great debate which continues still, and must for years to come. That is the importance of one small book in history. This search for presenting old truths in new and more contemporarily compulsive ways is the previously missing factor in the Church's performance of the reconciling task to which the Lambeth Conference of 1958 had called it. We have gone far to reconcile Christians with each other, and the New Theology has already had some share in this. There is still much, much further to go, but the outlook is hopeful. We have created at least the skeleton of an organization to contain the outreaching mission of Churches in process of being reconciled. But all this presupposes the reconciling of modern man with the God he does not know, and often does not even care to know. This has been the missing factor, not that attempts have not been made to provide it, but that those innumerable attempts have failed. The radical restatement of doctrine in the shapes of what have become commonly known as the New Morality and the New Theology has far to go, but it offers a new hope.

EPILOGUE

The Bubbling Cauldron

ONLY THIRTY-FOUR years now separate us from the coming of the second millennium of Christian history. This span of time is both long and short enough to tempt anyone who has lived uninterruptedly in the Church of England since this century began, and has tried to learn something of its history during the last sixty-odd years, to attempt to answer the question, 'Where do we go from here?', and to guess what its outward form and its inward disposition will be in AD 2000. This is a hazardous exercise of the imagination. An essentially mature religious society is working out its destiny in an adolescent age, big with all the pregnancies of revolution in every part of its life. The New Age of the New Man, now an assertion to be argued for, will then either be accepted as an unexamined axiom, or else be abandoned as the exploded claim of a few theological fanatics who made the 'sixties unquiet by their clamour. The former is more likely than the latter. Either way, the Church is, as always, being affected by the spirit of the age, and one consequence of this is that its sense of maturity is being both maimed and tempered by the tremendous revolutionary assumptions of contemporary society.

At present the Church of England is like a cauldron bubbling with deceptive steadiness over a slow fire. The fire is certainly alight and the cauldron is full. It simmers and a vapour rises from it, but it takes the form of an insubstantial question mark. A scent pervades the kitchen but it is not easy to identify it, nor even quite certain whether it tempts or discourages the appetite. That food of many kinds is being cooked in the cauldron is clear; we know what most of the ingredients are, but not what the stew they are going to make will look like and taste like. When the dinner is ready we can reasonably guess that there will be human beings who are eager to try it. But how many there will be, a handful or a multitude, and whether they will like it or, making a face, turn away from it, we cannot at present know.

The ingredients are many. Some are encouraging and some are ominous. Together they add up to changes greater rather than less. There is, first of all the reunion movement. While there are still Churches which, to all appearances, remain relatively undisturbed by it and seem to be unwelcoming towards it, the Church of England is not one of them, as the eagerness of its welcome to the proposals for union with the Methodist Church, shown by the voting in one diocesan conference after another, demonstrated. It is at least possible—more than that, it is likely—that by the end of the century the two Churches will be organically one single Church; and if so we shall then be in the thick of the rationalizing process by which many Methodist and Anglican churches will be closed so as to eliminate competition and redundancy. This is a process bound to be very uncomfortable which will put the reality of the union to the test.

The Roman Catholic Church has moved so fast, so far, in so short a time, towards ecumenical co-operation with other Churches and towards a position of real friendship with them that it must itself be feeling a little bewildered by having to assimilate changes so many and so great. Rome has entered the revolutionary age by promoting a revolution in her own structures and relationships. It is likely that she will now need a time of peaceful reflection to come to terms with her new look. Further dramatic changes before the end of the century seem unlikely. The changes now made will remain, and no doubt the Pope will continue to be an occasional world traveller. But it will be surprising if within the next thirty years the prospects of formal unity between the Roman Catholic and any other Church are more closely in sight than they are today. The vital change, however, has already been made, and, it would seem, irrevocably. The hostility of centuries is ended, a charitable friendship has taken its place, and this has been sealed by the removal of many old rocks of offence and the offer of co-operation in various fields of Christian witness. By the Church of England all this has been unreservedly welcomed, and she rejoices in the prospect of a new friendship and confidence with so many of her Roman Catholic neighbours. Much of what growth there may be in the Kingdom of God before the century ends will be due to this new friendship.

All this is modestly encouraging. But there are other ingredients in the cauldron which promise strife, and of these the first is the surprising but strong revival of biblical fundamentalism. There is no doubt of this, and one might speculate interminably on why it has come to be and yet not find a satisfying answer. It is dismaying to think that our successors of the twenty-first century may find themselves fighting the battle of biblical scholarship all over again.

There are of course many gradations within 'Conservative Evangelicalism'. The universities and colleges are full of Christian Unions based on a 'personal experience of Jesus Christ', but are also producing many ordained or lay missionaries for Britain and the world. Evangelical preaching and scholarship hold their own bravely; and a church like All Souls, Langham Place, where the work of this school is seen at its best, is rightly a power in the land. The stronger historic evangelicalism becomes, the better for Christendom it will be, for the true evangelical does not lose his sense of the authority of the Church, and does much to help forward the community of all its members.

But there is also a momentarily successful kind of protestantism which forms a dubious influence within the mainstream, and produces serious problems for us all by establishing its own missions all over the world. They immediately become thronged by disgruntled Christians with a grievance against their own Churches. These mushroom conventicles enjoy a momentary success for they lose members as fast as they entice them, and they bequeath them usually to sheer indifference. The conventicles die quickly but multiply yet faster. The more extreme and less creditable kinds of protestantism, far from being dead, are in fact fast reviving, and they will make a force to be seriously reckoned with in thirty years from now.

In England a parochial system changed in outward shape, and a ministry recruited under different conditions of service from those which have obtained for centuries, will have to grapple with all this. The separate independency of the parish is even now on the way out. Long before the century ends, current and contemporary trends will lessen the number of separate parishes, and so there will be many less incumbents than today. This will mean that assistant curates will have to wait far longer for a parochial charge of their own than has been true for many years. When at long last they have the chance to become vicars it seems unlikely that the Parson's Freehold will still be in existence to guarantee their freedom and independence. Furthermore the immemorial freedom of the Anglican clergy is almost certain to be whittled away at the beginning of a man's ministry. No one knows yet how much of Leslie Paul's revolutionary report, *The Deployment and Payment of the Clergy*, will be carried into effect, but it is at least likely that the part of it which suggests that for the first five years of the newly ordained man's ministry he must serve in whatever diocese and parish to which a staffing committee chooses to allot him will quite soon become the established practice of the Church of England. Thus he will lose his freedom to choose where he will work, and when he becomes a vicar he may well lose the protection of his freehold. The old tradition of Anglican freedom will have been seriously impaired.

The process of amalgamating two or more parishes together to form a single parochial unit has already been carried almost as far in rural areas as it can be. But in the towns it has not yet seriously begun, though there too it will be bound to come. The idea of the group ministry, the beginnings of which were described in a previous chapter, has spread at a triumphant speed. The appendix to the Archdeacon of Lincoln's 1965 report on the group ministry situation, *Team and Group Ministry*, published by the Church Information Office, lists no less than forty-nine schemes of the kind now in actual operation. That there will soon be many more can hardly be doubted. Then the plea that we need fewer and stronger parochial centres is backed by so strong a logic of events that the pressure to achieve it will be overwhelming.

These causes, and others, will reduce quite drastically the number of independent parishes, and so the newly ordained deacon of tomorrow is more likely to find himself the junior member of a team of clergy than the only curate of his vicar. This ministerial relationship of one curate to one vicar has been the normal pattern for many years. It looks now as if we shall soon be reverting to a still older traditional pattern that young deacons and priests learn their trade by belonging to a fleet of curates, and gradually working their way up the ladder of promotion until seniority takes them to what will then be the dizzy eminence of the senior curate. The period of apprenticeship which any priest must serve before he is appointed to be vicar of a parish of his own will be greatly lengthened. These changes, however, will apply only to the deacon who decides to start and to continue in parish work. If, as seems certain, the number of specialized and non-parochial ministries increases still further, it may well be necessary to recruit them by ordaining deacons directly into them, so that the ordination candidate will be able to choose whether he will serve the Church within the parochial system or outside it. But if so, some change in the law forbidding a bishop to ordain any man until he has a position or 'title' to offer him will be necessary. Hitherto a 'title' has meant, with few exceptions, a curacy in a parish. It may also have to mean something like an assistant chaplaincy in a non-parochial ministry.

The most influential adversary of the Church at present is the philosophic humanist. That he is also in so many ways an ally makes the strategy of defence very difficult. He seeks the assertion of the dignity of the person which is also a Christian purpose, and 'Christian humanists' is a genuine title of our Lord's people, and not a contradiction in terms. Moreover the right-wing humanist and the left-wing Christian are often indistinguishable. But humanism as a whole does postulate a world in which God is at best benevolently inactive, and turns its back on a religion which makes the psalmist's claim, 'The good that is done upon earth, God doeth it himself', which Jesus endorsed in a score of contexts. In the long run humanism and the Gospel are not compatible. The controversy between them, already tentatively begun, is likely to continue for a long time, and to widen and deepen. The alliance between the humanists and the academic philologists is very formidable, for the philologist, whose prestige is great, has rescued the humanist from wasting time in trying to score small points at the expense of the theologian, and has shifted the field of argumentative battle to that of the meaning (or meaninglessness, as he would claim) of credal and theological language. All this is among the most high minded and best tempered of Christian controversies, but it is one in which most of the initial advantages are with the humanists. It will therefore sway to and

fro for at least as long as the century lasts, and it is largely with this challenge that the academic theologians of the immediate future will have to
grapple.

The certainty of this controversy and the importance of its practical
implications makes it possible that the theologians will become less content
than at present they seem to be with their admissions that they do not know
many answers. They must be ready, they say, to begin all over again. The
most they can do at present is to ask the right questions, and anything like
the drawing of a theological map of the world is beyond their powers. The
admission has humility and there are reasons for it. But as the challenge of
a reinvigorated humanism presses upon them, their proper function of
defending vital Christian doctrine will assume an immediacy they may find
it impossible to gainsay. Our successors may well witness a theological
flight from the present principle of tentativeness, and quite a number of
attempts to put on the mantle of St Thomas Aquinas. Many will be abor-
tive and a few derisory, but times may well be coming when the reincarna-
tion of the Seraphic Doctor will seem to be the most urgent of necessities.

The personality and the wide and real scholarship of Dr Michael Ramsey, Archbishop of Canterbury since 1963, constitute what may well become
the most significant factor of all. He has grown in his office to the point
where his stature is influential now, and will become commanding in the
future. His characteristic message to the Church is the overwhelming importance of personal spirituality, and this he commends ceaselessly in
speech, print, and in his own person. The spirituality he expounds is very
deep and has the simplicity which is the fruit of long study and wide knowledge. It is classical and independent of momentary fashions, and it has
the power of communicating strength to the weak and comfort to the
tormented. Its quality can be seen by those who read his mission addresses
to the University of Oxford, published by the SCM Press under the title,
Introducing the Christian Faith. They are profound, simple, and, above all,
fortifying. He is likely to steady the Church when it is swaying distractedly,
by taking us back to the rock from which we were hewn. In the years in
front of us, this may be very important indeed.

These ingredients, and many others, seethe together in the cauldron. The
fire underneath it burns steadily. Many kinds of fuel combine to make this
molten mass, and they are a combination of the various revolutionary
pressures on the modern world, the twentieth-century man's excitement
over his sense of a recently achieved adulthood, the almost universal drive
for equality of every kind coupled with the decay of a sense of reverence
for past history and tradition and all upholders of it, and a concealed but
real fear that all futures and all ambitions might at any moment be destroyed by the total catastrophe of general atomic war. But side by side with
all this, interfused with every particle of it, is the unseen and immeasurable
pressure of the Holy Spirit which the Christian should never, but too often

does, forget. To guess too closely at his present purpose could be as impious as it is absurd. But at least this must be true, that the aim of the Holy Spirit is to bring the world through its present travails to the point of social development where the dignity of man as a child of God is refounded on a surer basis. The only possible path to that end leads through a continuance of the present revolution; short cuts and by-passes are all dead ends. The Church, being composed of human beings, is never unaffected by the current motions of the world, but shares them in its own body. It too is passing through its own revolution, and it has far still to go. By AD 2000 our successors may know if the revolution in the Church amounts to a new Reformation—to the only kind of Reformation worth having in which, in the words of *Alice in Wonderland*, everybody has won and all shall have prizes, and the road to the goal is not littered by broken hearts and maimed spirits. In any event Anglican Christians cannot expect a quiet and peaceable life during the next thirty years, and it is probably not the desire of the Holy Spirit that they should wish for it.

When the cooking of the meal is finished and the food is put on the table, who will be the guests? And will they like what is set before them and come back for a second helping? The new theologians and the new moralists are fond of writing about the 'appalling dangers' of what they preach. But that is all a manner of speaking. Their flesh does not really creep in the least. Yet there is indeed a frightening danger and it is that the New Man—the technologist, the manager, the merchant, the trade union official—may refuse to look at the Gospel which has been so laboriously simplified and re-stated for him, while the traditionalist, beaten down by AD 2000 into a state of acute inferiority, has lapsed into a despairing agnosticism. There are already signs that something like this may happen. The danger lies more in the field of the new theology than in that of the new morality, in so far as they can be separated. The new theologians are more shrill, and give the impression of being less sure of themselves, than the new moralists, who after all can call to their aid much of the authority of the Gospels and the epistles themselves.

This may not happen, but the danger is there and the possibility is real. The strongest bulwark against it is the charity which ought to exist between the radical and the conservative wings of the Church, and on this, more than on anything else, depends the question of whether the new Reformation will constitute a growth of charity all round, or whether it will turn out to be something we should all be much better without. But it is going to be very difficult. Charity is the easiest of all virtues to talk about and the hardest to practise.

Because of this difficulty, because of the possibility that the new Christian thinking may fail, and gradually be seen to fail, to reach the audience at which it is aimed, other methods of approach may have to be tried. Thus a strong revival of classical theology is evidently possible, and if theologians learn the lesson of their neglect and address themselves to the real situations in which men and women have nowadays to live, it is probable. In the long run it will be better for the multitudes who have unchurched themselves to have a choice between one dish and another of what is, after all, the same meal, spread before them by the same Lord. What is quite impossible is that the Church should ever be content that nothing is offered to them, or that they should continue indefinitely to refuse to partake of the whole wedding feast.

We must hope, then, that the all too possible rebirth of the old *odium theologicum* can be avoided. An obvious way of doing it is to stress more and more the eucharist theology in which all theologies of God and man and history are subsumed. For the eucharist is not only the supreme Christian act. It is also a rite which has a strong sociological significance, which ties it into the prevailing thought and aspiration of the world. Beyond this, it happens to be the most nearly universal of all Christian acts of worship which, in spite of all the quarrels once surrounding it, today causes almost no strife. Here the radical and the conservative Christian are at one, however much they differ over the creeds and the scriptures. The eucharist is at once peaceable and sociologically evangelistic, and the more the Church teaches about it and lays stress on it the fairer its future seems likely to be.

All these prophecies about the Church and the world in the next thirty years are no more significant than question marks. Like the modern theologians, one may hope to have asked the right questions but all answers are tentative and questioning. On the surface the coming changes may well be less dramatic and drastic, or at least more gradual, than we now expect. In a mature Church which has the roots of its being in a timeless permanence, thirty-odd years is a short time, even if they are the years of a continuing revolution. Worship, sacraments, prayer, preaching, scripture and all else which anchors us to the long traditions of history will, in all circumstances, go on; and those of us who continue to stand fast in the order of our service will find ourselves usable, and expendable too, in the service of the Kingdom. There is nothing to fear. The Kingdom the English Church serves is God's; his is its generating power; his its beauty and its glory. There may be no present reason to think that in 2000 it will be visibly stronger than now. But the promise is there: 'Fear not, little flock, it is your Father's good pleasure to give you the Kingdom.'

Index

Index